T0326384

Routledge Handbook of Environmental Conflict and Peacebuilding

The past two decades have witnessed the emergence of a large body of research examining the linkage between environmental scarcity, violent conflict, and cooperation. However, this environmental security polemic is still trying to deliver a well-defined approach to achieving peace. Studies are being undertaken to find the precise pathways by which cooperative actions are expected not only to pre-empt or moderate resource conflicts but also to help diffuse cooperative behaviour to other disputed issues. The recognition that environmental resources can contribute to violent conflict accentuates their potential significance as pathways for cooperation and the consolidation of peace in post-conflict societies.

Conceived as a single and reliable reference source which will be a vital resource for students, researchers, and policy makers alike, the *Routledge Handbook of Environmental Conflict and Peacebuilding* presents a wide range of chapters written by key thinkers in the field, organised into four key parts:

- **Part I:** Review of the concept and theories;
- **Part II:** Review of thematic approaches (resources, scarcity, intervention, adaptation, and peacebuilding);
- **Part III:** Case studies (Middle East, Iraq, Jordan, Liberia, Nepal, Colombia, Philippines);
- **Part IV:** Analytical challenges and future-oriented perspectives.

Enabling the reader to find a concise expert review on topics that are most likely to arise in the course of conducting research or policy making, this volume presents a truly global overview of the key issues and debates in environmental conflict and peacebuilding.

Ashok Swain is a Professor of Peace and Conflict Research, UNESCO Chair of International Water Cooperation, and Director of the Research School of International Water Cooperation at Uppsala University, Sweden. He has written extensively on new security challenges and democratic development issues.

Joakim Öjendal is Professor of Peace and Development Research at the School of Global Studies, University of Gothenburg, Sweden. He has been researching water management for twenty years and has published widely within water management as well as within regionalisation in East and Southeast Asia, and has been specialising in Cambodia studies.

Routledge Handbook of Environmental Conflict and Peacebuilding

Edited by Ashok Swain and Joakim Öjendal

from Routledge

Routledge
Taylor & Francis Group

LONDON AND NEW YORK

First published 2018 by Routledge

2 Park Square, Milton Park, Abingdon, Oxfordshire OX14 4RN

52 Vanderbilt Avenue, New York, NY 10017

Routledge is an imprint of the Taylor & Francis Group, an informa business

First issued in paperback 2020

British Library Cataloguing-in-Publication Data
A catalogue record for this book is available from the British Library

Library of Congress Cataloging-in-Publication Data
Names: Swain, Ashok, editor. | Öjendal, Joakim, editor.
Title: Routledge handbook of environmental conflict and peacebuilding /
    edited by Ashok Swain and Joakim Öjendal.
Other titles: Handbook of environmental conflict and peacebuilding
Description: Abingdon, Oxon ; New York, NY : Routledge, 2018. |
    Includes bibliographical references.
Identifiers: LCCN 2017051282| ISBN 9781138202528 (hardback) | ISBN
    9781315473772 (ebk)
Subjects: LCSH: Peace-building—Environmental aspects. | Peace-
    building—Environmental aspects—Case studies. | Conflict
    management—Environmental aspects. | Conflict management—
    Environmental aspects—Case studies. | War—Environmental aspects. |
    War—Environmental aspects—Case studies. | Natural resources—
    Management. | Natural resources—Management—Case studies.
Classification: LCC JZ1324 .R68 2018 | DDC 303.6/6—dc23
LC record available at https://lccn.loc.gov/2017051282

ISBN: 978-1-138-20252-8 (hbk)
ISBN: 978-0-367-52152-3 (pbk)

Typeset in Bembo
by Swales & Willis Ltd, Exeter, Devon, UK

Contents

Figures and tables

Figures

Tables

Contributors

Timothy Adivilah Balag'kutu is a PhD candidate of Global Governance and Human Security in University of Massachusetts Boston's John W. McCormack Graduate School of Policy and Global Studies. His doctoral research examines the role of and interaction between intergovernmental organizations and transnational advocacy networks in global mercury governance across scales. Based on the global process under the 2013 Minamata Convention on Mercury, his research studies governance of the use of mercury in artisanal and small-scale mining (ASM), with a focus on Ghana. Tim previously studied at Ohio University, where he obtained two masters degrees, in Political Science and International Affairs (African Studies). Prior to that, he studied at the University of Ghana, where he earned his first degree in a double major of Political Science and Swahili: he also studied language proficiency (Swahili) at the University of Dar es Salaam in Tanzania, in part-fulfillment of his first degree. His research interest is in environmental politics and governance, natural resource governance and the intersection between the two fields, as well as democratization and sustainable development. The regional focus of his research is Africa. He is currently an adjunct lecturer of African Studies in Babson College, Massachusetts, where he teaches two classes on a survey of contemporary Africa.

Karin Aggestam is professor of Political Science and holds the Samuel Pufendorf Endowed Chair by the Söderberg Foundations at Lund University, Sweden. She is the former director of Peace and Conflict Studies, Lund University, and presently visiting research professor at Monash University (2016–2018) and honorary professor at University of Queensland, Australia. She is also lead author for the International Panel on Social Progress and co-editor of Routledge book series Law, Conflict and International Relations.

Her interdisciplinary research interests include peace, conflict, negotiation, gender, hydropolitics and the Middle East. Some of her recent publications include *Gendering Diplomacy and International Negotiation* (2017, co-editor with A. Towns), Special section: Hydrology and peace in the Middle East (2016, *Hydrological Sciences Journal,* guest editor with R. Berndtsson), Desecuritisation of water and the technocratic turn in peacebuilding (2015, *International Environmental Agreement. Politics, Law and Economics), Rethinking Peacebuilding. The Quest for Just Peace in the Middle East and the Western Balkans* (2014, co-ed with A. Björkdahl) and Situating water in peacebuilding (2013, *Water International,* with A. Sundell).

Larissa M. Aldehoff has a Master's in International Studies/Peace and Conflict Studies from Frankfurt University and Technical University Darmstadt and a Bachelor's in Public Administration/European Studies from Münster University and Twente University. In her research she focuses on the role of water resources as a cause of conflict in the political relationship of riparian states with a focus on the Middle East.

Contributors

Peter Aldinger is an independent lawyer and consultant; he focuses on regulatory and institutional reform, improving natural resource management regimes and the tenure rights of rural communities, and the role of natural resources in conflict. Most recently he has been working in the Republic of Liberia to support the development and institutionalization of the community forestry program. Mr. Aldinger holds a BSc Econ/IR in International Relations from the University of Wales, Aberystwyth, an MPhil in International Relations from the University of Cambridge, an LLB from BPP University Law School, and an LLM from Harvard University Law School.

Saleem H. Ali is an environmental planner whose research and practice focuses on ways of resolving ecological conflicts through technical and social mechanisms, as well as exploring novel ways of peace-building between corporations, governments and communities. He holds the Blue and Gold Distinguished Professorship in Energy and the Environment at the University of Delaware, and is also a Senior Fellow at Columbia University's Center on Sustainable Investment and Georgetown University's Center for Australia, New Zealand and Pacific Studies. Professor Ali has held the Chair in Sustainable Resources Development at the University of Queensland's Sustainable Minerals Institute in Brisbane, Australia (where he retains professorial affiliation). Previously he was professor of Environmental Studies at the University of Vermont's Rubenstein School of Natural Resources where he was founding director of the Institute for Environmental Diplomacy and Security. His books include *Treasures of the Earth: Need, Greed and a Sustainable Future, Environmental Diplomacy* (with Lawrence Susskind), *Mining, the Environment and Indigenous Development Conflicts* and *Islam and Education: Conflict and Conformity in Pakistan's Madrassas*. He received his doctorate in Environmental Planning from MIT, a Master's degree in Environmental Studies from Yale University and Bachelor's degree in Chemistry from Tufts University (summa cum laude).

Randall Amster, J.D., Ph.D., is director and teaching professor in the Program on Justice and Peace at Georgetown University in Washington, DC. He serves as editor-in-chief of the *Contemporary Justice Review*, and was formerly the executive director of the Peace and Justice Studies Association. He teaches and publishes widely on subjects including peace and nonviolence, social and environmental justice, political theory and movements, and the impacts of emerging technologies. His recent books include *Peace Ecology* (2015), *Anarchism Today* (2012), *Lost in Space: The Criminalization, Globalization, and Urban Ecology of Homelessness* (2008), and the co-edited volume *Exploring the Power of Nonviolence: Peace, Politics, and Practice* (2013). Current research interests include environmental peacebuilding, climate justice, intersectionality and ecology, community and sustainability, and the justice implications of contemporary technology.

Jeremiah O. Asaka is a Global Governance and Human Security PhD candidate in the Department of Conflict Resolution, Human Security and Global Governance at the University of Massachusetts, Boston. He is also a lecturer in the Department of Global Studies and Human Geography at Middle Tennessee State University. Mr. Asaka is an alumnus of Pennsylvania State University's Sustainable Climate Risk Management (SCRiM) summer school and the University of Massachusetts Boston's National Science Foundation (NSF) funded Integrative Graduate Education and Research Traineeship (IGERT) fellowship. He has published in a few places including but not limited to the *Journal of Arid Environments*; *The Round Table: The Commonwealth Journal of International Affairs*; New Security Beat blog of the Woodrow Wilson International Center for Scholars' Environmental Change and Security Program; Adelphi's Environment, Conflict and Cooperation online platform; the Conversation; and a forthcoming

Routledge Handbook of the Resources Nexus. His areas of research interest include, among others, human dimensions of the environment, global environmental governance, climate change impacts and adaptation, human security, climate–security–resources nexus and sub-Saharan Africa.

Michael D. Beevers (PhD, University of Maryland) is an assistant professor in the Departments of Environmental and International Studies at Dickinson College. He teaches courses in global environmental politics, environmental peacebuilding and global environmental change and human security. Dr. Beevers was a Harrison Fellow at the University of Maryland, and Peace Scholar at the U.S. Institute of Peace in Washington, DC. He has served as a research associate at Princeton University and as a consultant for the United Nations Environment Programme and World Resources Institute. He also served as a Peace Corps volunteer in Niger, and worked in South Asia and West Africa on a range of development and environment issues. His recent work appears in *Global Governance, International Peacekeeping, African Conflict and Peacebuilding Review* and *The Extractive Industries and Society*, among others. His first book, *Natural Resources Governance and Peacebuilding in the Aftermath of Conflict* is due out in 2018.

Carl Bruch is an international environmental lawyer with more than 20 years of experience. A recognized authority on environmental governance and environmental peacebuilding, he has helped dozens of countries strengthen their environmental laws, institutions, and practices. He has conducted research, provided technical and legal assistance, and built capacity across Africa, the Americas, Asia and the Pacific, and Eastern Europe, and has worked in numerous conflict-affected countries, including Ivory Coast, Lebanon, Liberia, Myanmar, Sierra Leone, South Sudan, and Timor-Leste.

Since 2007, Carl has been a leader in a global effort to establish a new multidisciplinary field of environmental peacebuilding, which promotes environmental management to prevent, mitigate, resolve, and recover from conflict. He was a series editor of a six-volume set of books on post-conflict peacebuilding and natural resource management, with 150 chapters by 225 authors (2012–2016). With the United Nations Environment Programme and others, he established and leads the Environmental Peacebuilding Knowledge Platform, the Environmental Peacebuilding Community of Practice, the biweekly *Environmental Peacebuilding Update*, and the Environmental Peacebuilding Academy.

Carl has been quoted in more than 100 print, online, and radio media sources in English, Spanish, Portuguese, Japanese, and French, including *Science, Scientific American*, Inter Press Service, and Climate Wire.

Servio Caicedo is a professor and university researcher who has worked as a government and social organizations consultant. His approach to research and analysis of conflicts is guided by the theory of complexity and environmental justice. Its main research topics are environmental injustice in mining and oil exploitation, participatory water governance, and peacebuilding in communities affected by armed conflict.

His initial professional training is in Psychology, with studies in Sociology and Political Science, with a Master's degree in Development Planning and a Ph.D. in Humanities from San Buenaventura University in Colombia. Servio has worked as a lecturer at Rosario University, Javeriana University and Sabana University, in courses such as conflict resolution, environmental conflict; mediation; social and educational conflict. He has been an advisor and environmental consultant to the United Nations, Association of Regional Autonomous Corporations ASOCARS, the District's Water Company of Bogotá and the Foundation for the Defense of Public FUNDEPÚBLICO. He is currently a research professor at the Faculty of Juridical and Political Sciences at the San Buenaventura University, working as main researcher of the project called "Sumak Kawsay Bogotá Choachí". He has published in recent years the books: *Gobernanza del Agua en la Bogotá Humana* (2016) and *La Mediación como garante de Convivencia en la región del Carare y en la Comunidad Wayuu* (2014). His current topics of interest are: the construction of Good Living in rural communities; the transformation of socio-environmental conflicts; justice and environmental governance; formation of citizenship, conflict transformation.

Ken Conca is a professor of International Relations at American University. His research focuses on environment, conflict, and peacebuilding; water politics and governance; the political economy of climate adaptation; environmental human rights; and global institutions and the UN system. He is a member of the UN Environment Programme's Expert Advisory Group on Conflict and Peacebuilding. Previously, he served on the Scientific Steering Committee on Global Environmental Change and Human Security for the International Human Dimensions Program on Global Environmental Change. Dr. Conca is a two-time recipient of the International Studies Association's Harold and Margaret Sprout Award for best book on international environmental affairs and a recipient of the Chadwick Alger Prize for best book in the field of International Organization. His most recent book is *An Unfinished Foundation: The United Nations and Global Environmental Governance* (2015), and he is editor of the forthcoming *Oxford Handbook of Water Politics and Policy* (2018). He earned his Ph.D. from the Energy and Resources Group at the University of California, Berkeley.

Simon Dalby is CIGI Chair in the Political Economy of Climate Change at the Balsillie School of International Affairs, and professor of Geography and Environmental Studies at Wilfrid Laurier University, Waterloo, Ontario. Professor Dalby was educated at Trinity College Dublin and the University of Victoria, and holds a Ph.D. from Simon Fraser University. He is former coeditor of the journal *Geopolitics,* and (with Shannon O'Lear at the University of Kansas) coeditor of *Reframing Climate Change: Constructing Ecological Geopolitics* (2016). He is author of *Creating the Second Cold War* (1990), *Environmental Security* (2002) and *Security and Environmental Change* (2009). His articles have appeared in diverse scholarly journals including *Alternatives, Antipode, Australian Journal of International Affairs, Contemporary Security Policy, Geoforum, Geopolitics, Global Environmental Politics, Global Policy, Intelligence and National Security, International Politics, Political Geography, RUSI Journal, Society and Space* and *Studies in Political Economy.* Currently his research focuses on Anthropocene geopolitics, climate change discourse, globalization and bordering practices in a rapidly changing world.

Linda Holcombe is a current PhD student in the Global Governance and Human Security program at the McCormick Graduate School of Policy and Global Studies at University of Massachusetts Boston. Her academic background includes a Master of Arts in Global Governance and Human Security from UMass Boston, a Master of Environmental Science from the Yale School of Forestry and Environmental Studies, and a Bachelor of Science in Criminal Justice from Northeastern University. Prior to graduate school, she worked in animal husbandry and education at several nationally accredited aquariums, specializing in African penguin care and conservation. Through animal husbandry she was able to introduce various species of sharks, fish, mammals, reptiles, and penguins to the public through animal encounters and formal presentations, while finding creative ways to promote conservation messaging. This work continued into graduate school where she studied how South African residents and organizations perceived recent African penguin conservation efforts. During her MESc she also worked with various external organizations, researching eco-friendly certification systems for gorilla tourism, innovative fisheries enforcement approaches, and the effectiveness of recent anti-poaching operations. Her current research draws on her diverse academic and professional experience and centers on exploring illicit trade in Central Africa, specifically the nuances of illicit wildlife and mineral networks and how they influence local and international security issues.

Tobias Ide is Head of the Research Field Peace and Conflict at the Georg Eckert Institute in Braunschweig (Germany). Recently, he led a research project on environmental peacemaking and interstate reconciliation at the University of Melbourne. Tobias studied Political Science at the University of Leipzig and obtained his PhD in Geography from the University of Hamburg. His research focuses on environmental change, peace and conflict, particularly in the Middle East and East Africa. He has published in numerous well-known outlets, including *Global Environmental Change, Political Geography, WIREs Climate Change* and *Third World Quarterly*.

Anders Jägerskog PhD is Senior Water Resources Management Specialist at the Global Water Practice at the World Bank. His work focuses on the Middle East and North Africa region. Previously he was Counsellor for regional water resources in the MENA region at the Swedish Embassy in Amman, Jordan. He was Director, Knowledge Services, at the Stockholm International Water Institute (SIWI), where he headed the Transboundary Water Management Unit and was work area leader for applied research. He managed the UNDP Shared Waters Partnership which facilitates and promotes dialogue and cooperation on transboundary water resources. He is associate professor (docent) at Peace and Development Research, School of Global Studies, University of Gothenburg where his work focuses on global water issues. He worked for the Swedish Ministry for Foreign Affairs; at the Embassy of Sweden, Nairobi; and at Stockholm International Peace Research Institute (SIPRI). In 2003 he finished his PhD on the water negotiations in the Jordan River Basin at the Department of Water and Environmental Studies at Linköping University, Sweden. He has published over 100 scientific articles, book chapters, debate articles and reports on global water issues. The views expressed by Jägerskog are his own and do not represent the views of the World Bank Group.

David Jensen is the Head of the Environmental Peacebuilding Programme at UN Environment. He also co-directs the MapX platform that helps stakeholders map and monitor the sustainable use of natural resources using best available data.

The focus of his work is to address conflict risks and peacebuilding opportunities from renewable and non-renewable natural resources. In particular, to improve access to information, benefit sharing and risk mitigation during the life cycle of major natural resource investments. A summary of his work is available here: http://postconflict.unep.ch/publications/ECP/ECP_final_report_Nov2016.pdf. David has worked with all of the key peace and security actors of the UN, including the peacebuilding (PBC/PBSO), peacekeeping (DPKO/DFS), and mediation (DPA) communities, as well as UN country teams, Resident Coordinators and Special Representatives of the Secretary General.

David's programme has worked with a range of partners to produce a knowledge base of 150 case studies on natural resources and peacebuilding organized in six thematic books. This material covers 60 conflict-affected countries and 12 natural resource categories. The cases can be freely downloaded from www.environmentalpeacebuilding.org. David's work on natural resources and peacebuilding was featured in a TEDx event hosted in Geneva: https://youtu.be/-csxGMxyqxw. David is also one of the lead lecturers in a new Massive Open Online Course on Environmental Security and Sustaining Peace offered by the SDG Academy. David's recent publications include a new UN guide on mediating natural resource conflicts, as well as a book of case studies on *Assessing and Restoring Natural Resources in Post-Conflict Peacebuilding*.

David holds an MSc in Biology from Oxford University (UK) and an undergraduate degree in Geography from the University of Victoria (Canada). He is an Alumnus of the Peace Mediation Platform (Swiss Federal Department of Foreign Affairs) and a Beahrs' Environmental Leadership Fellow at the University of California, Berkeley. He was also certified as a Project Management Professional (PMP) in 2009.

McKenzie Johnson is a visiting assistant professor in the Department of Political Science at Purdue University. Her research explores the interactions between global governance norms, domestic resource politics, and human security in transitional, fragile, and conflict-affected states. Her areas of expertise include: (global) environmental politics, environmental and human security, and the politics of natural resource management. Dr. Johnson's current book manuscript examines how the diffusion of global governance institutions has shaped domestic resource politics in Ghana and Sierra Leone, focusing specifically on conflict over minerals and forest resources. She has also published in the *European Journal of International Relations*, *Global Environmental Change*, and *Biological Conservation*. McKenzie received her PhD in Environmental Policy from Duke University, her MA in Conservation Biology from Columbia University, and her AB in Environmental Studies from Vassar College. She has worked and conducted research in numerous countries including Afghanistan, South Sudan, India, and most recently Ghana and Sierra Leone.

Florian Krampe is a researcher in SIPRI's Climate Change and Risk Project. He specializes in peace and conflict research, international relations and political ecology. His primary academic interest is the foundations of peace and security, especially the processes of building peace after armed conflict. Currently, he focuses on climate security and the post-conflict management of natural resources with a specific interest in the ecological foundations for a socially, economically and politically resilient peace. His forthcoming book is *Understanding Environmental Peacebuilding* (2018/19).

Dr Krampe is an affiliated researcher at the Research School for International Water Cooperation at the Department of Peace and Conflict Research at Uppsala University and the UNESCO Centre on International Water Cooperation hosted by the Stockholm International Water Institute (SIWI).

Amanda Kron works as legal advisor to the Post-Conflict and Disaster Management Branch of UN Environment Programme. She holds an LL.M from Uppsala University (Sweden) with a specialization in international law. Prior to joining UN Environment Programme, Amanda served as research assistant at the International Law Commission, where she focused on protection of the environment in relation to armed conflicts. In addition to her work at UN Environment Programme, Amanda serves as member and Swedish representative of the International Law Association Committee on the Role of International Law in Sustainable Natural Resource Management for Development. She has also held positions at the Centre for International Sustainable Development Law, Amnesty International, the European Law Students' Association, and the Permanent Mission of Sweden to the United Nations in Geneva.

James R. Lee is a researcher-in-residence at the School of International Service with American University (Washington, DC). He was associate director in American University's Center for Teaching, Research, and Learning where he directed the training of faculty teaching online and hybrid courses. He also managed the Social Science Research Lab on campus. Before that, he was a full-time faculty member in the School of International Service. He has policy experience at the US Environmental Protection Agency and the Office of the U.S. Trade Representative.

He has also published numerous articles, reports, and research papers on trade, environment, conflict, and culture and taught courses on these subjects. His recent articles are "Situating Australia in a World of Climate and Conflict" (edited by Peter Dennis) and "Climate Change, Conflict, and Moving Borders" (with Kisei Tanaka). His books include *Climate Change and Armed Conflict: Hot and Cold Wars* and *Exploring the Gaps: The Vital Links Between Trade, Environment and Culture.*

Jason J. McSparren is a PhD candidate in the Global Governance and Human Security program at the McCormack Graduate School, University of Massachusetts, Boston. He is also a Pre-Doctoral Fellow (2017–18) for the West African Research Association/Center (WARA/C) Boston/Dakar. His dissertation research is a case study of the political–institutional norms of governance at the state and sub-state levels of natural resource governance in Mali, entitled, "Seeking a Nexus between Transparency, Accountability and Sustainable Development in the Extractive Industries: Evaluating Capacity of Civil Society Organizations in Mali". Jason is also a research assistant for a multi-year project funded by the Qatar National Research Foundation titled, *Natural Resource Governance in Africa, Promoting a Qatari Perspective and Economic Diversification.* His notable publications include: Jang, McSparren, Rashchupkina (2016), "Global Governance: present and future," *Palgrave Communications 2*; McSparren, Tok, Sanz (2015), "Contours of Qatar–Sub-Saharan Africa Relations: Shedding Light on Trends and Prospects," *London School of Economics Middle East Centre;* McSparren, Tok, Besada, Shaw (2015), "Inclusive Growth, Governance of Natural Resources and Sustainable Development in Africa from a Qatari Perspective," in *Africa and the Gulf Region: Blurred Boundaries and Shifting Ties.* His research interests include the political economy of natural resources, multi-stakeholder governance mechanisms, value chain management and development, and capacity building for improved governance, economic development and conflict management. Contact Jason at Jason.mcsparren001@umb.edu.

Richard A. Matthew (BA McGill; PhD Princeton) is Associate Dean for International Programs and Professor of Urban Planning and Public Policy at the University of California at Irvine. He is the founding director of the Center for Unconventional Security Affairs (www.cusa.uci.edu), the director of the Blum Center for Poverty Alleviation (http://blumcenter.uci.edu/), and co-principal investigator for the NSF-funded FloodRISE Project (http://floodrise.uci.edu).

His research focuses on understanding and addressing challenges at the intersection of severe environmental stress, extreme poverty and violent conflict. Over the past twenty years, he has done extensive fieldwork in conflict and disaster zones in Cambodia, the DRC, Mexico, Nepal, Pakistan, Rwanda, Sierra Leone and Swaziland. He currently is carrying out research in three areas: environmental peacebuilding, community-engaged flood hazard modeling, and the science and practice of compassion. His work is widely diffused beyond academic outlets to support the efforts of practitioners in the conservation and humanitarian communities.

Dr. Matthew is a Senior Fellow at the International Institute for Sustainable Development in Geneva, and a senior member of the United Nations Expert Group on Environment, Conflict and Peacebuilding. He has served on several UN missions, including two that he led to Sierra Leone, and he was the lead author of the UN policy report, *From Conflict to Peacebuilding: The Role of Natural Resources and the Environment,* and the UN technical report, *Sierra Leone:*

Environment, Conflict and Peacebuilding Assessment. He has given five TEDx talks and been a featured storyteller on The Moth twice. He has over 160 publications.

Hannah Moosa is a consultant at the UN Environment/Office for the Coordination of Humanitarian Affairs (OCHA) Joint Unit (JEU) in Geneva, Switzerland. Since May 2017, she has served as Event Manager for the 2017 Environment and Emergencies Forum and Green Star Awards Ceremony, which was held at the UN Office in Nairobi, Kenya, from 26–28 September 2017. The Forum, a biennial event organized by the JEU, brought together over 150 practitioners from 52 countries representing over 100 different organizations, to showcase innovations in environmental emergency preparedness and response, and to highlight current efforts to integrate environment in humanitarian action. Hannah previously worked as a consultant for UN Environment's Disasters and Conflicts sub-programme for two years, assisting on a collaborative project on strengthening post-conflict peacebuilding through natural resource management, and serving as assistant managing editor of *Assessing and Restoring Natural Resources in Post-Conflict Peacebuilding* (eds. David Jensen and Steve Lonergan, 2012). She has additional experience with the Forum of Federations and USIP, working on constitutional and institutional design in post-conflict societies, and assisting with capacity-building and policy-development workshops in Sudan and Ethiopia. Hannah has also assisted the UN DPI and UNDP Azerbaijan in organizing two international-level Model UN Conferences in Geneva and Baku; and she has served as a young water professional and junior rapporteur for the Stockholm International Water Institute's 2013 and 2015 World Water Weeks. Hannah has an Honours B.A. in international affairs and economics from the University of Toronto Mississauga, and an M.A. in International Relations from the Munk School of Global Affairs and Department of Political Science, University of Toronto. She has completed six years of doctoral work in comparative politics and international relations, focusing on transboundary water cooperation, regional integration and conflict prevention in Southern Africa. moosa@un.org

Joakim Öjendal has been professor of Peace and Development Research since 2006 at the School of Global Studies, University of Gothenburg, Sweden. He has worked on resource politics, peacebuilding, and post-war democratisation for three decades in research, policy and education. He has published widely in leading journals and with international publishers. Öjendal was a co-editor of *Water Security,* a four-volume set, as well as *Transboundary Water Management and the Climate Change Debate,* both in 2014. His most recent publications have focused on qualities of peacebuilding and include *In Search of a Civil Society*, and 'From friction to hybridity in Cambodia', *Journal of Peacebuilding,* 'Statebuilding under friction: 20 years of unfinished peacebuilding'. In June 2015, he was a co-editor of a *Third World Quarterly* special issue on 'The "Local Turn" in Peacebuilding'. Öjendal has recently contributed to several handbooks within the environmental field such as 'Water management' in the *Handbook on Contemporary Cambodia* and *Handbook of Water Politics and Policy.* His most recent engagement is with a contribution to *Natural Resource Conflicts and Sustainable Development* (forthcoming 2018). He is currently leading two major research projects: 'The Local Turn of Peacebuilding' and 'Peacebuilding amidst Violence', both funded from Swedish Scientific Council.

Rebecca Pincus leads research at the Center for Arctic Study and Policy (CASP) at the U.S. Coast Guard Academy, where she also teaches government courses in the Humanities department. She holds an MS and PhD in environment and natural resources from the University of Vermont, as well as an MS in environmental law from the Vermont Law School. Her primary interests are in the nexus of climate change and national security, with a focus on the Arctic region. Dr. Pincus currently teaches on environmental, maritime, and security topics.

Peter Stoett (PhD Queen's) is Dean of Social Science and Humanities at the University of Ontario Institute of Technology in Oshawa, Canada; and from 2012–2017 he was the director of the Loyola Sustainability Research Centre at Concordia University in Montreal. His main areas of expertise include international relations and law, global environmental politics, and human rights. In 2012 he was a Fulbright Visiting Research Chair at the Woodrow Wilson International Center in Washington, DC; in 2013 he was Erasmus Visiting Scholar at the International Institute for Social Studies in The Hague; in 2016 he was Leverhulme Visiting Scholar in Climate Justice at the University of Reading, UK; and in 2017 he held a Provost Research Fellowship at the University of Tasmania. He has worked extensively with the United Nations Environmental Programme and is a Senior Research Fellow with the Earth Systems Governance Project of Future Earth. Recent publications include *Global Ecopolitics: Crisis, Governance, and Justice* (2012), *Regional Transnational Networks and Governance: Towards North American Environmental Policy?* (2017), and articles in *Global Governance* and *The Lancet Global Health*.

Vakur Sümer is the director of the Eurasian Research Institute (Akhmet Yassawi University), Almaty, Kazakhstan. He is a faculty member in the Department of International Relations, Selcuk University, Konya, Turkey. He received his Ph.D. on International Relations from Middle East Technical University, Ankara, Turkey. Sümer worked as a post-doctoral fellow at the Global Research Institute at University of North Carolina–Chapel Hill, NC, USA, and as a visiting scholar at the Department of Environmental Science and Policy, University of California–Davis, CA, USA. He was a researcher at the Max Planck Institute in Heidelberg, Germany in 2012. Sümer has published articles in journals such as *Uluslararası İlişkiler*, *Water International*, and *Journal of Peacebuilding and Development*. His books include the coedited, *Sustainable Water Use and Management* (2015) and *Water and Politics in Turkey: Structural Change and EU Accession* (2016). He also has attended a number of international and national academic conferences. He served as a referee/expert for the European Commission in evaluation of numerous projects. His areas of research include water issues, transboundary rivers, environmental politics, and Turkey's accession to the European Union. Sümer is a member of ISA (International Studies Association), Environmental Studies Section of ISA, and the International Water Association (IWA).

Ashok Swain is a Professor of Peace and Conflict Research, UNESCO Chair of International Water Cooperation, and Director of the Research School of International Water Cooperation at Uppsala University, Sweden. He received his PhD from the Jawaharlal Nehru University, New Delhi, in 1991, and since then he has been teaching at Uppsala University. He has been a MacArthur Fellow at the University of Chicago, visiting fellow at the UN Research Institute for Social Development, Geneva, and visiting professor at University Witwatersrand, University of Science, Malaysia, University of British Columbia, University of Maryland, Stanford University, McGill University, Tufts University and University of Natural Sciences and Life Sciences, Vienna. He has written extensively on new security challenges, water sharing issues, environment, conflict and peace, and democratic development issues. His publications include *The Environmental Trap* (1996), *International Fresh Water Resources: Conflict or Cooperation* (1997), *Managing Water Conflict: Asia, Africa and the Middle East* (2004), *Struggle against the State: Social Network and Protest Mobilization in India* (2010), *Understanding Emerging Security Challenges: Threats* *and Opportunities* (2012), *Transboundary Water Management and the Climate Change Debate* (2015), and *Emerging Security Threats in the Middle East: The Impact of Climate Change and Globalization* (2016). He has also edited/co-edited several volumes, including *Education as Social Action* (2005), *Islam and Violent Separatism* (2007), *Globalization and Challenges to Building Peace* (2007), *The Democratization Project: Opportunities and Challenges* (2009), *The Security–Development Nexus: Peace, Conflict and Development* (2013) and *Water Security*, four volumes (2014). He has also published more than 100 journal articles and book chapters. He has worked as a consultant on environment and development issues for various UN agencies, OSCE, NATO, EU, IISS, the Arab League, and the governments of Sweden, Netherlands, UK and Singapore.

Larry Swatuk is Professor of International Development and Director of the Master of Development Practice Program in the School of Environment, Enterprise and Development at the University of Waterloo, Ontario, Canada. He is also Extraordinary Professor in the Institute of Water Studies, University of Western Cape, South Africa. Dr. Swatuk holds a PhD in Political Science and International Relations from Dalhousie University, Halifax, Canada and has for the past twenty-five years worked on the political economy of natural resources govern-ance with a particular focus on sub-Saharan Africa. Among his most recent publications are a monograph entitled *Water in Southern Africa* (2017) and a co-edited collection (with Corrine Cash) entitled *Water, Energy, Food and People Across the Global South: The 'Nexus' in an era of Climate Change* (2018).

Dennis Tänzler is director of International Climate Policy at adelphi in Berlin, Germany. His research focuses on climate and energy policies as well as on peace and conflict studies. In 2007 and 2008 he served the Policy Planning Unit of the German Foreign Office as an expert on climate and energy policies. Tänzler has nearly twenty years of experience in the fields of global environmental policy, climate change policy and climate change and foreign policy.

Dennis Tänzler has undertaken research on climate protection and energy policies in the European Union, the United States and a number of developing and transition countries. Furthermore he has provided in-depth analysis on the security implications of climate change and contributed to interdisciplinary research on new methodologies for vulnerability assess-ments and the development of conflict-sensitive adaptation. Most recently he led a project to develop a dynamic training course on climate finance readiness and is advising different govern-ments on establishing governance structures for climate finance readiness. In 2014 and 2015 he coordinated an EU-funded project on the Climate Diplomacy Narratives and is one of the lead authors of the 2015 flagship report "A New Climate for Peace" dealing with climate change impacts on fragile states. In the area of energy policy, he currently deals with the interrelation-ship of energy transformation, local value creation and jobs.

Dennis Tänzler has been the programme director on the environment, conflict and coopera-tion platform (www.ecc-platform.org) since 2004. He holds masters degrees in Political Science as well as in North American Studies and Cultural Sciences.

Pedro Valenzuela (Colombia) has a B.A. in Political Science from Florida International University (USA) and a PhD in Peace and Conflict Research from Uppsala University, Sweden. He is a full professor at the School of Political Science and International Relations, Pontificia Universidad Javeriana, Bogotá. Dr. Valenzuela founded and directed on two occasions the first graduate program in conflict resolution in his native country, and has also been director of the Institute of Human Rights at Javeriana University. He has been a guest teacher/researcher in several European (Sweden, Norway, the Netherlands, Spain) and Latin American (Mexico,

Guatemala, Colombia, Ecuador, Peru, Chile, Argentina) universities. He has also been involved in dialogues leading to negotiations with some of the actors of the internal armed conflict in Colombia. His areas of research include peacebuilding and reconciliation at the grassroots level, comparative peace processes, and nonviolent resistance.

Stacy D. VanDeveer is professor and program director of the PhD program in Global Governance and Human Security in the McCormack Graduate School of Policy and Global Studies at the University of Massachusetts, Boston. His research interests include EU environmental and energy politics, global environmental policymaking and institutions, comparative environmental politics, connections between environmental and security issues, the roles of expertise in policymaking, and the global politics of resources and consumption. In addition to authoring and co-authoring almost 100 articles, book chapters, working papers and reports, he has co-edited or co-authored ten books.

Maria Vink works at the Stockholm International Water Institute (SIWI) as acting director of the Transboundary Water Management Unit. Maria has over 20 years of experience in the field of transboundary water management, water diplomacy and water supply, and of carrying out diplomatic work, programme management and facilitation of multi-stakeholder dialogues. She has worked in Sweden, Africa and Southeast Asia, and in particular in Southern and Eastern Africa. Previously, Maria has worked at the Swedish International Development Cooperation Agency (Sida) and served as a Swedish diplomat. Between 2011 and 2015 she was Deputy Head of Section for Regional Development Cooperation in Africa, based at the Swedish Embassy in Kenya, and during 2003–2008 she was stationed at the Swedish Embassy in Mozambique, responsible for coordination of programmes on Economic Development and Natural Resources Management. As water policy advisor at the European Commission DG Development between 2008 and 2011, her work focused on advancing the EU's policies in relation to water and development, on representing the EU in international settings and on the conceptual development of the EU Water Initiative, the Africa EU Infrastructure Partnership and the Africa Caribbean Pacific–EU Water Facility. Maria has a M.Sc. in Chemical and Environmental Engineering from the Royal Institute of Technology in Stockholm and, after finishing her M.Sc. thesis in Zimbabwe, she worked as advisor to Swedish municipalities at the Swedish Water & Wastewater Association.

Colin Walch is a post-doctoral researcher at the University of California, Berkeley, and an assistant professor at the Department of Peace and Conflict Research, Uppsala University. He is also a research affiliate at Centre of Natural Hazards and Disaster Science (CNDS). His work focuses on disaster management in situations of armed conflict and fragility, the links between climate change and conflict, environmental peacebuilding and international negotiation. He has conducted field research in Mali, Philippines, Myanmar, and India, and previously worked for various NGOs in Liberia and Colombia. His work has been published in *Political Geography*, *Journal of Peace Research*, *Nature Climate Change*, *International Negotiation* and other policy outlets such as the Wilson Center, the Social Science Research Council and *Humanitarian Exchange Magazine* of the Overseas Development Institute (ODI).

Erika Weinthal is the Lee Hill Snowdon Professor of Environmental Policy at the Nicholas School of the Environment at Duke University. Dr. Weinthal has a secondary appointment in the Sanford School of Public Policy, Duke University, and in the Environment Program at Duke Kunshan University, China. She received her Ph.D. in Political Science from Columbia

University. She specializes in global environmental politics with an emphasis on water and energy. Her book, *State Making and Environmental Cooperation: Linking Domestic Politics and International Politics in Central Asia* (2002), was the recipient of the 2003 Chadwick Alger Prize and the 2003 Lynton Keith Caldwell Prize. She has co-authored *Oil is not a Curse: Ownership Structure and Institutions in Soviet Successor States* (2010) and co-edited *Water and Post-Conflict Peacebuilding: Shoring Up Peace* (2014). Her forthcoming book is the co-edited *Oxford Handbook on Water Politics and Policy* (2018). She is a member of the UNEP Expert Group on Conflict and Peacebuilding. At Duke University, she is a member of the Bass Society of Fellows, and she chairs the Global Priorities Committee. Dr. Weinthal is an editor at the journal, *Global Environmental Politics*.

Sofia Yazykova is a staff attorney at the Environmental Law Institute. She has worked on projects related to international environmental law, climate change adaptation, environmental displacement, environmental migration, ocean resource management, marine spatial planning, marine protected areas, and marine litter. She holds a JD from Vermont Law School and is a member of the District of Columbia Bar.

Preface and acknowledgements

Immediately after the end of the Cold War in Europe, several studies started to point out with the help of case studies that environmental stress is one main catalyst that creates societal insecurities, which end up in creating conflicts. This argument receives increasing attention and support in the ongoing debate on climate change and its effects on conflicts. Notwithstanding the large volume of research on the relationship of environmental factors and armed conflict, the causality is not as direct as it was thought at the outset. However, there is no debate over the importance of the state of the environment in having a comprehensive security framework. Emerging as a critique of the one-sided research focus on environmental conflict in the 1990s, it is being argued that the link between resource scarcity and environmental conflict should not be seen as deterministic. There is now significant ongoing scholarship on cooperation over the management of scarce renewable resources. Human agency could see the rise of cooperative solutions even when natural resources are scarce.

The recognition that environmental resources constitute potential pathways for cooperation also leads to its significance in the consolidation of peace in post-conflict societies. Since the end of the Cold War, the international community has been increasingly adopting peacebuilding as strategy for addressing the problems of post-conflict societies. The emerging argument in peacebuilding is that taking environmental issues into post-conflict peacebuilding policies will contribute to sustainable peace. Decisions about the restoration, management, and protection of natural resources are considered to have vital consequences for short-term stability, long-term sustainable development, and hence successful peacebuilding. Environmental resources can contribute to peacebuilding through economic development and sustainable livelihoods, while cooperation over their management can also serve as an effective platform or catalyst for enhancing dialogue, building confidence, utilising shared interests and broadening cooperation between segmented and conflicting groups.

At present, there is not a single published book that deals comprehensively with this increasingly important and rapidly growing research field. Moreover, there is no handbook as such, which could serve as a comprehensive resource for policy makers and students/researchers alike. The aim of this handbook is to serve as a single and reliable reference on the topic. Besides a comprehensive introductory chapter by us, the handbook contains 22 chapters written by world-class researchers in the subject. We are extremely thankful to all the chapter authors for adhering to a tight deadline in contributing to this handbook and in responding to various queries and comments.

Several chapters were discussed in two panels organized for this handbook at the Annual Convention of International Studies Association, Baltimore, USA, 22–25 February 2017. A number of authors had also participated in the Presidential Theme Panel to debate on 'Environmental Peace' in the same convention. We would like to sincerely thank the discussants and participants of these panels for their comments and suggestions to improve the chapters of the handbook.

We are indebted to Barbara M. Teixeira and Jenna Faustino for their skilled research assistance to prepare the final manuscript. Deep appreciation goes to Annabelle Harris, Editor–Environment and Sustainability of Routledge and her editorial assistant Matt Shobbrook for having guided us through the review and editing processes and overseen the publication of this handbook. Finally, special and sincere thanks go to our respective families.

Environmental conflict and peacebuilding

An introduction

Ashok Swain and Joakim Öjendal

The past two decades have witnessed the production of a large body of research work examining the linkage between environmental scarcity, violent conflict, and cooperation. The growing threat of global climate change has also added strength to this area of academic investigation. However, this environmental security polemic is still trying to deliver a well-defined approach to achieving peace. Studies are being undertaken to find the precise pathways by which cooperative actions are expected not only to pre-empt or moderate resource conflicts but also to help diffuse cooperative behavior to other disputed issues. To date there has not been a comprehensive volume covering environmental conflict and peacebuilding. This handbook aims to rectify that by providing a state-of-the-art review of research on how utilization of environmental resources can cause conflicts and how it can be a catalyst for cooperation and peacebuilding.

The problem addressed in this handbook is anything but trivial. On the one hand, the struggle for limited resources is an age-old cause for conflict, on the other, civilizations and societies are built on cooperation over the same limited resources. Obviously, causality on environmental scarcities and the making of peace goes in both directions. As such the interconnection – and indeed the entire field – remains under-conceptualized and overly complex. This handbook recognizes this complexity and aims to make an inventory of issues and findings in the contemporary research in this field. As such it covers a broad section of views, findings, and experiences on the relation between environmental resources and conflict.

In addition to the issue of causality between environmental stress and conflict and how a limited set of actors approach this rivalry over scarce resources, the issue of limited resources has recently taken on global dimensions through overall unsustainability, global climate change, and the volatility of some particularly scarce and critical resources (such as water, forest, and energy). Thus, there is a now a global and collective concern on how to safeguard access to critical resources and to deal with global climate change. This is a historically qualitatively new dimension to the field of environmental studies. In conflict terms, this global dimension can be seen as a conflict multiplier creating a complex web of interests, rivalries, and vulnerabilities. The unsustainability of contemporary global resource utilization and the accelerating global climate change indicate that there will be severe environmentally related impacts that will increase overall risks and vulnerabilities with distinct actors and areas being particularly jeopardized. Hence security issues have entered the environmental field.

Traditionally, security has been typically defined by threats which challenge it. This attitude has kept the focus of security away from non-military threats that promise to undermine the stability of many countries in the coming years. Trans-boundary environmental issues are gradually beginning to challenge the sacred boundaries of national sovereignty. The end of the Cold War also provided a new opportunity to attain an effective global security system that can address the broader needs of security for the human population and the planet. Global security is only partly dependent upon military power. Environmental stress is one of the major elements among many political, economic, and social factors that contribute to instability and conflict. The global challenges mentioned above have increasingly shown that environmental issues need to be given higher priority.

As Conca and Dabelko argued already in 1998, the global environmental debate rapidly in the post-Cold War period started focusing on "not only economic issues of welfare, production, and livelihood but also political questions of international conflict, violence and geopolitics." For good reasons, this probed the conflictual dimension of environmental changes. Every year, the world population is increasing by 78 million, roughly the equivalent of another Germany. The world population is projected to reach 10 billion around the year 2050. While population growth has stagnated in the industrialized world, it is still extremely high in many developing countries of the South, where more than 90 percent of population growth takes place. Research has found population growth pressure to have a significant impact on the likelihood of a state becoming involved in interstate military conflicts (Swain 2012). It might, however, be a matter of debate whether the population growth directly affects the decision-making of the state to go to war or not (Urdal 2005), but it undoubtedly generates scarcity of resources in developing countries.

Availability of renewable natural resources is increasingly falling short of meeting human needs. The future predictions on population growth and economic activities have brought a distinct possibility of severely crippling the natural resource base on which human beings are dependent for survival. The decline in agriculture, desertification, decreasing green cover, freshwater scarcity, and extinction of species threaten the life and survival of present and future generations. Hence the interconnections between the global environmental resources, security, and violent conflict is a field of growing concern, locally, regionally, and globally.

In the next section we will review the debate on causality between violent conflict and environmental stress (and vice versa), followed by discussions on whether increasing scarcity and accelerating global climate change act as a conflict multiplier or rather as a mechanism for increased cooperation – the latter putting focus on how peacebuilding could be performed in order to trigger this rather than the former which is also discussed.

Violent conflict and environmental stress

Destruction of the environment is commonly seen as a repercussion of violent conflict or conflict-induced migration. Many studies in the post-Second World War period have focused on the environmental consequences of warfare.

Besides the direct adverse effects of conflict on the environment, it is also true that, in some cases, environmental change is carried out as the deliberate objective in conflict rather than being an unwanted by-product. Even in the time of 'peace,' the military preparedness heavily contributes to resource depletion and environmental destruction. The production, testing, and maintenance of conventional, chemical, biological, and nuclear weapons procreate vast amounts of toxic and radioactive substances, which contaminate soil, air, and water (Leaning 2000).

Besides major wars and their preparations, internal civil wars are also a major contributing factor to global environmental destruction (Gurses 2012). Large-scale environmental destruction has taken place in most parts of Africa, South Asia, and Central America, due to the presence of civil wars in those regions. This is not only a direct impact of warfare but also a result of more complicated connections: for instance, internal violence makes it impossible to develop sustainable agriculture; it leads to massive deforestation and the destruction of wildlife.

Refugee movement is the direct product of political conflicts and its consequences extend beyond the actors involved in the conflict (Swain & Jägerskog 2016). There are more than 21 million people recognized as refugees in the world today. Mentioning the most familiar cases, they originate from Syria, Afghanistan, Iraq, Palestine, Somalia, Burundi, Sri Lanka, Sudan, Western Sahara, Vietnam, Myanmar, and the former Yugoslavia. In most cases, they have moved to their poor neighboring countries. The pressure created by the presence of refugees in receiving countries can be considerable. Aside from their potential threat to the social, economic and political fabric of the host state and society, they can also be a major source of environmental destruction in the areas of their resettlement (Swain & Jägerskog 2016).

The poorest people in society are relatively more dependent for their livelihood on renewable resources and are less capable of following conservation procedures. Refugees, generally belonging to this category of society, are more likely to cause environmental destruction than others. Their uncertain residential status, lack of land ownership and desire to return to their native place reduce their incentive to protect the environment in which they unwillingly find themselves. The refugees' consumption of resources coupled with their unfamiliarity with the local ecosystem often multiplies the harm to the local environment. Three types of environmental destruction are associated with the refugees: deforestation, land degradation, and water pollution (Swain 2012). While the number of international conflicts has been reduced in the past few years, the world is now witnessing an increase of internal conflicts, e.g., civil wars, ethnic conflicts, etc. As a result, the number of refugee movements has increased and simultaneously amplified the threat to the environment in the regions of their settlement.

Environmental stress and violent conflicts

Environmental destruction, while not immediately intuitive, can also be the cause and not merely the consequence or premeditated consequence of violent conflicts. In the last decade, findings of several major research projects have proved that environmental scarcities are already contributing to violent conflicts, particularly in the developing world. Applying different methodologies and studying disparate cases, all these research efforts have tried to establish the conflict-inducing potential of environmental scarcity.

Environmental changes have drastically reduced the availability of cultivable land, green forests, freshwater, clean air, and fish resources. The effects of this reduction are becoming more acute due to the increasing demand for resources to meet the needs of a growing population, and changing consumption behavior. Conflicts over renewable natural resources have grown more potent as demand for essential commodities increases day by day and as the supply-side looks more and more insecure. Most states depend greatly on renewable resources – soil, water, fish, and forests – that sustain much of their economic activity. When one state works for 'development' by acquiring or exploiting more than its share of these resources, it often affects the interests of other states. Conflicts over renewable resources have already shown their presence in most parts of the world.

Besides fisheries, river water resources have the massive potential of bringing various state actors into a conflictual situation. Almost all the major river systems, which are the paramount suppliers of water to mankind, are shared by more than one state. When multiple countries are jointly dependent on the same river systems, upstream withdrawal, damming and pollution may lead to conflict with downstream countries. There are many interstate conflicts active among the users of international river basins in different parts of the world. Climate change has raised the specter of further flow variation in these rivers, raising the possibilities for further hostility between the disputing riparian countries (Swain 2004).

Threats to basic food supplies of a country have become cause for friction and tensions between countries in the past. Trade embargoes and other forms of political manipulation have been used to get access to food supplies. Due to the increasing loss of arable land in some countries, food production may substantially decline. Under conditions of a changing climate and growing population, the situation may become even more severe. Many developing countries spend more than half of their income on food, which makes them more vulnerable to increased food prices due to production shortfalls. Thus, changes in productivity of major grain importers and exporters may provoke international tensions and conflict (Swain 2012).

Not only scarcity of environmental resources, but also environmentally induced population migration is becoming a source of international conflicts. The loss of living space and source of livelihood due to environmental change could force the affected people to migrate. Environmental changes have already forced a large number of people to move across international borders. This phenomenon has been one of the growing concerns of the international community for some time. Arguably the mass movement of populations may create security concerns for a nation-state. Trans-border environmental migration has several conflict-inducing characteristics between the receiver and sender states (Swain 1996).

There have been several instances of intra-state armed conflict over scarce natural resources. But, armed conflict is not the only logical ending of environmental scarcity. Obviously, many different forms of action may follow from the moment environmental destruction occurs: debate, demonstrations, out-migration, action to remedy the damage, halting or eliminating the sources of destruction, as well as serious conflicts (Wallensteen & Swain 1997b). It might be argued, however, that a government's response is more determining than many other factors. In most of the cases, environmentally induced conflict typically ends with highly generalized recommendations for environmental cooperation, but primarily there is a lack of careful analysis of the specific mechanisms or pathways by which cooperation could be expected to forestall or mitigate conflict (Conca & Dabelko 2002).

Global climate change – an environmental conflict multiplier or process for triggering cooperation?

Several studies show that environmental stress is one main catalyst that creates societal insecurity that may result in conflict (Swain 1993; Gleditsch 1998; Homer-Dixon 2001; Machlis & Hanson 2008). Meanwhile, the relationship between climate change and armed conflict receives more and more attention. It is often assumed that climate change will intensify environmental stress and might even create new conflicts (Salehyan 2008; Lee 2009; Swain 2015).

Climate change is a global environmental problem caused by the build-up of greenhouse gases, particularly carbon dioxide and methane, in the Earth's atmosphere. The world is warming up faster than at any time in the previous 10,000 years. The predicted dramatic sea level rise caused by this climatic change may deprive millions of people of their living space and source of livelihood in the near future. The Inter-Governmental Panel on Climate Change (IPCC) has predicted that sea levels could rise an average rate of 6 centimeters per decade over the next century. A rise of this magnitude will no doubt threaten the densely populated low-lying countries and coastal zones in different parts of the world. Among other foreseeable impacts are increases in tropical cyclones. Increased cyclones would also enhance the risk of coastal flooding.

Climate change can also potentially alter the typical rainfall pattern, which may lead to increased flooding, drought and soil erosion in tropical and arid regions of the world.

The issue of climate change is high on the world's policy agenda at present. Agricultural production may become highly vulnerable to climate change, given the other multiple stresses that affect food systems in the South. Response to climate change can also affect particular societies' cultural norms and social practices related to food production. Moreover, some states and societies are better at formulating adaptation strategies for all aspects of land use practices to safeguard them against the negative consequences of climate change. To address the adverse effects of climate change, the effectiveness and coping abilities of existing institutions matter as well.

Climate change can be linked to conflict in various ways. These include: increased competition over reduced/uncertain water supply, increased competition over agricultural land in the face of reduced crop yields, desertification and rising food prices, large-scale migration as a result of sea level and weather changes, and diminished capacity of governments to provide services to their people in the face of increasing poverty (Lee 2009; Swain 2015). While the exact impact of climate change is not known, it is clear that it will not only impact access to shared resources but also overall availability of resources.

While climate change may not be the sole cause of conflict or large-scale population migration, it is considered a threat multiplier (Raleigh, Jordan, & Salehyan, 2008). Social, economic, and political factors will also affect the vulnerability or resilience of communities. In Africa, the ability to cope with climate change decreases, and the likelihood of conflict increases, as a result of factors that include: poverty, low levels of education/literacy, lack of skills, weak institutions, limited infrastructure, lack of technology and information, limited access to healthcare, poor access to resources, over-exploitation of resources, etc. Climate change is likely to exacerbate many of these problems.

Environmental stress exacerbated by global climate change may reduce the availability of natural renewable resources for human consumption. This resource scarcity can potentially cause competition among various groups in society, which may lead to conflicts. Moreover, environmentally induced resource scarcity might also lead to the loss of land or other basic needs that are requisite for survival, which may force the affected population to migrate.

To date studies that have been published in the field of environmental security have typically emphasized the emergence of conflict. However, scarcity could also provide valid explanations for cooperation. As resources dwindle, parties and groups may come to appreciate the necessity of pooling resources, rather than risking their destruction in a serious conflict. Thus, it has been argued that a number of the greatest civilizations have emerged to safeguard joint control over river water for irrigation, drinking, transportation, and production. Dynamic cultures have grown across river resources, like the Indus, Nile, and Euphrates. Thus, water also brings people together. Better use of water, as well as the need to control water, is an important input in joint human construction. Presently, there have been a number of individual cases where there are cooperative arrangements for the better use of available water resources (Wallensteen & Swain 1997a; Earle et al. 2015). Thus it has been logically compelling to ask why such aspects have been more or less absent from research. A major shift of focus is needed from environmentally induced conflict to environmentally induced peace.

Human survival has always depended on the ability to handle challenges and find solutions, more than simply fighting wars, defeating peoples and conquering territory. In fact, such behavior can help to address problems presently confronting humankind on a global scale. Thus, it is pertinent to ask, not only whether humans can cooperate, but also, *under what conditions* cooperative human behavior might appear. If environmental stress can lead to conflict, it can also bring cooperation. By realizing the dangers and threats of environmental scarcity, groups and countries may come together and collaborate in pursuit of a common goal. Cooperation is an interactive process, which turns a situation from potentially destructive conflict into a productive one. Cooperation does not only mean that there is an absence of conflict, but it also implies that there is a mutual will to address the conflict through communicative and peaceful means. In other words, cooperation generates willingness among the parties to think creatively about their problems, consider mutual problem-solving mechanisms, and negotiate commitments.

A nation-state is not capable of solving alone many of the environmental problems that it faces. It cannot prevent the destruction of the ozone layer, arrest the adverse effects of greenhouse gases, save endangered species, or even deal with some of its local environmental scarcities on its own. Air pollution, acid rain, water pollution and scarcity in international rivers are transboundary environmental problems that require a higher-level approach to deal with them, be it regional or global. Thus, a wide range of environmental issues requires nothing short of global cooperation (Swain 2012).

Environmental problems have created strong incentives for countries to come together at the global level. The past few decades have seen an explosion of international environmental agreements, ranging from narrow bilateral accords to ambitious attempts at global governance. There is an intensive effort taking place to negotiate international conventions that will handle many of the environmental challenges: at Earth Summit in 1992, the conventions on desertification in 1994, a protocol on Climate Change and convention on international freshwater sharing in 1997. Some of these conferences have resulted on the building of new international institutions.

The 1972 United Nations Conference on the Human Environment, which was held in Stockholm, placed the environment as a whole on the UN agenda. The same year, the UN General Assembly decided to establish the United Nations Environment Programme (UNEP) in Nairobi, Kenya, to encourage and coordinate environmental initiatives among member states and international organizations. UNEP analyzes the state of the global environment and assesses global and regional environmental trends – providing policy advice and early warning information on environmental threats, and promoting international cooperation and action based on the best scientific and technical capabilities available.

Following the Stockholm Conference, a number of international conferences were held in the 1970s under the auspices of the UN to address population, food, water, and housing problems. During and after the Stockholm Conference developed countries displayed a particularly increased interest for environmental issues. This brought suspicion to the minds of many developing countries as they thought the environmental concern might hamper their quest for economic development. The views of developing countries on global environmental issues are dominated by their desire for economic growth and fear of environmental protection costs. International initiatives to build global regimes on ozone depletion, climate change, loss of biodiversity, and conservation of endangered species are regarded by many developing countries as the Northern agenda. The environmental priorities of the developed countries are different: air pollution, scarcity of clean water, desertification of agricultural land, and toxic contamination. However, for most developing countries, economic growth, employment, and overcoming poverty have been the dominant concerns.

To address the doubts of developing countries regarding the UN's environmental initiatives, the UN established the World Commission on Environment and Development. The report of the Brundtland Commission became an intellectual guide for the proceedings at the 1992 United Conference on Environment and Development, held in Rio de Janeiro, 20 years after the Stockholm Conference. The Rio Conference, popularly called the Earth Summit, was attended by representatives from 178 nations. The Earth Summit and its resulting Agenda 21 stressed that achieving the global agenda of environmental sustainability requires the participation of developing countries as well as industrial nations, and that the North must play a major role in funding investments in sustainable development. Agenda 21 also entrusted particular responsibility to the United Nations system to pursue the idea of sustainable development. As a follow-up, the UN General Assembly, in a resolution in December 1992, created the Commission on Sustainable Development (CSD) to implement Agenda 21.

Since the Earth Summit, the Global Environment Facility (GEF) has become the primary institution through which financial support is provided to developing countries to undertake sustainable development projects. GEF was created in 1990 to provide funds to developing countries to support their environmental projects, which would bring an overall benefit to the globe. It did not provide any support to address localized environmental problems in developing countries. This tri-agency fund brought together the UNEP, United Nations Development Programme (UNDP), and World Bank and it was operated by a combination of grant-aid and low-interest loans.

GEF focuses its attentions upon political barriers that otherwise restrict international environmental cooperation. The South along with a number of nongovernmental organizations (NGOs) have a major input in its decision-making compared to their role in other Bretton Woods institutions. Continuing efforts of the international community since the Stockholm Conference have facilitated some cooperation among countries to address global environmental concerns. However, it has been largely effective in brokering the Paris Agreement in 2015 to manage climate change, which is undoubtedly the worst environmental problem confronting humanity at the present time. The outcome of international efforts through a series of UN-sponsored conferences to manage climate change at the global level has been both effective and ineffective. These conferences have raised global awareness and a generalized commitment to strive for environmentally sustainable development and limiting climate change.

The global community needs to move fast to translate concern for the environment into greater global cooperation. To transform concern to action, there is a need to strengthen international institutions, which possess the capacity to make binding decisions. It is also true that most developing countries are sensitive about compromising their sovereignty for global environmental issues, fearing that they will force a limit to their freedom to determine their own development strategies. To get the support of the South, the developed world should show real concern and undertake several concrete actions to build mutual trust and confidence (Grugel & Hammett 2016).

The serious threat of climate change makes a strong case for increasing international cooperation on environment and development matters. International relations have become significantly more global and interwoven since the beginning of the twenty-first century. The crude power of a state is no longer enough to meet the present challenges. Security defined in military terms is no longer a formula for prosperity and peace. The global environmental challenges affecting world security in this century, such as climate change, desertification, scarcity of clean water, food security, and prospects of massive environmental migration, need global solutions not ill-prescribed state attempts. Nation-states' efforts to address these threats will not succeed without being supported by cooperative action at the international level. The multidimensional nature of climate change and global environmental stress demands that an integrated approach be adopted.

Scrutinizing the literature on cooperation theory in international relations (Haas 1964; Keohane 1984; Nye & Welch 2012) and social capital theory in development studies (Putnam 2004; Swain 2010), it is not difficult to find a strong argument for the general proposition that cooperation over environmental resources between rivaling states can have positive spin-offs for peace in other contentious areas.

There are two pathways for peacemaking over environmental resources. The first path involves transforming the more immediate problems of mistrust, uncertainty, suspicion, divergent interests, and short time horizons that typically accompany conflictual situations. A second pathway, consistent with the broader understanding of peace as the unimaginability of violent conflict, focuses less on narrow, short-term interstate dynamics and more on the broader pattern of trans-societal relations. In other words, cooperation would be pursued as an objective in itself, diffusing from environmental resource across other areas of international interaction. Such "spill-over" advantages of environmentally induced cooperation have been witnessed in different parts of the world (Conca & Wallace 2009; Jensen & Lonergan 2012).

However, there is still a dearth of serious empirical research scrutinizing the types of institutional structures and cooperative approaches that might embody this theoretical potential, particularly at the bilateral level. We are aware that disputing states after signing the resource-sharing agreement might not be genuinely interested in pursuing sustainable resource management policies rooted in environmental and social justice. Rather, their newly acquired rights and legitimacy might simply yield more effective resource exploitation.

Understandably, environmental cooperation does not transpire easily, nor will it have spontaneous peace-diffusing effects when it does take place. Furthermore, the strengthening of state capacity and increased interstate interaction might not always lead to the transformation of state institutions allowing better bilateral relations. In this context, the form of resource-sharing cooperation between disputing states and the way of arriving at it will have significant influence on its peace-diffusing character.

Environmental cooperation may transform mistrust and suspicion among groups to bring opportunities for shared gains and establish a pattern of reciprocity. It can also pave the way for greater interaction, interdependence, and societal linkages. Does environmental cooperation always provide peace-enhancing effects? It is possible that national sovereignty and self-interest maximizing actors may act as obstacles to the appropriate evolution of environmental cooperation. However, if the stakes are so high, which is the case with many environmental problems, then the logic of cooperation might alter the existing relationship. The diffusion of bilateral cooperation from land and water resources to other areas is being regularly cited in the literature, which supports the environmentally induced peace approach. Establishing a bilateral commitment to share or protect the environment can help to overcome the existing mistrust or suspicion between two disputing countries, and create a milieu of reciprocal gains and estimation of national interests on a long-term basis. Cooperation on environmental issues may also bring people together resulting in trans-border civil society linkages and the building of norms of joint responsibility and bilateral cooperation.

Environmental peacebuilding

Since the end of the Cold War, the international community has been increasingly adopting peacebuilding as strategy for addressing the problems of post-conflict societies (Chandler 2010; Aggestam & Björkdahl 2013). Influenced by 'Democratic Peace' theory, the peacebuilding consensus assumes that liberally constituted societies are more peaceful; thus, the liberal peace has become a guiding norm in reconstructing societies (Mac Ginty 2006; Mandelbaum 2002). In this context, strengthening state capacity, the facilitation of democratic elections and a market economy, and the promotion of human rights, justice, good governance and civil society in post-conflict societies have become the foundations of the international community's intervention in conflict-ridden societies (Paris 2004; Richmond 2004; Öjendal et al. 2015). Several proponents of this technocratic approach claim that these policies are pursued in order to 'build peace' and 'alleviate human suffering' (Paris 2010; Swain 2016).

In recent years, critics have questioned the practice of liberal peacebuilding on different grounds. Some scholars question the normative assumptions of liberal peacebuilding (Duffield 2007; Swain 2012), seeing it as illiberal, hegemonic, and expansionist behavior of the West. Recently, the outcome of this external interventionism is being described as a hybrid peace that emerges in situations when external and domestic actors engage with each other within externally imposed frameworks (Richmond 2011; cf. Öjendal & Ou 2016). The positivist critique, while subscribing to the overall 'idea' of the liberal peace strategy, is concerned with problems of its implementation and outcomes and focuses on improving policy solutions that make up the strategy. Some prominent suggestions include: focusing on institution-building before allowing electoral competition in order to overcome societal divisions (Paris 2004); facilitating coordination among stakeholders (Paris & Sisk 2009); effective reforming of the security sector (Nilsson 2008), formulating a new constitution (Samuels 2009); and bringing balance in international and local participation in liberal peacebuilding projects (Richmond 2009). In recent years, the debate has shifted beyond hybridity. Some studies point out the resilience of local responses and strategies to external impositions of ideas and order (Hughes, Öjendal, & Schierenbeck, 2015). There have also been attempts in understanding the alternative spaces where locally driven peace is established outside the externally determined formal frameworks (Björkdahl & Höglund 2013). Undoubtedly, over the past two decades peacebuilding strategy and our understanding of what peace may entail have evolved into new concepts and operations. But have they been able to achieve the principal objectives, i.e., to prevent the start or resumption of violent conflict by creating a sustainable foundation for peace?

Peacebuilding strategies cannot eradicate all of the root causes of violent conflict. However, as Matthew (2014) points out, they now primarily aim at identifying and delivering the technical and non-technical capacities that a post-conflict country lacks and that are needed as the platform for recovery, stability, and sustainable development. In spite of learning and evolution, peacebuilding in post-conflict societies still fails to a large extent (Paris 2004; Swain & Krampe 2011; Mac Ginty & Sanghera 2013) due to narrowly defined development goals and the neglect of sustainability during post-conflict reconstruction. Peacebuilding strategies today are dominated by a neoliberal agenda that favors situational short-term economic growth solutions over long-term environmental and resource availability concerns. The significant overlap between countries with heightened vulnerability to resource availability and countries coming out of war provides a prima facie case for suggesting that integrating environment in peacebuilding activities might be prioritized. There can be no durable and sustainable peace if natural resources that sustain livelihoods and the ecosystem are destroyed or degraded (Brown 2013). Analysis of intrastate conflicts over the past six decades suggests that conflicts associated with natural resources are twice as likely to revert to conflict in the first five years. Nevertheless, less than a quarter of peace negotiations aiming to settle conflicts linked to natural resources have addressed resource management mechanisms (Binningsbø & Rustad 2008). This is highly surprising and a state of affairs that is not satisfactory.

Machlis and Hanson (2008: 734) see that the governance of environmental resources at the core of post-war efforts, "could help avert resource conflicts, reduce degradation of war-dominated ecosystems, and increase postwar restoration of ecosystem services, thereby encouraging peace and security." Environmental resources bear the potential for a swift economic recovery, while equally being considered triggers for conflicts if not managed smartly (Lujala & Rustad 2012). Jensen and Lonergan (2012: 9) conclude from over 20 case studies that "integrating natural resource management and environmental sustainability into peacebuilding" is the way to avert uncontrolled exploitation in the aftermath of conflict. The emerging argument in peacebuilding is that taking environmental issues into post-conflict peacebuilding policies will contribute to sustainable peace.

Decisions about the restoration, management, and protection of natural resources are considered to have vital consequences for short-term stability, long-term sustainable development, and successful peacebuilding (Jensen & Lonergan, 2012). However, political success of post-conflict reconstruction interventions and subsequent peacebuilding invariably lead to crude exploitation of natural resources, unsustainable environmental practices, and massive threat to resource-based local livelihoods. In fact, it would be hard to find even a single case among the several dozens of cases since the end of the Cold War where intervention followed by liberalization and (typically shallow) democratization have not produced a period of drastic resource exploitation, often driven by, and to the benefit of, external actors (Jensen & Lonergan 2012).

So, repeatedly, peace agreements, post-conflict reconstruction, and peacebuilding at large are pursued from short-term urgency, producing long-term unsustainability. Every state, including the ones recovering from a period of violent conflict, needs to both use and protect its vital natural resources such as water, land, and forest. The recognition that these environmental resources can contribute to the re-emergence of violent conflict accentuates the imperative of addressing the resource curse of peacebuilding at an early stage and finding strategies, mechanisms, and institutions which can prevent the far too common resource exploitation, environmental degradation, and broken livelihood systems which usually follow (Matthew, Brown, & Jensen 2009).

The structure of the handbook

The handbook contains 22 chapters besides this introductory chapter, which has introduced the concepts and provided an overview of the historical development of research in the field. In Part I, Review of the Concept and Theories, there are five chapters to review the developing theoretical concepts of environmental conflicts and cooperation, challenges of global climate change, and the environmental peacebuilding. Chapter 2 by James R. Lee examines the evolution of the environmental conflict as an area of research, while Peter Stoett's chapter (3) examines the importance of transnational environmental crime as an important environmental security threat. Simon Dalby in Chapter 4 discusses the global climate change and its implications for present and future environmental conflicts. Ken Conca and Michael D. Beevers in Chapter 5 analyze peacemaking potentials of environmental challenges, while Randall Amster's chapter (6) argues that though climate change poses existential threats, it also provides opportunity for environmental peacebuilding.

There are five chapters in Part II, Review of Thematic Approaches, which discusses issues concerning the type of natural resources, climate adaptation, technocratic approach and the role of the international organizations and their contributions to environmental conflicts and peacebuilding. Erika Weinthal and McKenzie Johnson in Chapter 7 examine the role of both renewable and non-renewable resources in contributing to different phases of the environmental conflict cycle and peacebuilding. Chapter 8 by Karin Aggestam critically analyzes the depoliticization of water resources and the preferred technocratic approach to use it for peacebuilding purposes. Richard A. Matthew's chapter (9) examines how and why climate change adaptation should be integrated into peacebuilding. David Jensen and Amanda Kron in their chapter (10) explore numerous entry points provided by natural resources for addressing risks and opportunities in conflict-affected environments, and highlight some of the ways in which the United Nations can contribute to peacebuilding at the local level. Chapter 11 by Peter Aldinger, Carl

Bruch, and Sofia Yazykova carefully analyzes the environmental and natural resources provisions in the UN Security Council Resolutions from 1946 to 2016.

Part III, Case Studies, carries seven chapters. While Tobias Ide, Vakur Sümer, and Larissa M. Aldehoff in their chapter (12) discuss environmental peacebuilding in the Middle East region, Hannah Moosa's chapter (13) analyzes environmental peacebuilding in Iraq and Anders Jägerskog's chapter (14) critically examines environmental peacebuilding through water cooperation in the Jordan basin. Michael D. Beevers's chapter (15) discusses environmental peacebuilding in Liberia; Florian Krampe's chapter (16) examines environmental peacebuilding from studying Nepal's micro-hydropower projects; Pedro Valenzuela and Servio Caicedo's chapter (17) discusses potential positive contributions of the 2016 Accord to address environmental problems in Colombia; and Colin Walch's chapter (18) is on how natural resource management has been a source of conflict and peace in the Philippines.

The final part of the handbook, Analytical Challenges and Future-oriented Perspectives, contains five chapters. Timothy Adivilah Balag'kutu, Jeremiah O. Asaka, Linda Holcombe, Jason J. McSparren, and Stacy D. VanDeveer in Chapter 19, through studying Kenya, suggest that there are many existing governance initiatives at local and other scales clearly engaging resource cooperation and institution-building which might teach us a lot about environmental peacebuilding across contexts. Maria Vink's chapter (20) explores the link between water diplomacy and peacebuilding; Dennis Tänzler's chapter (21) investigates how climate diplomacy can contribute to peace, while Saleem H. Ali and Rebecca Pincus in Chapter 22 examine the role of the military in conservation and peacebuilding. In the final chapter (23), Larry Swatuk critically reviews the potentials of environmental resource governance to achieve peace.

In all, we hope, these chapters will contribute to a comprehensive handbook that will remedy the neglect this field has hitherto experienced.

References

Aggestam, K. & Björkdahl, A. (2013) *Rethinking Peacebuilding: The Quest for Peace in the Middle East and the Western Balkans*, Routledge, New York.

Binningsbø, H. & Rustad, S. A. (2008) Resource Conflicts, Resource Management and Post-conflict Peace, PRIO working paper, Oslo.

Björkdahl, A. & Höglund, K. (2013) Precarious Peacebuilding: Friction in Global–Local Encounters, *Peacebuilding* 1(3): 289–299.

Brown, O. (2013) Encouraging Peacebuilding through Better Environmental and Natural Resource Management, Chatham House Briefing Paper, London.

Chandler, D. (ed.) (2010) *International Statebuilding*, Routledge, Abingdon.

Conca, Ken & Dabelko, Geoffrey D. (eds.) (1998) *Green Planet Blues: Environmental Politics from Stockholm to Kyoto*, Westview Press, Boulder, CO.

Conca, Ken & Dabelko, Geoffrey D. (eds.) (2002) *Environmental Peacemaking*, Johns Hopkins University Press, Baltimore.

Conca, Ken & Wallace, J. (2009) Environment and Peacebuilding in War-torn Societies, *Global Governance* 15(4): 485–504.

Duffield, M. (2007) *Development, Security and Unending War*, Polity Press, London.

Earle, Anton, Cascao, Ana Elise, Hansson, Stina, Jägerskog, Anders, Swain, Ashok, & Öjendal, Joakim. (2015) *Transboundary Water Management and the Climate Change Debate*, Routledge, London.

Gleditsch, Nils Petter. (1998) Armed Conflict and the Environment: A Critique of the Literature, *Journal of Peace Research* 35(3).

Grugel, Jean & Hammett, Daniel. (eds.) (2016) *The Palgrave Handbook of International Development*, Palgrave Macmillan, Basingstoke.

Gurses, Mehmet. (2012) Environmental Consequences of Civil War: Evidence from the Kurdish Conflict in Turkey, *Civil Wars* 14(2): 254–271.

Haas, Ernst B. (1964) *Beyond the Nation-State*, Stanford University Press, Stanford, CA.

Homer-Dixon, Thomas F. (2001) *Environment, Scarcity, and Violence*, Princeton University Press, Princeton, NJ.

Hughes, Caroline, Öjendal, Joakim, & Schierenbeck, Isabell. (2015) The Struggle versus the Song – The Local Turn in Peacebuilding: An Introduction, *Third World Quarterly* 36(5): 817–824.

Jensen, D. & Lonergan, S. (eds.) (2012) *Assessing and Restoring Natural Resources in Post-Conflict Peacebuilding*, Routledge, London.

Keohane, Robert O. (1984) *After Hegemony: Cooperation & Discord in the World Political Economy*, Princeton University Press, Princeton, NJ.

Leaning, Jennifer. (2000) Environment and Health: 5 Impacts of War, *Canadian Medical Association Journal* 163(9): 1157–1161.

Lee, James R. (2009) *Climate Change and Armed Conflict. Hot and Cold Wars*, Routledge, London.

Lujala, P. & Rustad, Siri A. (eds.) (2012) *High-Value Natural Resources and Post-Conflict Peacebuilding*, Routledge, London.

Mac Ginty, R. (2006) *No War, No Peace*, Palgrave Macmillan, Basingstoke.

Mac Ginty, R. & Sanghera, G. (2013) Hybridity in Peacebuilding and Development: An Introduction, *Journal of Peacebuilding & Development* 7(2): 3–8.

Machlis, G. E. & Hanson, T. (2008) Warfare Ecology, *BioScience* 58(8): 729–736.

Mandelbaum, M. (2002) *The Ideas that Conquered the World: Peace, Democracy, and Free Markets in the Twenty-first Century*, Public Affairs, New York.

Matthew, R. (2014) Integrating Climate Change into Peacebuilding, *Climatic Change* 123: 83–93.

Matthew, R., Brown, O., & Jensen, D. (eds.) (2009) *From Conflict to Peacebuilding. The Role of Natural Resources and the Environment*, UNEP, Nairobi.

Nilsson, A. (2008) *Dangerous Liaisons: Why Ex-Combatants Return to Violence: Cases from the Republic of Congo and Sierra Leone*. Uppsala: Uppsala University.

Nye Jr., Joseph S. & Welch, David A. (2012) *Understanding Global Conflict and Cooperation: An Introduction to Theory and History*, 9th edn, Pearson, Harlow.

Öjendal, Joakim et al. (eds.) (2015) The 'Local Turn' in Peacebuilding: The Liberal Peace Challenged, *Third World Quarterly*, special issue, June.

Öjendal, Joakim & Sivhuoch Ou. (2016) Statebuilding under Friction: 20 Years of Unfinished Peacebuilding, in A. Bjorkdahl et al. (eds.) *Peacebuilding under Friction*, Routledge, London.

Paris, R. (2004) *At War's End: Building Peace after Civil Conflict*, Cambridge University Press, New York.

Paris, R. (2010) Saving Liberal Peace, *Review of International Studies* 36: 337–365.

Paris, R. & Sisk, T. (eds.) (2009) *The Dilemmas of Statebuilding – Confronting the Contradictions of Postwar Peace Operations*, Routledge, New York.

Putnam, Robert D. (2004) *Democracies in Flux: The Evolution of Social Capital in Contemporary Society*, Oxford University Press, Oxford.

Raleigh, C., Jordan, L., & Salehyan, I. (2008) *Assessing the Impact of Climate Change on Migration and Conflict*, The World Bank, Washington, DC.

Richmond, O. P. (2004) UN Peace Operations and the Dilemmas of the Peacebuilding Consensus, *International Peacekeeping* 11(1): 83–101.

Richmond, O. (2009) Beyond Liberal Peace? Responses to Backsliding, in E. Newman et al. (eds.) *New Perspectives on Liberal Peacebuilding*, UNU Press, New York.

Richmond, O. (2011) *A Post-Liberal Peace*, Routledge, New York.

Salehyan, Idean. (2008) From Climate Change to Conflict? No Consensus Yet, *Journal of Peace Research* 45(3).

Samuels, K. (2009) Postwar Constitution Building: Opportunities and Challenges, in R. Paris & T. Sisk (eds.) *The Dilemmas of Statebuilding*, Routledge, New York.

Swain, Ashok. (1993) *Environment and Conflict: Analysing the Developing World*, Uppsala Universitet, Uppsala.

Swain, Ashok. (1996) Environmental Migration and Conflict Dynamics: Focus on Developing Regions, *Third World Quarterly* 17(5): 959–973.

Swain, Ashok. (2004) *Managing Water Conflict: Asia, Africa and the Middle East*, Routledge, London.

Swain, Ashok. (2010) *Struggle against the State: Social Network and Protest Mobilization in India*, Ashgate, Farnham.

Swain, Ashok. (2012) *Understanding Emerging Security Challenges*, Routledge, London.

Swain, Ashok. (2015) Climate Change: Threat to National Security, in Domonic A. Bearfield & Melvin J. Dubnick (eds.) *Encyclopedia of Public Administration and Public Policy*, 3rd edn, CRC Press, London.

Swain, Ashok. (2016) Water and Post-Conflict Peacebuilding, *Hydrological Science Journal* 16(7): 1313–1322.

Swain, A, & Krampe, F. (2011) Stability and Sustainability in Peace Building: Priority Area for Warfare Ecology, in G. E. Machlis, T. Hanson, Z. Špirić & J. E. Mckendry (eds.) *Warfare Ecology: Synthesis, Priorities and Policy Implications for Peace and Security*, NATO Science for Peace and Security, Springer, New York.

Swain, Ashok & Jägerskog, Anders. (2016) *Emerging Security Threats in the Middle East: The Impact of Climate Change and Globalization*, Rowman & Littlefield, Lanham, MD.

Urdal, Henrik. (2005) People vs. Malthus: Population Pressure, Environmental Degradation, and Armed Conflict Revisited, *Journal of Peace Research* 42(5): 417–434.

Wallensteen, Peter & Swain, Ashok. (1997) *Comprehensive Assessment of the Freshwater Resources of the World, International Fresh Water Resources: Conflict or Cooperation?*, Stockholm Environment Institute, Stockholm.

Wallensteen, Peter & Swain, Ashok. (1997) Environment, Conflict and Cooperation, in Dag Brune, D. V. Chapman, M. D. Gwynne & J. M. Pacyna (eds.) *The Global Environment: Science, Technology and Management, Vol. 2*, VCH, Weinheim, pp. 691–704.

Part I
Review of the concept and theories

2

Environment and conflict

James R. Lee

What is a field and why does it grow?

The rise of any field of learning is often in response to a real problem in society. Medicine evolved to improve human health and speed recovery from ailments. Geography grew in importance as the scope of the human experience expanded. Sociology emerged with the development of civil society and the rise of attendant social problems in rapidly growing urban centers.

"Environmental Conflict" is emerging because violent behavior is increasingly associated with environmental actions, as either cause or effect. This is because environment has loomed larger in terms of importance to society and because conflict too has changed.

First, when most industry was farming, the need for arable land and water was paramount. Such enduring natural factors are renewable resources. Non-renewable resources were often luxuries or reserved for very specific industrial or ceremonial purposes. The role of renewables was far more important at the time.

The importance of non-renewables was occasional. Gold was for wealth and copper was for smelting, particularly in making weaponry. Non-renewable resources are much more important today. Energy issues alone are important enough to make countries go to war. Coltan, a vital input into consumer electronics, is a driver of war in eastern Congo. Diamonds were used to fund civil war in West Africa.

Second, war's ability to impact the environment has also changed. Weaponry today is far more lethal and can literally move mountains. Bio-chemical agents can kill almost every living thing in a certain area. Nuclear weapons can change the planet's climate. In the past, conquerors did contaminate the wells of enemies, showing that war on the environment is not new. Yet, such acts pale in comparison to the hydrogen bomb tests in the Pacific that literally removed some islands from the map. War is becoming more lethal to the environment.

The evolution of the field of environmental conflict

There is ample reference to environmental conflict by ancient writers, though the terms they use may differ. Thucydides in *History of the Peloponnesian War* pointed out the competition over timber and minerals from Thrace as key causes of the first Peloponnesian war (460–446 BCE).

Sun Tzu's *The Art of War* emphasizes the need to maximize gains while minimizing resources (544–496 BCE). There is a long tradition of qualitative and informal research on environmental conflict. It is not until recently that the field has adopted a more formal or systematic approach.

Quincy Wright was an early scholar of this line of thinking. The development of environmental conflict parallels that of an earlier field, namely International Relations. Quincy Wright helped define the discipline in his classic *The Study of International Relations*. "International relations is today an emerging discipline manifesting little unity of method, logic, and convenience but much from that of necessity and history" (Wright 1955: 26).

Wright was a pacifist and believed that to avoid war one needs to understand it. This belief is at the core of environmental peacebuilding. Wright discusses resources in his landmark *Study of War* in 1942. He differentiated between all of nature and that set of natural resources that are important to livelihoods. He cites the livelihood needs of hunter-gatherers and those of modern people and how different they are. Wright also parses the phrase "the struggle among peoples for a set of limited resources provided by nature inevitably leads to war" (1942: 299). He concludes that the root of the conflict problem lies in livelihoods. Are they getting better or worse? Livelihoods, however, are not static but rather dynamic concepts tied to levels and types of economic development at a particular point in time. When competition over these resources is political, then conflict is often the result. But when the competition for them is economic, there is more likely to be cooperation.

The growing recognition of environment in daily life was reflected in the 1970s with the creation of commemorative rituals (Earth Day) and government institutions (U.S. Environmental Protection Agency). Books like *The Limits to Growth* (Meadows et al. 1972) presented a stark view of the future and the role of a deteriorating environment in it.

In the 1980s until the millennium, the field experienced huge growth. There was a real growing awareness that arose in several prominent cases, but also there were some alarmist treatises. The Toronto School focused solely on pathways to conflict. But these pathways still failed to "connect the dots" from environment to conflict, and back. Cooperation pathways went unexplored. Dire predictions, such as Robert Kaplan's "The Coming Anarchy" in the *Atlantic* (1994), painted resource and climate conflicts as looming war clouds.

It was good to recognize the dangers of environmental conflict. Aldinger, Bruch, and Yazykova's chapter (11) in this handbook, on United Nations resolutions, notes the rise of environmental issues in the Security Council since the end of the Cold War. Was it due to the change in the structure of the international system? Or, could it also be that research and reality began to convince countries about the validity, nuances, and threats posed by environmental conflict?

I see Environmental Conflict now where International Relations stood in the mid-twentieth century. The field has a rich history that has built a specific focus and expertise, but needs to create an aggregating work that unites and orients a field.

The two faces of environmental conflict: normative and objective

Fields have both knowledge and application dimensions. Medicine is based on the knowledge of biology, chemistry, and several other very scientific disciplines which test theories related to the human body. Research is highly technical and studies are conducted with extensive peer-review. The science of medicine is based on a set of physical findings.

The application of medicine is however an entirely different matter. Running a hospital or administering long-term health programs uses those findings as the basis for achieving certain health goals given the characteristics of individuals. Being a doctor involves decisions of science, but also of cost, time, resources, technology, and a host of other factors. They also include types of relationships that may be in conflict or cooperation. Likewise, there is an objective and a normative side in the field of environmental conflict. Environmental issues, like other social issues, are potential instances of conflict or cooperation. Perhaps the research side of the field ought to be called "Environment and Conflict Intersections" so as to not bias behavior towards either conflict or peace.

In the same way, we can view environmental conflict/cooperation studies as having both an objective and scientific basis of common understanding and one that is more practically oriented. The basis for common understanding could be some inventory of common cases that adherents believe are relevant. Using this knowledge for avoiding war, or peacebuilding, is however a normative matter.

Is there a field of environment and conflict?

The reality of the field and the coalescence of scholarly discourse often advance at differing rates. Quincy Wright defines a discipline around communitarian concepts. "Discipline implies consciousness by writers that there is a subject with some sort of unity; a concept of the scope and of the boundaries which separate it from other subjects, its organization, its methods, and some recognition of the persons who are expert on the subject and of the criteria for establishing such expertise" (Wright 1955: 23–24). There are however some disciplines that are more formal or objective than others. Naturally the knowledge in physics and dance are two entirely different concepts. "Some say a discipline exists only in so far as a body of data has been systemized by a distinctive analytical method" (Wright 1955: 23–24). Most disciplines today would not meet that standard, especially those in the social sciences.[1]

A field is a branch of knowledge characterized by accepted theories, data sources, methods, concepts, and studies shared by a community of experts. Can we call environmental conflict a field (or a sub-field)? If so, it would belong to a genre of inquiry that is inter-discipline and blends elements of the physical and the social worlds in the search for knowledge.

In a blended field, it is necessary to incorporate both disciplines into a single working research community. I would argue that environmental conflict belongs to a genre reflecting an inter-discipline relationship. In other words, each field makes a roughly equal contribution to the area of study and the result is a niche of research that has elements of each but together constitutes a unique field of examination.

Environmental conflict must be more than the notional blending of two differing realms: the world of people and the world of nature. The field should be seen as a singular entity that makes each part inseparable from the other. For example, we would not conceptualize the battle between male lions as "just" a territorial conflict. It is much more than that. The winners not only gain access to the territory, the prey on it, but also gain access to the females. The new males immediately kill off any cubs to control the future gene pool of the pride. Conflict behavior is a singular part of complex interactions with closely intertwined feedback.

There are several disciplinary homes to the separate fields of environment and of conflict research within higher education. No university is complete without departments of environmental science or ecology studies and there are faculty in political science and international relations who study conflict. Spill-over is common. Thus, we have fields such as bio-ethics, computational psychology, geo-spatial statistics, political geography, and forensic chemistry.

Peter Gleditsch (1998) cautions that the possible theoretical union between environment and conflict does not automatically mean there is an intellectual coherence. He notes at least seven shortcomings in theory-building: the absence of other important variables, untestable research models, the lack of a control group, the issue of reverse causality, using the future as evidence, foreign and domestic conflict influences, and levels of analysis problems (Gleditsch 1998: 388). These weaknesses however can be overcome. As a relatively new field, there are many areas of environmental conflict that have yet to adequately develop.

Does the community possess a critical mass? Yes. There are numerous conferences that include panels and papers on the topic and many others are organized solely around salient issues of conflict and environment. The same holds true for accepted journals and theories, where there are abundant examples that suggest a nexus of interest and knowledge. Needless to say, the existence of this handbook is itself an indicator of the research and researchers that constitute a field of knowledge. You will see in this handbook bibliographies that often use overlapping sources of citation.

Is the field here already? Probably as an idea, though it is still developing as a field of study. There are already university programs that integrate the two fields in their instructional requirements and faculty with dual appointments. The field will make advancements in theory but will always have an ongoing tension between differing qualitative and quantitative methods for theory-building.

To further understand the field, I will talk about the history of environment and conflict behavior and then go deeper into a discussion of the field and its characteristics. After that, I will explore types of cases of environment and conflict, and then weigh the future of this young field.

The history of nature in conflictual human behavior

The term environmental conflict is of a relatively new vintage in the academic and policy lexicon. The idea of it, and its reality as part of the human experience, dates back much further in time. Ancient accounts discuss wars fought over gold and silver mines, oases in the desert, herds of buffalo and aurochs, groves of fruit and nut-bearing trees, and even the wood from trees. These resources include the land on which they are found.

Human history is often driven by military conquest that seeks to control a resource. The search for gold and silver was a major driver in European seafaring exploration and colonization of the New World. Trade in spice was a major factor in Dutch annexation of Indonesia. The British carved out Belize from Guatemala after their defeat in the American Revolution in which they lost access to hardwood forests of North Carolina. This wood was vital for construction of the British fleet. The lucrative fur trade was a key factor driving British and French competition in North America.

Forest resources over time provide a good case study. The value of forests is recounted in the Babylonian Epic of Gilgamesh and the emergence of early city-states in ancient Mesopotamia. Written about 2,600 BC, the Gilgamesh Epic occurred during the Agricultural Revolution and the invention of writing.

As cities grew, sturdy wood was needed to build the first centers of civilization. The Epic of Gilgamesh is a story of the conflict between humans and the environment, the opening of trade, and the incorporation of these events into culture via mythology. One prominent and coveted wood that built these initial urban centers was cedar.

Gilgamesh was a king of the ancient Mesopotamian city of Uruk. He was a cruel monarch and his people cried out for relief. The gods answered by sending his physical and psychological equal – Enkidu. The two wage battle for days until both, exhausted from the ordeal, declare a truce and become friends. They agree to test their friendship by traveling to the west (modern-day Syria and Lebanon probably) and take the great cedar trees. This act would require they fight the protector of the forest, the creature Humbaba.

They venture to the forest and immediately begin cutting trees, enraging Humbaba. A struggle ensues but eventually the two gain the upper hand. Humbaba begs for his life, offering to become the servant of Gilgamesh. But Enkidu argues against it, saying that a war not done is a war never won. Gilgamesh slays the creature and they take the cedars, floating them down the Euphrates River to Uruk. A great city was built and Uruk became powerful.

Myths are of course part story and part history. Perhaps there was no Humbaba, Gilgamesh, or Enkidu. But there was a city-state of Uruk built in a region that lacked hardwoods necessary for construction materials. There were surely historical cases involving expeditions with both military forces and woodsmen who traveled long distances to bring home wood resources through the use of force. In fact, it is thought that Gilgamesh was based on the real-life figure King Enmebaragesi.

Uruk though is just the start of the role of cedar in conflict. From 2,600 BC to AD 138, Canaanites, Aegeans, Armenians, and Phoenicians built great civilizations in the Middle East. Through cities such as Sidon and Tyre, cedar was exported to Palestine and Egypt, areas with large populations and relatively little forest cover. To build their thalassocracy (maritime empire), the Phoenicians constructed enormous seafaring fleets for exploration, conquest, and trade, much like the British more than 2,000 years later. Control of forest resources is a cause of human conflict to this day.

Types of environmental conflict

How do we define environmental conflict? Let's take each part of the definition separately. The term conflict usually refers to the opposition of one group of people to another. These groups can break down in a number of ways: along tribal, ethnic, religious, national, socio-economic, political, and other lines. Disputes are often the result of incompatible goals (Dougherty and Pfalzgraff Jr. 1981: 82). The result of this opposition may have a peaceful or an adversarial outcome, the latter ranging from a mere disagreement to violence. In environmental conflict, we are often interested in those cases that are more violent and where environmental impacts are more direct.

Herbert Simon (1996) includes conflict behavior in the "artificial" world of humanity. He paired this world with the "natural" world in which we live and how the two interact. The natural world – the environment – is the resources of the universe and the territories on which people exist.

A key issue is the choice of words used to describe the field. Differing authors at differing times have referred to the concepts of "environment" and "conflict" in a wide variety of ways. Table 2.1 shows some of the terms in the literature that ostensibly refer to essentially the same phenomena. There is clearly a tendency to use some terms interchangeably, though there may be substantial differences in the application of the terms.

Table 2.1 Terms somewhat synonymous with environment and conflict

Environment synonyms	Conflict synonyms
Biosphere, habitat, earth systems, ecology, natural world, resources	War, violence, dispute, quarrel, hostility

It is possible to envision at least four differing types of relations between environment and conflict. First, environmental conflict often indicates violence over access to natural resources, or *territorial and resource conflict*.

Steve Libiszewski (1992) differentiates between resources and territorial conflict. He argues that resources (gold, oil, etc.) are economic in nature and dependent on the type of technological system in place. These resources are not environmental conflicts but rather economic ones over finite resources. Territorial or eco-system change refers to renewables such as arable land, forests, or fresh water, for example.

Many dispute Libiszewski. Territorial claims often have little to do with the environment and reflect ethnic, religious, or racial differences (among others) in addition to revanchist grievances based on historical events. Renewability is often not a given. A forest is not necessarily renewable because it can be eradicated, since a forest is more than just the trees and includes a gamut of complex relations between many species. It often takes hundreds or thousands of years to create a forest eco-system. Likewise, arable soils can be depleted, blown away by winds, or exhausted through overuse. Rivers can be diverted or polluted so that they are no longer potable. It will take millennia to return them to a viable eco-system.

Second, there are many resources that lie outside of recognized territorial domains of states. Claiming these resources may or may not necessarily lead to conflict, but these cases are different from resources disputes within a state's boundaries. Many of these resources are multilateral contestations rather than bilateral claims. This type of interaction might include islands that could either support people or possess valuable resources. It could also cover marine resources or seabed resources in international waters or in Antarctica. Last, it may well apply to claims of resources outside of the planet. These are *extra-territorial resource conflicts*.

Third, environment and conflict could also mean damage to the environment that is part of a warfare strategy against a general population. This strategy usually involves the tactic of denying or destroying a resource vital to a population or an army. For example, the U.S. Army attempted to deprive Native Americans of a key food source by exterminating the buffalo. This relationship is perhaps called *conflict using the environment*.

Fourth, environment and conflict could mean using nature to one's advantage in waging war. The cases are much shorter term in their conceptualization, perhaps even down to the battle level. By this I mean events such as the Iraqi dumping of oil into the Persian Gulf to foul the engines of Allied landing craft during the Gulf War. The U.S. Air Force has investigated "owning the skies", an effort to use weather during aerial warfare. This interaction might be called *environment in conflict* (see Table 2.2)

Table 2.2 Types of environment and conflict interactions

Type	Description	Direction of relationship	Example
1 Territorial and resource conflict	Access to resources	Environment to conflict	Wars fought over specific resources
2 Extra-territorial resource conflicts	Control of resources	Environment to conflict	Claims to resources outside of current state boundaries
3 Conflict using the environment	Destruction of environment in war	Conflict to environment	Denial of strategic resources in war
4 Environment in conflict	Use of environment to wage war	Conflict to environment	Impact of environment on battles

In a broader sense, environment and conflict can mix these four differing types along a temporal dimension. Machlis and Hansen (2008) examined the idea of warfare *ecology* that accumulates at differing stages over time, ranging from the onset of the dispute to the cessation of conflict and the aftermath. "We suggest that the broader taxonomy of warfare includes (1) preparations for war, (2) war (violent conflict), and (3) postwar activities" (Machlis and Hansen 2008). Here, resources of any type accumulate differing impacts from conflict.

Research in environment and conflict has widely disparate data needs. In conflict studies, most data are generally qualitative – usually nominal or ordinal. Interval data (like war casualties) are used but quite suspect in terms of reliability. In environment research, measurement is much more oriented towards interval data and a greater focus on quantitative indicators. The challenge is to incorporate both into theory-building. The field will always have an ongoing tension between qualitative and quantitative approaches.

There is actually a wealth of conflict case studies, dating back over 50 years. Most data-oriented conflict studies originate with the Correlates of War (COW) project, starting with J. David Singer's efforts in 1963. Its descendants include the Militarized Interstate Disputes (MID) dataset. The Uppsala Conflict Data Program (UCDP) provides yearly updates for global conflict on a country basis.

Environment is often an afterthought in constructing these conflict inventories. This add-on approach has its limitations in adequately integrating environment indicators. Rather, it may be necessary to completely re-imagine the basis for creating an inventory.

There are a variety of environmental dispute inventories. Research by R. B. Bilder (1975), Arthur Westling (1986), Thomas Homer-Dixon (1994), and others provides qualitative schemes to meld with conflict data. The Institute for Water and Watersheds at Oregon State University maintains the Transboundary Freshwater Dispute Database (TFDD). The Inventory of Conflict and Environment (ICE), from this author, explicitly attempts to integrate indicators from the two fields (see Mandala Projects 2017). Building this bicameral core of understanding will be key to the development of the field.

What are the latest conflict trends? UCDP data for the 1989–2014 period shows a high per year of about 100,000 conflict deaths and a low of about 12,000. Conflict deaths have been on the rise in the last few years, though most of this impact is due to the Syrian civil war. There were also peak periods around 1990 and 2000, but again these trends were driven by a handful of wars. Compared to historical levels, especially during the two world wars, we are now experiencing relatively low levels of global conflict.

Deaths from conflict, however, pale in comparison to deaths from environmental causes. On a country basis, the numbers are illustrative. "With nearly 1.4 million deaths a year, China has the most air pollution fatalities, followed by India with 645,000 and Pakistan with 110,000 . . . The United States, with 54,905 deaths in 2010 from soot and smog, ranks seventh highest for air pollution deaths" (Lelieveld, Evans, Frais, Gainnadaki, and Pozzer 2015). For comparison, the U.S. deaths per annum due to air pollution alone equals the total deaths by the U.S. in either the Korean or the Vietnam wars.

The characteristics of conflict and environment cases

Cases of environmental conflict cover an immense range of issue configurations. In spite of these many differences, there are some generally agreed-on modes and principles. Seven commonly held beliefs which are instructive in providing a tapestry of cases that populate the field are outlined here.

The role of the environment in conflict needs to exceed some threshold of significance in order to be a case of interest in the field

Environmental conflict is defined by the set of violence cases rather than the set of environment cases. Because of this anchoring in perspective, it can be said that the field is an offshoot of social science areas such as political science, international relations, or sociology. When is environment an important factor in a conflict case? It is difficult to gauge the importance of resources (real or not) in the calculations of decision-makers when it comes to making war. In the Liberia Civil War, diamonds were important to funding rebel movements but the essential causes for the war were far more complicated. It is impossible to put a quantitative number on this factor. But it is possible to generally rank order the role of environment in conflict as below or above some *de minimus* level in factors related to war. This level is probably more difficult to measure through a specific indicator. It would require identifying environmental cases whose strategic value far outweighs the value of a territory. Agreeing on the importance of conflict in an environment case may need to rely on some type of expert opinion mechanism or a complex indicator.

There are many factors other than environment that drive conflict behavior

An environment factor alone is rarely the sole or the most important reason for a conflict. Structural conditions are paramount. There needs to be an existing state of unfriendly relations between states that triggers conflict. War may have roots in the structural characteristics of *people* (race, ethnicity, class, or religion, for example) or factors of *societies* (size of population, historical grievances, or climate change, for example). War may not be the only outcome that is possible. Cooperation is theoretically equally likely to occur.

The link between environment and conflict is largely indirect

Environmental conflicts are longer term, civil in nature, protracted between a variety of players, and lead to many more indirect casualties in recent history. An environment factor rarely directly leads to war though it can add to the likelihood of conflict, along with other factors. These forces play out through the weakening of social institutions and family livelihoods. Linking environment and conflict is not a straightforward process. For example, it is not that drought itself causes conflict. Rather, drought leads to a slow, prolonged, and accumulating diminution of resources and quality of life. This reversal of fortune, often in the wake of increasing demands, leads to a resource imbalance. The greater the gap, the more likely that violence will occur.

Structures need a trigger to lead to violence

There is a tradition of treating environmental factors as deterministic. This worldview generally sees environmental conditions like they were markers for disease that show up in DNA analysis. Environment may create structural conditions that can push two sides into conflict or cooperation, depending on sparks that ignite either tendency. Conflicts require a trigger and the challenge is in managing the triggers. The assassination of a leader in the backdrop of deteriorating environmental resources along with ethnic grievances (as in Rwanda in 1994) led to conflict, but a water-sharing agreement demonstrated cooperation in an otherwise belligerent bilateral relationship (the Indus River Agreement between India and Pakistan).

Environment includes natural resources that may be either finite or renewable

History includes many examples of wars over access to specific resources (gold, silver, oil, uranium, etc.). The political differences between the specific and general resources (territories) in wars are in fact quite stark. The United States had, at differing times, an interest in gaining and maintaining access to bananas from Central America and oil from Iraq. But the United States had no interest in ruling these countries.

Conflict may arise due to the perceived scarcity or surplus of a resource

Countries go to war to acquire both specific and general resources. The former tends to be more short term because technology needs can often change quite rapidly. No one cared where reserves of uranium existed prior to about 1900. The definition of a strategic resource is time dependent, given the state of technology and prevailing economic system. Oil was never a usable resource without the technology to process it into gasoline and other products. In the 1700s, whale oil was a much more valuable resource.

In the nineteenth century, a key source of agricultural fertilizer was from bird guano. Islands off the west coast of South America were abundant in this resource deposited by flocks of birds feeding on the ample fish populations existing along the Humboldt Current. A competition between Britain, the United States, and other countries emerged over claims to islands rich in bird guano. It has little currency today, though the guano trade still exists and guano is touted as a natural fertilizer. While guano now has limited demand, the need for obscure rare earth minerals has become critical to industries such as computer and cell phone technologies. Tantalum, cobalt, and other minerals were largely unheard of until recently.

There is often a lag between the existence of an environmental driver and when conflict occurs

Environment and conflict often involve lags in behavior. A prolonged drought does not make people immediately take up arms and go to war. Consider the lifespan of a prolonged drought. In year 1, an agriculturally reliant family will adopt some short-term strategies for storing more water or using less of it. Agricultural output might be slightly lower but some excess farm or ranch output can still be sold for extra income.

In year 2 of the drought, these water-saving strategies intensify. Substantial declines in plant output start to occur and sustenance versus survival issues emerge. The lack of water begins to harm human health. In year 3, the depths of the drought begin to set in. Plant output continues to decline and there is a steep drop in the holding of animal assets. Some animals are sold to offset losses because it is simply no longer possible to feed them.

In year 4, there is only enough agricultural output for self-sufficiency. The loss of income leads to reduction in health care and education. Remaining animals are sold or consumed. In year 5, and increasing each year, survival and entreaties of radicalism begin to accumulate. It is not hard to imagine them eventually culminating in violence.

Key resources in conflict cases

There are two broad types of environmental conflict: general and specific. The role of resources is central to both. Table 2.3 lists some types of general environmental resources that can be a source of conflict.

Table 2.3 General resources related to conflict

General resource type	Categorical types
Land	Arable land
Biomass	Forests, grasses, etc. for direct and indirect use in an eco-system
Fresh water and glaciers	For irrigation, transportation, and personal use
Sea sovereignty	For transportation and navigation control

Table 2.4 Specific resources related to conflict

Specific resource type	Categorical types
Energy (finite)	Coal, oil, wood, charcoal, uranium, gas, and others
Animals and plants (renewable)	Whale, buffalo, beaver, cod, banana, tuna, elephant, rubber, spice, mahogany, cedar, and others
Minerals and metals (finite)	Gold, silver, cobalt, tantalum, uranium, tin, copper, and others

The general types include four groups: control over territory, biomass, fresh water, and sovereignty in sea areas. Territory and sea sovereignty cases are often the most violent. Within each general resource there are a variety of categorical types. These categories often differ depending on the researcher. Gleditsch sees five types of resources in environmental conflict cases: territory, strategic raw materials, energy, water, and food (Gleditsch 1998: 382–383).

Conflict over specific resources falls into three groups. First, there are energy sources, which could include wood, coal, oil, gas, and uranium as a starting list. Second, animals and plants are often sources of conflict, more so in the past than now. Sometimes it is general game and other times it is specific species (beaver fur or bird feathers). Finally, certain minerals and metals have been the source of conflict. Gold and silver have long held value as currencies. Other minerals like cobalt, tin, or lead have been in high demand at differing points in time (see Table 2.4).

Where are we going?

The growing overlap of environmental issues and their role in conflict is bound to hasten a focus on research and policy solutions. The reach of the discipline should however remain fairly limited to a specific set of circumstances. Think of this as an overlap of interests in terms of a Venn diagram that narrowly straddles the two fields. This corresponding slice of behavior is a unique and limited subset.

In the broad spectrum of cases in the separate fields of environment and conflict, there are many instances where the existence of the two occurs in tandem in a case. This convergence does not imply cause or that there is a significant relationship. Moreover, while the two co-occur on many occasions, there is not necessarily any particular feedback relationship between the two. The coverage suggests a limited portion of each field, but that does not underestimate its importance (see Figure 2.1).

The field will become very important in informing future policy-makers who will need to respond to the issue of environmental conflict in line with unfolding events. With a growing interest in both fields, in separate or in tandem, trends suggest a greater focus by researchers,

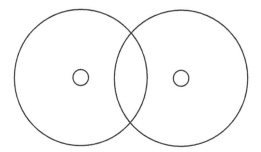

Figure 2.1   Venn diagram of environment and conflict cases

policy-makers, and the average person in the future. It will be a growth area for both under-standing and reconciling cases of conflict and environment.

Note

1 Defining a discipline also changes over time. Even in 1955, Wright noted the "proliferation of dis-ciplines during the last two centuries" (Wright 1955: 25). Wright says that there is evidence of a discipline when "progress in integrating the subject academically and professionally has been accom-panied by a great increase in the literature of all aspects of the field, and of the number of learned journals devoted to it, and in the analysis of the progress of international relations as a discipline" (Wright 1955: 28).

References

Bilder, R. B. ed. (1975) "International Environmental Disputes", *Recueil des Cours Academie de Droit International*, Paris.

Correlates of War Project. www.correlatesofwar.org/

Dougherty, J. E. and Pfalzgraff Jr., R. L. ed. (1981) *Contending Theories of International Relations: A Comprehensive Survey*, Harper & Row, New York.

Gleditsch, N. P. (1998) "Armed Conflict and the Environment: A Critique of the Literature", *Journal of Peace Research* 35(3): 381–400 (Special Issue on Environmental Conflict).

Homer-Dixon, T. F. (1994) "Environmental Scarcities and Violent Conflict: Evidence from Cases", *International Security* 19: 5–40.

Institute for Water and Watersheds, Oregon State University Transboundary Freshwater Dispute Database. www.transboundarywaters.orst.edu/database/DatabaseIntro.html [Accessed July 25, 2016].

Kaplan, R. (1994) "The Coming Anarchy", *The Atlantic*. Available at: www.theatlantic.com/magazine/archive/1994/02/the-coming-anarchy/304670/

Lelieveld, J., Evans, J. S., Frais, M., Gainnadaki, D., and Pozzer, A. (2015) "The Contribution of Outdoor Air Pollution Sources to Premature Mortality on a Global Scale", *Nature* 525: 367–371. doi:10.1038/nature15371, www.nature.com/nature/journal/v525/n7569/full/nature15371.html

Libiszewski, S. (1992) What is an *Environmental Conflict*? www.css.ethz.ch/content/dam/ethz/special-interest/gess/cis/center-for-securities-studies/pdfs/What_is_Environment_Conflict_1992.pdf [Accessed July 25, 2016].

Machlis, G. E. and Hansen, T. (2008) "Warfare Ecology", *BioScience* 58(8): 729–736. doi: 10.1641/B580809.

Mandala Projects. (2017) Inventory of Conflict and Environment Project. [online] Available at: http://mandalaprojects.com/wordpress/index.php/ice/ [Accessed December 5, 2017].

Meadows, D. H., Meadows, D. L., Randers, J., and Behrens III, W. W. (1972) *The Limits to Growth: A Report for the Club of Rome's Project on the Predicament of Mankind*, Universe Books, New York.

Militarized Interstate Disputes Dataset. *The Correlates of War Project.* http://cow.dss.ucdavis.edu/data-sets/ MIDs/mids

Simon, H. (1996) *Sciences of the Artificial*, MIT Press, Cambridge, MA.

Uppsala Conflict Data Program (UCDP) *Uppsala University.* www.ucdp.uu.se/

Westling, A. H. (1986) Appendix 2, "Wars and Skirmishes Involving Natural Resources: A Selection from the 20th Century", in Westling, A. H. (ed.) *Global Resources and International Conflict: Environmental Factors in Strategic Policy and Action*, Oxford, New York, 204–210.

Wright, Q. (1942) *A Study of War*, University of Chicago Press, Chicago.

Wright, Q. (1955) *The Study of International Relations*, Appleton-Century-Crofts, New York.

3

Transnational environmental crime

Peter Stoett

Introduction

Transnational environmental crimes (TECs) are severe threats to environmental security today. The sheer magnitude of TEC is staggering; the scope and level of complex organization surprising to even seasoned veterans of both environmental policy and law enforcement. Illegal logging alone is estimated to be a $30–100 billion industry, representing 10–30 percent of the global wood trade (Nelleman 2012). Indeed, a new field of "green criminology" (Stretesky, Long, and Lynch 2014; Bierne and South 2007; South and Brisman 2013; White 2008) has emerged in response to the rise of environmental crimes (a rise at least partly attributed to new legislation that outlaws formerly legal behavior). Taking green criminology to the international level, many authors and intelligence units are directing their focus onto the role played by multinational corporations, armed rebel groups, corrupt governments and/or bureaucracies, "environmental black market" dynamics (Brack and Hayman 2002), and other causal variables.

It is not difficult to argue that environmental crimes, which destroy natural capital and reduce ecosystem resilience (including the socio-ecological ecosystems of which humans are an integral part), are threats to national security (Ivanović 2010). It is important to note, however, that the more widespread and irreparable crimes, such as the estimated $20-billion illegal trade in wildlife (most of it destined now for Asia) or the emission of dangerous contaminants contrary to international conventions, are threats to global environmental security – to the biosphere (Banks et al. 2008). There is no other way to view, for example, massive illegal fishing operations that, coupled with habitual legal overfishing, drive fish stocks to near-extinction. And TECs are often linked to organized crime cartels (who are doubling-up on drug, arms, and human trafficking, money laundering, and/or other combinations) or are perpetrated by rebel groups such as the Lord's Resistance Army or Somalia's al-Shabaab militants seeking quick funding for arms and atrocity, which reinforces the internationalization of environmental crime today.

If TEC is tied inextricably to environmental security, it is also tied to environmental justice at the global level. For example, the shipping of hazardous waste to the southern hemisphere by industrial countries was considered an environmental injustice long before it was treated as a TEC, though it is clearly viewed as the latter today. In the same vein, we might suggest that climate justice issues will be legal ones in the future if the international climate change regime can evolve in a similar trajectory. However, we also need to be careful that, as TEC legislation and conventions proliferate in response to several coterminous ecological crises, we do not permit this to be used to the detriment to local communities for political gain. This too applies to environmental security in the broader sense, since it can be seen as a justification for greater state control and even military involvement; with TEC, however, it is a more acute problem: responses involve law enforcement and judicial consequences. For the greatest environmental crime, however, there is no punishment forthcoming.

The gravest TEC: ecocide?

There is an ongoing movement, especially visible in Europe, to have most environmental crimes – or even environmentally harmful acts that are still considered legal – declared acts of ecocide. This would entail utilizing a maximalist definition of the term ecocide.[1] While the movement has gained steam, it relies primarily on the idea of using the International Criminal Court (ICC) as a judicial body to pursue corporations and individuals committing acts of ecocide defined so broadly that we would need to expand the capacity of the ICC beyond any recorded institutional growth in history (see Higgins 2015). Nonetheless, ecocide remains a well-known word in the environmental security literature and it is generally viewed from a more specific, even minimalist, perspective.

Defined in the minimalist, military sense – the deliberate destruction of the environment for strategic gain – ecocide is bad for everyone involved: it rarely results in or even contributes to military victory; it leaves an indelible impression on local environments that takes generations to erase, if indeed it is even possible to "move on" from such catastrophic loss; it threatens fundamental ecosystem services and thus human security (food, water, liberty). Following the intentional attack on southeast Asian ecosystems by the United States in the late 1960s and early 1970s, an international agreement was reached that is designed to limit ecocide, which often has international origins: the Convention on the Prohibition of Military or Any Other Hostile Use of Environmental Modification Techniques (ENMOD).

If there is a global prohibition on ecocide, it is during wartime only. ENMOD remains the clearest pronunciation on this, though Additional Protocol I of the Fourth Geneva Convention also mentions it.[2] However, ENMOD is perhaps most famous for being nearly useless. It survives as a phantom convention: we know it exists but have never seen it in action. It lacks its own secretariat, being housed in the Chemical Weapons Convention in The Hague. Despite calls to use ENMOD as a behavior-altering mechanism, it languishes behind the priorities of national security and general strategic approaches to warfare today.

Environmental crime

Transnational environmental crime, on the other hand, has been the subject of numerous scholarly efforts to arrive at a common definition, and forms of it are already integrated into hundreds of national legislative efforts, though, as Mégret suggests, "[l]aws addressing environmental crimes are traditionally seen as an extension of public and administrative laws protecting the environment, rather than as a fully developed branch of criminal law" (2011: 200).

In a broader sense Wellsmith (2011) and others refer to "the field of eco-criminology"; a similar phrase, "green criminology," is used by Zaitch, Boekhou van Solinger, and Muller (2014). Wellsmith (2011: 127) adds:

There is no fixed definition of environmental crime, and the behaviours encompassed are varied including illegal waste discharges, fly tipping and illegal logging. Environmental law includes offences relating to neighbour noise, graffiti, littering, dog mess, wildlife and countryside, planning and rights of way, but many commentators concentrate on environmental offences concerning pollution and waste. In legal terms, then, the concept of the environment is much narrower than that considered by eco-criminologists, and offences involving nonhuman animals are rarely considered (perhaps with the exception of the illicit trade in endangered species, or the presence of nonhuman animals that may cause harm to the environment or public health).[3]

Forni places emphasis on "the trading and smuggling of plants, animals, resources and pollutants in violation of prohibition or regulation regimes established by multilateral environmental agreements and/or in contravention of domestic law" (Forni 2010: 34 in White 2011: 5). Wright suggests that transnational environmental crime can be split broadly into two categories: trafficking in natural resources and trafficking in hazardous substances. "The former includes the trade in endangered species (see Wyatt 2013), illegal logging and illegal exploitation and trafficking of mineral resources while the latter includes the illegal trade in ozone depleting substances and the dumping and trafficking of waste" (Wright 2011: 333). White (2011: 3, 7–8) offers what is perhaps the most extensive peer-reviewed list of TEC:

- Unauthorised acts or omissions that are against the law and therefore subject to criminal prosecution and criminal sanctions;
- crimes that involve some kind of cross-border transference and an international or global dimension; and
- crimes related to pollution (of air, water and land) and crimes against wildlife (including illegal trade in ivory as well as live animals).
- Transgressions that are harmful to humans, environments and non-human animals, regardless of legality per se; and
- environmental-related harms that are facilitated by the state, as well as corporations and other powerful actors, insofar as these institutions have the capacity to shape official definitions of environmental crime in ways that allow or condone environmentally harmful practices.

More specifically, he lists:

- illegal transport and dumping of toxic waste (see Clapp 2001);
- transportation of hazardous materials such as ozone-depleting substances;
- the illegal traffic in real or purported radioactive or nuclear substances;
- proliferation of 'e'-waste generated by the disposal of tens of thousands of computers and other equipment (see Gibbs, McGarrell, and Sullivan 2015);
- the unsafe disposal of old ships and aeroplanes;
- local and transborder pollution, that is either systematic (via location of factories) or related to accidents (e.g. chemical plant spills);
- biopiracy in which western companies are usurping ownership and control over plants developed using 'traditional' methods and often involving indigenous peoples in the third world;
- illegal fishing and logging.

Lorraine Elliott (2011: 2) offers an even more detailed list of potential TECs:

> the trafficking of illegally logged timber (sometimes called 'stolen' timber), the illegal trade
> in endangered and threatened species, the black market in ozone depleting substances and
> other prohibited or regulated chemicals, the transboundary dumping of toxic and hazard-
> ous waste, and illegal fishing. Other challenges such as carbon fraud and corruption with
> REDD projects (Reducing Emissions from Deforestation and Forest Degradation) are also
> now included under this rather broad heading.

Shover and Routhe (2005: 323) expand the litany further, including "littering, improper disposal of radioactive materials, taking game out of season, intentional discharge of hazardous substances into storm drains or waterways, and theft of flora, fauna, and natural resources." In terms
of domestic law, they differentiate between environmental "crime," which "requires prosecutors to demonstrate either that defendants knowingly, intentionally, or recklessly violated the
law or were negligent," and environmental "illegalities," which are "violations of rules that do
not require demonstration of intent to violate" (2005: 324). "Generally, illegalities are violations
of regulatory rules promulgated and enforced by environmental protection agencies. They are
regarded by many as substantially less serious than criminal acts, and they generally carry minor
civil penalties" (2005: 323–324). However, the accumulated impact of such illegalities can be
disastrous to local and global ecology.

I would suggest that the more clear-cut (pun unintended) violations of domestic and, even,
international environmental law, are not ecocidal in nature (or to nature, perhaps). Ecocide
demands a concerted, systemic effort with intent. But the broader category of environmental
injustice captures nicely the environmental harms described above, as well as the more specific, legally approachable cases of abject environmental negligence so often demonstrated by
humans in the pursuit of financial profit or political gain. However, since organized criminal
activity is by definition concerted and planned, we might stretch the definition a bit to include
transnational organized environmental crime. This deserves some attention, since most governments can at least agree that non-state-sanctioned criminal behavior is worth fighting. I
will return to this theme below with a short discussion of Interpol, but turn briefly now to
convention law and the ICC.

Treaty law and conventions

We do not have the space needed to delve at any depth into the sea of international conventions on the environment that exist today (see Stoett 2012). We should note that "there are
still areas of TEC that are not covered by an overarching international agreement, for example
illegal, unreported and unregulated fishing and logging" (Wright 2011: 337), though efforts to
overcome this are being made. Some of the major international initiatives that formally specify
certain activities as violations of international law, and which have been integrated with domestic legal regimes in cases where states have ratified them, include:

- UN Convention on the Law of the Sea, 1982, and the Convention for Prevention of
  Maritime Pollution by Dumping Wastes and Other Matters, 1972;
- Convention on International Trade of Endangered Species of Wildlife Fauna and Flora
  (CITES), 1973;
- International Tropical Timber Agreement, 1983;
- Vienna Convention for the Protection of the Ozone Layer, 1985;

- Montreal Protocol on Substances that Deplete the Ozone Layer, 1987;
- Basel Convention on the Control of Transboundary Movements of Hazardous Wastes and their Disposal, 1989;
- United Nations Framework Convention on Climate Change, 1992; and the Kyoto Protocol, 1997; and the Paris Agreement, 2015;
- Antarctic Treaty, 1959; and related protocols;
- Convention on Biological Diversity, 1992 (and two protocols);
- Convention to Combat Desertification, 1994;
- Agreement Relating to the Conservation and Management of Straddling Fish Stocks and Highly Migratory Fish Stocks, 1995;
- Rotterdam Convention on the Prior Informed Consent Procedure for Certain Hazardous Chemicals and Pesticides in International Trade, 1998;
- Minamata Convention on Mercury, 2013.

This is but a partial list. Yet as any casual observer of global environmental politics knows, the consequences of non-compliance are minimal in all cases. Most conventions have opt-out clauses, or graduated compliance time frames. While the overall body of treaty law is impressive, it presents limited opportunities for those concerned with pursuing environmental criminal law at the international level. There is utility in shaming countries that are habitually problematic, but this is not the same thing as charging someone with a crime. Treaty law is the foundation of TEC law, providing both legal precedent and normative context. But we need specific mechanisms to pursue TEC if it is to hinge on individual or even corporate responsibility, include ecocide during and out of wartime (international and non-international war), and deter/encourage human behavior across scales.

The ICC and the ICJ

As Freeland (2005: 358) reminds us, the Rome Statute (in force since 2002) "does not deal with acts that constitute a 'mere' violation of the over 200 International Environmental Agreements (IEAs) that exist: nor a breach of the domestic legislation in various jurisdictions that regulate the environment." He suggests that an environmental crime potentially giving rise to international criminal responsibility could be regarded as "a deliberate action committed with intent to cause significant harm to the environment, including ecological, biological and natural resource systems, in order to promote a particular military, strategic or other aim, and which does in fact cause such damage" (ibid.). There is scope within the definition of crimes in Part 2 of the Statute to pursue environmental war crimes. We've seen this utilized, to some extent, in the separate trial of deposed Liberian leader and war criminal Charles Taylor, which also took place in The Hague. But those concerned with a broader approach call for the adoption of a specific section on "Crimes Against the Environment" in the Rome Statute, thus enabling the ICC to deal effectively with the charge of ecocide. Within this context, some would include all forms of environmental harm, whereas others would limit this new obligation to wartime harm.

Even if there was some consensus that the ICC can move beyond property-related crimes with environmental consequences (the well-accepted "pillage" framework) and into the full-fledged prosecution of war leaders who have violated ENMOD or perpetrated other large-scale environmental crimes during war, this would hardly satisfy those who want to move toward a universal crimes against the environment regime, especially if the definition of ecocide they wish to employ is so broad it includes what many would consider distinctly national, and even regional, acts of pollution. Nor would it satisfy those concerned with transitional justice (which so often ignores environmental impacts of destructive behavior).[4] The ICC is in no condition to take on additional responsibilities, and it would be nothing short of a political miracle if this were allowed to occur in the first place (Security Council clearance, for example, would be necessary). Gilman's call for states to adopt universal jurisdiction statutes that encompass environmental war crimes as a way to "jumpstart the development of environmental war crime law" (2011: 470) is perhaps a more sensible way forward. Others suggest that relying on the ICC for environmental crime prosecution relieves the state of its responsibilities in the overall process of environmental degradation.[5]

Article 8(2)(b)(iv) of the Rome Statute now criminalizes as a war crime, in international armed conflict, "[i]ntentionally launching an attack in the knowledge that such attack will cause . . . widespread, long-term and severe damage to the natural environment which would be clearly excessive in relation to the concrete and direct overall military advantage anticipated."[6] However, beyond concerns over land grabs, it is unlikely the ICC will assume responsibility for ecocide as a crime, or even as a war crime. It will remain partially focused on property crimes and pillage during wartime (including civil conflicts), and thus there will be a small avenue toward integrating environmental concerns with international criminal law. But it would be chimerical to expect it to go any further under present circumstances, which include a virtual Security Council veto on specific cases, an overloaded set of extant demands, and limitations on funding and time. The establishment of a new world court mandated specifically to pursue charges of transnational environmental crime would seem, by default, the only way forward here. National governments can, of course, adopt ecocide legislation (including universal jurisdiction, as complicated as that will prove) and tighten their own environmental policy, but ultimately a new convention and court will need to be established. Pedersen (2012) covers the lobby for the establishment of an International Environmental Court in some detail; he ultimately rejects the idea but acknowledges there are long-term benefits to keeping the dream alive. Earlier efforts[7] cumulated in the development of an ICE Coalition, which "began campaigning for an international environmental court in the build-up to the United Nations Framework Convention on Climate Change (UNFCCC) Conference of the Parties 15 (COP15) meeting in Copenhagen in December 2009" (Pedersen 2012: 549). The UK-based Coalition has largely moulded its advocacy "on the experience of the Coalition for the International Criminal Court, which successfully advocated for the creation of the ICC" (Pedersen 2012: 549; see also Hinde 2003 on the role of NGOs and non-state actors in the prescribed court). An evolving definition of environmental justice can buttress the application of TEC law.

Meanwhile, the International Court of Justice will handle cases that many would consider to be ecocidal in nature if and when states request it to do so. The latest high-profile case (Australia/New Zealand vs. Japan) on Southern Ocean "scientific whaling" is exemplary: the court decided against Japan on the basis not that whaling or even whaling-for-science was against international norms, but that Japan was not conducting Convention-regulated scientific whaling but was running a small commercial whaling operation. Japan agreed to adhere to the decision, though it publicly retains the threat of leaving the International Whaling Commission altogether and has since resumed a minke whale hunt, much to the consternation of many observers. But, as in keeping with ICJ's mandate, no individuals were charged with any form of crime, and no sanctions have been placed on Japan despite decades of misconduct. The ICJ offers no hope as a venue to pursue transnational environmental crime other than when it is part of a treaty or border dispute, though it might be called on to offer more advisory opinions in the future. An advisory opinion on whether large greenhouse gas emitters are in breach of international law would be most welcome, for example – efforts to have the ICJ engage the issue were unsuccessful in the past but may have more chances now that the Paris Agreement on climate change received sufficient ratifications to enter into force in 2016.

It is painfully clear that at present the anti-TEC legal crusade is largely a European initiative.[8] Recent EU elections indicate there is mixed support within the EU itself for Union-wide projects. But Europe – as is so often the case with international law – is so far ahead of the rest of the world, it looks as if this is a European project. For example, there is already a European Network of Prosecutors for the Environment (ENPE). The International Network for Environmental Compliance and Enforcement does have its own Prosecutors Network, but the ENPE is the only advanced regional affiliation.[9] We can hypothesize that the Eurocentric character of this movement will harm the chances of a more global effort involving southern hemispheric states in particular. This is not to suggest the European efforts should be diminished in any way, but that all efforts must be made to circumvent the post-colonial charges a European-led initiative is bound to raise. This will be particularly important if there is a serious movement toward the establishment of a new world court.

Other responses

> CITES is a trade treaty—it wasn't designed to respond to organized crime. CITES meetings aren't the right forum to sit and discuss organized crime responses; the right people aren't in the room.
>
> You wouldn't appoint someone from the pharmaceutical industry to head a task force combating narcotic trafficking. So why assign a CITES administrator to lead the war against fauna- and flora-related criminal activity?
>
> If we agree, as I think we should and must, that organized crime now plays a major role in wildlife trafficking, then surely the issue for discussion is not illicit trade, it's crime?
>
> (John Sellar, former head of law enforcement
> for CITES in Steyn 2015)

The link between the illegal wildlife trade and terrorist organizations in operation mainly in Africa piqued the interest of several western states, but the link between TEC and transnational organized crime is, naturally enough, attractive to Interpol, which has adopted TEC as a new organizational focus:

> A significant proportion of both wildlife and pollution crime is carried out by organized criminal networks, drawn by the low risk and high profit nature of these types of crime. The same routes used to smuggle wildlife across countries and continents are often used to smuggle weapons, drugs and people. Indeed, environmental crime often occurs hand in hand with other offences such as passport fraud, corruption, money laundering and murder.
>
> (Interpol 2017)[10]

This assertion is, in my view, indisputable; anyone who has witnessed the illicit wildlife trade or toxic waste dumping knows intuitively that there are bigger forces, including corrupt and armed government forces, at work here.

On the enforcement side, national police and Interpol have begun at long last to take TEC more seriously, perhaps a reflection of rising western concern over links with terrorism, but also reflecting the growth of expertise and intelligence about environmental crimes in general (Blindell 2006). The advent of "situational crime prevention" (Graycar and Felson 2010) and "intelligence-led policing" (Gibbs et al. 2015; Elliott 2009) is of particular interest from a criminological perspective, part of a broader movement to combat transnational organized crime (Coyne and Bell 2011) and terrorism (McGarrell, Chermak, and Freilich 2007).

Interpol has branched out considerably into the TEC area in the preceding two decades; its interventions include the Interpol Wildlife Crime Working Group, Pollution Crime Working Group, and Fisheries Crime Working Group, all of which report to the umbrella Environmental Compliance and Enforcement Committee. Interpol has been active in establishing NESTs – National Environmental Security Task Forces – in many countries with recognized TEC issues. The NESTs are assisting in legislative, judicial, and enforcement measures, an unusual case of sovereign states collaborating with foreign advisors on such basic matters.[11]

A major innovation has been the recognition of the illegal exploitation of marine living resources (often referred to as "fisheries crime"). The Obama administration made this an American foreign policy priority as well in mid-2004. The key point in all these crimes is their transnational nature: they are

> either committed in more than one state or are committed in one state but with a substantial part of the preparation, planning, direction, or control taking place in another state. In effect, the products, the perpetrators, and often the profits move across borders with the knowing intention of obtaining illegal gain.
>
> *(Elliott 2012: 89)*

Today we can argue that TEC is a factor in the policy agenda of several international agencies such as the United Nations Environment Programme, the UN Office of Drugs and Crime, the Regional Intelligence Liaison Offices of the World Customs Organisation, the UN Commission on Crime Prevention and Criminal Justice, and Interpol. Transnational efforts integrating police and civil society forces include the Coalition Against Wildlife Trafficking (CAWT), the Asia Regional Partners' Forum on Combating Environmental Crime (ARPEC), the Multilateral Environmental Agreements Regional Enforcement Network (MEA–REN), the ASEAN Wildlife Enforcement Network (ASEAN–WEN), the South Asian Wildlife Enforcement Network (SA–WEN), and the International Network on Environmental Compliance and Enforcement (INECE). In March 2011, five international organizations – CITES, Interpol, the UN Office of Drugs and Crime, the World Customs Organisation and the World Bank – joined together to form the International Consortium on Combating Wildlife Crime (ICCWC) (Elliott 2011: 3). Since so many of the crimes they are involved in investigating are either causes of, or at the very least perpetuate, environmental injustice, they should be applauded (see Hoare 2007). They will not allow us to indict the state system for its complicity in global ecocide, of course, but they are establishing new boundaries in international legal enforcement.

Private security against TEC?

The role played by the private security sector is often overlooked. Make no mistake: many natural resources, especially mineral and oil/gas wealth, are closely protected already. This armed protection is supplied either by the state apparatus or by private security firms employed by states or corporations for this specific purpose. (Of course, this is the protection of private property, not of environmental health; the latter may be a pleasant side effect.) Another teasing possibility is that the private sector could begin to play a larger role here, as the rise of the private military/security (or renewed mercenary) industry suggests, and as some have called for in the responsibility to protect (R2P) context. As O'Reilly (2011) suggests, however, the "transnational security consultancy industry" has more to do with rescuing the rich than spreading environmental justice or human rights. Still, the potential contribution of the private sector to TEC management and enforcement should not be overlooked, especially in terms of forensic technology and other areas of research. And, of course, if a burgeoning international environmental law sector is before us, so is the proliferation of private law firms dealing partially or exclusively with it. Carbon trading, complete with the newest form of white collar environmental crime, carbon fraud, will be a bonanza for law firms and prosecutors alike if it involves the kind of money it promises to deliver to participants in the game.

A cautionary note: remembering environmental justice

Environmental security will not be a just pursuit if it is not rooted in human security and the respect for the individual and the community that term implies (Brisman 2008). Similarly, the pursuit of anti-TEC policies must be embedded within the context of respect for human rights lest it be misused for political gain. This is a sensitive issue in any decolonized context, or in the theatre of active conflicts where military presence is ubiquitous.

Ironically, perhaps, efforts at conserving nature are also possible sources of environmental injustice, and there is a little information on the level of displacement of both indigenous and non-indigenous persons caused by conservation projects (for historical treatments see Warner 2006, and Brockington and Igoe 2006, who refer to "eviction for conservation"). It is imperative that we retain human security, indigenous peoples' rights, women's rights, and other human rights-based themes in equal standing to anti-TEC measures lest they become convenient excuses for the spread of state power or the forceful economic disenfranchisement or physical dislocation of ethnic and other groups.

This is akin to the eco-global criminology now advocated by Robert White (2011, 2008), which insists that voices from the periphery are heard as we chart new paths towards the eradication of TEC; it echoes the work by Peluso and Watts (2001) and others who demand we avoid simplistic causal assumptions and look at the situational violence found in conflict zones before advocating one-size-fits-all solutions that could very well further marginalize local voices, especially under authoritarian regimes.

Another factor worthy of consideration is post-conflict justice: restitution for those who have suffered ecocide or, even, TEC outside of wartime (Carranza 2008; Drumbl 2009). If it is hard to deny the centrality of access to natural resources in environmental peacebuilding; it is equally obvious that transitional justice must reflect the recognition and compensation for egregious environmental crimes. We have a long way to go, however, in this normative shift.

Conclusion

Transnational environmental crime can no longer be considered a tangential threat to environmental security. The scale and scope are just too large and deep. Entire communities are often affected when resources are ransacked or permanently ruined by illegal loggers, miners, fishermen, and others. Often, the criminals involved are also trading in arms, drugs, and humans at the same time, and foreign investors from various organized criminal groups benefit at the expense of impoverished poachers, hazardous waste handlers, enslaved fishermen, and others caught up in the brutal trades of TEC. Efforts to break the complex links between poverty, markets for associated products, and criminal expertise are most welcome and Interpol and other organizations involved in the broader global governance context are playing an increasingly visible role.

At the same time, however, it is important to remember that environmental security is challenged by an array of actors and international economic and social structures, and that if TECs are defined in such a restricted manner that they only include egregious environmental crimes such as wildlife poaching, we are limiting its potential as an avenue toward increased environmental justice. Ecocide during wartime, legal but deleterious extractive industries, continued climate negligence by industrialized countries, dooming small island states to physical extinction: these, too, are the crimes of the century.

Notes

1 I have treated the question of defining ecocide at considerable length elsewhere, most notably in Stoett (2000), where I distinguish between minimalist (military action) and maximalist (neglectful environmental harm, such as air travel) definitional poles. In between we have military preparation and production and more conscious acts of ecological harm/sabotage outside of wartime, such as the dumping of toxic waste by organized criminals, which is a TEC.

2 ENMOD is the Convention on the Prohibition of Military or any Hostile Use of Environmental Modification Techniques, 10 December 1976. It prohibits Contracting Parties from engaging in "military or any other hostile use of environmental modification techniques having widespread, long-lasting or severe effects as the means of destruction, damage or injury to any other State Party." Generally, it is assumed that ENMOD applies to large-scale environmental disruption projects, and not to small-scale environmental destruction during wartime. Regardless, it is best known today as a phantom treaty that has never really had an impact on decision-making on or off the battlefield. Importantly, it would not even apply to civil war contexts, though many examples of widespread, long-lasting or severely impactful environmental alteration for military purposes have taken place during non-international wars.

3 Zaitch et al. (2014: 92) assert: "A green criminological perspective offers the possibility of simultaneously focusing on three interrelated issues. Firstly, the perspective allows us to analyze who the perpetrators of criminal or harmful behavior are, how legal/illegal mechanisms operate and intertwine at micro and macro levels, and why these practices take place. Secondly, such a perspective can reveal who the victims are and which social and environmental harms can be identified when it comes to the exploitation of natural resources. Finally, this perspective also pinpoints the 'rights' being violated (whether constitutional, human, environmental, social, etc.), the social initiatives that defend them (communities affected, NGOs), and the measures and interventions that are put in place (or not) by private, state or international actors to guarantee, protect and enforce those rights." White has his own conception, discussed below.

4 For example, enforced restitution for environmental harms is an under-studied necessity. Under the ICC, victims can access the Victims Trust Fund, but it is unlikely there is sufficient funding to restore ecologically devastated areas after severe conflict. See also Carranza (2008); more broadly on restitution from environmental crime see Skinnider (2011).

5 "There is currently no clear possibility that an international criminal prosecution of a state may be instigated in the ICC for any international crime, including actions that are intended to produce significant environmental degradation. Instead, states might have some degree of legal responsibility for the commission of international crimes under the principles of state responsibility or blame might be imputed to a state as a result of the commission of an international crime by one of its officials. However, this is quite a different level of culpability from accepting the possibility that a state itself may be *criminally responsible*. This distinction is more than a question of semantics – it carries with it the message that, irrespective of the degree of involvement by the machinery of a state, its culpability for actions that precipitate very serious consequences for humans and the environment is something less than the standards by which we judge individuals" (Freeland 2005: 347–348).

6 Though as Drumbl (2009: 9) notes, "other war crimes in the Rome Statute could incidentally address environmental harms. Examples include article 8(2)(a)(iv) (prohibiting extensive destruction and appropriation of property not justified by military necessity and carried out wantonly and unlawfully), article 8(2)(b)(xvii) (prohibiting the use of poison and poisoned weapons), and article 8(2)(b)(xviii) (prohibiting the employment of asphyxiating, poisonous, or other gases). These, however, are not environmental crimes *stricto sensu* but are 'anthropocentric'—that is, they criminalize things or practices that principally are inhumane and only incidentally have devastating effects on the environment." Note the language in Article 8(2)(b)(iv) borrows largely from ENMOD.

7 These include the drafting of a statute that, if it were ever accepted, would change the very nature of international law. Its scope was breathtaking, though it is probable those who drafted the statute were well aware of how unreachable their goals were. As described by Avgerinopoulou (2003: 16): "The International Court of the Environment is intended to be a permanent organ with global jurisdiction, comprised of 15 independent judges, elected by the United Nations General Assembly (UNGA) and paid out of the

budget of the United Nations. States and non-state actors, such as intergovernmental organizations, non-governmental organizations and individuals, will have access to the Court. The subject-matter jurisdiction of the court will include every environmental dispute that has caused or may cause substantial environmental damage at the international or national level and has not been settled through arbitration within a period of 18 months. The court will also be able to act preventively, by rendering preliminary measures. It will be able to carry out investigations and inspections either upon request or ex officio, in the case of urgency. It will provide services of arbitration and advisory opinions on global environmental issues. In addition, it will respond to requests of preliminary ruling by national courts, according to the successful example of the European Court of Justice. Civil remedies shall include interlocutory or perpetual injunction. The court will be able to issue orders for redress of an injured individual, for payment of the cost for the restoration of the damaged environment, or for payment into a World Environmental Fund. The UN Security Council will be entrusted with enforcement of the judgments."

8 This should not surprise us; the Council of Europe adopted a Convention on the Protection of the Environment Through Criminal Law as early as 1998, which is echoed in EU Parliamentary Directive 2008/99/EC. See Collantes (2001).

9 The Latin American Environmental Prosecutors Network is a partial exception.

10 See also Cook, Roberts, and Lowther (2002).

11 Curiously, unlike Interpol's fast immersion into TEC, EUROPOL has not yet followed suite; it does not include TEC on its lengthy list of official priorities, though Cigarette Smuggling and Outlaw Motorcycle Gangs make the grade.

References

Avgerinopoulou D.T. (2003) *The Role of the International Judiciary in the Settlement of Environmental Disputes and Alternative Proposals for Strengthening International Environmental Adjudication* Global Environmental Governance: the Post-Johannesburg Agenda, 23–25 October 2003, Yale Center for Environmental Law and Policy, New Haven, CT.

Banks D., Davies C., Gosling J., Newman J., Rice M., Wadley J., and Walravens F. (2008) *Environmental Crime – A Threat to the Future* Environmental Investigation Agency (EIA), London.

Bierne P. and South N. (2007) *Issues in Green Criminology: Confronting Harms against the Environment, Humanity, and Other Animals* Willan, Cullompton, Devon.

Blindell J. (2006) "21st Century Policing – The Role of Police in the Detection, Investigation and Prosecution of Environmental Crime" *Australasian Centre for Policing Research*, issue 2. http://citeseerx.ist.psu.edu/viewdoc/download?doi=10.1.1.121.9033&rep=rep1&type=pdf

Brack D. and Hayman G. (2002) *International Environmental Crime: The Nature and Control of Environmental Black Markets* Background paper for workshop, May, Sustainable Development Programme, Royal Institute of International Affairs.

Brisman A. (2008) "Crime–Environment Relationships and Environmental Justice" *Seattle Journal for Social Justice* 6(2): 727–817.

Brockington D. and Igoe J. (2006) "Eviction for Conservation: A Global Overview" *Conservation and Society* 4: 424–470.

Carranza R. (2008) "Plunder and Pain: Should Transitional Justice Engage with Corruption and Economic Crimes?" *International Journal of Transitional Justice*, 2: 310–330.

Clapp J. (2001) *Toxic Exports: The Transfer of Hazardous Wastes from Rich to Poor Countries* Cornell University Press, Ithaca, NY.

Collantes J.L. (2001) "The Convention on the Protection of the Environment through Criminal Law: Legislative Obligations for the States" *Revista Medio Ambiente y Derecho* no. 6. https://libros-revistas-derecho.vlex.es/vid/environments-through-legislative-states-231696

Cook D., Roberts M., and Lowther J. (2002) *The International Wildlife Trade and Organised Crime: A Review of the Evidence and the Role of the UK* World Wildlife Foundation-United Kingdom, Godalming, Surrey.

Coyne J. and Bell P. (2011) "The Role of Strategic Intelligence in Anticipating Transnational Organised Crime: A Literary Review" *International Journal of Law, Crime and Justice* 39(1): 60–78.

Drumbl M. (2009) "Accountability for Property Crimes and Environmental War Crimes: Prosecution, Litigation and Development" Transitional Justice and Development Project, International Center for Transitional Justice, November. www.ictj.org/sites/default/files/ICTJ-Development-PropertyCrimes-FullPaper-2009-English.pdf [Accessed 23 May 2013].

Elliott L. (2009) "Combating Transnational Environmental Crime: 'Joined Up' Thinking about Transnational Networks" in Kangaspunta K. and Marshall I.H. (eds) *Eco-Crime and Justice: Essays on Environmental Crime* Public Information Department, United Nations Interregional Crime and Justice Research Institute, Turin, 55–77.

Elliott L. (2011) "Transnational Environmental Crime: Applying Network Theory to an Investigation of Illegal Trade, Criminal Activity and Law Enforcement Responses" Transnational Environmental Crime Project Working Paper 1, Department of International Relations School of International, Political and Strategic Studies, Australian National University Canberra.

Elliott L. (2012) "Fighting Transnational Environmental Crime" *Journal of International Affairs* 66(1): 87–10.

Forni O. (2010) "Mapping Environmental Crimes" *Freedom From Fear Magazine* March. Turin: UN Interregional Crime and Justice Institute.

Freeland S. (2005) "Crimes against the Environment – A Role for the International Criminal Court?" in Costi A. and Sage Y-L. (eds) *Droit de l'Environnement dans le Pacifique: Problématiques et Perspectives Croisées/Environmental Law in the Pacific: International and Comparative Perspectives* New Zealand Association for Comparative Law/Association de Législation Comparée des Pays du Pacifique Tahiti, 335–372 (ISBN 0-473-10630-2).

Gibbs C., McGarrell E., and Sullivan B. (2015) "Intelligence-led Policy and Transnational Environmental Crime: A Process Evaluation" *European Journal of Criminology* 12(2): 242–249.

Gilman R. (2011) "Expanding Environmental Justice after War: The Need for Universal Jurisdiction over Environmental War Crimes" *Colorado Journal of International Environmental Law and Policy* 22(3): 448–471.

Graycar A. and Felson M. (2010) "Situational Prevention of Organised Timber Theft and Related Corruption" in Bullock K., Clarke R.V., and Tilley N. (eds) *Situational Prevention of Organised Crimes* Willan, Portland, OR, 81–92.

Higgins P. (2015) *Eradicating Ecocide: Laws and Governance to Stop the Destruction of the Planet* 2nd edition, Shepheard-Walwyn, London.

Hinde S.M. (2003) "The International Environmental Court: Its Broad Jurisdiction as a Possible Fatal Flaw" *Hofstra Law Review* 32: 727–757.

Hoare A. (2007) "International Environmental Crime, Sustainability and Poverty in the Growth and Control of International Environmental Crime" Background paper for Session1, Chatham House workshop, 10–11 December, UK.

Interpol (2017) *Environmental Crime* www.interpol.int/Crime-areas/Environmental-crime/Environmental-crime [Accessed 19 February 2018].

Ivanović A. (2010) *Environmental Crime as a Factor of Endangering National Security* Conference proceedings: 11th Slovenian Days of Criminal Justice and Security – A Modern Criminal Justice and Security Guidelines, ISBN 978-961-6821-05-6, University of Maribor, Faculty of Criminal Justice and Security, Ljubljana.

McGarrell E.F., Chermak S.M., and Freilich J.D. (2007) "Intelligence-led Policing as a Framework for Responding to Terrorism" *Journal of Contemporary Criminal Justice* 23(2): 142–158.

Mégret F. (2011) "The Problem of an International Criminal Law of the Environment" *Columbia Journal of Environmental Law* 36(2): 195–257.

Nellemann C., (2012) *Green Carbon, Black Trade: Illegal Logging, Tax Fraud and Laundering in the World's Tropical Forests. A Rapid Response Assessment* United Nations Environment Programme, GRID-Arendal, Birkeland Trykkeri AS, Norway.

O'Reilly C. (2011) "From Kidnaps to Contagious Diseases: Elite Rescue and the Strategic Expansion of the Transnational Security Consultancy Industry" *International Political Sociology* 5(2): 178–197.

Pedersen O.W. (2012) "An International Environmental Court and International Legalism" *Journal of Environmental Law* 4(3): 547–558. doi: 10.1093/jel/eqs022

Peluso N. and Watts M. (2001) *Violent Environments* Cornell University Press, Ithaca, NY.

Shover N. and Routhe A.S. (2005) "Environmental Crime" *Crime and Justice* 32: 321–371.

Skinnider E. (2011) *Victims of Environmental Crime – Mapping the Issues* International Centre for Criminal Law Reform and Criminal Justice Policy, Vancouver.

South N. and Brisman A. (eds) 2013 *The Routledge International Handbook of Green Criminology* Routledge, New York.

Steyn P. (2015) "As Animal Poaching Surges, Organized Crime Plays Bigger Role" *National Geographic.* http://news.nationalgeographic.com/2015/05/150526-wildlife-crime-elephant-rhino-poaching-organized-crime/

Stoett P. (2000) *Global and Human Security: An Exploration of Terms* University of Toronto Press, Toronto.

Stoett P. (2012) *Global Ecopolitics: Crisis, Governance, and Justice.* University of Toronto Press, Toronto.

Stretesky P., Long M., and Lynch M. (2014) *The Treadmill of Crime: Political Economy and Green Criminology* Routledge, London.

Warner R. (2006) "The Place of History in International Relations and Ecology: Discourses of Environmentalism in the Colonial Era" in Lafferière E. and Stoett P. (eds) *International Ecopolitical Theory: Critical Approaches* UBC Press, Vancouver, 34–51.

Wellsmith M. (2011) "Wildlife Crime: The Problems of Enforcement" *European Journal on Criminal Policy and Research* 17(2): 125–148.

White R. (2008) *Crimes against Nature: Environmental Criminology and Ecological Justice* Willan, Cullompton, Devon.

White R. (2011) *Transnational Environmental Crime – Toward an Eco-global Criminology* Routledge, Abingdon. ISBN 978-1-84392-804-1.

Wright G. (2011) "Conceptualising and Combating Transnational Environmental Crime" *Trends in Organized Crime* 14(4): 332–346. Available at SSRN: https://ssrn.com/abstract=1966744

Wyatt T. (2013) *Wildlife Trafficking: A Deconstruction of the Crime, the Victims, and the Offenders* Palgrave Macmillan, Basingstoke.

Zaitch D., Boekhou van Solinger T., and Muller G. (2014) "Harms, Crimes and Natural Resource Exploitation: A Green Criminological and Human Rights Perspective on Land-Use Change" in Bavink M., Pellegrini L., and Mostart E. (eds) *Conflicts Over Natural Resources in the Global South: Conceptual Approaches* CRC Press, London, 91–108.

4

Climate change and environmental conflicts

Simon Dalby

Climate security

The term 'climate security' has recently emerged as a shorthand expression for a broad range of issues that seemingly link conflicts, vulnerabilities and various forms of insecurity to global environmental change. In the United States in particular numerous retired military officers have made repeated public statements about the dangers climate change presents to specifically American national security, echoing increasingly alarming statements from the Pentagon and the White House (Holland 2016). British policy makers have repeatedly raised climate security arguments (Rothe 2016) along with their German counterparts (German Advisory Council on Global Change 2008). Climate has been discussed as a matter of security by the United Nations on a number of occasions now too, although many states prefer to discuss climate as a matter of development and adaptation rather than security (Dalby 2016a). Regardless, alarming statements about resource shortages caused by climate change causing conflicts, if not all-out wars, continue to garner numerous headlines.

Many of the themes in the climate discussion echo earlier discussions of environmental security, a theme that emerged in the late 1980s at the end of the Cold War as security analysts looked for new threats to the West after the demise of the Soviet threat and environmentalists tried to garner attention for pressing issues of tropical deforestation, stratospheric ozone depletion, radioactive pollution, biodiversity loss, water resource shortages and numerous other issues that had obvious global connections (Renner 1989). While it seemed that such difficulties would lead to conflict, that scarcities of key resources would cause conflicts and wars in future, it wasn't entirely clear in much of the discussion quite how this might come about.

As much of the rest of this chapter suggests, these formulations are often misleading, and indeed both climate and conflict issues might be better treated separately, not least because it is not at all clear that warnings about potential climate wars are efficacious in either preventing conflict or effectively mobilizing political action to deal with climate change (Meierling 2016). Nonetheless these formulations have persisted through the last few decades in updated versions of environmental security (Floyd and Matthew 2013) and repeated articulations of the dangers of climate-related disruptions to Western security. What is much less frequently noted is the simple point that in so far as climate change is a security threat, it's the Western states which generate alarms about climate in diverse and many inconsistent ways (Diez et al. 2016; Rothe 2016) that have historically produced most of the greenhouse gases that are causing climate change. In so far as solutions are to be found then remaking the global economy is far the most important theme that needs attention in climate security (Dalby 2013).

The question of how climate change might cause conflict, and if and when it does what should be done by whom to deal with the violence links the empirical questions in climate security to the policy ones, but the links are far from straightforward, not least because how the complicated empirical questions should be formulated and answered is in dispute among researchers (Scheffran et al. 2012). The rest of this chapter works through these difficulties suggesting that larger scale geopolitical issues and the interconnections in the global economy are the most important matters (Selby and Hoffmann 2014), ones that frequently get overlooked when local conflicts and their potential spread in a climate disrupted world are the dominant framing of the issue (O'Lear and Dalby 2016).

Environment, conflict and security

Research in the 1990s suggested that the relationships between environment, conflict and security were much more complex than policy analysts and media commentators frequently thought, and that while environmental change might indeed cause all sorts of displacements and insecurities, it wasn't necessarily a cause of conflict, and was unlikely to lead to international warfare (Homer-Dixon 1999). Indeed, it emerged that water shortages in particular often led to cooperation rather than conflict as shared resources required working together to manage and use them wisely. Shared infrastructures are hardly conducive to serious conflict as little advantage can be gained by destroying facilities that provide water for agriculture and urban use. While clearly low-level violence is related to some resource uses, especially where areas of fixed agriculture and nomadic herding overlap without carefully worked-out procedures to share the land and water supplies, alarmist fears of large-scale eco wars were discounted while many small-scale conflicts in areas of underdevelopment were highlighted (Baechler 1998; Lietzmann and Vest 1999).

But while these may have had fatalities and generated insecurity for local peoples, they clearly didn't rate as the kind of threat that the nuclear-armed superpower stand-off did in previous decades. It also became clear in the following decade that much of the political violence around the world was over control of resource supplies, not about matters of scarcity, a long-standing pattern sometimes obscured by the contemporary focus on environment and climate in particular (Le Billon 2012). Given the scale of climate change as a problem that has numerous dimensions that appear to be global in scope, and the growing recognition that the planet is being changed quite drastically as a result of the massive scale of carbon fuel use and, to a lesser degree, deforestation, land use patterns and other industrial and urban pollutants (Steffen et al. 2015), issues of conflict and security are not surprisingly back in the forefront of policy concern. After a few years when the war on terror occupied most security scholars' attention, environmental matters have returned to prominence in the discussion of security (Goldstein 2016).

In part, it seems that despite the renewed attention, some of the lessons from the 1990s haven't been learned. A confused debate about whether extreme weather is causing a rise in violence, and whether, if it is, this constitutes a clear link between climate change and conflict, continues despite conflicting findings and numerous methodological weaknesses that cast doubt on the whole enterprise (Buhaug 2015). Even if extreme weather is causing conflicts, it is not at all clear that the appropriate response to this in most cases is a military one. This is an old argument from the 1980s that, it seems, is still very pertinent (Deudney 1990). The more critical literature suggests that militarizing climate is likely to make everything worse (Marzec 2016), and indeed in some cases the military is itself actually a major culprit in causing climate change both directly by the carbon fuels it uses so profligately, and indirectly by supporting destructive corporate modes of state development that make people more vulnerable rather than safer (Buxton and Hayes 2016).

While there have been numerous attempts, especially in the Anglo-Saxon world, to deny the realities of climate change, or to downplay the dangers in favor of continued economic growth powered by fossil fuels (Jacques 2009), the obvious evidence of climate change and the increased frequency and severity of extreme weather events has now become widely accepted. In military circles in the United States, the self-evident rise in sea levels and the vulnerabilities of many societies to tropical storms, hurricanes, as they are called in the Atlantic, or typhoons, as they are known in the Pacific, have focused military planners' attention on the need to prepare to deal with disasters. They too have to plan for rising seas causing coastal facilities to be vulnerable to erosion and flooding.

In areas of political instability climate change has been posited repeatedly as a 'threat multiplier' (CNA 2007; Campbell et al. 2007) adding additional social stresses that lead to radicalization and declining state capacities in the face of droughts, floods, food shortages and the disruptions of migrants moving out of harm's way or seeking new means of livelihood when their agricultural systems are rendered unproductive. More recently, analysts in the United States have suggested that climate is more than a threat multiplier, being understood as a catalyst for conflict in many places (CNA 2014). This then requires the US military to be prepared to help provide security assistance to weakened regimes, many of which are, so the argument goes, increasingly vulnerable to terrorism and insurgencies as a result of the disruptions.

In search of some simple policy suggestions, the empirical question of where climate change can be seen to cause conflict appears to be the first and obvious question for researchers. A number of research projects have looked at meteorological data over the last few decades, and tried to draw correlations with conflict, suggesting that there is a causal connection if there is a pattern of weather extremes, heat, droughts, storms or some combination that coincides with political violence, all without coming to any clear consensus on the relationships of climate and conflict (Ide et al. 2016). The assumption is that there are discernable patterns, and hence, when linked to climate models it ought to be possible to predict likely security problems. These predictions in turn can lead to necessary policy actions and, in the worst case, preparations for military interventions. If the potential for violence is linked to larger political problems, insurgencies and terrorist networks, then clearly this is a matter of concern for military planners in the West too.

However, simple correlations, while suggestive, don't explain the complex causes of conflict in particular places (Selby 2014). While extreme weather, droughts, floods and related disruptions inevitably strain social systems, it is not at all clear that they necessarily cause violence, much less organized warfare. Detailed work trying to disaggregate national data and link much smaller scale analyses of weather and conflict produce no convincing evidence that a general causal link exists between fluctuating weather systems and organized violence (Buhaug 2015). As with the 1990s debate about environmental scarcities and acute conflict (Homer-Dixon 1999), other variables, not least the behavior of political elites in a crisis, whether they attempt to help, or instead benefit themselves, matter in terms of outcomes. The long-term history of prior conflict in a region is also a factor; fighting may resume when a social system is stressed by food shortages, drought or the failure of relief efforts to assist storm or flood victims in ways that allow grievances to be turned into issues for political mobilization by challengers for power.

History

Environmental history has, in the last few decades, generated numerous new insights into how human actions have changed landscapes and remade natural ecologies in the process of deforestation, agricultural innovations and the widespread elimination of species. These processes greatly accelerated as European imperialists extended their reach in the second half of the last millennium (Crosby 1986). Now, these processes are understood as part and parcel of the expansion of the global economy, only the latest manifestation of which is the matter of anthropogenic climate change (Hornborg et al. 2007). The paleo-ecological record, from tree ring analysis, pollen counts and numerous other indicators of past environmental conditions, makes clear that, while in comparison to earlier geological times, the last 10,000 years, known as the Holocene period, has had a remarkably stable climate, nonetheless there have been notable fluctuations.

Some of the obvious volcanic disasters in previous centuries, Tamboro in 1815, Krakatoa in 1885 and even Pinatubo in 1991, clearly affected agricultural production around the world in the years immediately after they lofted huge amounts of dust into the atmosphere providing temporary global cooling. Food shortages resulted and social stress followed, but these are short-term events, not a matter of longer-term climate change. While they may be dramatic historic episodes, they are not very good indications of how climate change might change things. The longer-term, more gradual history of climate change, notably in the 'little ice age' that began at the end of the European medieval period and lasted most of the way into the nineteenth century, clearly changed agricultural patterns (Fagan 2000).

The seventeenth century was a period of widespread famines in many parts of the world and a period of intense social change, and in Europe, in particular, much bloodshed in the Thirty Years War. Elsewhere, social change was accelerated by starvation and attempts by military and political elites to deal with the social dislocation part of the 'global crisis' (Parker 2013) that shaped many nascent modern institutions, including the international state system that is often simplistically dated to the Treaties of Westphalia. That the climate cooled isn't in doubt, and clearly food shortages were part of the tumult that changed the European political landscape quite dramatically. As Parker's (2013) analysis shows, however, it wasn't inevitable that shortages would lead to warfare; the regimes that took seriously their responsibilities to their subjects often fared better than those that went to war. It is also very much the case that armies frequently 'lived off the land', provisioning themselves by whatever food and fodder was locally available and leaving the local population in want once the soldiers moved on. Starvation too has long been a weapon of war and care has to be taken in imputing climate as a causal factor in famine during such times of conflict.

The last extensive famine in Western Europe, the Irish 'great hunger' in the 1840s, was caused when the widespread outbreak of potato blight eradicated the staple food for much of the poorer part of the island's population, but it did not lead to major political conflict (Fraser 2003). Given that meteorological conditions were especially conducive to the spread of the blight in the famine years, it's not too much of a stretch to suggest that a temporary climate aberration was partly to blame, but social arrangements, and the pernicious doctrines of contemporary political economy of the time, in which the poor were blamed for their own misery, and forced to work for minimal relief, explain much of the death and destitution that followed. This was insecurity and vulnerability, but not political conflict or a cause of war. Similar patterns of commercial disruption and neglect of vulnerable peoples by European imperial administrations later in the nineteenth century contributed greatly to famines that killed millions (Davis 2001). Likewise, the famines of the twentieth century in Eastern Europe during the early decades of the Soviet Union were caused by political struggles, not 'natural' phenomena. Great care has to be used in imputing climatological causes to human conflict, even if it is much easier to suggest them as a cause of immense suffering.

It is also the case that historical lessons might not be helpful in thinking about the likely future course of climate-related human difficulties. Since the Second World War, the global economy has rapidly expanded, industrial capabilities now dwarfing what could be built and produced in earlier periods. The rapid rise in carbon dioxide in the global atmosphere, which is now driving climate change, is because of this huge fossil fueled economic expansion (McNeill 2000). Part of this process is the rapid urbanization of the growing global population; we are now an urban species in that more than half of us live in towns and cities. The extraordinary transformation of rural landscapes that has happened simultaneously is in part about industrial agriculture expanding into many parts of the world to provide food and such things as palm oil to supply urban demands. This has displaced many subsistence farming systems, and rising commercial prices for farm land often preclude farmers from easily accessing new fertile land once they have been forced to move, whether by conflict, dispossession or drought (Parenti 2011).

The transportation systems, roads, railways and ships we now have to move materials into the cities and around the world also provide the capabilities for moving large quantities of food to areas facing famine, and do so on a scale and over distances that previous rulers often couldn't even contemplate. Globalization has changed the situation. Local climate changes, droughts, floods, storms and heatwaves may cause great distress among local populations of subsistence farmers, but now the world both knows these things are coming and has the ability, if frequently not the political will, to act in timely manner to help starving peoples. Likewise, unlike previous episodes of climate change, we also know that this too is accelerating even if we are yet unsure exactly how it will play out. As Jared Diamond's (2005) much discussed volume of over a decade ago made clear, 'collapse' is not the inevitable consequence of environmental change, at least not so if political systems can adapt to shape landscapes and trading systems to better prepare for future uncertainties and reduce the very wasteful current practices of food transportation and processing while simultaneously thinking of how to better protect ecosystems and people from extreme events.

Climate adaptation

Nonetheless, it is important to emphasize that climate mitigation measures are urgently necessary to slow the process of change to allow for easier adaptation. More extreme climates, more frequent storms and droughts will play out on landscapes that have been dramatically altered by human actions through history, changes that have been accelerated in recent decades by the globalization of food systems and the intrusion of commercial property markets and land grabs by distant corporations or states. These intrusions are frequently the cause of local conflict as people resist evictions, property right appropriations and landscape changes (Peluso and Watts 2001; Nixon 2011). Some of these are ironically driven by attempts to diversify food supply sources abroad in the face of increasing uncertainty about agricultural sustainability at home. Adaptations driven by international commercial arrangements may further marginalize subsistence food producers in distant lands (Dunlap and Fairhead 2014). If these dispossessed people are understood as a threat to peace and stability the irony is palpable, but such are the interconnections of a globalized world.

These geographies need to be worked into thinking about how to reduce insecurities of many sorts. Not least, this is because so many of the geopolitical frameworks used to specify climate dangers use very persistent formulations of distant dangers to metropolitan security. Thomas Malthus (1970) suggested that the pressure of population growth drove migrations from Asia into Europe, movements he argued that caused the collapse of the Roman Empire and the sack of Rome, and similar Malthusian tropes continue to appear in the environmental security discussion (Hartmann 2014). Threat multiplier arguments, where climate disruptions supposedly cause instabilities, terrorism and insurgencies, which threaten the West, often fail to grapple with the more complicated causes of rural trans-formation, agricultural change and disrupted traditional patterns of migration. In this they closely follow the similar mistaken arguments of imperial administrators in the last century (Watts 2015). Even more so they simply assume that patterns of economic growth fueled by combustion are inevitable, and the consequences will simply have to be managed by security agencies.

There are a number of ironies in all this, not least that vulnerabilities to extreme events are also affecting populations in the metropoles (Dalby 2009). In the United States, hurricane Katrina flooded much of New Orleans, a few years later super storm Sandy did much damage to New York and the summer of 2016 was marked both by extreme fires and flooding in many places. In Europe, floods and heatwaves have become more frequent too, although in none of these cases has serious violence resulted. Hence the vulnerabilities and what to do to adapt to them suggest that notions of human security and plans to adapt to reduce vulnerabilities are the key rather than military interventions, however useful some military equipment may be in rescue missions once disaster strikes.

Adaptation to climate change may take many forms but clearly one of the crucial themes is making habitats and ecosystems less vulnerable to extremes (Pelling 2011). Reducing vulner-abilities should also reduce social disruptions and, in so far as these are a source of conflict, hence improve security for all concerned. The difficulty here is that focusing only on some aspects of climate change, such as food supplies, to the exclusion of other ecological matters, or the eco-nomics of ensuring that people can actually buy the food that is available, fails to think through the multiple processes involved. Narrow technological fixes, such as breeding crops that are 'climate smart' so they can better resist droughts, may help feed some people, but if the fields are vulnerable to flooding, or because they facilitate rapid run-off of rainwater and hence flooding downstream, these measures alone aren't enough.

Likewise, questions of who owns land and what they choose, or are required, to grow, how much is forested, and which crops, what kind of plowing systems, what is irrigated and how, all have ecological effects that matter. Crucially, all these factors are currently in a period of flux regardless of climate effects as development conflicts play out across numer-ous landscapes (Taylor 2015). Frequently, one of the best methods of preventing floods is to ensure that there are forested areas in the headwaters of rivers upstream from vulnerable towns. These wooded areas often act as sponges absorbing rain and releasing it slowly into the ecosystem, hence slowing the flow in streams and rivers. If commercial farming, to increase food supplies or export crops, causes deforestation in uplands, then vulnerabilities downstream may be increased. All this suggests the need for comprehensive land use plan-ning of the sort that is often beyond the capabilities of developing states in particular, and runs into political opposition by landowners in many cases, so adaptive change isn't easy. Indeed, attempting to implement policies may be the cause of conflict; thinking through adaptation carefully is essential to prevent such 'backdraft' effects making things worse (Dabelko et al. 2013).

Vulnerability and resilience

Nonetheless, increasing the resilience of individuals and societies in the face of rapid change is a key priority for many policy makers. The resilience framework draws from ecological science discussions of environmental systems and their response to disruption (Gunderson and Holling 2002). Frequently disrupted ecosystems reconstruct themselves after the event, as is obvious in the case of forest fires where something resembling the forest prior to the fire eventually regrows. Resilience thinking, thus, tries to facilitate both surviving the disruption and reconstruction afterwards to reassemble societies and economies effectively, and hence avoid situations where destabilization might lead to conflict and violence. The ability to 'bounce back' quickly is emphasized as the best way to adapt to unavoidable disruptions, ones made more likely precisely by increasing climate change.

In so far as societies are vulnerable to extreme events, preparations to reassemble things after a storm or flood make policy sense, hence the focus on resilience. Much of the discussion of resilience is, however, about financial mechanisms to insure against commercial losses, and to ensure the continued function of government organizations in the aftermath of a storm that demolishes crucial infrastructure, and in the process, may also destroy sources of government revenue and the ability to collect it (Grove 2016). At the level of the household, resilience makes sense in terms of being prepared for a disaster by having water, food, batteries, a reliable radio, extra cellphones and a 'go bag' with essentials in it ready for an evacuation. Having insurance to facilitate rebuilding after a fire or flood is also a sensible precaution that reduces long-term vulnerabilities, although in many societies it is precisely the most vulnerable who either do not have assets that are insurable or, if they do, do not have the funds to allow them to purchase the policies they might need. All of which suggests that the resilience framework is much too limited in focus to deal with current necessities much less facilitate transitions to more sustainable and less vulnerable societies in future (Scheffran et al. 2012).

In terms of security, climate change now requires not just protecting and reconstructing the system but changing it and transforming landscapes, ecosystems, cities and trading arrangements so that they are both less vulnerable to obvious hazards and flexible enough to reinvent themselves when unpredictable crises occur (Pelling 2011). The political dangers and policy limitations of resilience thinking lie both in the assumptions that if people suffer it is their own fault for failing to be resilient, and in the transfer of focus from tackling aspects of the global economy that are causing enhanced extreme events to arguing that disasters are inevitable and many simply live in catastrophe's path (Cox and Cox 2016). The corollary is to assume that peripheral places are intrinsically violent, and hence climate disasters and related violence are nothing new, merely business as usual, a mode of understanding which facilitates either ignoring problems 'over there' or supporting military interventions (Welzer and Camiller 2012).

In addition, present implicitly if not explicitly in much of the related discussions of sustainability and transition strategies, is that climate change mitigation and smart growth policies will in the medium term, or at worst in the long term, be stopped and that new fairly stable circumstances will emerge where societies can assume that weather patterns will once again be predictable and hopefully something analogous to the recent past. The sheer speed of current climate change however makes this a doubtful possibility and certainly not a set of premises on which long-term thinking about policy options should rely (Dalby 2016b). Likewise, the interconnectedness of the global economy means that any serious discussion of the potential conflict consequences of climate change needs to address matters of changes in terms of the international system. Doing so, however, requires caution in drawing inferences from particular events, but clearly the largest dangers from climate change lie in disruptions to the global system, not in local environmental events, which might or might not spiral into violence.

Global change/local conflicts

The focus on local-scale causal mechanisms, and whether climate will cause conflicts in particular places due to proximate causes is a distraction from the larger patterns of change that, given both trading and political interconnections, and how these are managed, determine the security outcomes for much of the global population (Stiglitz and Kaldor 2013). The events of the global financial crisis in 2008 and the spikes in food prices at the same time, and again a couple of years later, focus attention on the long-distance interconnections that now matter in terms of global security much more than the preoccupation with small-scale violence that might be related to local climate changes. The drought in Russia in the summer of 2010 led to forecasts of a much-reduced harvest and caused alarm in Moscow. This resulted in a decision to stop exports of wheat as a precaution against likely future shortages. This in turn led to a spike in global grain prices as hoarding and speculation drove market behavior and other actors tried to buy what was available. Given how interconnected the global system now is, such complex causations are key to understanding global vulnerabilities (Homer-Dixon et al. 2015).

Did this spike in food prices cause the Arab spring indirectly, and with it all the political turmoil that resulted subsequently, not least the Libyan civil war and the violent implosion of Syria? The causations aren't that simple but there is a connection between the rise in food prices, the initial protests in Tunisia and subsequent events across the region. Was this, in the Syrian case, aggravated by a drought in the eastern region of the country, one that apparently was caused by climate change? Is therefore the Syrian civil war and the rise of ISIS caused by climate change? Once again, these simple causations miss the complicated social and political circumstances in the region (Swain and Jägerskog 2016). In particular they don't consider the particular political situation in these states, the complicated interplay of globalization, social change and trade that shaped the local conditions that made political elites see protests as a threat to their power rather than a cry for help to deal with injustices and poverty. There is little evidence that the displaced farmers were among the protestors in 2011, but once the protestors were portrayed by the regime as a challenge to its control, violent repression followed, which in turn escalated into further opposition to the government.

In the Syrian case, it is possible to make the case that while climate change was part of the complex dynamics prior to the outbreak of violence, the prior history of repression of opposition and the failures of agricultural development in the eastern part of the country were much more obviously the cause of difficulty than climate change induced droughts. The inadequate irrigation systems and the development model that introduced them into Eastern Syria meant that there was little resilience in the agricultural system when the weather changed (Gleick 2014). Numerous farm workers and farmers lost their livelihoods as a result and this economic problem led them to migrate to towns and cities. Once they protested about the failures of the Syrian political system to come to their aid, and were represented by the regime as a challenge to its control, violent repression followed, which in turn escalated into further opposition to the regime.

Such dynamics suggest parallels with many of the historical examples from earlier times that Davis (2001), Parker (2013) and other historians document, where regimes are more concerned with maintaining power than dealing with the economic plight of their peoples. Nothing makes political violence inevitable in the face of dire poverty and distress as the case of the Irish famine in the 1840s emphasizes, but the spiral of violence in the case of Syria replayed earlier revolts that had been violently defeated in previous decades. The protests across the region at the time were much more about politics than about climate, although food prices, partly driven by the international market fluctuations, were obviously a factor. In this sense, the discussion of threat multipliers or catalysts of conflict makes some sense, but clearly, as recent research emphasizes, it's the capabilities and willingness of existing regimes to respond appropriately to the stresses that are most important (Zografos et al. 2014). Governance matters in responding to changing times, in terms of both climate and global economic fluctuations. This is the key point in the climate security discussion that needs reinforcement in policy deliberations, rather than a focus on local environmental conditions and simple scarcity narratives as a causal mechanism for conflict.

Future conflicts?

As climate change accelerates in coming decades, large-scale destabilizations loom as an increasingly likely prospect. The relatively stable climate of the Holocene period, what is now increasingly understood as the 'safe operating space' for humanity, given that our agricultural systems and infrastructure are designed to operate in these conditions (Steffen et al. 2015), is now ending. What is coming is unclear given that there is no analogue situation in the recent climate record of the planet. The Holocene was remarkably unusual in just how stable the climate system was in comparison to earlier 'interglacial' warm periods. The future of the global climate system is much more likely to be a matter of increasingly unpredictable fluctuations; change is the new normal, and human actions are key to shaping the future.

Given the current trajectories of carbon fuel use and the so far unconvincing efforts on the part of large-scale users of carbon fuels to cut their usage and build non-carbon-based economies, the possibilities of artificially adjusting the earth's albedo to reflect more sunlight, and hence reduce the amount of warming that greenhouse gases are causing, are being increasingly seriously discussed (Hamilton 2013). Geoengineering solutions, as such technologies are now collectively called, only most obviously involving such things as plans to inject sulfate aerosols into the stratosphere or use iron filings to stimulate algal blooms in the ocean, are looming on the horizon as technical fixes to try to stave off the worst disruptions of climate change (Vaughan and Lenton 2011). However, given that it is not clear how such attempts might change regional climates, and do such things as disrupt the monsoon season in South and South East Asia, which brings the rains that rice and other crops there need to provide food for a substantial portion of humanity, the potential for conflict over attempts to artificially modify climate also looms.

While these uncertainties, and the obvious need to coordinate efforts rather than work at cross purposes, would seem to make cooperation more likely than conflict, it is not impossible to see that politicians faced with domestic difficulties related to food production shortages in the face of unusual weather events might choose to blame other states' geoengineering projects (Urpelainen 2012). The precedent has already been set when Iran's President Ahmadinejad blamed Iranian agricultural difficulties on the supposed use by external powers of cloud seeding technologies to deny Iran much needed rain (Dalby and Moussavi 2016). While no one took the president's claims seriously, as there is no evidence that such a strategy was even contemplated, much less implemented, the precedent is unnerving given that sulfate injection technology is relatively easy to produce and, by the standards of international security issues, very cheap.

In the face of such considerations, it is clear that what now needs to be secured both by individual states and by the United Nations system more generally is the ability to adapt while simultaneously building a global economy that doesn't use carbon-based fuels. This is particularly important because it is becoming easier to use climate change models of greater sophistication, and a longer meteorological record to attribute a climate change dimension to particular extreme events. This in turn is focusing the attention of victims of storms and, in the case of small island states, rising sea levels, on the responsibility of fossil fuel companies, and the states in which they operate, for the emissions of greenhouse gases (Vidas et al. 2015). In turn, this will lead to political demands for compensation and increasingly court claims to establish liability for damages attributed to extreme events, or for the territorial extinguishment of low lying states. While it isn't obvious that such legal actions will cause conflict, not least because poor vulnerable peoples have no military options, in so far as states resist the legal and political claims for compensation, international political tensions are inevitable given the obvious injustices the court cases highlight.

This point is crucial to thinking about the future of climate and conflict because the most obvious point in all this discussion that is frequently ignored is that those states that are most insecure due to climate change are often, though not exclusively, those that have done least to cause it. The overarching discussion of climate and conflict suggests that trouble in marginal parts of the global economy may spill over into metropolitan areas. But rarely, until relatively recently, has the obvious point that it is metropolitan consumption that has caused climate change, and hence is responsible for contemporary disruptions, been the focus of the climate security discussion. This is the key to climate insecurity and in so far as it can be linked to conflict, the indirect cause of climate violence. Getting this crucial point clearly in view is now key to thinking intelligently about both policy options for the future and how to conduct scholarly research with the appropriate contextualization to sensibly structure investigations.

References

Baechler, G. (1998) "Why Environmental Transformation Causes Violence: A Synthesis" *Environmental Change and Security Project Report* 4: 24–44.

Buhaug, H. (2015) "Climate–Conflict Research: Some Reflections on the Way Forward" *WIREs Climate Change* doi: 10.1002/wcc.336

Buxton, N. and Hayes, B. (eds.) (2016) *The Secure and the Dispossessed: How the Military and Corporations are Shaping a Climate Changed World* Pluto, London.

Campbell, K.M., Gulledge, J. McNeill J.R., et al. (2007) *The Age of Consequences: The Foreign Policy and National Security Implications of Global Climate Change* Center for Strategic and International Studies, Washington, DC.

CNA Corporation (2007) *National Security and the Threat of Climate Change* CNA Corporation, Alexandria, VA www.cna.org/cna_files/pdf/National%20Security%20and%20the%20Threat%20of%20Climate%20Change.pdf

CNA Military Advisory Board (2014) *National Security and the Accelerating Risks of Climate Change* CNA Corporation, Alexandria, VA.

Cox, S. and Cox, P. (2016) *How the World Breaks: Life in Catastrophe's Path, from the Caribbean to Siberia* The New Press, New York.

Crosby, A. (1986) *Ecological Imperialism: The Biological Expansion of Europe 900–1900* Cambridge University Press, Cambridge.

Dabelko, G., Herzer, L., Null, S., Parker, M., and Sticklor, R. (eds.) (2013) "Backdraft: The Conflict Potential of Climate Change Adaptation and Mitigation" Woodrow Wilson Center Environmental Change and Security Program Report 14(2).

Dalby, S. (2009) *Security and Environmental Change* Polity, Cambridge.

Dalby, S. (2013) "Climate Change: New Dimensions of Environmental Security" *RUSI Journal* 158(3): 34–43.

Dalby, S. (2016a) "Climate Change and the Insecurity Frame" in O'Lear, S. and Dalby, S. (eds.) *Reframing Climate Change: Constructing Ecological Geopolitics* Routledge, London, 83–99.

Dalby, S. (2016b) "Contextual Changes in Earth History: From the Holocene to the Anthropocene: Implications for the Goal of Sustainable Development and for Strategies of Sustainable Transition" in Brauch, H-G., Oswald Spring, U., Grin, J., and Scheffran, J. (eds.) *Sustainability Transition and Sustainable Peace Handbook* Springer-Verlag, Heidelberg, 67–88.

Dalby, S. and Moussavi, Z. (2016) "Environmental Security, Geopolitics and the Case of Lake Urmia's Disappearance" *Global Change, Peace and Security* 29(1): 39–55.

Davis, M. (2001) *Late Victorian Holocausts: El Nino Famines and the Making of the Third World* Verso, London.

Deudney, D. (1990) "The Case against Linking Environmental Degradation and National Security" *Millennium* 19: 461–476.

Diamond, J. (2005) *Collapse: How Societies Choose to Fail or Succeed* Viking, New York.

Diez, T., von Lucke, F., and Wellmann, Z. (2016) *The Securitization of Climate Change: Actors, Processes and Consequences* Routledge, London.

Dunlap, A. and Fairhead, J. (2014) "The Militarization and Marketization of Nature: An Alternative Lens to 'Climate–Conflict'" *Geopolitics* 19(1): 937–961.

Fagan, B. (2000) *The Little Ice Age: How Climate Made History 1300–1850* Basic Books, New York.

Floyd, R. and Matthew, R. (eds.) (2013) *Environmental Security: Approaches and Issues* Routledge, London.

Fraser, E. (2003) "Social Vulnerability and Ecological Fragility" *Ecology and Society* 7(2): 9.

German Advisory Council on Global Change (2008) *Climate Change as a Security Risk* Earthscan, London.

Gleick, P. (2014) "Water, Drought, Climate Change, and Conflict in Syria" *Weather, Climate and Society* 6: 331–340.

Goldstein, Joshua S. (2016) "Climate Change as a Global Security Issue" *Journal of Global Security Studies* (Advanced access 28 January) doi: 10.1093/jogss/ogv010

Grove, K. (2016) "Catastrophe Insurance and the Biopolitics of Climate Change Insurance" in O'Lear, S. and Dalby, S. (eds.) *Reframing Climate Change: Constructing Ecological Geopolitics* Routledge, London, 171–187.

Gunderson, L.H. and Holling, C.S. (eds.) (2002) *Panarchy: Understanding Transformations in Human and Natural Systems* Island Press, Washington, DC.

Hamilton, C. (2013) *Earthmasters: The Dawn of the Age of Climate Engineering* Yale University Press, New Haven, CT.

Hartmann, E. (2014) "Converging on Disaster: Climate Security and the Malthusian Anticipatory Regime for Africa" *Geopolitics* 19(4): 757–783.

Holland, A. (2016) "Preventing Tomorrow's Climate Wars" *Scientific American* June, 61–65.

Homer-Dixon, T. (1999) *Environment, Scarcity, and Violence* Princeton University Press, Princeton, NJ.

Homer-Dixon, T. et al. (2015) "Synchronous Failure: The Emerging Causal Architecture of Global Crisis" *Ecology and Society* 20(3): 6.

Hornborg, A., McNeill, J.R. and Martinez-Alier, J. (2007) *Rethinking Environmental History: World System History and Global Environmental Change* Rowman & Littlefield, Lanham, MD.

Ide, T., Link, P.M., Scheffran, J., and Schilling, J. (2016) "The Climate–Conflict Nexus: Pathways, Regional Links and Case Studies" in Brauch, H-G., Oswald Spring, U., Grin, J., and Scheffran, J. (eds.) *Sustainability Transition and Sustainable Peace Handbook* Springer-Verlag, Heidelberg, 285–304.

Jacques, P.J. (2009) *Environmental Skepticism: Ecology, Power and Public Life* Ashgate, Burlington, VT.

Le Billon, P. (2012) *Wars of Plunder: Conflicts, Profits and the Politics of Resources* Hurst, London.

Lietzmann, K.M. and Vest, G.D. (eds.) (1999) *Environment and Security in an International Context* NATO Committee on the Challenges of Modern Society Report No. 232, North Atlantic Treaty Organization, Bonn.

McNeill, J.R. (2000) *Something New Under the Sun: An Environmental History of the Twentieth Century World* Norton, New York.

Malthus, T. (1970) *An Essay on the Principle of Population* Penguin, Harmondsworth.

Marzec, R.P. (2016) *Militarizing the Environment: Climate Change and the Security State* University of Minnesota Press, Minneapolis.

Meierling, E. (2016) "Disconnecting Climate Change from Conflict: A Methodological Proposal" in O'Lear, S. and Dalby, S. (eds.) *Climate Change: Constructing Ecological Geopolitics* Routledge, London 52–66.

Nixon, R. (2011) *Slow Violence and the Environmentalism of the Poor* Harvard University Press, Cambridge, MA.

O'Lear, S. and Dalby, S. (eds.) (2016) *Reframing Climate Change: Constructing Ecological Geopolitics* Routledge, London.

Parenti, C. (2011) *Tropic of Chaos: Climate Change and the New Geography of Violence* Nation Books, New York.

Parker, G. (2013) *The Global Crisis* Yale University Press, New Haven, CT.

Pelling, M. (2011) *Adaptation to Climate Change: From Resilience to Transformation* Routledge, London.

Peluso, N. and Watts M. (eds.) (2001) *Violent Environments* Cornell University Press, Ithaca, NY.

Renner, M. (1989) *National Security: The Economic and Environmental Dimensions* Worldwatch Institute, Washington, DC.

Rothe, D. (2016) *Securitizing Global Warming: A Climate of Complexity* Routledge, London.

Scheffran, J., Brzoska M., Brauch H-G., Link P., and Schilling J. (eds.) (2012) *Climate Change, Human Security and Violent Conflict: Challenges for Societal Stability* Springer, Berlin.

Selby, J. (2014) "Positivist Climate Conflict Research: A Critique" *Geopolitics* 19(1): 829–856.

Selby, J. and Hoffmann, C. (eds.) (2014) *Rethinking Climate Change, Conflict and Security* Routledge, London.

Steffen, W. et al. (2015) "Planetary Boundaries: Guiding Human Development on a Changing Planet" *Science* 637(6223): 10.1126/science.1259855

Stiglitz, J.E. and Kaldor, M. (eds.) (2013) *The Quest for Security: Protection without Protectionism and the Challenge of Global Governance* Columbia University Press, New York.

Swain, A. and Jägerskog A. (2016) *Emerging Security Threats in the Middle East: The Impact of Climate Change and Globalization* Rowman & Littlefield, Lanham, MD.

Taylor, M. (2015) *The Political Ecology of Climate Adaptation: Livelihoods, Agrarian Change and the Conflicts of Development* Routledge, London.

Urpelainen, J. (2012) "Geoengineering and Global Warming: A Strategic Analysis" *International Environmental Affairs* 12(4): 375–389.

Vaughan, N.E. and Lenton, T.M. (2011) "A Review of Geoengineering Proposals" *Climatic Change* 109(3/4): 745–790.

Vidas, D., Zalasiewicz, J., and Williams, M. (2015) "What Is the Anthropocene – and Why Is It Relevant for International Law?" *Yearbook of International Environmental Law* 25(1): 3–23.

Watts, M. (2015) "Now and Then: The Origins of Political Ecology and the Rebirth of Adaptation as a Mode of Thought" in Perreault, T., Bridge, G., and McCarthy, J. (eds.) *Routledge Handbook of Political Ecology* Routledge, New York, 19–50.

Welzer, H. and Camiller, P. (2012) *Climate Wars: Why People Will Be Killed in the Twenty First Century* Polity, Cambridge.

Zografos, C., Goulden, M.C., and Kallis, G. (2014) "Sources of Human Insecurity in the Face of Hydro-climatic Change" *Global Environmental Change* 29: 327–336.

5

Environmental pathways to peace

Ken Conca and Michael D. Beevers

Introduction: environmental challenges as peace opportunities?

Over the past fifteen years, a growing body of scholarship and practice has embraced the possibility that the environment, so often identified as a source of conflict, can instead be a catalyst for peace. This research agenda – often referred to as 'environmental peacemaking' or 'environmental peacebuilding'[1] – developed to challenge the conventional wisdom that environmental degradation and natural resource scarcities were an important new trigger or driver of violent conflict. Its proponents suggested that if environmental dynamics create or increase the risk of conflict, then it must also be possible to use the environment proactively and cooperatively, as a point of departure for strengthening the conditions for peace. Such opportunities have been theorized to exist at all stages of the so-called 'conflict cycle', including conflict prevention, conflict management, conflict resolution, and post-conflict recovery. They have been posited to work through a range of mechanisms, including the reduction of grievances, the identification of opportunities for joint gains, the deepening of trust, the institutionalization of new practices and relationships that can channel disputes away from violence, and the transformation of conflict identities.

Much of this work has been based on the premise that environmental interdependencies have characteristics that make the environment a useful domain for bringing together parties engaged in or at risk of acute conflict (Conca 2000; Conca and Dabelko 2002). First, environmental issues ignore human-made boundaries and actively span the socially constructed barriers among groups that are at the heart of conflict. This makes it difficult, if not impossible, to address environmental issues unilaterally, and it supplies both opportunities and incentives for cooperation. Second, the technical complexity of environmental change and the challenges of monitoring and interpreting environmental data might make it possible for parties in or at risk of violent conflict to increase knowledge and understanding collaboratively, and in the process to reduce uncertainty and build trust. Third, the place-based character of human–environment relationships, and the deep interweaving of environment and culture, may make it possible to soften exclusionary identities by creating a common sense of place and purpose.

Of course, none of these outcomes is guaranteed, and specific instances of environmental cooperation may or may not have peace-enhancing effects. Indeed, ecological interdependencies, depending on how they are handled by social actors, may have precisely the opposite effects: they may encourage the creation or hardening of social boundaries rather than their transcendence, or produce rival bodies of knowledge that themselves become part of a conflict, or harden rather than soften conflict identities that are based on perceived inter-group grievances. Dawson (2000), for example, documents how environmental grievances in post-Soviet Eastern Europe overlay with inter-ethnic tensions in ways that threatened to make environmental mobilizations divisive rather than unifying. Thus, one characteristic of environmental peacemaking in practice – and one daunting challenge for scholars seeking to test for such effects – is that much depends on how human agency responds to whatever opportunities may be afforded.

Some of the early scholarship on the concept of environmental pathways to peace theorized the existence of such possibilities (Conca 2000, 2002; Lejano 2006) and/or identified cases in which such dynamics were seen to be at work (Conca and Dabelko 2002; Matthew et al. 2002; Ali 2007). Others took a more skeptical approach, arguing that environmental relationships reflected and were shaped by the state of political relationships rather than influencing or altering them (Brock 1991; Lowi 1995). There were also early cautions in the literature that transnational environmental cooperation may worsen conditions for those living closest to the resource base, thereby creating rather than ameliorating tensions around natural resource issues (Peluso 1993; Duffy 2000). Conca (2000) noted that nominally environmental international cooperation might constitute simply more efficient resource plunder, particularly if not leavened by strong transnational ties among local civil-society groups and the opening of closed institutions and processes. Again, this underscores that where peace is concerned, environmental cooperation should be viewed only as a possible means rather than an end, and that much depends on the form and content of cooperative engagements.

In the years since these early conceptual works, a growing community of practice has emerged driven by intergovernmental (IGO) and transnational non-governmental (NGO) organizations, bilateral donor agencies, and a wide array of local and regional groups working in specific settings. Figure 5.1, from a summary report by the Environmental Cooperation for Peacebuilding Programme of the United Nations Environment Programme (UNEP), illustrates the many types of initiatives that seek to enhance peace through coordinated environmental governance or cooperative natural resource management. The upper portion of the figure focuses on a set of conflict risks around natural resources and environmental change, traced along a continuum representing stages of the conflict cycle. Here, peace initiatives aim primarily to reduce the likelihood or consequences of conflict. The lower portion of the figure represents a similarly broad swath of opportunities, again spanning the entirety of the conflict cycle, in which resource and environmental relationships might be used to strengthen the positive aspects of peace.

The idea that there are environmental pathways to peace has also gained endorsement in some high political circles, with luminaries such as UN Secretaries-General Kofi Annan and Ban Ki-Moon, Liberian president Ellen Johnson Sirleaf, Costa Rican president Óscar Arias Sánchez, and Soviet president Mikhail Gorbachev hailing the potential of the environment to play a role in building peaceful societies. Bilateral and multilateral donor agencies have also begun to incorporate the concept into their programming. The US Agency for International Development, for example, has deployed a Water and Conflict Toolkit for its field operatives and project managers; it stresses not only the need for conflict sensitivity when doing water projects and programming, but also the importance of proactively identifying opportunities to strengthen positive, cooperative social ties in those same endeavors (USAID 2014). Several internationally active NGOs have also embraced the theme to varying extents in their work. Thus, conflict-resolution groups such as Search for Common Ground have used environmental activities to build inter-group trust (Jobbins et al. 2017), and conservation organizations such as Conservation International

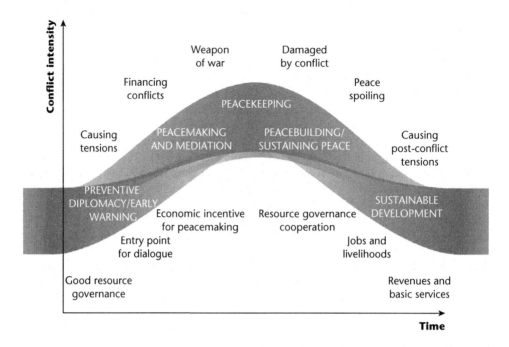

Figure 5.1 UN Environment Programme's conceptualization of "risks and opportunities from natural resources and the environment along the peace and security spectrum"

Source: United Nations Environment Programme, *Environmental Cooperation for Peacebuilding Programme: Final Report 2016*, p. 15. Nairobi: UNEP, 2016.

and World Wildlife Fund have launched initiatives that seek to "foster nature's role in resolving conflict" (CI n.d.) or tap "natural security" (Randall et al. 2010) to promote social resilience and disaster risk reduction. There are also several organizations whose *raison d'être* sits squarely at the juncture of environment, peace, and conflict, including EcoPeace (formerly known as Friends of the Earth Middle East), Green Cross International, International Alert, and the Center for Climate Security. They and others like them engage in activities that may include research and analysis, project implementation, policy advocacy, and second-track diplomacy.

Yet, the knowledge landscape for environment–peace linkages has been mapped in a limited and uneven way. The scholarly evidence for core theoretical claims remains uneven and fragmented, in several ways: some portions of the conflict cycle or dimensions of the posited relationship have received much more attention than others; some theorized opportunities have gained little in the way of empirical attention; and often-divergent methodologies – ethnographic inquiry, focused case comparison, statistical analysis – have been deployed with little conversation among them. Moreover, while many practitioner organizations have documented their work and the theories behind it (see for example EcoPeace/Friends of the Earth Middle East 2008), there have been only a handful of attempts to make systematic use of that body of material while also subjecting it to critical scrutiny (see for example Conca and Wallace 2009).

This chapter reviews the concept of environmental pathways to peace and summarizes what we think we have learned from the available body of scholarship and practice. It identifies conceptual and theoretical claims that remain contested or untested, points to research pathways to be explored, and flags both those aspects where we seem to have gained understanding and those where the largest knowledge gaps remain. The chapter then turns to a discussion of some specific opportunities for innovation in theoretical and empirical research on the topic. Throughout, we are conscious of the fact that peace is itself an essentially contested term. Our approach, following Conca (2000:226–277), is to conceive of peace as "a spectrum ranging from the absence of violent conflict to the inconceivability of such conflict," with the enhancement of peace consisting of moving in a positive direction along such a spectrum.

Historical context

In the late 1980s and early 1990s a body of scholarship began to emerge arguing that environmental problems were a growing factor in the risk or incidence of violent conflict. A team of researchers centered at the University of Toronto and led by Thomas Homer-Dixon (1991, 1994, 2010) theorized that various forms of environmentally induced scarcity triggered specific patterns of social response – including migration, livelihood effects, and resource capture – that increased risks of violent conflict. This work focused on impacts on renewable natural resources, including agricultural land, forests, fisheries, and freshwater resources, and found greater conflict risks at the intrastate, as opposed to interstate, level. The pathways to conflict that they conceptualized stressed the danger that environmentally induced scarcity and the resulting social responses to it would heighten tensions along existing patterns of social fragmentation, including cleavages around ethnicity, class, or religion. Around the same time, researchers led by Gunther Baechler of the Swiss Peace Foundation were developing a broadly similar conceptual framework, although paying more attention to the conflict risks of environmentally induced effects on unequal patterns of regional development (Baechler 1998).

Such claims remain contested among scholars. Early attempts to test eco-conflict hypotheses produced mixed results (e.g., Hauge and Ellingsen 1998; State Failure Task Force 1999; Urdal 2005), but seemed to suggest on balance that there was only limited support for core propositions linking environmental change and violent conflict, and that the economic and political drivers of violent conflict traditionally identified by conflict scholars had much stronger effects when tested alongside environmental variables. A more recent wave of statistical analysis of links specifically between climate change and armed conflict produced similarly weak-to-mixed results (Salehyan 2008; Theisen et al. 2013). As characterized in the "human security" chapter of the Fifth Assessment Report of the Intergovernmental Panel on Climate Change, "Some of these find a weak relationship, some find no relationship, and collectively the research does not conclude that there is a strong positive relationship between warming and armed conflict" (Adger et al. 2014: 772). Studies linking conflict specifically to cycles of drought and/or flooding, for example, have produced conflicting findings (e.g., Raleigh and Urdal 2007; Hendrix and Salehyan 2012; Slettebak 2012).

Statistical tests finding weak or no support for eco-conflict theses may not be definitive. Hendrix (2016; see also O'Lear 2006) notes several limits of statistical analysis in this context, including data limitations; the reverse causality problem (the fact that war and violence may cause the environmental scarcities theorized to drive war and violence, either directly or through mediating variables such as institutional performance); the limitations of using data that change only slowly over time to predict rapid-onset, rare events; and the tendency to lump together heterogeneous forms of political violence as the dependent variable, making it difficult to isolate on specific outcomes of concern or the mechanisms behind them. Ide and Scheffran (2014) note the role of terminological confusion and failure to integrate "the environmental peace perspective" as further barriers to a better understanding of environment/conflict dynamics.

In addition to differences between studies using 'like' methodologies, there are often notable differences in results across macro-statistical, sub-nationally georeferenced, and household-level scales of research (Linke et al. 2017).

Scholarly debate notwithstanding, the eco-conflict literature emerged at a time when the end of the Cold War was causing a rethinking of established security paradigms, practices, and institutions in several countries. This led some environmental policy entrepreneurs to perceive opportunities to gain attention to environmental concerns by linking them to a security framework. In his book *Earth in the Balance*, US Senator (and later Vice President) Al Gore (1992) invoked the possibility that environmental security threats could unify a fractious political system, overcoming the seemingly daunting barriers to collective action on unprecedented global environmental challenges. As 'environmental security' became a growing object of policymaker's attention, a critical literature on the implications of policy securitization also emerged (Waever 1993; Buzan et al. 1998), with the environment as a leading example of securitization risks (Deudney 1990; Tickner 1992; Conca 1994). Nor did the idea of environmental security impress developing countries in global policy debates: for many, it raised sensitivities that international efforts to protect the environment might infringe on sovereignty and hamper economic development, thereby creating a security rationale for sustaining an inequitable global political–economic system.

It was in this context that scholarship conceptualizing positive links between environmental protection and peace began to emerge. Central to the rationale for this work was the idea that focusing on positive opportunities for peace rather than negative threats to security might be a stronger strategic foundation to promote environmental cooperation (Conca 2000; Conca and Dabelko 2002; Matthew et al. 2002). As Conca (2002:3) noted around the time of the "Rio plus 10" summit in Johannesburg: "Recasting already contentious environmental debates in security terms – with the problematic connotations of intervention, unequal power, and a lack of voice in global institutions – has proven to be a diplomatic nonstarter." Conca (2002:4) also noted the de-linked character of existing work on environmental conflict and on environmental cooperation:

> Thus, for all that has been said and written, little has been done to investigate potentially important linkages between environmental conflict and environmental cooperation. It remains unclear whether and exactly how environmental cooperation can reduce the likelihood, scope, or severity of environmentally induced violence, or of violence and insecurity more generally. We have little knowledge of how to tailor environmental initiatives to speak specifically to the problem of violence. Even more important, we may be missing powerful peacemaking opportunities in the environmental domain . . .

In an effort to close that gap, Conca (2000) presented a deductive argument for the peacemaking potential of environmental cooperation. Focusing on the interstate level, he theorized two possible pathways. The first, rooted primarily in a game-theoretic conceptualization of the "contractual environment" for cooperation or conflict between states, suggested that the environment could be used to help transform barriers to cooperation and sources of insecurity such as mistrust, suspicion, uncertainty, competing interests, and short-time horizons (Conca 2000, 2002). Environmental peacemaking in this context meant leveraging environmental problems as an opportunity to alter these dynamics and bring countries together. Interdependence of ecological systems could be exploited as opportunities to work together toward mutual gains and, over time, establish cooperative practices. The complexity of environmental issues could be used to help states create shared knowledge in ways that could build trust and reduce suspicion. The long-term character of many environmental problems, while making cooperation difficult, could be stood on its head and embraced as a method of lengthening the "shadow of the future" in interstate relations and flagging the future stream of benefits from reduced hostilities and enhanced cooperation.

Conca's second path conceptualized peace as requiring more than just improved interstate relations, and stressed the importance of building a shared collective identity among people and groups such that violent conflict becomes less and less conceivable. This pathway, rooted in concepts of emergent "post-Westphalian" political practices and social identities, emphasized the strategic opportunities that environmental problems afforded to create or strengthen trans-societal non-state linkages, to foster new norms of cooperation and dispute resolution, and to transform security institutions that themselves constitute a barrier to peace.

Another early contribution was *Conserving the Peace* (Matthew et al. 2002), a book published as part of a joint initiative on environment and security by the International Institute for Sustainable Development (IISD) and the World Conservation Union (IUCN). Its case studies, authored primarily by conservation practitioners, identified ways that investment in conservation and better natural resource management could "conserve the peace" by addressing those root causes of violence and instability grounded in, or amplified by, poor environmental practices. It also argued that "conservation practices may provide a basis for bringing parties who have been or are engaged in conflict together to begin the process of peace building around common environmental concerns" (Matthew et al. 2002:5). By examining both the potential for environmentally induced conflict and the opportunities for peacebuilding dialogue, *Conserving the Peace* provided an important bridge between studies of environmental conflict and environmental cooperation. The book also reflected what would become a strong tendency in the literature on this topic: research that was driven by the perspectives, insights, and methods (as well as biases) of practitioners – either working in concert with more traditional scholars or taking the lead in publishing their own findings, often in non-peer reviewed reports and policy briefs targeting a policy audience.

One important strand in the conceptual foundations of environment/peace scholarship, implicit in early works such as *Environmental Peacemaking* and *Conserving the Peace*, but more fully developed by subsequent scholarship, is the recognition that socio-environmental interactions are social constructions. This means that whether such interactions catalyze cooperative or conflictive behavior is not inherent to the environmental circumstances and cannot be gleaned simply from the "incentive structure." Rather, such outcomes are shaped by the meaning and significance assigned to those interactions by human agents (Martin 2005; Ide and Fröhlich 2015). As Martin (2005:329) put it, "any resource use competition can be constructed in ways that engender either cooperative solutions or unproductive forms of conflict, including violence." Examining community-level discourses around water, cooperation and conflict in the context of the Palestinian–Israeli conflict, Ide and Fröhlich (2015:668) find a zero-sum, conflict-centered frame coexisting with a more cooperative frame stressing "largely (although not completely) inclusive identities and de-securitized situation assessments which highlight the need for water cooperation and more equitable water sharing."

Thus, challenging circumstances of the sort that a material scarcity thesis might predict to yield conflict could instead beget cooperative dynamics – as Martin (2005) documents in a case study of relations between a host community and a refugee camp. Research by Turner et al. in Niger among farmer and herder communities – so often cast as inherently in conflict due to climate-driven water scarcity across the Sahel – illustrates this point. Livelihood diversification adaptations, in which farmers engage in herding practices and vice versa, bring those communities into relations not simply of rivalry and conflict but also of enhanced social understanding, growing kinship ties, and opportunities for cooperation (Turner et al. 2011). Bogale and Korf (2007), while taking a more narrowly materialist view of the incentive structure, reach broadly similar conclusions in their study of agro-pastoralist communities in the "violence-prone" Somali Region of Ethiopia. Tubi and Feitelson (2016) find a similar pattern, with mixed conflictive/cooperative behavior that included extensive cooperation, in relations between Muslim Bedouin herders and Jewish agricultural settlements in the Negev during a historical episode of intensive drought.

An important corollary is that resource abundance may (and frequently does) fuel conflict, if actors with the ability to mobilize contention or violence feel themselves to be excluded from the benefits of abundance, to suffer disproportionately from the externalities of resource production, or to be inadequately consulted (Le Billon 2001). An emergent theme is that effective and equitable environmental and resource management can alleviate such tensions and enhance cooperation among the parties involved, reducing the potential for conflict (UNEP 2009).

Environmental cooperation as a peacebuilding tool: what have we learned?

The early conceptual works discussed previously essentially made two broad claims, grounded in a combination of deductive reasoning and observations from a handful of case studies. First, environmental initiatives could be exploited strategically to build or enhance peace; second, tapping such potential would depend on the specific characteristics of the initiative itself. Since then, we have not seen the emergence of a large, systematic body of research that seeks to test those core propositions in a cumulative, self-referential way. Rather, much of what we have learned has come by way of the trial-and-error methods of practitioners or from scholars seeking to answer other questions. Moreover, testing such propositions is no simple matter. As Carius (2006) has noted, there are several barriers to the clean measurement of the peace-enhancing effects of environmental cooperation. Peacebuilding goals are often implicit (and sometimes necessarily so, to avoid politicization of the issue), making it difficult to assess effectiveness relative to aims. Non-state actors often take the lead, making it difficult to evaluate effectiveness in terms of state commitments and compliance. Initiatives often do not include evaluation components and may not preserve necessary data.

A different sort of challenge is that much of the available theorizing was done at a specific level of analysis or in the context of a particular type of environmental phenomenon: for example, regional interstate dynamics for Conca and Dabelko's *Environmental Peacemaking* project, local conservation initiatives for the case studies in *Conserving the Peace*, and issue-specific transboundary dynamics in the sizable literatures on shared river basins (e.g., Wolf et al. 2003) and "peace parks" (e.g., Ali 2007). It is an open question as to whether any trust-building effects produced from building knowledge cooperatively will work the same way among, say, the riparian states in an international river-basin organization as they might among the local communities on opposite banks of that same river.

Much of the existing work on environmental peace has followed the organizational logic of the conflict cycle (e.g., Carius 2006). As a result, we have organized our discussion accordingly, while remaining sensitive to the ways in which a conflict-cycle framework can blur or elide conflict dynamics.

Preventing conflict

The thesis at the heart of the aforementioned eco-conflict literature was that material scarcities or rapid changes in the availability of natural resources or critical ecosystem services create grievances that can drive violent conflict. If this is correct, then it stands to reason that better environmental protection and resource management can forestall or diminish such conflict drivers. Thus, for example, Tir and Stinnett (2012) find that water cooperation mitigates the risk of water scarcity as a conflict driver. Griffin and Ali (2014) identify significant trust-enhancing effects associated with the Ramsar Convention (Convention on Wetlands of International Importance Especially as Waterfowl Habitats).

Grievances alone, however, are a poor predictor of violent outcomes: actors may lack the ability to mobilize grievances, or credible and legitimate institutions may effectively channel grievances into non-violent forms of political expression and problem solving. Indeed, the sizable literature on international cooperation and conflict over shared river basins casts considerable doubt on a simple scarcity-to-grievance-to-conflict model. An oft-cited study by Wolf and colleagues (2003), using a database of basin-specific episodes of interaction on water issues over a 54-year period across 122 international basins, found substantially more episodes of cooperation than conflict. They identified only a handful of episodes of "acute" conflict tied to water (including military or other hostile acts), most of which occurred between Israel and its neighbors. Moreover, acts of cooperation may lay a foundation for a cascade of deepened cooperation over time. Brochmann (2012; see also Dinar et al. 2016), studying shared river basins, found that signing water treaties correlated with later acts of water cooperation. Less clear, however, is whether the ability to find such cooperative solutions is channeling actions away from conflict; it may be that the conflict risk is not as great in practice as is often presumed.

The shared-basins literature provides stronger support for the second broad premise of environmental peace theorizing: that conflict outcomes depend not just on environmental cooperation, but also on its specific content. Tir and Stinnett (2012:223) analyze militarized conflict among river treaty signatories from 1950 to 2000 and find that "agreements supported by more extensive institutions tend to be better equipped to prevent conflicts from escalating." Dinar et al. (2015) find that treaties with water allocation mechanisms and treaties with a larger number of institutionalized mechanisms produce higher levels of cooperation. Mitchell and Zawahri (2015) find that treaties with provisions for information exchange and enforcement provisions are more effective in preventing the militarization of river claims among the parties.

Natural disasters, which are an extreme and abrupt form of environmental change, provide another domain for testing the conflict-prevention potential of environmental protection. There is some evidence in the literature, albeit no consensus, that natural disasters may create a subsequent heightened risk of civil war or other forms of large-scale violence. (They may also be a spur to conflict cessation when occurring in the midst of war, as discussed separately in the section on conflict termination, below.) If disasters create conflict vulnerabilities, then disaster risk reduction (DRR) can be thought of as a form of conflict prevention. In such instances, 'natural security' variants of DRR, such as the preservation of ecosystems that provide natural barriers against storm surges and inland flooding, may be considered a form of preventive environmental peacemaking.

However, the literature remains unclear as to the existence or importance of a disaster–conflict link. Nel and Righarts (2008) identify an increased conflict risk in the wake of disaster, with significant results for both the short and medium term, and across a range of income levels. Bergholt and Lujala (2012), however, find no such effect, even when allowing for an indirect pathway of disasters' impact on economic growth (which is considerable). In addition, Sletteback (2012) finds the opposite effect – that countries suffering disasters had (all else being equal) a lower risk of conflict. Similarly, Hendrix and Salehyan (2012), looking specifically at drought, find that periods of water abundance are more conducive to violent conflict than are periods of drought. They explain this finding in terms of the greater ease of mobilizing resources for political violence when basic needs are met than when such needs are more difficult to secure. It may also be that the well-documented impacts of disasters, which the latest IPCC assessment (Adger et al. 2014:762) identified in terms of "nutrition, economic stability, and threats to shelter and human health," create indirect pathways to conflict vulnerability that are difficult to tease out through the traditional statistical methods of conflict scholarship.

Another domain in which the conflict-prevention potential of environmental cooperation has been tested is that of transboundary protected areas or "peace parks" (Ali 2007). While it might be tempting to conclude that coordinating conservation activities in often-remote border regions would be a form of "low politics" with little in the way of broader political salience, it is interesting to note that agreements to establish transboundary protected areas are more likely to occur in interstate relationships that have been marked by militarized interstate disputes (Barquet et al. 2014). Borel (2008–09) notes the potential of such initiatives – to strengthen conservation, symbolize cooperative intent, redefine the symbolic meaning of borders, and reduce tensions through joint activity – while also allowing for the potential to heighten disparities or trigger tensions among local communities. Walters and Ali (2017) stress the potential for experiential learning in border landscapes, through experiences of personal empowerment, "the conscious use of symbolism and ritual to create meaningful images, metaphors, and experiences," and real-world experiences across identity groups that serve to counter existing stereotypes.

Whether transboundary conservation can have peace-enhancing effects appears to be highly sensitive to context: Barquet et al. (2014) found that transboundary protected areas led to an increased risk of militarized interstate disputes in Latin America, in contrast to a positive effect of lessening such dispute risk in other regions. They speculate that the difference is explained by the weaker tendency in Latin America than in other regions to use transboundary conservation as a tool of regional economic integration, and the lower overall risk of serious interstate conflict in the region (which may suggest a lower cost to allowing interstate disputes to become militarized). Further exploring the conflict risk of transboundary conservation, Barquet (2015:14) found that in the case of Costa Rica and Nicaragua, transboundary conservation provided "arguments for maintaining or even strengthening conflicts rather than fostering peace," including strengthening the state's presence in sensitive border regions. Van Ameron and Buscher (2005) reach similar conclusions regarding peace parks in southern Africa, cautioning that they heighten interstate tensions around power imbalances and trigger fears about inability to control borders, in ways that may undermine rather than stimulate cross-border cooperation and regional integration. Even when effects are positive, there are challenging questions about the capacity to sustain transboundary conservation activities. In a review of the experience of marine transboundary protected areas, Mackelworth (2012) found that sustaining governmental attention was a key determinant of long-term effectiveness.

Studies of highly localized dynamics also provide a domain for examining environment–peace links. Obviously, caution must be exercised in exporting theory or models of causal mechanisms across levels of analysis or different scales of social aggregation – whether it be in the personification of the state as an individual agent of choice or the presumption that localized conflicts share characteristics with, say, civil war. More useful is the integration of levels to gain a more complete understanding of complex, multi-level dynamics. Deligiannis (2012), for example, points out that much of the eco-conflict literature focused on regional and national dynamics, and failed to account for the (in)ability to make livelihood adjustments at the household or community level. Much like the interstate literature, a key message emerging from studies of localized dynamics is the importance of the institutional context. Linke et al. (2017) conducted surveys in Kenya that explored respondents' views about both the institutional context for natural resource use and personal attitudes about the use of violence, which they then linked to data on drought patterns. They found that there was a link between drought and support for the use of violence, but that this effect was mitigated by the respondents' perception that there was a stronger set of local (formal and informal) rules in place governing resource use and access. This finding is consistent with a growing body of research showing that links between natural resources and conflict dynamics are mediated by a wide range of localized contextual factors, ranging from the availability of livelihood adaptation options to the way in which markets function (see Linke et al. 2017 for several examples).

Ending interstate conflicts

A second key domain in which to test environmental peace premises is the ability of cooperative environmental ties to help end conflict. Several authors have pointed to the possibility that dialogue around environmental and resource issues may provide a channel for ongoing communication during periods of tension or even violent conflict (e.g. Carius 2006; Dabelko 2008). One variant of this argument is that the environment may be perceived as "low politics," and thus a relatively safe operating space for dialogue during conflict. Thus, during the latter stages of the Cold War, the United States, Norway, and the Soviet Union openly discussed the dumping of radioactive wastes in the Arctic Ocean. The Indus Waters Treaty, signed by India and Pakistan in 1960, persisted intact through three wars between India and Pakistan, with the Permanent Indus Commission meeting to resolve issues, share (some) data, and cooperate on other plans for the river (Alam 2002). Evidence suggests communication remained open even during times of high tension in the relationship, because the water stakes to both countries was high.

A famous example is the so-called "picnic table" talks that took place between Israelis and Jordanians while their two countries remained in a formal state of war, and which created a foundation for including water issues as a centerpiece of the 1994 peace treaty (Dabelko 2008). Kibaroglou and Scheumann (2013), tracing the evolution of transboundary water relations in the Tigris–Euphrates basins, identify distinct periods of nation building (with limited external policy development), competition (driven by uncoordinated development of large water projects), complexity (with multiple water links to security issues), and cooperation (centered on interactions of water bureaucracies). They find that the "partial institutionalization" of water cooperation in the latter two periods, along with the growth of both governmental and non-governmental transnational dialogue networks, "have continued to serve as open channels for easing the tensions." While cautioning that water relations remain hostage to larger political relations, they note that the building of institutionalized channels for water dialogue made it possible to put water at the center of a framework for regional cooperation when relations improved after the Iraq War.

The challenge is to connect any such elements of sustained dialogue around environmental and resource relationships to conflict transformation. Dialogue may be a form of managerialism that runs in parallel to conflict, allowing specific issues to be managed for more efficient resource extraction, but without transforming the conflict status quo. The World Bank catalyzed the Nile Basin Initiative with a similar hope that seeding water-cooperative ties could defuse tensions, create channels for dialogue, and seed wider efforts for regional development cooperation centered on common interests around water and energy needs. Almost two decades after its launch in 1999, it remains unclear whether the water glass is half-empty or half-full. On the positive side, several cooperative initiatives are moving forward, the basin states have discussed and drafted a modern water accord, and the primary axis of tension – Egypt's fears about Ethiopian dam building – has (for the most part) tilted from recrimination into dialogue.

Less positively, the terms of the draft accord have themselves become quite polarizing between upstream and downstream states. And the resource-extractive, infrastructure-developing model of water management implicit in the cooperative dialogue bodes ill for the basin's broader human-security and climate-adaptation needs.

Water ties between Israel and Palestine during that protracted, asymmetric conflict also reflect both opportunities for dialogue and its limits. The Oslo Accords elevated water to the level of a 'final-status' issue in the conflict (along with such politically thorny problems as the status of Jerusalem and Palestinians' right of return), and Israel and the Palestinian Authority set up a joint water committee to make decisions about water and sewage infrastructure in the occupied territories. The hope was that working together in this manner would build out and normalize cooperative dialogue during the push to a final settlement of the conflict. Rather, as the Oslo framework foundered and settled into additional decades of protracted conflict, water dialogue fared no better. The joint committee was the subject of a 2009 World Bank report highly critical of Israel for the frequent rejection of and long delays in processing Palestinian project proposals for the West Bank. The committee entered a de facto suspension of activities in 2010 (although a deal to revive it was struck at the time of this writing, in early 2017). Aggestam and Sundell-Eklund (2014) argue that "technical framing" of the water issues between the parties has had the effect of blurring power asymmetries at the heart of the conflict (see also Zeitoun and Warner 2006).

At the non-state level, non-governmental organizations have also sought to foster water dialogue, most famously including the "Good Water Neighbors" project of EcoPeace (formerly Friends of the Earth Middle East). Their activities, while falling well short of transforming that conflict, have succeeded in sustaining contact among Israeli, Palestinian, and Jordanian civil society. They have also had some success in mobilizing mayors of communities with shared water needs to come together across the conflict divide and exert upward pressure on the political process (EcoPeace/FOEME 2008). On a more localized scale, the conflict-transformation NGO Search for Common Ground reports some success with using a community clean-up project to bring together conflict factions around a common, place-based, cooperative effort (Jobbins et al. 2017).

Ending civil wars

Turning from interstate to intrastate conflict, a key consideration is the centrality of natural resources – as a point of contention, a source of revenue to sustain conflict, or an incentive to avoid peace lest control of resources become threatened by a return to civil governance and state-based regulation. Resource and environmental provisions, thus, may be central to the way that war transitions into peace.

The emphasis in scholarship has been on how either intentional actions or external shocks may alter the incentive structure in ways that favor a cessation of hostilities. In a review of 94 civil-war peace agreements from 27 countries, complemented by detailed case studies from Guatemala, the Democratic Republic of Congo, Sierra Leone and Sudan, Mason et al. (2016) found that the inclusion of natural resource provisions in peace agreements had mixed outcomes. Resources could be useful as bargaining chips in the cessation of hostilities, but the resource provisions in peace agreements often did not survive subsequent political developments. They also found instances of resource provisions that proved to be destabilizing (for example, market-based land mechanisms in Guatemala that failed to account for equity and the non-market values of land). Accords were generally ineffective instruments for addressing the broader transnational dimensions of resource use in which local practices are embedded.

More generally, it may be tempting to use resource access as a lure for peace, particularly in cases where control of resource revenue streams prolongs conflict (and perhaps creates incentives to sustain conflict). Promising former combatants control of resource-rich territory or government positions that manage natural resources may create an incentive to come to the negotiating table, but the evidence suggests that such efforts typically fail to consolidate peace effectively (Le Billon 2012). (Several years ago, one of the authors of this chapter (Conca) attended a meeting of an international river-basin commission, including a riparian state emerging from a protracted period of civil conflict. When the head of the delegation from that state was asked about his country's experiences with coordinating land-use and water-management policies, he replied, "Integrated water resources management is a lovely academic idea. But in the peace negotiations, we kept the water ministry and gave the (redacted) rebels the land ministry. We don't talk much.")

United Nations sanctions on "conflict" natural resources (those that provide funding streams allowing conflict to be sustained) provide an example of third-party attempts to shift the incentive structure for conflict (Conca 2015). Between 1992 and 2005, the UN imposed sanctions on timber, diamonds, and oil in Angola, Cambodia, Liberia, Sierra Leone, Angola, and Cote d'Ivoire. International initiatives like the Kimberley Process Certification Scheme were also implemented to curtail the trade of resources like diamonds and timber from conflict zones and thereby persuade combatants to negotiate for peace (Grant 2012). Sanctions and certification schemes have gotten mixed reviews and have been largely ineffective at ending conflicts by themselves, although improvements in terms of monitoring resources and their revenues have been helpful (Le Billon and Nicholls 2007).

Another entry point for examining how environmental change may alter the incentive structure for conflict is found in the shock effects of natural disasters and the wider debate around "disaster diplomacy." Kreutz (2012:482) found that disasters "can produce a ripe moment for conflict resolution because governments faced with the demand for effective disaster relief have incentives to offer concessions to separatist challengers." The case of the Aceh separatist struggle in Indonesia, and the impacts of the 2004 tsunami in catalyzing movement toward a peace agreement, has been widely cited as an example (e.g., Gaillard et al. 2008). Akcinaroglu et al. (2011), in case studies of interstate conflict involving India/Pakistan and Greece/Turkey, note the "audience costs" to the state of failing to seek warmer relations, given public sentiments of compassion. They also find, however, that communal violence can suppress such public sentiments. In the most thorough treatment of the topic to date, Kelman (2011) finds a mix of outcomes across cases, including some short-term gains (e.g., avenues for diplomacy), challenges to sustaining long-term gains as memory of both the event and the response fade, and harmful consequences from efforts that backfire in still other instances. In a review of the case-study literature, Maciver (2012) finds an important limitation in the failure to examine local dynamics, in both interstate and intrastate case studies.

Beyond shifting the incentive structure lies the harder question of softening, if not transforming, conflict identities. Focusing on the conflict in Cyprus, Zikos et al. (2015) identify opportunities to use water as a foundation for a shared social identity, as opposed to traditional discourse that has securitized water in the context of the ongoing conflict. However, Akçali and Antonsich (2009), in a case analysis of United Nations Development Programme (UNDP) efforts in Cyprus, identify skepticism about UNDP's "nature knows no boundaries" discourse, particularly among Turkish Cypriots. Noting that there is also widespread support for "bi-communal" environmental cooperation, they conclude that cooperation providing tangible benefits to both sides is a better pathway forward than efforts to construct a shared identity of place.

Building peace in the aftermath of violent conflicts

The environment has been identified as a key ingredient for building a sustainable peace in war-torn societies. The challenges are immense in the aftermath of war, as public order and security, political reconciliation, reconstruction, economic recovery, livelihoods, and humanitarian relief all command priority attention. As Conca and Wallace (2009) describe it: "Environmental challenges create high-stakes choices in war-torn societies. Handled well, they may create a solid foundation for peace and sustainable development; handled poorly, they risk undercutting an already tenuous peace." UNEP (2009) identifies fostering dialogue, promoting economic recovery, and supporting sustainable livelihoods as three potential peace-strengthening roles for environmental and resource-management policies in such settings.

Accumulated evidence suggests that tapping such opportunities while avoiding pitfalls is a challenging agenda for the community of IGOs, NGOs, donor agencies, and local actors seeking to strengthen peace through environmental initiatives. Carius (2006), in a review of 17 environmental peacebuilding projects/programs in a mix of "post-conflict" and "fragile state" settings, identifies significant participatory and institutional requirements for success. These include the institutionalization of legal or quasi-legal frameworks, adequate resources, integrative mechanisms to coordinate across diverse actors and issues, and institutionalized channels for broad stakeholder participation. Beginning in 2008, UNEP, the Environmental Law Institute, the University of Tokyo, and McGill University oversaw a project that accumulated 150 case studies on various aspects of post-conflict environmental peacebuilding, as well as a series of policy briefs summarizing lessons learned across this knowledge landscape (www. environmentalpeacebuilding.org). The project paid particular attention to the management of natural resources in ways that would minimize conflict relapse, promote sustainable livelihoods, and proactively tap opportunities to build trust and enhance dialogue. A policy brief emerging from the project identified nine "success factors" for natural resource management (NRM) programming in post-conflict settings:

1 Align NRM with peacebuilding priorities;
2 Address the conflict economy and the illicit use of natural resources;
3 Rebuild NRM governance, institutions, and capacities;
4 Design programs that can adapt to volatility, rapid change, and persistent insecurity;
5 Focus on rebuilding sustainable and resilient livelihoods;
6 Recognize legal pluralism and work to clarify resource rights;
7 Strengthen gender equity in NRM;
8 Use shared natural resources as a platform for cooperation and reconciliation;
9 Adopt conflict-sensitive approaches to NRM programs.

One underlying challenge in executing such strategies has been engaging and sustaining the attention of the international donor community to the environmental and natural resource dimensions of peacebuilding and recovery work. Kovach and Conca (2016) evaluated which types of environmental and natural resource issues received sustained attention across the increasingly institutionalized process that marks peacebuilding efforts, with distinct stages of post-conflict needs assessment, economic policy planning, and the establishment of multi-donor trust funds. Looking at the path through these stages charted by the donor community in seven country cases of post-conflict recovery efforts, they found evidence of a bias in favor of urban and infrastructural issues, with less attention to extractive industries and a set of predominantly rural issues around ecosystem services and nature-based livelihoods.

A second challenge has been the risk of taking a technocratic, managerialist approach that fails to actively manage conflict and exploit opportunities for dialogue. Aggestam and Sundell-Eklund (2014) caution against a "technocractic turn" in peacebuilding that may suppress one of the chief aims of de-securitization, namely the return of normal politics as means of managing social conflict. Conca and Wallace (2009) note that the price of admission for the UN Environment Programme to do post-conflict environmental work has been to tread cautiously around politicized issues and stress its technical expertise as a neutral party, which may in turn limit its ability to engage with inherently conflictive questions around competing resource uses. Krampe's (2016) assessment of water/peacebuilding dynamics in Kosovo identifies important limits of the technocratic approach. He argues that water in Kosovo has been treated as a narrowly technical issue "to the neglect of its complex political nature." Problematic consequences of this approach, from a peacebuilding perspective, include the separation rather than collaborative linking of conflict parties around water infrastructure systems and their governance, a failure to actively manage inevitable conflicts over water, and supplanting the role of local actors in favor of external ones.

Moreover, even well-framed international strategies must be matched by conducive conditions on the ground. In a detailed case study of UNDP's environmental peacemaking efforts in Cyprus, including extensive survey and interview work in both the Greek Cypriot and Turkish Cypriot communities, Akçali and Antonsich (2009) identify a challenging set of conditions: "successful environmental peacemaking strategies are dependent on widespread environmental awareness, trust in the 'third party' (UNDP), and civil society's empowerment, which, however, should complement and not substitute for intervention at a state level."

Another emerging insight relates to inherent contradictions across key elements of the environmental peacebuilding agenda in post-conflict settings. Beevers (2015 and forthcoming), drawing on field research of the forestry sector in Liberia and mining sectors in Sierra Leone, found that international efforts to transform so-called 'conflict resources' into 'peace resources' has proved to be a mixed blessing. While initiatives have helped to curb the worst elements of resource plunder in both countries, a peacebuilding approach based on restarting extractive industries has led to tensions with local groups, and intensified historical disputes linked to land ownership, environmental quality, and alternative livelihoods.

Conclusion: looking forward

There are several challenges to drawing inferences from the available research on environment/peace linkages. Much of the literature cited in this chapter was written for other purposes, making it necessary to tease out implications indirectly. Moreover, most of the empirical material available to test or assess premises about environment/peace linkages consists of case-study and comparative case-study research. Problems of case (non)comparability are well known across the social sciences. More to the point, the complexity of causal mechanisms at work, and the recognition that much depends on how actors construct and extract meaning from socio-ecological relationships, raises real questions about whether "structured, focused comparison" is even possible here. Finally, we note the disproportionate amount of scholarly emphasis on nominally 'post-conflict' cases, in part because the greater attention to that part of the conflict cycle by governments, IGOs and NGOs has given us much more empirical material with which to work.

Still, it is possible to gain insight from what is now almost two decades of research on the topic, which can in turn shape any future research agenda. Two such insights seem particularly salient. First is the now well-documented capacity of social actors to construct a wide range of meanings from the same set of environmental parameters or conditions of resource access and availability, which suggests the need to incorporate constructivist insights more effectively into theory. Second is the heterogeneity of actors and multiplicity of scales on which many of the best-documented cases play out, which suggests the need to move beyond some simple dichotomies established by some of the earlier conceptual work. What follows is a set of brief observations about how to incorporate these observations into scholarship moving forward.

Beyond structure. Two observations – the many and growing examples of cooperative activity, and the frequent absence of violent conflict in what simple scarcity models would suggest are conflict-ripe settings – indicate that structural models of environmental peacemaking are unlikely to fare any better than structural models of eco-conflict. One implication of this: rather than trying to identify favorable or unfavorable conditions as the basis for comparative, most likely, or critical case studies, we would do better to pursue cases that are more fine-grained – perhaps even at the level of actor perceptions – and that incorporate multiple cycles of socio-ecological engagement in a particular ecosystemic or resource-based context.

Politics, both high and low. Much of the early scholarship sought to distinguish between instances in which environmental change constituted "high" politics with concomitant conflict risk (in which case, peacemaking meant forestalling or lessening risks of conflict) and those in which it constituted "low" politics (in which case environmental issues might provide a safe space for dialogue, with little risk of politicization). Yet, constructivist insights suggest the limited utility of seeking to categorize environmental peacemaking opportunities as "high" or "low" politics. While such instances clearly exist at each end of a conceptualized high/low political spectrum, the domain is also replete with instances where one actor's low politics is a very high-stakes matter to another. Indeed, social movement campaigns are often designed precisely to redefine issues previously of little political salience to elites, through mobilization and contention. Using what may seem like "low" politics to elites as a basis for dialogue may have unintended consequences, if the societal stakes are high for actors who may not have access to the conversation. By the same token, presumption that forestalling conflict is the sole purpose of "high" politics engagements may miss transformative opportunities around common interests.

State and society – and . . . ? Some of the early theorizing drew a sharp distinction between state-based and societally based peace efforts – in particular, to caution against emphasizing the former at the expense of the latter. The continuing retreat of the state in many parts of the world, and the complex IGO/NGO/state partnerships we have seen in many of the applied environmental peace efforts, suggests that this dichotomy may be of limited usefulness. To cite one example, EcoPeace's efforts to mobilize Palestinian and Israeli mayors whose towns share common watershed interests have pointed both 'upwards' toward national political elites and 'outward' toward societal engagement. There are now many documented cases in which purely state-based efforts have exacerbated social conflicts or increased vulnerability for elements of society; and there are few examples of purely societally based efforts having a sustained transformative impact on violent conflict risks.

The ambiguities of peace. Much of the scholarship on this topic has taken both environmental protection and peace as unambiguously good outcomes, with the primary question then being how to marry the two strategically, for maximum efficacy in attaining both. Research in settings marked by asymmetric conflict, 'hydro-hegemony,' and/or uneven distributions of financial, institutional, or knowledge-based power, however, has made clear that some relevant actors may value justice more than peace and change more than a stability that reinforces the status quo. Israeli–Palestinian water relations provide probably the best-documented example. At the intrastate/sub-state level, contention around extractive industries is a particularly salient example for post-conflict peacebuilding. For scholarship, how much different actors value peace, and what they understand it to consist of, must be treated as a critical variable rather than a constant.

The politics of cooperative knowledge. The building of shared knowledge through cooperative means has, much like peace, generally been assumed to promote better relations among actors by enhancing trust. Much less attention has been paid to whether and how better information or deeper understandings may lead actors to see "knowledge" in increasingly politicized or contested terms. Similarly, there is too often a presumption that it is enough to work on reducing knowledge gaps in a common institutional setting, without paying attention to the specific social dynamics that can enhance trust or soften exclusionary identities. There is a parallel here to emerging critiques of the 'social learning' literature, which has tended to downplay the role of power and the potential for what we might term 'uncooperative' learning that challenges dominant structures, confronts differences within a group, and integrates new kinds of knowledge (Muro and Jeffrey 2008).

Multi-stage analysis. As Ide and Scheffran (2014) point out, both "sociological" and "functionalist" variants of environment/peace scholarship assume conceptually that peace is built in multiple stages. Moreover, the literature tends to assume that conflict and cooperation are polar opposites when, as Martin et al. (2011) document in the Virunga transboundary region in East Africa, conflict and cooperation frequently coexist. Shifting from a dichotomous success/failure or conflict/cooperation rubric to one that takes intermediate, staged accomplishments seriously would shed more light on both the specific mechanisms at work and the barriers to sustaining gains. Staged analysis would also make it easier to document and interpret the coexistence of conflict and cooperation.

Note

1 There is no consensus in the literature on the distinction between these two terms. It is common, though far from universal, to use the term peacebuilding to refer exclusively to post-conflict settings. This follows UN terminology, which typically refers to peacebuilding as a post-conflict process distinct from conflict prevention or conflict management. As we discuss, this 'conflict cycle' perspective has both advantages and disadvantages, both conceptually and empirically.

References

Adger, W.N., Pulhin, J.M., Barnett, J., Dabelko, G.D., Hovelsrud, G.K., Levy, M., et al. (2014) "Human Security" in Field, C.B. et al. (eds.) *Climate Change 2014: Impacts, Adaptation, and Vulnerability. Part A: Global and Sectoral Aspects* Cambridge University Press, Cambridge, 755–791.

Aggestam, K. and Sundell-Eklund, A. (2014) "Situating Water in Peacebuilding: Revisiting the Middle East Peace Process" *Water International*, 39(1):10–22.

Akçali, E. and Antonsich, M. (2009) "'Nature Knows No Boundaries': A Critical Reading of UNDP Environmental Peacemaking in Cyprus" *Annals of the Association of American Geographers*, 99(5):940–947.

Akcinaroglu, S., DiCicco, J.M., and Radziszewski, E. (2011) "Avalanches and Olive Branches: A Multimethod Analysis of Disasters and Peacemaking in Interstate Rivalries" *Political Research Quarterly*, 64(2):260–275.

Alam, U.Z. (2002) "Questioning the Water Wars Rationale: A Case Study of the Indus Waters Treaty" *Geographical Journal*, 168(4):341–353.

Ali, S. (ed.) (2007) *Peace Parks: Conservation and Conflict Resolution* Cambridge University Press, Cambridge.

Baechler, G. (1998) "Why Environmental Transformation Causes Violence: A Synthesis" *ECSP Report*, (4):24–44.

Barquet, K. (2015) "Yes to Peace? Environmental Peacemaking and Transboundary Conservation in Central America" *Geoforum*, 63:14–24.

Barquet, K., Lujala, P., and Rød, J.K. (2014) "Transboundary Conservation and Militarized Interstate Disputes" *Political Geography*, 42:1–11.

Beevers, M.D. (2015) "Governing Natural Resource for Peace: Lessons from Liberia and Sierra Leone" *Global Governance*, 21(2):227–246.

Beevers, M.D. (Forthcoming) *Peacebuilding and Natural Resource Governance after Armed Conflict* Palgrave, New York.

Bergholt, D. and Lujala, P. (2012) "Climate-related Natural Disasters, Economic Growth, and Armed Civil Conflict" *Journal of Peace Research*, 49(1):147–162.

Bogale, A. and Korf, B. (2007) "To Share or Not to Share? (Non-)Violence, Scarcity and Resource Access in Somali Region, Ethiopia" *Journal of Development Studies*, 43(4):743–765.

Borel, R. (2008–09) "Peace Parks: Conservation and Conflict Resolution (book review)" *ECSP Report*, 13:110–112.

Brochmann, M. (2012) "Signing River Treaties: Does It Improve River Cooperation?" *International Interactions*, 38(2):141–163.

Brock, L. (1991) "Peace through Parks: The Environment on the Peace Research Agenda" *Journal of Peace Research*, 28(4):407–423.

Buzan, B., Wæver, O., and De Wilde, J. (1998) *Security: A New Framework for Analysis* Lynne Rienner, Boulder, CO.

Carius, A. (2006) *Environmental Cooperation as an Instrument of Crisis Prevention and Peacebuilding: Conditions for Success and Constraints* Adelphi Consult, Berlin.

Conca, Ken (1994) "In the Name of Sustainability" *Peace & Change*, 19(2):91–113.

Conca, K. (2000) "Environmental Cooperation and International Peace" in Diehl, P. and Gleditsch, N.P. (eds.) *Environmental Conflict* Westview Press, Boulder, CO.

Conca, K. (2002) "The Case for Environmental Peacemaking" in Conca, K. and Dabelko, G.D. (eds.) *Environmental Peacemaking* Johns Hopkins University Press, Baltimore, 1–22.

Conca, K. (2015) *An Unfinished Foundation: The United Nations and Global Environmental Governance* Oxford University Press, New York.

Conca, K. and Dabelko, G.D. (eds.) (2002) *Environmental Peacemaking* Johns Hopkins University Press, Baltimore.

Conca, K. and Dabelko, G.D. (2002b) "The Problems and Possibilities of Environmental Peacemaking" in Conca, K. and Dabelko, G.D. (eds.) *Environmental Peacemaking* Johns Hopkins University Press, Baltimore, 220–233.

Conca, K. and Wallace, J. (2009) "Environment and Peacebuilding in War-torn Societies: Lessons from the UN Environment Programme's Experience with Postconflict Assessment" *Global Governance*, 15(4):485–505.

Conservation International (CI) (n.d.) "Conservation and Peace." www.conservation.org/projects/Pages/Conservation-and-peacebuilding.aspx [Accessed 17 April 2017].

Dabelko, G.D. (2008) "An Uncommon Peace: Environment, Development and the Global Security Agenda" *Environment*, 50(3):32–45.

Dawson, J. (2000) "The Two Faces of Environmental Justice: Lessons from the Eco-nationalist Phenomenon" *Environmental Politics*, 9(2):22–60.

Deligiannis, T. (2012) "The Evolution of Environment–Conflict Research: Toward a Livelihood Framework" *Global Environmental Politics*, 12(1):78–100.

Deudney, D. (1990) "The Case against Linking Environmental Degradation and National Security" *Millennium*, 19(3):461–476.

Dinar, S., Katz, D., De Stefano, L., and Blankespoor, B. (2015) "Climate Change, Conflict and Cooperation: Global Analysis of the Effectiveness of International River Treaties in Addressing Water Variability" *Political Geography*, 45:55–66.

Dinar, S., Katz, D., De Stefano, L., and Blankespoor, B. (2016) "Climate Change and Water Variability: Do Water Treaties Contribute to River Basin Resilience?" World Bank Group, Policy Research Working Paper 7855, October.

Duffy, R. (2000) *Killing for Conservation: Wildlife Policy in Zimbabwe* James Currey, Oxford.

EcoPeace/Friends of the Earth Middle East (2008) *Environmental Peacebuilding: The Good Water Neighbors Project.* Available at http://foeme.org/uploads/publications_publ93_1.pdf

Gaillard, J.-C., Clave, E., and Kelman, I. (2008) "Wave of Peace? Tsunami Disaster Diplomacy in Aceh, Indonesia" *Geoforum*, 39(1):511–526.

Gore, A. (1992) *Earth in the Balance* Houghton Mifflin, New York.

Grant, J.A. (2012) "The Kimberley Process at Ten: Reflections on a Decade of Efforts to End the Trade in Conflict Diamonds" in Lujala, P. and Rustad, S. (eds.) *High-Value Natural Resources and Peacebuilding* Earthscan, Abingdon, 159–179.

Griffin, P.J. and Ali, S.H. (2014) "Managing Transboundary Wetlands: The Ramsar Convention as a Means of Ecological Diplomacy" *Journal of Environmental Studies and Sciences*, 4(3):230–239.

Hauge, W. and Ellingsen, T. (1998) "Beyond Environmental Scarcity: Causal Pathways to Conflict" *Journal of Peace Research*, 35(3):299–317.

Hendrix, C. (2016) *Putting Environmental Stress (Back) on the Mass Atrocities Agenda.* Policy Analysis Brief, Stanley Foundation, October.

Hendrix, C.S. and Salehyan, I. (2012) "Climate Change, Rainfall, and Social Conflict in Africa" *Journal of Peace Research*, 49(1):35–50.

Homer-Dixon, T. (1991) "On the Threshold: Environmental Scarcities as Causes of Acute Conflict" *International Security*, 16(2):76–116.

Homer-Dixon, T. (1994) "Environmental Scarcities and Violent Conflict: Evidence from Cases" *International Security*, 19(1):5–40.

Homer-Dixon, T. (2010) *Environment, Scarcity, and Violence* Princeton University Press, Princeton, NJ.

Ide, T. and Scheffran, J. (2014) "On Climate, Conflict and Cumulation: Suggestions for Integrative Cumulation of Knowledge in the Research on Climate Change and Violent Conflict" *Global Change, Peace & Security*, 26(3):263–279.

Ide, T. and Fröhlich, C. (2015) "Socio-environmental Cooperation and Conflict? A Discursive Understanding and its Application to the Case of Israel and Palestine" *Earth System Dynamics*, 6:659–671.

Jobbins, M., Covington, W., and Puleo, V. (2017) *Natural Resources, Conflict and Humanitarian Challenges: Lessons from Community-based Conflict Transformation.* Search for Common Ground, Washington. Available at www.sfcg.org/wp-content/uploads/2017/04/Lessons-from-Community-based-conflict-transformation_032317.pdf

Kelman, I. (2011) *Disaster Diplomacy: How Disasters Affect Peace and Conflict* Routledge, London.

Kibaroglu, A. and Scheumann, W. (2013) "Evolution of Transboundary Politics in the Euphrates–Tigris River System: New Perspectives and Political Challenges" *Global Governance*, 19(2):279–305.

Kovach, T. and Conca, K. (2016) "Environmental Priorities in Post-Conflict Recovery: Efficacy of the Needs-Assessment Process" *Journal of Peacebuilding & Development*, 11(2):4–24.

Krampe, F. (2016) "Water for Peace? Post-conflict Water Resource Management in Kosovo" *Cooperation and Conflict*, Published online 15 June.

Kreutz, J. (2012) "From Tremors to Talks: Do Natural Disasters Produce Ripe Moments for Resolving Separatist Conflicts?" *International Interactions*, 38(4):482–502.

Le Billon, P. (2001) "The Political Ecology of War: Natural Resources and Armed Conflicts" *Political Geography*, 20(5):561–584.

Le Billon, P. (2012) *Wars of Plunder: Conflicts, Profits and the Politics of Resources* Columbia University Press, New York.

Le Billon, P. and Nicholls, E. (2007) "Ending 'Resource Wars': Revenue Sharing, Economic Sanction or Military Intervention?" *International Peacekeeping*, 14(5):613–632.

Lejano, R.P. (2006) "Theorizing Peace Parks: Two Models of Collective Action" *Journal of Peace Research*, 43(5):563–581.

Linke, A.M., Witmer, F.D.W., O'Loughlin, J., Terrence McCabe, J., and Tir, J. (2017) "Drought, Local Institutional Contexts, and Support for Violence in Kenya" *Journal of Conflict Resolution*, Published online 12 April.

Lowi, M. (1995) *Water and Power: The Politics of a Scarce Resource in the Jordan River Basin* Cambridge University Press, Cambridge.

Maciver, C. (2012) *Disaster Diplomacy: A Brief Review* Strategic Applications International, Washington, December. Available at http://sai-dc.com/wp-content/uploads/2014/07/Disaster-Diplomacy-FINAL-Lit-Review.pdf

Mackelworth, P. (2012) "Peace Parks and Transboundary Initiatives: Implications for Marine Conservation and Spatial Planning" *Conservation Letters*, 5(2):90–98.

Martin, A. (2005) "Environmental Conflict between Refugee and Host Communities" *Journal of Peace Research*, 42(3):329–346.

Martin, A., Rutagarama, E., Cascão, A., Gray, M., and Chhotray, V. (2011) "Understanding the Co-existence of Conflict and Cooperation: Transboundary Ecosystem Management in the Virunga Massif" *Journal of Peace Research*, 48(5):621–635.

Mason, S.J.A., Sguaitamatti, D.A., and Gröbli, M.P.R. (2016) "Stepping Stones to Peace? Natural Resource Provisions in Peace Agreements" in Bruch, C., Muffett, C., and. Nichols, S.S. (eds.) *Governance, Natural Resources, and Post-Conflict Peacebuilding* Earthscan, Abingdon.

Matthew, R.A., Halle, M., and Switzer, J. (eds.) (2002) *Conserving the Peace: Resources, Livelihoods and Security* International Institute for Sustainable Development, Winnipeg.

Mitchell, S.M. and Zawahri, N.A. (2015) "The Effectiveness of Treaty Design in Addressing Water Disputes" *Journal of Peace Research*, 52(2):187–200.

Muro, M. and Jeffrey, P. (2008) "A Critical Review of the Theory and Application of Social Learning in Participatory Natural Resource Management Processes" *Journal of Environmental Planning and Management*, 5(3):325–344.

Nel, P. and Righarts, M. (2008) "Natural Disasters and the Risk of Violent Civil Conflict" *International Studies Quarterly*, 52(1):159–185.

O'Lear, S. (2006) "Resource Concerns for Territorial Conflict" *GeoJournal*, 64:297–306.

Peluso, N. (1993) "Coercing Conservation" in Lipschutz, R.D. and Conca, K. (eds.) *The State and Social Power in Global Environmental Politics* Columbia University Press, New York, 46–70.

Raleigh, C. and Urdal, H. (2007) "Climate Change, Environmental Degradation and Armed Conflict" *Political Geography*, 26(6):674–694.

Randall, J., Stolton, S., and Dolcemascolo, G. (2010) "Natural Security: Protected Areas and Hazard Mitigation" in Stolton, S. and Duffy, N. (eds.) *Arguments for Protected Areas: Multiple Benefits for Conservation and Use* Earthscan, Abingdon, 97–111.

Salehyan, I. (2008) "From Climate to Conflict? No Consensus Yet" *Journal of Peace Research*, 45(3):315–326.

Slettebak, R.T. (2012) "Don't Blame the Weather! Climate-related Natural Disasters and Civil Conflict" *Journal of Peace Research*, 49(1):163–176.

State Failure Task Force (1999) "State Failure Task Force Report: Phase II Findings" *ECSP Report*, 5:49–72.

Theisen, O.M., Gleditsch, N.D., and Buhaug, H. (2013) "Is Climate Change a Driver of Armed Conflict?" Climatic Change, 117(3):613–625.

Tickner, J.A. (1992) *Gender in International Relations: Feminist Perspectives on Achieving Global Security* Columbia University Press, New York.

Tir, J. and Stinnett, D.M. (2012) "Weathering Climate Change: Can Institutions Mitigate International Water Conflict?" *Journal of Peace Research*, 49(1):211–225.

Tubi, A. and Feitelson, E. (2016) "Drought and Cooperation in a Conflict Prone Area: Bedouin Herders and Jewish Farmers in Israel's Northern Negev, 1957–1963" *Political Geography*, 51:30–42.

Turner, M.D., Ayantunde, A.A., Patterson, K.P., and Patterson III, E.D. (2011) "Livelihood Transitions and the Changing Nature of Farmer–Herder Conflict in Sahelian West Africa" *Journal of Development Studies*, 47(2):183–206.

United Nations Environment Programme (UNEP) (2009) *From Conflict to Peacebuilding: The Role of Natural Resources and the Environment* UNEP, Nairobi.

United Nations Environment Programme (UNEP) (2016) *Environmental Cooperation for Peacebuilding Programme. Final Report 2016* UNEP, Nairobi.

United States Agency for International Development (USAID) (2014) *Water and Conflict: A Toolkit for Programming* USAID, Washington, DC.

Urdal, H. (2005) "People vs. Malthus: Population Pressure, Environmental Degradation, and Armed Conflict Revisited" *Journal of Peace Research*, 42(4):417–434.

Van Amerom, M. and Buscher, B. (2005) "Peace Parks in Southern Africa: Bringers of an African Renaissance?" *Journal of Modern African Studies*, 43(2):159–182.

Wæver, O. (1993) *Securitization and Desecuritization* Centre for Peace and Conflict Research, Copenhagen.

Walters, T. and Ali, S.H. (2017) "Borders as Zones of Experiential Learning: The Case of the Balkans Peace Park Initiative" in Grichting, A. and Zebich-Knos, M. (eds.) *The Social Ecology of Border Landscapes* Anthem Press, London.

Wolf, A.T., Yoffe, S.B., and Giordano, M. (2003) "International Waters: Identifying Basins at Risk" *Water Policy*, 5(1):29–60.

World Bank (2009) *West Bank and Gaza. Assessment of Restrictions on Palestinian Water Sector Development* Sector Note April, Report No. 47657-GZ, World Bank, Washington, DC.

Zeitoun, M. and Warner, J. (2006) "Hydro-hegemony: A Framework for Analysis of Trans-boundary Water Conflicts" *Water Policy*, (8):435–460.

Zikos, D., Sorman, A.H., and Lau, M. (2015) "Beyond Water Security: Asecuritisation and Identity in Cyprus" *International Environmental Agreements: Politics, Law and Economics*, 15(3):309–326.

6

Environment, climate change, and peace

Randall Amster

Introduction

The connections among environmental issues, conflict, and peacebuilding have been well explored in academic and policy spheres alike, yet there is no consensus on the precise nature of the relationships. On one hand, myriad accounts of "resource wars" (Klare 2002) have infused the discourse with a perspective that is equal parts empirical and predictive, citing examples of historical and contemporary conflicts that project ahead toward continuing crises over resources including water, arable land, minerals, and of course energy sources. On the other hand, in recent years a parallel body of literature has arisen, drawing upon numerous case studies and theoretical assessments that indicate a more complex picture in which environmental concerns (including resource allocations) can be drivers of peace between parties rather than conflict. In both cases, the centrality of the environment is viewed as a critical juncture for security considerations.

As such, it is important to explore these issues in light of challenges emerging in the present era. Specifically, with climate change coming to the fore as a matter of global concern – and with due regard to an increasing cognizance of the existential threat that it poses to humankind – it is imperative to consider the role it may play in terms of serving as a driver of conflict or peace. Climate change is increasingly viewed as a galvanizing ecological force that both subsumes and informs the analysis of nearly every other extant environmental issue (e.g., food, water, energy, biodiversity, forest integrity, ocean health, arctic ice melt, atmospheric quality, temperature and weather patterns, etc.). As well, the urgent need for collective action to mitigate and/or adapt to climate change can have demonstrable repercussions at levels from the local to the international.

Against this backdrop, an exploration of climate change and its implications for peacebuilding or conflict begins with acknowledging a set of core principles that transect the dialogue. First, climate change is widely viewed as a fundamental security issue both within and among nation-states. Second, it necessitates engagement from political, economic, scientific, and cultural spheres in order to fully understand its impacts and develop coherent responses. Third, whatever outcomes are anticipated, it is generally agreed that climate change will be a "threat multiplier" (Arria-formula 2015) of nascent crises at all levels. Fourth, the leading edge of climate change's effects are already being experienced, from more frequent and severe storms to patterns of desertification and flooding across a range of geographies. Fifth, efforts to mitigate the impacts of climate change have thus far been insufficient, yielding greater emphasis on adaptive strategies. Ultimately, climate change necessitates coordinated engagement at the global scale.

Drawing upon these premises, this chapter will explore the expanding impacts of climate change and associated environmental issues as factors of continuing conflict or potential peace. This analysis is grounded in the central tenets of emerging frameworks including "environmental peacemaking" and "environmental peacebuilding" that have adduced important lessons for considering the conditions under which environmental issues can facilitate processes of dialogue, mutual engagement, and capacity building among actors that might otherwise lapse into conflict. The essential teachings of these developing frameworks are summarized at the outset, followed by an analysis of their application to climate change, and concluding with an assessment of the efficacy of these integrative processes for addressing environmental crises and cultivating peace.

Lessons of environmental peacebuilding

A central tenet of peace studies and environmental studies alike is that crises can also serve as opportunities for change. Too often, environmental issues are depicted as either inevitable with a sense of fatalism, or as trivial in the sense that we can simply "green" our individual practices but leave the basic arrangements of society firmly in place. Likewise, issues of violence and conflict in the sociopolitical realm are often met with tepid solutions at best, and ones that further enflame the roots of the problem at worst. Nonetheless, despite these limitations as a function of misapplication, the potential for practices of peacebuilding and sustainability to transform even intractable challenges is palpable – even more so when the two spheres are seen as intertwined.

It is this nexus of environmentalism and peacebuilding that has begun to draw increasing attention from scholars and practitioners, with the recognition of emerging crises such as climate change implicating a range of related issues, from geopolitics and activism to atmospheric chemistry and energy production. Simply put, mounting global challenges require full-spectrum approaches, and it is becoming apparent that neither peace nor sustainability will be possible without the other. Still, the question remains: how do we engage these sorts of issues without generating more apathy or greater disempowerment in the process? What tools, techniques, and strategies can be utilized to engage potentially existential threats such as climate change, species extinctions, the loss of biodiversity, toxification, and rampant degradation, among other crises?

This is where the work of building a portfolio of best practices is most germane. In Ken Conca and Geoffrey Dabelko's landmark book *Environmental Peacemaking* (2002), the aim was to ascertain "the cooperative triggers of peace that shared environmental problems might make available," surmising that even conflicting parties might find common ground through exploring mutual ecological concerns. The cases presented in this volume indicated that there were two key elements for the success of any such environmental peacemaking effort: (1) it must create minimum levels of trust, transparency, and cooperative gain, and (2) it must strive to transform the nation-state itself, which is often marked by dysfunctional institutions and practices that become further obstacles to peaceful coexistence and cooperation. The operative principle running through the cases presented was that an environmental crisis/conflict can be transformed into an opportunity for peace when it can be demonstrated that there is more to be gained by cooperating than by competing, and when the impetus of peaceful cooperation transcends the interests and aims of nation-states that are generally focused on security as a function of control.

Later treatments extended this logic that environmental issues can yield opportunities for trust-building and cooperation, and further that the presence of common ecological concerns could serve to provide pathways toward a more robust and durable "peace" among conflicting parties. Thus, Alexander Carius (2006:63) has discerned:

> As a mechanism for peace, the environment has some useful, perhaps even unique qualities that are well suited for peacebuilding and conflict resolution. Environmental problems ignore political borders. They require a long-term perspective, encourage participation by local and non-governmental organizations, help build administrative, economic and social capacities for action and facilitate the creation of commonalities that transcend the polarization caused by economic relations.

Encapsulating this sensibility, Ashok Swain (2002:81) affirmed that "most environmental issues are transboundary in nature" and thus that "a nation-state alone is not capable of solving [them]," concluding that "environmental cooperation may in turn spill over" to promote wider forms of peacebuilding.

This work suggests a synergistic framework in which peacebuilding and environmentalism are mutually reinforcing, and how efforts in one sphere benefit the other. As Saleem Ali (2007:2) has posited, we thus begin to see "how environmental issues can play a role in cooperation – regardless of whether they are part of the original conflict." Examining international conservation efforts, Ali's work on "peace parks" confirms the underlying logic that "positive exchanges and trust-building gestures are a consequence of realizing common environmental threats," by weaving together strands of environmentalism, conflict resolution, psychology, and resource management. Entities such as the Peace Parks Foundation seek to establish a network of protected areas linking ecosystems across international borders; such projects suggest that conflictual hotspots can be redefined as "sources of peace" through joint conservation efforts.

The role of water in geopolitics merits particular consideration here. Often construed as a locus of potential global conflict – through the lens of looming "water wars" and the coding of water as the "new oil" (Engelke and Sticklor 2015) – another take is equally palpable. In declaring the year 2013 as the "International Year of Water Cooperation," the United Nations (UNESCO 2012) drew upon a basic tenet of environmental peacebuilding: "Water is a shared resource and its management needs to take into account a wide variety of conflicting interests. This provides opportunities for cooperation among users." Similar insights had been proffered by related global agencies: "History has often shown that the vital nature of freshwater is a powerful incentive for cooperation and dialogue, compelling stakeholders to reconcile even the most divergent views. Water more often unites than divides people and societies" (UNDESA 2014). Scholars such as Shlomi Dinar (2009, 2011) have likewise observed that the costs of armed conflict over shared waters often outweigh the benefits of potential victory, and moreover that the transboundary locus, essential nature, and scarcity of freshwater render it rife with potential for cooperation.

There are myriad points of engagement with such perspectives in policymaking and academic spheres alike. The site "Environmental Peacebuilding" (www.environmentalpeace building.org) offers a robust set of case studies, publications, testimonials, research, and other resources in support of the proposition that "natural resources are one of a country's most critical assets for peacebuilding." The materials on the website coalesce around a cohesive framework in which environmental issues (including access to and management of resources) often are located at the core of conflicts both within and among states and associated actors, and likewise how such issues are critical to include in any peace process if it is to have a chance to succeed. As we have seen throughout the development of this integrative field, the drivers of conflict can become opportunities for peacebuilding when sufficient attention is paid to underlying environmental issues. And nowhere is this insight more salient than with regard to the crisis of climate change.

Applications in the face of climate change

The set of intersecting issues under the umbrella of climate change presents a quintessential case for gauging the efficacy of an environmental peacebuilding perspective. As a problem registering at the global scale, climate change is a borderless phenomenon that can serve to cultivate a sense of mutual struggle and, potentially, mutual obligation to address it. To some extent, this has transpired in unprecedented levels of international engagement with climate issues, culminating most recently in the Paris Agreement that sets the most aggressive carbon limits to date – even as it is clear that much more needs to be done in order to avert the full implications. Moreover, the fact that these issues transcend borders does not necessarily mean that the impacts are evenly distributed, raising concerns of environmental justice that are less prominent in the discourse.

The nature of the problem

The emerging realities of living in a world with a destabilizing climate are sobering to consider in their full magnitude. While the technical aspects often elude public perception, the consensus of credible science is overwhelming, and the urgency of their warnings is increasing. As a central locus for considering how environmental issues are interlinked, concerns over climate bring to the fore the myriad ecological thresholds being broached with regard to diminishing biodiversity, eroding soil nutrients, ocean acidification, and other critical factors. As a host of scientists (Steffen et al. 2015) recently warned in *Science*:

> There is an urgent need for a new paradigm that integrates the continued development of human societies and the maintenance of the Earth system (ES) in a resilient and accommodating state. . . . There is increasing evidence that human activities are affecting ES functioning to a degree that threatens the resilience of the ES – its ability to persist in a Holocene-like state in the face of increasing human pressures and shocks.

An independent report commissioned by the G7 members, titled "A New Climate for Peace" (2015), devolves upon the notion of climate change serving as a "threat multiplier" and conveys the sense of requisite urgency with the succinct observation that "climate change will stress the world's economic, social, and political systems." The report identifies "seven compound risks that emerge as climate change puts pressure on states and societies in fragile situations: local resource competition, livelihood insecurity and migration, extreme weather events, volatile food prices and provision, transboundary water management, sea-level rise and coastal degradation, and unintended effects of climate policies" (Risi 2015). These sentiments follow those issued by the UN Security Council in 2013 on "The Security Dimensions of Climate Change," as to which it was noted by a commentator that "climate change now poses the greatest risk to both national and international security. Climate change causes droughts, storms, fires and sea level rise. These all lead to increased vulnerability, famine, poverty, migration and conflicts" (Maman 2013).

There are myriad other reports making similar assertions, but the overarching point when they are taken together is, in essence, that the window of time in which to act is rapidly closing – not in geological time, but potentially in the span of our lifetimes. The conjoined nature of the emerging crises in our midst raises the specter of an existential threat to the continuation of human societies on the planet, and likewise raises profound questions of justice in terms of who bears responsibility and who suffers most acutely from the impacts. Nonetheless, despite the scope and scale of the impending threat, there may also be the potential for synergistic and collaborative solutions. The question, then, becomes whether climate issues are more likely to spur conflict or cooperation, and what studies of environmental crises can tell us about this.

Climate, conflict, and security

Whereas the consensus on the reality of climate change as a profound threat is demonstrable, there is less agreement as to what the precise impacts will be, how they will be distributed, and whether they will operate as a direct driver of conflict. In a sense, these concerns are less about causality than correlation, since there has yet to be an undisputed occurrence of what might be coded as a "climate war." At present, however, there have been numerous references to climate change serving to exacerbate environmental conditions (e.g., protracted drought conditions) that are cited as critical factors undergirding conflicts in places including Syria and Sudan, among others. Discussions about potential "climate refugees" are emerging with greater frequency and urgency, as low-lying areas and island nations are seeing the leading effects of rising waters. Contests among global powers for resources in arctic regions and elsewhere are keyed to climate; geopolitical conflicts over fossil fuel resources are likewise implicated within this framework.

Still, the analysis over climate and conflict remains unresolved in the literature, generally breaking along the same lines in which "resource scarcity" in general is viewed as either a driver of ruthless competition and expanding antipathies or as an impetus toward innovation, development, and more robust governance (e.g., Nordås and Gleditsch 2007; Salehyan 2008; Gartzke 2012; Gleditsch 2012; Tir and Stinnett 2012). Some view the issues more in terms of associated risks and vulnerabilities, as is often noted in an "environmental security" framework (Brauch 2002; Barnett 2015). And from an institutional governance perspective, it is generally understood that

> climate change may exacerbate other drivers of insecurity and sources of conflict. It is not only an environmental factor; it is a highly complex phenomenon that interacts with a wide range of global risks. Against the backdrop of an increasing demographic pressure and conflicts over resources due to, among others, the decrease of arable land, water scarcity or the reduction of food stocks, could be worsened by [its] effects.
>
> *(Arria-formula 2015)*

In all of these formulations, the recognition of the seriousness of the challenge is unquestioned, with the ensuing debate over the appropriate responses rather than the gravity of the situation. It is therefore apparent why climate change often is viewed as a security issue in a wide range of spheres, with due regard for its emerging and potential impacts on a global scale – including prolonged droughts and severe floods, mass displacement and refugeeism, and the limitations of existent institutional structures to manage more frequent and intense disasters overall. Thus, initiatives such as the "Climate Security Consensus Project" (CCS 2016) opine that "the current trajectory of climatic change presents a strategically-significant risk to U.S. national security," reflecting a consistent arc of not only US policy but that of international entities including NATO, the EU, and the UK (e.g., Liberatore 2013). Acknowledging the nexus of potential risks, other formulations have queried the climate–security causal chain while advocating the creation of a "global security community" to address the extant issues (Scheffran and Battaglini 2010).

Taking up this implicit sense of caution regarding the invocation of a security framework for managing climate-related issues, others have expressed even more pointed concerns about the limitations (and potential tribulations) of a security-centric discourse. Christian Parenti (2012:13–20) highlights the presence of a "security–industrial complex" that is "planning for a world remade by climate change," while cautioning that "planning too diligently for war can preclude peace" – depicting a troubling scenario in which "climatological collapse" leads to the rise of "fortress societies" that protect their own at the expense of others. Betsy Hartmann (2010:242) further cautions against the convenient invocation of monolithic references to "climate refugees" and "climate conflict" that can fuel the militarization of climate policy – instead recommending more robust forms of public and democratic engagement with the issues. Likewise, Eric Bonds (2015:209) advises resistance to viewing climate change through a militarized lens, arguing that such a posture "may provide a new legitimation for U.S. global militarism, just at the time when the United States needs to shift public resources from funding soldiers and weaponry to instead building the green infrastructure that is required to meaningfully address the climate crisis."

Similar themes have emerged in studies investigating what ensues in the aftermath of a so-called "natural disaster" – a paradigm which in itself is precipitated by the ravages of a rapidly changing global climate. The burgeoning analysis of post-disaster settings reveals the tendency to adopt a conflictual lens that can support the necessity of a militarized response, even as such a framework generally is belied by the actuality of experiences on the ground (Amster 2015). In particular, the aftermath of disasters such as hurricanes and floods is often marked by profound demonstrations of courage and compassion among the survivors, including a reclaiming of community-based processes and resilient capacities that largely had been dormant before the crisis fully emerged (e.g., Ride and Bretherton 2011). Despite media frames emphasizing criminality and chaos, more often these crises adduce patterns of solidarity and sustainability that are important components of peace and that fit within the ambit of environmental peacebuilding.

Implications for the cultivation of peace

Bringing all of these strands together, a pathway emerges in which the demonstrable challenges of climate change might serve as powerful stimuli toward the creation and maintenance of peace. As suggested by the lessons and practices highlighted under the rubric of environmental peacebuilding, the presence of ostensible tensions can likewise point toward potential avenues for peace – even in a world increasingly animated by the existential challenges connected with climate change. The precise formula for determining when an environmental crisis will spark conflict or cooperation, violence or peace, or ruination rather than resilience remains elusive, even as important touchstones of peacebuilding have emerged in recent analyses. Taken together, these formulations indicate that peace can be cultivated in the presence of seemingly intractable challenges when there is a confluence of factors present including robust institutional capacities, mutually beneficial opportunities, a sense of shared struggle, and an ethos toward education.

Indeed, it has been observed that a common threat can actually help "create peaceful relations between people," that people confronted with a profound crisis not only can "bounce back" but can actually "bounce forward," and that we can learn episodically from these experiences to cultivate greater resilience and peacebuilding capacities (Ride and Bretherton 2011:6, 191). Focusing on the long-term implications of climate change "should contribute to a process of political learning and cooperation" if they are viewed as a set of non-military security challenges that are coupled with "*anticipatory learning* and *forward looking* foreign policy strategies" (Brauch 2002:100, emphases in original). A commitment to being more proactive than reactive and to thinking on a longer time horizon than the urgings of the media cycle can help yield more opportunities for reducing vulnerabilities and promoting equities, leading to a prospective world in which "climate change is doing more to build peace than cause violence" (Barnett 2015:4).

As Kent Shifferd (2011:111) has observed, creating peace requires the development of a "social system that at all levels produces abundant life and justice, a system in which . . . basic human needs are met, including the right to life, to food and clean water;" as with a healthy ecosystem, such a social system must be "layered, redundant, resilient, robust, and proactive. Its various parts must feed back to each other so the system is strengthened and the failure of one part does not lead to systems failure." These insights help frame the ecological dimensions of peace and justice, the peaceful potentials of ecology, and in the end, the overarching impetus toward a sustainable and just peace: "A sustainable society must also be an equitable society, locally, nationally and internationally [since] social justice and environmental sustainability are inextricably linked" (Agyeman et al. 2003:323–25). Work in one sphere is simultaneously work in the other sphere, necessitating not only the absence of conflict but the presence of justice.

Building from these insights and informed by lessons of "environmental justice," a movement toward "climate justice" has arisen in recent years (Tokar 2014). Central tenets of this emerging framework are that the benefits (i.e., security, profitability) and burdens (i.e., vulnerability, exploitation) resulting from the accelerated threats posed by climate change are being skewed along preexisting lines of political and economic power, and moreover that it is often those contributing the least to the problems who bear the brunt of their impacts most directly. Object lessons in this regard are presented by the small-island nations facing potential inundation from rising ocean waters due to glacial melt that is precipitated by rising global temperatures, raising the prospect of the displacement and deterritorialization of entire peoples. The implications of this are sobering and present myriad challenges on both practical and ethical levels at once, serving as a necessary reminder that these issues exceed mere scholarly or policy interventions.

The authors of the report on "A New Climate for Peace" (G7 2015:vii–xiii) likewise took note of these interlocking concerns: "While all will feel the effects of climate change, the people in the poorest countries – and the most vulnerable groups within those countries – are the most threatened. In places affected by fragility and conflict, people face especially challenging obstacles to successful adaptation. If they fail to adapt to the effects of climate change, the risk of instability will increase, trapping them in a vicious cycle." As the report noted, "demand for food, water, and energy is increasing, particularly where the population or the economy is growing rapidly. . . . In fragile regions, persistent inequality, political marginalization, and unresponsive governments exacerbate these stresses, increasing the potential for instability and conflict. Adding the impacts of a changing climate on water, food, and land will multiply these pressures and strain countries' ability to meet their citizens' needs." Importantly, rather than advancing a set of security recommendations, the report focused on measures including adaptive capacity, sustainable development and humanitarian aid, and "climate sensitive peacebuilding."

Conclusions

In the final analysis, we come to see that the existential threat posed by climate change also presents a remarkable opportunity to proactively engage issues of justice and sustainability that draw us closer to the root causes of the mounting crises in the first place. This, in fact, is the larger lesson of environmental peacebuilding, namely that work in one sphere benefits the other and that the strategies utilized to address conflicts in the present can also help mitigate those that may develop in the future. It is this sort of spatio-temporal breadth that renders environmental peacebuilding uniquely situated to confront the nexus of social and ecological challenges, of which climate change is a quintessential example, with the grounded optimism that it is possible to "collectively articulate and implement a way of being in the world that does not make us the enemies of each other and the balance of life on the planet" in the process (Amster 2013:478).

As Lauret Savoy (2011) observes: "To face the increasingly urgent challenges of global climate change, freshwater shortages, persistent fossil fuel dependence, cascading extinctions, and inequities behind the spread of poverty and food insecurity will require the best of human imagination and responsibility because, at end, they are moral crises." The moment in which we find ourselves is beyond just navigating security considerations or technologically managing ecological boundaries, in the sense that "our fight is not simply with the carbon in the sky, but with the powers on the ground" (Smith 2014). In this light, the "solution" to climate change is not merely strategic or scientific, but has structural roots that go to the core of how our societies are configured and how we see ourselves vis-à-vis the world around us. This parallels the peacebuilding perspective, in which conflicts are recognized as being grounded in myriad patterns and practices in a given society rather than confined to a single actor or institution.

Despite the cautions expressed about securitizing and/or militarizing the response to climate change, there nevertheless remains a tendency to continue thinking in such terms as we move rapidly into a world facing escalating patterns of environmental destabilization and sociopolitical strife. Invocations of climate-confronting measures akin to the Marshall Plan that was instantiated after World War II are sometimes cited as potential mechanisms for promoting integrative engagement and exchanges among experts for discerning best practices and cultivating cooperation (Brauch 2002:101). Even more pointedly, some cutting-edge formulations posit climate change as literally constituting a "world war" in the sense of the requisite marshaling of resources needed to convert immediately (akin to World War II industrial conversion for the war effort) from a climate-destabilizing economy to a sustainable one (McKibben 2016). Nevertheless, as Vandana Shiva (2010) urges, while we may well be engaged in a collective "war against the planet," it is also the case that "the war against the earth begins in the mind" and, further, that "violent thoughts shape violent actions" and beget "violent tools."

The essential task of environmental peacebuilding is to strive to develop and deploy tools that are both sustainable and nonviolent, seeking to integrate the means and ends as much as possible in managing current crises and projecting forward to a more stable, equitable future. Climate change – as the galvanizing point for bringing deeply rooted sociopolitical and environmental issues to the fore – draws our work toward the inherent interconnection of sustainability and peace in terms that are simultaneously pragmatic and visionary. The nexus of the environment, climate, and peace offers potential for navigating emergencies and cultivating emergence alike.

References

Agyeman, J., Bullard, R. D., and Evans, B. (2003) *Just sustainabilities: Development in an unequal world* MIT Press, Cambridge, MA.

Ali, S. H. (ed.) (2007) *Peace parks: Conservation and conflict resolution* MIT Press, Cambridge, MA.

Amster, R. (2013) "Toward a climate of peace" *Peace Review* 25: 473–79.

Amster, R. (2015) *Peace ecology* Routledge, New York.

Arria-formula (2015) "Concept note: Open Arria-formula meeting on the role of Climate Change as a threat multiplier for Global Security" United Nations. www.spainun.org/wp-content/uploads/2015/06/Concept-Note_ClimateChange_20150630.pdf [Accessed 20 July 2016].

Barnett, J. (2015) "From vicious to virtuous cycles" *Environmental Peacebuilding Perspectives* Environmental Law Institute, Washington, DC. http://environmentalpeacebuilding.org/assets/Documents/EnvPerspectives2-5.7.4.pdf [Accessed 2 September 2016].

Bonds, E. (2015) "Challenging global warming's new 'security threat' status" *Peace Review* 27: 209–16.

Brauch, H. G. (2002) "Climate change, environmental stress and conflict" in *Climate Change and Conflict*, Federal Ministry for the Environment (Germany), Berlin, 9–112.

Carius, A. (2006) *Special report: Environmental peacebuilding: Conditions for success* Wilson Center, Washington, DC. www.wilsoncenter.org/sites/default/files/CariusEP12.pdf [Accessed 30 September 2016].

CCS (2016) "Climate Security Consensus Project" Center for Climate and Security. https://climateandsecurity.org/consensus [Accessed 31 October 2016].

Conca, K. and Dabelko, G. D. (eds.) (2002) *Environmental peacemaking* Johns Hopkins University Press, Baltimore, MD.

Dinar, S. (2009) "Scarcity and cooperation along international rivers" *Global Environmental Politics* 9(1): 109–35.

Dinar, S. (ed.) (2011) *Beyond resource wars: Scarcity, environmental degradation, and international cooperation* MIT Press, Cambridge, MA.

Engelke, P. and Sticklor, R. (2015) "Water wars: The next great driver of global conflict?" *National Interest*. http://nationalinterest.org/feature/water-wars-the-next-great-driver-global-conflict-13842 [Accessed 30 September 2016].

G7 (2015) *A new climate for peace: Taking action on climate and fragility risks.* www.newclimateforpeace.org [Accessed 30 September 2016].

Gartzke, E. (2012) "Could climate change precipitate peace?" *Peace Research* 49(1): 177–92.

Gleditsch, N. (2012) "Whither the weather: Climate change and conflict" *Peace Research* 49(1): 3–9.

Hartmann, B. (2010) "Rethinking climate refugees and climate conflict: Rhetoric, reality and the politics of policy discourse" *Journal of International Development* 22: 233–46.

Klare, M. T. (2002) *Resource wars: The new landscape of global conflict* Owl Books, New York.

Liberatore, A. (2013) "Climate change, security and peace: The role of the European Union" *Review of European Studies* 5(3): 83–94.

McKibben, B. (2016) "A world at war" *New Republic*. https://newrepublic.com/article/135684/declare-war-climate-change-mobilize-wwii [Accessed 31 October 2016].

Maman, J. (2013) "It's no secret: Climate change is a threat to peace and security" *Greenpeace*. www.greenpeace.org/international/en/news/Blogs/makingwaves/itsnosecretclimatechangeisathreattop/blog/44040 [Accessed 19 September 2016]

Nordås, R. and Gleditsch, N. P. (2007) "Climate change and conflict" *Political Geography* 26: 627–38.

Parenti, C. (2012) *Tropic of chaos: Climate change and the new geography of violence* Nation Books, New York.

Ride, A. and Bretherton, D. (2011) *Community resilience in natural disasters* Palgrave Macmillan, New York.

Risi, L. H. (2015) "How to create a new climate for peace: Preventing climate change from exacerbating conflict and fragility" *New Security Beat*. www.newsecuritybeat.org/2015/06/create-climate-peace-g7-report-aims-prevent-climate-change-exacerbating-conflict-fragility/ [Accessed 19 September 2016].

Salehyan, I. (2008) "From climate change to conflict? No consensus yet" *Peace Research* 45(3): 315–26.

Savoy, L. (2011) "Desegregating nature" *Terrain.org* 27. www.terrain.org/columns/27/savoy.htm [Accessed 17 September 2016].

Scheffran, J. and Battaglini, A. (2010) "Climate and conflicts: The security risks of global warming" *Regional Environmental Change* 11: S27–S39.

Shifferd, K. D. (2011) *From war to peace: A guide to the next hundred years* McFarland, London.

Shiva, V. (2010) "Time to end the war against the earth" *Common Dreams*. www.commondreams.org/views/2010/11/07/time-end-war-against-earth [Accessed 17 September 2016].

Smith, D. (2014) "Why the climate movement must stand with Ferguson" *350.org*. https://350.org/how-racial-justice-is-integral-to-confronting-climate-crisis [Accessed 1 August 2016].

Steffen, W. et al. (2015) "Planetary boundaries: Guiding human development on a changing planet" *Science* 347(6223). http://science.sciencemag.org/content/347/6223/1259855 [Accessed 23 August 2016].

Swain, A. (2002) "Environmental cooperation in South Asia" in Conca, K. and Dabelko, G. D. (eds.) *Environmental peacemaking* Johns Hopkins University Press, Baltimore, MD, 61–85.

Tir, J. and Stinnett, D. M. (2012) "Weathering climate change: Can institutions mitigate international water conflict?" *Peace Research* 49(1): 211–25.

Tokar, B. (2014) *Toward climate justice: Perspectives on the climate crisis and social change* New Compass Press, Porsgrunn, Norway.

UNDESA (2014) "International Decade for Action: 'Water for Life' 2005–2015" United Nations Department of Economic and Social Affairs. www.un.org/waterforlifedecade/water_cooperation.shtml [Accessed 31 October 2016).

UNESCO (2012) "World Water Day 2013: International Year of Water Cooperation" United Nations Educational, Scientific and Cultural Organization. www.unwater.org/water-cooperation-2013/water-cooperation/en [Accessed 31 October 2016].

Part II
Review of thematic approaches

7

Post-war environmental peacebuilding

Navigating renewable and non-renewable resources

Erika Weinthal and McKenzie Johnson

Since the 1990s, the environmental security and peacebuilding community has sought to understand the mechanisms by which the environment can produce conflict and foster peace and security. The early literature on environmental security largely emphasized the conflict-producing aspects of the relationship between environmental degradation and violence (e.g., Homer-Dixon 1994; Baechler and Spillmann 1996; Diehl and Gleditsch 2001).[1] To the international relations specialist broadly, the lack of attention to the environment as a mechanism for building peace and/or fostering cooperation stemmed from the widespread skepticism about the environment's ability to help resolve some of the most difficult internal and interstate conflicts. Drawing upon the Middle East experience, the prevailing assumption was that cooperation over low politics (i.e., the environment or economic issues) was unlikely to bring about cooperation over high politics (i.e., security and political conflict). In particular, Miriam Lowi (1993) eloquently argued that in the absence of resolving the larger political conflict between Israel and its Arab neighbors, it was unlikely that the parties to the conflict would be able to settle their water-sharing disputes over the Jordan River basin. In short, the environment (in this case, water) was unlikely to be the spark to bring about peace.

In the late 1990s, scholars such as Aaron Wolf (1998) found that empirically water was, however, more likely to bring about cooperation than conflict. The subsequent publication of *Environmental Peacemaking* (Conca and Dabelko 2002) further sought to turn this assumption about the environment as a source of conflict on its head through examining the mechanisms by which "environmental cooperation can trigger broader forms of peace" (Conca 2002:9). In particular, scholars in the volume shed light on the ways in which environmental cooperation could change the strategic climate and bolster post-Westphalian governance (Conca and Dabelko 2002). Whereas the majority of case studies in the *Environmental Peacemaking* volume inadvertently converged around water at the regional level (e.g., Weinthal 2002; Swain 2002; Swatuk 2002), subsequent work spearheaded by the United Nations Environment Programme (UNEP) has looked more broadly at natural resource management in post-conflict peacebuilding settings, which has entailed examining intrastate as well as bilateral and regional cases across multiple resource sectors (Lujala and Rustad 2012; Jensen and Lonergan 2012). A growing body of scholarship has sought then to not only understand the ways in which the environment might foster conflict and/or facilitate peace, but also the extent to which the environment might play a role in rebuilding livelihoods at war's end, sustain trust and cooperation among formerly warring parties, and reinforce the peace process once peace agreements have been signed.

As it became increasingly evident that many of the civil conflicts of the 1990s were linked to a broad array of natural resources, including oil, diamonds, cocoa, minerals, and timber (UNEP 2009), scholarly work on environment and peacebuilding more broadly moved beyond early scholarship on environmental peacemaking that looked almost exclusively at water and has instead sought to examine the role of both renewable and non-renewable resources in generating conflict and promoting peace. Research has aimed to embrace greater complexity in the relationship between the environment, peace, and security by determining how different resources contribute to the full conflict cycle, ranging from preventing conflict to peacemaking to peacekeeping to sustaining peace (UNEP 2015). Thus, while the environment is often not the sole cause of violent conflict, scholarship in the area of post-war environmental peacebuilding, for example, finds that different natural resources are likely to play different roles in different phases of the conflict cycle and introduce different opportunities for peacebuilding after the cessation of conflict (UNEP 2015).[2] In particular, natural resources can contribute to the start of conflict through generating grievances about inequities; sustain conflict through helping to finance military groups; and undermine peacemaking efforts in the aftermath of a peace settlement (UNEP 2009:8). On the flip side, sustainable use and conservation of renewable resources has been cited as a necessary element for peace in post-conflict societies while good governance of non-renewable resources – especially oil – may contribute to economic growth and development. Having a better understanding of the role of natural resources in conflict production and resolution, as well as linkages to other variables such as economic conditions is thus vital for post-war peacebuilding more generally.

To date, however, scholars and practitioners have tended to overly concentrate on either renewable or non-renewable resources (or to fragment resources into specific categories such as water, extractives, and land) in their work and research. We argue, instead, for a better integration of renewable and non-renewable resources into the environmental peacebuilding framework given the intersectoral connections that exist; for example, it is impossible to separate water and energy in many production processes and both are necessary for the production of food. Yet, one cannot overlook, too, that owing to the variation in the types of natural resources – water is often a shared resource among many users and states and thus requires cooperation whereas oil and gas may be located within one state and finite – different types of policies may be needed to manage these resources in post-war peacebuilding efforts. As such, this chapter provides a cursory survey of how different types of natural resources affect post-war environmental peacebuilding in order to demonstrate the importance of factoring in sustainable management of both renewable and non-renewable resources at the end of conflict. Additionally, we explore how scholars are beginning to think about the relationship between renewable and non-renewable resources, and the ways those connections contribute to conflict and/or peace. We highlight, for example, literature that examines the role of forests and minerals – both singly and through their interactions – in contributing to conflict in West Africa, as well as how those resources should be utilized in the peacebuilding process. Ultimately, we contend that environmental peacebuilding as a field requires more research targeted at explicating how natural resource interplay impacts the risk of conflict as well as peacebuilding objectives.

The rest of the chapter proceeds as follows: owing to the prominent role that water played in the early literature on environmental peacemaking, we begin with a focus on renewable resources with a particular focus on water. The chapter then shifts to examine the ways in which non-renewable resources have become increasingly important to post-war environmental peacebuilding efforts, as many of these resources, especially from the extractives sector, play a critical role in different phases of the conflict cycle. The chapter concludes with identifying ways in which to better integrate renewable and non-renewable natural resources in post-war peacebuilding efforts so as to help societies avoid the conflict trap and build a sustainable peace.

Post-war environmental peacebuilding

At the same time that the link between water and interstate conflict has never been direct, when it comes to natural resources more broadly, UNEP (2009) found that natural resources have played an increasing role in contributing to conflict, especially in the growing number of internal conflicts since World War II. From the mid-twentieth century into the first decade of the 2000s, approximately 40 percent of all intrastate conflicts have had a link to natural resources; more so, between 1990 and 2009, 18 conflicts were fueled by exploitation of natural resources (UNEP 2009). As such, scholars of environmental peacebuilding increasingly begin with the premise that if natural resources are a root cause of conflict and/or can fuel conflict, in the aftermath of conflict or what this volume refers to as post-war environmental peacebuilding, natural resources must then be included in programming efforts to build a sustainable peace.

Post-war environmental peacebuilding or what has been referred to as post-conflict peacebuilding more generally is one phase of the conflict cycle that extends from assessing conflict risks to building a sustainable peace. Post-conflict peacebuilding often begins following a peace treaty or the cessation of hostilities between adversaries (Call and Cousens 2008). While many acute conflicts have persisted for decades, post-conflict peacebuilding may also continue for decades and be punctuated with intermittent periods of conflict. Where conflicts are usually seen to end formally with the conclusion of a peace treaty or the withdrawal of armed forces, the rebuilding of war-torn societies and failed states usually does not have a clearly defined endpoint; states may experience periods of recidivism as international peacebuilding efforts fail to quell hostilities, as has characterized the Democratic Republic of Congo (DRC) (Autesserre 2010).

At the same time that international activities in post-conflict settings have focused on convening elections, rebuilding economies, reintegration of combatants, and nation building, UNEP's Environmental Cooperation for Peacebuilding (ECP) programme has elevated the often-overlooked role of the environment and natural resources in preventing conflict and building peace. In doing so, they have carried out post-conflict environmental assessments (Afghanistan, Sudan, DRC) to tease out the linkages between environment, conflict, and peacebuilding with a focus on both renewable and non-renewable resources (for an overview see, Jensen 2012; Conca and Wallace 2012). The assessment process has allowed UNEP to work with a range of development partners to prioritize environmental issues that should be addressed in the reconstruction phase (Conca 2015). These assessments underscore that the environment is often one of the greatest casualties of war; for example, in Afghanistan, the civil war damaged large tracts of agricultural land as well as forests (Jensen 2012). Likewise, assessments have highlighted the role different natural resources have played in fueling conflict, as well as the role of both renewable and non-renewable resources in post-war environmental peacebuilding. Assessments are used to help prioritize interventions in the natural resource and environmental sectors to foster the rebuilding of the economy, restore land tenure, and sustainable livelihoods, as well as to complement other priorities pertaining to security sector reform, assist displaced persons, and promote disarmament and demobilization (Jensen and Lonergan 2012).

Given the importance of understanding the different ways in which natural resources and the environment should be managed immediately at war's end and the impacts of these decisions on short- to long-term economic recovery and peacebuilding (Conca and Wallace 2012;

Jensen and Lonergan 2012), the rest of this chapter explores the ways different types of natural resources have been harnessed to strengthen peace agreements and to rebuild war-torn societies at war's end.

Renewable natural resources and post-war environmental peacebuilding

The renewable resource most often associated with conflict and peacebuilding is water (Gleick 1993). When it comes to post-war environmental peacebuilding, water has also been found to be vital for building a sustainable peace and for providing immediate societal benefits (Weinthal et al. 2014). For countries emerging from conflict, the provision of safe water and sanitation is considered to be one of the greatest priorities for government and humanitarian efforts given that war often disrupts the provision of basic water services, leaving civilians at risk for water-borne illnesses. For example, during Liberia's first civil war, Charles Taylor's rebel forces shut off the water and electricity flowing to the country's capital in 1990 by seizing control of the country's only hydroelectric facility, the Mount Coffee Water Plant (UNEP 2004). More so, as was the case in Afghanistan, internally displaced persons moved to urban centers, putting additional pressure on overstretched water systems (UNEP 2003). More recently, there are also no short-ages of examples from the new wars in the Middle East in which government forces, regional powers, and militias have targeted directly water and sanitation systems as a way to harm civilian life (Sowers et al. 2017). Projects devoted to ensuring clean drinking water in conflict-ridden regions thus become even more pertinent for maintaining human health since death and disease are likely to increase after a civil war ends (Ghobarah et al. 2003) and are a core component of post-war environmental peacebuilding.

Because in many parts of the world water is also considered a basic human right, the ability of states to provide access to water and sanitation thus becomes a critical marker of moving from conflict to peace. Case studies on water and post-conflict peacebuilding found that in order to meet heightened expectations for improvements in social welfare (i.e., also poverty alleviation) at war's end, governments and international efforts must give precedence to renewable resources such as water and land, as livelihoods restoration is also linked to accessing these resources (Weinthal et al. 2014). Yet, providing water is complicated because governance mechanisms are often also wiped out during conflict, especially as water engineers and staff flee conflict zones; as such, despite progress made across the globe in extending water and sanitation vis-à-vis the Millennium Development Goals (MDGs), fragile and conflict-affected countries remained the furthest from meeting the MDGs (UN ECOSOC 2010).

Because there are no substitutes for water, as there are for other natural resources such as energy, the immediate provision of water at war's end is also vital for rebuilding economic live-lihoods and ensuring food security. In particular, a focus on renewable resources such as water along with other resources such as land can facilitate government resettlement of refugees and displaced persons. Cases from post-war Japan and post-partition India and Pakistan underscore the importance of early efforts to reconstruct irrigation and drainage systems in the agricultural sector as part of post-war environmental peacebuilding (Sugiura et al. 2014; Zawahri 2014).

Addressing water use and distribution in post-war environmental peacebuilding is also nec-essary for preventing new conflicts over access to water. While scholars have found that water is increasingly less likely to be a source of conflict at the interstate level, water is increasingly more likely to be an aggravating force within post-conflict states. Afghanistan provides a vivid illustration of the importance of addressing water at war's end: whereas water was not a source of the conflict in Afghanistan, by 2008 (after 30 years of conflict), Oxfam found that water was the second most contentious issue at the local level after land (Waldman 2008).

That water is a shared resource makes it necessary for states to cooperate, especially if the users are highly dependent upon the water (Zawahri forthcoming). More so, in some parts of the world, as in the Middle East, water has remained a source of tension throughout the twentieth century. Thus, when the Israelis and Palestinians and Israelis and Jordanians, respectively, sat down to negotiate a cessation of hostilities in the 1990s (i.e., Declaration of Principles on Interim Self-Government Arrangements in 1993 – also known as the Oslo Accords – and the 1994 Peace Treaty between Israel and Jordan), the importance of water and environmental issues did not go unnoticed. Both the Oslo Accords and the 1994 Peace Treaty included sections that were solely devoted to these topics. One of the lessons learned from studying water and post-conflict peacebuilding is that it can help to build trust among former adversaries if addressed as a core component in the peace process. For Israel and Jordan, the inclusion of water in the 1994 Peace Treaty committed the countries to joint planning and development of their water resources and even when political tensions have increased in the region, they have continued to abide by the spirit of the treaty (Haddadin 2014).

In addition to water, forests constitute a renewable resource that can serve as an important source of conflict, as well as a potential opportunity for environmental peacebuilding. In terms of conflict, high-value timber species have served as a critical source of financing for war, as was the case in the protracted conflict between the Khmer Rouge and government forces in Cambodia in the 1990s (Le Billon 2000; Davis 2005). In Liberia, Charles Taylor utilized high-value timber resources to finance the civil war: he ultimately exported hundreds of millions of dollars of timber in order to purchase weapons (Beevers 2015). Forests also provide an important base for insurgencies, which often take shape in rural areas where inequalities that drive civil conflict persist. For example, the Gola forest in Sierra Leone is considered "the cradle of the war" (Mokuwa et al. 2011:339) in that it provided a base for the Revolutionary United Front (RUF). The rainforest sheltered RUF soldiers from government forces and provided remote access routes to Liberia for smugglers financing the civil conflict through the illicit diamond trade. Richards (2001:72) deemed the communities around Gola as the "masterless classes – especially young men excluded from the wider society by the exigencies of diamond mining." Finally, illicit extraction of lootable natural resources in forest areas, whether through artisanal mining or harvesting timber, fuel informal economies that can increase tension within communities and contribute to local grievances that drive larger conflict (Johnson 2017a). In Ghana and Sierra Leone, for example, illicit timber and mineral extraction have degraded forest areas in ways that negatively impact local livelihoods and contribute to conflict risk (Johnson 2017a).

Understanding the mechanisms linking forest resources to conflict can help the state realize opportunities for building – and sustaining – peace. Beevers (2012), for example, argues that forest resources should be considered as one component within the broader mosaic of natural resource management. Specifically, he argues "sustainable livelihoods are generally considered low-stakes elements of the informal economy; hence, livelihoods receive little attention in peacebuilding efforts" (Beevers 2012:386). For Beevers (2012), building a sustainable peace includes prioritizing the preservation and management of forest resources that sustain local livelihoods while simultaneously promoting the extraction of non-renewable resources that drive wider economic growth. Recognizing and addressing social inequalities in forest zones, such as the ability to access and utilize forest resources, is another important avenue for redressing local grievances that fuel conflict (Ribot 1998; Ribot and Peluso 2003). After the civil war in Liberia, for example, the state worked closely with international partners to develop a Community Rights Law which empowered communities to engage in the sustainable management of forest resources. Bruch et al. (2009:68) note that the "new government of Liberia and the United Nations placed a priority on establishing a strong, effective, and sustainable legislative and institutional framework to manage the resources whose theft and abuse had for so long provided the engine of war." Such legislative remodeling was done not only to remove a primary source of conflict in Liberia but also to promote peace by enhancing community voice in the management and use of forest resources. These examples emphasize the importance of considering renewable and non-renewable resources as integral components of the peacebuilding process.

Non-renewable natural resources and post-war peacebuilding

Cited as drivers of conflict in the so-called "new wars" in Angola, the Democratic Republic of Congo, Liberia, Sierra Leone, and Sudan/South Sudan in the 1990s (Kaldor 2012), high-value non-renewable resources have become a critical priority in post-war environmental peacebuilding. However, similar to renewable natural resources, the challenge is determining how to manage these resources so that they can facilitate peacebuilding through improving livelihoods and restoring trust and confidence in government. For countries like Nigeria, Chad, or Angola this means ensuring that the population enjoys the social welfare benefits of oil and gas development and that such high-value resources support human development, fuel employment, and contribute to the government budget. Instead, countries have often turned to discoveries of new high-value natural resources to feed government coffers and build up militaries rather than to diversify the economy, which has contributed to increasing social inequality and environmental degradation. Beevers (2015) and Johnson (2017a) argue that, without proper management, the extraction of non-renewables can often exacerbate rather than alleviate the underlying causes of conflict. Similarly, Rustad et al. (2012) warn in their work on high-value resources that relying upon mineral wealth is likely to impede long-term economic development and stymie peacebuilding efforts.

A substantial literature on the role of non-renewable resources as a source of conflict and peacebuilding has thus emerged that pays explicit attention to the ways in which the physical and social characteristics of specific resources impact conflict risk. For example, Le Billon (2012:4) argues that certain characteristics of resource sectors such as "relative location, level of economic dependence, mode of production and transport, industry structure and revenue accessibility matter a great deal" in influencing conflict. For example, point source resources, like oil wells, located at a distance from the state may incite secession conflicts (e.g. Sudan and South Sudan) whereas diffuse resources in proximity to the state may cause rioting or uprisings (e.g. chronic small-scale conflict over gold in Ghana) (Le Billon 2001; Auty 2004). Similarly, high-value lootable resources may contribute to warlordism or help to finance rebel activity (Le Billon 2001; Lujala et al., 2010).

The non-renewable resource most associated with conflict is oil (Ross 2004, 2012, 2015). Broadly, the argument goes that countries that are rich in oil and gas resources are often most likely to experience a broad array of negative political and economic effects associated with the so-called resource curse, including not only conflict, but authoritarian regimes, unbalanced economic growth, corruption, and Dutch disease (Ross 2012; Jones Luong and Weinthal 2010).[3] Because oil has been directly linked to a number of conflicts globally, understanding these linkages becomes essential for devising interventions as part of the post-conflict peacebuilding efforts. Consider Nigeria where conflict has lingered for decades, especially in the oil-rich Niger Delta concerning disputes over revenue sharing from the production of oil as well as the lingering effects on the environment and on the local economy (Watts 2004; UNEP 2011). Part of building a sustainable peace in such conflicts where non-renewables have played a role in fueling the conflict thus requires that government leaders and the international community deal with the way that the revenue is used and distributed as well as focusing on economic livelihoods (UNEP 2009). More so, the impacts of oil exploitation on other renewable resources such as water resources and fisheries in the Niger Delta requires a more comprehensive and integrated approach to natural resource management in peacebuilding.

However, other research suggests that an overemphasis on oil can mask conflict risks inherent in the extraction of other high- and medium-value natural resources – such as conventional minerals like gold or gemstones (Johnson 2017a). Because diamonds (or the trade in diamonds), for example, helped to finance the war in Sierra Leone (Silberfein 2004), it would be impossible to foster post-war peacebuilding without targeting the management of these non-renewable resources. Yet, building a durable peace requires focusing on the financial aspect of managing diamond extraction so that the revenue generated does not end up in coffers of a few political elites (Lujala et al. 2010). The high-profile role of diamonds or "blood diamonds" in the civil conflict thus helped fuel transparency initiatives such as the Kimberly Process Certification Scheme, which, through a multi-stakeholder initiative that traced the production and sale of diamonds from conflict zones, made it more difficult for such diamonds to be sold on the global market and hence provide a source of funding (Grant 2012). Given the prevalence of non-renewable high-value commodities in fueling civil conflicts, such certification schemes increasingly play an important role in enhancing post-war peacebuilding through providing information to consumers about their purchases and how these purchases may fuel conflict or enhance peacebuilding efforts.

In contrast with many non-renewable resources, citizens do not require access to minerals for their basic survival; yet these resources are often seen as belonging to the state and as such there is an expectation that society should benefit from the exploitation of these resources (Jones Luong and Weinthal 2010). Post-war environmental peacebuilding must confront how best to allocate the revenue generated through extraction so that society also shares in the benefits of these resources. Few countries have succeeded in doing so; the ones that have been successful are countries that have strong institutions and have not experienced conflict (e.g., Norway). Post-war environmental peacebuilding efforts have thus concentrated on supporting transparency initiatives such as the Extractive Industries Transparency Initiative that seeks to bolster revenue management and mitigate corruption through making the revenue generated more transparent (Rustad et al. 2017). Thus, while transparency is vital to mitigate corruption, transparency schemes, however, only work if all the parties involved adhere to best practices. Enhancing transparency of revenue flows into the state is only part of the solution; governments also need to manage expenditures so that funds are directed toward human development, poverty alleviation measures, and economic diversification. Yet, devising such revenue management programs to address poverty alleviation is often difficult, as with the World Bank's model effort in Chad which floundered owing to the pervasiveness of patronage politics and corruption (Gould and Winters 2012).

In addition to addressing issues of benefit sharing and transparency in the management of extractive resources, another issue that has become critically important for post-war environmental peacebuilding is that of equity of access to non-renewable resources. In its effort to generate revenue streams, the state often cedes large tracts of land to international companies in the period after conflict for the purpose of natural resource exploration or extraction (Hilson 2002, 2013). For example, after the conflict in Sierra Leone, Brown et al. (2012) estimate that the government allocated some 82 percent of land to mineral exploration and/or exploitation licenses. While large mining corporations provide valuable revenue to the state, such revenue does not readily flow to those communities most impacted by extractive activities (Dupuy 2017).

Furthermore, communities lose livelihood opportunities as lands used for agriculture, artisanal mining, and other livelihood activities are surrendered for large-scale mineral extraction. As a result, the informal mineral economy in which local miners operate outside of formal regulatory channels has expanded rapidly across much of Africa, South America, and Asia – creating significant tension between formal and informal actors, as well as local communities ravaged by the impacts of both legal and illegal mining (Hilson 2013; Johnson 2017a). A number of studies document that large-scale human rights violations and significant instances of conflict have taken place as individuals, the state, and private companies have clashed over access rights and benefits, and as the state has increasingly employed security forces to remove artisanal miners from formal concessions (Hilson and Yakovleva 2007; Tschakert 2010; Johnson 2017a). Others argue that current mineral policies risk aggravating underlying grievances that could result in more conflict (Beevers 2011; Johnson 2017a). While the state and international actors have attempted to address such inequities in access and benefits through regulatory measures – especially assigning more land for artisanal and small-scale mining – these measures have struggled to enable widespread access to non-renewable resources critical for livelihoods. The ability of non-renewable resources to produce a sustained peace will thus depend on the ability to balance the state's need for revenue from large-scale extraction with communities' need to generate livelihoods through sustainable access.

Lastly, as with renewable resources, including non-renewable natural resources in the peace agreements is essential for building a sustainable peace, especially where resources such as oil, minerals, and diamonds were one of the drivers of the conflict. In the few cases in which non-renewable natural resources have been addressed in a peace process, it has been through wealth-sharing arrangements (Wennmann 2012). One of the reasons for why it is attractive to address the use and distribution of the revenues from high-value resources is so as to preclude new conflicts from erupting over their allocation, but also to devise early on new governance mechanisms for managing these resources and revenue generated so as to ensure that the revenue is directed toward economic recovery (Wennmann 2012). Thus, because oil was one of the drivers of the conflict between Sudan and South Sudan, it was vital to include a revenue-sharing mechanism in the 2005 Comprehensive Peace Agreement (CPA); yet for a number of other reasons, including boundary demarcation disputes over the oil-rich Abyei region, disagreement and distrust over implementation of the CPA – especially the sharing of revenues between Sudan and the Government of South Sudan (GOSS) – continued ethnic conflict, and mismanagement and corruption by political elites in both countries, merely focusing on wealth sharing without dealing with other longstanding grievances undermined the building of a sustainable peace. Additionally, competition among political elites to control oil revenue further deepened political and ethnic divisions in the newly designated South Sudan, which breathed new life into historical grievances and disputes. Patey (2010:628), for example, noted that insecurity increased dramatically in the five years after the signing of the CPA and highlighted that fiscal mismanagement and corruption "fed resentment among local populations as unprecedented amounts of oil revenue flow into GOSS coffers." All of these factors contributed to the resurgence of conflict in South Sudan in December 2013. More so, the peace process between Sudan and South Sudan was further encumbered through the absence of including water in the agreement (Salman 2014).

Conclusion

Through contextualizing the role of both renewable and non-renewable resources in contributing to different phases of the conflict cycle, with a particular focus on post-war environmental peacebuilding, this chapter has sought to not only highlight the complexity of these relationships, but also demonstrate the importance of considering both renewable and non-renewable resources for building a sustainable peace at the end of conflict.

While the environmental peacemaking literature began with a heavy focus on water, evidence from the field of post-war environmental peacebuilding has underscored the importance of examining all natural resources and their relationships, as their effective management contributes to fostering human development and economic livelihoods. As such, while resources might differ in the ways in which they affect conflicts, having a robust understanding of their role in post-conflict peacebuilding may prevent recidivism and help societies rebuild livelihoods and reduce poverty as well as foster trust and confidence in institutions that are vital for governance.

To ensure that both renewable and non-renewable natural resources are integrated into post-war peacebuilding efforts, it is essential that they are also addressed at that stage in which peace negotiations are taking place; to raise concerns, for example, about water allocation or revenue-sharing schemes. Further, creating a cohesive management plan to realize those peace-building opportunities associated with both renewable and non-renewable resources should be consistently prioritized in the post-conflict period. The international community increasingly has turned its attention to building or reinforcing state and local institutions, as well as introducing regulatory measures such as Environmental Impact Assessments, to foster the sustainable management of natural resources, reduce conflict risk, and encourage processes that promote dialogue and cooperation among stakeholders (Campbell 2006, Johnson 2017a, 2017b). While these efforts have helped increase transparency (to address revenue distribution), participatory and community governance initiatives (to address resource access and benefits), and government accountability (to improve institutions weakened through conflict), they often address natural resource management in a fragmented rather than integrated manner.[4] In particular, responsibility for specific resources tends to be allocated across distinct government bodies that then advocate for the management of those resources as a zero-sum game (Johnson 2017a). More research highlighting how integrated resource planning can contribute to environmental peacebuilding opportunities and sustainable development is needed.

Lastly, effective management of renewable and non-renewable natural resources at war's end must also consider climate change impacts, as climate variability is expected to affect water availability, for example. As such policy makers will need to make decisions about managing natural resources that take into account greater uncertainty and adaptive management so that efforts to rebuild sustainable livelihoods are not undermined at war's end. This means that post-conflict states face a double-pronged challenge in their efforts to rebuild after conflict: they must introduce governance measures that promote growth and development without sacrificing the flexibility in resource-use policies that climate variability will require. Many post-conflict countries continue to struggle with this delicate balance in that the future is heavily discounted in order to deal with the immediate and pressing problems that emerge in the aftermath of conflict. The field of environmental peacebuilding would thus benefit from research that pays greater attention to how policy makers can balance such competing objectives.

Notes

1 For a more recent and nuanced survey of this relationship, see Bernauer et al. (2012).
2 This chapter uses interchangeably the terms post-war environmental peacebuilding and post-conflict environmental peacebuilding. While the Handbook is focused on post-war environmental peacebuilding, a larger body of environmental peacebuilding literature often uses post-conflict environmental peacebuilding. Broadly, peacebuilding is defined as, "the identification and support of measures needed for

transformation toward more sustainable, peaceful relationships and structures of governance, in order to avoid a relapse into conflict" (see UNEP 2009:7).

3 Though both Jones Luong and Weinthal (2010) and Ross (2012) find that it is state ownership or nationalization that often leads to many of these outcomes and not simply oil wealth.

4 The volumes on natural resource management and post-conflict peacebuilding have sought to address these limitations by examining ways of sequencing interventions. See https://environmentalpeace building.org/publications/books/

References

Autesserre, S. (2010) *The Trouble with the Congo: Local Violence and the Failure of International Peacebuilding* Cambridge University Press, New York.

Auty, R. M. (2004) "Natural Resources and Civil Strife: A Two-Stage Process" *Geopolitics* 9:29–49.

Baechler, G. and Spillmann, K. R. (eds.) (1996) *Environmental Degradation as a Cause of War: Regional and Country Studies* Swiss Peace Foundation/Swiss Federal Institute of Technology, Berne.

Beevers, M. (2011) *Sustaining Peace? Environmental and Natural Resource Governance in Liberia and Sierra Leone* University of Maryland, College Park.

Beevers, M. D. (2012) "Forest Resources and Peacebuilding: Preliminary Lessons from Liberia and Sierra Leone" in Lujala, P. and Rustad, S. A. (eds.) *High-Value Natural Resources and Post-Conflict Peacebuilding* Earthscan, London.

Beevers, M. D. (2015) "Governing Natural Resources for Peace: Lessons from Liberia and Sierra Leone" *Global Governance* 21:227–246.

Bernauer, T., Böhmelt, T., and Koubi, V. (2012) "Environmental changes and violent conflict" *Environmental Research Letters* 7(1).

Brown, O., Hauptfleisch, M., Jallow, H., and Tarr, P. (2012) "Environmental Assessment as a Tool for Peacebuilding and Development: Initial Lessons from Capacity Building in Sierra Leone" in Jensen, D. and Lonergan, S. (eds.) *Assessing and Restoring Natural Resources in Post-Conflict*, 327–342, Earthscan, New York.

Bruch, C., Jensen, D., Nakayama, M., Unruh, J, Gruby, R., and Wolfarth, R. (2009) "Post-Conflict Peace Building and Natural Resources" *Yearbook of International Environmental Law* 19:58–96.

Call, C. T. and Cousens, E. M. (2008) "Ending Wars and Building Peace: International Responses to War-Torn Societies" *International Studies Perspectives* 9:1–21.

Campbell, B. (2006) "Good Governance, Security and Mining in Africa" *Minerals & Energy* 21:31–44.

Conca, K. (2002) "The Case for Environmental Peacemaking" in Conca, K. and Dabelko, G. D. (eds.) *Environmental Peacemaking* Johns Hopkins University Press, Baltimore, MD.

Conca, K. (2015) *An Unfinished Foundation: The United Nations and Global Environmental Governance* Oxford University Press, Oxford.

Conca, K. and Dabelko, G. D. (eds.) (2002) *Environmental Peacemaking* Johns Hopkins University Press, Baltimore, MD.

Conca, K. and Wallace, J. (2012) "Environment and Peacebuilding in War-torn Societies: Lessons from the UN Environment Programme's Experience with Post-conflict Assessment" in Jensen, D. and Lonergan, S. (eds.) *Assessing and Restoring Natural Resources in Post-conflict Peacebuilding* Earthscan, New York.

Davis, M. (2005) "Forests and Conflict in Cambodia" *International Forestry Review* 7(2):161–164.

Diehl, P. F. and Gleditsch, N. P. (2001) *Environmental Conflict* Westview, Boulder, CO.

Dupuy, K. (2017) "Corruption and Elite Capture of Mining Community Development Funds in Ghana and Sierra Leone" in Williams, D. A. and Le Billon, P. (eds.) *Corruption, Natural Resources and Development: From Resource Curse to Political Ecology*, 69–80, Edward Elgar, Cheltenham.

Ghobarah, H. A., Huth, P., and Russett, B. (2003) "Civil Wars Kill and Maim People, Long after the Fighting Stops" *American Political Science Review* 97(2):189–202.

Gleick, P. H. (1993) "Water and Conflict: Fresh Water Resources and International Security" *International Security* 18:79–112.

Gould, J. and Winters, M. S. (2012) "Petroleum Blues: The Political Economy of Resources and Conflict in Chad" in Lujala, P. and Rustad, S. A. (eds.) *High-Value Natural Resources and Peacebuilding* Earthscan, London.

Grant, J. A. (2012) "The Kimberly Process at Ten: Reflections on a Decade of Efforts to End the Trade in Conflict Diamonds" in Lujala, P. and Rustad, S. A. (eds.) *High-Value Natural Resources and Peacebuilding* Earthscan, London.

Haddadin, M. J. (2014) "The Jordan River Basin: A Conflict Like No Other" in E. Weinthal, E., Troell, J., and Nakayama, M. (eds.) *Water and Post-conflict Peacebuilding* Earthscan, London.

Hilson, G. (2002) "Land Use Competition between Small- and Large-Scale Miners: A Case Study of Ghana" *Land Use Policy* 19:149–156.

Hilson, G. (2013) "'Creating' Rural Informality: The Case of Artisanal Gold Mining in Sub-Saharan Africa" *SAIS Review of International Affairs* 33:51–64.

Hilson, G. and Yakovleva, N. (2007) "Strained Relations: A Critical Analysis of the Mining Conflict in Prestea, Ghana" *Political Geography* 26:98–119.

Homer-Dixon, T. F. (1994) "Environmental Scarcities and Violent Conflict: Evidence from Cases" *International Security* 19(1):5–40.

Jensen, D. (2012) "Evaluating the Impact of UNEP's Post-conflict Environmental Assessments" in Jensen, D. and Lonergan, S. (eds.) *Assessing and Restoring Natural Resources in Post-conflict Peacebuilding* Earthscan, New York.

Jensen, D. and Lonergan, S. (2012) "Natural Resources and Post-conflict Assessment, Remediation, Restoration, and Reconstruction: Lessons and Emerging Issues" in Jensen, D. and Lonergan, S. (eds.) *Assessing and Restoring Natural Resources in Post-conflict Peacebuilding* Earthscan, New York.

Johnson, M. (2017a) "Strong Institutions in Weak States: Institution Building, Natural Resource Governance, and Conflict in Ghana and Sierra Leone" PhD Dissertation, Duke University, Durham, NC: http://hdl.handle.net/10161/14411

Johnson, M. (2017b) "Institutional Change in a Conflict Setting: Afghanistan's Environment Law" *European Journal of International Relations* 23(1):168–191.

Jones Luong, P. and Weinthal, E. (2010) *Oil Is Not a Curse: Ownership Structure and Institutions in Soviet Successor States* Cambridge University Press, Cambridge.

Kaldor, M. (2012) *New and Old Wars: Organized Violence in a Global Era* Stanford University Press, Stanford, CA.

Le Billon, P. (2000) "The Political Ecology of Transition in Cambodia 1989–1999: War, Peace and Forest Exploitation" *Development and Change* 31:785–805.

Le Billon, P. (2001) "The Political Ecology of War: Natural Resources and Armed Conflicts" *Political Geography* 20:561–584.

Le Billon, P. (2012) *Wars of Plunder: Conflicts, Profits, and the Politics of Resources* Hurst, London.

Lowi, M. (1993) *Water and Power: The Politics of a Scarce Resource in the Jordan River Basin* Cambridge University Press, Cambridge.

Lujala, P. and Rustad, S. A. (eds.) (2012) *High-Value Natural Resources and Post-Conflict Peacebuilding* Earthscan, London.

Lujala, P., Rustad, S. A., and Le Billon, P. (2010) "Valuable Natural Resources in Conflict-Affected States" in Berdal, M. and Wennmann, A. (eds.) *Ending Wars, Consolidating Peace: Economic Perspectives* Routledge, London.

Mokuwa, E., Voors, M., Bulte, E., and Richards, P. (2011) "Peasant Grievance and Insurgency in Sierra Leone: Judicial Serfdom as a Driver of Conflict" *African Affairs* 110:339–366.

Patey, L. A. (2010) "Crude Days Ahead? Oil and the Resource Curse in Sudan" *African Affairs* 109:617–636.

Ribot, J. C. (1998) "Theorizing Access: Forest Profits Along Senegal's Charcoal Commodity Chain" *Development and Change* 29:307–341.

Ribot, J. C. and Peluso, N. L. (2003) "A Theory of Access" *Rural Sociology* 68:153–181.

Richards, P. (2001) "Are 'Forest' Wars in Africa Resource Conflict? The Case of Sierra Leone" in Peluso, N. L. and Watts, M. (eds.) *Violent Environments: Social Bonds and Racial Hubris* Cornell University Press, Ithaca, NY.

Ross, M. L. (2004) "What Do We Know about Natural Resources and Civil War?" *Journal of Peace Research* 41(3):337–356.

Ross, M. L. (2012) *The Oil Curse: How Petroleum Wealth Shapes the Development of Nations* Princeton University Press, Princeton, NJ.

Ross, M. L. (2015) "What Have We Learned about the Resource Curse?" in Levi, M. and Rosenblum, N. (eds.) *Annual Review of Political Science* 18:239–259.

Rustad, S., Lujala, P., and Le Billon, P. (2012) "Building or Spoiling Peace? Lessons from the Management of High-value Natural Resources" in Lujala, P. and Rustad, S. A. (eds.) *High-Value Natural Resources and Peacebuilding* Earthscan, London.

Rustad, S. A., Le Billon, P., and Lujala, P. (2017) "Has the Extractive Industries Transparency Initiative Been a Success? Identifying and Evaluating EITI Goals" *Resources Policy* 51:151–162.

Salman, S. M. A. (2014) "Water Resources in the Sudan North–South Peace Processes and the Ramifications of the Secession of South Sudan" in Weinthal, E., Troell, J., and Nakayama, M. (eds.) *Water and Post-Conflict Peacebuilding* Earthscan, London.

Silberfein, M. (2004) "The Geopolitics of Conflict and Diamonds in Sierra Leone" *Geopolitics* 9(1): 213–241.

Sowers, J., Weinthal, E., and Zawahri, N. (2017) "Targeting Environmental Infrastructures: International Law and Infrastructural Wars in the Middle East and North Africa" *Security Dialogue* 48(5):410–430.

Sugiura, M., Toguchi, Y., and Funiciello, M. (2014) "Irrigation Management and Flood Control in Post–World War II Japan" in Weinthal, E., Troell, J., and Nakayama, M. (eds.) *Water and Post-conflict Peacebuilding* Earthscan, London.

Swain, A. (2002) "Environmental Cooperation in South Asia" in Conca, K. and Dabelko, G. D. (eds.) *Environmental Peacemaking* Johns Hopkins University Press, Baltimore, MD.

Swatuk, L. A. (2002) "Environmental Cooperation for Regional Peace and Security in Southern Africa" in Conca, K. and Dabelko, G. D. (eds.) *Environmental Peacemaking* Johns Hopkins University Press, Baltimore, MD.

Tschakert, P. (2010) "Digging Deep for Justice: A Radical Re-Imagination of the Artisanal Gold Mining Sector in Ghana" in Holifield, R., Porter, M. and Walker, G. (eds.) *Spaces of Environmental Justice*, 118–152, Wiley-Blackwell, Oxford.

United Nations Economic and Social Council (ECOSOC) (2010) *Joint Special Event of the Economic and Social Council (ECOSOC) and the Peacebuilding Commission (PBC) on MDGs in Countries Emerging from Conflict* Issues Note. New York, July 19.

United Nations Environment Programme (UNEP) (2003) *Afghanistan Post-Conflict Environmental Assessment* UNEP, Nairobi.

United Nations Environment Programme (2004) *Desk Study on the Environment in Liberia* UNEP, Geneva.

United Nations Environment Programme (2009) *From Conflict to Peacebuilding: The Role of Natural Resources and the Environment* UNEP, Nairobi.

United Nations Environment Programme (2011) *Environmental Assessment of Ogoniland* UNEP, Nairobi.

United Nations Environment Programme (2015) *Addressing the Role of Natural Resources in Conflict and Peacebuilding: A Summary of Progress from UNEP's Environmental Cooperation for Peacebuilding Programme 2008–2015* UNEP, Nairobi.

Waldman, M. (2008) *Community Peacebuilding in Afghanistan: The Case for a National Strategy* Oxfam International, Oxford.

Watts, M. (2004) "Resource Curse? Governmentality, Oil and Power in the Niger Delta, Nigeria" *Geopolitics* 9(1):50–80.

Weinthal, E. (2002) "The Promises and Pitfalls of Environmental Peacemaking in the Aral Sea Basin" in Conca, K. and Dabelko, G. D. (eds.) *Environmental Peacemaking* Johns Hopkins University Press, Baltimore, MD.

Weinthal, E., Troell, J., and Nakayama, M. (eds.) (2014) *Water and Post-conflict Peacebuilding: Shoring Up Peace* Earthscan, London.

Wennmann, A. (2012) "Sharing Natural Resource Wealth during War-to-peace Transitions" in Lujala, P. and Rustad, S. A. (eds.) *High-Value Natural Resources and Peacebuilding* Earthscan, London.

Wolf, A. T. (1998) "Conflict and Cooperation along International Waterways" *Water Policy* 1:251–265.

Zawahri, N. A. (2014) "Refugee Rehabilitation and Transboundary Cooperation: India, Pakistan, and the Indus River System" in Weinthal, E., Troell, J., and Nakayama, M. (eds.) *Water and Post-conflict Peacebuilding* Earthscan, London.

Zawahri, N. A. (Forthcoming) "Managing Transboundary Rivers to Avert Conflict and Facilitate Cooperation" in Conca, K. and Weinthal, E. (eds.) *The Oxford Handbook of Water Politics and Policy* Oxford University Press, Oxford.

8

Depoliticisation, water, and environmental peacebuilding

Karin Aggestam

Introduction

This chapter addresses the politics of water and the interplay between depoliticisation, technocracy and peacebuilding. Water scarcity is often framed with a dual emphasis on the conflictual and cooperative dimensions. Hence, water is an important and prioritised area of environmental peacebuilding (Conca and Dabelko 2002). At the same time, there is something puzzling about the interaction between water and politics. While water quality and quantity is at the top of the political agendas in basins, such as the Nile and the Jordan River, strategies to resolve water conflicts tend to be framed in depoliticised and technical ways.

Even though most analyses and forecasts about water wars have proven exaggerated and misguided, the water conflict scenario is still highly present in the framing of scholars, policy makers and practitioners (see, for example, Chellaney 2013; Kliot 1994; Soffer 1994, 1999). One reason for this is that it provides a preventive rationale for initiating water infrastructural projects to avert future water conflicts. These kinds of projects are often being channelled through bilateral and multilateral foreign aid assistance by international organisations and institutions.[1]

While technical innovations, such as desalination, and engineering solutions are of huge importance for water development and systems, this chapter analyses some of the problematic effects of technocracy in water development and peacebuilding. Many hydro-projects focus on technical solutions of water management whereas politically more sensitive questions about water rights, equity and redistribution are avoided. Such technical framing of water management and peacebuilding has, for instance, been observed in the Middle East peace process (MEPP) where international donor assistance for a long time has been extensively involved in improving water infrastructure in the Palestinian territories (Aggestam and Sundell 2013).

The overarching aim of this chapter is to elaborate on some of the general patterns of depoliticisation in policy and practice of environmental peacebuilding. It analyses depoliticisation as part of the technocratic turn in peacebuilding and discusses to what extent it interacts with liberal peacebuilding practices. It illuminates these conceptual discussions by focusing specifically on the politics of water in relation to environmental peacebuilding and with empirical examples from the Middle East. By way of conclusion, three remarks are made. First, technocracy tends to be perceived among policy makers and practitioners as an impartial and less controversial way of resolving conflict. Second, the tendency to exclude politics may prevent alternative ideas and practices of water management. Third, the technocratic turn in peacebuilding may empower some actors while marginalising others.

(De)politicisation in policy and practice

In many parts of the world, the politics of uncertainty and insecurity has become central to governance. Some scholars argue that this has resulted in an overall depoliticisation with a rapid decline in political participation and shifts towards technocratic governance (Flinders and Wood 2014). To become politicised, an issue has succeeded in gaining public attention and high salience, which reflects the human capacity to influence, deliberate and contest. Hence, politicisation underlines choice and contestation of diverse political positions, policies and ideologies. Depoliticisation, on the other hand, is about "displaced and submerged politics – a politics occurring elsewhere, typically beyond sites and arenas in which it is visible to nonparticipants" (Hay 2014: 302). Hence, the study of politicisation and depoliticisation raises basic questions about how we understand and conceptualise politics. An important distinction is between the "political", which refers to the ontological underpinnings, and the "politics", which includes institutions and set of practices (Mouffe 2005). As such, politics concerns power, authority and processes, which open political space for public deliberation and political actors gaining capacity to make an impact (Byrne, Kerr and Foster 2014). As Colin Hay (2007) points out, politicisation and depoliticisation should be seen as parallel processes, which reflect the fluctuations between functions, powers and responsibilities in diverse political domains and arenas across and between society. Politicisation also refers to processes where an issue can "travel" and gain a high level of political salience, which then is open for public deliberation and contestation. This indicates an acceptance and recognition of pluralism where distinct and often polarised political positions can be expressed. In such ways, conflicting and competing alternatives are publicly discussed and debated. By raising political questions in diverse arenas, the political agenda can be expanded, deliberated and contested between various actors (Zürn 2014: 50). Consequently, politicisation includes the ever-presence of antagonism, agonism and power relations, which according to Chantal Mouffe (2005) are integral parts of the ontological premise of the political.[2]

At the same time, we can notice a strong depoliticised trend in politics, triggered by the growing complexities in national and transnational governance. Depoliticisation is associated with delegation of issues and policy functions, where deliberation and decision making take place elsewhere away from the public and governmental spheres to semi-official and private arenas. This trend can be observed in many policy domains, which are reframed as areas dominated by technology, economics and science. Obviously, such framing favours solutions sought among technocrats, bureaucrats and experts. As such, depoliticisation becomes associated with "scientisation", which underlines how an issue is framed, but also how an issue in the long run becomes part of a discursive institutionalisation (Hajer 1985). Politicisation and depoliticisation can thereby either serve to close down or open up an area for contestation of various competing positions (Hay 2007). For example, an issue can be framed and reformulated not as a political problem, but more as an "illness", which in its most extreme form will direct attention towards scientific solutions. Decision-making power is thereby delegated to technocrats and experts who come to gain hegemonic status (Mac Ginty 2012).

Furthermore, depoliticisation seems to generate consensus-seeking solutions; thus, downplaying conflicts and antagonism as technological rationality and apolitical outcomes take precedence (Flinders and Wood 2014). The expression of such hegemonic power according to Kenis and Lievens (2014) is often disguised by a specific kind of politics that mostly focuses on inefficiency and bureaucracy rather than competing alternatives. As such, depoliticisation strategies are inherently framed as "anti-political" as they preclude conflict, contestation and plurality (Beveridge and Naumann 2014). However, depoliticisation does not mean less, but a different kind of politics occurring elsewhere, typically beyond traditional sites and arenas for politics, that is less visible and exposed to other diverse external actors. In short, depoliticisation is a different type of political rationality as Colin Hay (2014: 300–306) underlines; thus, it is inherent in political actions, for instance, as a tool of government and statecraft.

The study of depoliticisation is a rapidly growing field of research whereas re-politicisation has gained much less attention. We have limited knowledge of how and where re-politicisation takes place and which kinds of processes it entails. Re-politicisation brings attention to the capacity and power that political actors have or gain in order to reframe and turn an issue visible for public contestation. This indicates a dynamic and fluid interplay between de- and re-politicisation (Beveridge and Naumann 2014). Kuzemko (2014) also points out that the research field needs to broaden and include insights from securitisation theory. What happens politically when we speak security she asks? This implies an interplay between securitisation and desecuritisation processes, and their political consequences. In this regard, the seminal work of the Copenhagen School provides a theoretical framework to analyse how processes of securitisation frame an issue in "exceptional terms" and how it consequently moves outside the rules of decision making of "normal" politics due to national security considerations (Waever 2011). Consequently, the concern for security may close down political debates and move an issue away from public scrutiny, debates and domains, so it becomes less transparent. Desecuritisation, on the other hand, assumes that an issue may be transferred back to "normal" politics of deliberation, transparency and democratic processes of decision making. Yet, what is "normal" politics in an age of depoliticisation is contestable (Browning and McDonald 2011).

Other scholars argue that securitisation and politics mean different things at different times. For instance, securitisation may indicate a more extreme version of politicisation, a kind of "hyperpoliticisation" of an issue seen as politically controversial combined with heightened public attention (Flinders and Wood 2015, 2014; Kuzemko 2014). In sum, depoliticisation and re-politicisation are here understood as two forms of fluctuating political processes that are distinct but also intertwined (Flinders and Wood 2014). In the section below we will discuss how depoliticisation impacts peacebuilding practices.

Depoliticisation and the technocratic turn in peacebuilding

Since the mid-1990s, the international community has attempted to manage contemporary conflicts, which most often have been framed as in fragile, failing or dysfunctional states. Consequently, most of the peacebuilding efforts have centred on transforming these states into strong robust liberal democracies. Against this background, it may be argued that peacebuilding has developed into state building (Chandler 2010; Call and Wyeth 2008). This means that the peacebuilding agenda has expanded greatly to include economic development, institution building and regional cooperation as well. Hence, peace support operations from the early 1990s have grown dramatically not only in numbers, but also in their multifunctional tasks and mandates (Heldt and Wallensteen 2006).

As part of this trend, peace expertise is also increasingly in demand particularly among western policy makers. Peace professionals have expanded in numbers and are often recruited from peace NGOs and academia in the global north. This development reflects the overall and widespread ambition and optimism after the end of the Cold War about the possibility of building peace globally. To note, it was at the time a response to the growing number of internal and destructive conflicts, which some scholars came to label as "new wars", distinct from the "old wars" (Duffield 2001; Kaldor 2012). With the devastating ethnic cleansing and genocide witnessed in the last decades, there were growing concerns and public calls for international intervention, demanding a more proactive stance to engage in contemporary conflicts and to build sustainable peace.

Since then policy makers and international organisations have commissioned numerous assessment studies and evaluation programmes about peacebuilding practices with the aim of generating lessons learned and of improving efficiency and best practices. Most of these policy reports tend to conclude that contexts matter; they also stress the need of local ownership, institutions and capacity building (United Nations 2010). A significant part of the scholarly field of peacebuilding has also striven to generate policy-relevant research, which is reflected in the large number of practical handbooks and toolboxes on peacebuilding strategies (Ho-Won 2005). Various theories on how to build a durable and sustainable peace have been tested and combined with diverse methodological approaches ranging from large N-studies to ethnographic studies (Mac Ginty 2012). Yet, despite the growth of the academic field of peacebuilding the cumulative knowledge is still limited. Both scholars and practitioners are struggling with a whole range of problems and challenges, such as those posed by collapsed peace processes (Mac Ginty 2006), the non-implementation of negotiated peace agreements (Stedman et al. 2002), the resurgence of violence in post-conflict societies by so-called peace spoilers (Newman, Paris and Richmond 2009; Darby 2001) and widespread peace fatigue in long-drawn-out peace processes where conflicts tend to be frozen (Perry 2009). Some scholars, such as David Chandler (2017), even argue that the era of liberal peacebuilding is over.

As conflicts are framed and analysed in technocratic and depoliticised terms, such as "complex emergencies", the core problems are delineated to state structures, institutions and economic development. In addition, to reduce and manage these complexities the international community has continuously worked towards a standardised, professionalised and technocratic methodology for peacebuilding, in which scientific and rational approaches dominate (Mac Ginty 2012). This means a greater reliance on what is seen as an impartial and professional peace expertise, which stresses universal, managerial, economic and bureaucratic solutions. Peacebuilding practices are also set against some limited time horizons; thus providing strong incentives to demonstrate progress and short-term results. This indicates an intricate relationship between the political on the one hand and economics, science and technocracy on the other (Unsworth 2009).

In several peacebuilding missions, calls are made for an increase of "technical assistance". Today such peace expertise includes a broad range of state actors, international institutions and NGOs that seek to contribute in building peace worldwide. Working globally, international actors and peace experts often perceive themselves as neutral and impartial because their practices are couched in technocratic, scientific and rational language, and anchored in bureaucracy, law and administration (Mac Ginty 2012: 296). As a consequence, a specialist and technocratic terminology of peacebuilding has developed at various organisational levels. Again, this pattern can be observed in the growing number of toolboxes, handbooks and best prescribed practices, which are embedded in the liberal peace paradigm and promoted globally (Goetschel and Hagmann 2009; Mac Ginty 2012).

Technocracy and liberal peacebuilding

Liberal peacebuilding includes a highly ambitious and comprehensive programme, which is illustrated in the *Agenda for Peace* launched by the former UN Secretary-General Boutros Boutros-Ghali (1992). This document highlights the responsibility of the international community to prevent, manage and resolve conflicts. The liberal peacebuilding paradigm can also be traced to some broad agreements that have emerged in recent decades among liberal states, multilateral organisations and western NGOs (Peterson 2013).

To promote and implement such an ambitious peacebuilding agenda, technocracy and depoliticisation have been one way of reducing the complexity of conflict dynamics, but also of limiting the contestation about alternative political visions. It is a strategy to foster consensual ideas about peace formation, which are anchored in some dominant liberal peacebuilding norms. However, such technical framing of conflict frequently fails to acknowledge the depth and entrenchment of specific complexities and challenges involved in external peacebuilding intervention. It also fails to take locally driven processes of change into account. Accordingly, such narrow political analyses can backfire in practice. At the same time evaluations of peacebuilding practices frequently fail to recognise the necessity of bringing in the political as they are assessed against some well-established international project logics, which are limited in time and space (Carey 2012).

An additional problem is the outsourcing and privatisation of peacebuilding, development aid and donor assistance from western states to NGOs and local civil society organisations (Carey 2012). Such a trend corresponds with some of the goals stipulated in the liberal peacebuilding paradigm, which has as an overriding ambition to strengthen broader processes of democracy and civil society that are distinct from the state. For instance, civil society organisations (CSOs) are seen as vital partners in most peacebuilding projects and provide alternatives to faltering state structures and institutions. As such, the CSOs have been able to benefit from generous funding because they are important agents in contributing towards normalisation and stabilisation of societal relations in conflict-ridden societies. At the same time, the standards and logics of these kinds of civil society projects tend to emanate from the global north. This is, for instance, reflected in the broad usage of policy terms and western buzz words, such as Security Sector Reforms (SSR), Disarmament, Demobilisation and Reintegration (DDR) and democracy promotion, which are programmes adopted by local NGOs in order to compete successfully in what has become a highly competitive market of funding and donor schemes (Smillie 1997). These concepts are also used in other fields, such as development and security, which reflect the intertwined nexus of peace–security–development. For instance, the usage of value-laden notions, such as "good governance" and "empowerment", in international policy documents can be seen as anchoring practices (Sending and Neumann 2011). Furthermore, these notions serve as a type of moral authority by virtue of the persuasive, normative and governable power they enshrine, and provide justification and legitimacy for international intervention (Cornwall and Brock 2005).[3]

At the same time, these terms are deeply contested and practitioners are often confronted with the political realities on the ground while trying to implement peacebuilding and development projects (Unsworth 2009). There are also local political actors that are not able to benefit from international donor assistance as they are not capable of establishing an agreeable fit with the liberal peacebuilding paradigm. This exclusion and lack of political space may cause insecurity, fear and even violence between some actors, who in peacebuilding jargon are labelled as "peace spoilers" (Newman and Richmond 2006; Stedman 1997). Hence, wider societal and local participation may paradoxically be seen as an obstacle to be overcome. In this regard, technocracy may offer a way of bypassing such a problem by depoliticising the conflict (Mac Ginty 2012).

The expansion of the peacebuilding field has mostly occurred in the post-conflict phases and been situated within post-political contexts that seek to foster a liberal peace consensus. As such, politics is often seen as "messy" as it may interfere and clash with a presumed universal rationality entailed by standardised peacebuilding programmes (Warner and Wegerich 2010). This trend has been deepened by the parallel expansion of privatisation in the peacebuilding spheres by delegating and outsourcing to private actors (Carey 2012). Consequently, the political nature of peacebuilding tends to be bracketed. In the section below, we will illustrate how this political dynamic may play out in the water sector.

Framing water conflict and peace

The framing of water conflict is to a large extent influenced by dominant worldviews and discourse structures, which guide actors in their interpretation and construction of meaning and reality (Barnes and Alatout 2012; Frölich 2012). The theory of securitisation, as mentioned above, provides great insights into the ways water scarcity can be framed as an existential security threat, which concerns survival of a referent object, such as the nation state, the global economy or the environment. While there have been numerous studies on water security, few scholars have studied the contents of desecuritisation, which is central to peacebuilding (Aggestam 2015). Bezen Coskun (2008; 2009) points out that desecuritisation is basically about transforming and reframing an issue as asecurity and non-security. In her view, this can be done by widening participation beyond the elite-based groups in water management by including so-called desecuritising actors, such as NGOs, experts and international actors.

Two distinct and parallel international trends of framing and (de)securitising water conflict have been dominating in the last decades. First, in the early 1990s there was a drastic increase in the number of statements by influential policy makers about the linkage of water scarcity and the potential of future wars (Amery 2002; Scheumann and Schiffler 1998; Trottier 2003). Second, a similar development evolved in academia with a growing number of scholars theorising about the causal linkage between water scarcity and war (Homer-Dixon 1999). Departing from neo-Malthusian and realist positions, they argue that conflict may erupt in basins and areas where states are suffering from water scarcity, lack of trust and cooperative institutional means to seek joint solutions to manage shared water resources (Dinar 2002; Lowi 1995).

A region frequently mentioned in the context of water conflict and securitisation is the Middle East as it suffers from volatile politics, unfavourable demographic trends, droughts and limited quantities of freshwater (Kliot 1994). By way of illustration, the former UN Secretary-General Boutros Boutros-Ghali stated after the first Gulf War in the early 1990s that the next war would more likely be over water than oil. At the time, this seemed like a plausible scenario as the region had suffered from several recent droughts. Obviously, climate change adds severity to the urgent problem of water scarcity. With increased uncertainty about the effects of rising temperature and decreased precipitation, it is assumed that evaporation of surface water will intensify while the renewal of groundwater will slow down. This will have dire consequences on economic growth, social stability and food security in the region (Brown and Crawford 2009). For instance, some policy makers, scholars and analysts imply that one of the major causes to the outbreak of civil war in Syria was the droughts related to climate change, which have plagued the country in recent years (Selby and Hulme 2015).

While water conflict and water security dominated in the early 1990s, there was also a noticeable discursive turn in the latter part of the 1990s and early 2000. This reframing of water countered the water-war thesis by emphasising the linkage between water and peace. The basic argument here is that water scarcity triggers cooperation rather than war and thereby holds greater prospect for peace (Katz 2011). The seminal work of Aaron Wolf and his colleagues, for instance, shows through extensive historical analyses of interstate water disputes how rare water wars actually have been in history whereas cooperation overwhelmingly has dominated among riparians (Wolf et al. 2003). Since then a number of studies have been conducted, which suggest different technological and diplomatic strategies that make cooperation more likely as an outcome of water scarcity (Alam 2002; Dolaytar and Gray 2000). As a consequence, the water sector turned into a strategic and potential area for peacebuilding in the 1990s. In contrast to other areas of high politics, water cooperation between adversaries was now seen as a catalyst for building peace. Furthermore, it provided a suitable rationale for water development to become part of the liberal peacebuilding agenda in its overarching effort to strengthen institution building and state capacity. Shared functional interests in scarce water resources and technological innovations were expected to trigger cooperation and create confidence and trust between warring parties. Part of that framing was also a tendency to stress water cooperation as conflict prevention. The potential dangers and risks of failing to take action in regard to water security were underlined, thus encouraging investments in water development and infrastructures, such as pipelines, desalination plants, wastewater treatment, drip irrigation systems, to mention a few (Katz 2011).

Shared functional ideas about water management have also been supported by some core assumptions in functionalist theory (Haas 2008). The theory in short prescribes and expects cooperation in areas of low politics to spill over to high politics and ultimately result in stability, peace and integration. Functionalist ideas were for instance reflected in the initial phases of the Middle East peace process where water constituted one of the prioritised areas of the multilateral negotiations,[4] aiming to foster long-term regional cooperation and sustainable peace (Jägerskog 2003; Peters 1996). The water–peace discourse also dominated among practitioners and diplomats, who consequently favoured the water sector as an area for donor assistance. Following on from this, a whole range of hydro-cooperative projects between Israelis and Palestinians were launched and received generous funding under the assumption that water, economic development and peace are strongly interrelated. Particularly for the Palestinians, with their underdeveloped and inefficient water sector, a broad range of technical hydro-projects, such as irrigation systems, pipelines and wastewater plants, were initiated and funded in an effort to develop additional and new water supplies (Selby 2003, 2004).

Depoliticisation of water and peace

Water development and peacebuilding in general concerns a wide range of activities and actors. At the same time, the drive to make water development and cooperation more "rational", politics and wider societal participation are often seen as inhibiting efficiency. As discussed above, technical framing of conflict results in technical solutions; politics can therefore be seen as negatively influencing rationality and scientific reasoning. Furthermore, several peacebuilding projects are centred on the creation of new water, locating alternative resources and improving efficient use; while hydro-political concerns tend to be avoided, such as equitable benefit sharing and redistribution of existing water resources. Wider social participation can therefore be seen as a challenge to water development as in theory the technocratic system does not favour popular input. By depoliticising water conflict, local political participation can be bypassed because of the technocratic nature of water management (Mac Ginty 2012). But as Ole Waever (2011) rightly points out, desecuritisation that transforms into technocratic management depoliticises at least as much as securitisation does. Thus, if desecuritisation of water is likely to lead to the depoliticisation of conflict, it can have unforeseen consequences regarding ownerships, power dynamics and contextual sensitivity.

Water development is inherently a political process with contested meanings of water, which includes diverse actors with unequal powers to confront, negotiate and cooperate (Mollinga 2008). Warner and Wegerich (2010) underline that we need to acknowledge that water scarcity is a conflict-induced area of political contestation. As such, we need to adopt a sensitive political gaze in order to critically engage with depoliticised discursive constructions of water and the distinct characteristics of water politics in relation to scarcity (Warner and Wegerich 2010).

Particularly troublesome is depoliticisation in peacebuilding processes that concern asymmetric water conflicts. In the Israeli–Palestinian case, the Israeli government has consistently favoured a depoliticised and technocratic approach to water cooperation as part of the peace process, which avoids any questions related to hydro-politics, historical contexts, water rights and redistribution (Zeitoun 2011). For instance, the Israeli government has only been willing to negotiate agreements that are limited to shared management of existing resources, conservation and joint development of new water supplies (Weinthal and Marei 2002). Claims and demands made by the Palestinians regarding access to the Mountain Aquifer have been rejected. Being the weaker party, the Palestinians have consistently tried to argue for their water rights as well as for a greater share of and access to water resources[5] by making references to the Helsinki Rules and the 1997 Convention on the law of the non-navigational uses of international watercourses. These international conventions underscore equitable share of water and that neither party should cause "significant harm" to another user. The Palestinians have for a long time sought Israeli recognition of these water rights, but to no avail (Schlütter 2005). As such, the Israeli framing of water development in the Middle East peace process has come to dominate and guide water negotiations.

The efforts to reframe water conflict in a more technical–managerial manner provide much leverage to water managers and experts. Yet, their significant dispositional power of expertise is seldom studied and analysed critically (Warner and Wegerich 2010: 6). As part of the peacebuilding intervention, international actors often conduct dual roles by assisting and funding water development projects. At the same time, these actors are inclined to focus more narrowly on water issues and privilege technical solutions, description and prescription that are non-context-specific. Some of the actors also lack substantial knowledge of local circumstances, but as the "new" peacemakers and "experts" they frame their ideas and models as impartial based on "liberal reasons" (Selby 2004: 44; 2013; Stetter et al. 2011).

In particular, development brokers fulfil important roles in mediating between local and international discourses on peace and water development. For instance, Julie Trottier (2006) shows in her in-depth empirical studies of water management in the Israeli–Palestinian conflict how development brokers shape and constrain agendas according to a presumed universal project rationality, which emanates from the global north. She points out how development brokers in many ways are indispensable as go-betweens between local organisations and international actors by speaking the "right" technical languages and using the appropriate language and terminology to fit the project logic of the international donors. The development brokers are usually local actors who have insights and networks with donor organisations while their local social positions enable them to act as go-betweens between the local population targeted by donors and the donors themselves (Trottier 2006). As there is fierce competition for international funds among many local agencies some actors are empowered whereas others become disempowered. In short, this pattern feeds into a more general trend in recent decades of development and peacebuilding towards increasing privatisation and outsourcing of donor assistance.

Conclusion

This chapter has analysed the interplay between technocracy, water and depoliticisation in environmental peacebuilding. By way of conclusion, three remarks can be made. First, technocracy is viewed as a constructive way of resolving water conflict because it downplays politics and instead puts strong emphasis on professionalism, standardisation and rational problem-solving. Yet, as argued in this chapter, such technical framing of conflict in the water sector tends to downplay hydro-politics in general and power dynamics in particular. To ignore politics and asymmetrical relations runs the risk of strengthening the status quo rather than resolving water conflict. Second, the exclusion of politics may prevent alternative ideas and practices as they may divert too much from the universal blueprints of water development and peacebuilding. Third, the technocratic turn in peacebuilding practices tends to empower some actors while marginalising others. New peacemakers have been introduced in their capacities of being water experts and development brokers. These actors play critical roles locally and have come to gain significant power in water management; still their power is rarely assessed as they are assumed to act impartially on the basis of their technical and/or scientific knowledge and competence. Hence, there is a need for more studies that critically assess what the effects of technocracy and depoliticisation are on the norms and practices of environmental peacebuilding.

Notes

1 Some examples are the World Bank support for adaptation to water scarcity in the Middle East and North Africa through pipeline and infrastructure projects and technical assistance programs (World Bank website: http://www.worldbank.org).
2 This is also the main reason why she argues that the idea of a "perfectly reconciled and harmonious society has to be abandoned" (Mouffe 2013: xi). In her view, the denial of the political in its antagonistic dimension is the reason why liberal theory is not able to envisage politics in an adequate way and can even be dangerous in its consensus-seeking drive as it cannot cope with growing extremism.
3 David Chandler (2014) argues that this shift towards a societal framing is an expression of post-liberalism, which provides a new domain for policy intervention and governance. Consequently, intervention is justified as a way of empowering individuals and groups with a focus on capacity building, resilience and societal practices in everyday life.
4 The framework of the Middle East peace process was structured along two tracks of bilateral and multilateral negotiations.
5 Palestinians demand the rights to most of the water in the West Bank, both groundwater and rights to the Jordan River, which are embedded within a historical context and international law.

References

Aggestam, Karin (2015) Desecuritisation of water and the technocratic turn in peacebuilding, *International Environmental Agreements: Politics, Law and Economics* 15(4): 327–340.

Aggestam, K. and Sundell, A. (2013) Situating water in peacebuilding, *Water International* 39(1): 10–22.

Alam, U. Z. (2002) Questioning the water wars rationale: A case study of the Indus Waters Treaty, *Geographical Journal* 168(4): 341–353.

Amery, H. A. (2002) Water wars in the Middle East: A looming threat, *Geographical Journal* 168(4): 313–323.

Barnes, J. and Alatout, S. (2012) Water worlds: Introduction to the special issue of Social Studies of Science, *Social Studies of Science* 42(4): 483–488.

Beveridge, R. and Naumann, M. (2014) Global norms, local contestation: Privatisation and de/politicisation in Berlin, *Policy and Politics* 42(2): 275–291.

Boutros-Ghali, Boutros (1992) *An Agenda for Peace*. Available at un-documents.net

Brown, O. and Crawford, A. (2009) *Rising Temperatures, Rising Tensions. Climate Change and the Risk of Violent Conflict in the Middle East*, IISD (International Institute for Sustainable Development), Winnipeg.

Browning, C. and McDonald, M. (2011) The future of critical security studies: Ethics and the politics of security, *European Journal of International Relations* 19(2): 235–255.

Byrne, C., Kerr, P. and Foster, E. (2014) What kind of 'Big Government' is the Big Society? A reply to Bulley and Sokhi-Bulley, *British Journal of Politics and International Relations* 6(3): 471–478.

Call, C. T. and Wyeth, V. (2008) *Building States to Build Peace*, Lynne Rienner, Boulder, CO.

Carey, H. (2012) *Privatizing the Democratic Peace: Policy Dilemmas of NGO Peacebuilding*, Palgrave Macmillan, Basingstoke.

Chandler, D. (2010) R2P or not R2P? More statebuilding, less responsibility, *Global Responsibility to Protect* 2(1): 161–166.

Chandler, D. (2014) *Resilience. The Governance of Complexity*, Routledge, Abingdon.

Chandler, D. (2017). *Peacebuilding. The Twenty Years' Crisis, 1997–2017*, Palgrave, Basingstoke.

Chellaney, B. (2013) *Water, Peace, and War. Confronting the Global Water Crisis*, Rowman & Littlefield, Plymouth.

Conca, K. and Dabelko, G. D. (eds.) (2002) *Environmental Peacemaking*, Johns Hopkins University Press, Baltimore, MD.

Cornwall, A. and Brock, K. (2005) What do buzzwords do for development policy? A critical look at 'participation', 'empowerment' and 'poverty reduction', *Third World Quarterly* 26(7): 1043–1060.

Coskun, Bezen (2008) Analysing desecuritisations: Prospects and problems for Israeli–Palestinian reconciliation, *Global Change, Peace & Security* 20(3): 393–408.

Coskun, Bezen (2009) Cooperation over water resources as a tool for desecuritisation: The Israeli–Palestinian environmental NGOs as desecuritising actor, *European Journal of Economics and Political Studies* 2: 97–115.

Darby, J. (2001) *The Effects of Violence on Peace Processes*, United States Institute of Peace, Washington, DC.

Dinar, S. (2002) Water, security, conflict and cooperation, *SAIS Review* 22(2): 229–253.

Dolaytar, M. and Gray, T. S. (2000) *Water Politics in the Middle East – A Context for Conflict or Co-operation?* Macmillan, London.

Duffield, M. (2001) *Global Governance and the New Wars*, Zed Books, London.

Flinders, M. and Wood, M. (2014) Depoliticisation, governance and the state, *Policy & Politics* 42(2): 135–149.

Flinders, M. and Wood, M. (2015) When politics fails: hyper-democracy and hyper-depoliticization, *New Political Science* 37(3): 363–381.

Frölich, C. (2012) Security and discourse: The Israeli–Palestinian water conflict, *Conflict, Security & Development* 12(2): 123–148.

Goetschel, L. and Hagmann, T. (2009) Civilian peacebuilding: Peace by bureaucratic means? *Conflict, Security, Development* 9(1): 55–73.

Haas, Ernst (2008) *Beyond the Nation State. Functionalism and International Organization*, ECPR Press, Colchester.

Hajer, Maarten (1985) *The Politics of Environmental Discourse. Ecological Modernization and the Policy Process*, Oxford University Press, Oxford.

Hay, Colin (2007) *Why We Hate Politics*, Polity Press, Cambridge.

Hay, Colin (2014) Depoliticisation as process, governance as practice: What did the 'first wave' get wrong and do we need a 'second wave' to put it right? *Policy & Politics* 42(2): 293–311.

Heldt, B. and Wallensteen, P. (2006) *Peacekeeping Operations: Global Patterns of Intervention and Success, 1948–2004*, Vol. 2, Edition 2, Folke Bernadotte Academy Publications, Stockholm.

Ho-Won, J. (2005) *Peacebuilding in Postconflict Societies: Strategy & Process*, Lynne Rienner, Boulder, CO.

Homer-Dixon, T. (1999) *Environment, Scarcity and Violence*, Princeton University Press, Princeton, NJ.

Jägerskog, A. (2003) *Why States Cooperate over Shared Water: The Water Negotiations in the Jordan River Basin*, Linköping Arts and Science, Linköping.

Kaldor, M. (2012) *New and Old Wars*, Polity Press, London.

Katz, D. (2011) Hydro-political hyperbole: Examining incentives for overemphasizing the risks of water wars, *Global Environmental Politics* 11(1): 12–35.

Kenis, A. and Lievens, M. (2014) Searching for 'the political' in environmental politics, *Environmental Politics* 23(4): 531–548.

Kliot, N. (1994) *Water Resources and Conflict in the Middle East*, Routledge, London.

Kuzemko, C. (2014) Politicising UK energy: What 'speaking energy security' can do, *Policy & Politics* 42(2): 259–274.

Lowi, M. R. (1995) *Water and Power: The Politics of a Scarce Resource in the Jordan River Basin*, Cambridge University Press, Cambridge.

Mac Ginty, R. (2006) *No War, No Peace. The Rejuvenation of Stalled Peace Processes and Peace Accords*, Palgrave, Basingstoke.

Mac Ginty, R. (2012) Routine peace: Technocracy and peacebuilding, *Cooperation and Conflict* 47(3): 287–308.

Mollinga, P. P. (2008) Water Policy – Water Politics. Social Engineering and Strategic Action in Water Sector Reform, in Sheumann, W. et al. (eds.) *Water Politics and Development Cooperation*, Springer Verlag, Berlin.

Mouffe, C. (2005) *On the Political*, Routledge, London.

Mouffe, C. (2013) *Agonistics. Thinking the World Politically*, Verso, London.

Newman, E. and Richmond, O. (2006) *Challenges to Peacebuilding. Managing Spoilers during Conflict Resolution*, United Nations University Press, Tokyo.

Newman, E., Paris, R. and Richmond, O. (eds.) (2009) *New Perspectives on Liberal Peacebuilding*, United Nations University Press, Tokyo.

Perry, V. (2009) At cross purposes? Democratization and peace implementation strategies in Bosnia and Herzegovina's frozen conflict, *Human Rights Review* 10: 35–54.

Peters, Joel (1996) *Pathways to Peace? The Multilateral Arab–Israel Peace Talks*, Royal Institute of International Affairs, London.

Peterson, J. (2013) Creating space for emancipatory human security: Liberal obstructions and the potential of agonism, *International Studies Quarterly* 57: 318–328.

Scheumann, W. and Schiffler, M. (eds.) (1998) *Water in the Middle East: Potential for Conflicts and Prospects for Cooperation*, Springer, Berlin.

Schlütter, B. (2005) Water rights in the West Bank and in Gaza, *Leiden Journal of International Law* 18: 621–644.

Selby, Jan (2003) Dressing up domination as 'co-operation': The case of Israeli–Palestinian water relations, *Review of International Studies* 29(1): 121–138.

Selby, Jan (2004) *Water, Power and Politics in the Middle East: The Other Palestinian–Israeli Conflict*, I.B. Tauris, London.

Selby, J. (2013) Cooperation, domination and colonisation: The Israeli–Palestinian Joint Water Committee, *Water Alternatives* 6(1): 1–24.

Selby, J. and Hulme, M. (2015) Is climate change really to blame for Syria's civil war? *The Guardian* 29 November.

Sending, O. and Neumann, I. (2011) Banking on Power: How Some Practices in an International Organization Anchor Others, in Adler, E. and Pouliot, V. (eds.) *International Practices*, Cambridge University Press, Cambridge.

Smillie, I. (1997) NGOs and development assistance: A change in mind-set? *Third World Quarterly* 8(3): 563–577.

Soffer, A. (1994) The relevance of Johnston Plan to the reality of 1993 and beyond, *Studies in Environmental Science* 58: 107–121.

Soffer, A. (1999) *Rivers of Fire – The Conflict over Water in the Middle East*, Rowman & Littlefield, Lanham, MD.

Stedman, S. J. (1997) Spoiler problems in peace processes, *International Security* 22(2): 5–53.

Stedman, S., Rothchild, D. and Cousens, E. (2002) *Ending Civil Wars: The Implementation of Peace Agreements*, Lynne Rienner, Boulder, CO.

Stetter, S., Herschinger, E., Teichler, T. and Albert, M. (2011) Conflicts about water: Securitizations in a global context, *Cooperation and Conflict* 46(4): 441–459.

Trottier, J. (2003) Water Wars: The Rise of a Hegemonic Concept, in *Water Security and Peace: A Synthesis of Studies Prepared under the PCCP–Water for Peace Process*, UNESCO–Green Cross International, Paris.

Trottier, J. (2006) Donors, modellers and development brokers: The pork barrel of water management research, *Reconstruction: Studies in Contemporary Culture* 6(3).

United Nations (2010) *Monitoring Peace Consolidation. United Nations Practitioners' Guide to Benchmarking*, United Nations, New York.

Unsworth, Sue (2009) What's politics got to do with it? Why donors find it so hard to come to terms with politics, and why this matters, *Journal of International Development* 21: 883–894.

Waever, Ole (2011) Politics, security, theory, *Security Dialogue* 42(4–5): 465–480.

Warner, Jeroen and Wegerich, Kai. (2010) Is Water Politics? Towards International Water Relations, in Wegerich, Kai and Warner, Jeroen (eds.) *The Politics of Water*, Routledge, London.

Weinthal, E. and Marei, A. (2002) One resource two visions, *Water International* 27(4): 460–467.

Wolf, A. T., Yoffe, S. and Giordano, M. (2003) International waters: Identifying basins at risk, *Water Policy* 5(1): 29–60.

Zeitoun, M. (2011) The global web of national security, *Global Policy* 2(3): 286–296.

Zürn, Michael (2014) The politicization of world politics and its effects: Eight propositions, *European Political Science Review* 6(1): 47–71.

9

Climate change adaptation and peacebuilding

Richard A. Matthew

Introduction[1]

This chapter examines how and why climate change adaptation should be integrated into peacebuilding. It begins with a brief overview of climate science, and summarizes real and potential climate change impacts. It then reviews how scholars have sought to link environmental stress generally to the conflict cycle, work that has provided a strong platform for investigating the role of climate change across the conflict cycle. I argue that based on what we know about climate change impacts, there are at least six compelling and robust claims about the relationship between climate change and the conflict cycle that together provide a strong rationale for integrating climate change into peacebuilding programs. After a short discussion of the concept of peacebuilding, I identify obstacles to and entry points for this integration.

Climate change science

The science of climate change has matured in a matter of decades into a domain of human knowledge in which there is a very high level of confidence. Scientists have measured changes in several variables that affect the planet's climate: the proportion of carbon in the earth's atmosphere, the rate at which glaciers and permafrost are melting, the extent of forest cover, and so on. They have compiled data sets extending back hundreds, hundreds of thousands, and, in some cases, millions of years. They have observed upward trends in global average temperatures, and they have determined that weather patterns are changing worldwide. Most importantly, they have identified strong correlations between these changes and human activities, such as the use of fossil fuels and the modification of land cover for agriculture, settlement, and other purposes. Scientists around the world have considered very carefully other possible explanations for trends such as global warming, and they have concluded that human behavior is indeed driving contemporary climate change.

In the past three decades, scientists have provided extensive details about the complex relationships between human activities and climate change. Through this research, we know that greenhouse gas (GHG) emissions are the key driver of climate change because they trap solar heat on the earth's surface. Carbon dioxide is the primary GHG contributing to climate change, but methane, nitrous oxide, and other gases are also important (IPCC 2014). Anthropogenic emissions come primarily from the use of fossil fuels for electricity, heat, and transportation, but agricultural and industrial practices, forestry, and land cover change are also significant drivers of climate change (IPCC 2014).

The cumulative impact of human behavior has been to increase the atmospheric concentration of carbon dioxide by 40 percent since the 1700s, from 280 parts per million (ppm) to 400 ppm in 2013 (IPCC 2014). This level of carbon dioxide is higher than it has been in at least the past three million years and average global temperature has increased as a result by approximately 0.8 degrees Celsius (IPCC 2014). In a business as usual scenario, carbon dioxide levels will exceed 450 ppm by 2040, and global warming will increase by 2.6 to 4.8 degrees Celsius by 2100 (IPCC 2014).

Typically when scientists discover something important about the non-human material world, their findings simply enrich our symbolic order – the way we understand the world we inhabit. But also, typically, these findings do not call into question our behavior to the extent that climate science does. In this sense, resistance to this branch of science is entirely predictable, especially by those who are doing well in the status quo. The findings of climate science are controversial in some measure because they have broad, transformative implications for our practices, institutions, beliefs and values, and thus they generate spirited and anxious debate. In a sense, climate change is not only a scientific phenomenon; it is also a social one.

Popular media has focused much attention on one small area of controversy – whether science has adequately established that humans are the primary drivers of contemporary climate change. In academic and practitioner circles, one finds little of this type of discussion; there is instead wide agreement that "human influence on the climate system is clear" (IPCC 2014: 15). The scientific controversy instead focuses on the social implications of this reality. How is climate change affecting disasters, public health, human security, and different forms of violent conflict from riots to war? What might happen in vulnerable areas as the planet warms further, and floods, droughts, and heat waves increase in frequency and intensity? What are the best strategies for adaptation and mitigation? How should the costs of managing climate change be allocated, especially given vast inequalities in the emissions of different countries, and in their capacity to address this global challenge?

Climate change impacts

According to the 2014 Intergovernmental Panel on Climate Change's (IPCC) Fifth Assessment Report, climate change today confronts humankind with an unacceptably high risk of severe, long-term, and global impacts, including "substantial species extinction, global and regional food insecurity, consequential constraints on common human activities and limited potential for adaptation in some cases" (IPCC 2014: 19). There are, however, some challenges in assessing climate change impacts. On the environmental side, climate change often amplifies phenomena that occur naturally. Take the example of flooding. Around the world, flood zones are generally demarcated by the concept of a 100- or 500-year flood event. The idea is that the flood zone includes all of the land that could be flooded by an event that has a 1 percent or 0.2 percent chance of happening in any given year. This can then be used as the basis for flood insurance systems, building codes, evacuation strategies, and so on. But this is a somewhat problematic baseline as there is clearly some artificiality in using 100 years or 500 years. There may or may not be any real change, for example, in the risk of flooding considered as a 95-year or 120-year event. But in the latter case people might settle into an area that is not identified as a flood zone, and the flood defenses designed for that baseline might be a poor fit for the reality of that particular space. Many people flooded by Hurricane Harvey were living outside the 500-year flood zone. Moreover, projections of risk typically do not account for human adaptation and intervention, which is evident throughout the course of human history, and can increase or decrease sensitivity to flooding.

Still the idea does provide a baseline that can be useful for demonstrating the extent to which climate change might be forcing more frequent flooding, even though this baseline is not fixed and immutable. But it is convenient to note that under conditions of climate change, 100- or 500-year events are becoming far more frequent – say, becoming 10- or 50-year events. However, this, too, is a difficult calculation for several reasons. First, severe flood events may be univariate, multivariate, or compound events. For example, the environmental drivers of coastal flooding include sea level, winds, tides, and precipitation – a dramatic increase in one of these variables (e.g. unusual rainfall) could cause a severe flood, or several of these variables converging (e.g. hurricane and rainfall) could cause a severe event. But often coastal flooding will also be affected by riverine flooding, itself the product of a set of variables, or by an earthquake. These are compound events, and their probability is very hard to establish, although progress is being made on this front.

Second, flooding is also affected by changes in topography. Human behavior, such as draining wetlands, paving roads, and building piers and seawalls, can all have significant impacts on the area's hydrology and can alter flood dynamics – creating, for example, spaces where the flow of water might deepen and speed up, or where water might pool for extended periods, or where water flows may be dissipated and diverted.

So in the same sense that a sharp increase in unemployment (X) might be associated with a significant increase in certain types of crime (Y), but it can be very difficult to say that X caused Y in any particular case, it is difficult to identify specific events as "caused" by climate change. Nonetheless, scientists have become very sophisticated at establishing "natural" rates for different hazards, and at accounting for types of human behavior that might contribute to phenomena such as flooding, heat waves, and drought but not to climate change per se, and types of behaviors that contribute to climate change – which in turn alters the historical patterns of those same events. And they are also able to assess with great accuracy the extent to which climate change is in an overall sense contributing to univariate, multivariate, and compound events. The broadly supported conclusion of all of this research is that anthropogenic climate change is contributing to a variety of observed phenomena, including the frequency and intensity of extreme weather events, glacial melt, changes in animal and plant migration, and sea level rise. Moreover, regardless of what people do in terms of mitigation, there are latent climate change impacts that will continue to emerge over decades. And, perhaps most alarming, left unabated, further climate change will tend overwhelmingly to create conditions that adversely affect human and non-human life, and could ultimately pose an existential threat. On the policy side of the equation, it may be enough for most policy innovation and risk management to know about trends in dangerous events like floods and droughts, and to know that anthropogenic climate change affects these trends, regardless of where we stand on the issue of attribution.

What is important, then, is that according to the IPCC's Fifth Assessment Report (2014), under business as usual scenarios, global temperatures are projected to increase by between 2.6 and 4.8 degrees Celsius by 2100 compared to pre-industrial levels, and by at least two degrees with strong mitigation efforts. Under the most optimistic scenario, then, the world will experience increases in food insecurity and water scarcity, changes in disease vectors, and more costly events such as floods, cyclones, heat waves, droughts, and wildfires (IPCC 2014). Sea level rise will expand flood extent in much of the world, leading to widespread displacement that in some cases will be permanent (IPCC 2014).

Although linking population displacement and climate change is very challenging, because people move for many reasons, the concern expressed by the IPCC that hundreds of millions of people might be forced to evacuate coastal areas for part of each year or permanently is reasonable based on the evidence at hand (IPCC 2014). Considerable research has demonstrated the enormous probable impact of climate change on extreme weather events, and there is no obvious reason to assume people would not consequently be displaced in increasingly large numbers (Mirza 2003; Lehner et al. 2006; Hirabayashi et al. 2008, 2013; Hallegatte et al. 2013; Hinkel et al. 2014). Indeed, in recent years tens of millions of people have been displaced by weather events, and especially by flooding.

Moreover, climate change will also lead to increases in less extreme weather events such as nuisance flooding, which can impose considerable costs on a society. Moftakhari et al. (2017) have shown that in some cases, over time, the cumulative effect of nuisance flooding could equal or exceed that of extreme events. According to an estimate developed by Hallegatte et al. (2013), severe flooding alone could impose costs of US $1 trillion by mid-century – an enormous and unprecedented number that, in the wake of Hurricanes Harvey and Irma, in 2017, seems now quite plausible. Minor flooding would add substantially to that figure.

While considerable attention has focused on climate change and extreme weather events, and flooding is emerging as the hazard with the greatest potential to cause widespread harm and displacement, climate change is having a variety of other impacts, and the trends for these are also alarming. Arid regions of the world are likely to experience increasing water stress and extended droughts. In many projections, sub-Saharan Africa could experience steep declines in precipitation (IPCC 2014). Crop yields are also likely to decrease in parts of the world, which would expand food insecurity (IPCC 2014). Fish stocks, which are a primary source of protein for many countries, could decline dramatically under conditions of ocean warming and acidification (IPCC 2014).

There is another important aspect of climate change impacts that merits attention. As climate science improves, the sense of shared fate that helped unify global concern in the 1990s may be eroding, as it becomes clear that climate change could confer some benefits. Russia, Scandinavia, Canada, and the United States, for example, all could gain arable land, longer growing seasons, better access to natural resources in the Arctic, and new trade routes. Ironically, primary beneficiaries tend to be powerful countries, with well-developed economies – and high emission rates. This is in sharp contrast to the countries typically identified as in the front lines of negative climate change impacts, such as those in South Asia, the Middle East, and sub-Saharan Africa. This has led a number of analysts to explore the ways in which climate change might affect regions where poverty, instability, and violent conflict could make adaptation more challenging. This is not to say that these regions lack understanding or ingenuity, but rather that their capacity to act might be stretched very thin by immediate social needs or being consumed by long-term violent conflict.

Climate change and the conflict cycle

There is a long history of linking environmental stress and competition over natural resources and land to violent conflict and other forms of social vulnerability such as poverty. In antiquity, Thucydides (*The Peloponnesian War*) and Plato (*The Republic*) argued that states living within their ecological limits would be more stable and secure than those relying on imports. This line of thinking about ecological limits received a more explicit treatment in the work of Thomas Malthus, who, in 1798, argued that population growth would lead to resource scarcities that would in turn generate disaster and conflict. In the twentieth century, Fairfield Osborn drew on Malthus to explain World War II: "When will it be openly recognized that one of the principal causes of the aggressive attitudes of individual nations and of much of the present discord among groups of nations is traceable to diminishing productive lands and to increasing population pressures?" (Osborn 1948: 200–201).

Arguments linking resource scarcity to violent conflict picked up momentum as evidence of environmental stress improved in the 1970s and were popularized through works such as Garrett Hardin's article "The Tragedy of the Commons" (1968), Paul Ehrlich's *The Population Bomb* (1968), and Donella Meadows et al.'s *Limits to Growth* (1972). In 1977 Lester Brown argued that environmental issues were matters of national security; Richard Ullman (1983) contended that environmental stress should catalyze a rethinking of the concept of national security; and Norman Myers (1986) described environmental security as 'ultimate security.' Over the past thirty years, these seminal arguments have served as the platform for the subdiscipline of environmental security, a protean concept that has supported a wide range of thinking, discussion, and policymaking. One perspective that has received considerable attention examines linkages between the environment and the so-called conflict cycle – pre-conflict, conflict, and post-conflict. Of course, some forms of conflict always exist in society; here the emphasis is on unusually violent forms of conflict such as war.

A compelling finding of this research is that environmental factors can be significant across the conflict cycle – for example, contributing to the outbreak of war (the desire by the Revolutionary United Front (RUF) to gain control of diamond fields in Sierra Leone); funding war (the imposition of levies on cacao in Côte d'Ivoire by both rebel and government forces to raise funds to purchase weapons and ammunition); and as an element of peacebuilding in post-conflict countries (such as the reform of the diamond and forest sectors in the early days after the war in Liberia by President Johnson Sirleaf).

Influential work on how environmental variables could contribute to the onset of violent conflict has been carried out by, among others, Homer-Dixon (1991, 1994, 1996, 1999) and Kahl (2006), focusing on resource scarcity. At the same time, scholars such as de Soysa (2000), Klare (2001), Collier and Hoeffler (2002), and Collier (2008) argued that an abundance of high value natural resources could also contribute to violent conflict. Early critiques of these arguments (e.g. Peluso and Watts 2001; Korf 2006), emphasized the complexity of war and dismissed this wave of scholarship as simplistic, an observation largely accommodated in more recent research (see Floyd and Matthew 2012).

In recent years, linkages have been tested using large data sets. Hanson et al., for example, conclude that between 1950 and 2000, "118 of 146 conflicts (81 percent) took place wholly or partially within biodiversity hotspots. When we used the historical percentage of land covered by hotspots to generate an expected value, this proportion was highly significant (one-tailed; $\chi2 = 456$, $p < 0.01$, df = 1)" (2009: 580).

Once violent conflict erupts, natural resources can be used to finance war (or accumulated for personal gain), the environment may be targeted by combatants (such as the destruction of water systems by the RUF during the civil war in Sierra Leone), environmental management may be disrupted, and civilians fleeing the violence may place enormous pressure on the urban, protected or fragile environments to which they relocate (Le Billon 2004, 2005, 2012; Brown 2013). Finally, the role of the environment in the post-conflict period has also been examined through research identifying how environmental factors can be fruitfully integrated into conflict resolution and peacebuilding processes (Conca and Dabelko 2002; Matthew, Halle and Switzer 2002; Ali 2007).

This research has served as the platform for studies focused on how climate change might affect the conflict cycle. These have tended to be quite speculative although they are beginning to be more data-driven. For example, Hsiang et al. have written that

Using data from 1950 to 2004, we show that the probability of new civil conflicts arising throughout the tropics doubles during El Niño years relative to La Niña years. This result, which indicates that ENSO [El Niño Southern Oscillation] may have had a role in 21 percent of all civil conflicts since 1950, is the first demonstration that the stability of modern societies relates strongly to the global climate.

(Hsiang et al. 2011: 438)

But much of the work to date builds on projections and speculation in IPCC (2007, 2014) reports, where considerable attention is given to how climate stress could amplify problems in turbulent regions of South Asia and Africa. The planet's mid-latitude countries have heightened exposure to many natural hazards, and they also often have greater sensitivity due to poverty and low governance capacity. They are, in a sense, the contemporary antithesis of sustainable development. This assessment lends itself, unfortunately, to the easy integration of negative impressions of these regions that are not scientifically informed, so one must be alert to the possibility that some reports unwittingly fuse climate science to popular Western impressions of Africa and South Asia and consequently exaggerate vulnerability and underestimate ingenuity and capacity.

With this caveat in mind, some of the most familiar and influential assertions include:

- "Climate change acts as a threat multiplier for instability in some of the most volatile regions of the world" (CNA 2007: 6–7).
- "Climate change will overstretch many societies' adaptive capacities within the coming decades" (German Advisory Council on Global Change 2008: 1).
- There are "46 countries – home to 2.7 billion people – in which the effects of climate change interacting with economic, social and political problems will create a high risk of violent conflict" (Smith and Vivekananda 2007: 3).
- "Over the next few years – driven by a combination of natural variability, a warmer climate from the effects of greenhouse gases, and a more vulnerable world in general – the risk of major societal disruption from weather and climate-related extreme events can be expected to increase. These stresses will affect water and food availability, energy decisions, the design of critical infrastructure, use of the global commons such as the oceans and the Arctic region, and critical ecosystem resources." The authors add "They will affect both poor and developed nations with large costs in terms of economic and human security" (McElroy and Baker 2012: 4).
- "The impact of climate change will challenge and reduce the resilience of people and communities to varying degrees. . . . In some contexts, this can increase the risk of instability or violence. This is a particular problem in conflict-prone or conflict-affected contexts where governance structures and institutions are often weak, regardless of climate change" (Vivekananda 2011: 8).

Opposing this speculation, Sletteback (2012: 175), among others, writes:

Rather than over-emphasizing conflict as a result of climate change, I would recommend keeping the focus on societal development, including building resilience against adverse effects of climate change. While this promises the possibility of alleviating the danger of climate change, it can also lead to strengthened societies in the face of natural disaster and civil war.

Against this context, there are a handful of claims that have emerged that seem compelling and robust. First, in large measure anthropogenic climate change amplifies phenomena such as floods, droughts, and heat waves that occur naturally. The impacts of such phenomena on human societies are partly determined by where people settle, the defense systems they build, and so on. We have an increasingly crowded planet with a great deal of brittle infrastructure and metropolitan space rapidly expanding on coastal and riverine flood plains, as well as in arid regions. As noted earlier, it is very difficult to distinguish between "natural" severe weather events and those "caused" by climate change. Together, this suggests that when exploring linkages to the conflict cycle, it would be more accurate to replace "climate change" with a more inclusive term such as "anthropogenic climate change and natural climate variability." Admittedly, this is a bit unwieldy.

Second, the vast literature on violent conflict makes it clear that simple causal models are very misleading. Violent conflict has links to deep structural issues such as poverty, inequality, regime type and identity as well as to more immediate variables such as recession and corruption. Individuals and groups at different levels can also play critical roles, as can military plans and technological innovations. Human psychology may provide important insights into the propensity for group violence. When many variables shape outcomes, small changes in one might have enormous impact (complexity science) but it may also be very hard to isolate the signal of any given variable. Even a very large effect could be hard to identify. So at this point in time, it is perhaps most accurate to suggest that links between anthropogenic climate change and natural climate variability, on the one hand, and the conflict cycle, on the other, may very well vary from case to case. And often, climate impacts will be indirect, amplifying variables related to war such as poverty and weak governance capacity.

Third, and related to the above point, recent research is expanding the dependent variable to include a broader range of negative social outcomes. The idea is that climate change might contribute to many other forms of violence, such as human insecurity, crime, murders, protests, riots, pandemics, and terrorism. Insofar as peacebuilding is concerned, the conflict cycle is a logical starting point, but we should be aware of other relationships to violence, and the types of adaptation and resilience responding to these might require, that might be possible within the context of peacebuilding.

Fourth, climate change is a global phenomenon, which suggests that in some sense it is introducing turbulence at a planetary level. For example, if tens of millions of people are displaced by drought and flood in many parts of the planet, then this might influence how any one society responds to migratory pressure on its own borders – and this response might differ (e.g. it might be much more aggressive) from what it would have been if the broader pattern of displacement did not exist. A sort of general system-wide climate effect might lead to less generous particular responses.

Fifth, earlier I noted how some countries could benefit from climate change. One important example is the potential of Arctic nations to gain access to the vast mineral wealth that has for millennia been locked under an impenetrable sheet of ice. This suggests that climate change could be highly disruptive in other contexts as well, by changing the value of assets such as land and water. The implications for current power relationships are potentially enormous.

Sixth and finally, the concept of winners and losers has another variant. Some countries, and regions within countries, have more capacity to adapt than others. The state of California recently experienced a five-year drought. Many wealthy coastal communities had responded to an earlier drought by investing in water efficiency and were largely self-sufficient and unaffected by the recent drought. Poor communities, on the other hand, had not adapted to the likelihood of more frequent drought events and they experienced enormous hardship. It is easy to imagine this scenario playing out globally, at which point the arguments of Harald Welzer (2012) – that where extreme poverty and climate hardship intersect, violence could erupt – seem very reasonable.

Peacebuilding

At the end of the Cold War, seeing new hope for international cooperation and alarmed by violent civil wars being fought in places like Angola, Rwanda, Sierra Leone, and Somalia, Boutros Boutros-Ghali introduced the concept of peacebuilding in *An Agenda for Peace* (1992). Since that time, the concept has evolved through deliberation and practice, especially inside the United Nations (United Nations 2001, 2006; UNDP 1994; UNGA 2009). While there is not a single definition used by everyone, the following statement captures current thinking quite well:

> Peacebuilding involves a range of measures targeted to reduce the risk of lapsing or relapsing into conflict by strengthening national capacities at all levels for conflict management, and to lay the foundations for sustainable peace and development. Peacebuilding strategies must be coherent and tailored to specific needs of the country concerned, based on national ownership, and should comprise a carefully prioritized, sequenced, and therefore relatively narrow set of activities aimed at achieving the above objectives.
>
> *(United Nations 2007, website)*

A 2004 study carried out by the Peace Research Institute of Oslo identified four aspects of peacebuilding based on a review of 336 projects that were funded by Germany, the Netherlands, Norway, and the United Kingdom (Smith 2004). This framework for organizing peacebuilding into a set of core functions was adopted by the Organization for Economic Cooperation and Development (OECD) in 2008, and by a variety of UN agencies (e.g. UNEP 2009). The framework organizes peacebuilding into four functional domains: (1) social, economic, and environmental; (2) governance and political; (3) security; and (4) truth and reconciliation. Other researchers have weighed in with slightly different frameworks. Barnett et al. (2007: 49) focus on stability creation, restoration of state institutions, and socio-economic recovery. De Coning (2008: 47) identifies security and rule of law, politics and governance, socio-economic recovery, and human rights.

These theorizations do capture the format of early peacebuilding initiatives, and make clear that in the 1990s peacebuilding was largely about prompting post-conflict states towards something that resembled Sweden or Canada. But the early track record was not especially successful. Following the first round of peacebuilding, so to speak, Hun Sen assumed full control over Cambodia; UN peacekeepers watched helplessly as an incredibly brutal genocide took place in Rwanda; and Charles Taylor played a key role in three wars after the UN mission left Liberia. The UN failed forward, and peacebuilding has improved over time. It shifted its focus to capacity building for both government and civil society. It sought to avoid areas in which other donors were active, and focus on meeting needs where they were not. It made clear that post-conflict programs had to be largely designed and led by the people they would affect, and that the character of peacebuilding would inevitably be highly contextual.

Has the evolution of peacebuilding been successful? Assessments vary (Berdal 2009; Call and Cousens 2008; Chetail 2009; Doyle and Sambanis 2006; Fortna 2008; Howard 2008; Tschirgi 2004). Many argue that there is a huge gap between resources and needs (United Nations 2013). Others contend that peacebuilding is shaped by Western agendas and ideology, and needs to have more local input and content (Chandler 1999; Chopra 2000). For some, post-conflict societies are simply being recolonized with Western institutions and values (Bendaña 2005; Pugh 2008).

But two things are certain. First, almost no one else is rallying to help post-conflict states meet immediate needs and build capacity for sustainable development. So the role of the UN remains critical. Second, although much has been written about the links between climate change and the conflict cycle, climate change adaptation has not been integrated into peacebuilding except in ad hoc and piecemeal ways.

Climate change adaptation and peacebuilding

Thus there is an opportunity, especially through the United Nations, and a need, given the ways in which climate change has been linked to the conflict cycle, to focus on the prospects for integrating climate change adaptation into peacebuilding activities. In earlier work with Anne Hamill (2010) and alone (Matthew 2014), we identified two major obstacles to this integration. First, there is considerable tried and true programming, generally adaptable to local contexts, for many peacebuilding priorities – disarming, demobilizing and reintegrating (DDR) combatants, crafting conditions attractive to foreign investors, building capacity in core civil society and government areas, establishing reconciliation processes, and so on. There is considerably less proven content for climate change adaptation in post-conflict states.

Second, the timescales for conventional peacebuilding and climate change adaptation are not easy to align. Donors and societies emerging from war typically have immediate and pressing needs, and are looking for fairly quick results, whereas climate change adaptation may impose costs early on, with the promise of benefits in the future.

To this I would now add a third obstacle. In 2015, the Paris Agreement created a general framework for climate action designed to be globally inclusive, but this has not yet matured into clear policies, programs, and funding opportunities for post-conflict states. Under such conditions of uncertainty, climate change adaptation is easily delayed in peacebuilding operations.

Nonetheless in earlier work we developed an approach to thinking about how climate change adaptation could be integrated into conventional peacebuilding areas (see Table 9.1).

We further argued that principles for this integration ought to be established, perhaps modeled on the OECD's (2007) principles for effective engagement in fragile states, and that an inventory of appropriate adaptation tools and best practices needs to be created. To this I would add that climate change adaptation is not likely to succeed if it is not fully responsive to the needs, values, experiences, knowledge, and assets of the communities that will be affected by it. While a national climate action plan is essential, in the context of peacebuilding, trusted and inclusive community-based development of climate change adaptation projects and programs is critical.

The costs of not acting are becoming increasingly clear. In 2017, for example, mudslides in Freetown, the capital of Sierra Leone, destroyed homes and killed as many as a thousand people. The area received three times its normal rainfall in July 2017, creating a lot of mud in the hills. Unfortunately, during the post-conflict era, deforestation and unplanned and unregulated construction amplified vulnerability considerably, transforming a natural hazard into a flood and mudslide disaster. It is well known, however, that mud and rain are a deadly combination in a hilly city where people build in areas of heightened vulnerability. Mud flows very quickly and being at least twice the weight of water it is extremely difficult to stop and can overwhelm neighborhoods, destroying houses and killing people, in a matter of minutes. If some attention had been given to climate resilience, then perhaps this tragedy

Table 9.1 Opportunities for integrating Climate Change Adaptation (CCA) and Climate Change Mitigation (CCM) into peacebuilding

Peacebuilding area CCA/CCM type	Socio-economic recovery	Politics and governance	Security and rule of law	Human rights
Identification and assessment of climate-sensitive sectors	Vulnerability of agricultural livelihoods	Integration into national plan for reconstruction	Areas vulnerable to climate-related disasters	Impacts of water scarcity on women
Climate-sensitive general capacity building	Transportation	Screening tools for government agencies	Community resilience and response	Property rights
Climate change specific CCA and CCM capacity building	Urban flood dynamics modeling	Energy policy	Dedicated disaster response programs	CCA and CCM education
CCA and CCM capacity building requiring bilateral, regional or global cooperation	Regional trade associations	Transboundary water management	Regional response planning	Participation in climate justice dialogues

Source: Adapted from Matthew (2014: 89).

would not have happened. This is a story playing in different parts of the planet, as war and disaster overlap.

Looking ahead, several things seem essential to this integration. First, as the case of Sierra Leone suggests, building community level resilience, and harnessing the ingenuity and assets of a community to this effort, is essential. Second, this in turn requires improvements in the ability to quickly assess climate vulnerability, build adequate warning systems, and access funds to support climate action in post-conflict settings. Third, climate change affects variables associated with instability and conflict such as poverty, water access and food security, and therefore a particular focus on building climate-sensitive capacity in these areas, where immediate needs are being met, is especially important. Fourth, during consultations around plans for post-conflict recovery, points of intersection need to be identified and trade-offs need to be openly discussed so that informed decisions can be made that are broadly understood. Fifth, absent a more concrete framework for coordinating and funding global climate action, there is no easy reference point for this integration – it is held hostage by broader forces of inertia, which seems remarkably unfair given the heightened sensitivity to climate impacts in post-conflict states.

Note

1 This chapter has benefited from work carried out while preparing another edited volume and especially the chapter Goodrich, K. and Nizkorodov, E. (2016) "The Science of the Anthropocene" in Matthew, R., Harron, C., Goodrich, K., Maharramli, B., and Nizkorodov, E. (eds.) *The Social Ecology of the Anthropocene*, World Scientific/Imperial Press, London, 3–32; from previous work done on climate change and peacebuilding with Anne Hammill; and from informal conversations about what we know about the links between climate change and conflict with Marc Levy.

References

Ali S. (2007) *Peace parks: Conservation and conflict resolution*, Cambridge: MIT.

Barnett M., Kim H., O'Donnell M., and Sitea L. (2007) "Peacebuilding: What is in a name?" *Global Governance*, 13: 35–58.

Bendaña A. (2005) "From peacebuilding to statebuilding: One step forward and two steps back?" *Development*, 48(3): 5–15.

Berdal M. (2009) *Building peace after war*, London: International Institute for Strategic Studies.

Boutros-Ghali B. (1992) *An agenda for peace: Preventive diplomacy, peacemaking and peacekeeping* http://journals.sagepub.com/doi/abs/10.1177/004711789201100302 [Accessed 1 September 2017].

Brown L. (1977) "Redefining national security" Worldwatch Institute Paper 14.

Brown O. (2013) "Encouraging peacebuilding through better environmental and natural resource management" Chatham House Briefing Paper.

Call C. and Cousens L. (2008) "Ending wars and building peace: International responses to war-torn societies" *International Studies Perspectives*, 9: 1–21.

Chandler D. (1999) *Bosnia: Faking democracy after Dayton*, London: Pluto.

Chetail V. (ed.) (2009) *Post-conflict peacebuilding: A lexicon*, Oxford: Oxford University Press.

Chopra J. (2000) "The UN's kingdom in East Timor" *Survival*, 42(3): 27–40.

CNA (2007) *National security and the threat of climate change* www.cna.org/cna_files/pdf/National%20Security%20and%20the%20Threat%20of%20Climate%20Change.pdf [Accessed 1 September 2017].

Collier P. (2008) *The bottom billion: Why the poorest countries are failing and what can be done about it*, Oxford: Oxford University Press.

Collier P. and Hoeffler A. (2002) "Greed and grievance in civil war" Working Paper, Oxford, Centre for the Study of African Economies.

Conca K. and Dabelko G. (eds.) (2002) *Environmental peacemaking*, Washington, DC: Woodrow Wilson Center.

De Coning C. (2008) "Understanding peacebuilding: Consolidating the peace process" *Conflict Trends*, 4: 45–51.

De Soysa I. (2000) "The resource curse: Are civil wars driven by rapacity or paucity?" In Berdal M. and Malone D. (eds.) *Greed & grievance: Economic agendas in civil war*, Boulder, CO: Lynne Rienner, 113–135.

Doyle M. and Sambanis N. (2006) *Making war and building peace: United Nations peace operations*, Princeton, NJ: Princeton University Press.

Ehrlich, P. (1968) *The population bomb*, San Francisco: Sierra Club/Ballantine Books.

Floyd R. and Matthew R. (eds.) (2012) *Environmental security: Frameworks for analysis*, Oxford: Routledge.

Fortna V. (2008) *Does peacekeeping work? Shaping belligerents' choices after civil war*, Princeton, NJ: Princeton University Press.

German Advisory Council on Global Change (2008) *World in transition: Climate change as a security risk*, London: Earthscan.

Hallegatte S., Green C., Nicholls R.J. and Corfee-Morlot J. (2013) "Future flood losses in major coastal cities" *Nature Climate Change*, 3(9): 802–806.

Hammill A. and Matthew R. (2010) "Peacebuilding and climate change adaptation" *St. Antony's International Review*, 5(2): 89–112.

Hanson T., Brooks T. M., Fonseca G. A. B., Hoffmann M., Lamoreux J. F., Machlis G., et al. (2009) "Warfare in biodiversity hotspots" *Conservation Biology*, 23: 578–587.

Hardin G. (1968) "The tragedy of the commons" *Science*, 162: 1243–1248.

Hinkel J. D., Lincke A. T., Vafeidis M., Perrette R. J., Nicholls R. S. J., Tol B., et al. (2014) "Coastal flood damage and adaptation costs under 21st century sea-level rise" *Proceedings of the National Academy of Sciences*, 111(9): 3292–3297.

Hirabayashi Y., Kanae S., Emori S., Oki T., and Kimoto M. (2008) "Global projections of changing risks of floods and droughts in a changing climate" *Hydrological Sciences Journal*, 53(4): 754–772.

Hirabayashi Y., Mahendran R., Koirala S., Konoshima L., Yamazaki D., Watanabe S., et al. (2013) "Global flood risk under climate change" *Nature Climate Change*, 3(9): 816–821.

Homer-Dixon T. (1991) "On the threshold: Environmental changes as causes of acute conflict" *International Security*, 16: 76–116.

Homer-Dixon T. (1994) "Environmental scarcities and violent conflict: Evidence from cases" *International Security*, 19: 5–40.

Homer-Dixon T. (1996) "Debate between Thomas Homer-Dixon and Marc A. Levy" *Environmental Change and Security Project Report*, 49–60.

Homer-Dixon T. (1999) *Environment, scarcity, and violence*, Princeton, NJ: Princeton University Press.

Howard L. (2008) *UN peacekeeping in civil wars*, Cambridge: Cambridge University Press.

Hsiang S. M., Meng K. C., and Cane M. A. (2011) "Civil conflicts associated with global climate change" *Nature*, 476: 438–441.

Intergovernmental Panel on Climate Change (IPCC) (2007) *Working group II report: Climate change impacts, adaptation, and vulnerability* www.ipcc.ch/report/ar5/ [Accessed 1 September 2017].

IPCC (2014) *Climate change 2014: Synthesis report. Contribution of Working Groups I, II and III to the Fifth Assessment Report of the Intergovernmental Panel on Climate Change*, Geneva.

Kahl C. H. (2006) *States, scarcity, and civil strife in the developing world*, Princeton, NJ: Princeton University Press.

Klare M. (2001) *Resource wars: The new landscape of global conflict*, New York: Henry Holt.

Korf B. (2006) "Cargo cult science, armchair empiricism and the idea of violent conflict" *Third World Quarterly*, 27(3): 459–476.

Le Billon P. (ed.) (2004) *The geopolitics of resource wars: Resource dependence, governance and violence*, London: Frank Cass.

Le Billon P. (2005) *Fuelling war: Natural resources and armed conflict*, Adelphi paper no. 373, Oxford: Routledge.

Le Billon P. (2012) *Wars of plunder: Conflicts, profits and the politics of resources*, London: Hurst.

Lehner B., Döll P., Alcamo J., Henrichs T., and Kaspar F. (2006) "Estimating the impact of global change on flood and drought risks in Europe: A continental, integrated analysis", *Climate Change*, 75(3): 273–299.

McElroy M. and Baker D. J. (2012) *Climate extremes: Recent trends with implications for national security* http://environment.harvard.edu/sites/default/files/climate_extremes_report_2012-12-04.pdf [Accessed 10 September 2017].

Malthus T. (1798) *An Essay on the Principle of Population* http://oll.libertyfund.org/titles/malthus-an-essay-on-the-principle-of-population-1798-1st-ed [Accessed 10 September 2017].

Matthew R. (2014) "Integrating climate change and peacebuilding" *Climatic Change*, 123: 83–93.

Matthew R., Halle M., and Switzer J. (eds.) (2002) *Conserving the peace: Resources, livelihoods and security*, Geneva: IUCN/IISD.

Meadows D.H, Meadows D.L, Randers J., and Behrens III W.W. (1972) *Limits to growth*, New York: New American Library.

Mirza, M. M. Q. (2003) "Climate change and extreme weather events: Can developing countries adapt?" *Climate Policy*, 3(3): 233–248.

Moftakhari H. R., AghaKouchak A., Sanders B. F., and Matthew R. A. (2017) "Cumulative hazard: The case of nuisance flooding" *Earth's Future*, 5: 214–223.

Myers N. (1986) "The environmental dimension to security issues" *The Environmentalist*, 6: 251–257.

Organization for Economic Cooperation and Development (OECD) (2007) *Principles for good international engagement in fragile states* www.oecd.org/dac/governance-peace/conflictfragilityandresilience/ principlesforgoodinternationalengagementinfragilestates.htm [Accessed 15 September 2017].

Osborn F. (1948) *Our plundered planet*, New York: Grosset & Dunlap.

Peluso N. and Watts M. (eds.) (2001) *Violent environments*, Ithaca, NY: Cornell University Press.

Pugh M. (2008) "Corruption and the political economy of liberal peace" International Studies Association annual convention paper, San Francisco.

Slettebak R. T. (2012) "Don't blame the weather! Climate-related natural disasters and civil conflict" *Journal of Peace Research*, 49: 163–176.

Smith D. (2004) *Towards a strategic framework for peacebuilding: Getting their act together: Overview report of the Joint Utstein Study of Peacebuilding* www.regjeringen.no/upload/kilde/ud/rap/2004/0044/ddd/pdfv/210673-rapp104.pdf [Accessed 15 September 2017].

Smith D. and Vivekananda J. (2007) *A climate of conflict: The links between climate change, peace and war*, London: International Alert. www.international-alert.org/sites/default/files/ClimateChange_ ClimateOfConflict_EN_2007_0.pdf [Accessed 15 September 2017].

Tschirgi N. (2004) *Post-conflict peacebuilding revisited: Achievements, limitations, challenges*, New York: International Peace Academy.

Ullman R. (1983) "Redefining security" *International Security*, 8(1): 129–153.

United Nations (2001) *No exit without strategy. Report of the Secretary-General S/2001/394*, New York: United Nations.

United Nations (2006) *Note of guidance on integrated missions*, New York: United Nations.

United Nations (2007) *Secretary General Policy Committee statement* Reported on Peacebuilding Initiative website www.un.org/en/peacebuilding/pbso/pbun.shtml [Accessed 5 September 2016].

United Nations (2013) *Financing peacekeeping*, New York: United Nations. www.un.org/en/peacekeeping/ operations/financing.shtml [Accessed 15 September 2017].

United Nations Development Programme (UNDP) (1994) *Human development report 1994*, Oxford: Oxford University Press.

United Nations Environment Programme (UNEP) (2009) *From conflict to peacebuilding: The role of natural resources and the environment*, Nairobi: UNEP.

United Nations General Assembly (UNGA) (2009) *Report of the Secretary-General on peacebuilding in the immediate aftermath of conflict*, 11 June, A/63/881–S/2009/304.

Vivekananda J. (2011) *Practice note: Conflict-sensitive responses to climate change in South Asia*, International Alert. www.international-alert.org/sites/default/files/publications/201110IfPEWResponsesClimChan geSAsia.pdf [Accessed 15 September 2017].

Welzer H. (2012) *Climate wars: Why people will be killed in the 21st century*, Cambridge: Polity Press.

10

Environmental peacebuilding and the United Nations

David Jensen and Amanda Kron

Introduction: recent United Nations milestones on environmental peacebuilding

Environmental peacebuilding responding to contemporary peace and security challenges

Resolving natural resource conflicts is a defining peace and security challenge of the twenty-first century. The geopolitical stakes are high as the survival or authority of states may depend on securing access to key natural resources. A range of national, multinational and state-backed companies seek to capitalize on emerging demand and supply dynamics. In some cases, elite actors monopolize control over resource revenues, concentrating their personal wealth at the expense of local citizens.

At the same time, some communities are becoming hostile to resource investments and may revoke companies' social license to operate. This is the case especially if benefits and burdens are not shared equitably, human rights are violated, environmental damage is significant or expectations are not met. In addition, armed groups and criminal networks increasingly use revenues from illicit resource exploitation and trade to finance their activities (UN Environment–INTERPOL 2016). A wide range of natural resources are affected, from land and water to minerals.

For countries recovering from violent conflict, natural resources often offer the first opportunity to help stabilize and revive livelihoods and other economic activity. When governments manage their environment and resources well and integrate them across a range of peacebuilding activities, natural resources can provide an important pathway to lasting peace and poverty reduction.

At the turn of the millennium, the UN's evolving peacebuilding architecture did not reflect the broad and complex role of natural resources across the peace and security continuum (UN Environment 2015a). As a result, the UN was insufficiently prepared to support lasting resolutions to resource conflicts or capitalize on the peacebuilding potential of natural resources and the environment. However, over the last 17 years significant progress has been made by the

UN in terms of adopting new policies, programs and practices to help Member States address these challenges in a more coherent and coordinated manner. While there is still much work to accomplish, this chapter reviews some of the major international policy milestones in the evolution of the field of environmental peacebuilding and summarizes some of the key lessons learned. The chapter is based on the policy and field work conducted by the UN Environment Programme (UN Environment) since 1999, when it established dedicated capacity to conduct post-conflict environmental assessments and support governments in environmental clean-up, restoration, governance and peacebuilding.

The chapter is structured in the following manner: After a brief introduction to the emerging field of environmental peacebuilding, the chapter introduces key international policy milestones that have advanced the field and prompted new programs and practices at the country level, focusing on the period 1999–2017. Following this overview, the chapter focuses on key lessons learned by UN Environment and partners in the efforts to catalyze a UN-wide approach to addressing the environment and natural resources in conflict and peacebuilding. The final section concludes with suggestions for future work and research in this area.

Defining environmental peacebuilding

Environmental peacebuilding provides a framework for understanding the different positive and negative roles that natural resources and the environment can play throughout the different parts of the conflict lifecycle – also known as the peace and security continuum. In general, environmental peacebuilding is divided into three main areas:

- preventing natural resources and the environment from contributing to or fueling violent conflict,
- protecting natural resources and the environment from damage and illegal exploitation during conflict, and
- promoting the use of natural resources and the environment to support recovery, cooperation and post-conflict peacebuilding.

Environmental peacebuilding is unique in that it combines technical, social and political perspectives together with their historical context. It is one of the first interdisciplinary fields that explicitly includes a temporal element, and requires an understanding of how these three areas interconnect in the design and implementation of policies and programs to govern and use natural resources in a sustainable and peaceful manner.

Historical background

Prior to outlining the key policy developments that have taken place over the last two decades, it should be noted that the importance of protecting the environment in times of armed conflict is not a new concept. Even in ancient times, rules can be found on the need to ensure access to natural resources essential for survival, such as clean water, lands and forests, in times of warfare (Deutoronomy 20:19 in Carson 2013).[1]

In the twentieth century, a series of international crises and events contributed to increased awareness by the international community of the consequences of armed conflict to the environment and the risks to human health, livelihoods and security. The international outcry following the Vietnam War resulted in the first two international legal instruments that focus specifically on preventing and prohibiting harm to the environment during armed conflicts:

a) First, the Convention on the Prohibition of Military or Any Other Hostile Use of Environmental Modification Techniques (ENMOD Convention), adopted in 1976, prohibited environmental modification as a method of warfare. The Convention focuses on the modification of natural processes as a weapon of war, with a focus on weather modification. As regards UN engagement with the process, UN Environment helped convene the negotiations that led to ENMOD – but does not manage it or monitor enforcement (UN Environment 2009a);

b) Second, the Additional Protocol I to the 1949 Geneva Conventions, adopted in the following year, included two articles (35 and 55) prohibiting warfare that may cause "*widespread, long term and severe damage to the natural environment.*" This legal instrument was brokered by the International Committee of the Red Cross (UN Environment 2009b).

Both of these instruments were critical in terms of bringing some measure of international attention to protection of the environment during conflict. However, they did not specifically address natural resources as a driver of conflict or as an opportunity for post-conflict peacebuilding.

In addition to these initial legal developments on environmental protection, there has been a gradual progression in terms of addressing the different dimensions of environmental peacebuilding at the international policy level.

The environmental implications of the first Gulf War, including oil leaks and burning oil fields that took months to extinguish, sparked international concern which catalyzed an international policy debate. In 1992, the UN General Assembly held an important meeting on the protection of the environment in times of armed conflict, where the Member States of the Assembly expressed their "deep concern about environmental damage and depletion of natural resources, including the destruction of hundreds of oil-well heads and the release and waste of crude oil into the sea, during recent conflicts."

While the meeting did not call for a new convention or any new protection measures, the resulting resolution urged Member States to take all measures to ensure compliance with existing international law on the protection of the environment during armed conflict (UNGA 1992). It also recommended that States take steps to incorporate the relevant provisions of international law into their military manuals and ensure that they are effectively disseminated.

While this was an important starting point, international policy development on this topic then waned. It was not until 1999 that a range of policy innovations began to emerge which placed the issue back in the international spotlight.

International policy milestones

This section outlines the major international policy advances that have been made since 1999, and demonstrates the increasing emphasis placed by the UN and the international community on addressing the risks and opportunities presented by natural resources and the environment for conflict and peacebuilding.

The policy development is outlined in four distinct tracks:

1) The first track began in 1999 and involved establishing standing UN capacity to assess and address the environmental causes and consequences of conflict.
2) The second track began in 2009, focusing on recognizing and integrating environment, conflict and peacebuilding linkages within key peace and security reports and policies.
3) The third track began in 2015, and has focused on stocktaking and creating new approaches towards understanding the role of the environment and climate change in state fragility as

well as implementing the peace and security dimensions of the Sustainable Development Goals.

4) The fourth and final track is ongoing as of 2016 and consists of formal adoption of new norms and resolutions which reinforce the existing tools and instruments and permanently place the issue on the international policy agenda.

1999>: Standing UN capacity to conduct independent and scientific assessments of the environmental causes and consequences of conflict

In 1999, the international policy landscape on environmental peacebuilding began to shift. Following the conflict in former Yugoslavia, then UN Secretary-General Kofi Annan requested UN Environment and UN-HABITAT to undertake an independent and scientific assessment of the impacts of the conflict on the environment and human settlements. In order to carry out this assessment, a specific Balkans Task Force was created in 1999, and hosted by UN Environment. This task force was eventually transformed into a dedicated unit that would focus on conducting post-conflict environmental assessments and helping countries address environmental clean-up, recovery, governance and peacebuilding. Successful desk and field assessment work was conducted in the Balkans (UN Environment 2004a), Afghanistan (UN Environment 2003a), Iraq (UN Environment 2003b), the Occupied Palestinian Territories (UN Environment 2003c) and Liberia (UN Environment 2004b).

Recognizing the impacts of armed conflict on the environment, on 5 November 2001, the UN General Assembly declared 6 November of each year as the International Day for Preventing the Exploitation of the Environment in War and Armed Conflict (UNGA 2001).

In 2002, the environmental aspects of international criminal law came to the forefront of the international debate. That year saw the entry into force of the Rome Statute of the International Criminal Court. Article 8 (b) (iv) of the Statute prohibits as war crimes actions that correspond to "intentionally launching an attack in the knowledge that such attack will cause incidental loss of life or injury to civilians or damage to civilian objects or widespread, long-term and severe damage to the natural environment which would be clearly excessive in relation to the concrete and direct overall military advantage anticipated" (Rome Statute 1998).[2]

In 2005, UN Environment was requested by its Governing Council of Member States to further increase its capacity to conduct post-conflict operations by establishing a dedicated branch with core funding. The new branch worked on major field assessments in Iraq, the Gaza Strip, Lebanon and Sudan (UN Environment 2007).

In 2008, at the 10th Special Session of the UN Environment Governing Council, Member States endorsed a further advancement, whereby assessing and addressing the environmental causes and consequences of conflicts and disasters would become one of six new strategic priorities for the organization. Further assessments were conducted in Rwanda, DR Congo, Nigeria, Sierra Leone, Haiti and Côte d'Ivoire (UN Environment 2015b). In total, UN Environment has undertaken more than 20 post-conflict environmental assessments since the 1999 decision, and raised over USD 200 million in funding to help national environmental authorities address priority issues and build their institutional capacity.

On the basis of these incremental changes in UN Environment's mandate, the scope of UN Environment's work also began to expand from an exclusive focus on field assessments and capacity building, to also addressing UN-wide policies and practices at the global level. Indeed, one of the first priorities for UN Environment following the promotion of disasters and conflicts as an institution-wide priority in 2008 was to begin sharing lessons learned on the role of natural resources and the environment in conflict and peacebuilding with the broader UN peace and security architecture. UN Environment, together with the International Institute for Sustainable Development, established an Expert Group on Peace and Security consisting of ten leading academics and experts to provide policy and strategic advice as well as technical expertise. This area of work was managed by a new UN Environment program known as Environmental Cooperation for Peacebuilding (UN Environment 2015a; UN Environment 2016).

2009>: Recognition and integration of environment, conflict and peace linkages in international reports, policies and fora

The year 2009 represented three important steps forward in terms of international policy development on environmental peacebuilding. These shifts built on a process which started in 2008, when the newly established Peacebuilding Commission and its secretariat requested assistance from UN Environment to explore the natural resources, conflict and peace nexus. In May 2008, a working group on lessons learned was organized for members of the Peacebuilding Commission, where a combination of academic and field evidence was presented by UN Environment and members of its Expert Group on Peace and Security. The core issues raised during the debate were eventually published in a joint policy report in 2009 by UN Environment and the Peacebuilding Commission Support Office entitled "*From Conflict to Peacebuilding: The Role of Natural Resources and the Environment*" (UN Environment 2009a). This publication was the first major milestone in terms of formally recognizing the role of natural resources and the environment in conflict and peace.

"*From Conflict to Peacebuilding*" has been widely cited across a range of UN publications as well as in academic literature. Most importantly, it helped to ensure that the successive reports by the UN Secretary-General on Peacebuilding in the Immediate Aftermath of Conflict in 2009, 2010, 2012 and 2014 addressed natural resources. Within this series of reports, the most important policy tipping point came in the 2010 report, when the Secretary-General formally called on Member States and the United Nations system "to make questions of natural resource allocation, ownership and access an integral part of peacebuilding strategies" (UNGA and UNSC 2010). On the basis of this call, the UN Development Group (UNDG) and the Executive Committee on Humanitarian Affairs (ECHA) adopted a joint guidance note in 2013 on addressing natural resources in post-conflict transitional settings (UNDG and ECHA 2013), which was endorsed by 38 different UN entities. The intent of the UN guidance note was to improve joint analysis and joint programming for UN country teams in order to translate the call for action into tangible changes on the ground.

The second important policy development began with the publication of a joint report by UN Environment, the International Committee of the Red Cross (ICRC) and the Environmental Law Institute entitled "*Protecting the Environment During Armed Conflict: An Inventory and Analysis of International Law.*" Among the findings and recommendations, the report called on the International Law Commission (ILC) to undertake further study on the international legal protection of the environment during armed conflicts (UN Environment 2009b).

This recommendation prompted the ILC to place the topic "*Protection of the environment in relation to armed conflicts*" on its program of work in 2013, and to appoint Dr. Marie G. Jacobsson of Sweden as Special Rapporteur (UNGA 2013). Dr. Jacobsson adopted a three-year work program for 2014–2016, focusing on identifying and analyzing legal provisions and potential gaps for protecting the environment before, during and after armed conflicts.

The three reports that have been issued by the ILC Special Rapporteur in 2014, 2015 and 2016 respectively provide an overarching analysis of the state of environmental protection and suggestions for further development (ILC 2014, 2015, 2016). The work has helped to document the practices of states and international organizations in this area. As such, it serves as an important source of information submitted by numerous states on their national legislation and means of implementation of their obligations under international law.

The third major policy milestone that was achieved in 2009 relates to the UN Secretary-General's report to the General Assembly entitled "*Climate Change and Its Possible Security Implications*" (UNGA 2009). The report recognizes that increasing competition over climate-sensitive natural resources could increase the risk of domestic conflict as well as have international repercussions. Following the publication of the report, a UN Security Council debate was held on the topic in 2011, where UN Environment's Executive Director was invited to directly address the Council. This set a new precedent within the Council in terms of welcoming the head of the UN Environment Programme to talk about the links between environment, peace and security. The thematic debate resulted in a Security Council Presidential Statement on climate change and the maintenance of international peace and security (UNSC 2011). In the statement, the Council requested the Secretary-General to report on the possible security implications of climate change when such issues are drivers of conflict, represent a challenge to the implementation of Council mandates or endanger the process of consolidation of peace (UNSC 2011). This statement was particularly important as it requires peacekeeping missions to more actively monitor and report to the Secretary-General on climate change and security dynamics.

2015>: Stocktaking and adopting new frameworks for analysis, action and prevention

In 2015, three high-level reviews – on peacekeeping, peacebuilding and a global study on Security Council Resolution 1325 on women and peace – all included the idea that natural resources can be a structural driver of conflict, but can nonetheless play an important role in stabilization and peacebuilding. The 1325 review also acknowledged that natural resources can offer an entry point for women's economic, social and political empowerment, if managed in a sustainable manner (Advisory Group of Experts 2015; "Report of the High-level . . . 2015; UN Women 2015). These reports were complemented by a fourth report commissioned by the G7 Foreign Ministers entitled "*A New Climate for Peace.*" The report observed that climate change exacerbates and amplifies existing risks, particularly in fragile states (Rüttinger et al. 2015). One of the seven compound climate-fragility risks highlighted by the report focused on increasing resource competition from climate change and resource scarcity. Together with other factors, this competition can lead to instability and even violent conflict, particularly in the absence of effective dispute resolution. The need for more integrated programming focusing on building resilience to multiple shocks and stresses as well as investing more in conflict prevention was a common theme of all four reports.

The year 2015 also saw the adoption of the 2030 Agenda for Sustainable Development and the Sustainable Development Goals (SDG) by the General Assembly in September (UNGA 2015). Agenda 2030 provides numerous entry points for environmental peacebuilding (see Figure 10.1), e.g. on transparency, participation and access to information (SDG 16), equitable access to resources for men and women (SDG 5) and combating illegal wildlife crime (SDG 15). The key challenge will be measuring the contribution of natural resources and the environment to the various goals in a manner that demonstrates whether conflict was prevented or peace enhanced.

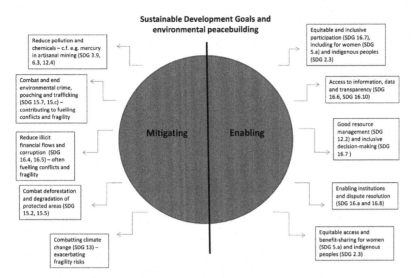

Environmental peacebuilding entry points in the Sustainable Development Goals. Unsustainable management of the environment and natural resources can contribute to the outbreak of conflict, fuel and finance existing conflicts, and increase the risk for conflict relapse. Conversely, natural resources can serve as vehicles for durable peace, confidence building and poverty reduction when governments manage their resources well and integrate them into peacebuilding activities and strategies. Similarly, the Sustainable Development Goals serve to both mitigate fragility, corruption and environmental hazards on the one hand, and enable good governance on the other.

Figure 10.1   Sustainable Development Goals and environmental peacebuilding

2016>: Adoption of new international guidelines and resolutions

The policy advances on environmental peacebuilding that have been made since 1999 culminated in 2016 in the UN Environment Assembly resolution on *"Protection of the Environment in Areas Affected by Armed Conflict"* in May 2016. The resolution, which was adopted unanimously by the universal membership of the Assembly, stressed *"the critical importance of protecting the environment at all times, especially during armed conflict, and of its restoration in the post-conflict period"* (UNEA 2016). It called on all Member States to implement applicable international law related to the protection of the environment in situations of armed conflict and to consider the application of other relevant international agreements. Perhaps the single most important impact of the resolution is that it provides a vehicle for States, international organizations and civil society to discuss, debate and engage with conflict and the environment in the context of the UN Environmental Assembly. This is a key political milestone in international efforts to afford greater environmental protection and consideration in areas affected by armed conflicts. The ILC Special Rapporteur remarked that this was the most significant UN resolution of its kind since 1992 and will serve as a critical instrument for international cooperation on this issue going forward (ILC 2016).

Also in 2016, the ILC Special Rapporteur proposed a set of draft principles as part of her tenure to improve protection of the environment before, during and after armed conflict. They include provisions on access to and sharing of information, post-conflict environmental assessments and protection of zones of major environmental and cultural interest (see e.g. ILC 2016). These draft principles were discussed among UN Member States at the Sixth Committee of the General Assembly, in the fall of 2016, and continues to be elaborated within the Commission.

The final important development of 2016 was that the Organization for Economic Cooperation and Development (OECD) launched a new a multidimensional fragility framework. Importantly, the OECD recognized that fragility is the accumulation and combination of multiple risks stemming from security and political dimensions, to economic and social, to also including environmental and climatic (OECD 2016b). This was the first recognition by OECD that environmental issues may contribute to fragility. The new framework will attempt to measure and monitor this risk on an ongoing basis as part of the annual OECD report on the topic.

Conclusions

As has been outlined above, the international policy and normative framework on environmental peacebuilding has tackled the issue on an incremental basis in a series of four "pulses" over the past two decades.

Perhaps the most progress has been made in terms of establishing UN capacity to assess and address the environmental consequences of conflict through systematic environmental assessments and recovery programs. There has also been an important recognition of the need to use natural resources in a strategic and conflict-sensitive manner to support stabilization and peacebuilding goals. While the programming and coordination mechanism to accomplish this goal remains elusive, the fact that the UN system and Member States recognize the risks and opportunities from natural resources is important. Indeed, UN Environment has observed that many decision makers now acknowledge that in the absence of policy on natural resources during periods of transition, decisions will be made by the most powerful stakeholders. When such structures become institutionalized, it may take decades to undo them (UN Environment–DPA 2015, UNDG–ECHA 2013). Early decisions about resource governance can be critical, in the long run, in affecting whether social relations follow a peaceful or a violent path.

On the other hand, further progress is required in terms of preventing resource conflicts from escalating to violent outcomes. This is primarily because natural resource governance decisions are under the sovereign domain of each Member State and any UN program in this area is politically sensitive. The engagement of UN's good offices in a specific resource dispute can signal that it might be beyond the capacity of domestic actors to resolve leading to uncertainty and potential capital flight. For these and other reasons, some Member States have seen the conflict prevention mandate of the UN as controversial.

This perception is starting to change with the recommendations of the UN peacebuilding architecture review, as well as the focus on peace and conflict prevention in the 2030 Agenda for Sustainable Development and in the "Sustaining Peace" resolutions adopted by the General Assembly and UN Security Council (UNGA 2016a; UNSC 2016). These resolutions were developed in response to the three reports on peacekeeping, peacebuilding and Security Council Resolution 1325 on women and peace, and highlight the importance of "a comprehensive approach to sustaining peace, particularly through the prevention of conflict and addressing its root causes."

In addition, conflict prevention is one of the key focus areas of the new Secretary-General Antonio Guterres. At a UN Security Council debate on 10 January 2017, Secretary-General Guterres underlined that conflict prevention "is not merely a priority, but the priority."

While these policy shifts are important and promising, the changes have yet to trickle down to conflict prevention over natural resources and the environment within or between states. One of the key challenges in conflict prevention is that successful interventions are not only about building good governance and dispute resolution processes, but also about building trustful and resilient relationships between resource stakeholders in a manner which ensures that disputes are resolved in constructive and non-violent ways.

In conclusion, the policy framework for environmental peacebuilding remains a patchwork of different initiatives and frameworks that operate in a largely disconnected manner. The temporal nature of environmental peacebuilding – in terms of understanding the role of natural resources and the environment across the conflict lifecycle – poses a serious policy challenge, particularly when such policies are themselves fragmented among different fora and implementing institutions.

In the next section, the chapter will outline lessons learned from the three temporal phases of environmental peacebuilding: before, during and after conflicts. Field examples will serve to highlight responses and strategies by the UN in all three phases.

Lessons learned and the role of the United Nations in addressing natural resources and the environment in peacebuilding

The lessons learned and experiences of UN Environment's work on environmental peacebuilding can be divided into three main areas, following the different stages of the conflict lifecycle as outlined in the introduction:

(i) the role of natural resources as potential conflict drivers;
(ii) impacts of armed conflict on natural resources and their governance; and
(iii) the role of natural resources in consolidating and sustaining peace.

While outlining the experiences, challenges and opportunities that natural resources often provide for local communities and stakeholders in conflict-affected states, this section provides observations on the current and potential role of the United Nations, as well as efforts made to establish an integrated UN-wide approach to addressing natural resources throughout the different phases of conflict and peacebuilding.

Lessons on the role of natural resources as conflict drivers

a) Natural resources contribute to conflict through many unique pathways: distinguishing between means versus motivation

First, at an overarching level, it is important to distinguish between violent conflicts where natural resources act as an economic *means* for financing conflict versus situations where natural resources contribute to the social and political *motivation* for conflict. This difference is critically important in terms of designing prevention and resolution strategies.

In effect, where natural resources act as a means for funding the activities of armed groups, they must be secured and restricted from entering the market and generating revenue. Tools include commodity sanctions and trade restrictions, certification schemes and due diligence requirements around specific resources known to finance conflict such as diamonds or other metals and minerals. Examples include UN timber and diamond sanctions in Liberia, the Kimberly process certification scheme and the Dodd–Frank Act. In the case of Sierra Leone, for example, it is estimated that USD 25–125 millions' worth of raw diamonds were smuggled out per year (UN Environment 2010). Similarly, in the Angola conflict, so-called blood diamonds are estimated to have been worth USD 3–4 billion (UN Environment 2009a).

In contrast, conflicts that are motivated by grievances around natural resources need to be tackled in an entirely different manner. These conflicts typically revolve around one or more drivers that need to be addressed: disputes over ownership; restrictions on resource access; exclusion from consultation and decision making; and/or inequitable distribution of the benefits and risks associated with extraction and use.

One of the complicating factors is that these drivers often occur at different scales and interact in ways that are nested and interconnected at local, regional, national and sometimes transboundary levels. For example, the civil war in Darfur had a series of interconnected resource drivers, ranging from changes in land administration, to competition over resource access, to lack of voice for pastoral groups in decision-making processes. Chronic conflict over natural resources, occurring primarily at the local level, was also interlinked with issues of tribal and state governance (UN Environment 2014). This situation was compounded by the multiple concurrent drivers of change, including climate, population, urbanization, conflict and economic development that livelihoods were adapting to.

In addressing this challenge, the UN has acted as an impartial third party to convene stakeholders and help conduct a conflict analysis in order to identify core drivers. The UN can also conduct scientific assessments and can provide all parties with equal access to impartial information to inform their dialogue and decision making. For example, in Sudan, UN Environment provided all three of these functions to stakeholders in Sudan and South Sudan prior to independence.

b) Social grievances and disputes over natural resources are rarely, if ever, the sole cause of violent conflict

The drivers of violence are most often multidimensional, including a range of social, political and economic grievances as well as opportunistic motivations. Resource conflicts can be an important driver, but are rarely, if ever, the sole source of violent conflict.

What determines whether a resource conflict escalates to the point of violence is more related to: (i) how they become politicized, instrumentalized and connected to other political movements; (ii) the degree to which the prevailing political economy and supporting institutions are based on patronage systems, social marginalization and exclusion (geographic, ethnic, religious or other factors); (iii) the perceived legitimacy of the state and ability to protect and extend its authority across national sovereign territory; (iv) respect for the rule of law and degree of impunity for violations of domestic laws and human rights; and (v) the prevailing security situation, including history of violence and access to arms. Therefore, technical responses are part of the solution but they need to be connected to a broader political response which aims to help states build and communicate a social contract (UN Environment–UN DPA 2015).

For example, in Bougainville, the Panguna mine was the flashpoint for starting the decade-long civil war. Most analysts agree that the conflict drivers included environmental damage from the mine combined with the inequitable distribution of benefits, including both revenues and jobs. However, the disputes around the mine were also politicized to amplify a long-standing desire for cultural self-determination and autonomy of Bougainville from Papa New Guinea.

The UN has worked with countries to help identify early warning indicators and areas of high vulnerability to resource conflicts. For example, the Office of the High Commissioner for Human Rights is undertaking an initiative to better understand how violations of economic, social and cultural rights are causes, consequences and even predictors of violence, social unrest and conflict. Rights to natural resources such as water are a prominent part of the study (OHCHR 2016).

c) Preventing and resolving resource conflicts depends on effective institutions, good governance and a shared vision

The prevention and peaceful resolution of social conflicts over natural resources requires effective institutions and good governance that are based on the principles of inclusion, transparency, accountability, equitable benefit sharing and sustainability. A shared vision on how natural resources can contribute to sustainable development at the local or national level is also an important process and outcome. Communities and other stakeholders should be included within key decisions around natural resources, and there must be some level of equity in the distribution of benefits, costs and risks. This process should be supported by access to authoritative information and transparent monitoring frameworks on compliance and performance. Grievance redress mechanisms and dispute resolution processes are equally essential to address rising discontent before it can turn violent.

While few countries have all of these measures and tools in place, countries such as Liberia and East Timor have used these overarching principles as the basis for major institutional and governance reforms in the resource sector. In fact, the UN peacekeeping mission in Liberia was provided an explicit mandate in 2003 to "*assist the transitional government in restoring proper administration of natural resources*" while the peacekeeping mission in Timor-Leste was mandated in 1999 to "*assist in the establishment of conditions for sustainable development*." In practice, this included transitional administration of lands and natural resources. At a local level, both UNDP and UN Environment have worked with stakeholders in Sudan to help establish joint visions for sustainable resource management. These visions have become the foundation for resource management planning and sustainable use in a range of different localities, such as e.g. Dar Es Salaam and Kilamendo (UN Environment 2014).

d) Each natural resource has a distinct set of characteristics that can drive conflicts in different ways

Different types of natural resources such as minerals, oil and gas, timber, land and water can generate unique kinds of conflict between stakeholders, often at different spatial and political scales (cf. e.g. European Union and United Nations Interagency Framework Team for Preventive Action, 2010–2012). Typically, the potential for natural resources to generate risks and vulnerabilities that drive conflict depends on the magnitude and distribution of revenues and benefits they generate, the number of livelihoods they directly support or the scale of negative impacts they cause. Natural resources can also play different roles in the onset and escalation of violent conflict, with the potential to act as a trigger of conflict, as a means of conflict financing and as an incentive to prolong conflict and spoil peace. Many resources are influenced by a range of natural, economic and social factors leading to a high level of complexity and uncertainty in their availability, quality and value that is always context specific.

In Côte d'Ivoire for example, land played an important role as a conflict driver, while natural resources such as coffee and cocoa provided conflict financing and also undermined peace incentives (UN Environment 2015b). Land tenure reform is an important priority in peacebuilding and reconstruction processes generally, while also harnessing the specific potential of extractive resources such as minerals.

In addressing this challenge, the UN has helped local stakeholders identify conflict risks and suitable mitigation measures. For example, in Sierra Leone (UN Environment 2010) and along the border region between Haiti and the Dominican Republic

(UN Environment–UNDP–WPF 2013), UN Environment worked with local actors to identify key conflict drivers linked to natural resources and helped to develop conflict resolution strategies by resource sector, including integrated water resource management and disaster risk reduction measures.

Lessons on the impacts of armed conflicts on natural resources and the environment

a) Natural resources are a livelihood lifeline during violent conflicts when basic services of society break down

Natural resources frequently become an important economic lifeline for local populations and displaced people during violent conflicts. Coping strategies are often based on short time horizons and insecure access rights that lead to unsustainable practices. In many cases, conflict economies emerge, consisting of several distinct but intertwined segments: (i) the remains of the formal economy; (ii) an expanding informal economy; (iii) the international aid economy; and (iv) often an illicit criminal economy (Conca and Wallace 2012). The main challenge for peace consolidation and UN programming is to understand how these strands provide support to different livelihoods, and how incentives can be used to promote a gradual return to regulated and sustainable resource use. In the majority of cases, it is the formal and aid economies that get most attention from donors and ministries, whereas many people are actually earning a post-conflict living from natural resources in the illicit and informal economies.

The most common activities include artisanal and small-scale mining (ASM), charcoal production and wood supply, fisheries and wildlife. Such coping strategies and survival livelihoods for local populations and displaced persons during, and after, violent conflicts can have extensive impacts on the environment and such practices often last long into peacebuilding processes.

One such example is the Eastern DRC, where artisanal mining is widespread. In 2015, the International Peace Information Service (IPIS) noted that approximately 80 percent of an estimated 221,500 artisanal miners active in the mining sites visited in the Eastern DRC were digging for gold (IPIS 2015). Mercury is often used to separate the gold from the ore in artisanal gold mining, which can contaminate drinking water and threaten human health.

Similarly, UN Environment's research demonstrates that in general, 50 80 percent of former combatants return to agriculture following the end of a conflict, and thus require access to land (UN Environment–UNDP 2013). UNDP has begun to use employment and livelihood opportunities from natural resources as part of reintegration strategies for ex-combatants. Such projects have been undertaken e.g. in Afghanistan to combine combating deforestation with demobilization, demilitarization and reintegration programs (UN Environment 2003a). Similarly, in the Province of Aceh, Indonesia, UNDP supported the development of coffee production value chains in conflict-affected areas and linked this with certification efforts, including the establishment of a geographic indication of origin for the area.

One of the most significant UN-backed studies on coping and survival strategies used by different livelihood groups was conducted on the camel herding nomads in Darfur known as the Northern Rizaygat. Their notoriety as part of the Janjaweed militia obscured from view how their lives and livelihoods were affected by conflict and how they adopted maladaptation strategies for coping with livelihood collapse (Abusin et al. 2009). The study helped transform the way in which livelihood support programs were being designed and implemented.

b) Assessing both direct and indirect environmental damage from conflict

When assessing the environmental damage from conflict, it is useful to consider both direct and indirect impacts from armed conflict. Direct impacts arise from military action during or immediately after conflict. They comprise direct targeting of the environment and scorched earth tactics, incidental damage, impacts from weapons and military operations, toxic hazards from damage to infrastructure and industry, as well as financing of conflict through looting of the environment and conflict resources.

Direct damage is often more acute and site-specific. Direct damage seems to be more extensive in international armed conflicts where the military forces of opposing states are using modern weaponry and tactics to strike strategic targets and infrastructure. One example of such direct impacts on the environment occurred during the Kosovo conflict, when hundreds of industrial sites and municipal infrastructure were targeted by NATO forces, with collateral damage including major chemical spills into the environment and at least 100 bomb craters inside national parks and protected areas in Serbia.

Indirect impacts refer to secondary impacts that can be credibly sourced to the conflict, such as coping and survival strategies of local populations, profiteering and legacies of the conflict economy, breakdown of institutions and local governance, impact of peacekeeping and humanitarian operations, as well as temporary settlements and infrastructure. These impacts may in turn affect human health, livelihoods and displacement. Indirect impacts are often more chronic, widespread and long term. Examples include Rwanda, where population displacement caused deforestation, and Darfur, where demands for bricks increased five times due to international operations which in turn contributed to significant deforestation (over 50,000 trees per year) (UN Environment 2012).

As noted above, UN Environment has been given an increasingly strong mandate to conduct post-conflict environmental assessments at the request of governments to identify direct and indirect impacts and risks to human health, livelihoods and security. The assessments help prioritize key risks, opportunities and resource governance needs during post-conflict peacebuilding and recovery.

c) Armed conflicts destroy resource governance arrangements, undermine social relationships and weaken resilience

One of the most significant long-term indirect impacts of violent conflict is the tendency to undermine resource governance arrangements, as well as social relationships and trust between resource stakeholders. This combination of impacts often weakens resilience to different shocks and stresses, be they natural, social or economic. For instance, in Afghanistan, a wide-scale collapse of local level environmental governance systems led to reduced and unreliable water supply through uncontrolled well drilling. In addition, the water quality suffered through contamination from waste dumps, chemicals and open sewers (UN Environment 2003a). Similarly, in Iraq, land registration documents, environmental information, materials and laboratories were destroyed during the conflicts, leaving governance structures vulnerable (Conca and Wallace 2012).

In this context, it is critical to ensure that vulnerable and marginalized groups are protected in the aftermath of conflicts. In particular, women often lack formal access to land, which in turn provides access to other resources and rights, such as water and food security (UN Environment–PBSO–UN Women–UNDP 2013). For example, in Uganda, a joint UN study found in 2013 that while women were responsible for growing 80 percent of the food crops in the country, only 7 percent of landowners were women (UN Environment–PBSO–UN Women–UNDP 2013). Unfortunately, less than 2 percent of official development assistance (ODA) from OECD countries that is invested in the productive sectors – including the agricultural sector, in which women are particularly active globally – targets women's equality or empowerment (UN Environment–PBSO–UN Women–UNDP 2013). Thus, while women are responsible for an overwhelming majority of crop production in certain countries and regions, men nonetheless receive the majority of donor support in the agricultural sector, whether in the form of extension packages, inputs or credits (UN Environment–PBSO–UN Women–UNDP 2013).

Providing fair access to natural resources supports women as agents of change in their communities, and provides pathways to empowerment through equal and effective resource governance. Consequently, sustainable and inclusive peacebuilding will require more equitable support to the endeavors of civil society organizations and local communities led by women as well as by men.

The UN can support and provide platforms for stakeholders to develop more inclusive and participatory processes and help identify options to modify existing mechanisms. When developing plans to use natural resources – either through large-scale commercial investments or for local livelihoods, stakeholders can be assisted in understanding the shocks and stresses that might occur, for instance shifts in commodity prices, natural hazards or impacts related to climate change and developing a shared vision for joint management.

d) The resource governance vacuum that occurs during armed conflict can make natural resources particularly vulnerable to pillage and looting

Natural resources are particularly vulnerable to pillage and looting during the governance vacuum that often follows in the wake of armed conflict. During violent conflict, the resulting resource governance and institutional vacuum is almost systematically exploited. Extensive resource theft tends to take place by a combination of predatory individuals, armed groups and transnational criminal networks. Such activities include land grabbing, illegal wildlife trade and the looting of high-value resources. In many cases, the revenues from the illegal resource exploitation and trafficking of natural resources are used to perpetuate and sustain instability and violence. The international system has developed tools for addressing such "conflict resources," ranging from voluntary transparency regimes, to certification mechanisms, to targeted commodity sanctions (UN Environment 2015a). However, these instruments require context-specific application and improved strategic coordination to be able to respond to the complexity of global supply chains and the dynamic nature of transboundary resource flows. In particular, the geographic and technical intricacy of these chains, as well as their ability to adapt to and thwart regulation, often confound international and domestic legal frameworks, resulting in an unregulated space between the two levels (Conca 2015). While the existing range of tools are useful, they need to be linked to a broader anti-trafficking approach, information exchange and institutional strengthening to be more effective.

These tendencies are particularly troubling given the rise of environmental crime over the last few decades. In 2015, UN Environment undertook a joint study on illegal exploitation and trade in natural resources in Eastern DRC together with the peacekeeping mission (MONUSCO) and with the Special Envoy of the Secretary-General for the Great Lakes Region. The study found that 98 percent of revenues from illegal resource theft goes to transnational organized criminal networks, rather than to armed groups (UN Environment–MONUSCO–OSESG 2015). Recent estimates by UN Environment and INTERPOL place the total value of environmental crime, such as wildlife poaching, illegal logging and illegal extraction of minerals, at up to USD 259 billion, which corresponds to twice the amount of global ODA in 2015 (OECD 2016a). Sadly, this number is increasing as environmental crime rises by up to 5–7 percent annually, an increase 2–3 times the rate of growth of the global economy (UN Environment–INTERPOL 2016). More generally, recent estimates from the High-Level Panel on Illicit Financial Flows from Africa show that Africa is losing at least USD 50 billion annually in illicit financial outflows (IFF 2015).

Lessons on the role of natural resources in consolidating and sustaining peace

a) Post-conflict economic recovery strategies should include a blended approach involving both renewable and non-renewable natural resources

A number of post-conflict countries are rich in high-value natural resources that could support a range of different extractive investments. However, extractive resources also carry a number of inherent risks that need to be managed by policy makers. While extractive industries are often seen as an important opportunity for post-conflict countries to kick-start economic growth, create jobs and generate revenues, they seldom live up to these expectations and should never be used as the only pathway out of fragility. In most cases, the immediate employment generated by commercial extractives is minimal, with the majority of the population continuing to depend on small-scale subsistence livelihoods. Overreliance on a single extractive industry also heightens vulnerability to price shocks and market downturns. For example, the recent slump in oil prices has contributed to Nigeria's lowest growth rate in almost 20 years (e.g. IMF 2016a; Bloomberg 2016; BBC 2015), while Sierra Leone suffered serious economic setbacks from falling prices in iron ore (IMF 2016b).

Given these challenges, any economic development plan should be geared towards supporting the recovery and improved production of rural livelihoods based on other renewable natural resources, notably agriculture, fishing, livestock and community forestry. This can maximize employment, including for ex-combatants and women, and contribute to food security. Furthermore, an initial focus on rural livelihoods buys the time needed for countries to build the internal capacity, legal framework and infrastructure to develop their extractive sector in a more strategic and effective manner.

Where extractive resources form an important part of the economic recovery strategy, countries should consider adopting a resource transformation and economic growth model based on six core elements: (i) building the institutions and good governance of the resource sector; (ii) developing infrastructure that can be shared with other economic sectors; (iii) ensuring robust fiscal policy and competitiveness; (iv) supporting local employment and value chains; (v) deciding how to share and spend a resource windfall wisely; and (vi) transforming resource wealth into broader economic development and diversification (McKinsey Global Institute 2013). The Natural Resource Charter (NRGI 2014) also provides a sound framework for the good governance of the extractive sector.

In this context, the UN can help secure, demilitarize and restore access to resource-rich sites. Across the range of different mandates given to peacekeeping missions on addressing natural resources, the most comprehensive was given to the mission in Liberia, where the mission was given a mandate to restore administration over natural resources (UN Environment 2004b). This included securing high-value resource-rich areas, such as rubber plantations, that had been taken over by ex-combatants (UN Environment 2004b). Moreover, peacekeeping forces have supported national forces in taking over mining sites in Eastern DRC, and the mission in South Sudan has also protected oil installations and infrastructure (UN Environment 2012). Thus, where natural resources have financed conflict, and may continue to contribute to escalation of tension and hostilities, peacekeeping missions should be given a clear mandate to secure and/or demilitarize affected areas.

b) Collaboration around natural resources can be used as an entry point for dialogue and for confidence building

Depending on the country context, environmental issues such as pollution, habitat degradation, deforestation, protected areas or shared natural resources such as water can be an initial entry point for dialogue and confidence building between divided groups and communities. Local peacebuilding may be promoted using natural resources as the basis for rebuilding key relationships if mutual benefits can be identified and a common vision agreed. Over time, cooperation over natural resources can have important "spillover" effects, leading to cooperation in other domains and establishing a basis of trust for continued joint action. Some natural resources or environmental issues seem to have more cooperation and peacebuilding potential than others – much depends on how "politicized" the resource is within the prevailing political context combined with the historical levels of conflict and cooperation around the specific resource.

UN Environment's program in Darfur is founded on the idea that shared natural resources can be used to both rebuild relationships between communities and also establish new systems of local governance. By assisting the government in developing mediation and governance strategies for different actors and different resources, the program has contributed to enhanced local governing of water resources (UN Environment 2014).

c) Access to neutral and authoritative information is essential for good decision making

Information around natural resources in conflict-affected countries is often highly contested, and having an impartial third party, such as the UN, contributing to establish a neutral set of facts that all parties can trust can contribute to overcoming impasses in mediation and conflict resolution processes. Equalizing the information available to all stakeholders is a critically important tool in moving from problem analysis to inclusive and equitable action (UN Environment 2015c).

The possibility for confidence building and conflict resolution based on impartial information was tested in Ogoniland, Nigeria. In 2006 the government of Nigeria requested that UN Environment undertake a comprehensive environmental assessment of the oil contamination of Ogoniland, a region with a long history of resource-based conflict. At the time, the government was trying to mediate between the community and the oil producer. UN Environment provided the first independent baseline assessment of the contamination using a scientific methodology to measure the environmental impacts and corresponding risks. To ensure objectivity, this effort was led by international experts; but to ensure transparency and buy-in, local institutions also participated. The environmental implications of the oil spills were immense, with some regions experiencing levels of benzene 900 times higher than the recommendations of the World Health Organization (UN Environment 2011). The assessment ultimately provided a common information base to the parties and a solid technical basis on which they could negotiate a clean-up program.

In order to strengthen transparency and access to information on the sustainable development of natural resources, and upon request from the g7+ group of fragile states, UN Environment,

GRID–Geneva and the World Bank have developed an online geospatial platform called MapX. The MapX mission is to support the sustainable use of natural resources by increasing access to the best available geospatial information, technology and monitoring tools. The MapX process focuses on generating actionable insights from geospatial data to inform dialogue and enable evidence-based decisions.

In so doing, MapX integrates a range of best available information into an online geospatial platform, and offers a combination of analytical and monitoring tools to support stakeholder dialogue and decision making on benefit sharing and risk mitigation. MapX is being designed to build trust among stakeholders, improve transparency, reduce conflict and improve the contribution of natural resources toward the achievement of the Sustainable Development Goals.

MapX is currently being implemented on a pilot basis in DR Congo and Afghanistan. It is also providing support to the implementation of the Minamata Convention on Mercury, in terms of mapping and assessing mercury use by artisanal and small-scale gold miners.[3]

d) Resilient natural resource programs depend on considering multiple shocks and stresses, including from climate change

Repetitive stresses and shocks from disasters and conflicts gradually undermine positive development gains and fundamentally reduce community resilience over time. Climate change has the potential to increase the frequency and magnitude of disasters, as well as contribute to increased competition and conflict over scarce natural resources. The interplay between disasters, conflicts and climate change, as well as the cumulated effects, requires integrated responses to successfully increase community resilience and protect the viability of resource-dependent livelihoods. The recently revised OECD multidimensional fragility framework is a step in the right direction in terms of understanding the multiple risks that interact to amplify fragility: political, social, economic and environmental (see e.g. OECD 2016c).

Future directions and recommendations

Building on these lessons, a number of opportunities and challenges can be identified for further work and research.

First, it remains to be seen how environmental peacebuilding efforts will contribute to informing the realization of Sustainable Development Goal 16, as well as the implementation of the 2030 Agenda for Sustainable Development more broadly. An integrated approach is necessary to deliver on the 2030 Agenda, and opportunities for collaboration and joint programming between UN agencies and other actors will be crucial. As mentioned above, a guidance note on natural resource management in transition settings was developed by the UNDG and ECHA in 2013 (UNDG–ECHA 2013). Building on and implementing the recommendations of this note could help to consolidate a UN strategic approach to addressing these challenges and further joint analysis and approaches to addressing natural resources in peacebuilding processes.

Second, while the importance of addressing climate change and fragility risks has been identified and emphasized at the global policy level, additional research and analysis is needed to identify local, national and regional programs and actions that contribute to resilience through adopting a climate risk management lens to peacebuilding programs, as well as a conflict-sensitivity lens to climate change adaption programs. Developing and furthering such projects and actions could also contribute to operationalizing the 2011 Presidential Statement of the Security Council, as well as the recommendations of a series of policy reports, including "A New Climate for Peace – Taking Action on Climate and Fragility Risks" commissioned by the Group of 7.

Third, participatory processes combined with access to data, information and transparency are not only crucial for post-conflict environmental assessments and reviews, but will also be critical to realizing global sustainable development objectives. Further analysis and action on public participation and access to information are warranted, particularly in post-conflict contexts where natural resource allocation and management is often characterized as being undertaken in an *"ad hoc, decentralized, or informal manner"* (UN Environment 2009c). Tools such as the UN Environment–World Bank geospatial platform MapX can contribute to strengthening transparency and access to information on the financial, social and environmental performance of natural resource development.

Finally, protected areas and zones of particular significance to sensitive ecosystems should receive particular attention. In this context, it is promising that the UNEA resolution speaks to the importance of protecting World Heritage Sites affected by armed conflicts, and recommends further collaboration between UN Environment, UNESCO and other relevant stakeholders to this end (UNEA 2016). Similarly, the proposed and provisionally adopted set of draft principles of the International Law Commission on protection of the environment in relation to armed conflicts contains two draft principles on the protection of zones of major environmental and cultural importance before, during and after armed conflicts (UNGA 2016b).

All of these efforts will require extensive collaborations between the UN, civil society, states, the private sector and other stakeholders to collect good practice and lessons learned. The collaboration between Environmental Law Institute and UN Environment and a range of other universities and partners serves as one such example, which has led to the development and publication of 150 case studies covering more than 60 post-conflict countries. This work has involved over 225 experts from all over the world, and all of the material is freely available online (Jensen and Lonergan 2012; Lujala and Rustad 2012; Unruh and Williams 2013; Weinthal et al. 2014; Young and Goldman 2015; Bruch et al. 2016).[4] This work is now being transformed into a Massive Open Online Course on Environmental Security and Sustaining Peace that is being offered by the SDG Academy as of 2018.

The lessons outlined in this chapter demonstrate that natural resources provide numerous entry points for addressing risks and opportunities in conflict-affected environments, and highlight some of the ways in which the United Nations can contribute to these efforts by providing information, support and platforms for stakeholders to develop solutions informed by the local context. Despite significant progress, research is still needed to show how these endeavors can be further integrated into the global agenda for sustainable development, and connected to climate change adaption efforts.

Notes

1 "When thou shalt besiege a city a long time, in making war against it to take it, thou shalt not destroy the trees thereof by forcing an axe against them: for thou mayest eat of them, and thou shalt not cut them down (for the tree of the field is man's life) to employ them in the siege."

2 Interestingly, in September 2016, the Office of the Prosecutor of the International Criminal Court issued an interpretation document for case selection and prioritization, which notes the following regarding determining the gravity of cases (which is one of the criteria in case selection):

> 41. The impact of the crimes may be assessed in light of, inter alia, the increased vulnerability of victims, the terror subsequently instilled, or the social, economic and environmental damage inflicted on the affected communities. In this context, the Office will give particular consideration to prosecuting Rome Statute crimes that are committed by means of, or that result in, inter alia, *the destruction of the environment, the illegal exploitation of natural resources or the illegal dispossession of land.*
>
> *(Office of the Prosecutor of the International Criminal Court 2016; emphasis added).*

3 For more information about the Mapping and Assessing the Performance of Extractive Industries (MapX) partnership, see www.mapx.org

4 More information at www.environmentalpeacebuilding.org

References

Abusin, A. M., Young, H., Osman, A. M., Asher, M., and Egemi, O. (2009) *Livelihoods, Power and Choice: The Vulnerability of the Northern Rizaygat, Darfur, Sudan* Feinstein International Centre, Tufts University. Available at http://fic.tufts.edu/assets/Livelihoods-Power-Choice-2009.pdf

Advisory Group of Experts (2015) Review of the United Nations Peacebuilding Architecture, *The Challenge of Sustaining Peace*, 29 June. Available at www.un.org/en/peacebuilding/pdf/150630%20 Report%20of%20the%20AGE%20on%20the%202015%20Peacebuilding%20Review%20FINAL.pdf

BBC (2015) "Nigeria Raises Borrowing in Budget as Oil Prices Fall," 22 December. Available at www.bbc.com/news/business-35162111

Bloomberg (2016) "Nigeria Revenue Drops to 5-Year Low as Tax, Oil Income Fall," 22 April. Available at www.bloomberg.com/news/articles/2016-04-22/nigeria-s-revenue-drops-to-five-year-low-as-tax-oil-income-fall

Bruch, C., Muffett, C., and Nichols, S. (eds.) (2016) *Governance, Natural Resources, and Post-Conflict Peacebuilding* Routledge, Abingdon.

Carson, T. (2013) "Advancing the Legal Protection of the Environment in Relation to Armed Conflict: Protocol I's Threshold of Impermissible Environmental Damage and Alternatives" *Nordic Journal of International Law* 82(1): 83–101.

Conca, K. (2015) *An Unfinished Foundation: The United Nations and Global Environmental Governance* Oxford University Press, Oxford.

Conca, K. and Wallace, J. (2012) "Environment and peacebuilding in war-torn societies: lessons from the UN Environment Programme's experience with post-conflict assessment" in Jensen, D. and Lonergan, S. (eds.) *Assessing and Restoring Natural Resources in Post-Conflict Peacebuilding* Earthscan, London.

European Union and United Nations Interagency Framework Team for Preventive Action, *Toolkits and Guidance Notes for Preventing and Managing Land and Natural Resource Conflicts*, 2010–2012. Available at www.un.org/en/land-natural-resources-conflict/

Illicit Financial Flows (IFF) (2015) Report of the High-Level Panel on Illicit Financial Flows from Africa, Commissioned by the AU/ECA Conference of Ministers of Finance, Planning and Economic Development. Available at www.uneca.org/sites/default/files/PublicationFiles/iff_main_report_26feb_en.pdf

International Law Commission (ILC) (2014) *Preliminary report of the Special Rapporteur*, Submitted by Marie G. Jacobsson, Special Rapporteur, UN Doc. A/CN.4/674 and Corr. 1.

International Law Commission (ILC) (2015) *Second report of the Special Rapporteur*, Submitted by Marie G. Jacobsson, Special Rapporteur, UN Doc. A/CN.4/685.

International Law Commission (ILC) (2016) *Third report on the protection of the environment in relation to armed conflicts*, Submitted by Marie G. Jacobsson, Special Rapporteur, UN Doc. A/CN.4/700.

International Monetary Fund (IMF) (2016a) *Nigeria: Selected Issues*, IMF Country Report No. 16/102, April. Available at www.imf.org/external/pubs/ft/scr/2016/cr16102.pdf

International Monetary Fund (IMF) (2016b) *Sierra Leone: Selected Issues*, IMF Country Report No. 16/237, July. Available at www.imf.org/external/pubs/ft/scr/2016/cr16237.pdf

International Peace Information Service (IPIS) (2015) Infographic – Mapping Mining Areas in Eastern DRC, January 28. Available at http://ipisresearch.be/2015/01/infographic-mapping-security-human-rights-mining-areas-eastern-drc/

Jensen, D. and Lonergan, S. (eds.) (2012) *Assessing and Restoring Natural Resources in Post-Conflict Peacebuilding* Earthscan, London.

Lujala, P. and Rustad, S. A. (eds.) (2012) *High-Value Natural Resources and Post-Conflict Peacebuilding* Routledge, Abingdon.

McKinsey Global Institute (2013) *Reverse the Curse: Maximizing the Potential of Resource-driven Economies*, December. Available at www.mckinsey.com/industries/metals-and-mining/our-insights/reverse-the-curse-maximizing-the-potential-of-resource-driven-economies

Natural Resource Governance Institute (NRGI) (2014) *Natural Resource Charter* (Second Edition). Available at http://resourcegovernance.org/sites/default/files/documents/nrcj1193_natural_resource_charter_19.6.14.pdf

Organization for Economic Cooperation and Development (OECD) (2016a) *Development Aid Rises Again in 2015, Spending on Refugees Doubles*, 13 April. Available at www.oecd.org/dac/development-aid-rises-again-in-2015-spending-on-refugees-doubles.htm

Organization for Economic Cooperation and Development (OECD) (2016b) *States of Fragility 2016: Highlights*, September. Available at www.oecd.org/dac/conflict-fragility-resilience/docs/Fragile-States-highlights-2016.pdf

Organization for Economic Cooperation and Development (OECD) (2016c) *Towards a Multidimensional Fragility Framework for the OECD: Working Paper Outlining the Methodology for the OECD's Monitoring of Fragility*. Available at www.oecd.org/dac/governance-peace/conflictfragilityandresilience/Multidimensional%20Fragility%20Framework%20OECD.pdf

Office of the High Commissioner for Human Rights (OHCHR) (2016) *Early Warning and Economic, Social and Cultural Rights*. Available at www.ohchr.org/Documents/Issues/ESCR/EarlyWarning_ESCR_2016_en.pdf

Office of the Prosecutor of the International Criminal Court (2016) *Policy Paper on Case Selection and Prioritization*. Available at www.icc-cpi.int/itemsDocuments/20160915_OTP-Policy_Case-Selection_Eng.pdf

Report of the High-level Independent Panel on Peace Operations on uniting our strengths for peace: politics, partnership and people (2015) UN Doc. A/70/95–S/2015/446. Available at www.un.org/sg/pdf/HIPPO_Report_1_June_2015.pdf

Rome Statute (1998) Article 8 (b) (iv) Available at http://legal.un.org/icc/statute/romefra.htm

Rüttinger, L., Smith, D., Stang, G., Tänzler, D., and Vivekananda, J. with Brown, O., et al. (2015) *A New Climate for Peace: Taking Action on Climate and Fragility Risks* An Independent Report Commissioned by the G7 Members. Available at www.newclimateforpeace.org

United Nations Development Group (UNDG) and Executive Committee on Humanitarian Affairs (ECHA) (2013) *Natural Resource Management in Transition Settings*, Guidance Note. Available at https://undg.org/wp-content/uploads/2014/06/UNDG-ECHA_NRM_guidance_Jan20131.pdf

UN Environment–INTERPOL (2016) "The Rise of Environmental Crime – A Growing Threat to Natural Resources Peace, Development And Security" *UNEP–INTERPOL Rapid Response Assessment* United Nations Environment Programme and RHIPTO Rapid Response – Norwegian Center for Global Analyses.

UN Environment–MONUSCO–OSESG (2015) *Experts' Background Report on Illegal Exploitation and Trade in Natural Resources Benefitting Organized Criminal Groups and Recommendations on Monusco's Role in Fostering Stability and Peace in Eastern DR Congo*, April. Available at http://postconflict.unep.ch/publications/UNEP_DRCongo_MONUSCO_OSESG_final_report.pdf

UN Environment–PBSO–UN Women–UNDP (2013) *Women and Natural Resources. Unlocking the Peacebuilding Potential*. Available at http://postconflict.unep.ch/publications/UNEP_UN-Women_PBSO_UNDP_gender_NRM_peacebuilding_report.pdf

UN Environment–UN DPA (2015) *Natural Resources and Conflict: A Guide for Mediation Practitioners*. Available at http://postconflict.unep.ch/publications/UNDPA_UNEP_NRC_Mediation_full.pdf

UN Environment–UNDP (2013) *The Role of Natural Resources in Disarmament, Demobilization and Reintegration: Addressing Risks and Seizing Opportunities*, December. Available at http://postconflict.unep.ch/publications/UNEP_UNDP_NRM_DDR.pdf

UN Environment–UNDP–WPF (2013) *Haiti – Dominican Republic: Environmental Challenges in the Border Zone*. Available at http://postconflict.unep.ch/publications/UNEP_Haiti-DomRep_border_zone_EN.pdf

United Nations Environment Assembly (UNEA) (2016) *Protection of the Environment in Areas Affected by Armed Conflict*, 27 May, UNEP/EA.2/Res.15

United Nations Environment Programme (2003a) *Afghanistan Post-Conflict Environmental Assessment*. Available at www.unep.org/pdf/afghanistanpcajanuary2003.pdf

United Nations Environment Programme (2003b) *Desk Study on the Environment in Iraq*. Available at www.unep.org/pdf/iraq_ds.pdf

United Nations Environment Programme (2003c) *Desk Study on the Environment in the Occupied Palestinian Territories*. Available at http://postconflict.unep.ch/publications/INF-31-WebOPT.pdf

United Nations Environment Programme (2004a) *From Conflict to Sustainable Development: Assessment and Clean-up in Serbia and Montenegro*. Available at http://postconflict.unep.ch/publications/sam.pdf

United Nations Environment Programme (2004b) *Desk Study on the Environment in Liberia*. Available at http://postconflict.unep.ch/publications/Liberia_DS.pdf

United Nations Environment Programme (2007) *UNEP in Iraq: Post-conflict Assessment, Clean-up and Reconstruction*. Available at http://postconflict.unep.ch/publications/Iraq.pdf

United Nations Environment Programme (2009a) *From Conflict to Peacebuilding: The Role of Natural Resources and the Environment*. Available at www.unep.org/pdf/pcdmb_policy_01.pdf

United Nations Environment Programme (2009b) *Protecting the Environment during Armed Conflict: An Inventory and Analysis of International Law*. Available at http://postconflict.unep.ch/publications/int_law.pdf

United Nations Environment Programme (2009c) *Integrating Environment in Post-Conflict Needs Assessments*, Guidance note. Available at http://postconflict.unep.ch/publications/environment_toolkit.pdf

United Nations Environment Programme (2010) *Sierra Leone: Environment, Conflict and Peacebuilding Assessment*. Available at http://postconflict.unep.ch/publications/Sierra_Leone.pdf

United Nations Environment Programme (2011) *Environmental Assessment of Ogoniland*. Available at http://postconflict.unep.ch/publications/OEA/UNEP_OEA.pdf

United Nations Environment Programme (2012) *Greening the Blue Helmets: Environment, Natural Resources and UN Peacekeeping Operations*, May. Available at www.un.org/en/peacekeeping/publications/UNEP_greening_blue_helmets.pdf

United Nations Environment Programme (2014) *Relationships and Resources: Environmental Governance for Peacebuilding and Resilient Livelihoods in Sudan*, June. Available at http://postconflict.unep.ch/publications/UNEP_Sudan_RnR.pdf

United Nations Environment Programme (2015a) *Addressing the Role of Natural Resources in Conflict and Peacebuilding: A Summary of Progress from UNEP's Environmental Cooperation for Peacebuilding Programme 2008–2015*. Available at www.unep.org/disastersandconflicts/Introduction/Environmental CooperationforPeacebuilding_/ECPProgressReport/tabid/1060787/Default.aspx

United Nations Environment Programme (2015b) *Côte d'Ivoire Post-conflict Environmental Assessment*. Available at http://postconflict.unep.ch/publications/Cote%20d'Ivoire/UNEP_CDI_PCEA_EN.pdf

United Nations Environment Programme (2015c) *Natural Resources and Conflicts: A Guide for Mediation Practitioners*, February. Available at http://postconflict.unep.ch/publications/UNDPA_UNEP_NRC_Mediation_full.pdf

United Nations Environment Programme (2016) *Environmental Cooperation for Peacebuilding: Final Report*. November. Available at http://postconflict.unep.ch/publications/ECP/ECP_final_report_Nov2016.pdf

United Nations General Assembly (UNGA) (1992) *Protection of the Environment in Times of Armed Conflict*, Resolution, 25 November, UN Doc. A/RES/47/37.

United Nations General Assembly (UNGA) (2001) *Observance of the International Day for Preventing the Exploitation of the Environment in War and Armed Conflict*, Resolution, 5 November, UN Doc. A/RES/56/4.

United Nations General Assembly (UNGA) (2009) *Climate Change and Its Possible Security Implications: Report of the Secretary-General*, UN Doc. A/64/350, 11 September. Available at www.un.org/ga/search/view_doc.asp?symbol=A/64/350

United Nations General Assembly (UNGA) (2013) Official Records, Sixty-Eighth Session, Supplement No. 10, UN Doc. A/68/10.

United Nations General Assembly (UNGA) (2015) *Transforming Our World: The 2030 Agenda for Sustainable Development*, 25 September, UN Doc. A/RES/70/1.

United Nations General Assembly (2016a) *Review of the United Nations Peacebuilding Architecture*, 12 May, UN Doc. A/RES/70/262. Available at http://undocs.org/A/RES/70/262

United Nations General Assembly (UNGA) (2016b) Seventy-first Session, Supplement No. 10, *Report of the International Law Commission: Sixty-eighth session (2 May–10 June and 4 July–12 August)*, UN Doc. A/71/10, footnote 1039.

United Nations General Assembly (UNGA) and United Nations Security Council (UNSC) (2010) *Progress Report of the Secretary-General on Peacebuilding in the Immediate Aftermath of Conflict*, Report, 16 July, UN Doc. A/64/866; UN Doc. S/2010/386 para. 44.

United Nations Security Council (UNSC) (2011) *Statement by the President of the Security Council*, 20 July, UN Doc. S/PRST/2011/15. Available at https://undocs.org/S/PRST/2011/15

United Nations Security Council (UNSC) (2016) *Resolution 2282 (2016)*, 27 April, UN Doc. A/RES/70/262. Available at www.un.org/en/ga/search/view_doc.asp?symbol=S/RES/2282(2016)

UN Women (2015) *Preventing Conflict, Transforming Justice, Securing the Peace: A Global Study on the Implementation of United Nations Security Council Resolution 1325*. Available at http://wps.unwomen.org/pdf/en/GlobalStudy_EN_Web.pdf

Unruh, J. and Williams, R. (eds.) (2013) *Land and Post-conflict Peacebuilding* Routledge, Abingdon.

Weinthal, E., Troell, J., and Nakayama, M. (eds.) (2014) *Water and Post-conflict Peacebuilding* Routledge, Abingdon.

Young, H and, Goldman, L. (eds.) (2015) *Livelihoods, Natural Resources, and Post-conflict Peacebuilding* Routledge, Abingdon.

11

Revisiting securitization

An empirical analysis of environment and natural resource provisions in United Nations Security Council Resolutions, 1946–2016

Peter Aldinger, Carl Bruch, and Sofia Yazykova[1]

Introduction

There is a robust debate regarding whether the environment be addressed as a matter of international peace and security. When an issue such as the environment is securitized, it may be removed from regular politics and, more broadly, from the public sphere (Buzan, Ole, and de Wilde 1995; Taureck 2006). In the United Nations, environmental issues have historically fallen within the purview of the UN General Assembly, while peace and security issues have been the realm of the UN Security Council (Conca 2015). Many countries have been loath to have environmental issues discussed in the Security Council, as that moves the issue from the democratic General Assembly (universal membership with each country holding one vote) to the non-democratic Security Council (comprising 15 countries, with 5 having permanent vetoes), and the Security Council has substantially more power to intrude into national sovereignty.

The term "environment" encompasses a host of issues, including the adverse effects of pollution on human health and welfare, natural resource abundance and the resource curse, resource scarcity and population growth, natural disasters, and climate change (Floyd and Matthew 2013). The wide variety of ways in which the environment can be linked to security has led many to question whether it is useful to talk of environmental security as a subject or subdiscipline (Deudney 2015). Some suggest that it may be more appropriate to

> "desecuritize" the environment – reintegrate it into regular politics – as this would represent "a recognition of social–political responsibilities for changes in the quality of environmental conditions" (Buzan et al. 1995:15). There are also concerns that securitizing the environment may in fact dilute the concept of security, since many such issues cannot be addressed effectively by the military
> *(Græger 1996)*.

Notwithstanding the various concerns, there are clear linkages between the environment (and especially natural resources) and the onset, financing, conduct, conclusion, and recovery from armed conflict. The United Nations Environment Programme (UNEP) has observed that the "exploitation of natural resources and related environmental stresses can be implicated in all phases of the conflict cycle, from contributing to the outbreak and perpetuation of violence to undermining prospects for peace" (UNEP 2009:5). The Security

Council recognized this on June 12, 1998, when it adopted Resolution 1173, which aimed to prevent the União Nacional para a Independência Total de Angola (UNITA) from using revenues from diamond exports to finance the protracted civil war.[2] While a number of earlier UNSC Resolutions addressed natural resources in different contexts, this Resolution was the first time the Council had made a direct link between natural resources and conflict. Since then, it has recognized a wide range of natural resources that have been used to finance fighting, has expanded its approach to preventing natural resources from being used in this manner, and has recently begun to require environmental impact assessments and other environmental measures for peace operations.

The number of Resolutions that address natural resources and other environmental issues has dramatically increased. Through the end of 2016, 336 Security Council Resolutions (14.4 percent of all Resolutions) had addressed natural resources or the environment.[3] The substantial number and diversity of instances in which the Security Council has recognized the importance of natural resources and the environment highlights the clear fact that historic political divisions between environment and security are seriously outdated. Securitization of the environment and environmentalization of security are here to stay.

This chapter reviews how the Security Council, the preeminent interpellator of threats to international peace and security, has addressed the environment and natural resources in its Resolutions. It aims to provide empirical data and analysis on how the environment has been securitized: when, how, and in what context it emerged as an issue for the Security Council, how the Security Council has addressed the issue and adapted to changing conflict dynamics and politics, and how it has expanded its approach.

The first section examines the effects of the Cold War on the Security Council and the Security Council's response to threats to international peace. The second section provides a brief overview of the linkages between the natural resources and conflict. The third section surveys how the Security Council has viewed natural resources in the past, how its perception has changed over the years, and how it has addressed various natural resources in its Resolutions. The final section explains how the Security Council, with the means it has available, has addressed natural resources and conflict in chronological context. This includes a discussion of how the Council has used sanctions, sanctions committees, expert panels, UN-led peacekeeping missions, and UN-sanctioned peacekeeping missions to address the perpetuation of conflict through the illicit exploitation of natural resources and in the post-conflict stage, and how it has focused on natural resources for purposes of peacebuilding.

The Cold War, its end, and civil conflict

The institutional architecture of the Security Council enshrined the dominant post-World War II positions of the Republic of China, France, the Soviet Union (now the Russian Federation), the United Kingdom, and the United States of America. Under the 1945 Charter of the United Nations, these five states became permanent members of the Security Council. Per Article 24(1) of the Charter, the Security Council was vested with the "primary responsibility for the maintenance of international peace and security," and the permanent members could veto any non-procedural Resolution pursuant to Article 27(3).

With the advent of the Cold War, the purpose of the Security Council became framed by the geopolitical contest between the United States and the Soviet Union. The Security Council rarely authorized an action that could be considered interference in the "domestic jurisdiction" of a Member State (Matheson 2006:41). Article 2(7) of the Charter explicitly prohibited such intervention, in recognition of the primary importance of State sovereignty.[4] The ideological camps "proved willing to use their Security Council vetoes to block resolutions in order to stymie the wishes and interests of their opponents" (Pilbeam 2015:295). During the Cold War, the superpowers provided financial and material support to authoritarian regimes[5] and concerned themselves with actions taken by proxies, especially with regard to anything that could affect the existing balance of power (Mearsheimer 1990a) or lead to the use of armed force (Enuka 2012; Sotiropoulou 2004).

With the end of the Cold War, the United States and newly formed Russian Federation had substantially less interest in supporting their erstwhile proxies. As the allegiance of controversial allies became unnecessary, they withdrew financial and material support (Rustad et al. 2008; Le Billon 2005). The days of coordinating proxies in a larger ideological struggle, where the ends justified the means, were (largely) over.

One of the best indicators of how the relationship between the United States and the Soviet Union's successor changed after the Cold War, and how it affected the workings of the Security Council, is the number of Resolutions the Security Council passed. While the Security Council only adopted 646 Resolutions from 1946 through the end of 1989 (an average of 14.6 per year), it passed 1,690 Resolutions between 1990 and the end of 2016 (an average of 62.6 per year) – an annual increase of more than four-fold.

Various commentators predicted an increase in civil conflict at the end of the Cold War (Mearsheimer 1990b), in part due to an expected rise in nationalism (Mearsheimer 1990a; Wimmer 2004). However, research conducted by the Department of Peace and Conflict Research at Uppsala University in 2014 revealed that the "end of the cold war saw a marked drop in the number of conflicts" (*The Economist* 2013). Also, the International Peace Institute has shown that while civil conflicts have been the norm, rather than the exception since 1945, "until the end of the Cold War, the Security Council rarely qualified civil wars as a threat to international peace and security" (Cockayne, Mikulaschek, and Perry 2010:6). It may therefore be more accurate to say that the defining characteristic of the post-Cold War era is the increased willingness of the Security Council to intervene in civil wars and intrastate conflicts. The increase in the adoption of Resolutions by the Security Council does not, therefore, represent a correlative increase in conflict. Rather, it represents the Security Council's recognition that threats to international peace and security can emanate from intrastate conflict, and its newfound willingness to engage.[6]

The theory that conflicts emerging from the end of the Cold War could primarily be explained by "ethnic" or "tribal" grievances has also been debunked. James Fearon and David Laitin have shown that the most important causal factor is state fragility: "financially, organizationally, and politically weak central governments render insurgency more feasible and attractive due to weak local policing or inept and corrupt counterinsurgency practices" (Fearon and Laitin 2003:75–76). Researchers have since established that economic factors, most notably the quality of natural resource governance, are significant factors in explaining and predicting the occurrence of civil conflict (Collier and Hoefler 2004; Ross 2003; Ross 2004; Brunnschweiler and Bultey 2009).

Natural resources in conflict – theoretical underpinnings

Research on the resource curse shows that overreliance on natural resources for economic growth and government revenues can lead to structural problems and inhibit the development of higher forms of manufacturing (Auty 1994). This can adversely affect the investment environment and employment levels, what is sometimes termed "Dutch disease," leading to lower standards of living and higher rates of inequality and poverty. Paul Collier and Anke Hoeffler have argued that "primary commodity exports substantially increase conflict risk" (Collier and Hoeffler 2004:588), and could be linked to two motivational factors: insurgent groups may seek to control and extract valuable natural resources for their own personal gain (greed), and opposition may emerge as a form of protest against poverty and poor governance (grievance) – a function of the country's dependence upon primary commodities and the effects of the resource curse (Collier and Hoeffler 2004).

With the end of the Cold War and the associated financing for proxy wars, rebel groups needed to secure alternative sources of financing (Garrett and Piccinni 2012). Governments had taxation, concession revenues, and foreign assistance. In many cases, rebels resorted to the exploitation of domestic natural resources, often high-value, lootable resources with limited capital requirements (Le Billon 2005). For example, in Angola, UNITA relied upon the sale of rough diamonds to continue to fund its armed opposition to the newly elected government (Ross 2003); at the same time, the government financed its martial efforts through oil in what has been termed "the quintessential resource conflict" (Paes 2009). This was the first time the Security Council recognized the role natural resources play in financing and driving conflict.

The logic that affected the Angolan civil war can be applied to civil conflicts more broadly: groups wishing to pursue a military campaign must either receive financial and/or material support from an external backer or secure the necessary funds to purchase weapons and materiel and pay fighters on their own (Ross 2003). Since the Angolan civil war, direct links between natural resources and conflict have been made in Sierra Leone, Liberia, Côte d'Ivoire, Cambodia, Colombia, and the Democratic Republic of the Congo (DRC), to name a few. This has led some, such as the advocacy group Global Witness, to call for the Security Council to adopt an established definition of the term "conflict resources," as well as a legal and institutional framework to more consistently address conflict resources (Global Witness 2010)[7] – but the Security Council has shown limited interest in doing so, preferring to take an ad hoc approach.

Evaluation of Security Council Resolutions, 1946–2016

Almost from its inception, the Security Council has recognized the importance of natural resources to the development and prosperity of nations. Having awarded trusteeships to the victorious Allies following the end of World War II, the Security Council emphasized the fiduciary duty of these trustees to promote development and to "regulate the use of natural resources; encourage the development of fisheries, agriculture, and industries; [and] protect the inhabitants against the loss of their lands and resources" (UNSC 1947, art. 6(2)). The Security Council also recognized the potential for conflict over natural resources in 1973, when it expressed "deep concern" about "the existence and use of coercive measures which affect the free exercise of permanent sovereignty over natural resources of Latin American countries," and stated "that the use or encouragement of the use of coercive measures may create situations likely to endanger peace and security in Latin America" (UNSC 1973, pmbl.).

By granting the Security Council the authority to enforce "measures not involving the use of armed force, [which] may include complete or partial interruption of economic relations" (UN 1945, art. 41), the UN Charter provided a mandate for using natural resource-related sanctions where there are threats to peace. Initially, the Security Council applied such sanctions to State actors. For instance, Resolution 253 made it illegal for any country to import primary commodities, including iron ore, chrome, copper, and agricultural products, from what was then Southern Rhodesia, now Zimbabwe, so as to pressure the country's administration and ruling elite to alter its policy of apartheid (UNSC 2013l).

The end of the Cold War saw not only a dramatic rise in the use of conflict resources by rebel groups, but also significant growth in international cooperation and collective action – including through the Security Council – to address conflict resources and the broader implications of natural resources to international peace and security. Security Council Resolution 1173, adopted in 1998, introduced sanctions on rough diamonds from Angola (UNSC 1998a). In 2000, the Security Council expressed its concern over "reports of the illegal exploitation of the [DRC's] assets and the potential consequences of these actions on security conditions and the continuation of hostilities" (UNSC 2000a). Less than a month later, the Security Council noted "the role played by the illicit trade in diamonds in fuelling the conflict in Sierra Leone" (UNSC 2000b). It established an expert panel to investigate the "illegal exploitation of natural resources and other forms of wealth" in the DRC (UNSC 2000a), and held "exploratory hearings" to "assess the role of diamonds in the Sierra Leone conflict and the link between trade in Sierra Leone diamonds and trade in arms and related materiél" (UNSC 2000b). Both inquiries concluded that the illicit exploitation and sale of natural resources were fuelling conflict (UNSC 2001c).

Since then, the Council has recognized direct links between natural resources and conflict in Liberia, Côte d'Ivoire, Somalia, the Central African Republic, Afghanistan, as well as at the regional level, such as in the Mano River Basin and the African Great Lakes area (UNSC 2001a, 2005, 2006a, 2006b). Between 1946 and 1989, only 17 Resolutions addressed natural resources and/or the environment – an annual average of 0.4. With the end of the Cold War, this rose dramatically. Between 1990 and 2016, 319 Resolutions contained such references – an approximate annual average of 12. Put another way, only 2.6 percent of the Resolutions between 1946 and 1989 contained references to natural resources and the environment, in contrast to 19 percent of the Resolutions passed between 1990 and 2016. Overall, natural resources and environmental issues were mentioned in slightly more than 14 percent of Resolutions between 1946 and 2016. While numbers fluctuate from year to year, there is a strong upward trend in the number of Resolutions addressing natural resources or the environment: from 5 times in 1992, to 12 times in 2002, to 29 times in 2016 (see Figure 11.1).

The overwhelming majority – 89 percent – of the 336 Resolutions that mention natural resources and the environment are operational. That is, the Security Council "demands," "directs," "encourages," and/or "urges" some kind of action be taken, either by Subject States, Member States, or one of the UN bodies (usually a UN-led peacekeeping mission, agency, or subsidiary body). These actions include, for example, cooperating with expert panels, preventing harm to marine life, or taking action to prevent corporations from coercing states to exploit natural resources. Where there is no mention of Member States, Subject States, or UN Agency/ Mission, the operational aspect may call for action from terrorist groups (UNSC 2012d) or demand that the illicit exploitation of natural resources cease (UNSC 2001d). Approximately 60 percent of the 336 Resolutions direct Subject States to take some form of action in relation to the environment and natural resources; 60 percent address action by Member States; and 67 percent direct a UN body to take some kind of action.

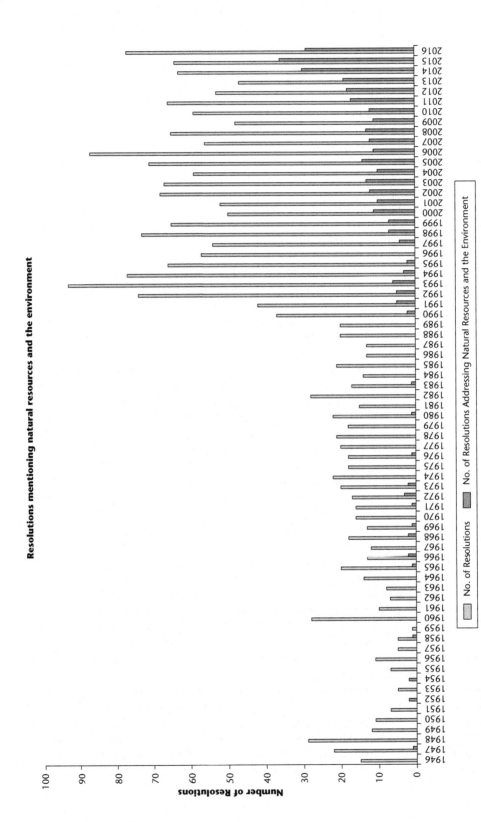

Figure 11.1 UN Security Council Resolutions mentioning natural resources and the environment

Natural resources in Security Council Resolutions

Within the 336 Resolutions mentioning natural resources and the environment, references to oil and gas, minerals, forestry, wildlife and biodiversity, land and real property, agriculture, narcotics production, water, ocean resources, and other general environmental terms appear over 450 times. These are considered in turn.

Hydrocarbons

Oil and natural gas dominate national economies of many fragile and conflict-affected states, and many territorial disputes and secessionist movements relate to territory rich in oil and gas (Lujala and Rustad 2012; Yergin 2008). Examples include Sudan/Southern Sudan, Sudan/ South Sudan/Abyei, Iraq/Kurdistan, Argentina/United Kingdom, Nigeria/Biafra, and the South China Sea. Hydrocarbons also provide opportunities for conflict financing by rebel movements through direct exploitation (as with the Islamic State in Iraq and Syria, or ISIS) and through extortion of oil companies and ransoming kidnapped oil workers (as with rebel groups in Colombia) (USAID 2011). Reflecting these dynamics, it appears that oil and gas reserves make it more difficult to resolve conflicts – and lead to longer conflicts (Lujala 2009).

Ninety-four Resolutions[8] address hydrocarbons, including mention of oil, natural gas, natural gas products, petroleum, petroleum products, oil infrastructure, oil installations, oil facilities, gas infrastructure, oilfields, and pipelines. The Security Council has mentioned this type of resource more often than any other (see Figure 11.2). In most cases, the Security Council has addressed the role of hydrocarbons in conflict in a relatively direct manner. Eight involve embargoes aimed at preventing armed groups from accessing petroleum and related products, which could otherwise be used in pursuance of military objectives, as in Angola and Sierra Leone, or to pressure illegitimate governments, as in Southern Rhodesia and Haiti. Forty Resolutions relate to Iraq's invasion of Kuwait and the subsequent efforts to prevent Saddam Hussein from acquiring weapons of mass destruction, which was achieved by restricting how Iraq's oil revenues could be spent – the "Oil-for-Food" programme. In these situations, the Security Council utilized embargoes and targeted sanctions to mitigate conflict, coerce belligerents and illegitimate regimes to alter their behavior, and prevent threats to international peace and security.

The Security Council has similarly adopted Resolutions to prevent terrorists and non-state armed groups from using the proceeds from the sale of illicitly acquired oil to finance terrorism, for example in response to the emerging threat from ISIS in Iraq and Syria (UNSC 2014m), and insurgent and terrorist groups in Libya (UNSC 2014e). In some cases, targeted sanctions have been applied to individuals who are "providing support for armed groups or criminal networks through the illicit exploitation of crude oil" (UNSC 2014n).

Since 2011, the Council has also begun to focus upon the effects of attacks on oil infrastructure and the oil industry, and the importance of oil revenues for economic growth, peacebuilding, and development. It has, for instance, "underscored" "the important role oil revenue could play in the economy of South Sudan" (UNSC 2013d), and has mandated United Nations Interim Security Force for Abyei (UNISFA) to, "[w]hen necessary and in cooperation with the Abyei Police Service, provide security for oil infrastructure in the Abyei Area" (UNSC 2011c). Interestingly, none of the Resolutions calling for groups to refrain from attacking oil infrastructure mention the danger of environmental damage; the emphasis is clearly on the adverse effects of economic disruption on the State in question. Finally, the Council has, in very limited circumstances, warned of petroleum becoming a potential source of conflict and encouraged the State in question – Somalia – "to mitigate properly against the risk of the petroleum sector . . . becoming a source of increased tension" (UNSC 2013e).

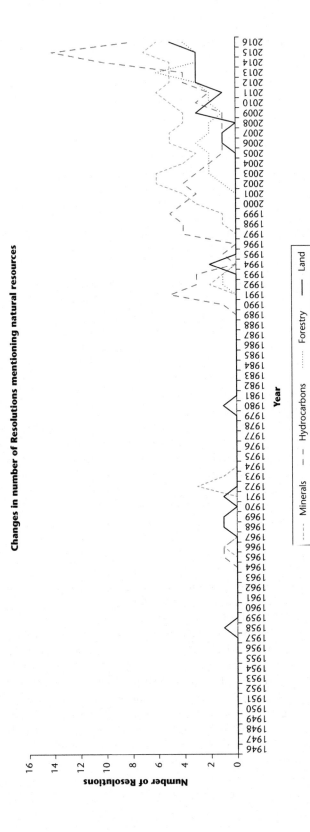

Figure 11.2 UN Security Council Resolutions mentioning particular types of natural resources

Minerals

Minerals – including gold, diamonds, iron ore, cassiterite, coltan, and wolframite, among others – are an important source of revenue for governments and rebel movements, as well as a source of artisanal livelihoods. Unlike oil and gas, minerals do not require substantial capital for infrastructure. Their ready lootability and high value have made diamonds and other minerals the "guerrilla's best friend," and a frequent conflict resource (Malaquias 2001).

The Security Council has addressed minerals in 93 Resolutions.[9] The overwhelming focus has been on the role of minerals in financing groups considered to pose a threat to international peace and security, beginning in the 1960s with what was then Southern Rhodesia, now Zimbabwe. In most cases, the Security Council has targeted high-value minerals such as gold or diamonds coming from conflict-affected countries; in 1992, though, it banned the export of coal, iron, steel, and other metals *to* the Former Federal Republic of Yugoslavia (UNSC 1992a). Since then, it has largely focused on preventing high-value minerals from being sold to finance conflict.

The Security Council started introducing sanctions on minerals at the end of the 1990s, after it recognized the "linkage between the illicit trade in rough diamonds from certain regions of the world and the fuelling of armed conflicts that affect international peace and security," and supported the establishment of the Kimberley Process Certification Scheme (UNSC 2003a).[10] At the end of 2008, the Security Council encouraged Member States to adopt measures requiring companies to exercise due diligence to ensure that they are not sourcing minerals from the DRC that fund rebel groups (UNSC 2008d). The 2014 U.S. conflict minerals rule adopted pursuant to the Dodd–Frank Wall Street Reform Act and the pending EU conflict minerals legislation respond to this call for due diligence. The Security Council has also imposed due diligence requirements in relation to mining in Eritrea (UNSC 2011g). By focusing on certification and chain of custody regimes, the Council has attempted to cut off funding to insurgents, while allowing State-sanctioned groups to continue to exploit natural resources.

Forestry[11]

Forestry is an important sector in the economies of many developing countries, especially those endowed with large swathes of forestland, such as Brazil, Indonesia, and Cameroon. It is also often a source of contestation between indigenous groups, local communities, and the government. Timber, charcoal, and other forest products have been utilized as conflict resources in Cambodia, Liberia, Somalia, and elsewhere (USAID 2005).

Forty Security Council Resolutions address forestry resources, including timber, timber products, round logs, logs, and charcoal. As with minerals, the Security Council's overriding concern with forestry products is that they may be used to finance conflict. Having recognized the role of timber in conflict financing, the Security Council imposed sanctions on the export of logs from Cambodia in 1992 (UNSC 1992b), logs from Liberia in 2003 (UNSC 2003b), and on charcoal from Somalia in 2012 (UNSC 2012a). It has encouraged the adoption of voluntary measures, such as in DRC, where it recommended that regional States "regularly publish full import and export statistics for natural resources including . . . timber . . . and charcoal and enhance information sharing and joint action at the regional level to investigate and combat regional criminal networks and armed groups" (UNSC 2010d).

The Security Council imposed sanctions on importation of timber and round logs from Liberia, and extended the sanctions after the peace agreement had been signed to ensure that Liberia adopted the necessary reforms to ensure that forestry resources did not lead to a relapse to conflict (UNSC 2004a). The Security Council noted "that Liberia's progress in the timber sector is held back by the absence of appropriate forestry legislation, and urg[ed] speedy adoption of the necessary laws" (UNSC 2006c). But even after the National Forestry Reform Law (NFRL) was passed and sanctions were lifted (Altman, Nichols, and Woods 2012), the Council remained engaged, as it called on the newly elected government to ensure "the effective implementation of the Forestry Reform Law" (UNSC 2006d). It also directed the Panel of Experts on Liberia to "assess the extent to which forestry and other natural resources are contributing to peace, security and development rather than to instability and to what extent relevant legislation . . . is contributing to this transition" (UNSC 2009b). In 2013 – nearly eight years after sanctions on timber and round logs had been lifted – the Security Council still remained seized of the matter, encouraging the "Government of Liberia to continue to make progress through effective implementation and enforcement of the National Forestry Reform Law" (UNSC 2013k). The Security Council's series of Resolutions addressing forestry resources in Liberia demonstrates that it is able and, under certain circumstances, willing to remain engaged for many years to ensure the necessary legislative and institutional reforms for more effective resource management are undertaken to prevent a return to conflict and lay the foundation for long-term peace.

Wildlife and biodiversity

Armed groups have financed themselves through the illegal exploitation of wildlife for decades. For example, illicit ivory trade has provided financing for the Janjaweed in Sudan, the Lord's Resistance Army in Uganda, various armed groups operating in the eastern DRC, al-Qaeda, al-Shabaab, and Boko Haram (Vira and Ewing 2014; Rao 2013). The Security Council did not explicitly recognize this until the end of 2013, following the eruption of violence in the Central African Republic. Initially, the Security Council only condemned "the devastation of natural heritage and not[ed] that poaching and trafficking of wildlife are among the factors that fuel the crisis in the CAR" (UNSC 2013h; UNSC 2013j), but later it imposed targeted sanctions on individuals who were deemed to be "providing support for armed groups or criminal networks through the illicit exploitation of natural resources, including . . . wildlife and wildlife products" (UNSC 2014a). Soon after, the Security Council imposed sanctions on "[i]ndividuals or entities supporting armed groups in the DRC through illicit trade of natural resources, including . . . wildlife as well as wildlife products" (UNSC 2014b). Through these Resolutions, the Security Council thus addressed illegal exploitation of wildlife and wildlife products in the same way as other conflict resources.

The only post-conflict peacebuilding context in which the Security Council has addressed wildlife and conservation is Liberia. In 2007, the Security Council stressed that "Liberia's progress in the timber sector must continue with [among other things] . . . the conservation and protection of biodiversity" (UNSC 2007e; UNSC 2008a; UNSC 2008c). This was the first time since 1983 that the Security Council had mentioned the importance of non-human life. Overall, wildlife, conservation, and biodiversity have not been priorities for the Security Council and were mentioned in only 16 Resolutions.[12]

Land and real property

Property rights are notoriously problematic, especially when two or more systems overlap. Due to colonial imposition, many States have plural legal systems, which include both statutory and customary regimes (Unruh and Williams 2013b). Additionally, more than one customary system may exist. In Liberia, for instance, there are 16 distinct ethnic groups, each with its own subdivisions. This legal overlap and lack of clarity over tenure rights often creates a great deal of uncertainty, which provides an opportunity for conflict. Moreover, in Guatemala, Nepal, and other countries, grievances related to historically inequitable allocation of land helped to motivate the conflict (Unruh and Williams 2013a).

The Security Council has addressed land and property issues in the context of certain ongoing conflicts, most clearly when one nation has invaded and occupied the territory of another.[13] Initially, the Security Council's main concern was that occupying forces were violating international law by expropriating the land and real property of those occupied. This was the case with Israel's occupation of the Palestinian territories in the 1950s and 1960s, wherein the Security Council emphasized that "unless otherwise mutually agreed, Israelis should not be allowed to use Arab-owned properties and Arabs should not be allowed to use Israeli-owned properties" (UNSC 1958). In an attempt to prevent this from occurring, the Security Council directed the UN Chief of Staff "to conduct a survey of property records with a view to determining property ownership in the [occupied] zone" (UNSC 1958). Similarly, following the disintegration of the Former Federal Republic of Yugoslavia (FFRY), the Security Council "[r]eaffirm[ed] its support for the established principles that all declarations and actions made under duress, particularly those regarding land and ownership, are null and void, and that all displaced persons should be enabled to return in peace to their former homes" (UNSC 1994b).

Outside of these examples, the Security Council has addressed land issues only in the context of post-conflict peacebuilding. The Security Council usually addresses land issues in general terms, except when prior arrangements have been made, as in the case of El Salvador (UNSC 1994c). It has exhorted governments and authorities to work toward the "resolution of land and tenure rights" (Liberia) (UNSC 2006e); "regulat[e] land and property titles and ownership" (Timor-Leste) (UNSC 2011a); "address the underlying causes of tension and conflict including with respect to land and nationality" (Côte d'Ivoire) (UNSC 2014k); and "address issues of land ownership with a view to establishing mutually beneficial arrangements for local communities and the private sector" (Sierra Leone) (UNSC 2013a). In Burundi, the Security Council encouraged the national government and the "Commission Nationale des Terres et autres Biens (CNTB) to handle land grievances and disputes in a non-partisan manner and to also address land tenure in the broader context of socioeconomic development, bearing in mind the need to foster reconciliation and national cohesion" (UNSC 2014c). Overall, however, the Council has not felt the need to impose mandatory measures in any of the 32 Resolutions that mention land.[14]

Agriculture

Most civil conflicts occur in poor, agrarian societies (Ross 2004), yet agriculture is rarely considered to be a cause or significant contributor. Rebel groups in many countries have relied on licit and illicit agricultural products as conflict resources, including, for example, cacao in Côte d'Ivoire (Global Witness 2007).

The Security Council has addressed agriculture in 9 Resolutions.[15] Agricultural products have, in the past, been the target of sanctions during conflict. In Southern Rhodesia, the import bans imposed by the Security Council on sugar, meats, and hides were part of a comprehensive package, which also included minerals. The objective was to coerce the Smith Administration into changing its policy on apartheid. In Guinea-Bissau, following the coup by General Ansumane Mane, the Security Council focused on "the need for urgent demining of affected areas to pave the way for the return of refugees and displaced persons and for the resumption of agricultural activities" (UNSC 1999a). More recently the Security Council expressed its "concern at the large-scale contraband of natural resources, in particular cocoa, cashew nuts, cotton, timber, gold and diamonds, which are illegally exported from or imported into Côte d'Ivoire"

(UNSC 2013c). By lumping agricultural products together with timber, gold, and diamonds – natural resources that have been used to finance various West African conflicts – the Security Council has implicitly recognized the potential danger of conflict financing from cocoa, cashew nuts, and cotton.

Narcotics production

A number of insurgent groups – including the Sendero Luminoso in Peru, the FARC in Colombia, and the Taliban in Afghanistan – have financed their armed activities through illicit drug production and trade (Cornell 2005; Felbab-Brown 2005; UNODC 2012). While they are agricultural products, the high value of illicit drugs means that they are often lumped together with "lootable" resources, such as alluvial diamonds. Illicit drug production may increase the duration of a conflict by effecting a change in the motivations of the rebels, as drug production becomes a primary objective, rather than a means to an end (Cornell 2005).

Of the 37 Resolutions that deal with the production and trafficking of illicit drugs,[16] 31 relate directly to Afghanistan, and the remaining 6 are concerned with "Threats to International Peace and Security Caused by Terrorist Acts." Prior to the United States' invasion of Afghanistan – following the attacks on September 11, 2001 – the Security Council had expressed its concern with "the growing cultivation, production and trafficking of drugs in Afghanistan," and "demanded" that "the Taliban, as well as others, halt the cultivation, production and trafficking of illegal drugs" (UNSC 1998b). In subsequent Resolutions, the Security Council has manifested concern that drug production and trafficking provide financing for the Taliban and other terrorist groups, which lead to "threats to the local population, including children, national security forces and international military and civilian personnel" (UNSC 2012b). The Council has also imposed sanctions on "Al-Qaida and other individuals, groups, undertakings and entities associated with them," who derive their funding from the "illicit cultivation, production and trafficking of narcotic drugs and their precursors" (UNSC 2012h). As with other conflict resources, the main concern of the Security Council is to prevent individuals and groups that pose a threat to international peace and security from financing themselves through the illicit production and sale of narcotics.

Water

Despite water's importance to life, health, communities, and economies, only 8 Resolutions mention it.[17] The most notable of these Resolutions was passed in 1980, in relation to the Occupied Territories, when the Security Council asked the designated Commission to "investigate the reported serious depletion of natural resources, particularly the water resources, with a view to ensuring the protection of those important natural resources of the territories under occupation" (UNSC 1980). This also appears to be the first time that the Security Council directed a UN body to look into the depletion of natural resources, and one of the few times that it explicitly linked a subsidiary body's mandate with the protection of natural resources. However, since this Resolution, the only other references to water have been made in relation to Sudan, Syria, Iraq, and Haiti. In Sudan, the Security Council called upon the parties to the Darfur conflict, as well as the United Nations Assistance Mission in Darfur (UNAMID) and other UN bodies, to comply with commitments made at the Darfur International Conference on Water (UNSC 2011e). With regard to Haiti, the Security Council requested the United Nations country team to assist the Government of Haiti to address the "structural weaknesses, in particular in the water and sanitation systems" (UNSC 2014p).

Ocean resources

As the world's population grows and large segments become wealthier, the demand for seafood is dramatically increasing, in some cases putting extreme pressure on fisheries. As fish stocks are depleted, commercial competition is increasing, leading to illegal fishing (Kaye 2015).

The Security Council has addressed ocean resources in two ways with regard to conflict. First, in the Iran–Iraq war, it called on the warring parties to "refrain from any action . . . that may endanger marine life in the region of the Gulf" (UNSC 1983) – one of the few times the Security Council has explicitly exhorted belligerents to consider the environmental effects of military action in a Resolution. Years later, the Security Council also urged Member States to "avoid causing harm to the marine environment" as they inspect vessels to enforce an arms embargo on Libya (UNSC 2016d). In relation to piracy off the coast of Somalia, where some argued that the illegal, unreported, and unregulated (IUU) fishing and the illegal dumping of toxic waste contributed to the emergence of piracy off the Horn of Africa (UNODC 2010), the Security Council stated that "concerns about protection of the marine environment as well as resources should not be allowed to mask the true nature of piracy off the coast of Somalia which is a transnational criminal enterprise driven primarily by the opportunity for financial gain" (UNSC 2012f). Outside of these cases, the main concern with marine resources seems to be development and the possible destabilizing effects of IUU. In all, the Security Council has addressed ocean resources 20 times.[18]

General terms

General terms, such as "natural resources," "commodities," and "sustainable development," appear in 162 Resolutions, although in most cases they are mentioned in conjunction with a specific resource. By themselves, general terms appear in 59 Resolutions.[19] Up until 1994, the general term favored by the Security Council was "commodities," which denoted a host of primary products (including iron and chrome ore) and agricultural products (such as sugar and animal products). The Security Council restricted the import and export of commodities from various countries – including what was then Southern Rhodesia, and from the FFRY, Iraq, and Haiti – in order to coerce the respective governments into altering their policies that were deemed to threaten international peace. Since 1994, the Security Council has eschewed mention of commodities, focusing instead on "natural resources." Another general term increasingly used by the Security Council is "sustainable development," which is widely understood to have an environmental component. The Security Council referred to "sustainable development" or some variant in 21 of its Resolutions (UNSC 1999c; UNSC 2015c).[20]

As with specific resources, the Security Council has made general links between the illicit exploitation of natural resources and the financing of conflict. In the DRC, the Security Council focused on natural resources, and specifically on minerals and due diligence guidelines; it has also provided UN-led peacekeeping missions with general mandates to assist national governments "in restoring proper administration of natural resources" (UNSC 2003c). The Council also passed Resolutions of general applicability, raising the issue of "the link between the illegal exploitation of natural resources, illicit trade in such resources and the proliferation and trafficking of arms as a major factor fuelling and exacerbating many conflicts" (UNSC 2013g).

Natural resources across the conflict lifecycle

The Security Council tends to respond to threats as they emerge. Once a conflict has begun and clear links between natural resources and the conflict are established, the Security Council will often encourage or even require the reform of governance structures and institutions. It will often continue to push for governance reform after the fighting has stopped (Cockayne et al. 2010), in order to ensure that the conflict cannot be reignited through the illicit exploitation of natural resources. This section examines different ways in which the Security Council addresses natural resources during conflict and afterward.

During conflict[21]

Once the Security Council recognizes a threat to international peace and security, halting the fighting becomes the priority. One common strategy is to remove the means with which to conduct armed attacks through arms embargoes. To address the fact that belligerents can be adept at evading arms embargoes, the Security Council has increasingly focused on preventing belligerents from acquiring the means to finance a military campaign, with an emphasis on conflict resources.

Of the 336 Resolutions that mention the environment and natural resources, 182 were passed while a conflict was ongoing – approximately 54 percent of all relevant Resolutions. Of these, 157 relate to civil conflicts, while the remaining 25 relate to interstate fighting, the reason for which can be linked to the nature of financing civil wars.

Sanctions and voluntary measures

The imposition of sanctions under Chapter VII, Article 41 of the UN Charter is the most common way that the Security Council has sought to prevent belligerents from benefiting from the illegal exploitation of natural resources. In 2015, the Security Council published a report on its utilization of sanctions related to natural resources (UNSC 2015d). From 1946 to the end of 1989, only 7 Resolutions addressed natural resource-related sanctions during conflict; since then, the Security Council has adopted 72 such Resolutions (including Resolutions that address existing measures).

The Security Council has also imposed "targeted sanctions," so as to minimize adverse effects on innocent parties.[22] These include measures that are intended to permit the legitimate exploitation and sale of natural resources by authorized groups, such as public authorities under the control of the internationally recognized State government, while choking off a source of rebels' funding. The most obvious example of this is the Security Council's approach to diamonds, the foundations of which were laid in 1998, when it prohibited "the direct or indirect import from Angola . . . of all diamonds . . . not controlled through the Certificate of Origin regime of the Government" (UNSC 1998a). This ad hoc system, as well as ones in Sierra Leone and Liberia, was eventually replaced by the Kimberley Process Certification Scheme (UNSC 2000b).

The Security Council called on Member States to ensure that companies exercise due diligence to address conflict minerals in eastern DRC (UNSC 2009a). More recently, the Security Council has called on "the Ivorian authorities to participate in the OECD-hosted implementation program with regard to the due diligence guidelines for responsible supply chains of minerals from conflict-affected and high-risk areas, with a special attention to gold" (UNSC 2014h). As a consequence of the Council's actions, various States have introduced legislation to ensure that nationally based corporations do not inadvertently introduce conflict minerals into their supply chains.[23] The Security Council's Resolutions explicitly address the link between financing and conflict, and they attempt to break the connection by imposing internationally verifiable governance regimes, while conflict is ongoing.

Sanctions committees and expert panels

Sanctions are not always effective. For instance, in the immediate aftermath of the Rwandan genocide, weapons were still delivered to the country, despite the imposition of an arms embargo (UNSC 1994a). This resulted in the establishment of an International Commission of Inquiry (UNICOI) "to investigate and report on violations of the arms embargo to the Rwanda Sanctions Committee" (Vines 2003:248). However, sanctions committees consist of representatives of the Security Council, with each member nominating a representative (UNSC 2013l). Thus, the same dynamics and considerations that affected decision-making in the Security Council are reflected at the committee level.

In response to these institutional problems, the Security Council and sanctions committees began engaging panels of independent experts. For example, in May 1999, the Security Council authorized the establishment of two panels of experts to investigate "the violation of the measures imposed against UNITA with respect to arms and related matériel, petroleum and petroleum products, diamonds and the movement of UNITA funds" (UNSC 1999b). Now, most sanctions regimes include, together with a sanctions committee, a "panel" or "group" of experts – small groups of civilians with subject-matter expertise, usually field-based – tasked with sanctions monitoring and making recommendations as to how regimes may be strengthened (Farrall 2009).

Panels have been used in innovative ways, including by "investigating the link between the trade in natural resources and the trade in arms that fuel conflict" (Farrall 2009:201). Expert panels are often requested to make recommendations on how to address important issues affecting a given conflict (UNSC 2001a), for example by developing "guidelines for the exercise of due diligence by the importers, processing industries and consumers of mineral products" from the DRC (UNSC 2009c). The Security Council established expert panels in Angola, Sierra Leone, Liberia, the DRC, Côte d'Ivoire, Somalia, Central African Republic, and Libya to monitor and report on the links between natural resources and conflict. Of the 79 Resolutions that include sanctions relating to natural resources, and passed during conflict – during and after the Cold War – 69 contain references to a subsidiary body, such as a sanctions committee, while 44 contain references to expert panels. It should, however, be noted that all references to "expert panels" or "groups of experts" occur after 1999, following the sanctions imposed on diamonds in Angola.

The UN Environment Programme has found that expert panels "have made a major contribution towards understanding how natural resources finance arms and armed groups, how illicit resources are traded both regionally and internationally, and how sanctions have curtailed conflict financing and illegal resource exploitation" (UNEP 2012:54). However, UN peacekeeping missions are rarely required to support the work of expert panels in the context of the environment and natural resources. Such mandates, for example, took place in Liberia, DRC, Côte d'Ivoire, Sudan/South Sudan, and Central African Republic.

Embargoes[24]

The Security Council has also issued embargoes – bans on exports to the subject of the embargo – on natural resources and commodities, usually petroleum and petroleum products, since these quite literally fuel military activities. For example, with regard to UNITA in Angola, the Security Council decided that "States shall prevent the sale or supply, by their nationals or from their territories . . . of petroleum and petroleum products" (UNSC 1993). Similar measures have been applied against Bosnia-Herzegovina, Cambodia, Haiti, and Sierra Leone.[25] Overall, 17 Resolutions have addressed embargoes on natural resources and commodities during conflict.

UN-led peacekeeping[26]

Of the 182 Resolutions relating to the environment and natural resources that were passed during conflict, 73 mention peacekeeping missions, and of these 36 deal with the missions in the DRC: the United Nations Organization Mission in the Democratic Republic of the Congo (MONUC) and the successor mission, the United Nations Organization Stabilization Mission in the Democratic Republic of the Congo (MONUSCO). Moreover, only 57 of the 73 Resolutions contain "operational" provisions that require action by a UN body.

Resolution 1925 mandated that MONUSCO "support the [DRC] Government's efforts and enhance its capabilities . . . to prevent . . . support derived from illicit economic activities and illicit trade in natural resources" (UNSC 2010a). In later Resolutions, the Security Council also called upon MONUSCO to "carry out spot checks and regular visits to mining sites, trade routes and markets, in the vicinity of the five pilot trading counters" (UNSC 2011d). The Security Council has grown more confident in mandating peacekeeping missions to address some of the security problems posed by natural resources,[27] as when it directed the United Nations Operation in Côte d'Ivoire to prevent rough diamonds from being exported (UNSC 2010b). It also recently authorized MONUSCO to "[e]ncourage the consolidation of an effective national civilian structure to control key mining activities and to manage in an equitable manner the extraction and trade of natural resources in eastern DRC" (UNSC 2014f). These examples suggest that where peacekeeping missions encounter active conflict situations, they may be required to address the illicit exploitation of natural resources by using military measures, and by supporting institutional and legal reform of existing governance structures.

UN-sanctioned peacekeeping

In addition to UN-led peacekeeping, the Security Council has authorized regional organizations and multinational coalitions to carry out action under its authority during ongoing conflict, as permitted by Articles 52 and 53 of the UN Charter. It directed such UN-sanctioned peacekeeping missions to explicitly address natural resources in Afghanistan ("addressing the illicit production of and trafficking in drugs") (UNSC 2008b), and in Somalia (preventing the export of charcoal) (UNSC 2013e).

Environmental protection during conflict

There are relatively few Resolutions that explicitly address wartime pollution or spoliation. The first mention of the need to protect the environment during armed conflict was in 1983, when the Security Council asked Iran and Iraq to "[r]efrain from any action that may endanger peace and security as well as marine life in the region of the [Persian] Gulf" (UNSC 1983). Later Resolutions express concern about the targeting of oil installations, pipelines, and other facilities, but the emphasis appears to be on the economic aspects – "the damage to economic infrastructure, in particular oil installations" (UNSC 2012c) – rather than the environmental impacts of targeting oil facilities.[28] A number of Resolutions on Somalia (UNSC 2010c; UNSC 2011b; UNSC 2011f; UNSC 2012f; UNSC 2013j) express concern about illegal fishing and illegal dumping of hazardous waste, stressing the "importance of preventing, in accordance with international law, illegal fishing and illegal dumping, including toxic substances" (UNSC 2010c). This is a different kind of spoliation from targeting the environment for military purposes, especially since the Security Council expressed concern that "allegations of illegal fishing and dumping of toxic waste in Somali waters have been used by pirates in an attempt to justify their criminal activities" (UNSC 2011b).

After conflict

The Security Council has emphasized "the need for coherence between, and integration of, peacekeeping, peacebuilding, and development to achieve an effective response to post-conflict situations" (UNSC 2013f). The challenge the Security Council faces in addressing most contemporary post-conflict situations is that it is not enough to restore the *status quo ante bellum*, but it must instead address the root causes of the conflict and thereby prevent a return to conflict.

Of the 336 Resolutions that mention the environment and natural resources, 122 were passed within ten years from the end of a conflict. Between 1946 and 1989, 76 percent of the Resolutions that mentioned the environment and natural resources were passed during conflict, while 6 percent were passed after conflict. In contrast, between 1990 and 2016, 53 percent of the Resolutions that mentioned the environment and natural resources were passed during conflict, while 38 percent were passed after conflict. Comparing the number of Resolutions in absolute terms passed during the post-conflict stages, before and after the ending of the Cold War, leads to even starker results: only 1 Resolution that mentioned the environment and natural resources was passed after conflict through the end of 1989, while 121 were passed between 1990 and 2016. These results echo research by the International Peace Institute, which suggests that "after the end of the Cold War the Security Council has gradually become much more active in guiding and sustaining peace processes after the end of fighting" (Cockayne et al. 2010:11).

Sanctions and voluntary measures

Sanctions are more commonly associated with active conflicts, since they are measures used to address threats to international peace and security. However, the underlying issue that a sanction regime is intended to address rarely disappears with the signing of a peace accord. This is certainly the case with natural resources, as the poor governance and lack of government control, which so often creates a context in which rebel groups can extract and sell resources to finance their campaign, is unlikely to have improved. The Security Council has recognized this and sought to address it in two ways.

For threats emanating from States under the effective control of a national government, the Security Council has severely restricted the manner in which revenues derived from natural resources can be used until the target State takes the necessary measures. For example, with the Oil-for-Food Programme in Iraq, the Security Council limited use of oil revenues to humanitarian products, such as food and medical supplies (UNSC 1991b).

Second, the Council has required the internationally recognized authorities of a State to reform its governance structures and exert control over resource productive territories. The primary concern here is that the same or similar groups will continue to use natural resources to finance their armed struggle. In Angola, for example, sanctions were maintained for three months after the demobilization of UNITA's armed forces. A secondary purpose is to ensure that the State, as it emerges from conflict, is able to capture important sources of revenue for development and strengthen its governance institutions. This was also the case in Liberia (UNSC 2003b), where sanctions on timber exports remained in place until the Administration of newly elected Ellen Johnson-Sirleaf imposed a moratorium on "timber exports and new timber concessions pending the passage by the Liberian legislature of forestry legislation" among other measures (UNSC 2006c). Similarly, the sanctions imposed on the export of diamonds from Liberia, which began in 2001 (UNSC 2001a), remained in place until 2007 (UNSC 2007c), when the government demonstrated that it had met all requirements of the Kimberley Process Certification Scheme.[29]

In total, the Security Council has passed Resolutions containing sanctions related to natural resources during the post-conflict stage on 61 occasions, the majority of which address Iraq, Liberia, and Côte d'Ivoire.

Sanctions committees and expert panels

The Security Council has used expert panels to identify threats to the peace through the illicit trafficking of natural resources (UNSC 2014h), and to assess and improve governance structures in post-conflict situations (UNSC 2006e; UNSC 2007d; UNSC 2007e). Recognizing the importance of timber, diamonds, and other natural resources in post-conflict peacebuilding in Liberia, the Security Council directed the Liberian Panel of Experts to assess how natural resources are contributing to peace (UNSC 2009b). In later Resolutions, the Panel had "to provide recommendations, if appropriate, on how such natural resources could better contribute to the country's progress towards sustainable peace and stability" (UNSC 2010e; UNSC 2011h; UNSC 2012g). Expert panels have been explicitly mentioned in 44 post-conflict Security Council Resolutions that address the environment and natural resources, but these panels often focus on other issues, such as the arms trade.

UN-led peacekeeping/peacebuilding

Post-conflict peacekeeping measures utilized by the Security Council include assisting national governments to exercise effective control over natural resources and the productive regions in which they are contained, as well as assisting national governments in the development and implementation of institutional and legal reforms affecting natural resource governance.[30] Of the 122 Resolutions relating to the environment and natural resources that have been passed after conflict, 69 refer to peacekeeping missions. Of these, 48 contained operational provisions requiring action by a UN body – greater rates than such Resolutions passed during conflict.

A good example of the Security Council's approach is the United Nations Mission in Sierra Leone (UNAMSIL), which when revised, had "the overall objective of assisting the Government of Sierra Leone to re-establish its authority throughout the country, including the diamond-producing areas" (UNSC 2001b). Later, UNAMSIL was asked to assist the government of Sierra Leone "to accelerate the restoration of civil authority and public services throughout the country, in particular in the diamond mining areas" (UNSC 2002b), and "to support the Sierra Leone armed forces and police in patrolling the border and diamond-mining areas, including through joint planning and joint operations where appropriate" (UNSC 2004b). Similarly, UNMIL was mandated "to assist the transitional government in restoring proper administration of natural resources" (UNSC 2003c) which entailed "helping the Government establish its authority throughout the country, particularly in the diamond and timber-producing regions" (UNSC 2008a). More recently, MINUSCA was mandated to "advise the Transitional Authorities on efforts to keep armed groups from exploiting natural resources" (UNSC 2014g).

The Security Council has also explicitly asked UN peacekeeping missions to support the process of reforming the institutional and legal infrastructures governing natural resources. For example, the Security Council determined that UNMIL's broad mandate to help the transitional government of Liberia restore "proper administration" of natural resources included, "ensuring the effective implementation of the Forestry Reform Law [and] the continuing commitment to the Government and Economic Management Program" (UNSC 2006d).

In a unique case, at least since the end of the trusteeship system, the Security Council authorized a UN-led peacekeeping mission to assume direct control over the administration of Timor-Leste, which included control and reform of natural resources.[31] The mandate for the United Nations Transitional Authority in East Timor (UNTAET) included "establish[ing] an effective administration . . . support[ing] capacity-building for self-government . . . [and] assist[ing] in the establishment of conditions for sustainable development" (UNSC 1999c). Similarly, the Governance and Economic Management Assistance Program (GEMAP) in Liberia, endorsed in Resolution 1647, provided the donor community with the authority "to forcefully intervene to manage assets and expenditures, as well as build the capacity of Liberian government" (Clark 2008:26), though it was distinct from UNMIL.

Environmental impact and assessment

The Security Council has sometimes demanded that parties refrain from causing environmental harm, in both interstate conflict (e.g., Iran/Iraq) and intrastate conflict (e.g., Somalia). However, until recently it had not mandated, or even mentioned, the need for peacekeeping operations to consider the environmental impacts of deployment or action. This changed in 2013, when Resolution 2100 requested the UN Secretary-General to consider the "environmental impacts of the operations of MINUSMA" (UNSC 2013b). Later that year, the Security Council asked the Monitoring Group tasked with overseeing sanctions in Somalia to provide "further detailed information . . . on possible environmentally sound destruction of Somali charcoal" (UNSC 2013e). The implicit requirement that the environmental impact of the disposal of seized charcoal be considered became explicit in 2014, when the Security Council requested "Member States to dispose of any charcoal, weapons or military equipment seized pursuant to paragraph 17, in an environmentally responsible manner" (UNSC 2014q).

The Security Council continued to request consideration of environmental impacts in 2015 and 2016. For example, in 2015, it requested the UN Secretary-General to carry out an "environmental baseline study and regular environmental impact assessments of the operations of UNSOM and UNSOS" (UNSC 2015a). It also urged Member States to "avoid causing harm to the marine environment" as they carry out its instructions related to Libya (UNSC 2015b; UNSC 2016d).

Environmental damage

Few Resolutions address the issue of environmental damage. The primary example is Resolution 687 (UNSC 1991a). Following the end of the 1990–1991 Gulf War, the Security Council created the United Nations Compensation Commission (UNCC) to oversee the review and payment of compensation claims associated with Iraq's invasion of Kuwait (UNSC 1991a). The Security Council determined that under the UN Charter, Iraq was liable *inter alia* for "environmental damage and the depletion of natural resources" (UNSC 1991a). Later Resolutions – 692, 986, 1153, 1483, and 1546 – were indirectly relevant to the issue of environmental damage, but only because they related to the general operation of the UNCC.

Climate change

As effects of climate change are gaining attention, the Security Council has considered the significance of climate change to international peace and security in a number of debates and meetings,
particularly with regard to challenges faced by small island developing states (SIDS) and in the
Sahel region.[32] With regard to SIDS, for example, the Permanent Representative of New Zealand
noted that "sea-level rise and other adverse impacts of climate change . . . represent the gravest of
threats to [SIDS'] survival and viability" and that "Climate change acts as a risk multiplier, making
existing security and development challenges more severe [which] [o]ver time . . . will increase
competition for scarce resources and therefore the potential for armed conflict" (UNSC 2015e).
The Security Council has also begun to mention climate change in its Resolutions, as it did in
Resolution 2242, relating to Women and Peace and Security (UNSC 2015c).

An evaluation of the core dynamics

Resolutions that mention natural resources address some types of resources significantly more
often than others. For example, while hydrocarbons are mentioned 94 times, water (which is
a resource crucial for survival) is only mentioned 8 times. This discrepancy may be attributed
to the core dynamics that characterized the context in which the Security Council passed these
Resolutions. They are: causes of conflict, conflict financing, attempts to pressure repressive
regimes, peacekeeping, conduct of conflict, and recovery after conflict. Due to the inherent differences of various natural resources, some of them had less connection to these core dynamics
that were at play and subsequently received less attention from the Security Council.

With regard to the causes of conflict, the Security Council has acknowledged that petroleum, land, and forestry can become sources of conflict (UNSC 2009b; UNSC 2013e; UNSC
2014k). So far, it has made no such connection to agriculture, water, or other natural resources,
even though it did note in one Resolution that the "global context of peace and security" is
changing, in particular as it relates to climate change (UNSC 2015c). It is likely that the result
would be different, however, if territorial disputes were included in the dataset.

Conflict resources and conflict financing occupy a significant portion of Resolutions relating to natural resources. The Security Council has established a direct link between conflict
financing and hydrocarbons, minerals, forestry, wildlife, narcotics, and, implicitly, agricultural
products.[33] Various armed groups have used these resources to finance their operations, and
the Security Council has sought to restrict trade in conflict resources to end the conflict, often
through sanctions and embargoes (UNSC 2001d; UNSC 2014e; UNSC 2014m). Water, ocean
resources, and land, on the other hand, are not the types of resources that provide substantial
revenues to armed groups.

Another core dynamic has to do with the Security Council's attempts to apply pressure on
repressive regimes. These Resolutions relate to Iraq's invasion of Kuwait and the Oil-for-Food
Programme, as well as embargoes the Security Council imposed on minerals, oil, and agricultural products (UNSC 2013l). Water, land, ocean resources, wildlife, and narcotics are not as
amenable to such pressure.

In contrast to the other dynamics, UN Resolutions addressing peacekeeping operations
refer to a wide range of resources, including minerals, hydrocarbons, land, forestry, narcotics,
wildlife, water, agriculture, and ocean resources.[34] The breadth of resources is due to two key
dynamics. First, Resolutions provide mandates for peacekeeping missions to help countries
manage resources to keep disputes over the resources from precipitating a relapse to conflict (often relating to conflict resources, including minerals, forestry, and narcotics). Second,

Resolutions direct peacekeeping missions to limit their environmental impacts (their "boot-print"), addressing water, land, and other resources.

The Security Council has also addressed all of these types of resources in the context of ongoing conflicts.[35] The Security Council's goals during conflict are wide in range and include preventing illegal armed groups from utilizing conflict resources; encouraging the use of natural resources to stabilize governments and build peace; providing protection for natural resources; and, increasingly, avoiding harm to the environment.

Lastly, Resolutions relating to post-conflict recovery also mention all of these various types of resources. The Security Council has recognized the important part some natural resources, such as oil and minerals, play in generating revenues for economic growth and development of the State, and has sought to protect those natural resources (UNSC 2011c; UNSC 2013d). It has also addressed the role land, forestry, agriculture, minerals, water, ocean resources, and wildlife play in peacebuilding and overall recovery.[36] As evidenced from these Resolutions, state sovereignty and economic development are of particular concern to the Security Council.

Conclusion

The end of the Cold War has had a profound effect on the frequency and diversity of Security Council Resolutions addressing natural resources and the environment. With the end of the Cold War, insurgent groups and proxies could no longer rely on funding from the superpowers and many started relying largely on revenues from minerals, timber, and other natural resources, which led to the proliferation of conflict resources. Once the Security Council recognized the connection between natural resources and conflict financing, it adopted a range of measures to reduce the ability of insurgents to illicitly exploit these resources to finance their campaigns.

In many respects, the Security Council appears to have adopted a similar approach to addressing natural resources during and after conflict: using sanctions, expert panels, and peacekeeper mandates, among other tools. By imposing certain governance systems during conflict, the Security Council has sought to prevent insurgents from benefiting from the illicit exploitation of natural resources, while permitting licensed operators to continue producing and providing the government with a source of sustainable revenue. Similarly, by focusing on these systems after conflict, the Security Council has made it more difficult for non-state armed groups to financially benefit from the illicit exploitation of natural resources, which might otherwise provide the means to restart the conflict.

A diversity of actors – particularly governments and NGOs – have lobbied for (and against) particular environmental measures in Security Council Resolutions. Global Witness has played an important role in raising awareness of the use of conflict resources and lobbying for sanctions regimes. It has been relatively successful in addressing particular conflict resources in specific countries, but struggled to convince the Security Council to adopt a broader regime addressing conflict resources generally (Taylor and Davis 2016). More frequently, Security Council Member States sponsor and lobby for specific provisions. For example, the United States has played a leading role in establishing, sustaining, and ultimately removing natural resource-related sanctions and monitoring measures in Security Council Resolutions addressing Liberia – a country with which the United States enjoys historical connections (UN 2004; UN 2016; UNSC 2016b; Sengupta 2016).

The Security Council's Resolutions reveal that it has continued to expand its approach to the environment and natural resources in recent years. It has expanded the list of conflict resources from minerals and timber to include wildlife and wildlife products. Although it has not explicitly stated that agricultural products are being used to finance conflict, it has placed cocoa, cashew nuts, and cotton in the same category as gold and diamonds, and expressed concern about the role of these resources in the context of the conflict in Côte d'Ivoire.

The Security Council has demonstrated its willingness to entertain arguments linking environmental degradation to the onset of conflict. Although it did not agree that IUU fishing and illegal dumping of toxic waste led to the emergence of piracy off the Horn of Africa, it felt obliged to respond to the assertion.

The Security Council has begun emphasizing the positive role of natural resources in the post-conflict peacebuilding process by, for example, directing the Liberian Panel of Experts to assess the extent to which forestry contributes to peace (UNSC 2009b). The Security Council has granted mandates to a growing number of peacekeeping missions to address natural resource issues important to post-conflict peacebuilding; it also has requested peacekeeping missions such as MINUSMA to consider their environmental impacts (UNSC 2013b; UNSC 2014l).

It is time to stop debating *whether* the Security Council should securitize the environment, and to focus rather on *when* and *how*. Experience from dozens of countries around the world shows that environment is essential to peace and security, with grievances over inequitable land distribution or allocation of oil revenues contributing to the onset of conflict, diverse natural resources being exploited to finance armed conflict, and natural resources and the environment being an important input or other dimension to most post-conflict peacebuilding priorities. Natural resources and the environment have an important role to play across the conflict lifecycle, and ignoring that reality greatly complicates peacebuilding.

After years of debate, there is finally a critical mass of experience that is driving new policy approaches. The inclusion of peace in the 2015–2030 Sustainable Development Goals was an important complement to the numerous Security Council Resolutions; it was also a major step for UN agencies in recognizing that sustainable development depends on a peaceful society, further blurring the line between the General Assembly and the Security Council.

This is not to say that the concerns about securitization are without merit. Further consideration is warranted to determine under what circumstances and how natural resources and the environment should be treated as a matter of international security. With years of experience, hindsight, and more than 300 Security Council Resolutions on the topic, there is a good foundation for starting to address these issues in an informed manner.

Notes

1 The authors are grateful to Jonathan Cohen, Bethany Pereira, Sangmin Shim, and Supriya Kanal for their research assistance.
2 As discussed below, a number of earlier UNSC Resolutions addressed natural resources in different contexts, but the link to conflict was not as explicit.
3 These Resolutions applied to the following states: Afghanistan, Angola, Burundi, Cambodia, Central African Republic, Côte d'Ivoire, Democratic People's Republic of Korea, Democratic Republic of the Congo, El Salvador, Eritrea, Former Federal Republic of Yugoslavia, Great Lakes (Central Africa), Guinea-Bissau, Haiti, Iran–Iraq, Iraq, Iraq–Kuwait, Israel/Occupied Territories, Liberia, Libya, Mali, Pacific islands previously under Japanese control, Sierra Leone, Somalia, Southern Rhodesia/Zimbabwe, Sudan/Abyei, Sudan/Darfur, Sudan/South Sudan, Syria, Syria/Iraq, Timor-Leste, and Yemen. Some Resolutions were also of general applicability.
4 This was further bolstered by the protection provided by the Charter, which codified the principle of collective self-defense under Article 51. This provided that Member States may assist another Member State when it has been subject to an illegal act of aggression. Would-be belligerents, it was supposed, would therefore be deterred from perpetrating acts of aggression.

5 Talking of Anastasio Somoza, the authoritarian leader of Nicaragua in 1939, President Franklin Delano Roosevelt is alleged to have said, "Somoza may be a son of a bitch, but he's our son of a bitch" (Cavendish 2011).

6 There is also a question of whether protracted civil conflicts are more difficult to resolve and therefore require greater and more prolonged engagement.

7 Global Witness has proposed the following definition: "natural resources whose systematic exploitation and trade in a context of conflict contribute to, benefit from or result in the commission of serious violations of human rights, violations of international humanitarian law or violations amounting to crimes under international law" (Global Witness 2006).

8 These include: 3 related to Angola, 1 Former Federal Republic of Yugoslavia, 1 Haiti, 1 Sierra Leone, 45 Iraq, 9 Libya, 3 Somalia, 2 Southern Rhodesia/Zimbabwe, 7 Sudan/Abyei, 13 Sudan/South Sudan, 1 Syria/Iraq, 2 Yemen, 4 Threats to International Peace and Security, 1 Cambodia, and 1 Non-Proliferation. Of the 94 Resolutions, 80 were associated with countries considered to be within the Middle East and North Africa (MENA), 6 in Sub-Saharan Africa, 1 in Europe, 1 in the Caribbean, 1 in Southeast Asia, and 5 were of general applicability.

9 These include: 1 in Afghanistan, 6 Angola, 2 Cambodia, 6 Central African Republic, 12 Côte d'Ivoire, 16 DRC, 1 Eritrea, 1 Former Federal Republic of Yugoslavia, 21 Liberia, 15 Sierra Leone, 2 Democratic People's Republic of Korea, 5 Southern Rhodesia/Zimbabwe, and 5 of general application. Of the 93 Resolutions, 81 focused on countries in Sub-Saharan Africa, 2 in South East Asia, 2 in Northeast Asia, 1 in Central Asia, 1 in MENA, 1 in Europe, and 5 applied generally.

    Coverage includes diverse provisions mentioning minerals, mineral products, mineral resources, iron ore, chrome, copper, asbestos, cassiterite, coltan, wolframite, gems, semi-precious stones, diamonds, rough diamonds, diamond mining, diamond mining activities, diamond production, diamond producing areas, diamond fields, diamond industry, diamond trade, rough diamond smuggling, illicit diamond trade, conflict diamonds, the Kimberley Process Certification Scheme, gold, precious metals, and gold sector. In addition, the dataset includes two Resolutions that mentioned "extractive industries" or "extractive sectors" in geographic areas known for mineral extraction.

10 The Security Council has recognized diamonds as an important source of financing for rebel groups in Cambodia, Angola, Sierra Leone, Liberia, Côte d'Ivoire, and the Democratic Republic of Congo, and has mentioned them in relation to Afghanistan.

11 This includes mention of timber, timber products, round logs, logs, and charcoal.

12 This includes mention of biodiversity, wildlife, trafficking, poaching, wildlife products, and natural heritage. Of the 16 Resolutions, 7 were in reference to Central African Republic, 3 Liberia, 3 DRC, and 3 Threats to International Peace and Security. All but three of the Resolutions focus on Sub-Saharan African countries.

13 The dataset for this chapter does not include territorial disputes between States. Still, there is clearly an argument that Resolutions addressing the issue could be included, as "the possession of land means access to many other resources, such as minerals, timber, and animals" (USIP 2007:5) and is essential for nearly all types of agricultural activities. Territories or lands, are, in this sense, foundational for other natural resources. If territorial disputes were included in the dataset, a further 96 Resolutions could be included – increasing the number of Resolutions to 432. These include Resolutions that address the India–Pakistan dispute over Kashmir; the UK–Argentina dispute over the Falklands/Malvinas; the question of Western Sahara; Iraq's invasion of Kuwait; the break-up of the Former Federal Republic of Yugoslavia; boundary disputes between Eritrea and Ethiopia, and Eritrea and Djibouti; the status of the Occupied Territories under Israel; and the boundary dispute between the Republic of the Sudan and the Republic of South Sudan, among others.

    The dataset for this chapter also does not include Resolutions that only implicitly refer to natural resources or the environment. For example, Resolutions that extend, end, or just refer to sanctions related to natural resources but do not explicitly mention natural resources in the text of the Resolution, such as Resolution 1395, are not included in the dataset (UNSC 2002a).

14 The 32 Resolutions include those mentioning land ownership, land grievances, land disputes, land rights, land tenure, tenure rights, land title, land reform, public land, property, property rights, property title, and property ownership. Of the 32 Resolutions referring to land and real property, 1 relates to Burundi, 3 to Côte d'Ivoire, 1 to El Salvador, 1 to FFRY, 6 to Israel/Occupied Territories, 14 to Liberia, 1 to Sierra Leone, 2 to Timor-Leste, 2 to Sudan/South Sudan, and 1 to Women and Peace and Security. By region, this breaks down as, 17 in Sub-Saharan Africa, 10 in the Middle East and North Africa, 2 in South East Asia, 1 in Latin America, 1 in Europe, and 1 with general applicability.

15 The 9 Resolutions include mention of meat and meat products, leather, cocoa, cashew nuts, cotton, and agriculture generally. These include 1 Resolution on Côte d'Ivoire, 1 on Guinea-Bissau, 1 on Libya, 1 on Pacific Islands, 1 on Southern Rhodesia/Zimbabwe, 2 on Timor-Leste, 1 on Somalia, and 1 on Democratic People's Republic of Korea.

16 These Resolutions mention drug production, illicit production, opium cultivation, poppy crop, and poppy production. It should be noted that Resolutions dealing solely with drug trafficking have not been included, as it is the cultivation and processing of the raw materials (such as poppies, coca, marijuana) that brings narcotics production into the category of a "natural resource."

17 This includes mention of water, water resources, sanitation, water, and sanitation supplies.

18 Of the 20 Resolutions mentioning fisheries, illegal fishing, marine life, and offshore natural resources, 5 apply to Guinea-Bissau, 1 to Iran–Iraq, 11 to Somalia, 1 to Libya, 1 to Pacific Islands Previously under Japanese Control, and 1 to Maintenance of International Peace and Security.

19 Some Resolutions, which contain potentially relevant terms, have not been included in the dataset and results because they are not explicitly tied to natural resources. These include Resolutions 283 and 301, which relate to Namibia and the Security Council's call for the imposition of voluntary measures relating to "concessions" and "economic relations."

20 Of these Resolutions, 14 contain the term "sustainable development," and the remaining 7 Resolutions mention related terms, such as "sustainable exploitation of natural resources," "environmentally sustainable business practices," "sustainable growth," "sustainable peace and security," and "sustainable solutions." Of the 21 Resolutions referring to sustainable development, 2 apply to Afghanistan, 1 to Cambodia, 2 to the Democratic Republic of Congo, 2 to Guinea-Bissau, 1 to Haiti, 2 to Iraq, 3 to Liberia, 1 to Sudan/South Sudan, 2 to Timor-Leste, and 5 are of general applicability.

21 For purposes of determining at what stage of the conflict lifecycle a Resolution was passed, the UCDP/PRIO Armed Conflict Dataset of Uppsala University was used (www.pcr.uu.se/research/ucdp/datasets/ucdp_prio_armed_conflict_dataset/) for Resolutions passed from 1946 through 2014. Resolutions passed in 2015 and 2016 were analyzed on a case-by-case basis to determine whether the conflict was ongoing or whether the fighting had stopped.

22 The most common actions include severance of diplomatic relations, travel bans, asset freezes, arms embargoes, and commodity interdiction. See UNSC (2013l).

23 Examples include Section 1502 of the 2010 Wall Street Reform and Consumer Protection Act, better known as the Dodd–Frank Act; draft EU legislation; and proposed legislation in Canada (which was rejected by Parliament).

24 For the purposes of the research and the chapter, only Resolutions that explicitly prohibit or limit the export of a natural resource (such as oil, minerals, or timber) from the State which is the subject of the Resolution to other Member States are included in this category. Resolutions that impose embargoes on various commodities, but do not explicitly mention the terms "commodities" or "natural resources," or name natural resources affected by the embargoes, such as Resolution 970, for example, are not included in the dataset (UNSC 1995). Embargoes preventing the importation of a natural resource, such as oil, into a Subject State are dealt with separately. Other types of sanctions, such as travel bans, asset freezes or seizures, or arms embargoes, have not been included.

25 As with sanctions, for the purpose of the study only mandatory embargoes have been included in the "Sanctions" category.

26 Peacekeeping is understood to be the means through which an established peace is maintained, and usually includes the implementation of measures agreed upon by the warring factions. For the purposes of the chapter, and for recording statistical data, peacekeeping operations are those that have been and are "conducted under the direction of the United Nations Secretary-General, and planned, managed, directed and supported by the United Nations Department of Peacekeeping Operations (DPKO) and the Department of Field Support (DFS)" (UN 2008:8). The United Nations deploys a variety of missions. For the purposes of the research and chapter, a mission has been categorized as "UN Led Peacekeeping" if it meets the above criteria and is authorized and has the capacity to use force in self-defense or defense of a mission's mandate (UN n.d.).

27 In some cases, the Security Council has directed peacekeeping missions to help implement a peace agreement, and a growing number of peace agreements contain natural resource-related provisions. This is the case with Resolutions 1590 and 1870, and Resolution 1769, which deal with the conflict between Sudan and South Sudan, and South Sudan and Darfur, respectively. They have not been included in this dataset, as we have focused upon explicit references to the environment and natural resources, in order to draw categories as clearly as possible.

28 Sudan/South Sudan/Abyei: Resolutions 2046, 2075, 2126, 2155, 2156, 2178; Middle East: Resolution 2051; Yemen: Resolution 2140 (UNSC 2012c; UNSC 2012e; UNSC 2013i; UNSC 2014i; UNSC 2014j; UNSC 2014o; UNSC 2012d; UNSC 2014d).

29 Another example is Côte d'Ivoire, which had sanctions imposed upon diamond exports in 2005, after fighting between the Gbagbo government and northern groups had ceased. The sanctions were lifted in 2013, once the Kimberley Process "recognized that Côte d'Ivoire fulfilled KP Certification Scheme minimum requirements" (UNSC 2014h).

30 It should be noted that although natural resources and UN peacekeeping are often mentioned within the same Resolution, it is not always the case that missions have a mandate to address environmental and natural resources issues.

31 The United Nations Transitional Authority in East Timor (UNTAET) was "endowed with overall responsibility for the administration of East Timor and ... empowered to exercise all legislative and executive authority, including the administration of justice" (UNSC 1999c).

32 See, e.g., UNSC 2007a; UNSC 2007b; UNSC 2011i; UNSC 2015e; UNSC 2015f; UNSC 2016c. See also Warren (2015).

33 See UNSC 1992b; UNSC 1998a; UNSC 1998b; UNSC 2000a; UNSC 2000b; UNSC 2001a; UNSC 2001c; UNSC 2003b; UNSC 2005; UNSC 2006a; UNSC 2006b; UNSC 2012a; UNSC 2012b; UNSC 2013c; UNSC 2014a.

34 See, e.g., UNSC 2008b; UNSC 2011d; UNSC 2013e.

35 See UNSC 1958; UNSC 1980; UNSC 1983; UNSC 1992b; UNSC 1994b; UNSC 1998a; UNSC 1999a; UNSC 1999b; UNSC 2011e; UNSC 2016d.

36 See UNSC 1994c; UNSC 2004a; UNSC 2006c; UNSC 2006e; UNSC 2007e; UNSC 2008a; UNSC 2008c; UNSC 2011a; UNSC 2013c; UNSC 2014k; UNSC 2014p; UNSC 2016a.

References

Altman, S. L., Nichols, S. S. and Woods, J. T. (2012) "Leveraging High-Value Natural Resources to Restore the Rule of Law: The Role of the Liberia Forest Initiative in Liberia's Transition to Sustainability" in Lujala, P. and Rustad, S. A. (eds.) *High-Value Natural Resources and Post-Conflict Peacebuilding* Routledge, London.

Auty, R. (1994) "Industrial Policy Reform in Six Large Newly Industrializing Countries: The Resource Curse Thesis" *World Development* 22 (1):11–26.

Brunnschweiler, C. N., and Bultey, E. H. (2009) "Natural Resources and Violent Conflict: Resource Abundance, Dependence, and the Onset of Civil Wars" *Oxford Economic Papers* 61:651–674.

Buzan, B., Ole, W. and de Wilde, J. H. (1995) Environmental, Economic and Societal Security. *Working Papers, No. 10* Centre for Peace and Conflict Research, Copenhagen.

Cavendish, R. (2011) "General Somoza Takes Over Nicaragua" *History Today* 61 (6). Available at: www. historytoday.com/richard-cavendish/general-somoza-takes-over-nicaragua#sthash.E7TgA10V.dpuf

Clark, M. A. (2008) "Combating Corruption in Liberia: Assessing the Impact of the Governance and Economic Management Assistance Program (GEMAP)" *Journal of Development and Social Transformation* 5:25–32. Available at: www1.maxwell.syr.edu/uploadedFiles/moynihan/dst/Clark.pdf?n=5122

Cockayne, J., Mikulaschek, C. and Perry, C. (2010) *The United Nations Security Council and Civil War: First Insights from a New Dataset.* International Peace Institute, New York.

Collier, P. and Hoeffler, A. (2004) "Greed and Grievance in Civil War" *Oxford Economic Papers* 56 (4):563–595.

Conca, K. (2015) *An Unfinished Foundation: The United Nations and Global Environmental Governance.* Oxford University Press, Oxford.

Cornell, S. E. (2005) "The Interaction of Narcotics and Conflict" *Journal of Peace Research* 42 (6):751–760.

Deudney, D. (2015) "The Case against Linking Environmental Degradation and National Security" in Conca, K. and Dabelko, G. (eds.) *Green Planet Blues: Critical Perspectives on Global Environmental Politics* Westview Press, Boulder, CO.

The Economist (2013) "Inner Turmoil: The 100 Deadliest Civil Wars and Armed Conflicts since the Second World War" *The Economist*, November 9. Available at: www.economist.com/content/inner-turmoil

Enuka, C. (2012) "Post-Cold War Conflicts: Imperative for Armed Humanitarian Intervention" *Global Journal of Human Social Science Interdisciplinary* 12 (9):17–26.

Farrall, J. (2009) "Should the United Nations Security Council Leave it to the Experts? The Governance and Accountability of UN Sanctions Monitoring" in Farrall, J. and Rubenstein, K. (eds.) *Sanctions, Accountability, and Governance in a Globalised World* Cambridge University Press, Cambridge.

Fearon, J. D. and Laitin, D. D. (2003) "Ethnicity, Insurgency, and Civil War" *American Political Science Review* 97 (1):75–90.

Felbab-Brown, V. (2005) "The Coca Connection: Conflict and Drugs in Colombia and Peru" *Journal of Conflict Studies* 25 (2):104–128.

Floyd, R. and Matthew, R. A. (2013) "Environmental Security Studies: An Introduction" in Floyd, R. and Matthew, R. A. (eds.) *Environmental Security: Approaches and Issues* Routledge, London.

Garrett, N. and Piccinni, A. (2012) *Natural Resources and Conflict: A New Security Challenge for the European Union* Stockholm International Peace Research Institute, Stockholm, Sweden.

Global Witness (2006) *The Sinews of War: Eliminating the Trade in Conflict Resources* Global Witness. Available at: www.globalwitness.org/en/archive/sinews-war

Global Witness (2007) *Hot Chocolate: How Cocoa Fuelled the Conflict in Côte d'Ivoire* Global Witness. Available at: www.globalwitness.org/archive/hot-chocolate-how-cocoa-fuelled-conflict-cte-divoire/

Global Witness (2010) *Lessons UNlearned: How the UN and Member States Must Do More to End Natural Resource-Fuelled Conflicts* Global Witness. Available at: www.globalwitness.org/en/reports/lessons-unlearned/

Græger, N. (1996) "Environmental Security?" *Journal of Peace Research* 33 (1):109–116.

Kaye, M. (2015) "Indonesia Sinks 41 Foreign Vessels in a Single Day to Counter Illegal Fishing" *Mongabay*, May 21. Available at: http://news.mongabay.com/2015/05/indonesia-sinks-41-foreign-vessels-in-a-single-day-to-counter-illegal-fishing/

Le Billon, P. (2005) *Fuelling War: Natural Resources and Armed Conflict,* Adelphi Paper No. 357 International Institute for Strategic Studies, London.

Lujala, P. (2009) "Deadly Combat over Natural Resources: Gems, Petroleum, Drugs, and the Severity of Armed Civil Conflict" *Journal of Conflict Resolution* 53 (1):50–71.

Lujala, P. and Rustad, S. A. (2012) "High-Value Natural Resources: A Blessing or a Curse for Peace?" in Lujala, P. and Rustad, S. A. (eds.) *High-Value Natural Resources and Post-Conflict Peacebuilding* Routledge, London.

Malaquias, A. (2001) "Diamonds Are a Guerilla's Best Friend: The Impact of Illicit Wealth on Insurgency Strategy" *Third World Quarterly* 22 (3):311–325.

Matheson, M. J. (2006) *Council Unbound: The Growth of UN Decision Making on Conflict and Postconflict Issues after the Cold War* United States Institute of Peace Press, Washington, DC.

Mearsheimer, J. (1990a) "Back to the Future: Instability in Europe after the Cold War" *International Security* 15 (1):5–56.

Mearsheimer, J. (1990b) "Why We Will Soon Miss the Cold War" *Atlantic Monthly* 266 (2):35–50.

Paes, W.-C. (2009) "From Failure to Success: The Impact of Sanctions on Angola's Civil War" in Brozska, M. and Lopez, G. A. (eds.) *Putting Teeth in the Tiger: Improving the Effectiveness of Arms Embargoes* Emerald, Bingley.

Pilbeam, B. (2015) "The United Nations and the Responsibility to Protect" in Hough, P., Malik, S., Moran, A. and Pilbeam, B. (eds.) *International Security Studies: Theory and Practice*, Routledge, London.

Rao, P. (2013) "Elephants are the Latest Conflict Resource" *Africa Renewal*. Available at: www.un.org/africarenewal/magazine/december-2013/elephants-are-latest-conflict-resource

Ross, M. (2003) "The Natural Resource Curse: How Wealth Can Make You Poor" in Bannon, I. and Collier, P. (eds.) *Natural Resources and Violent Conflict: Opinions and Actions*, International Bank for Reconstruction and Development/The World Bank, Washington, DC. Available at: www-wds.worldbank.org/servlet/WDSContentServer/WDSP/IB/2004/05/24/000012009_20040524154222/Rendered/PDF/282450Natural0resources0violent0conflict.pdf

Ross, M. (2004) "What Do We Know about Natural Resources and Civil War?" *Journal of Peace Research* 41 (3):337–356.

Rustad, S. C. A., Rød, J. K., Larsen, W. and Gleditsch, N. P. (2008) "Foliage and Fighting: Forest Resources and the Onset, Duration, and Location of Civil War" *Political Geography* 27 (7):761–782.

Sengupta, S. (2016) "Last Liberia Sanctions, Vestige of Civil War, Are Lifted" *New York Times*, May 25. Available at: www.nytimes.com/2016/05/26/world/last-liberia-sanctions-vestige-of-civil-war-are-lifted.html?_r=0

Sotiropoulou, A. (2004) *The Role of Ethnicity in Ethnic Conflicts: The Case of Yugoslavia* Hellenic Foundation for European and Foreign Policy (ELIAMEP), Athens. Available at: www.isn.ethz.ch/Digital-Library/Publications/Detail/?ots591=0c54e3b3-1e9c-be1e-2c24-a6a8c7060233&lng=en&id=26506

Taureck, R. (2006) "Securitization Theory and Securitization Studies" *Journal of International Relations and Development* 9:53–61.

Taylor, M. B., and Davis, M. (2016) "Taking the Guns out of Extraction: UN Responses to the Role of Natural Resources in Conflicts" in Bruch, C., Muffett, C. and Nichols, S. S. (eds.) *Governance, Natural Resources, and Post-Conflict Peacebuilding* Routledge, London.

United Nations (UN) (1945) Charter of the United Nations.

United Nations (UN) (2004) Security Council Renews Liberia Sanctions on Arms, Travel, Timber, Diamonds, Unanimously Adopting Resolution 1579 (2004). Press Release. December 21. Available at: www.un.org/press/en/2004/sc8275.doc.htm

United Nations (UN) (2008) United Nations Peacekeeping Operations Principles and Guidelines.

United Nations (UN) (2016) Security Council Terminates Sanctions Regime on Liberia, Unanimously Adopting Resolution 2288. Meetings Coverage. May 25. Available at: www.un.org/press/en/2016/sc12373.doc.htm

United Nations (UN) (n.d.) "What Is Peacekeeping?" Available at: www.un.org/en/peacekeeping/operations/peacekeeping.shtml

United Nations Environment Programme (UNEP) (2009) *From Conflict to Peacebuilding: The Role of Natural Resources and the Environment* UNEP, Nairobi. Available at: www.unep.org/pdf/pcdmb_policy_01.pdf

United Nations Environment Programme (UNEP) (2012) *Greening the Blue Helmets: Environment, Natural Resources and UN Peacekeeping Operations* UNEP, Nairobi. Available at: www.un.org/en/peacekeeping/publications/UNEP_greening_blue_helmets.pdf

United Nations Office on Drugs and Crime (UNODC) (2010) *The Globalization of Crime: A Transnational Organized Crime Threat Assessment*. Available at: www.unodc.org/documents/data-and-analysis/tocta/TOCTA_Report_2010_low_res.pdf

United Nations Office on Drugs and Crime (UNODC) (2012) *World Drug Report*. Available at: www.unodc.org/documents/data-and-analysis/WDR2012/WDR_2012_web_small.pdf

Unruh, J. and Williams, R. C. (2013a) "Land: A Foundation for Peacebuilding" in Unruh, J. and Williams, R. C. (eds.) *Land and Post-Conflict Peacebuilding* Routledge, London.

Unruh, J. and Williams, R. C. (2013b) "Lessons Learned in Land Tenure and Natural Resource Management in Post-Conflict Societies" in Unruh, J. and Williams, R. C. (eds.) *Land and Post-Conflict Peacebuilding* Routledge, London.

United Nations Security Council (UNSC) (1947) Resolution 21 S/RES/21 (1947). April 2, New York.

United Nations Security Council (UNSC) (1958) Resolution 127. S/RES/127 (1958). January 22, New York.

United Nations Security Council (UNSC) (1973) Resolution 330 S/RES/330 (1973). March 21, New York.

United Nations Security Council (UNSC) (1980) Resolution 465. S/RES/465 (1980). March 1, New York.

United Nations Security Council (UNSC) (1983) Resolution 540. S/RES/540 (1983). October 31, New York.

United Nations Security Council (UNSC) (1991a) Resolution 687. S/RES/687 (1991). April 3, New York.

United Nations Security Council (UNSC) (1991b) Resolution 706. S/RES/706 (1991). August 15, New York.

United Nations Security Council (UNSC) (1992a) Resolution 787. S/RES/787 (1992). November 16, New York.

United Nations Security Council (UNSC) (1992b) Resolution 792. S/RES/792 (1992). November 30, New York.

United Nations Security Council (UNSC) (1993) Resolution 864. S/RES/864 (1993). September 15, New York.

United Nations Security Council (UNSC) (1994a) Resolution 918. S/RES/918 (1994). May 17, New York.

United Nations Security Council (UNSC) (1994b) Resolution 941. S/RES/941 (1994). September 23, New York.

United Nations Security Council (UNSC) (1994c) Resolution 920. S/RES/920 (1994). May 26, New York.

United Nations Security Council (UNSC) (1995) Resolution 970. S/RES/970 (1995). January 12, New York.

United Nations Security Council (UNSC) (1998a) Resolution 1173. S/RES/1173 (1998). June 12, New York.

United Nations Security Council (UNSC) (1998b) Resolution 1214. S/RES/1214 (1998). December 8, New York.

United Nations Security Council (UNSC) (1999a) Resolution 1233. S/RES/1233 (1999). April 6, New York.

United Nations Security Council (UNSC) (1999b) Resolution 1237. S/RES/1237 (1999). May 7, New York.

United Nations Security Council (UNSC) (1999c) Resolution 1272. S/RES/1272 (1999). October 25, New York.

United Nations Security Council (UNSC) (2000a) Resolution 1304. S/RES/1304 (2000). June 16, New York.

United Nations Security Council (UNSC) (2000b) Resolution 1306. S/RES/1306 (2000). July 5, New York.

United Nations Security Council (UNSC) (2001a) Resolution 1343. S/RES/1343 (2001). March 7, New York.

United Nations Security Council (UNSC) (2001b) Resolution 1346. S/RES/1346 (2001). March 30, New York.

United Nations Security Council (UNSC) (2001c) Resolution 1355. S/RES/1355 (2001). June 15, New York.

United Nations Security Council (UNSC) (2001d) Resolution 1376. S/RES/1376 (2001). November 9, New York.

United Nations Security Council (UNSC) (2002a) Resolution 1395. S/RES/1395 (2002). February 27, New York.

United Nations Security Council (UNSC) (2002b) Resolution 1400. S/RES/1400 (2002). March 28, New York.

United Nations Security Council (UNSC) (2003a) Resolution 1459. S/RES/1459 (2003). January 28, New York.

United Nations Security Council (UNSC) (2003b) Resolution 1478. S/RES/1478 (2003). May 6, New York.

United Nations Security Council (UNSC) (2003c) Resolution 1509. S/RES/1509 (2003). September 19, New York.

United Nations Security Council (UNSC) (2004a) Resolution 1549. S/RES/1549 (2004). June 17, New York.

United Nations Security Council (UNSC) (2004b) Resolution 1562. S/RES/1562 (2004). September 17, New York.

United Nations Security Council (UNSC) (2005) Resolution 1643. S/RES/1643 (2005). December 15, New York.

United Nations Security Council (UNSC) (2006a) Resolution 1653. S/RES/1653 (2006). January 27, New York.

United Nations Security Council (UNSC) (2006b) Resolution 1659. S/RES/1659 (2006). February 15, New York.

United Nations Security Council (UNSC) (2006c) Resolution 1689. S/RES/1689 (2006). June 20, New York.

United Nations Security Council (UNSC) (2006d) Resolution 1712. S/RES/1712 (2006). September 29, New York.

United Nations Security Council (UNSC) (2006e) Resolution 1731. S/RES/1731 (2006). December 20, New York.

United Nations Security Council (UNSC) (2007a) 5663rd Meeting. S/PV.5663. April 17, New York.

United Nations Security Council (UNSC) (2007b) 5663rd Meeting (Resumption). S/PV.5663 (Resumption 1). April 17, New York.

United Nations Security Council (UNSC) (2007c) Resolution 1753. S/RES/1753 (2007). April 27, New York.

United Nations Security Council (UNSC) (2007d) Resolution 1760. S/RES/1760 (2007). June 20, New York.

United Nations Security Council (UNSC) (2007e) Resolution 1792. S/RES/1792 (2007). December 19, New York.

United Nations Security Council (UNSC) (2008a) Resolution 1819. S/RES/1819 (2008). June 18, New York.

United Nations Security Council (UNSC) (2008b) Resolution 1833. S/RES/1833 (2008). September 22, New York.

United Nations Security Council (UNSC) (2008c) Resolution 1854. S/RES/1854 (2008). December 19, New York.

United Nations Security Council (UNSC) (2008d) Resolution 1857. S/RES/1857 (2008). December 22, New York.

United Nations Security Council (UNSC) (2009a) Resolution 1896. S/RES/1896 (2009). November 30, New York.

United Nations Security Council (UNSC) (2009b) Resolution 1903. S/RES/1903 (2009). December 17, New York.

United Nations Security Council (UNSC) (2009c) Resolution 1986. S/RES/1896 (2009). November 30, New York.

United Nations Security Council (UNSC) (2010a) Resolution 1925. S/RES/1925 (2010). May 28, New York.

United Nations Security Council (UNSC) (2010b) Resolution 1946. S/RES/1946 (2010). October 15, New York.

United Nations Security Council (UNSC) (2010c) Resolution 1950. S/RES/1950 (2010). November 23, New York.

United Nations Security Council (UNSC) (2010d) Resolution 1952. S/RES/1952 (2010). November 29, New York.

United Nations Security Council (UNSC) (2010e) Resolution 1961. S/RES/1961 (2010). December 17, New York.

United Nations Security Council (UNSC) (2011a) Resolution 1969. S/RES/1969 (2011). February 23, New York.

United Nations Security Council (UNSC) (2011b) Resolution 1976. S/RES/1976 (2011). April 11, New York.

United Nations Security Council (UNSC) (2011c) Resolution 1990. S/RES/1990 (2011). June 27, New York.

United Nations Security Council (UNSC) (2011d) Resolution 1991. S/RES/1991 (2011). June 28, New York.

United Nations Security Council (UNSC) (2011e) Resolution 2003. S/RES/2003 (2011). July 29, New York.

United Nations Security Council (UNSC) (2011f) Resolution 2020. S/RES/2020 (2011). November 22, New York.

United Nations Security Council (UNSC) (2011g) Resolution 2023. S/RES/2023 (2011). December 5, New York.

United Nations Security Council (UNSC) (2011h) Resolution 2025. S/RES/2025 (2011). December 14, New York.

United Nations Security Council (UNSC) (2011i) Statement by the President of the Security Council. S/PRST/2011/15. July 20, New York.

United Nations Security Council (UNSC) (2012a) Resolution 2036. S/RES/2036 (2012). February 22, New York.

United Nations Security Council (UNSC) (2012b) Resolution 2041. S/RES/2041 (2012). March 22, New York.

United Nations Security Council (UNSC) (2012c) Resolution 2046. S/RES/2046 (2012). May 2, New York.

United Nations Security Council (UNSC) (2012d) Resolution 2051. S/RES/2051 (2012). June 12, New York.

United Nations Security Council (UNSC) (2012e) Resolution 2075. S/RES/2075 (2012). November 16, New York.

United Nations Security Council (UNSC) (2012f) Resolution 2077. S/RES/2077 (2012). November 21, New York.

United Nations Security Council (UNSC) (2012g) Resolution 2079. S/RES/2079 (2012). December 12, New York.

United Nations Security Council (UNSC) (2012h) Resolution 2083. S/RES/2083 (2012). December 17, New York.

United Nations Security Council (UNSC) (2013a) Resolution 2097. S/RES/2097 (2013). March 26, New York.

United Nations Security Council (UNSC) (2013b) Resolution 2100. S/RES/2100 (2013). April 25, New York.

United Nations Security Council (UNSC) (2013c) Resolution 2101. S/RES/2101 (2013). April 25, New York.

United Nations Security Council (UNSC) (2013d) Resolution 2109. S/RES/2109 (2013). July 11, New York.

United Nations Security Council (UNSC) (2013e) Resolution 2111. S/RES/2111 (2013). July 24, New York.

United Nations Security Council (UNSC) (2013f) Resolution 2116. S/RES/2116 (2013). September 18, New York.

United Nations Security Council (UNSC) (2013g) Resolution 2117. S/RES/2117 (2013). September 26, New York.

United Nations Security Council (UNSC) (2013h) Resolution 2121. S/RES/2121 (2013). October 10, New York.

United Nations Security Council (UNSC) (2013i) Resolution 2126. S/RES/2126 (2013). November 25, New York.

United Nations Security Council (UNSC) (2013j) Resolution 2127. S/RES/2127 (2013). December 5, New York.

United Nations Security Council (UNSC) (2013k) Resolution 2128. S/RES/2128 (2013). December 10, New York.

United Nations Security Council (UNSC) (2013l) *Special Research Report on UN Sanctions*. Available at: www.securitycouncilreport.org/atf/cf/%7B65BFCF9B-6D27-4E9C-8CD3-CF6E4FF96FF9%7D/special_research_report_sanctions_2013.pdf

United Nations Security Council (UNSC) (2014a) Resolution 2134. S/RES/2134 (2014). January 28, New York.

United Nations Security Council (UNSC) (2014b) Resolution 2136. S/RES/2136 (2014). January 30, New York.

United Nations Security Council (UNSC) (2014c) Resolution 2137. S/RES/2137 (2014). February 13, New York.

United Nations Security Council (UNSC) (2014d) Resolution 2140. S/RES/2140 (2014). February 26, New York.

United Nations Security Council (UNSC) (2014e) Resolution 2146. S/RES/2146 (2014). March 19, New York.

United Nations Security Council (UNSC) (2014f) Resolution 2147. S/RES/2147 (2014). March 28, New York.

United Nations Security Council (UNSC) (2014g) Resolution 2149. S/RES/2149 (2014). April 10, New York.

United Nations Security Council (UNSC) (2014h) Resolution 2153. S/RES/2153 (2014). April 29, New York.

United Nations Security Council (UNSC) (2014i) Resolution 2155. S/RES/2155 (2014). May 27, New York.

United Nations Security Council (UNSC) (2014j) Resolution 2156. S/RES/2156 (2014). May 29, New York.

United Nations Security Council (UNSC) (2014k) Resolution 2162. S/RES/2162 (2014). June 25, New York.

United Nations Security Council (UNSC) (2014l) Resolution 2164. S/RES/2164 (2014). June 25, New York.

United Nations Security Council (UNSC) (2014m) Resolution 2170. S/RES/2170 (2014). August 15, New York.

United Nations Security Council (UNSC) (2014n) Resolution 2174. S/RES/2174 (2014). August 27, New York.

United Nations Security Council (UNSC) (2014o) Resolution 2178. S/RES/2178 (2014). September 24, New York.

United Nations Security Council (UNSC) (2014p) Resolution 2180. S/RES/2180 (2014). October 14, New York.

United Nations Security Council (UNSC) (2014q) Resolution 2182. S/RES/2182 (2014). October 24, New York.

United Nations Security Council (UNSC) (2015a) Resolution 2245. S/RES/2245 (2015). November 9, New York.

United Nations Security Council (UNSC) (2015b) Resolution 2240. S/RES/2240 (2015). October 9, New York.

United Nations Security Council (UNSC) (2015c) Resolution 2242. S/RES/2242 (2015). October 13, New York.

United Nations Security Council (UNSC) (2015d) UN Sanctions: Natural Resources. New York. Available at: www.securitycouncilreport.org/atf/cf/%7B65BFCF9B-6D27-4E9C-8CD3-CF6E4FF96FF9%7D/research_report_4_sanctions_2015.pdf

United Nations Security Council (UNSC) (2015e) Letter Dated 15 July 2015 from the Permanent Representative of New Zealand to the United Nations Addressed to the Secretary-General. S/2015/543 (2015). July 16, New York.

United Nations Security Council (UNSC) (2015f) 7499th Meeting. S/PV.7499. July 30, New York.

United Nations Security Council (UNSC) (2016a) Resolution 2267. S/RES/2267 (2016). February 26, New York.

United Nations Security Council (UNSC) (2016b) Resolution 2288. S/RES/2288 (2016). May 25, New York.

United Nations Security Council (UNSC) (2016c) 7699th Meeting. S/PV.7699. May 26, New York

United Nations Security Council (UNSC) (2016d) Resolution 2292. S/RES/2292 (2016). June 14, New York.

United States Agency for International Development (USAID) (2005) *Forests & Conflict: A Toolkit for Intervention.* Available at: http://pdf.usaid.gov/pdf_docs/Pnade290.pdf

United States Agency for International Development (USAID) (2011) *Oil and Conflict*, Technical Brief. Available at: http://pdf.usaid.gov/pdf_docs/pnadz960.pdf

United States Institute for Peace (USIP) (2007) *Natural Resources, Conflict, and Conflict Resolution* United States Institute for Peace, Washington, DC. Available at: www.usip.org/sites/default/files/file/08sg.pdf

Vines, A. (2003) "Monitoring UN Sanctions in Africa: The Role of Panels of Experts" *Verification Yearbook.* Verification Research, Training and Information Centre (VERTIC). Available at: www.isn.ethz.ch/Digital-Library/Publications/Detail/?lang=en&id=13412

Vira, V. and Ewing, T. (2014) *Ivory's Curse: The Militarization & Professionalization of Poaching in Africa* Born Free USA and C4ads, Washington, DC.

Warren, D. (2015) *Climate Change and International Peace and Security: Possible Roles for the U.N. Security Council in Addressing Climate Change* Columbia Law School. Available at: https://web.law.columbia.edu/sites/default/files/microsites/climate-change/warren_-_cc_and_international_peace_and_security_-_roles_for_the_un_security_council.pdf

Wimmer, A. (2004) "Introduction: Facing Ethnic Conflicts" in Wimmer, A., Goldstone, R., Horowitz, D., Joras, U. and Schetter, C. (eds.) *Facing Ethnic Conflicts: Toward a New Realism*, Rowman & Littlefield, Lanham, MD.

Yergin, D. (2008) *The Prize: The Epic Quest for Oil, Money & Power* Free Press, New York.

Part III
Case studies

12

Environmental peacebuilding in the Middle East

Tobias Ide, Vakur Sümer, and Larissa M. Aldehoff

Introduction

The potential links between environmental stress or resource scarcity and armed conflict have received considerable political and academic attention since the early 1990s (Brauch 2009; Homer-Dixon 1999). From 2007 on, the discussion gained additional currency as concerns about the security implications of climate change began to grow (McDonald 2013). The Middle East has been a focal point in these discussions for several reasons. First, the region suffers from several environmental problems such as the overuse and pollution of rivers and groundwater resources or soil degradation. Table 12.1 shows that, according to the Falkenmark Water Stress Index (Falkenmark et al. 1989), most countries in the region were water scarce in 2014. Israel, Jordan, the Palestinian territories and the states of the Arab Peninsula even suffered from absolute water scarcity.[1]

Table 12.1 Freshwater availability in selected countries of the Middle East in 2014

Country	Renewable freshwater (m³/person/year)	Falkenmark classification
Iran	1,732	water vulnerability
Iraq	2,467	water vulnerability
Israel	221	absolute water scarcity
Jordan	123	absolute water scarcity
Lebanon	770	water scarcity
Oman	312	absolute water scarcity
Palestinian territories	195	absolute water scarcity
Saudi Arabia	76	absolute water scarcity
Syria	908	water scarcity
Turkey	2,690	sufficient water
United Arab Emirates	16	absolute water scarcity
Yemen	78	absolute water scarcity

Source: FAO (2016).

Table 12.2 Battle-related deaths in selected countries of the Middle East (2010–2014) and active armed conflicts in 2014/2015

Country	Battle-related deaths	Conflict active 2014/2015?
Iran	302	no
Iraq	16,912	yes
Israel	1,812	yes
Jordan	0	yes
Lebanon	126	yes
Oman	0	no
Palestinian territories	no data	no data
Saudi Arabia	0	yes
Syria	119,117	yes
Turkey	1,768	yes
United Arab Emirates	0	no
Yemen	5,887	yes

Source: UCDP (2016).

Second, climate change is predicted to aggravate water scarcity in many parts of the Middle East due to higher temperatures, reduced rainfall, and seawater intrusion into groundwater aquifers (Feitelson et al. 2012). Finally, the Middle East already suffers from intense political tensions and armed conflicts, such as the civil wars in Syria and Yemen, political unrest in Lebanon and Iraq, tensions between Israel and several Arab states, and the geopolitical rivalry between Iran and Saudi Arabia. Table 12.2 illustrates the immense numbers of battle-related deaths and the high frequency of armed conflict in the region. Water plays a key role in several of these disputes, including the ones between Turkey, Iraq, and Syria, between Israel and the Palestinians, or between Israel and Syria (Amery 2002; Kibaroglu and Scheumann 2013; Selby 2013).

However, from the early 2000s onwards, several streams of literature argued that environmental stress also has the potential to facilitate peace and cooperation between adversary groups or states. These approaches have been termed "environmental peace perspective" (Ide and Scheffran 2014:273) or "environmental peacebuilding" (Schoenfeld et al. 2015:173). A focus on environment–cooperation links rather than on the environment–conflict nexus is promising for at least two reasons. Discursively, it avoids making securitizing and potentially self-fulfilling prophecies of future conflicts about scarce resources (Brzoska 2009; Feitelson et al. 2012). And empirically, it might guide policies which address important environmental problems and contribute to the transformation of intense conflicts simultaneously (Carius 2006).

This chapter provides a comprehensive discussion of the environmental peacebuilding literature with a special focus on the Middle East. We first review the different streams of research which contribute to our understanding of environmental peacebuilding. We also formulate some suggestions for the theoretical integration of the different approaches. Afterwards, the – rather mixed – results of several key studies on environmental peacebuilding are presented. In the fourth section, we present two case studies which illustrate and extend the potentials and pitfalls of environmental peacebuilding in the Middle East: interactions between Turkey, Syria, and Iraq concerning the Euphrates and Tigris river basin(s); and water-related cooperation between Israel and Jordan. The key lessons of the chapter are summarized in the conclusion.

Research streams and theoretical integration

Maas et al. (2013:103) point out that

> [e]nvironmental peacebuilding is neither a coherent theoretical school nor a concrete and distinct set of practical activities. Instead, it should be considered as an umbrella term that covers a wide range of aspects, which are united by their focus on the relationship between environment, conflict and peace.

Several major research streams have contributed to the genesis of an environmental peacebuilding perspective. First, proponents of environmental peacemaking claim that environmental problems are cross-border, long-term, important and largely de-securitized issues on which significant epistemic communities exist. They are therefore well suited to initiate cooperation even between adversary parties. This cooperation can, in turn, facilitate processes of building mutual trust and understanding (Conca 2002). Drawing on the literature of common pool resources (Ostrom 1990), Dinar (2011) also explores how cross-border water problems can be addressed by cooperation rather than escalating into conflict.

Second, a closely related strand of literature focuses on so-called peace parks. This label refers to cross-boundary, protected areas which are managed in a coordinated or even integrated way by adversary groups (Ali 2007). These areas can serve as a buffer zone between the groups in conflict, thus increasing the security of each while decreasing the chances for border incidents (Lejano 2006). Similar to the environmental peacemaking hypothesis, the joint management of cross-border ecosystems might also facilitate further processes of cooperation and trust building (Ali 2011).

Third, disaster diplomacy scholars ask whether "disaster-related activities induce cooperation amongst enemy countries?" (Kelman 2006:215). It is hypothesized that disaster prevention, preparation, management, and reconstruction activities provide opportunities for functional cooperation, but also that disasters can create solidarity and empathy with the victims. Although disaster diplomacy research has initially mainly focused on inter-state relations, its strongest empirical case is the peace process between the government of Indonesia and the separatist Free Aceh Movement after the 2004 Indian Ocean tsunami (Le Billon and Waizenegger 2007).

Fourth, peace ecology aims to develop environmental peacebuilding further. Specifically, it focuses on all kinds of ecological issues (rather than just on environmental problems) and on positive peace (rather than the mere absence of violence). It also aims to employ a combination of critical, positivist, and constructivist approaches in order to develop a comprehensive framework of the interlinkages between ecology and peace (Kyrou 2007). So far, few studies have drawn on the peace ecology approach, and its conceptual and empirical advantages vis-à-vis related approaches remain to be shown (Brauch et al. 2016).

Finally, environmental issues have gained prominence in the literature on post-conflict peacebuilding during recent years. Societies recovering from wars are often particularly vulnerable to suffering from environmental problems and related conflicts. The reasons for this are manifold and include a lack of operative infrastructure and adequate management institutions, a strong dependence of the economy on natural resources, lack of security and human capital, and migration processes (Troell and Weinthal 2014). Various researchers have therefore investigated how post-conflict societies can manage natural resources, especially water and land, in an ecologically sustainable, conflict sensitive, and economically sound way (Krampe 2016; Unruh and Williams 2013).

The first four streams of research are primarily interested in how environmental peacebuilding can take place in and contribute to the resolution of ongoing conflicts, while the fifth approach deals with ways to avoid the re-eruption of hostilities after an armed conflict has largely ceased. In the introduction, we have shown that the Middle East is characterized by a number of ongoing and often violent conflicts. Therefore the remainder of this chapter focuses on the potential of cross-boundary environmental problems to facilitate cooperation and understanding in ongoing disputes.

Following Ide and Scheffran (2014:274–276) and Lejano (2006), one can distinguish two broad theoretical approaches regarding the links between perceived environmental problems and the promotion of peace: sociological and liberal.

The sociological approach claims that (especially large-scale) environmental degradation and natural disasters produce a sense of shared vulnerability and/or empathy towards those hardest hit. In the words of Fritz (1996:29–30), such problems might create a symbolic "community of sufferers . . . characterized by a strong feeling of mutual suffering and in-group solidarity." In turn, political, social, or ethnic cleavages at least temporarily lose their salience, thus opening windows of opportunity for cooperation. Greek–Turkish cooperation after the 1999 Izmit earthquake is a case in point (Akcinaroglu et al. 2011). In a second phase, regular interaction and cooperation between people from adversary groups can create mutual understanding and trust, thus increasing the chances for further cooperation. Over the long term, this might transform those dominant worldviews of the parties involved which sustain the conflicts and impede the realization of peace (Conca 2002).

The liberal approach argues that (perceived) ecological interdependence and shared environmental degradation provide incentives even for hostile groups to cooperate. This allows them to realize material gains, for instance when several riparians work together to manage a shared river in a sustainable way or to preserve a cross-border ecosystem (Conca et al. 2005). Working together on shared ecological challenges might then stimulate spillover processes, that is, actors will widen or deepen their cooperation in order to realize additional benefits. In other words, environmental cooperation "will set in motion economic, social and political progresses which generate pressures towards further integration" (Tranholm-Mikkelsen 1991). Eventually, advanced cooperation and integration is also considered to have the potential to transform confrontational worldviews and identities (Conca 2002).

Figure 12.1 illustrates the two theoretical approaches described. In most studies, as well as in practice, elements of the sociological and the liberal approach are usually intertwined.

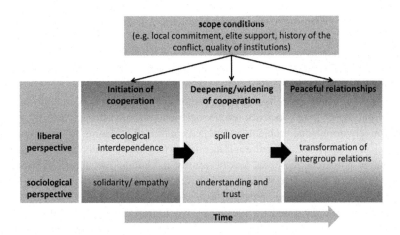

Figure 12.1 Theoretical approaches on environmental peacebuilding

Source: Modified from Ide and Scheffran (2014:276).

Furthermore, environmental peacebuilding can fail at the initial phase or before entering the second or third phase. Finally, researchers have identified a number of scope conditions which facilitate or impede processes of environmental peacebuilding. These include, but are not limited to, local commitment, the support of political elites, international mediation and funding, the absence of recent political violence, and adequate institutionalization (Feil et al. 2009; Kelman 2012; Mackelworth 2012).

Findings of the empirical literature

Empirical findings relevant for environmental peacebuilding are provided by a number of research streams employing different theoretical and methodological approaches. In general, these findings are hardly integrated and largely inconclusive. Some large-N studies from the environmental security literature, for instance, find a significant and robust link between environmental stress/degradation and violent conflict (e.g. Nardulli et al. 2015; Tir and Stinnett 2012; von Uexkull 2014). Other studies, by contrast, claim that water scarcity (Dinar et al. 2011; Hendrix and Glaser 2007), natural disasters (Slettebak 2012) or land degradation (Rowhani et al. 2011) reduce the risk of violent conflict. However, some of these studies argue that difficult environmental conditions simply provide bad opportunities, or points in time, to wage violence (Salehyan and Hendrix 2014), thus not necessarily supporting the environmental peacebuilding perspective.

No large-N investigations but several case studies are available which focus specifically on environmental peacebuilding in the Middle East. These fall into three different categories. First, several researchers analyze the performance of projects explicitly aiming at environmental peacebuilding. Most of them focus on trilateral efforts between Israel, Jordan, and Palestine such as the Good Water Neighbors project, the Arava Institute, or the Regional Water Databank project. These projects are usually conducted by academics, NGOs, and committed citizens in a bottom-up manner. Several researchers find that within this scope, environmental peacebuilding efforts have a positive impact on mutual understanding and transnational cooperation (Djernaes et al. 2015; Ide and Fröhlich 2015; Schoenfeld et al. 2015). Other scholars object that due to the lack of political support, the protracted conflict situation, vast power asymmetries, and their depoliticized approach, environmental peacebuilding efforts largely fail to facilitate wider processes of cooperation and reconciliation (Aggestam and Sundell-Eklund 2014; Kramer 2008; Reynolds 2016).

Second, there is a large literature investigating whether states manage competing river claims in a cooperative way or whether dysfunctional conflict is the predominant response. So far, it shows that river-related disputes tended to worsen the already tense relationships between Israel and Palestine (Selby 2013), Israel and Syria (Amery 2002), and Israel and Lebanon (Zeitoun et al. 2013). By contrast, Israel and Jordan signed a water treaty in 1994 as part of a broader peace treaty which was largely successful in formalizing existing and even stimulating new water cooperation (Jägerskog 2003). Water relations between Turkey, Syria, and Iraq in the Euphrates and Tigris basins oscillated between intense conflicts, periods of minor tensions, and efforts to establish and extend water-related cooperation (Kibaroglu and Scheumann 2013). The securitization of water, the focus on water quantity (rather than quality) problems, and the dominance of zero-sum thinking are key obstacles to the further success of environmental peacebuilding between states in the region (Sümer 2014; Zeitoun et al. 2013).

Third, research on environmental conflicts provides several studies of cases in which environmental problems stimulated inter-group tensions or, conversely, facilitated collaboration and the improvement of relationships. Tubi and Feitelson (2016) find that during the 1957–1963

Negev drought, conflict and cooperation occurred simultaneously between Bedouin nomads and Israeli farmers. Power inequalities, adaptation/mediation efforts by the state, and especially the involvement of Kibbutzim communities made significant cooperation to cope with the drought more likely. By contrast, the 2006–2010 Mediterranean drought seems to have eroded social relationships in Syria and made conflict more likely than cooperation (de Châtel 2014). In Yemen, sinking groundwater levels have in some cases urged groups to cooperate in order to preserve the aquifers. But when community relations are already very tense and no shared external threat (such as water grabbing by the state or a drought) is identified, competing water claims in the context of environmental degradation tend to escalate existing conflicts (AbuZaid and Abdel-Meguid 2006; Weiss 2015).

Case studies

In this section, we present two in-depth case studies which illustrate and extend the theoretical and empirical issues discussed in the two preceding sections. By doing so, we aim to deepen the understanding of the dynamics, potentials, and pitfalls of environmental peacebuilding in the Middle East.

The conundrum of the Euphrates–Tigris Basin: evolution of the hydropolitics between Turkey, Syria, and Iraq

Euphrates and Tigris are two significant transboundary rivers in southwest Asia. Three major riparians of the Euphrates–Tigris River basin are Turkey, Syria, and Iraq. The water question emerged as a significant political issue in the region when the three riparians, after consolidating their newly established statehood, initiated major water development projects in the 1960s almost simultaneously in an uncoordinated fashion. These projects came to completion in the 1970s and raised tensions about transnational water, especially about the Euphrates.

Therefore, starting from the 1970s, several crises occurred in the basin. The first of these happened when Turkey started impounding the Keban Reservoir on the Euphrates in early 1974. This coincided with the completion of the biggest dam in Syria, namely the Tabqah Dam. By 1975, impounding of both dams resulted in a highly reduced flow to Iraq which was strongly protested by this country. Exchanging harsh statements, Iraq and Syria came to the brink of a war which was averted at the last minute when Saudi Arabia mediated and convinced Syrian authorities to release extra water to Iraq.

Completion of the Ataturk Dam, the biggest reservoir in the Euphrates–Tigris River basin, triggered another crisis in 1990. Trying to fill the reservoir, Turkey temporarily reduced the flow of the Euphrates River. The Syrian and Iraqi governments made official complaints, and consequently called for an agreement to share the waters of the Euphrates, as well as for a reduction of the impounding period. In 1996, after Turkey started construction of the Birecik Dam on the Euphrates, both Syria and Iraq sent official notes to the Turkish government objecting to the construction on the grounds that it would affect the quantity and quality of waters flowing into their countries. The issue became an international affair when Syria and Iraq requested that Arab League countries cease financial aid to Turkish projects and boycott European companies that had financed the dam (Scheumann 2003).

However, even in the face of these intense conflicts, efforts were made to solve water disputes peacefully, to establish mechanisms of coordinated water governance, and even to use water as a tool to facilitate reconciliation and further cooperation. Negotiations between Turkey and Iraq on the development of the Euphrates' water had already started in the 1940s (Kibaroglu 2002).

In the context of several water development projects implemented in the 1960s, the downstream riparians, particularly Iraq, insisted on guaranteed flows to be released by Turkey during the impounding period of the Keban Reservoir. At the end of negotiations, Turkey guaranteed to undertake all necessary measures to maintain a discharge of 350 cubic meters per second immediately downstream from the dam.

The cooperation attempts among the Euphrates–Tigris riparian countries gained momentum when Iraq and Turkey agreed to form a permanent "Joint Technical Committee" (JTC) in 1980. The JTC was established to discuss and – if possible – settle the water issue among the riparians. Syria joined the JTC in 1983 and the three countries continued to negotiate thereafter. However, after sixteen meetings it became apparent that the JTC process was not able to proceed further. There were strong disagreements between the three riparians whether the Euphrates and the Tigris should be considered as a single water system, about the status of the Euphrates as an international or transboundary watercourse, and about the principles according to which water would be shared between the countries. There were also uncertainties and inadequacies relating to the data on water as well as land resources. In 1984, Turkey proposed the "Three-Stage Plan for Optimum, Equitable and Reasonable Utilization of the Transboundary Watercourses of the Tigris–Euphrates Basin." But both Iraq and Syria rejected the Three-Stage Plan on the ground that it was nothing more than a mere reflection of the position of Turkey (Kibaroglu and Scheumann 2013; Sümer 2016:144).

Despite the lack of a final agreement on allocations, two interim bilateral accords were concluded in 1987 and 1990 between Syria and Turkey and between Iraq and Syria, respectively. With the 1987 Protocol, Turkey agreed to release on average 500 cubic meters of water per second from the Euphrates at the border with Syria. The Syrian–Iraqi Water Accord allocates the water of the Euphrates River according to a fixed ratio of 42 percent to Syria and 58 percent to Iraq.

Although the JTC process ended in futility amidst the political setting caused by the Iraqi invasion of Kuwait, the 2000s witnessed another wave of cooperation, particularly between Syria and Turkey and to some extent between Iraq and Turkey. Following the Adana Protocol signed in 1998, Turkey–Syria (water) relations improved significantly. In 2001, a joint communiqué was signed, followed by fifty Memoranda of Understanding (MoU) in 2009, four of which related to water issues. One of the MoUs was related to the construction of a so-called "Friendship Dam" on the Orontes River. Another one was on pumping waters from the Tigris to northeastern Syria. The third MoU aimed at efficiency in water utilization and at combating drought in the two countries, while the fourth was on water quality. In a similar fashion, a MoU was signed between Turkey and Iraq in October 2009, stipulating that the two sides agreed to exchange hydrological and meteorological information as well as exchanging expertise in these fields (Kibaroglu and Scheumann 2013).

Outbreak of war in Syria in 2011 and the subsequent deterioration of Syrian–Turkish relations halted the operationalization of all initiatives of cooperation between these countries. Similarly, ebbs and flows in Iraqi–Turkish relations resulted in a five-year-long suspension of ratifications of the MoUs by the Iraqi side. These cases demonstrate that the high-level political atmosphere between countries is a very strong determinant of the fate of water cooperation in particular and environmental peacebuilding in general. The current unstable political situation in both downstream states, Iraq and Syria, renders future collaboration quite difficult.

On the non-governmental level, the establishment of the Euphrates–Tigris Initiative for Cooperation (ETIC) in 2005 by a group of scholars and professionals from the three major riparian countries can be seen as one of the most significant developments towards promotion of cooperation in the basin. As a "voluntary, non-official, nonbinding, non-profit seeking and non-governmental" network of professionals, ETIC aims at organizing joint training and capacity building programmes and research activities (Kibaroglu and Scheumann 2013). However, it remains to be seen whether the initiative can gain the support from high-ranking policy makers and facilitate formal water cooperation, especially in the face of significant political instability.

To conclude, the Euphrates–Tigris case features a hybrid track record whereby securitization of water and water conflicts went hand in hand with continued attempts at consensus building and cooperation. Despite the existence of an apparent power asymmetry at the expense of downstream states, sometimes labeled as "hydro-hegemony" (Zeitoun and Warner 2006:435), and a clear disagreement over fundamental terms, parties were able to maintain a semi-institutionalized dialogue for more than a decade and to reach a number of bilateral agreements. Examples such as ETIC show that an epistemic community also recently emerged. This demonstrates that even in unfavorable conditions there is room for dialogue and concrete results. However, there is still no basin-wide agreement. Also, water cooperation is strongly dependent on the support of political elites as well as on good and stable political relations within and between Turkey, Syria, and Iraq.

A trust building process in the Jordan River Basin: the water regime of Jordan and Israel

The trust building process between Israel and Jordan can be roughly divided into three steps: (1) establishing a water regime, (2) institutionalizing the regime by a joint water committee based on the peace treaty, and (3) implementing the regime with a joint desalination project, based on game changing technological innovation.

With the Jewish immigration at the end of the nineteenth and the beginning of the twentieth centuries, water became a political issue long before the founding of the state of Israel (Dolatyar and Gray 2000:94ff.). The Israeli settlers had financial resources for and knowledge about developing and establishing irrigation systems to cultivate land. In Jordan, at that time part of the British Mandate, there were virtually no investments in such projects (Jägerskog 2003:76ff.). After the 1948 Arab–Israeli War, a ceasefire agreement was signed but the state of war had not been put to an end. There was no agreement or any kind of coordination concerning the distribution of the Jordan River's water resources. At the beginning of the 1950s, the issue of water resource allocation, especially between Israel and Jordan, worsened because they planned competing water projects (Dombrowsky 2008).

A regional plan by the UN and the USA for the use of the Jordan River's resources from September 1953 was refused by both sides, as was the Eric Johnston Jordan Valley Project proposed by the USA in the same year (Kliot 1994:198ff.). The Arab League did not want to recognize the existence of the State of Israel indirectly through the ratification of the Johnston Plan, and Israel saw it as an "American mandate" that would prefer Jordan's interests. At the end of 1955, there was a revised draft of the Johnston Plan that Israel, Jordan, and Egypt were willing to accept after several months of discussions. But Syria and Lebanon still refused to approve the plan and the Arab League remained ambivalent as well. Eventually, Israel decided not to wait any longer and stated a unilateral-oriented use of the Jordan River's resources in March 1956 (Ma'oz 2006).

Even though Israel and the Arab League as a whole could not find an agreement about an institutionalized framework, Israel and Jordan felt obliged – after some diplomatic efforts by the USA – to comply with the second draft of the Johnston Plan. In the aftermath of this informal mutual adherence to the plan, secret water discussions on technical matters between the two parties took place regularly. In the literature this is often referred to as the "Picnic Table Talks." This process not only reduced the tensions, but also built trust between the two parties and is even claimed as the beginning of an Israeli–Jordanian water regime (Jägerskog 2003).

The political developments in the region and the growing water scarcity made a renegotiation of the Johnston Plan necessary, at least from the Jordanian perspective. Thus, the distribution of the resources was discussed within the negotiations of the peace treaty between Israel and Jordan in 1994.[2] The agreement defines mutually recognized water allocations for the Jordan River and its major tributary, the Yarmouk, as well as the groundwater resources from Wadi Araba.

For implementing and monitoring its water clauses, the peace treaty prescribes the establishment of a Joint Water Committee (JWC).[3] It includes three members of each country and is able to call experts whenever necessary (Schmoll 2008:218). Meanwhile, the committee has become a platform for regular exchange of information and opinions both on the diplomatic and on the expert levels, where both sides work together constructively. Over the years, the JWC's fields of work has extended, for example by establishing a subcommittee that is working on the rehabilitation of the Jordan River (Aldehoff 2016). The water clauses were very controversial and were critically discussed before and even after the peace treaty was signed (Dombrowsky 2008; Jägerskog 2003). Nonetheless, the peace treaty and especially the founding and development of the JWC strengthened the Israeli–Jordanian water regime as they institutionalized their existing water relationship. The constant exchange of information not only reduced uncertainty but also strengthened the process of trust building (Jägerskog 2003; Schmoll 2008).

Even though the regime had established formal coordination and cooperation to share shrinking water resources, it still functioned according to the logic of a zero-sum game. This changed when Israel enhanced its water management by improved desalination technology, wastewater recycling, and new conservation as well as efficiency techniques. Israel started operating its first large-scale seawater desalination plant in Ashkelon in 2005. To date there are five major desalination plants along the Israeli Mediterranean coast and half of Israel's freshwater needs can be covered by desalinated seawater. Thus, desalination already has a great impact on Israel's domestic water situation and it even influences the water relations to other countries. The use of desalination reduces the water scarcity which allows overcoming the zero-sum logic, thus having a positive impact on the Israeli–Jordanian water regime (Aviram et al. 2014).

In the aftermath of the 1994 peace treaty, a working group for the development of the Jordan River basin carried out a study on a canal project linking the Red Sea and the Dead Sea in 1996. The goal of this project is to provide new water resources by desalination and to stabilize the level of the rapidly shrinking Dead Sea. In May 2005, Israel, Jordan, and the Palestinian Authority signed an agreement to develop this idea further with a feasibility study. After a long and still ongoing debate about technical and political issues, an agreement on the Red Sea–Dead Sea project was signed in Washington in December 2013.

On the one hand, the project is a water swap: Jordan desalinates water from the Red Sea in Aqaba and delivers part of it to the south of Israel and the West Bank. In exchange, Israel delivers water from the Jordan River and Lake Tiberias to the north of Jordan (Demilecamps 2013; Salameh and Haddadin 2006). On the other hand, a 180-km long canal from the desalination plant in Aqaba to the Dead Sea (where another desalination plant is envisioned) will convey the brine water that results from the desalination process to the Dead Sea in order to raise its level. The 400 meter drop in elevation can be used for installing a hydroelectric generator which provides energy for the pumping, the desalination process, and surplus energy for the three countries involved in the project (Demilecamps 2013; Hübschen 2014:129f.).

The project will produce water and energy resources and is envisioned to positively affect agro-industry and tourism. Moreover, it is likely to strengthen the trust between Israel and Jordan. It will also deepen the mutual dependence of both sides and thus further develop their common water regime. Nevertheless the "Peace Canal" is controversial, especially since neither its funding nor its environmental impacts are clear yet (Demilecamps 2013; Donnelly 2014).

To conclude, the case of the Jordan River basin has featured a process of trust building between the riparians Israel and Jordan for several decades. This process resulted in the (still ongoing) formation of a water regime and was even institutionalized by establishing the JWC. Both sides realized that cooperation concerning the Jordan River's water resources is more fruitful than conflict. Thus, even an overcoming of zero-sum-game assumptions between both parties became possible as the Red Sea–Dead Sea project indicates. However, this cooperation depends on the political elites and there is still no chance for a basin-wide agreement.

Conclusion

Environmental peacebuilding, in its different variances, is a concept and practice which utilizes ecological interdependencies and shared environmental problems to facilitate cooperation, trust building, and reconciliation. It thus frames the environment–security nexus in a more constructive manner than the environmental security literature. However, as the findings of previous empirical studies and the two case studies presented in greater detail show, the empirical record of environmental peacebuilding in the Middle East is mixed.

On the one hand, the process of environmental peacebuilding often remains in the initiation stage and rarely proceeds to the second stage of the framework presented in this chapter (the deepening or widening of cooperation; see Figure 12.1). In particular, competing discourses about water demands and ecological scales (Harris and Alatout 2010; Ide 2016) as well as political instability and a lack of elite support inhibit environmental peacebuilding. On the other hand, the Israeli–Jordanian JWC and Turkish–Syrian water relationships during the 2000s show that during political windows of opportunity, lasting progress towards environmental cooperation, common problem solving, and trust building can be made. On the non-state, civil society level, successful instances of environmental peacebuilding like Good Water Neighbors or ETIC are even more prevalent. However, none of these have had a significant impact on the transformation of intergroup relationships (the final stage of the framework) so far.

Overall, we would like to encourage future research to gain a deeper understanding of the factors and pathways which facilitate and inhibit environmental peacebuilding. Due to the considerable amount of environmental stress and political instability it faces, but also due to the considerable number of past environmental peacebuilding projects, the Middle East is a region particularly interesting to study in this context.

Notes

1 Please note that these data include transboundary water flows (which are not always guaranteed). Data on renewable internal water resource per capita show different values for several countries (http://data.worldbank.org/indicator/ER.H2O.INTR.PC), but overall confirm the impression of the Middle East as a water scarce region.
2 Article 6 and Annex II of the Treaty of Peace between the State of Israel and the Hashemite Kingdom of Jordan, available online: https://peacemaker.un.org/sites/peacemaker.un.org/files/IL%20JO_941026_PeaceTreatyIsraelJordan.pdf
3 Article VII of Annex II.

References

AbuZaid, K. and Abdel-Meguid, A. (2006) *Water conflicts and conflict management mechanisms in the Middle East and North Africa region.* CEDARE, Cairo.

Aggestam, K. and Sundell-Eklund, A. (2014) "Situating water in peacebuilding: revisiting the Middle East peace process" *Water International* 39:10–22.

Akcinaroglu, S., DiCicco, J. and Radziszewski, E. (2011) "Avalanches and olive branches: a multimethod analysis of disasters and peacemaking in interstate rivalries" *Political Research Quarterly* 64:260–275.

Aldehoff, L. M. (2016) *Smoke on the water? Zur Wirkung von Wasserknappheit als Konfliktgegenstand am Beispiel des Jordanbeckens,* unpublished MA thesis, Goethe University, Frankfurt.

Ali, S. (2007) "A natural connection between ecology and peace?" in Ali, S. (ed.) *Peace parks: conservation and conflict resolution.* Cambridge University Press, Cambridge, 1–18.

Ali, S. (2011) "The instrumental use of ecology in conflict resolution and security" *Procedia Social and Behavioral Sciences* 14:31–34.

Amery, H. (2002) "Water wars in the Middle East: a looming threat" *Geographical Journal* 168:313–23.

Aviram, R., Katz, D. and Shmueli, D. (2014) "Desalination as a game-changer in transboundary hydropolitics" *Water Policy* 16:609–624.

Brauch, H. G. (2009) "Securitizing global environmental change" in Brauch, H. G., Spring, Ú. O., Grin, J., Mesjasz, C., Kameri-Mbote, P., Behera, N. C., et al. (eds.) *Facing global environmental change: environmental, human, energy, food, health and water security concepts.* Springer, Berlin, 65–104.

Brauch, H. G., Oswald Spring, Ú. and Scheffran, J. (2016) "Conceptualizing sustainable peace in the anthropocene: a challenge and task for an emerging political geoecology and peace ecology" in Brauch, H. G., Oswald Spring, Ú., Grin, J. and Scheffran, J. (eds.) *Handbook on sustainability transition and sustainable peace.* Springer, Heidelberg.

Brzoska, M. (2009) "The securitization of climate change and the power of conceptions of security" *Security & Peace* 27:137–145.

Carius, A. (2006) *Environmental peacemaking: environmental cooperation as an instrument of crisis prevention and peacebuilding: condition for success and constraints.* Adelphi, Berlin.

Conca, K. (2002) "The case for environmental peacemaking" in Conca, K. and Dabelko, G. (eds.) *Environmental peacemaking.* John Hopkins University Press, Baltimore, 1–22.

Conca, K., Carius, A. and Dabelko, G. (2005) "Building peace through environmental cooperation" in Worldwatch Institute (ed.) *State of the world 2005: redefining global security.* Worldwatch, Washington, DC, 144–157.

de Châtel, F. (2014) "The role of drought and climate change in the Syrian uprising: untangling the triggers of the revolution" *Middle Eastern Studies* 50:521–535.

Demilecamps, C. (2013) "The Red Sea–Dead Sea Canal" in Ababsa, M. and Kohlmayer, C. (eds.) *Atlas of Jordan: history, territories and society.* Presse de l'Ifpo, Beirut, 433–436.

Dinar, S. (2011) "Resource scarcity and environmental degradation: implications for the development of international cooperation" in Dinar, S. (ed.) *Beyond resource wars: scarcity, environmental degradation and international cooperation.* MIT Press, Boston, 289–305.

Dinar, S., Dinar, A. and Kurukulasuriya, P. (2011) "Scarcity and cooperation along international rivers: an empirical assessment of bilateral treaties" *International Studies Quarterly* 55:809–833.

Djernaes, M., Jorgensen, T. and Koch-Ya'ari, E. (2015) "Evaluation of environmental peacemaking intervention strategies in Jordan–Israel–Palestine" *Journal of Peacebuilding & Development* 10:74–80.

Dolatyar, M. and Gray, T. (2000) *Water politics in the Middle East: a context for conflict or co-operation.* St. Martin's Press, New York.

Dombrowsky, I. (2008) "Konflikt und Kooperation an grenzüberschreitenden Flüssen" in Franzke, J. (ed.) *Wasser: Zukunftsressource zwischen Menschenrecht und Wirtschaftsgut, Konflikt und Kooperation.* Brandenburgische Landeszentrale für politische Bildung, Potsdam, 57–69.

Donnelly, K. (2014) "The Red Sea–Dead Sea Project update" in Gleick, P. H. (ed.) *The World's Water, volume 8.* Island Press, Washington, DC, 153–158.

Falkenmark, M., Lundquist, J. and Widstrand, C. (1989) "Macro-scale water scarcity requires micro-scale approaches: aspects of vulnerability in semi-arid development" *Natural Resources Forum,* 13:258–267.

FAO (2016) "Aquastat" Available at: www.fao.org/nr/water/aquastat/main/index.stm (12/04/2016).

Feil, M., Klein, D. and Westerkamp, M. (2009) *Regional cooperation on environment, economy and natural resource management: how can it contribute to peacebuilding?* Initiative for Peacebuilding, Brussels.

Feitelson, E., Tamimi, A. and Rosenthal, G. (2012) "Climate change and security in the Israeli–Palestinian context" *Journal of Peace Research* 49:241–257.

Fritz, C. E. (1996) *Disasters and mental health: therapeutic principles drawn from disaster studies.* Disaster Research Center, Newark, DE.

Harris, L. M. and Alatout, S. (2010) "Negotiating hydro-scales, forging states: comparison of the upper Tigris/Euphrates and Jordan River basins" *Political Geography* 29:148–156.

Hendrix, C. S. and Glaser, S. M. (2007) "Trends and triggers: climate, climate change and civil conflict in Sub-Saharan Africa" *Political Geography* 26:695–715.

Homer-Dixon, T. (1999) *Environmental scarcity and violence.* Princeton University Press, Princeton, NJ.

Hübschen, K. (2014) *Integrated water resources management as a governance challenge for countries of the Middle East with special focus on Yemen, Jordan and Syria.* Logos, Berlin.

Ide, T. (2016) "Space, discourse and environmental peacebuilding" *Third World Quarterly* 37.

Ide, T. and Fröhlich, C. (2015) "Socio-environmental cooperation and conflict? A discursive understanding and its application to the case of Israel/Palestine" *Earth System Dynamics* 6:659–671.

Ide, T. and Scheffran, J. (2014) "On climate, conflict and cumulation: suggestions for integrative cumulation of knowledge in the research on climate change and violent conflict" *Global Change, Peace & Security* 26:263–279.

Jägerskog, A. (2003) *Why states cooperate over shared water: the water negotiations in the Jordan River basin.* Linköping University, Linköping.

Kelman, I. (2006) "Acting on disaster diplomacy" *Journal of International Affairs* 59:215–240.

Kelman, I. (2012) *Disaster diplomacy: how disasters affect peace and conflict.* Routledge, London.

Kibaroglu, A. (2002) "Settling the dispute over the waters of the Euphrates–Tigris river basin" in Bogardi J. C. S. (ed.) Selected papers of the International Conference from Conflict to Co-operation in International Water Resources Management. UNESCO–IHP, Delft, 329–343.

Kibaroglu, A. and Scheumann, W. (2013) "Evolution of transboundary politics in the Euphrates–Tigris river system: new perspectives and political challenges" *Global Governance* 19:279–305.

Kliot, N. (1994) *Water resources and conflict in the Middle East.* Routledge, London.

Kramer, A. (2008) *Regional water cooperation and peacebuilding in the Middle East.* Adelphi Research, Berlin.

Krampe, F. (2016) "Water for peace? – Post-conflict water resource management in Kosovo" *Cooperation and Conflict* 51.

Kyrou, C. N. (2007) "Peace ecology: an emerging paradigm in peace studies" *International Journal of Peace Studies* 12:73–92.

Le Billon, P. and Waizenegger, A. (2007) "Peace in the wake of disaster? Secessionist conflicts and the 2004 Indian Ocean tsunami" *Transactions of the Institute of British Geographers* 32:411–427.

Lejano, R. (2006) "Theorizing peace parks: two models of collective action" *Journal of Peace Research* 43:563–581.

Ma'oz, M. (2006) "The Jordan Valley's water: a source of conflict or a basis for peace?" in Hambright, K. D., Ragep, F. J. and Ginat, J. (eds.) *Water in the Middle East: cooperation and technical solutions in the Jordan Valley.* Sussex Academic Press, Brighton, 11–22.

Maas, A., Carius, A. and Wittich, A. (2013) "From conflict to cooperation? Environmental cooperation as a tool for peacebuilding" in Floyd, R. and Matthew, R. A. (eds.) *Environmental security: approaches and issues.* Routledge, London, 102–120.

McDonald, M. (2013) "Discourses of climate security" *Political Geography* 33:42–51.

Mackelworth, P. (2012) "Peace parks and transboundary initiatives: implications for marine conservation and spatial planning" *Conservation Letters* 5:90–98.

Nardulli, P. F., Peyton, B. and Bajjalieh, J. (2015) "Climate change and civil unrest: the impact of rapid-onset disasters" *Journal of Conflict Resolution* 59:310–335.

Ostrom, E. (1990) *Governing the commons: the evolution of institutions for collective action.* Cambridge University Press, Cambridge.

Reynolds, K. M. (2016) "Unpacking the complex nature of cooperative interactions: case studies of Israeli–Palestinian environmental cooperation in the greater Bethlehem area" *Geo Journal* DOI 10.1007/s10708-016-9708-0.

Rowhani, P., Degomme, O., Guha-Sapir, D. and Lambin, E. (2011) "Malnutrition and conflict in East Africa: the impacts of resource variability on human security" *Climatic Change* 105:207–222.

Salameh, E. and Haddadin, M. J. (2006) "The population–water resources equation" in Haddadin, M. J. (ed.) *Water resources in Jordan: evolving policies for development, the environment, and conflict resolution.* Routledge, London, 7–27.

Salehyan, I. and Hendrix, C. (2014) "Climate shocks and political violence" *Global Environmental Change* 28:239–250.

Scheumann, W. (2003) "The Euphrates issue in Turkish–Syrian relations" in Brauch, H. G., Liotta, P. H., Marquina, A. and El-Sayed, S. M. (eds.) *Security and environment in the Mediterranean: conceptualising security and environmental conflicts*. Springer, Berlin, 745–760.

Schmoll, M. C. (2008) *Die Kooperation zwischen Israel und Jordanien: ein Sicherheitsregime als Weg zur Lösung eines Sicherheitskonflikts*. Lit, Berlin.

Schoenfeld, S., Zohar, A., Alleson, I., Suleiman, O. and Sipos-Randor, G. (2015) "A place of empathy in a fragile contentious landscape: environmental peacebuilding in the eastern Mediterranean" in McConnell, F., Megoran, N. and Williams, P. (eds.) *Geographies of peace*. I. B. Tauris, London, 171–193.

Selby, J. (2013) "Cooperation, domination and colonisation: the Israeli–Palestinian joint water committee" *Water Alternatives* 6:1–24.

Slettebak, R. T. (2012) "Don't blame the weather! Climate-related natural disasters and civil conflict" *Journal of Peace Research* 49:163–176.

Sümer, V. (2014) "A chance for a pax aquarum in the Middle East? Transcending the six obstacles for transboundary water cooperation" *Journal of Peacebuilding and Development* 9:83–89.

Sümer, V. (2016) *Water and politics in Turkey: structural change and EU accession*. I. B. Tauris, London.

Tir, J. and Stinnett, D. M. (2012) "Weathering climate change: can institutions mitigate international water conflict?" *Journal of Peace Research* 49:211–225.

Tranholm-Mikkelsen, J. (1991) "Neo-functionalism: obstinate or obsolete? A reappraisal in the light of the new dynamism of the EC" *Millennium* 20:1–22.

Troell, J. and Weinthal, E. (2014) "Shoring up peace: water and post-conflict peacebuilding" in Weinthal, E., Troell, J. and Nakayama, M. (eds.) *Water and post-conflict peacebuilding*. Earthscan, London, 1–23.

Tubi, A. and Feitelson, E. (2016) "Drought and cooperation in a conflict prone area: Bedouin herders and Jewish farmers in Israel's northern Negev, 1957–1963" *Political Geography* 51:30–42.

UCDP (2016) "Uppsala Conflict Data Program" Available at: http://ucdp.uu.se/ (26/07/2016).

Unruh, J. and Williams, R. C. (2013) "Land: a foundation for peacebuilding" in Unruh, J. and Williams, R. C. (eds.) *Land and post-conflict peacebuilding*. Earthscan, London, 1–20.

von Uexkull, N. (2014) "Sustained drought, vulnerability and civil conflict in Sub-Saharan Africa" *Political Geography* 43:16–26.

Weiss, M. (2015) "A perfect storm: the causes and consequences of severe water scarcity, institutional breakdown and conflict in Yemen" *Water International* 40:251–272.

Zeitoun, M. and Warner, J. (2006) "Hydro-hegemony: a framework for analysis of trans-boundary water conflicts" *Water Policy* 8:435–460.

Zeitoun, M., Talhami, M. and Eid-Sabbagh, K. (2013) "The influence of narratives on negotiations and resolution of the upper Jordan river conflict" *International Negotiation* 18:293–322.

13

Environmental peacebuilding in Iraq

Restoring the Iraqi Marshes and the ancient *kahrez* systems in the northern governorates

Hannah Moosa

Introduction

Water resources in Iraq: a brief introduction

Iraq depends primarily on the waters from the Tigris and Euphrates, which provide an estimated 98 per cent of the country's water supply. Despite low levels of average annual rainfall, estimated at 154mm, the country has good renewable water resources, estimated at 3,287m³/capita/year, due to the flows from these two rivers, and their tributaries. The Tigris and Euphrates are now the main sources of potable and agricultural water for the country ("Iraq's shared water resources" 2016).

Iraq's ancient underground aqueducts, popularly known as *kahrez*, have contributed importantly to the country's water supply for centuries, providing an essential lifeline for communities in northern and eastern Iraq. These man-made structures have provided a reliable supply of water for both irrigation and consumption purposes, particularly in Iraqi Kurdistan. It is estimated that at least 380 *kahrez* were still in use in the early 2000s (NCCI OP-ED 2010).

Water uses in Iraq

Some 75 per cent of Iraq's overall water resources are consumed by the agricultural sector. The country's remaining water resources go towards municipal and industrial needs, the Mesopotamian Marshlands, the Gulf via the Shatt al-Arab River, and fish farms and livestock ("Water uses in Iraq" 2016).

While Iraq's annual active groundwater recharge rate is not fully understood, the government, in cooperation with UNESCO, continues to study the country's aquifers in order to more fully understand their potential. Iraq's groundwater is primarily used in the agricultural, industrial and municipal sectors ("Water uses in Iraq" 2016). There are over 88,000 wells across the country, which supply families, cities and industries with water, though detailed information about consumption rates is not always available. Iraq also has an undetermined number of illegal wells ("Water uses in Iraq" 2016).

The impacts of human conflict and war on Iraq's water resources

While much of Iraq is arid, the country has for centuries successfully thrived despite the limited water resources available. The chronic water crisis Iraq currently faces has emerged over the past few decades, largely due to years of war, armed conflict, international sanctions and embargoes. These factors, together with persistent neglect of infrastructure, and limited environmental awareness, have undermined the country's water resource management system. ("Republic of Iraq Emergency Baghdad. . ." n.d.; NCCI OP-ED 2010)

Prior to the first Gulf War in the 1990s, Iraq had arguably the most highly developed water service delivery mechanisms in the region, and largely met the basic water needs of its people. Throughout the 1970s, the government used the proceeds from the nationalised oil revenue to invest in the water sector and other infrastructure projects (World Bank PID 2004; NCCI OP-ED 2010). While investments declined during the Iran–Iraq War from 1980 to 1988, by 1990, the country had constructed impressively modern water, electrical and sewerage systems. Prior to the first Gulf War in 1991, the Iraqi population enjoyed a relatively high level of water supply and sanitation services (World Bank PID 2004). Over 95 per cent of the urban population and over 75 per cent of the rural population had access to safe potable water. Water quality in Iraq was fairly good, as reflected by the estimated 218 water treatment plants and 1,200 compact water treatment units operating throughout the country. Sanitation services covered roughly 75 per cent of urban communities and 40 per cent of rural communities. However, following the Iraqi occupation of Kuwait in 1990, the country's water supply and sanitation sector has declined significantly (World Bank PID 2004).

UN-imposed sanctions on Iraq in 1991 blocked the importation of specialised equipment and chemicals, including chlorine for water purification. The 13-year-long sanctions further hindered the country's ability to repair damaged water treatment plants and pipes. During 'Operation Desert Storm', water treatment plants and power plants, as well as other key infrastructural elements, were deliberately targeted and destroyed. The capacity of the state to continue water delivery services at pre-war levels deteriorated, and this led to serious health consequences ("Rebuilding Iraq. . ." 2006; NCCI OP-ED 2010; Boyer-Souchet et al. 2011).

The water resources of the country were further devastated following the 1991 Gulf War when the government of Saddam Hussein began to destroy the Marshes through aerial bombing, the burning of villages, and the building of extensive drainage structures to dry out the wetlands and force migration away from the Marshes (Lonergan 2012:226; Managing for Change 2010; Aoki et al. 2014; Reiss n.d.).

In the early 1990s then, Iraq failed to maintain an adequate supply of potable water for agriculture and human consumption. It is estimated that by 1996, over 500,000 Iraqi children had died from preventable diseases under the period of sanctions. According to UNICEF estimates, between 1990 and 2000, the average per capita share of potable water decreased from 330 litres to 150 litres in Baghdad and from 180 litres to 65 litres in rural areas ("Rebuilding Iraq. . ." 2006; NCCI OP-ED 2010).

The 2003 invasion of Iraq caused additional devastation to the country's water sector. During the attacks, water and electrical plants were bombed, and pumping stations, dams, canals, water desalination plants and sewage facilities became military targets (Boyer-Souchet et al. 2011). Iraq's energy production and distribution infrastructures were significantly damaged, and the frequent electricity shortages made it increasingly difficult to run the remaining water treatment plants. By 2004, only 73 per cent of the urban population and 43 per cent of rural communities had access to safe drinking water (Boyer-Souchet et al. 2011).

In 2007, an epidemic of cholera broke out in southern Iraq, bringing to light the deteriorating quality of water and sanitation services in the region. By 2010, ICRC estimated that one in four Iraqis were living without access to safe drinking water, and those with access only had scarce and unreliable supplies. In addition, an estimated 80 per cent of discharged sewage was untreated due to frequent power outages, which debilitated pumping stations and sewage treatment plants. This posed serious health consequences, with diarrhoea and other preventable illnesses spreading rapidly across many regions (Boyer-Souchet et al. 2011; NCCI OP-ED 2010; "Republic of Iraq Emergency Baghdad. . ." n.d.).

Iraq's water sector continues to suffer as a result of the ongoing volatile security situation in the country created by the Islamic State (IS) insurgency. Water infrastructures on the Tigris and Euphrates rivers have been an important dimension of IS's expansion strategy and a specific target. By 2015, IS had gained control of six dams along the rivers. By controlling major water infrastructure, IS has used water resources for military purposes, such as flooding areas and contaminating drinking water ("What does the future hold for water in Iraq?" 2016). Since 2013, the group has launched almost 20 major attacks against Iraqi and Syrian water infrastructure, including closing dam gates in Ramadi and Fallujah, and cutting off water supplies to Mosul. Throughout 2016, IS lost a significant amount of its territory as well as the water infrastructure it had captured, however, the dangerous environment created by the persistent armed conflict in the country, coupled with the damage to water facilities and the contamination of water sources, have further harshly impacted the country's water supply ("What does the future hold for water in Iraq?" 2016). In the context of such a volatile political and security environment, the rehabilitation of water resources, and rebuilding and modernisation of vital water infrastructure, poses significant challenges to Iraq's Ministry of Water Resources ("What does the future hold for water in Iraq?" 2016).

Today, Iraq's water sector is characterised by ageing infrastructure, leaking water and sewage networks and canals, poor drainage, wasteful irrigation practices and poorly maintained equipment (Zolnikov 2013). Corruption, low levels of investment in the water sector, electricity shortages, low technical capacity and a lack of qualified workers further exacerbate the situation. Years of armed conflict, war, embargoes and sanctions have also contributed significantly to poor water quality throughout the country. Hazardous chemicals, such as sulphate, carbonates, chlorides and nitrates have been discovered in various sources (Zolnikov 2013). Drinking water in many regions contains high levels of toxic minerals, suspended solids and salinity, and several groundwater sources of drinking water are brackish or contain excess saline. Increasingly frequent and persistent drought conditions due to climate change, coupled with agricultural development, population growth, industrial development, dam construction and other water diversion plans by upstream riparians Syria, Turkey, and Iran continue to further devastate the country's already fragile water sector and natural ecosystem (Zolnikov 2013).

Chapter outline

Against the backdrop of myriad contemporary challenges in the Iraqi water sector, coupled with the history of armed conflict and war, the ongoing volatile security situation and a fragile geopolitical environment, this chapter will explore two cases in which invaluable water resources were managed, restored and protected in the post-conflict context. First, the chapter will take an in-depth look at the restoration of the Iraqi Marshlands. Importantly, the chapter will focus on various restoration efforts, the links between restoration projects and peacebuilding, economic development and sustainable livelihoods, as well as challenges to ongoing restoration efforts. Second, the chapter will consider the rehabilitation of the *kahrez* systems in northern

Iraq, its impacts on sustainable livelihoods and community development, its links with conflict resolution and peacebuilding, and its contribution to a more reliable and sustainable source of groundwater for communities living in northern Iraq and Iraqi Kurdistan.

Restoration of the Iraqi Marshlands

The Mesopotamian Marshlands, often referred to as the Iraqi Marshes, were once among the largest wetlands in the world, covering over 10,500km² (Lonergan 2012:223). The famous Marshlands, in the lower floodplains of the Tigris and Euphrates, were home to an estimated 500,000 people and supported a diverse range of flora and fauna (Managing for Change 2010; "Conserving and restoring. . ." 2016; Coast 2003). The Iraqi Marshlands consist of the interconnected wetland systems of the Central Marsh, Hammar Marsh and Hawizeh Marsh, and are located in the areas around the confluence of the Tigris and Euphrates rivers in the governorates of Basra, Maysan and Dhiqar in southern Iraq (Aoki et al. 2014:117–118).

Significance of the Marshes

The Iraqi Marshlands, the largest wetland ecosystem in the Middle East, are of historical, ecological and sociocultural importance (Lonergan 2012:224).

The history of the indigenous marsh dwellers, the Ma'dan, or Marsh Arabs, can be traced back at least 5,000 years (Reiss n.d.). The lives and livelihoods of the Marsh Arabs have for centuries centred around a healthy marsh ecosystem, which provided drinking water, building materials and transportation, and enabled marsh dwellers to engage in fishing and agricultural activities (Lonergan 2012:223). Many also consider the Iraqi Marshes the cradle of civilisation, and the site of the biblical Garden of Eden (Lonergan 2012:224).

Apart from their historical and ecological significance, the Marshes have also been of strategic importance to the government of Iraq. During the 1980s, the Marshes were the sites of fighting in the Iran/Iraq war, and subsequent invasions in 1991 and 2003 by US and coalition forces went through the Marshes (Lonergan 2012:224).

One of the world's largest oil fields, the Majnoon Oil Field, is also located in the Marshes, adding further to the socioeconomic, political and strategic importance of the area ("Conserving and restoring. . ." 2016).

The destruction of the Marshes

Plans to drain the Marshes in order to reclaim the land for agricultural purposes were developed by the British from 1951. However, it was only following the 1991 Gulf War that systematic efforts to destroy the Marshes actually began, initially through aerial bombing and the burning of villages (Lonergan 2012:226; Managing for Change 2010). The government of Saddam Hussein followed up these efforts with the building of extensive drainage structures in order to dry out the wetland ecosystem, and force migration away from the Marshlands, which had become a haven for political factions opposed to his regime (Reiss n.d.; Aoki et al. 2014:118; Lonergan 2012; Managing for Change 2010).

The international community became aware of the true extent of the Marshlands' destruction when, in 2001, UNEP released satellite images which showed that an estimated 90 per cent of the Marshes had already been destroyed (UNEP 2007; Aoki et al. 2014:117; Managing for Change 2010:1). By the fall of Saddam's regime in 2003, the Iraqi government's construction of dams and hundreds of drainage canals resulted in the Marshes being reduced to less than 10 per cent of their pre-1990 size. It had also displaced most of the Marsh Arabs, reducing the population in the Marshes from an estimated half a million to less than 80,000 people, and causing immeasurable damage to the livelihoods of local residents (Managing for Change 2010:1; Reiss n.d.; Lonergan 2012:226; France 2006; Aoki et al. 2014; UNEP 2007; Charbonneau 2009). In a little over a decade then, the Marsh Arabs had been persecuted, forced into exile or pushed onto the drained lands on the margins, left with limited services and a ruined economy (Reiss n.d.). The draining of the Marshes was identified as a major environmental and humanitarian disaster by the UN and the World Bank (Managing for Change 2010:1; Lonergan 2012:226).

Rehabilitation and restoration of the Iraqi Marshes

With the fall of the Saddam regime in 2003, an opportunity emerged for Iraqi and international actors to assess the damage to the Marshlands and begin restoration efforts. The Iraqi government, working in collaboration with various actors, including the governments of Canada, Italy, Japan and the USA, as well as UNEP and UNDP, initiated a range of habitat restoration projects ("The New Eden Project. . ." 2014). The sections below will provide a brief overview of several of these restoration projects.

Italian restoration efforts

Launched in June 2003 within the framework of the Italian and Iraqi governments' cooperation agreement, the New Eden Project has played an integral role in restoration efforts in the Marshlands. Established under the auspices of the Washington DC-based Free Iraq Foundation, the day-to-day running of the project was then handed over to Nature Iraq, an Iraqi-based NGO ("The New Eden Project. . ." 2014).

The Italian Ministry for the Environment, Land and Sea (IMELS) worked in collaboration with international donors including UNEP, UNDP, UNOPS (United Nations Office for Project Services), USAID (United States Agency for International Development), CIDA (Canadian International Development Agency), the US State Department and JICA (Japan International Cooperation Agency), to assist the Iraqi ministries of Environment, Water Resources and Municipalities and Public Works in the coordination of the New Eden Team project ("The New Eden Project. . ." 2014).

The New Eden Project study area encompasses 40,000 km^2 in southern Iraq, in the three governorates of Basrah, Missan and Thi Qar, and comprises an estimated five million people ("The New Eden Project" 2009).

Through the New Eden Project, the IMELS has invested over 20 million euros in projects and works related to the restoration of the Iraq Marshlands ("The New Eden Project. . ." 2014). Notable achievements of the project include: the reflooding and re-naturalisation of a large part of the Marshlands, from the initial 7 per cent to an estimated 40–60 per cent, depending on yearly climatic conditions; the erection of structural facilities such as buildings, laboratories, water regulators, monitoring networks and fisheries; and the return of a significant number of the native population ("The New Eden Project. . ." 2014).

In addition, in July 2013, the Iraqi Council of Ministers approved in principle the establishment of Iraq's Central Marshes as a National Park. Over 350 people participated in the preparation of the New Eden Master Plan for Integrated Water Resources Management in the Marshlands (2004–2007), (including 115 scientists – 45 Italian and 70 Iraqi), which aimed to assist Iraqi policy makers by providing sound information and analytical tools with which to make reasoned choices regarding environmental management and water resource allocation decisions ("The New Eden Project" n.d.). Over the past ten years, over 60 capacity building sessions/workshops/courses have been carried out in Iraq, as well as in Canada, Italy, Jordan, Syria and Kuwait, training over 500 individuals in various topics including environmental monitoring and surveys, geographic information system (GIS) and hydrological modelling, the management of protected areas, water and sanitation planning, environmental impact assessment (EIA) and biodiversity field training ("The New Eden Project" n.d.).

Through the second five-year memorandum of understanding between Nature Iraq and the Italian and Iraqi ministries of Environment, beginning in 2010, efforts have also been directed at providing technical support to the Iraqi Ministry of Environment, primarily with regards to Iraq's obligations under the Convention on Biological Diversity (CBD), the Ramsar Convention on Wetlands, the Cartagena Protocol on Biosafety, and the UN Framework Convention on Climate Change (UNFCCC) ("New Eden Projects – Nature Iraq" n.d.). To this end, Nature Iraq has assisted in compiling Iraq's first Greenhouse Gas Inventory, prepared the chapter on biodiversity in Iraq's first national communication to the UNFCCC and assisted in the first national report on biodiversity to the CBD ("New Eden Projects – Nature Iraq" n.d.).

USAID restoration efforts in the Iraqi Marshlands

In 2003, USAID began its involvement in the restoration efforts, with the funding of the Iraq–Marshlands Restoration Program (IMRP) (IMRP–DAI n.d.). Implemented by DAI, the project, which ran between May 2003 and November 2006, aimed to (i) restore the region and make it environmentally sustainable and economically profitable for marsh dwellers, (ii) improve the management of existing and newly reflooded Marshlands, and (iii) expand restoration activities (IMRP–DAI n.d.).

The IMRP worked on two tracks. At the national level, the IMRP developed the first hydrologic model of the Tigris and Euphrates river basins to simulate water allocation and flood control, established a Marshlands monitoring system, re-established water and soil laboratories at the University of Basra and in the Ministry of Water Resources in Baghdad, and helped the government articulate a comprehensive marsh restoration policy (Aoki et al. 2014; Reiss n.d.; IMRP–DAI n.d.). The IMRP led to the reflooding of more than half of the Marshes. At the regional level, DAI worked in five priority areas: agriculture, fishing, livestock and dairy, integrated marsh management, and primary health care (IMRP–DAI n.d.). Through the project, at the regional level, cultivated land for sorghum and barley increased from 4,860ha to 21,590ha; eight nurseries were planted with 1,500 palm seedlings; 21,000 patients were served through two health clinics; 300,000 fish fingerlings were restocked; and 9,972 animals were treated through veterinary extension services (IMRP–DAI n.d.)

Through project implementation, DAI trained provincial government employees and university staff skilled in and able to apply the fundamentals of marsh restoration and wetland management; and identified committed provincial government employees who could carry forward livestock and agricultural efforts, as well as a team of veterinary graduates with experience working with livestock in marsh villages (IMRP–DAI n.d.) The IMRP helped create ownership by the Marsh Arab tribes, as evidenced by their adoption of program interventions, particularly in the areas of agriculture, public health and livestock (IMRP–DAI n.d.)

Overall, the project, which demonstrated the potential of a complex, multidisciplinary USAID program led and operated exclusively by Iraqis in-country, was considered a model for others in sustainable development (Reiss n.d.).

CIMI restoration efforts

Established in 2004, the Canada–Iraq Marshlands Initiative (CIMI) was a project designed to partner with local, regional and national organisations to better understand, restore and manage the Iraqi Marshes (Managing for Change 2010; Null 2010). The project aimed to train Iraqi wetland scientists and work with universities in the three southern governorates of Iraq in order to enhance their scientific capabilities. Meetings were held twice a year with local sheikhs, university researchers, governorate officials and national ministry representatives (Lonergan 2012:225).

The first phase of the CIMI project focused on enhancing the scientific capacity of Iraqi researchers and universities in environmental monitoring and analysis. The second phase, which was initiated in 2007 and ran until March 2010, prioritised wetlands planning and management, and meeting the basic needs of the marsh residents. Led by the University of Victoria, in cooperation with the University of Waterloo, the Fraser Basin Council of British Columbia and Iraqi partners, the second phase of the initiative was funded by CIDA (Managing for Change 2010; Lonergan 2012; Null 2010).

Four key themes were central to the Canada–Iraq Marshlands Initiative and hence the sustainability of the Marshes: (Managing for Change 2010:vi; Lonergan 2012):

1   The importance of a formal mechanism between Turkey, Syria, Iran, and Iraq to facilitate discussions on transboundary water issues.
2   The need for continued learning and capacity building in wetlands management.
3   The importance of designating the healthiest marshes as a Category IV Protected Area under international guidelines to allow for the maintenance of the existing habitat and the protection of biological communities including existing human settlements.
4   The need to put in place and maintain a collaborative decision-making model capable of taking action on all factors outlined in the CIMI report (Managing for Change 2010:vi).

Through the CIMI, two key outputs emerged:

1   *Managing for Change: The Present and Future State of the Marshes of Southern Iraq*: a report which provides a scientific basis for the creation and adoption of management strategies for the sustainable development of the Marshes. Importantly, the report developed an index of ecosystem health to better understand the spatial variability in water and soil quality in the Marshes, identified key factors that influenced the restoration of the Marshes, and using these factors and the data on ecosystem health, presented possible scenarios for the future (Managing for Change 2010:vi).
2   *An Atlas of the Marshes*, which comprises satellite photos, maps and pictures used in or developed by the project (Managing for Change 2010:vi; Lonergan 2012).

UNEP restoration efforts

UNEP's involvement in the Iraqi Marshlands dates back to 2001, when it began monitoring changes in the Marshlands using satellite data, and established the Iraqi Marshlands Observation System to provide information to the international community (UNEP 2007). In 2004, the UNEP Iraqi Marshlands Project was established as part of the UN Assistance Mission for the Reconstruction of Iraq. This project, which serves as one of the largest restoration efforts undertaken in the Iraqi Marshlands, focused on wetland rehabilitation and improving water supply to marsh residents (Aoki et al. 2014:120; Lonergan 2012).

The purpose of wetland rehabilitation was to revive life in the Marshlands and prevent further deterioration of the socioeconomic conditions of the people, as well as improve security and stability in the region (Aoki et al. 2014:129). In order to restore the Marshlands, reflooding was necessary. The UNEP Iraqi Marshlands Project focused specifically on two aspects of wetland rehabilitation. In the first phase, project interventions focused on environmentally sound technologies (ESTs) for restoring degraded areas of the wetlands; while in the second phase, interventions focused on ESTs to improve the quantity and quality of water available for reflooding (Aoki et al. 2014:129).

The Iraqi Ministry of Environment, which was established in 2003, took the lead on the project, and worked in collaboration with the Ministry of Water Resources and the Ministry of Municipalities and Public Works (Aoki et al. 2014:120). The project also involved representatives from the governorate councils from Basra, Maysan and Dhiqar, local groups, universities and NGOs (Aoki et al. 2014:121).

Key project outcomes were:

- The project provided drinking water for up to 25,000 rural residents and demonstrated sanitation and wetland management practices for replication, and thus contributed importantly to improving the living conditions of the local communities (Aoki et al. 2014:125).
- The project also pioneered the use of modular reverse osmosis container units for water purification in rural areas, and the number of these units funded by the Iraqi government and donors in the Marshlands increased significantly (Aoki et al. 2014:125).
- The project generated important data on marshland conditions: through water-quality and biodiversity monitoring, baseline data was established and limited trend analysis of marshland conditions was conducted (Aoki et al. 2014:125).
- Over 2,000 participants were involved in project initiatives, thereby increasing the level of community engagement in marshland management (Aoki et al. 2014:125).
- Through the project, a number of training sessions were held: 14 international training sessions involved 314 participants, 10 in-country training sessions brought together 141 participants, and 2 study tours were organised with 22 participants (Aoki et al. 2014:126).
- The project involved relevant ministries in developing data collection and analysis methods, and in preparing survey reports (Aoki et al. 2014:125).

UNEP's Iraqi Marshlands Project thus demonstrated environmentally sound technologies (ESTs) and management practices for rehabilitating wetlands and maintaining water quality, and provided pilot-scale sanitation services and access to safe and improved drinking water to residents in selected rural communities (Aoki et al. 2014:117).

Links to peacebuilding

The UNEP Iraqi Marshlands Project played a significant role in the socioeconomic dimension of reconstruction and peacebuilding, as it provided relief and basic social services, and support for the return of displaced populations (Aoki et al. 2014:129). Notably, the project's drinking water interventions helped the rural area accommodate the projected number of returning displaced people (Aoki et al. 2014:129). In addition to rehabilitating the wetlands and providing access to safe drinking water, the project further contributed to peacebuilding efforts by helping address residents' frustration and desperation, and increasing trust and partnership between public authorities and local communities (Aoki et al. 2014:130).

UNEP's Iraqi Marshlands Project was one of the first and largest environmental management initiatives implemented with UN support following the establishment of the Iraqi Ministry of Environment. To this end, the project importantly served as a platform for on-the-job training in international cooperation, environmental management and domestic coordination for the ministry and its staff (Aoki et al. 2014:133). Furthermore, it provided a practical context for establishing cooperative working relations with other ministries, the governorates, universities, local groups, and international and non-governmental organisations (Aoki et al. 2014:133).

Through the project's various interventions and their successful impacts, UNEP's Iraqi Marshlands Project further contributed to Iraq's environmental policy-making efforts, as well as the country's involvement in international environmental regimes. At the national level, the positive impacts of the project extended to the development of new water law and policy (Aoki et al. 2014:133; UNEP 2009a, 2009b). On a broader scale, through the project, the Iraqi people and institutions gained a deeper appreciation of the global value of the Iraqi Marshlands and the country's natural environment. The project further influenced the Iraqi Ministry of Environment's efforts for Iraqi accession to various multilateral environmental agreements (MEAs) including the Convention on Biological Diversity, the Ramsar Convention and the UN Framework Convention on Climate Change (Aoki et al. 2014:133; UNEP 2009a, 2009b).

Challenges in implementing the various marshland restoration projects

Despite the broad successes of the marshland restoration projects detailed above, each faced numerous challenges, and various factors had negative impacts on the project intervention outcomes. Most significant among these challenges was the security situation on the ground in the post-war period. Worsening security and continued acts of terrorism at the local level presented immense security and accountability challenges for all stakeholders involved in the various restoration projects (Aoki et al. 2014:128). In the case of the UNEP Iraqi Marshlands Project, for example, interventions related to basic services, such as electricity generation or water treatment, had to be halted on many occasions due to security concerns and, in some cases, these interventions were destroyed by terrorism (Aoki et al. 2014:128). In addition, the limited availability of human, financial, technical and other resources, in part due to the decade-long sanctions against the government, as well as the instability of the telecommunications infrastructure and limitations on the electricity supply, further hindered the effective and efficient implementation of project interventions (Aoki et al. 2014:129; UNEP 2009a, 2009b).

Marshland restoration projects: links to post-conflict peacebuilding, economic development and sustainable livelihoods

Despite the many challenges, the partial restoration of the Mesopotamian Marshes through the efforts of various international and local actors has been heralded as one of the few success stories to emerge in the post-war Iraqi peacebuilding environment (Schwartzstein 2015). Importantly, these projects did not focus solely on restoring the marshland habitats; they also prioritised environmental sustainability, socioeconomic development and livelihoods, and thus contributed significantly to the post-conflict peacebuilding project in Iraq. Interventions were geared towards restoration efforts as well as providing basic services, training and capacity building, and making living conditions more conducive for displaced populations returning to the Marshlands.

Across the restoration efforts, project interventions prioritised the training and capacity building of a range of stakeholders (including government employees, researchers, scientists, technical experts, academics, students). In addition, restoration efforts were all done in collaboration with relevant local, regional and national stakeholders across various sectors and, to the extent possible, project interventions ensured local ownership from the outset.

Restoration efforts also contributed to advancing Iraqi law and policy-making in the areas of environmental restoration, rehabilitation and sustainable development. Furthermore, through the various project interventions and their outcomes, international actors provided support and guidance to Iraqi ministries as they sought accession to various MEAs and worked to meet their obligations under international environmental regimes.

Progress in recent years

Iraq's accession to international environmental agreements

In early 2008, Iraq became a party to the Convention on Wetlands of International Importance, commonly known as the Ramsar Convention. Under this convention, the Hawizeh Marsh is listed as a site of international importance (Lonergan 2012:229). In July 2009, Iraq became party to the UNFCCC and the Kyoto Protocol, and in October 2009, the country became party to the Convention on Biological Diversity. Iraq has also become a member of the Global Environment Facility (GEF), and since 2010, the country has been eligible for GEF financing in the fields of climate change and biodiversity (Aoki et al. 2014:135; Lonergan 2012:229).

Continued restoration efforts

In recent years, restoration efforts in the Iraqi Marshlands have continued through a number of initiatives. Most notable among them has been the joint UNEP–UNESCO project, launched in 2009, to assist in transitioning from short- and medium-term interventions in the post-conflict period, to implement a longer-term sustainable management framework in the Iraqi Marshlands ("Iraq Project – Background" n.d.). Building upon the experiences and outcomes of the UNEP project for environmental management of the Iraqi Marshlands, this joint project focused on emerging priority needs to promote longer-term sustainable management practices that reflect the unique historical, cultural, environmental, hydrological and socio-economic characteristics of the Marshlands ("Iraq Project – Background" n.d.). In particular, the project used the World Heritage inscription process as a tool to develop and implement a sustainable management framework, and prepare a World Heritage nomination file for the Marshlands ("Iraq Project – Background" n.d.). With funding from the government of Italy, the project sought to implement key practices for resource efficiency and sustainable production/consumption, build capacity and raise awareness among the local population to ensure their participation for ecosystem management and site preservation ("Iraq Project – Background" n.d.).

The 2011–2014 UN Development Assistance Framework (UNDAF) for Iraq also gave priority to water resource management, particularly in the Iraqi Marshlands and those which involved transboundary issues (Aoki et al. 2014:135). Furthermore, UN programming has focused on addressing climate change by strengthening institutions and institutional frameworks, assessing Iraq's vulnerability to climate change, and identifying opportunities for climate change mitigation measures that have economic, social and environmental benefits, including the potential for the development of green jobs (UN 2010; Aoki et al. 2014:135).

In January 2014, the government of Iraq signed a landmark five-year Strategic Cooperation Agreement with UNEP, aimed at strengthening the country's attempts to overcome its many environmental challenges, speeding up environmental recovery and supporting peacebuilding efforts ("UN to help Iraq. . ." 2014). Areas of cooperation defined by the agreement will focus on: biodiversity conservation; cleaner production; combating dust storms; climate change reporting, mitigation and adaptation; environmental legislation and regulations; green economy; and resource efficiency ("UN to help Iraq. . ." 2014).

Iraqi Marshlands – a UNESCO World Heritage Site

On August 17, 2016, the Iraqi Marshlands was officially inscribed on the UNESCO World Heritage List at the 40th Session of the World Heritage Committee in Istanbul, Turkey. The inscription of the property known as "The Ahwar of Southern Iraq: Refuge of Biodiversity and the Relict Landscape of the Mesopotamian Cities" serves as an international recognition of its outstanding universal value ("UN Environment helps Arab negotiators. . ." n.d.; "Iraqi Marshlands named. . ." 2016; "The Marshlands of Iraq. . ." 2016). The Ahwar of Southern Iraq have been recognised by UNESCO as one of the world's largest inland delta systems, within a desert landscape (in an extremely hot and arid environment). The area named comprises seven sites in southern Iraq: the three Sumerian Mesopotamian archaeological sites of Ur, Uruk and Eridu, and four wetland marsh areas – Huwaizah, East and West Hammar and the Central Marshes. The inscription is considered 'unprecedented' as it is the first time a World Heritage dossier of mixed property and serial nomination has been listed ("UN Environment helps Arab negotiators. . ." n.d.; "Iraqi Marshlands named. . ." 2016; "The Marshlands of Iraq. . ." 2016).

The country has been seeking World Heritage Status for the Marshes since 2003, and the recent inscription of the Marshes on the World Heritage List serves as a significant milestone and impetus for Iraq's continued efforts to promote and advance the sustainable management of the Ahwar's natural and cultural components, in collaboration with the international community ("UN Environment helps Arab negotiators. . ." n.d.; "Iraqi Marshlands named. . ." 2016; "The Marshlands of Iraq. . ." 2016). It is also hoped that this important step will now pave the way for exemplary conservation of Iraq's natural ecosystems, create new opportunities for the community and maintain sustainable livelihoods. The Iraqi Marshlands are the fifth site from Iraq to be included in the World Heritage List, after Ashur, Hatra, Samarra Archaeological City and Erbil Citadel ("UN Environment helps Arab negotiators. . ." n.d.; "Iraqi Marshlands named. . ." 2016; "The Marshlands of Iraq. . ." 2016).

Ongoing restoration efforts and current realities

In the post-war period, restoration efforts by international actors, including UNEP, UNDP, the USA, Japan, Italy and Canada, working in collaboration with Iraqi nationals at the regional and local levels, contributed to a remarkable comeback of the Marshes from 2003 to 2008 (Null 2010).

However, despite efforts in recent years, today, the Marshes are only a fraction of their former size, they no longer provide appreciable sustenance at the national level, and support less than 10 per cent of their original number of inhabitants (Null 2010). In addition, the greatly reduced water flows of the Tigris and Euphrates, the two rivers that feed the Marshes, are once again threatening the livelihoods of some of the area's inhabitants (Schwartzstein 2015). From a high of approximately 75 per cent restored in 2008, the wetlands were at 58 per cent of their average pre-drained level in 2015, and expected to continue shrinking during the summer months (Schwartzstein 2015).

A 2014 report on the State of Environment and Outlook in Iraq, prepared by the government of Iraq, with support from UNEP, UNDP and the WHO, highlighted key facts and figures on current socioeconomic and environmental challenges that are threatening the sustainable management, restoration and preservation of Iraq's natural ecosystems, including the Marshlands. First amongst these issues is increasing population growth, which is adding significant pressure to existing food, energy and water resources ("Landmark agreement. . ." 2014). The report predicts that by 2030, the population is expected to grow to almost 50 million people, further exacerbating these problems. Sustainable access to safe water and sanitation continues to be a challenge: an estimated 83 per cent of Iraq's wastewater is left untreated, contributing further to the pollution of Iraq's waterways and the environment ("Landmark agreement. . ." 2014). Decades of violence and conflict have led to chemical pollution and unexploded ordnances, which are affecting the lives and safety of an estimated 1.6 million Iraqis. The drought of 2005–2009 further reduced already limited water supplies ("Landmark agreement. . ." 2014). Between 1977 and 2009, the amount of water available per person per year is estimated to have decreased from 5,900 cubic metres, to 2,400 cubic metres. The report further warns that, if current conditions prevail, the Tigris and Euphrates, two of the country's major surface water sources, may dry up ("Landmark agreement. . ." 2014).

Despite the emergence of promising longer-term initiatives and the inscription of the Iraqi Marshlands on the UNESCO World Heritage List, current and emerging environmental threats, together with socioeconomic, political and security conditions in the country, are negatively impacting on the improvements in natural resource management that have been achieved thus far, and threaten to continue undermining ongoing restoration efforts in the Marshlands (Aoki et al. 2014:135).

Threats to ongoing restoration efforts

Harsh natural conditions

Harsh natural conditions are severely impeding restoration efforts in the Iraqi Marshlands (Schwartzstein 2015). The drought of 2008–2009 significantly reduced the water flow and vegetative cover in the wetlands and the availability of water around the country. By the fall of 2009, the size of the Marshes had approached that of 2002 (Lonergan 2012:228). The drought and resulting desertification, attributed to climate change, have had significant negative impacts on the country's economic development and the quality of the life of the people (Aoki et al. 2014:134). With greater climate variability expected to persist in the future, longer and more severe droughts in the region are expected, which will further impact the already declining quality and quantity of water, and shock this vulnerable ecosystem (Lonergan 2012:238).

Upstream concerns

Increasing demand for water for non-agricultural uses and infrastructure developments upstream have reduced and continue to severely reduce the flow of water to the Marshes. Since 2006, Iran has dammed many of the small rivers which provided water to the Hawizeh Marsh. In the spring of 2009, Iran completed the construction of a six-metre high dike along its border with Iraq, which divided the Hawizeh Marsh, the largest of the three areas, into two

(Lonergan 2012:228; Null 2010). According to the UN, dam construction in Turkey and Iran has reduced the combined volumes of the rivers by up to 60 per cent (Schwartzstein 2015). Furthermore, with increasing withdrawals of water upstream, from both Turkey and Iran, as well as other sectors within Iraq, it is unlikely that there will ever be enough water to replenish the Marshes to the extent they reached prior to 1990 (Schwartzstein 2015; Lonergan 2012; Null 2010). The increasing withdrawals of water and infrastructure developments have led to greater controlling of the flow of water upstream, which is eliminating the annual pulse of water that cleansed the Marshes of salt and other pollutants. In addition, the reduced flow of water from Iran is posing increasing problems to the extent and health of the Hawizeh Marsh (Schwartzstein 2015; Lonergan 2012; Null 2010).

Broader socioeconomic and environmental concerns

Despite restoration efforts in the Marshes after 2003, and continued efforts by the government to rebuild the lost communities of Marsh Arabs, the wetlands continue to suffer from a lack of water, poor health in some areas and a lack of economic opportunities once provided by the ecosystem services (e.g. fishing, reeds for weaving and construction, the sustenance for buffalo) (Managing for Change 2010:1). While it is likely that water levels in the Marshes will continue to fluctuate in wet and drought years, much of the original Southern Marshes have been converted into agricultural lands by the Iraqi government, and are unlikely to ever return to wetlands. There are also plans to develop oil resources under some of the existing and former marshes (Null 2010; Lonergan 2012:237). Low rainfall levels and wasteful irrigation practices in the country further suggest that the Marshes will remain at only a fraction of their original size (Schwartzstein 2015).

Marsh Arabs returning to the region must now also contend with the declining quality of water. While residents once drank directly from the Marshes, they must now buy water from treatment plants. Waterborne diseases, particularly those causing skin and gastrointestinal problems, are increasing, and the lack of doctors or medical facilities nearby makes it increasingly challenging for displaced communities now returning to the wetlands to seek basic health care (Schwartzstein 2015).

Political factors

In recent years, the government of Iraq has demonstrated a continued commitment to the ongoing restoration of the Marshes, for both ecological and humanitarian reasons. The inscription of the Iraqi Marshes on the UNESCO World Heritage List has given further impetus to government bodies at the local, regional and national levels not only to continue improving the infrastructure and ensuring basic service delivery for marsh residents, but to also pay greater attention to the ecology of the Marshes. However, greater intergovernmental coordination is needed, and a better balance between prioritising economic development needs and ecological restoration is necessary in the Marshlands (Lonergan 2012:230). The lack of interest of neighbouring states in the restoration of the Marshes is equally concerning, and with existing socioeconomic and environmental pressures, a lack of increased efforts by the Iraqi government to build stronger collaboration for the ecological restoration and sustainable management of the Marshes with neighbouring countries is likely to further negatively impact upon the wetland ecosystem and the livelihoods of returning communities (Lonergan 2012:238).

Security concerns – the spread of IS across Iraq

The Islamic State's stronghold in northern and western Iraq poses significant additional challenges for the continued restoration efforts in the Marshes, as well as to the communities trying to rebuild their lives in the wetlands. Marsh Arabs trying to sustain livelihoods have been deprived of selling in the areas now under IS control, such as the markets in Tikrit and Ramadi, amongst other places, and are limited to selling across the impoverished south of Iraq (Schwartzstein 2015).

Over the past several years, IS has repeatedly used water as a weapon across the country, seizing control over dams including those at Fallujah, Ramadi and Mosul (Schwartzstein 2015). IS control of the upper reaches of the Euphrates River has enabled them to further reduce the water flow to the Marsh Arabs, whom IS also considers enemies due to their minority status as adherents to Shia Islam (King 2016).

The impacts on the wetlands have not only been from further upstream, as IS has also in the past few years controlled territory surrounding the wetlands, such as in 2014 when it was operating a cell near Lake Hamrin (Mironova and Hussein 2017).

The destructive effects of IS's activities on the country's scarce water resources and its shrinking wetlands are likely to continue, further hindering the sustainable management of the Marshes and jeopardising the livelihoods of the returning Marsh Arabs (Mironova and Hussein 2017).

Thus, despite impressive efforts since 2003 to restore the wetlands and implement sustainable management practices and policies, given current and unfolding socioeconomic, political and security conditions, coupled with climate variability and harsh natural conditions, the future of the Iraqi Marshes and the livelihoods of the Marsh Arabs appear bleak (Lonergan 2012:238).

Rehabilitation of the *kahrez* in northern Iraq

What are the kahrez?

Kahrez in Kurdish, or 'Qanats' in Arabic (Aflaj in the Arabian Peninsula), are a system of ancient underground aqueducts that bring infiltrated groundwater, surface water or spring water to the surface using only the earth's gravitational force ("Rehabilitation and conservation. . ." n.d.).

Through this ancient water conveyance and irrigation system, water is collected in underground canals at the foot of rocky hills, and then carried to neighbouring fields, where it is drawn off by strategically located well shafts ("Rehabilitation and conservation. . ." n.d.).

For centuries, *kahrez* have played an integral role in supplying irrigation and drinking water to communities around the world, particularly in the Middle East and North Africa, and Central and West Asia (Wessels 2014). These underground water tunnels have provided an essential lifeline for communities in northern and eastern Iraq, particularly in the Iraqi Kurdistan region. Up until the early 2000s, it is estimated that at least 380 *kahrez* were still in use in Iraq (NCCI OP-ED 2010).

Kahrez not only provide water to rural communities in a sustainable manner, but they also play an indispensable role in village social life, one that pump-wells cannot replicate. While these man-made underground aqueducts are centuries old, they are by no means obsolete (Wessels 2014). Cleared *kahrez* systems can significantly assist in mitigating the water security challenges in Iraq, providing increased amounts of water for irrigation and household purposes, as well as preserving Iraqi Kurdistan cultural and historical values ("Rehabilitation and conservation. . ." n.d.; Wessels 2012, 2014; NCCI OP-ED 2010; Boyer-Souchet et al. 2011; External Evaluation Report 2011).

Unfortunately, over the past few decades, against the backdrop of years of violent conflict, displacement of populations and droughts, the *kahrez* in northern Iraq have been rapidly drying up and being abandoned by rural communities. This has resulted in decay and damage to the historical structures, which are no longer sustainable, as well as a significant loss of traditional knowledge needed to maintain the systems ("Restoring the ancient Kahrez system. . ." 2009).

A study conducted by UNESCO found that the drought of 2005–2009, coupled with the lack of *kahrez* upkeep, resulted in the drying up of an estimated 70 per cent of the *kahrez* system, and contributed to the displacement of an estimated 100,000 people in northern Iraq (Walther 2011; Wessels 2014, 2012; "Restoring the ancient Kahrez system. . ." 2009; Boyer-Souchet et al. 2011).

The rehabilitation of the kahrez system

Recognising the urgent need for the rehabilitation of the *kahrez* system in order to improve water security in northern Iraq, in April 2007, UNESCO launched a project to rehabilitate the *kahrez* (Wessels 2014).

The project was implemented by the UNESCO Iraq Office, working in collaboration with the Iraqi Ministry of Irrigation and Water Services, the International Organization for Migration (IOM), the Kurdistan Regional Government (KRG) and UNESCO's International Centre for Qanat and Hydraulic Studies (Yazd, Iran) between April 2007 and March 2011. Funding for the project was granted by the EU in late 2006, through the UN Development Group Iraq Trust Fund (UNDG ITF), a multi-donor trust fund established in 2004 to channel resources for the reconstruction efforts ("Rehabilitation and conservation. . ." n.d.; External Evaluation Report 2011; Boyer-Souchet et al. 2011).

Aims and objectives of the project

Through the rehabilitation and conservation of *kahrez* water systems, the UNESCO project aimed to improve the supply of drinking water and water for irrigation in the rural areas of northern Iraq. In addition, the project aimed to generate both short-term skilled and unskilled employment, build the technical capacity of communities and government officials in long-term rehabilitation and maintenance of the systems, and build networks with regional and international *kahrez* experts and institutions to exchange information and expertise (External Evaluation Report 2011:3–4). Through rehabilitation of the *kahrez* and an improvement in the water supply, the project also hoped to entice communities to continue living in their villages, rather than moving to the urban areas (External Evaluation Report 2011:3–4).

Rehabilitation efforts

Following initial project delays, in 2009, scientific surveys were conducted in order to select sites for *kahrez* rehabilitation. In total, 20 *kahrez* systems in the Erbil and Sulaimaniyah governorates were selected for the project (External Evaluation Report 2011).

One of the pilot sites was the *kahrez* system in the village of Sheikh Mamudian, which lies north of the town of Shaqlawa in the Erbil Governorate (Wessels 2014). During the Al-Anfal Campaign of 1986–1990, the village was attacked by the regime of Saddam Hussein. Most of the homes were destroyed, although the residents had managed to flee before the arrival of the Iraqi army (Walther 2011; Wessels 2012:7). It was only in 1991 that some of the residents returned to the village, and began to restore their homes and clean out the *kahrez* tunnel, which had not been destroyed during the campaign. With the American invasion in 2003, many more villagers returned to establish their livelihoods in their communities. Despite their efforts, however, the years-long drought, which began in 2005, further harshly impacted the socioeconomic situation of the village (Wessels 2012:7).

The village of Sheikh Mamudian was selected as one of the pilot sites for *kahrez* rehabilitation, as the groundwater table had not yet plummeted and water could still be seen in the tunnel. However, there was an accumulation of debris inside the tunnel, as it had not been properly cleaned for many years (Wessels 2012:8). The rehabilitation of the underground water system required a change in the outlet point inside the irrigated fields. As the *kahrez* is community owned, the effects of the rehabilitation project were carefully considered in consultation with the village *mukthar* (local leader), a religious representative of the mosque, as well as the 50 families who owned a water irrigation right (Wessels 2012, 2014).

Rehabilitation of the *kahrez* system in Sheikh Mamudian was carried out under the supervision and guidance of experts from the UNESCO Centre on Qanats and Historic Hydraulic Structures (ICQHS). Following a feasibility study, the experts supervised the rehabilitation work, and offered guidance during the process. The *kahrez* was finally inaugurated in 2010 (Wessels 2012:9; Walther 2011; Wessels 2014).

Project outcomes

After a delay of 29 months following the project start date, the rehabilitation of the 20 selected *kahrez* systems was successfully achieved (External Evaluation Report 2011:7). While the KRG Ministry of Agriculture and Water Resources (MoAWR) was initially selected as the main implementing partner of the UNESCO Iraq Office, due to a lack of capacity within the ministry, UNESCO then brought in *kahrez* rehabilitation experts to conduct the first rehabilitation. Subsequently, rehabilitation of 4 of the sites was subcontracted to a local construction company, while 15 were completed by the IOM, which also brought in a *kahrez* rehabilitation expert to conduct and manage the process (External Evaluation Report 2011:7–8).

Following one year of project implementation, in 2010, the IOM had completed restoration of 15 *kahrez* systems in the governorate of Sulamaniyah, thereby providing easier access to water for both household and irrigation purposes, to 256 families and 50 hectares of cultivated land in 10 villages. The rehabilitation of the *kahrez* systems in Erbil also saw increases in water quantity and quality (Wessels 2014; IOM 2010; External Evaluation Report 2011).

Implementation challenges

UNESCO's *kahrez* rehabilitation project was the first of its kind in Iraq, and consequently posed several challenges during the project design and implementation phases. Key challenges included: a lack of knowledge of the locations, the implementation context and the nature of the *kahrez* systems in northern Iraq (External Evaluation Report 2011:5). In addition, at the outset, UNESCO was unfamiliar with the capacity of the Kurdistan Regional Government's Ministry of Agriculture and Water Resources, its primary implementing partner (External Evaluation Report 2011).

A number of external factors further impacted upon project implementation. These included: flooding, the drought in northern Iraq, the absence of the KRG's Ministry of Water Resources for several months, as well as UN Department of Safety and Security (UNDSS) security regulations for international UN staff working in Iraq (External Evaluation Report 2011:7).

Together, these challenges led to several delays, five project extensions and project completion 36 months after the original end date. However, after the first 18 months, project management and implementation improved markedly, and remained sound until the end of the project (External Evaluation Report 2011:4). Project evaluations also revealed that, overall, UNESCO responded well to problems as they occurred, by adopting alternative methods so as not to substantially affect project implementation. In the end, the project was completed within the budget and according to the original objectives (External Evaluation Report 2011:7).

Impacts of the kahrez rehabilitation project

The *kahrez* rehabilitation project in northern Iraq had a number of positive impacts on the communities.

Employment generation

An estimated 111 community members gained short-term employment through the rehabilitation projects. Additional local employment was generated through 19 rehabilitation sites, which were subcontracted to an Iraqi construction company, a local *kahrez* rehabilitation company and the IOM. This short-term employment led to income generation for community members and increased their *kahrez* rehabilitation skills (External Evaluation Report 2011:8).

Improvements in living conditions

Kahrez rehabilitation led to improvements in both the quality and quantity of water available for household, agricultural and/or livestock use in communities. This in turn had an indirect positive impact on living conditions in most communities, as many of the *kahrez* had no water for a number of years prior to the project (External Evaluation Report 2011). As a result, most of the communities increased their water usage from the *kahrez*. While the amount of water from the *kahrez* was insufficient for all the communities' water needs, it did lead to plans for expanding agricultural production for personal and/or business purposes in a number of communities (External Evaluation Report 2011; Wessels 2014).

Participatory approach

The *kahrez* rehabilitation project in northern Iraq adopted a participatory approach, involving local communities and villagers in the interventions from the outset. Integrating local leadership, culture and customary systems of governance in the rehabilitation process helped ensure a more sustainable and successful outcome. In addition, this participatory approach served to indirectly raise awareness of the importance of *kahrez* systems and their rehabilitation in nearby communities (External Evaluation Report 2011; Wessels 2012).

Capacity building

The rehabilitation project increased the capacities of MoAWR in *kahrez* rehabilitation and maintenance in several ways. First, the technical capacity of MoAWR staff was enhanced through two comprehensive training sessions, a study tour and guidelines in the UNESCO Kahrez Manual (External Evaluation Report 2011:9). This Manual, together with a Concept Note and Kahrez Survey, was developed as part of UNESCO's comprehensive plan for further *kahrez* rehabilitation and conservation in Iraq (External Evaluation Report 2011:9). The Kahrez Survey provided MoAWR with in-depth information on the location and nature of the *kahrez* systems in northern Iraq, which could facilitate further rehabilitation work. In addition, the Kahrez Survey revealed population movements related to the decline of *kahrez*, which did not exist in other *kahrez* countries. This in turn led to work on environment-related displacement in Iraq (External Evaluation Report 2011:11; Wessels 2012).

By connecting MoAWR staff with regional and international *kahrez* experts, and enabling MoAWR to participate in existing regional and international *kahrez* networks, the project facilitated the sharing of information and experience on *kahrez* rehabilitation, conservation and management in the region (External Evaluation Report 2011:11).

The project also indirectly increased MoAWR's support of *kahrez* for rural water management, and indirectly raised awareness of the cultural heritage of the *kahrez* systems (External Evaluation Report 2011:11).

Local *kahrez* rehabilitation skills were also built through the subcontracting of 19 sites for rehabilitation work. Most notably, the IOM provided training and skills development for local community members, particularly younger workers, in the art of *kahrez* restoration and rehabilitation (IOM 2010; Wessels 2014).

Shortcomings of the project

Despite the noteworthy impacts of *kahrez* rehabilitation in northern Iraq, the project was not without its shortcomings. At some rehabilitation sites, tensions were created between community members over the selection of *kahrez* to be restored, and individuals who received livelihood support from the IOM. However, these factors did not significantly decrease the overall positive impacts of the project (External Evaluation Report 2011:11–12).

While the rehabilitation projects built the capacity of MoAWR in many ways, the practical training could have been further developed. In addition, the technical capacity of community members in long-term *kahrez* rehabilitation and maintenance could have been significantly strengthened. In only one instance of restoration did the subcontractors deliver sufficient technical training to community members on how to operate and maintain the *kahrez*, as well as on the proper use of these systems. While some community members gained this experience through employment on the rehabilitation sites, not all communities had members employed, and this did not include formal training (External Evaluation Report 2011:9).

Finally, operating policies and procedures for managing the rehabilitation of *kahrez* were also lacking, with only guidelines developed in the Kahrez Manual (External Evaluation Report 2011:9).

Kahrez *rehabilitation: links to peacebuilding, economic development and sustainable livelihoods*

Kahrez rehabilitation, community development and conflict resolution

Through close collaboration with rural communities, UNESCO's *kahrez* rehabilitation project contributed importantly to local community development and conflict resolution. Through this project, it became evident that the act of rehabilitating *kahrez*, conducted under the guidance of local leaders with traditional knowledge and a deep understanding of the cultural heritage of these ancient underground aqueducts, can contribute to preventing water conflicts, particularly in the context of drought and climate change, which are further harshly impacting upon already scarce water resources in northern Iraq (Wessels 2012:12; Wessels 2014). In addition, successful rehabilitation of *kahrez* systems contributes to community revitalisation: it promotes the settlement of people, strengthens social cohesion and local development, and can also lead to an increase in tourism in the area (Wessels 2012:12). The sustainable maintenance of *kahrez*, on the other hand, serves as a preventative measure, preserving the symbiotic relationship between the water systems and the villages that depend upon them (Wessels 2012:11; Wessels 2014).

Governance of kahrez systems

Kahrez rehabilitation in northern Iraq and other parts of the Middle East has revealed that strong local leadership is necessary to ensure the effective management of *kahrez* as a common water resource in communities. Where there is a lack of local leadership, internal divisions and a history of disagreements over common water resources, the improper management of and disputes over *kahrez* systems are likely (Wessels 2012:11).

Having a clear definition of ownership of the *kahrez* systems, and hence having responsibility for their maintenance in place, is essential, as is a defined system of rights, controls and regulations on water. These systems and definitions are necessary in order to avoid conflict following *kahrez* rehabilitation, when water increases or begins to flow once again (Wessels 2012:11).

With respect to the maintenance of the *kahrez* systems, restoration efforts across northern Iraq and the Middle East have demonstrated important links with customary systems of governance (Wessels 2012:11). Where local governance has a long uninterrupted history, and is still intact, *kahrez* are regularly maintained, whereas, in instances where the local history of governance is not that old, or has been severely interrupted (for example by years of conflict, drought or migration), local institutions are relatively weak. It is these *kahrez* systems that are most vulnerable to socioeconomic transformations of the modern world, such as the introduction of diesel power-operated pumps, which negatively impact upon *kahrez* maintenance, and in turn affect the integral role which *kahrez* play in strengthening social cohesion and protecting the cultural heritage of these communities (Wessels 2012:11).

Rehabilitation efforts – lessons learned

Selection of kahrez rehabilitation sites

Future projects should allocate a greater amount of time to select the *kahrez* sites for rehabilitation. This would enable *kahrez* of varying difficulty, size and nature to be selected, as well as those that would have the largest impact on the targeted community (External Evaluation Report 2011:14). In order to minimise tensions, relevant government bodies and local communities should be involved in the selection process, and actively support and participate in the project, particularly if work is conducted in the Disputed Internal Boundaries. Involvement of relevant local and government stakeholders would also ensure consideration of the particular environmental, socioeconomic and political contexts as sites are selected for rehabilitation (External Evaluation Report 2011:14).

Collaboration

Future *kahrez* rehabilitation projects should ensure collaboration across all related projects, sectors and levels of governance. Importantly, restoration efforts should be done in conjunction with other integrated resource management efforts (External Evaluation Report 2011:12). Projects should continue to involve regional and international *kahrez* experts, working in collaboration with local counterparts from the outset. This would help ensure a more sustainable effort, as traditional knowledge and customary systems of governance would be integrated in the process from its initiation. This would also assist implementing partners in exploring ways to more effectively combine traditional and new sustainable rehabilitation techniques (External Evaluation Report 2011:15). At the same time, the relevant government counterparts, local leaders and communities involved in the rehabilitation and restoration process would benefit from the knowledge and experience of *kahrez* experts. To this end, further practical training on *kahrez* rehabilitation, maintenance and management should be provided to communities, local leaders and governments (External Evaluation Report 2011:14).

The need for continued kahrez rehabilitation efforts

In recent years, groundwater levels in northern Iraq have been decreasing due to a lack of dams in the region, lack of rainfall and the illegal drilling of wells ("Groundwater in Iraqi Kurdistan. . ." 2017). In the context of growing regional water scarcity, an increased frequency of droughts due to climate change, a volatile security situation and the persistent use of water as a weapon by IS, the ancient underground aqueduct systems are an invaluable source of sustainable water resources for communities and villages across northern Iraq. The restoration and rehabilitation of the *kahrez* have demonstrated their capacity to contribute to sustainable livelihoods, conflict resolution and community development. Drawing upon the lessons from this first project, the rehabilitation, restoration and maintenance of *kahrez* systems offer a unique opportunity to further integrate natural resource management efforts, and provide a sustainable source of groundwater resources to communities and villages across northern Iraq and Iraqi Kurdistan.

References

Aoki C., Al-Lami, A., and Kugaprasatham, S. (2014) "Environmental management of the Iraqi Marshlands in the post-conflict period" in Weinthal, E., Troell, J. and Nakayama, M. (eds.) *Water and Post-Conflict Peacebuilding* Earthscan, London, 117–136.

Boyer-Souchet, I., Floch K., Lagrée P., and Le Gall, L. (2011) "Water Resources and War in Iraq" *L'eau en Irak*. Available at: http://eau3e.hypotheses.org/files/2011/11/Leau-en-Irak.pdf Accessed September 2016.

Charbonneau, L. (2009) "Canadian project has contributed to Iraqi marshes restoration" *University Affairs*. Available at: www.universityaffairs.ca/news/news-article/canadian-project-has-contributed-to-iraqi-marshes-restoration/ Accessed August 2016.

Coast, E. (2003) "Demography of the Marsh Arabs" in Nicholson, E. and Clark, P. (eds.) *The Iraqi Marshlands: A Human and Environmental Study*, 2nd ed. Politico's Publishing, London.

"Conserving and restoring the iconic marshes of Southern Iraq" (2016) *Wetlands International*. Available at: www.wetlands.org/casestudy/conserving-and-restoring-the-iconic-marshes-of-southern-iraq/ Accessed September 2016.

External Evaluation Report – Rehabilitation and Conservation of Karez Systems in the Northern Governorates of Iraq (2011) UNESCO Kahrez External Evaluation Report. Available at: www.unesco.org/fileadmin/MULTIMEDIA/FIELD/Iraq/pdf/Publications/Kahrez.pdf Accessed January 2016.

France, R. (ed.) (2006) *Sustainable Redevelopment of the Iraqi Marshlands* Routledge, Oxford.

"Groundwater in Iraqi Kurdistan has decreased, ministry says" (2017) *Kurd Net – Ekurd.net Daily News*. Available at: http://ekurd.net/groundwater-kurdistan-decreased-2017-01-12 Accessed February 2017.

International Organization for Migration (IOM) (2010) *Iraq Newsletter*, Volume I.

Iraq–Marshlands Restoration Project (IMRP)–DAI: International Development (n.d.) *DAI*. Available at: www.dai.com/our-work/projects/iraq-marshlands-restoration-project-imrp Accessed August 2016.

"Iraq Project – Background" (n.d.) *UNEP/IETC – UNEP–UNESCO Iraqi Marshlands Project – Background*. Available at: www.unep.or.jp/ietc/IraqWH/background.html Accessed August 2016.

"Iraqi Marshlands named as Unesco world heritage site" (2016) *The Guardian*. Available at: www.theguardian.com/environment/2016/jul/18/iraqi-marshlands-named-as-unesco-world-heritage-site Accessed September 2016.

"Iraq's shared water resources" (2016) *Fanack Water of the Middle East and North Africa*. Available at: https://water.fanack.com/iraq/iraqs-shared-water-reources/ Accessed February 2017.

King, M. D. (2016) "The weaponisation of water in Syria and Iraq" *Washington Quarterly* 38(4): 153–169.

"Landmark agreement sets in motion action to restore Iraq's environment as new study outlines magnitude of deterioration" (2014) *UNEP*. Available at: www.unep.org/NewsCentre/default.aspx?DocumentID=2758&ArticleID=10701&l=en Accessed August 2016.

Lonergan, S. (2012) "Ecological restoration and peacebuilding: The case of the Iraqi marshes" in Jensen, D. and Lonergan, S. (eds.) *Assessing and Restoring Natural Resources in Post-Conflict Peacebuilding* Earthscan, London, 223–239.

Managing for Change: The Present and Future State of the Marshes of Southern Iraq (2010) Victoria, BC: Canada–Iraq Marshlands Initiative.

Mironova, V. and Hussein, M. (2017) "The new ISIS insurgency – what jihadists do after losing territory" *Foreign Affairs*. Available at: www.foreignaffairs.com/articles/iraq/2017-01-09/new-isis-insurgency Accessed February 2017.

NCCI OP-ED (2010) "NCCI OP-ED: Iraq – Water scarcity in the land of two ancient rivers" *ReliefWeb*. Available at: http://reliefweb.int/report/iraq/ncci-op-ed-iraq-water-scarcity-land-two-ancient-rivers Accessed February 2017.

"New Eden Projects – Nature Iraq" (n.d.) *Nature Iraq*. Available at: www.natureiraq.org/new-eden-project.html Accessed August 2016.

Null, S. (2010) "Iraq: Steve Lonergan on the Southern Marshes" *New Security Beat*. Available at: www.newsecuritybeat.org/2010/09/iraq-at-the-crossroads-steve-lonergan-on-the-southern-marshes/ Accessed August 2016.

"Rebuilding Iraq: U.S. achievements through the Iraq Relief and Reconstruction Fund. U.S." (2006) Department of State. Available at: https://2001-2009.state.gov/documents/organization/60952.pdf Accessed September 2016.

"Rehabilitation and conservation of Kahrez water systems in Iraqi Kurdistan" (n.d.) UNESCO Office for Iraq. Available at: www.unesco.org/new/en/iraq-office/natural-sciences/water-sciences/karez-rehabilitation Accessed January 2017.

Reiss, P. (n.d.) "The re-greening of Iraq: restoring Marshlands" DAI Developments. Available at: http://dai-global-developments.com/articles/the-re-greening-of-iraq-restoring-marshlands/ Accessed August 2016.

"Republic of Iraq Emergency Baghdad Water Supply and Sanitation Project, Project Information Document (PID)" (n.d.) World Bank Baghdad Draft PID V3 Amman. Available at: http://siteresources.worldbank.org/IRFFI/64168382-1092418978875/20266690/Baghdad-Draft-PID-V3-Amman.pdf Accessed February 2017.

"Restoring the ancient Kahrez system in Iraqi Kurdistan" (2009) United Nations Educational, Scientific and Cultural Organization. Available at: www.unesco.org/new/en/iraq-office/about-this-office/single-view/news/restoring_the_ancient_kahrez_system_in_iraqi_kurdistan/ Accessed February 2017.

Schwartzstein, P. (2015) "Iraq's famed marshes are disappearing – again" *National Geographic*. Available at: http://news.nationalgeographic.com/2015/07/150709-iraq-marsh-arabs-middle-east-water-environment-world/ Accessed August 2016.

"The Marshlands of Iraq inscribed on UNESCO's World Heritage List" (2016) United Nations Educational, Scientific and Cultural Organization. Available at: www.unesco.org/new/en/iraq-office/about-this-office/single-view/news/the_marshlands_of_iraq_inscribed_on_unescos_world_heritag/ Accessed September 2016.

"The New Eden Project" (2009) The Italian Ministry for the Environment, Land and Sea UNEP/UNESCO Meeting, Amman. Available at: www.estis.net/includes/file.asp?site=marshlands&file=DFF153E7-7789-4DB9-9BEB-42D0655052B7 Accessed August 2016.

"The New Eden Project" (n.d.) Presentation at International Workshop. Available at: http://marshlands.unep.or.jp/includes/file.asp?site=marshlands&file=5AD64E91-49C6-4E3E-8381-3ED24DEC5A3F Accessed August 2016.

"The New Eden Project Executive Summary – 2003–2013 Activities" (2014) Italian Ministry for the Environment, Land and Sea and Nature Iraq. Available at: www.natureiraq.org/uploads/5/2/9/9/52997379/report_new_eden.pdf Accessed August 2016.

"UN Environment helps Arab negotiators of the region to prepare for COP22" (n.d.) UNEP Regional Office for West Asia. Available at: www.unep.org/westasia/un-environment-helps-arab-negotiators-region-prepare-cop22 Accessed February 2017.

"UN to help Iraq with environmental restoration" (2014) *ENS*. Available at: http://ens-newswire.com/2014/01/26/un-to-help-iraq-with-environmental-restoration/ Accessed September 2016.

United Nations (UN) (2010) *United Nations Development Assistance Framework for Iraq: 2011–2014*. UNDP, New York.

United Nations Environment Programme (UNEP) (2007) *UNEP in Iraq: Post-conflict Assessment, Clean-up and Reconstruction*. UNEP, Nairobi. Available at: http://postconflict.unep.ch/publications/Iraq.pdf Accessed August 2016.

United Nations Environment Programme (UNEP) (2009a) *Lessons Learned on Mainstreaming Pilot Projects into Larger Projects DTI/1241/JP* UNEP, Osaka, Japan.

United Nations Environment Programme (UNEP) (2009b) *Support for Environmental Management of the Iraqi Marshlands, 2004–2009* UNEP, Osaka, Japan. Available at: www.unep.or.jp/Ietc/Publications/Water_Sanitation/Support_for_EnvMng_of_IraqiMarshlands_2004-9.pdf Accessed August 2016.

Walther, C. (2011) "Rehabilitation and conservation of Kahrez systems in the northern governorates" Project Reports UNESCO, Iraq.

"Water uses in Iraq" (2016) *Fanack Water of the Middle East and North Africa*. Available at: https://water.fanack.com/iraq/water-uses-in-iraq/#_ftn1 Accessed February 2017.

Wessels, J. (2012) "Qanat rehabilitation as a viable tool for collective action for social development and conflict resolution in rural communities in arid areas" Paper presented at the International Conference on Traditional Knowledge for Water Resources Management. UNESCO ICQHS, Yazd, Iran. Available at: www.academia.edu/3487207/Qanat_rehabilitation_as_a_viable_tool_for_collective_action_for_social_development_and_conflict_resolution_in_rural_communities_in_arid_areas Accessed February 2016.

Wessels, J. (2014) "Qanats and water cooperation for a sustainable future" Middle East Institute. Available at: www.mei.edu/content/qanats-and-water-cooperation-sustainable-future Accessed January 2017.

"What does the future hold for water in Iraq?" (2016) *Fanack Water of the Middle East and North Africa*. Available at: https://water.fanack.com/iraq/what-does-the-future-hold-for-water-in-iraq/#_ftn2 Accessed February 2017.

World Bank PID (2004) "Project Information Document (PID) Concept Stage – Emergency Baghdad Water Supply" World Bank Documents Report No.: AB5197.

Zolnikov, T. R. (2013) "The maladies of water and war: addressing poor water quality in Iraq" *American Journal of Public Health* 103(6): 980–987. Available at: www.ncbi.nlm.nih.gov/pmc/articles/PMC3698740/pdf/AJPH.2012.301118.pdf

14

Are there limits to environmental peacebuilding?

A critical reflection on water cooperation in the Jordan basin

Anders Jägerskog

Introduction

In the last decades, it has been noted that environmental change may lead to conflicts of various sorts. Water scarcity, among other environmental stresses, was highlighted as a source of conflict and even war (e.g. Starr 1991; Falkenmark 1986; Shiklomanov 1990; Homer-Dixon 1994). As noted elsewhere in this volume, the prophecies later emerged as being overly deterministic in their prediction of conflict and wars. Later in the debate,[1] and as a result of significant undertakings in establishing a quantitative understanding, for example, of water, conflict and war pioneered by Aaron Wolf and colleagues at the Oregon State University (Wolf et al. 2005), it has been shown that conflicts over transboundary water (be it groundwater or surface water in rivers and lakes) tend to lead to cooperative outcomes rather than, as first assumed, to deeper conflict and wars (Transboundary Freshwater Database, Oregon State University). It has been shown, at the global level, that around two-thirds of the interactions over transboundary water have been of a cooperative nature and about one-third of a more conflictive nature. In the last decade or so that insight has been further developed and broadened as a range of scholars (Zeitoun 2006; Zeitoun and Warner 2006) have been deconstructing what *type* of cooperation has emerged, asking questions such as: "does the cooperation produce equitable outcomes?" and "can the cooperation be seen as fair and just?" The so-called Hydro-Hegemony theory has highlighted the need to analyze and understand how power asymmetries are affecting the outcomes in river basins in which countries "share" transboundary waters.

It is the *aim* of this chapter to provide a critical analysis of the limits to environmental peacebuilding through studying a specific case in the Middle East and North Africa (MENA) region – the Jordan basin. Does water resources management contribute to peacebuilding? If so, are there specific parameters that enable (or disable) peacebuilding processes to happen? The chapter will draw on earlier studies of conflict and cooperation over water in the MENA region *with a particular focus on transboundary water management*, and discuss it from a peacebuilding perspective (importance of legitimacy in post-conflict settings; the building of institutions, etc.). As such, the peacebuilding theory offers perspectives that are important as a basis for analysis.

In post-conflict societies, access to water, and functioning and well-managed ecosystems providing livelihood opportunities through for example farming, represent important tenets of peacebuilding. These aspects are all important when considering the key (as defined by Troell and Weinthal 2014) peacebuilding objectives: 1) establishing security; 2) restoring basic services; 3) revitalizing the economy and enhancing livelihoods; and 4) rebuilding governance and inclusive political processes. Needless to say, the provision of water in both conflict and post-conflict societies represents a key tenet for allowing the rebuilding to occur, but it also contributes to installing legitimacy. It is clear that equitable and efficient water resources management and delivery can assist in meeting these objectives. Both during and in the direct aftermath of conflict, water must be available to people and, in moving from humanitarian support and provision of services, such as access to water, to reconstruction and rebuilding of societies, efficient measures for the provision of water need to be put in place. While there is a need to renew water governance frameworks within countries, the added challenge of relying on transboundary waters further adds complexity. In the case of the MENA region, where water is scarce as well as to a high degree of a transboundary nature, the complexity is even greater than in most other places. As Swain (2015:1317) notes: "A major challenge for peacebuilding projects, particularly in the Middle East, is how to manage the critical natural resource base such as freshwater and pursue sustainable policies of growth and development." The example analyzed in this chapter represents a case which can be argued to be both conflict as well as post-conflict. As a matter of fact, it is perhaps best described as a combination of conflict and post-conflict.

As noted by Krampe (2016) many studies of transboundary water management highlight the cooperation potential it represents and how it can provide for broader cooperation (beyond water) between countries sharing the resource (e.g. Conca 2006; Sadoff and Grey 2002; Haftendorn 2000; Wolf et al. 2005). At the same time, there is limited theoretical understanding of how water resource management relates to peacebuilding more specifically. Often an overly straight line is made between basic cooperation over water, without much focus on the *quality* of the cooperation, and general development of improved political relations which then pave the way for reconstruction and peacebuilding. But is such a path dependency supported by evidence or is it merely hypothetical? Furthermore, are there variations between regions in this respect? It is argued here that the link may not be so strong and in particular not in situations where the level of securitization is high, such as is the case in the Middle East (Jägerskog 2009). Arguably, a key reason for this is that the politics of water is not addressed in many of these cases. Aggestam (2015) and Aggestam and Sundell (2014) argue that water has been treated more as a technical aspect and dealt with primarily through technocrats. As noted by Swain (2015), there has been a relatively great interest from both policy-makers and researchers in the link between cooperation over water and peacebuilding. While work on major rivers such as the Nile and the Mekong has not provided clear outcomes (at least not yet), the policy and analytical work is ongoing. In this respect, more often than not regime/functionalist/institutional perspectives are either consciously or subconsciously employed while more realist perspectives figure more rarely. It is argued in this chapter that for a deeper understanding, a more critical perspective that analyzes the limits to environmental peacebuilding is needed, which has to include input from distinctly different schools of thought.

The chapter will first discuss theoretical underpinnings and perspectives drawing on international relations theory and peacebuilding theory. Then it will move on to critically discussing the Middle East and North Africa (MENA) region and in particular focusing on the Jordan

River Basin before attempting to draw conclusions, from a theoretical perspective as well as relating to the case as such.

Theoretical framework

In this section, a number of perspectives drawn from different schools of thought will be outlined with the view to provide a useful perspective with which to analyze the key questions as outlined above.

In the debate on whether transboundary water was a source of conflict or of cooperation, a number of phases can be identified. First, during the 1980s and 1990s scholars such as Homer-Dixon (1994), Starr (1991) and Cooley (1984) focused on water as being a source of conflict and even wars. They largely based their ideas on the situation in the MENA region where a number of countries were already in a situation where they did not have enough water to sustain the food production that they needed to be self-sufficient. Added to that were belligerent statements coming out from political leaders saying the next war in the region will be about water. The basic theoretical perspectives were those of realism where the security of the state is the primary objective. To view the sharing of water through a realist perspective means that it is a zero-sum competition between states sharing the resources. Needless to say, a zero-sum perspective encourages a conflict mindset also on the resource of water. What the analyses did not take into account were the perspectives provided by political economy. The countries in the MENA region had, when they were "running out of water," accessed the shortfall in their domestic water availability not through waging war on their neighbors, but instead through importing water-intensive foodstuff (virtual water) on the global market to cover for the shortfall. The 'solution' was therefore not found through a realist thinking but through the analytical approaches that are entertained within political economy. Thus, the ameliorating factor that the market provided assisted countries in maintaining a certain level of water security. Thus, it was shown that rather than transboundary water resources leading to armed conflict and wars, states globally, but also in the MENA region, cooperated (at some level) over them.

The debate in the late 1990s and early 2000s focused more on transboundary water as a source of cooperation (Wolf et al. 2005; Wolf 1995, as well as a collection of articles on the topic in Jägerskog et al. 2014). The theoretical underpinnings of the debate focusing on cooperation took on a distinct functionalist perspective. A functionalist perspective in principle argues that cooperation on 'low politics,' such as water, may be something that can spur cooperation in other more sensitive political areas. In addition, within this paradigm, cooperation is seen as something that leads to more cooperation. A particular strand of the functionalist approach is the regime theory whereby the formal and informal rules that are being developed over time through interaction between actors (states) coalesce into a 'regime' by which cooperation can happen and become further institutionalized. In regime theory, the specific focus is the normative institution which deals with a specific issue which states create and subscribe to voluntarily, as a means of self-regulation in the international arena (Mayer et al. 1993). Keohane (1984:97) furthermore holds that:

> International regimes are useful to governments. Far from being threats to governments (in which case it would be hard to understand why they exist at all), they permit governments to attain objectives that would otherwise be unattainable. They do so in part by facilitating intergovernmental agreements. Regimes facilitate agreements by raising the anticipated costs of violating others' property rights, by altering transaction costs through the clustering of issues, and by providing reliable information to members. Regimes are relatively efficient institutions, compared with the alternative of having a myriad of unrelated

agreements, since their principles, rules, and institutions create linkages among issues that give actors incentives to reach mutually beneficial agreements. They thrive in situations where states have common as well as conflicting interests.

In a similar vein, John Waterbury (2002:35), when analyzing conflict and cooperation in the Nile basin, argues that "the process of regime formation itself – legislating, data-gathering, formal institution-building and negotiating – can provide momentum, the creation of new institutional interests and expertise, and, occasionally, 'tipping' moments that lead to formal co-operation." One of the core features in regime formation is the view that through putting a focus on technology, science and innovation, cooperation can be encouraged and instigated and politics more or less avoided. However, as Aggestam and Sundell (2014) note, issues surrounding water in the Middle East are not primarily technical but rather political at their core. Thus, a purely technical perspective, avoiding (or at least trying to avoid) politics, risks leading to misguided analytical, as well as policy, perspectives.

In the last decade or so, parallel to a continued focus on water as a source of cooperation in and beyond water (see e.g. Conca and Wallace 2009), a theoretical perspective that aims to analyze the *quality* of the cooperation has emerged. Zeitoun and Warner (2006) emphasized the need to understand how power asymmetries (and not only riparian position) contribute to equitable outcomes (or most often do not) when they pioneered the so-called Hydro-Hegemony framework, which provides tools for analysis of power differences in areas such as economic, military, human resources, etc. This approach has provided a nuanced perspective and shows that just achieving any type of cooperation may be misguided or, even worse, bad for the people as well as the environment.

Coupled to these perspectives are the broader environmental peacebuilding perspectives pioneered by, among others, Conca and Dabelko (2002). Their work is a systematic attempt to understand if, and if so how, cooperation over environmental issues can bring about or catalyze cooperation and peace beyond the environment. The basic idea is functionalist (or regime theory), arguing that environmental cooperation can positively affect other variables such as trust, and perception of the 'other' in a positive way so that shared norms and systems are developed. While they do not claim to firmly establish that environmental cooperation leads to peace they argue that environmental cooperation can provide for entry points for wider political dialogue. While the argument can be seen to be supported by empirical examples from cooperation over transboundary water (see e.g. Jägerskog et al. 2014) it can be argued that it is not a given that it works in settings that are more *securitized* than others. Troell and Weinthal (2014:428) draw on the fact that most (around two-thirds) of the transboundary water interactions that have been studied are of a cooperative nature and also on cases such as the Indus Rivers Commission between India and Pakistan that has withstood two wars when they suggest that "these incentives can be harnessed to build trust and confidence among former adversaries following interstate conflict and facilitate reconciliation and peacebuilding." But is that the case where securitization is still prevailing? Jägerskog (2009) argues that it is hard to establish that cooperation over transboundary waters, drawing on the cases of Israel–Jordan and Israel and Palestine, leads to broader cooperation beyond water. While technical solutions may be possible and lead to some form of cooperation, the securitized nature of a river basin like the Jordan does not seem to lend itself to such outcomes. Having said that, it is of course important to note that the cooperation that may become institutionalized over water can, if also taking into account equitability aspects, be positive in and of itself.

Buzan (1995) and Buzan, Wæver and de Wilde (1998) argue that states and societies 'securitize' issues to highlight their urgency. This has been the case with the environment and particularly water in the MENA context. Buzan et al. (1998) argue that security is *socially constructed*. They argue that security is not an objective feature of threats, which is in contrast to the traditional approach in security studies. Within security studies the predominant approach has traditionally been to view security from an 'objective' standpoint. In other words, what is seen as a clear threat to the stability and security of the state is what matters. It traditionally focuses on external threats such as military ones. From a peacebuilding perspective, it is argued here that, as a complement to the functionalist approaches that dominate the theorization of the field, the addition of securitization perspectives, following Buzan and colleagues, would assist as this would enable a deeper (and arguably more comprehensive) analysis of the situation in particular in regions like the MENA. This would also allow *politics* to be brought back in as the securitization is the 'ultimate' outcome of a politicization. This would be in line with the argument raised by Krampe (2016) as well as Swain (2015), who both point out that technocratic approaches lead to a disconnect when trying to understand peacebuilding in politicized and/or securitized realities. It is argued that perspectives that try to avoid politics and address the issue from a purely technical perspective will not succeed in regions like the MENA, as water is seen as being very political and also intimately connected to national security.

Jordan basin[2]

It may be argued that the Jordan basin has a unique set of characteristics in order for it to be able to say something in the area of peacebuilding and transboundary waters. However, it is the most water scarce part of the world; water is at the center of many of the discussions in the region, and furthermore, it is argued that by cooperating over a 'technical' issue such as water, one may be able to achieve cooperation also in other sectors/areas. The Jordan River Basin covers areas in Israel, Palestine (West Bank), Jordan, Syria and Lebanon. The basin is more important for Jordan and Israel (and arguably to Palestine when they have had their equitable water rights established) than for Syria and Lebanon, which get more water from other sources. Still, it is considered to be of importance for all of the five riparian states. Between Israel and Palestine, the water is also one of the five final status issues to be negotiated which primarily focus on the groundwater in the West Bank and Israel (for more details of the issues in the basin see e.g. Jägerskog 2003). Basin-wide cooperation (and even basic coordination) is largely absent in the Jordan basin and has been so for a long time due to the Arab–Israeli political conflict (Jägerskog 2003).

From a peacebuilding perspective, grand ideas such as the Red Sea–Dead Sea Water Conveyance scheme are highlighted as one avenue in the nurturing of peace in the region (Aggestam and Sundell 2014). Many development agencies have focused on water in the region supporting cooperation over the Jordan River. It is however not always clear that supporting projects in this area will bring about the four peacebuilding objectives as outlined by Troell and Weinthal (2014): 1) establishing security; 2) restoring basic services; 3) revitalizing the economy and enhancing livelihoods; and 4) rebuilding governance and inclusive political processes. The assumed, from a functionalist perspective as outlined above, positive cooperative results spurred by assumed technical cooperation over water in the region should spill over into other sectors. This, however, is hard to establish when looking at the cooperation in the Jordan basin (Jägerskog 2009). Even if there has been basin cooperation and coordination between Israel and Palestine, as well as between Israel and Jordan, it is not evidenced that the cooperation has encouraged (spilled over to) other sectors. In addition, it is also possible to discuss the 'quality' of the cooperation as has been done by, for example, Jägerskog (2003), Selby (2003, 2013) and Zeitoun (2006) where it is noted that Israel dominates the cooperation (particularly in relation to Palestine).

It is argued that water has indeed been securitized in the Jordan basin by all parties, meaning it has moved up in terms of political priority and is seen as an issue of national security. This is in clear contrast to the more technically oriented focus of peacebuilding theory where water is seen as a technical matter that should be 'apolitical.' Arguing along the lines of Krampe (2016), who analyzes a politicized context in Kosovo, and Swain (2015), politics needs to be included in the discussion in geographies and contexts such as the Jordan River Basin. Water in the region is inherently political and unless addressed from such a perspective, important insights and considerations are lost. Employing a purely technical perspective in the relations over water between Israel and Palestine would not allow a deep understanding of the underlying power asymmetries between the parties which lead to inequitable outcomes (Selby 2013, 2003; Zeitoun 2006).

It is argued here, based on an analysis and understanding of the situation in the Middle East region, that the cooperation over water has not shown that it has functioned as a source of future cooperation on other issues. Arguably this is since water has become securitized and is deeply political. Still, from a realist perspective, it can be argued that 'high' politics (such as national security concerns) decide what is agreed upon in areas of 'low' politics (such as water) (Lowi 1993). It is argued, however, that in the case of Israel and Palestine the evidence suggests that water cooperation, noting that it has not been a cooperation among equals, has not been able to instigate wider cooperation beyond the water itself (Selby 2003, 2013; Jägerskog 2009). In addition, as dependence on domestic agriculture is declining in the region and reliance on imports of water-intensive foodstuff is increasing the rationale that water would act as a bridge between states can be seen as decreasing (Aggestam and Sundell 2014). However, one can also argue that as water scarcity (measured by per capita water availability) is decreasing, the reason to cooperate would increase. That said, from a realist power perspective it could lead to increased competition and conflict. Noting the power asymmetry between the parties and the inequality it leads to when it comes to relations over water, it is noted that it has negative impacts for the cooperative outcomes, which tend to favor the stronger party or hegemon (Zeitoun 2006; Selby 2013; Jägerskog 2003, 2009). While cooperation over water in the Jordan basin might be the best possible solution for all riparian parties, it is still Israel, which is in the hegemonic position, that dictates to a great extent what is acceptable and what is not. The power asymmetry between the parties, with Israel being the stronger on issues such as human resources, military power and economics, is also an obstacle for the Palestinians in obtaining the best possible outcome, while it naturally presents itself as an opportunity for Israel to push its interests even harder.

For the situation depicted above to move to one in which peacebuilding is institutionalized, technocratic approaches that address water from an apolitical perspective seem unlikely to lead to the benefits that are aimed at through peacebuilding. This is particularly the case in highly politicized and/or securitized contexts such as the one discussed above. Through de-emphasizing politics in the basin, such as Palestinian water rights (including division and allocation of the scarce water resource), while focusing on increasing supply, it is unlikely that the intended outcomes of a peacebuilding approach (such as improving security; strengthening livelihoods; restoring basic services, etc.) will be achieved. Thus, the *quality* of the cooperation achieved or the *regime formation* is unlikely to be strong enough to provide the outcomes aimed for in the peacebuilding approach. In the case of Israel and Palestine, one may argue that none of the four objectives of a peacebuilding approach has been established. Neither security, restoring basic services, revitalizing the economy and enhancing livelihoods nor rebuilding governance and inclusive political processes has been comprehensively achieved. It is possible to argue that parts of this have been achieved but clearly not in a broad manner that has assisted in establishing Palestinian sovereignty over its resources. Indeed, as noted in the 2009 World Bank report on the Palestinian water sector, the Israeli dominance and occupation has in principle denied Palestine the possibility to develop its own water sector (World Bank 2009).

Concluding discussion

This chapter has tried to shed some light on the 'limits' of environmental peacebuilding. It is limited in the sense that it only looks at one geographic case – the Jordan River Basin – but some lessons going beyond that case can possibly still be identified. One of the conclusions of the chapter is that the effort to analyze, as well as implement, peacebuilding methods through an 'apolitical' approach is not helpful as that leads to key aspects being de-emphasized in a manner that makes solutions unsustainable, thereby siding with other research (Swain 2015; Krampe 2016). The functionalist perspectives, which peacebuilding work builds upon, overemphasize the ability of technocratic approaches in establishing security and development. Functionalist approaches contribute to our understanding of how water cooperation might come about but only provide part of the picture. A critique of the functionalist/regime theory perspective is that it is somewhat blind to the fact that water may be subordinate to much more important areas of dispute. An objection from a realist perspective to the focus on how water can bring about cooperation in other areas would be that the political/security perspective, as well as, importantly, power perspectives are left out of (or at least de-emphasized in) the analysis.

Kütting (2000) pointedly notes that functionalist regime theory concentrates too much on action and behavior and thereby misses the wider social and historical process. While a regime in which cooperation and coordination takes place may exist, it does not offer a complete perspective of the cooperation. On the contrary, it may even obstruct an understanding of the underlying political processes and power asymmetries that are often at the core of a dispute over water, even if states are cooperating over the resource. It is therefore argued that rather than fixing oneself on a single theoretical approach and perspective, a broader perspective should be applied. It is argued here that peacebuilding theory would be informed by perspectives other than the functionalist such as the 'constructivist' approach that Buzan et al. (1998) offer when they discuss securitization. This, in itself, represents a call for bringing politics into the core of peacebuilding, and not trying to avoid it and treat issues and processes as 'apolitical' or purely technical. If such an approach could be incorporated into peacebuilding theory, important perspectives relating to equitability and power would render more sustainable approaches.

That said, it is also important to bring in the time perspective. Transboundary processes are by nature complex. This requires a long-term, process-oriented approach in which the outcomes (of a potential cooperative nature) may take decades to achieve. Thus, viewing them as processes that can achieve results is important.

An approach that would bring politics more clearly to the center of the peacebuilding agenda would also require improved understanding of a number of issues. Up front there would have to be an increased focus – combining quantitative analysis from a peacebuilding perspective of cases which are securitized and cases which are not. This is also in line with the conclusion that Krampe (2016) has drawn. He argues that deeper theoretical and empirical understanding of the politics connects water management with peacebuilding and post-conflict reconstruction.

In conclusion, the chapter notes that the continued development (theoretical as well as empirical) would do well to pay further attention to perspectives and approaches that encourage *politics* to be brought back in. In situations such as the Jordan River Basin where water (along with many other issues) is being securitized and seen primarily as a political perspective, the technocratic and functionalist peacebuilding approach will be misguided and lead to analysis that misses important issues, such as, in this case, Palestinian water rights. A research agenda that includes perspectives inspired by realist and power politics as well as social constructivism (seeing security not as 'objective' but as something that is 'created or constructed within the discourse') would help further inform the peacebuilding approach and agenda.

Notes

1 For a more elaborate discussion of the global debate over water as a source of conflict (or war) and cooperation please see Jägerskog, Swain and Öjendal, 2014.
2 This section draws partly on Jägerskog, 2003. It shall be noted that the discussions in this section not only relate to the hydrologically defined Jordan River Basin but also include the groundwater aquifers that are shared between Israel and Palestine.

References

Aggestam, K. (2015) "Desecuritization of water and the technocratic turn in peacebuilding" *International Environmental Agreements: Politics, Law and Economics* 15(3):327–340.

Aggestam, K. and Sundell, A. (2014) "Depoliticizing water conflict: functional peacebuilding in the Red Sea–Dead Sea Water Conveyance Project" *Hydrological Sciences Journal* 61(7):1302–1312.

Buzan, B. (1995) "The levels of analysis problem in international relations reconsidered" *International Relations Theory Today* Polity Press, Cambridge.

Buzan, B., Waever, O. and de Wilde, J. (1998) *Security: A New Framework for Analysis* Lynne Rienner, Boulder, CO.

Conca, K. (2006) *Governing Water: Contentious Transnational Politics and Global Institution Building* MIT Press, Cambridge, MA.

Conca, K. and Dabelko, G. (eds.) (2002) *Environmental Peacemaking* Woodrow Wilson Centre Press and John Hopkins University Press, Washington, DC.

Conca, K. and Wallace, J. (2009) "Environment and peacebuilding in war-torn societies: Lessons from the UN Environment Programme's experience with postconflict assessment" *Global Governance* 15(4):484–504.

Cooley, J. K. (1984) "The war over water" *Foreign Policy* (54):3–26.

Falkenmark, M. (1986) "Freshwater: Time for a modified approach" *Ambio* 15(4):192–200.

Haftendorn, H. (2000) "Water and international conflict" *Third World Quarterly* 21(1):51–68.

Homer-Dixon, T. (1994) "Environmental scarcities and violent conflict" *International Security*, 19/1.

Jägerskog, A. (2003) *Why states cooperate over shared water: The water negotiations in the Jordan River Basin*, Linköping University, PhD Dissertation, Linköping Studies in Arts and Science.

Jägerskog, A. (2009) "Functional water co-operation in the Jordan River Basin: Spillover or spillback for political security" in Brauch, H. G., Oswald Spring, U., Grin, J., Mesjasz, C., Kameri-Mbote, P., Chadha Behera, N., et al. (eds.) *Facing Global Environmental Change: Environmental, Human, Energy, Food, Health and Water Security Concepts* Springer-Verlag, Berlin.

Jägerskog, A., Swain, A. and Öjendal, J. (2014) *Water Security – Origins and Foundations, Volume I* in Jägerskog, A., Swain, A. and Öjendal, J. (eds.) *Water Security* 4 vols. Sage Publications, London.

Keohane, R. (1984) *After Hegemony* Princeton University Press, Princeton, NJ.

Krampe, F. (2016) "Water for peace? Post-conflict water resource management in Kosovo" *Cooperation and Conflict* 52(2):1–19.

Kütting, G. (2000) *Environment, Society and International Relations: Towards More Effective International Agreements* Routledge, London.

Lowi, M. (1993) *Water and Power: The Politics of Scarce Water Resources in the Jordan River Basin* Cambridge University Press, London.

Mayer, P., Rittberger, V. and Zürn, M. (1993) "Regime theory: State of the art and perspectives" in Rittberger, V. (ed.) *Regime Theory and International Relations* Clarendon Press, Oxford, 391–430.

Sadoff, C. W. and Grey, D. (2002) "Beyond the river: The benefits of cooperation on international rivers" *Water Policy* (4):389–403.

Selby, J. (2003) "Dressing up domination as 'co-operation': the case of Israeli–Palestinian water relations" *Review of International Studies* 29(1):121–138.

Selby, J. (2013) "Cooperation, domination and colonisation: The Israeli–Palestinian Joint Water Committee" *Water Alternatives* 6(1):1–24.

Shiklomanov, I. A. (1990) "Global Water Resources" *Nature and Resources* 26(3):34–43.

Starr, J. R. (1991) "Water wars" *Foreign Policy* (82):17–36.

Swain, A. (2015) "Water and post-conflict peacebuilding" *Hydrological Sciences Journal* 61(7):1313–1322.

Troell, J. and Weinthal, E. (2014) "Harnessing water management for more effective peacebuilding: Lessons learned" in Weinthal, E., Troell, J. and Nakayama, M. (eds.) *Water and Post-Conflict Peacebuilding* Earthscan/Routledge, London.

Waterbury, J. (2002) *The Nile Basin: National Determinants of Collective Action* Yale University Press, New Haven, CT.

Wolf, A. (1995) *Hydropolitics along the Jordan River: Scarce Water and its Impact on the Arab–Israeli Conflict* United Nations University Press, Tokyo.

Wolf, A., Kramer, A., Carius, A. and Dabelko, G. D. (2005) "Managing water conflict and cooperation" in *State of the World: Redefining Global Security* World Watch Institute, Washington, DC.

World Bank (2009) *West Bank and Gaza: Assessment of restrictions on Palestinian Water sector development*, Sector Note, Middle East and North Africa Region – Sustainable Development. *Report No. 47657-GZ.* International Bank for Reconstruction and Development/World Bank, Washington, DC.

Zeitoun, M. (2006) *Power and Water in the Middle East: The Hidden Politics of the Palestinian–Israeli Water Conflict* I. B. Tauris, London.

Zeitoun, M. and Warner, J. (2006) "Hydro-Hegemony a Framework for Analysis of Transboundary Water Conflicts" *Water Policy* (8):435–460.

15

Environmental peacebuilding in Liberia

Michael D. Beevers

Introduction

Natural resources and the environment have emerged as an important part of the peacebuilding agenda. This is no coincidence. As this book highlights, a significant body of research suggests that natural resources can, under certain conditions, stimulate, aggravate or lengthen violent conflicts. For example, high-profile work has argued that renewable resources like water and arable land, made scarce by growing populations and elite "resource capture," trigger instability (Homer-Dixon 1994, 1999). Other work found that a country's dependence on high-value natural resources, such as oil, timber, minerals, oil and diamonds, can undermine economic progress, intensify poverty and foster corruption in ways that increase the odds of armed conflict (de Soysa 2002; Ross 2004). And finally, prominent and often-cited research has argued that rebel groups, and their warlord leaders, loot natural resources to fund rebellion and are motivated to fight for economic reasons related to personal enrichment, rather than any political reasoning (Collier and Hoeffler 2004).

Although the precise causal links between natural resources and armed conflict remain ambiguous and contested, a range of international interventions developed to end and mitigate conflicts perceived to be linked to natural resources, and more specifically, to resource-derived revenue (Le Billon 2012). The future spoils of natural resources have been used by negotiators to broker peace agreements. UN sanctions have been enacted by the Security Council to disrupt and curtail the trade of so-called "conflict resources" to deprive rebel groups of the funds that can fuel war. International mechanisms have also been established to help track and regulate the trading of natural resources believed to finance conflict and beget violence. The most advanced in this regard is the Kimberley Process Certification Scheme (KPCS), which was designed in 2003 to regulate the global trade in rough diamonds (Grant 2012).

Natural resources such as timber, diamonds, minerals, oil and cash crops have also emerged as critical for building peace; not just as a tool to end wars (Lujala and Rustad 2012). Natural resources can help to foster economic growth, alleviate poverty, provide jobs and fill state coffers with revenue to fund basic services and post-war reconstruction. If natural resources can be leveraged effectively, they can also send a signal to potential peace "spoilers" that the benefits of peace outweigh the costs. The paradox is that countries that are particularly weak and war-torn, and have an abundance of natural resources, tend to be most susceptible to conflict relapse. This is largely because governance and management of natural resources is often ineffective, deeply fractured and lacking in legitimacy in the aftermath of armed conflict, and resources and their revenues can be the focus of deep-seated and violent disputes among a variety of actors (Bruch, Muffett and Nichols 2016).

Beyond natural resources, the environment itself has been recognized as vital for sustaining peace. In the aftermath of conflicts, people struggle to acquire clean water, sanitation, shelter, food and energy resources (Matthew et al. 2002; UNEP 2009; Conca and Wallace 2009). Moreover, conflicts disrupt land ownership patterns and lead to contested access to resources in ways that deepen poverty and make the attainment of sustainable livelihoods more challenging (Unruh and Williams 2013). Such challenges can undercut peacebuilding since they increase tensions among actors, threaten social and political reconciliation, and stymie robust economic development.

For over a decade now, the idea that natural resources, and to a lesser extent the environment, can help the difficult task of peacebuilding has been common refrain in international peacebuilding circles. But understanding the links between natural resources, conflict and peacebuilding or environmental peacebuilding broadly conceived is more than an academic exercise. Research shows that peace can be much shorter when natural resources are involved (Rustad and Binningsbø 2012). Nor is it by any means believed to be a thing of the past. Peacebuilding operations are on the rise and the United Nations Environment Programme (UNEP) has stated that violent conflict associated with the environment and natural resources will only increase in the decades ahead, especially as climate change intensifies (UNEP 2009:8).

Based on my own research, this chapter examines environmental peacebuilding to date in Liberia. The country in many respects is the veritable "poster child" of so-called resource conflicts, and also an exemplar of attempts to leverage natural resources for peace. As I discuss in the next section, despite a complex array of causes, natural resources emerged as a dominant explanation for the conflict, and because of this, international actors placed a priority on ensuring resources would not contribute to conflict relapse. Given Liberia's vast repositories of timber and minerals, I also discuss how large-scale resource extraction – as well as industrial agriculture – emerged as the key to spurring the economic growth and development deemed crucial to peace and stability. I would argue, however, that the Liberian case starkly demonstrates the challenges and complexities inherent in leveraging resources for peace and development. I highlight that while attention to natural resources did help to end the outright plunder of Liberia's resources and begin the vital process of legal and regulatory reform, disagreements over the specifics of resource extraction and how it is felt on the ground remain deeply contentious and hard to overcome. As a result, issues related to land ownership, community rights, sustainable livelihoods, grassroots development and environmental protection have emerged as just as vital to peacebuilding success.

Natural resource extraction – from plunder to peace

The causes of the conflict in Liberia defy simple explanation. However, it has been widely linked to the country's vast natural resources. The seeds of the conflict were sewn deep in Liberia's history when a small group of Americo-Liberians established the country, and with it the rules governing land ownership and political rights in ways that fostered almost continuous violence over access to land and resources (Levitt 2005). The conflict's roots also rested in Liberian leadership that ruled with utter dysfunction, authoritarianism and oppression, and used this political order to damage the environment and exploit the country's resources and land for the benefit of a few (Sawyer 1992; Somah 1995). Not surprisingly, this dynamic was a source of continued resistance as local people were exploited and garnered few, if any, benefits from resource extraction. This dynamic intensified in the twentieth century as Liberia began to sell off large chunks of land and resources to foreign companies (Sawyer 1992). In 1926, for example, the Firestone Rubber and Tire Company was granted a 99-year lease on roughly 4 percent of the country's land area. And by the 1970s, timber extraction and iron ore mining had become fundamental to the country's economy growth. The problem was that the exploitation of resources and land was predatory, arranged with no transparency, and the profits accrued overwhelmingly to a small cadre of land owners, foreign businesses and political elites. The country remained largely impoverished and undeveloped (Clower et al. 1966). The result of which has been entrenched opposition to concessionary agreements, and the notion that the government, as opposed to the people, controls the land and resources (Sawyer 1992:242). In short, Liberia's history, and its conflicts as well, are deeply entangled in contestation over the control, access and benefits of land and natural resources.

International actors were essentially oblivious of the resource predation and persistent violence and conflict that traditionally characterized Liberia's resource base. It was only after scholars and non-governmental organizations began to pay attention to the role of "conflict resources" in fueling armed conflict in places like Angola and Sierra Leone that international attention began to shift. Evidence emerged, for example, that Sierra Leonean diamonds were transiting through Liberia and the revenues were fueling the war (UN Panel of Experts 2000). In response, the UN Security Council passed sanctions on all diamonds originating in Liberia (UNSC 2001). But as the world's attention focused on diamonds, Liberia's president turned his attention to the timber sector to procure weapons and fund other illicit activities (UN Panel of Experts 2000:12; UN Panel of Experts 2001:13). Of equal concern was that local communities were being subjected to human rights abuses by timber companies and government security forces. Timber extraction was also being done hastily and unsustainably, leaving the country's forests in crisis (Global Witness 2001). After much debate, the UN eventually imposed a ban on all timber and timber products originating in Liberia in the hope of ending the Liberian conflict and bringing stability to the region (UNSC 2003). A UN Panel of Experts suggested the sanctions should remain in place until "peace and stability are restored" and the forest governance is "participatory, transparent, accountable, effective and equitable, and ... promote[s] the rule of law" (UN Panel of Experts 2003:26–30).

A host of contingent factors led to the end of hostilities in Liberia in 2003. But relief that the war had ended quickly gave way to immense challenges of building peace. Not surprisingly, the governance of natural resources developed into an international peacebuilding priority. At one level, international actors understood that if resource revenues, from timber extraction for example, were to fall into the hands of rebel groups (or potential rebel groups) or corrupt officials there would be a possibility of conflict relapse. At another level, natural resources were viewed as fundamental for a quick post-war recovery since resource extraction can help to foster economic growth, lead to more employment and less poverty, and provide revenue that the government can allocate to development priorities (Bannon and Collier 2003). The rub, of course, is that natural resources must be managed effectively, transparently and in ways that ensure revenues are not stolen or siphoned off, and genuinely benefit all of the Liberian people.

Below, I discuss efforts to leverage natural resources (timber, iron ore and agricultural land) in Liberia in an effort to trigger broad-based economic development and by extension set the foundation for sustainable peace.

Forests and timber extraction

Timber extraction was perceived by international actors to be a threat to Liberia's peace and security. It had funded illicit activities and weapons smuggling during the conflict and led to the widespread plunder of Liberia's forests and the harassment of its local communities. A report published two years after the war uncovered that all timber concessions awarded between 1985 and 2004 were illegal, covered vast expanses of the country and left communities with impaired livelihoods (FCRC 2005). As a result, a vigorous effort by international actors to reform Liberia's forests sector emerged (Beevers 2016; Altman, Nichols and Woods 2012). In 2006, Ellen Johnson Sirleaf became president and promptly canceled all existing timber concessions. She also renewed calls to lift the UN sanctions on timber, noting that extraction was vital for Liberia's transition from conflict to development. Advocacy organizations like Global Witness suggested that lifting of the sanctions was premature and questioned the idea that timber extraction would by itself bring peace or development (Global Witness 2006). Regardless, the UN lifted the sanctions, conditional on the "speedy adoption" of the necessary forest laws (UNSC 2006).

The National Forest Reform Law (NFRL) was passed in late 2006. It was squarely focused on restarting timber extraction, but also noted the importance of community forests and the conservation of ecologically valuable areas. Estimates suggested timber exports could generate upwards of $50 million, provide 7,000 jobs and spur economic recovery (IMF 2008:63). The law set the qualifications for timber companies, established the rules for the bidding and issuing of timber contracts, and put in place tax, fee and royalty payment. The law also set rules for public participation, required the establishment of a community rights law and laid the groundwork for a protected areas network, among other things. Starting in 2008, bids for large-scale timber concessions opened up and that is where problems began. First, finding qualified timber companies was difficult. A number of companies were found to be involved in the armed conflict in some way, and owed back taxes to the government. Other timber companies that bid for contracts were found to be devoid of any investment capital, had virtually no experience at all in the timber sector or did not disclose their true ownership. Second, bidding documents were found to be illicitly altered, and companies were accused of predatory logging in other locations around the world (UN Panel of Experts 2008, 2009; Global Witness 2009).

Not surprisingly, these difficulties, along with accusations of collusion, corruption and disregard for Liberian law, brought efforts to "jump start" timber extraction to a standstill. However, this stimulated a substantial increase in "private use permits" (PUP), which allowed private land owners and timber companies to extract timber in ways that circumvent the NFRL. While PUPs required assessments and a social agreement with affected communities, there was no open bidding process or restriction on the size or duration of the contract, and fees to the government and local communities were not required. Between 2010 and 2012, at least 70 PUPs were issued covering nearly a quarter of the country's land area (Global Witness 2012; SIIB 2012). The problem was that a large majority of the PUPs were bogus, illegal and approved without community involvement. The UN called PUPs an "unregulated route to substantial concessions holdings" and there was evidence that officials within the Forest Development Authority were complicit (UN Panel of Experts 2012:233; SIIB 2012). In response, President Sirleaf placed a moratorium on PUPs citing them as a threat to Liberia's natural heritage and local communities.

In places where timber companies were granted timber concessions or PUP, tensions with communities were high. Companies frequently failed to follow up on promised benefits like infrastructure, clinics and schools, or did not pay the required fees (Harris et al. 2013). Social agreements that were meant to incorporate local voices and negotiate access rights and benefits were contentious, with many communities excluded from decisions or having agreements breached (Harris et al. 2013; UN Panel of Experts 2008). Communities complained vigorously about the lack of information to make effective decisions and of not being consulted by the government or companies about activities on what they considered their land. All of this highlights deep disagreements that have emerged about how forests are managed and ultimately who has the right to make decisions about land (Wily 2007). In the Liberian Constitution, all land (except if defined as communal or private and deeded) is held in trust by the government. That means that the land set aside for timber extraction was determined by the government regardless of the fact that all concessions have people living in them and there are overlapping ownership claims (Alforte et al. 2014).

Over a relatively short period, the government, again with the help of international actors, passed numerous legal and regulatory reforms related to the timber sector. Liberia enacted the Forestry Policy and Implementation Strategy, Ten Core Regulations and Community Rights to Forest Lands Law. Liberia has signed on to the Extractive Industries Transparency Initiative, that requires extractive companies to publish what they pay to government, and the government to publish the revenues they receive. Liberia also signed a Voluntary Partnership Agreement with the EU to help guarantee that timber exported to Europe is compliant with Liberian law and an agreement with the Government of Norway to improve forest governance (EU/FLEGT 2014; Government of Norway 2014). However, increasingly, the problems related to timber extraction discussed above have altered the terms of the debate. Questions have arisen about the dominance of the concession-based extraction model to benefit the people of Liberia. First, research has begun to show that concession-based models do a poor job of bringing development to local communities and contribute little to GDP compared to small-scale extraction (World Bank 2012). Second, such models have historically led to environmental destruction and poor outcomes for local communities where rights to land and their interests were not the central concern. This has led to a move to place "communities to the center" of forest policy.

The current "Land Rights Policy" and a much-debated "Land Right Act," for example, would recognize community land rights and codify community ownership of Liberia's land including forests. In short, communities would own and be responsible for managing forests with the support and expertise of the government. Critics have argued that such an arrangement would lead to mismanagement, lead to conflicts over land and put at risk Liberia's national development. Others, however, have argued that sustainable forest management and the improvement of people's livelihoods will only advance if local communities – and not timber companies or the government that have historically provided little in the way of benefits – genuinely control Liberia's forests.

Certainly, the view that restarting timber extraction will bring peace and development has been tempered by the complexities of restarting the timber industry and the historically rooted tensions and mistrust that surround the sector. There is a clear effort now to rethink how Liberia's forests are managed, but it remains to be seen precisely how the forest sector will develop in the years ahead.

Iron ore mining

Attention to the security threat posed by diamonds and timber dominated resource-based policies following the conflict. More recently, however, attention has turned to the iron ore mining sector as a way to foster economic recovery and put the country on a sustainable path to peace. Liberia was Africa's largest exporter of iron ore and the fifth largest producer of iron in the world before the conflict. The industry was crippled during the war, but once the conflict ended the mining sector was viewed as critical to economic growth, employment and the alleviation of poverty. The 2008 Poverty Reduction Strategy noted that transforming the economy was essential for putting the country on a path to peace, and iron ore would be an important engine of that economic recovery (IMF 2008).

Since the end of the conflict, five iron ore concessions have been signed in Liberia. Estimates suggest that over time the sector could produce upwards of $13 billion and create thousands of jobs (Ministry of Internal Affairs 2014). ArcelorMittal, the world's largest producer of steel, was granted a 25-year mining license and began operations in 2010. By 2014, the company had shipped an estimated 4.1 million tons of iron ore abroad, and is expected to export three times that amount at full capacity (ArcelorMittal 2013). Likewise, China-Union, a Chinese government-owned enterprise, holds a 25-year license to mine iron ore. In 2014, the company began exports, with a target to ship 10 million tons by 2016 (Reuters 2014). ArcelorMittal has committed to investing at least $1.5 billion and China-Union $2.6 billion, and social contributions made by mining companies to the counties has been estimated to be nearly $40 million (Sustainable Development Institute 2014). In 2011 and 2012 iron ore contributed to 8 percent of the country's GDP and 58 percent of tax revenues from the extractive industries (LEITI 2016).

International actors have stressed the need to make the sector more participatory, internationally competitive, transparent and sensitive to social and environmental impacts of mining (World Bank 2003). Liberia has been revising the Minerals and Mining Law, which was enacted in 2000 by then President Charles Taylor. Although the law was amended in 2004 in part to meet Kimberley Process Certification Scheme requirements and again in 2010 to meet Exploration Requirements, the law is widely viewed as outdated in terms of internationally recognized standards to boost state revenues while maximizing transparency, accountability and public participation. The current reforms will align with the African Mining Vision – a framework designed to ensure that mining not only raises revenues for the state, but contributes to development at local, national and regional levels (UN Economic Commission of Africa 2009). The reforms would ensure that the mining law is in accord with other Liberian laws including the Public Procurement and Concession Act, Revenue Code, Extractive Industries Transparency Initiative, and the Environmental Protection and Management Law, among others.

Despite legal and regulatory accomplishments, however, there remain significant concerns about whether the iron ore sector will truly benefit all Liberians. Historically, negotiations with mining companies were carried out in secret without input from civil society groups or mining communities. The government did not secure the best possible agreements, in terms of royalties and taxes, which deprived the country of much-needed revenue. The revenue collected was poorly managed and corrupt policies ensured that the benefits from the sector accumulated to national elites and foreign entities, thus depriving the country of robust development.

Controversy over the transparency of mining agreements and revenues suggests that similar problems have begun to resurface. Agreements between the government and mining companies contained what many maintain were overly generous clauses and tax rates that do not allow Liberia to capitalize on the value of the iron ore (Sustainable Development Institute 2014). One school of thought is that since Liberia is a risky venture for extractive companies generous tax rates and other concessions are needed to attract investors. However, others have suggested that it is a bad precedent, and that the government should seek as much revenue as possible given Liberia's development and infrastructure needs, and the fact that once extracted iron ore is non-renewable and has environmental costs (Sustainable Development Institute 2014). ArcelorMittal, for example, paid $8 million in total taxes to the government in 2013 despite the determination by various advocacy organizations that the company should have paid upwards of $23 million in royalties alone (Sustainable Development Institute 2010). In fact, there is little in the way of public information or oversight mechanisms to make tax obligations, or how royalties are calculated, open and transparent.

There is also increasing tension related to iron ore companies failing to meet obligations established in mining development agreements (MDA). Poor working conditions, environmental impacts, lack of employment opportunities, issues of displacement and resettlement, and a general lack of promised benefits in mining communities have been reported (Sustainable Development Institute 2014). More concerning is a growing threat of violence in communities that endangers not only mining operations, but peace and stability itself. Demonstrations by workers in China-Union's concession area resulted in a police response that included live ammunition and the dismissal of chiefs that supported protestors (Sustainable Development Institute 2014). The company has also been accused of abusive labor practices with workers reporting physical cruelty, low wages, extended working hours and a lack of the benefits to which they were entitled. In addition, many of the benefits promised to affected communities have not been forthcoming, and general improvements in standard of living and development outcomes have not been met.

The Ebola outbreak in 2013, and lower worldwide demand for iron ore, have led to layoffs of workers and a reduction in exports. This highlights both the complexity of conducting business in Liberia and the difficulty of leveraging natural resources for peace and development when prices are volatile and unpredictable. When prices are high and exports in demand, fiscal returns can lead to palpable development outcomes and a higher standard of living. Alternatively, when prices drop and exports contract, reductions in government spending, employment and investment, as well as gaps in people's expectations about the development potential of resources, can create uncertainty and even raise tensions. Regardless of the potential for "boom and bust" cycles, Liberia's mining sector is widely viewed as underperforming. Liberia is not fully explored and is still transitioning from small-scale mining activities to industrial mining (Alix 2014). The expectation is that global demand for iron ore will increase and as such revenues from the sector will continue to grow.

That said, the view that prevailed in the years following the conflict that restarting the iron ore sector would spur development and consolidate peace is being questioned. Indeed, iron ore is a valuable asset that if managed effectively can bring employment and economic growth that can genuinely address the country's endemic poverty, poor infrastructure and meager basic services. But there is also the possibility, which many insist is more and more likely, that iron ore extraction will bring back a system that benefits only the few, leaving people in areas near mining areas open to exploitation and violence. The legal and regulatory reforms are certainly an improvement. Transparency and accountability are essential if agreements with companies and the revenues from extraction are going to improve the lives of all of Liberia's people. Beyond this, there is a move to put people first. Rather than a mining sector that treats people as passive beneficiaries (or expendables), the sector needs to give people more rights. That is, active participation in decisions that affect their livelihoods and access to resources, directly make positive contributions to poverty alleviation and do no harm in terms of social and environmental costs of extraction. In short, it is becoming obvious that iron ore extraction rooted in corruption and the exploitation of people will not bring development or peace.

Land and palm oil plantations

Along with forests and the mining of iron ore, agriculture is an integral part of Liberia's strategy for long-term peace and development. Agriculture is vital to a vast majority of the Liberian people and in the aftermath of the conflict it was essential that people could satisfy their food and livelihood needs through traditional subsistence agriculture. Agriculture is certainly key to Liberia's economy. The sector makes up an estimated 42 percent of GDP and is the primary livelihood resource for nearly an estimated 75 percent of the population (World Food Programme 2013). As President Sirleaf has noted, "if Liberia can grow its own food and be self-sufficient, and we have the potential to do so due to the large territorial farmable soils, the tropical climate and abundant water resources, the country would be insulated from the effects of soaring global food prices" (Sirleaf 2010). However, even as agriculture and access to food is noted as vital for alleviating poverty and providing thousands of jobs, only 2 percent of Liberia's national budget is allocated to institutions and activities in the sector (Sirleaf 2010). Moreover, Liberia remains a net importer of food and half of the country has been identified as food insecure (World Food Programme 2013).

As the peace consolidation process moved forward, the importance of food security and traditional agriculture gave way to an emphasis on mechanization and increased production (IMF 2008). Large-scale, mechanized agriculture – dependent on foreign investment and the private sector similar to that in the timber and mineral sectors – was believed to be a "win–win" for Liberia because it would bring the market to small landowners, provide jobs and enhance food security. Specifically, there emerged a growing emphasis on developing the palm oil industry. International investors began buying up Liberia's fertile and cheap land in response to the global food and fuel crisis in 2008 in which countries, businesses and investors acquired land to secure future food security or invest in biofuels. Liberia was considered a good investment, touted for its cheap labor and low-cost water. Sensing an opportunity to attract foreign investors, the government advertised its vast amounts of "available" land. Since 2009, three large palm oil companies have begun operations in Liberia. These include Sime Darby, Equatorial Palm Oil and Golden Veroleum that between them have concessions on nearly 8 percent of Liberia's land area. Between the companies, investment dollars are projected to be in the billions, bringing in hundreds of millions in royalties and taxes, and upwards of 80,000 jobs (International Trade Center 2013).

President Sirleaf has touted the land deals, but significant problems have started to emerge. First, there has been little information about how land is identified by the government as "available for investors" given that most of Liberia's land is customarily owned and people live on virtually all of the land in question. Like most of Liberia's history, there was little consultation with local communities that depend on the land for their livelihoods and well-being. The agreement with Sime Darby, one of the world's largest producers of palm oil, is a case in point. The company signed a 63-year lease with the government in 2009 with the understanding that the land could be used "free of encumbrances." The problem is that people live on the land, and despite a commitment to resettle displaced communities, there are many that question how people will be able to procure food and livelihoods (Siakor 2012). Another problem has been that farmers are paid for crops only and not for the use of their land, since many do not hold a clear title (FOE 2013). Communities also are concerned that wages are too low and that many of the people have not been hired by the company. Finally, as a society dependent on agriculture, the transformation of vast amounts of land into palm oil plantations has raised concerns how people will meet their livelihood needs. Proponents of these agreements suggest they will help the country's national development, critics suggest that they will simply undermine livelihoods, take land away from people and create environmental destruction.

Although palm oil development is only in the beginning stages, protests and violence are on the rise (Stokes 2015). Workers at Golden Veroleum seeking assurances about a salary increase detained a company official in 2015 and another similar protest over a lack of community consultation resulted in violence and looting (UNSC 2015). In both instances, UN peacekeepers and Liberian security forces intervened. In Senaii Town, local people organized against the company to protest rumors that the company was about to clear-cut farmland. Reports suggested that bulldozers showed up without warning and started to demolish communal lands. However, in response to the protest the company fired hundreds of "troublemakers." The town in response put together a list of demands that included the ability to consent to the expropriation of land. Tensions between the company and aggrieved landowners were so acute that President Sirleaf visited the area. In a local newspaper, she was quoted as admitting that the town had not been consulted properly, but suggested that all Liberians will benefit from Sime Darby. The president warned, for example, that the town risked alienating investors and also undermining the government.

Regardless, communities have argued that large agricultural concessions like that of Sime Darby are not only taking over lands and forest used by communities for their livelihoods, but have been able to do so without consultations, consent or adequate compensation. Where communities have consented to plantations, reports have surfaced that they have been "pressured to sell" with some even being threatened with violence. Local communities are increasingly looking to the pending Land Rights Act that would grant rights to communities to ensure that communities are able to manage their land and are not deprived against their will of keeping their land and benefiting from concessions. Much like the forest and iron ore mining discussed above, the idea that natural resource extraction will quickly support peace and development goals has been revised. While increased transparency and accountability, and the legal and regulatory environment have been a priority, increasingly, people have raised concerns about how such concessions impact the ability of people to meet their access to land and livelihood needs. There is a reluctance to believe that land deals involving palm oil can improve the lives of the population or enhance their benefits. For instance, how is poverty to be reduced and food security improved without land or other vital opportunities for alternative livelihoods?

From extraction to rights – an evolving agenda?

The most egregious aspects of resource plunder that characterized the Liberian conflict have been addressed. Due in part to the efforts of international actors, the revenues from natural resources like timber, rubber or diamonds no longer go to buy weapons or openly fuel armed conflict. However, it is increasingly clear that leveraging natural resources for peace and development is at best complex and at worst deeply contentious. There have been a barrage of new laws and regulations to lure foreign investors and negotiate and implement concessionary agreements but on several fronts these efforts have fallen short. Although mechanisms for transparency and accountability have been improved, one look at the forest, iron ore or palm oil sectors suggests that corruption and collusion are a problem. A range of issues have surfaced, for example, in the negotiating of contracts and agreements. Local communities desperately want their land and resources to fuel improvements in their well-being, but many feel left out of the decision-making process as deals with companies get done "behind closed doors."

The slow pace of development and a lack of concrete benefits in communities endowed with natural resources also create the perception of a lack of transparency and accountability. Without experiencing tangible benefits or improvements in basic services the perception of mismanagement and corruption within the government and among companies vying for natural resources remains high, reinforcing the enduring perception that the government, along with some local authorities, colludes with the private sector without consideration of the people's needs. As the cases illustrate, communities have little say in issues of resettlement, compensation for land and crops, or the protection of the environment. This not only needs to be improved, but the government needs to improve its capacity to provide communities with necessary information to make informed decisions.

Liberia's growing population has little access to sustainable livelihoods and access to land is a problem. Current trends, however, suggest that livelihoods linked to land and traditional agriculture may be more difficult to acquire and establish as mining operations and land deals threaten to convert arable land. Recent estimates suggest that at least a quarter of the country's land area, or about 1.2 million hectares, is being leased or in the process of being leased to investors in the rubber, agriculture and timber sectors (Siakor 2012). Mining accounts for an additional 30 percent, which suggests that at least half of Liberia's land area is a part of concession areas that carry leases of between 25 and 99 years.

Economic desperation, caused partly by a lack of viable livelihoods, was an important factor in rebel recruitment during the conflict. At issue is whether a country with food insecurity should be leasing its land for palm oil or using it to grow food for local consumption. What happens to the farmers that have their lands leased and become displaced? With unemployment rampant does reducing available land make sense? If communities are going to have land appropriated for new mines, then, there needs to be some thought about how people will meet their livelihood needs. What alternatives to farming on traditional land exist?

Many are hoping that the pending Land Rights Act will help solve all these problems. The Act as currently written would add another level of protections for local communities when it comes to resource extraction. It would force the government to recognize customary rights of communities and allow these communities to obtain legal title to their land. With title in hand, communities would be authorized to make decisions about how the land will be used, what benefits will accrue to the people, and require that communities provide free, prior and informed consent before concessions or contracts are awarded. The government would provide support and information required for communities to make their own decisions. The hope is that the Act will empower communities that have historically been left out, reduce tensions about land and land acquisition and enable development that is "people-centered." Liberian activists have warned that a failure to pass the Act could result in more conflict and jeopardize peace and security (Civil Society Working Group on Community Land Rights 2016). However, the Act remains in a state of limbo because many people, including elites and companies, who stand to benefit from the current situation are opposed. International actors are also wary that the Act could jeopardize resource extraction and negatively affect national development.

Conclusion

Significant progress has been made in Liberia. Conventional indicators of peace consolidation, such as the demise of rebel groups, disarmament and peaceful elections, are indicative of positive change. Post-war reconstruction continues apace and the traumas inflicted by war are gradually healing. The economy is expected to continue growing despite challenges caused by Ebola and worldwide commodity prices. The UN mission in Liberia is also winding down, signaling an improvement in the overall security situation. However, Liberia remains fragile and a future of peace and prosperity is still uncertain. The case of Liberia demonstrates that how natural resources relate to peace is complex. Peacebuilding strategies defined in terms of natural resources extraction are being questioned. So too is the preoccupation with an emphasis on legal and regulatory reforms that stress transparency and accountability. The case illuminates that in order to truly leverage natural resources for peace and development another approach is necessary. This approach takes seriously issues related to land ownership, sustainable livelihoods and environmental protection, and acknowledges that the rights of people and communities are vital for building peace.

References

Alforte, A., Angan, J., Dentith, J., Domondon, K., Munden, L., Murday, S., and Pradela, L. (2014) "Communities as Counterparties: Preliminary Review of Concessions and Conflict in Emerging and Frontier Market Concessions" The Munden Project, New York.

Alix, Y. (2014) "The Liberia Mining Law Reform and the Impact of the Ebola Crisis" Legal Briefing, Herbert, Smith FreeHills, Liberia.

Altman, S. L, Nichols, S. S., and Woods, J. T. (2012) "Leveraging High-Value Natural Resources to Restore Rule of Law: The Role of the Liberia Forest Initiative in Liberia's Transition to Stability" in Lujala, P. and Rustad, S. A. (eds.) *High-Value Natural Resources and Post-Conflict Peacebuilding* Routledge, New York, 337–365.

ArcelorMittal (2013) Annual Report.

Bannon, I. and Collier P., (eds.) (2003) *Natural Resources and Violent Conflict* World Bank, Washington, DC.

Beevers, M. (2016) "Forest Governance and Post-Conflict Peace in Liberia: Emerging Contestation and Opportunities for Change" *Extractive Industries and Society* 3:320–328.

Bruch, C., Muffett, C., and Nichols, S. S. (2016) *Governance, Natural Resources and Post-Conflict Peacebuilding* Routledge, New York.

Civil Society Working Group on Community Land Rights in Liberia (2016) Statement.

Clower, R. W., Dalton, G., Harwitz, M., and Walters, A. A. (1966) *Growth without Development: An Economic Survey of Liberia* Northwestern University Press, Evanston, IL.

Collier, P. and Hoeffler, A. (2004) "Greed and Grievance in Civil War" *Oxford Economic Papers* 56(4):563–595.

Conca, K. and Wallace, J. (2009) "Environment and Peacebuilding in War-Torn Societies: Lessons from the UN Environment Programme's Experience with Post-Conflict Assessment" *Global Governance* 15(4):185–205.

de Soysa, I. (2002) "Ecoviolence: Shrinking Pie or Honey Pot" *Global Environmental Politics* 2(4):1–34.

EU/FLEGT (2014) Voluntary Partnership Agreement between the European Union and the Republic of Liberia.

Forest Concession Review Committee (FCRC) (2005) *Forest Concession Review: Phase III, Report of the Forest Concession Review Committee.*

Friends of the Earth (FOE) (2013) "Sime Darby and Land Grabs in Liberia" Friends of the Earth Europe.

Global Witness (2001) *Taylor-Made: The Pivotal Role of Liberia's Forests in Flag of Convenience in Regional Conflict* Global Witness, London.

Global Witness (2006) *Cautiously Optimistic: The Case for Maintaining Sanctions in Liberia* Global Witness, London.

Global Witness (2009) *Liberia Poised to Hand Forests to Timber Pirates* Global Witness, London.

Global Witness (2012) *Signing Their Lives Away: Liberia's Private Use Permits and the Destruction of Community-Owned Forests* Global Witness, London.

Government of Norway (2014) Liberia and Norway Launch Climate and Forest Partnership.

Grant, J. A. (2012) "The Kimberley Process at Ten: Reflections on a Decade of Efforts to End the Trade in Conflict Diamonds" in Lujala, P. and Rustad, S. A. (eds.) *High-Value Natural Resources and Post-Conflict Peacebuilding* Routledge, New York, 159–179.

Harris, R., Higgins, J., Kennedy, J., Kingsley, D., and Riley, L. (2013) "Assessing the Forestry Sector: Community Benefit Sharing and Participation in Forest Governance" Liberia Social Audit 2012/2013.

Homer-Dixon, T. (1994) "Environmental Scarcities and Violent Conflict: Evidence from Cases" *International Security* 19(2):5–40.

Homer-Dixon, T. (1999) *Environment, Scarcity and Violence* Princeton University Press, Princeton, NJ.

International Monetary Fund (IMF) (2008) *Liberia: Poverty Reduction Strategy Paper.* IMF, Washington, DC.

International Trade Center (2013) *The Republic of Liberia National Export Strategy: Oil Palm 2014–2018* ITC, Geneva.

Le Billon, P. (2012) *Wars of Plunder: Conflicts, Profits and the Politics of Resources* Columbia University Press, New York.

Levitt, J. I. (2005) *The Evolution of Deadly Conflict in Liberia: From Paternalitarianism to State Collapse* Carolina Academic Press, Durham, NC.

Liberia Extractive Industries Transparency Initiative (LEITI) (2016) EITI Report for the Year Ended 30 June 2014.

Lujala, P. and Rustad, S. A. (eds.) (2012) *High-Value Natural Resources and Post-Conflict Peacebuilding* Routledge, New York.

Matthew, R., Halle, M., and Switzer, J. (2002) *Conserving the Peace: Resources, Livelihoods and Security* IISD, Geneva.

Ministry of Internal Affairs (2014) "Analysis on Country's Social Development Contribution, Distribution, Disbursement from 2005–2014" Government of Liberia, Monrovia.

Reuters (2014) "China-Union Makes First Shipment of Iron Ore from Liberia" 13 February.

Ross, M. (2004) "How Do Natural Resources Influence Civil War? Evidence from Thirteen Cases" *International Organization* 58(1):35–67.

Rustad, S. A. and Binningsbø, H. (2012) "A Price Worth Fighting For? Natural Resources and Conflict Recurrence" *Journal of Peace Research* 49(4):531–546.

Sawyer, A. (1992) *The Emergence of Autocracy in Liberia* Institute for Contemporary Studies, San Francisco.

Siakor, S. K. (2012) *Uncertain Futures: The Impacts of Sime Darby on Communities in Liberia* SDI, Monrovia.

Sirleaf, E. J. (2010) "The Role of Agriculture in Post-Conflict Recovery – The Case of Liberia" Available at: http://allafrica.com/stories/201005240880.html

Somah, S. L. (1995) *Historical Settlement of Liberia and its Environmental Impact* University Press of America, Lanham, MD.

Special Independent Investigative Body (SIIB) (2012) *Report on the Issuance of Private Use Permits (PUP)* Government of Liberia, Monrovia.

Stokes, E. (2015) "Riot on the Plantation: In Liberia, Palm Oil Has Set Off a Dangerous Scramble for Land" *Al Jazeera America* 4 October.

Sustainable Development Institute (2010) *Working for Development? ArcelorMittal's Mining Operations in Liberia* SDI, Monrovia.

Sustainable Development Institute (2014) *Liberia: Poverty in the Midst of Plenty: How Post-War Iron Ore Mining is Failing to Meet Local People's Expectations* SDI, Monrovia.

United Nations Economic Commission of Africa (2009) Africa Mining Vision.

United Nations Environment Programme (UNEP) (2009) *From Conflict to Peacebuilding: The Role of Natural Resources and the Environment* UNEP, Geneva.

United Nations (UN) Panel of Experts (2000) Report Pursuant to Security Council Resolution 1306 (2000), Paragraph 19, in Relation to Sierra Leone. S/2000/1195.

United Nations (UN) Panel of Experts (2001) Report Pursuant to Security Council Resolution 1306 (2000), Paragraph 19, Concerning Liberia. S/2001/1015.

United Nations (UN) Panel of Experts (2003) Report Pursuant to Paragraph 25 of Security Council Resolution 1478 (2003), Concerning Liberia. S/2003/937.

United Nations (UN) Panel of Experts (2008) Report Pursuant to Paragraph 1 of Security Council Resolution 1819 (2008) Concerning Liberia. S/2008/785.

United Nations (UN) Panel of Experts (2009) Report Pursuant to Paragraph 4(e) of Security Council Resolution 1854 (2008). S/2009/640.

United Nations (UN) Panel of Experts (2012) Final Report Pursuant to Paragraph 5(f) of Security Council Resolution 2025 (2011). S/2012/901.

United Nations Security Council (UNSC) (2001) Resolution 1343. S/RES/1343.

United Nations Security Council (UNSC) (2003) Resolution 1478. S/RES/1478.

United Nations Security Council (UNSC) (2006) Resolution 1689. S/RES/1689.

United Nations Security Council (UNSC) (2015) Thirtieth Progress Report of the Secretary General on the United Nations Mission in Liberia. S/2015/620.

Unruh, J. and Williams, R. C. (2013) *Land and Post-Conflict Peacebuilding* Routledge, New York.

Wily, L. A. (2007) *Who Owns the Forest? An Investigation into Forest Ownership and Customary Land Rights in Liberia* Sustainable Development Institute, Brussels.

World Bank (2003) *Global Mining: Mining Reform and the World Bank: Providing a Policy Framework for Development* World Bank, Washington, DC.

World Bank (2012) *Liberia Forest Sector Diagnostic: Results of a Diagnostic on Advances and Learning from Liberia's Six Years of Experience in Forest Sector Reform* World Bank, Washington, DC.

World Food Programme (2013) *Comprehensive Food Security and Nutrition.* Survey. WFP, Rome.

16

Environmental peacebuilding in Nepal

Lessons from Nepal's micro-hydropower projects

Florian Krampe

Introduction

Located in the southern Himalayan region, Nepal offers dramatic diversity in terms of topography, ecology and its people. Beginning at Nepal's southern border with India, the world's highest peaks demark its northern frontier facing the Tibetan plateau and China. Along this ascent the ecology changes from the fertile plains of the Terrai, to the subtropical forests of the Nepali Hill Region, leading up to the scarce montane grass and shrublands summiting with the glaciers and rock of the central Himalaya mountain range. This diversity translates to the more than 26 million people inhabiting this multiethnic, multireligious and multilingual country.

Nepal suffered under a disruptive civil war between 1996 and 2006 fought by Maoist rebels against the Nepali government and monarchy. After the peace agreement in 2006, Nepal successfully transitioned from a monarchy to a republic and despite some degree of political violence has not seen a return to war since. Among others the reintegration process of Maoist rebels has been largely successful. However, up to 2015, Nepal had not moved much beyond these initial steps. While it had seen two elections for its constituent assembly, it took the elected members of this interim parliament seven years to draft a constitution that came into force in September 2015. After strong popular demand a transitional justice and reconciliation process is emerging, but progress remains slow.

The accumulation of slow socioeconomic development, the impact and legacy of the civil war, and Nepal's exposure to environmental and geological risks challenge the task of rebuilding the country and reducing the vulnerability of the Nepali population. Nepal's vulnerability to the impact of climate change is further exacerbating this task. Today, increased and changing rainfall patterns are already causing extreme floods and landslides. In the first half of 2013 alone, 59 people lost their lives and over 12,000 were displaced.[1] Geopolitically, transboundary water relations with India are generally good. But India's dominance in these bilateral relations often raises mistrust from the Nepali population that questions the intentions of India for instance in the development of Nepal's unmatched hydropower potential.

As difficult as these challenges might be, the impact of the 2015 earthquakes that hit Nepal remains unparalleled. The violent tremors left over 8.5 thousand people dead and 3.5 million homeless, causing damage of over 10 billion USD and wiping out priceless historical and cultural artifacts.

Given this daunting situation for Nepal, caught in the interaction between social, political, and ecological processes, this chapter focuses on the aftermath of the civil war and the possibilities of environmental peacebuilding interventions for facilitating the building of peace. I conceive of environmental peacebuilding as interventions in post-war peace processes of a country by domestic or international actors that are geared towards the sustainable management and governance of natural resources and the environment with the intention to improve livelihoods and resilience by reducing vulnerability to environmental risks. After a brief overview of the Nepali civil war and peace process, the main challenges for Nepal's development are outlined. Afterwards a micro level perspective is offered in a case study of the development of micro-hydropower projects in Baglung district in Western Nepal's development region. The micro view highlights the chances and challenges for local communities that stem from this environmental peacebuilding intervention.

Conflict and peacebuilding in Nepal

Nepal's peace process started shortly after the civil war took a significant turn in 2005. By 2005, Maoist rebels, today's United Communist Party of Nepal–Maoist (UCPN–M), had waged a nine-year insurgency against the Nepali government and monarchy largely by attacking police and army facilities throughout western parts of the country. In February 2005, King Gyanendra abolished the government and took full autocratic rule over Nepal. In response, seven of the former parliamentary parties, including the two strongest – Nepali Congress (NC) and Communist Party of Nepal–Unified Marxist Leninist (UML) – formed the Seven Party Alliance (SPA) and sought talks with the Maoist rebels to gain their support. A 12-point understanding reached between the seven political parties and Nepal Communist Party (Maoists) was signed on 22 November 2005. The signatories mobilised successful mass demonstrations that stopped all public life in Nepal for several months. Following increasing public pressure, the King reinstated the parliament in April 2006. Parliament successively curbed the King's power, and the new government aimed to end the civil war. After peace negotiations between the government under G. P. Koirala (NC) and UCPN–M, a comprehensive peace agreement was signed in November 2006, ending the then ten-year civil war in Nepal. UCPN–M, the former rebels, formally became members of parliament (Baral 2012). On the 23 January 2007, the United Nations established a political mission to Nepal. The United Nations Mission in Nepal (UNMIN) was authorised by the United Nations Security Council on request of the Nepali government to monitor the peace process (UNSC 2007). Through the pressure of UCPN–M, eventually the Nepali monarchy was abolished in December 2007, Nepal became a republic, and the path for democratic elections became free. In the 2008 elections to the constituent assembly (CA) UCPN–M won a majority. The former government parties that served under the King, NC and UML, only won a few districts throughout the country.

The peacebuilding process in Nepal suffers – like many others – from a lack of accountability of those in power. The link of "society to the public sphere for articulation of public action" is widely missing (Dahal and Bhatta 2010). This became ever clearer as the first constituent assembly elected in 2008 had not managed to produce a new constitution by the end of its term in 2013. Inter and intra party power struggles continuously paralysed politics in Nepal for over nine years (Pyakurel 2015). The gap left by state actors had been filled by over 56,000 officially registered NGOs in the country by 2010 (Baral 2012:70).

Agreement on a new constitution in 2015 overcame the shortfall of the first constituent assembly, but again caused new internal and regional tensions. Protests by the Madheshi ethnic group against the new constitution at the border to India caused major disruptions. Unofficially supported by India, which traditionally wants to maintain influence on Nepali politics, a fuel supply blockade to landlocked and import-dependent Nepal increased tensions across the border and pushed Nepal closer towards trade with China.

Social, political, and environmental challenges and successes in post-war Nepal

Aside from the internal and regional challenges that remain in Nepal's statebuilding process, there are notable successes and achievements since the end of the civil war (see Table 16.1).

In particular, the transition from monarchy to republic has been successful. In the Polity IV Individual Country Regime Trends this change is clearly reflected by a change from autocracy in 2006 to democracy in 2008 and 2010. Similarly, the World Banks' Political Stability and Absence of Violence/Terrorism indicator shows Nepal clearly improving in the initial five years after the end of the civil war. In the first five years after the war, Nepali's civil liberties and political rights improved, with Freedom House, a US-based think tank, ranking it as partly free, after it was ranked not free at the end of the civil war. Despite this positive development, Nepal's government effectiveness score decreased by 0.72, which is a World Bank governance indicator of the "perceptions of the quality of public services, the quality of the civil service and the degree of its independence from political pressures, the quality of policy formulation and implementation, and the credibility of the government's commitment to such policies".

Nepal's population gained in terms of both human development and income per capita in the first five years after the conflict, which is clearly reflected in the later micro perspective analysis. With a Human Development Index of 0.536, Nepal ranked among the highest countries in the Low Human Development category. Similarly, income per capita almost doubled in the first five years according to World Bank data. However, still 25 per cent of the Nepali population lived under the national poverty line in 2010.

In terms of environmental performance, Nepal also progressed in the first five years after the end of the civil war, which was important to reduce the vulnerability of the country's population to future impacts of environmental and climate change. The Environmental Performance Index (EPI) from Yale and Columbia University, which assesses a country's environmental performance through measurable outcomes such as emissions or deforestation rates, shows a small, yet important, improvement of 0.82. Especially in terms of environmental health, that is variables measuring environmental stresses to human health, Nepal made important progress (see Table 16.2).

Table 16.1 Political development since settlement

	Regime type (Polity IV)	Freedom in the World (Freedom House)	Political Stability and Absence of Violence/Terrorism: estimate (World Bank)	Government Effectiveness: estimate (World Bank)
Settlement	−6	Not free	−1.919	−0.788
2yrs	6	partly free	−1.837	−0.769
5yrs	6	partly free	−1.593	−0.861
Change 0–5	*12*	*−1.50*	*0.325*	*−0.072*

Source: Adapted from Polity data, World Bank Governance Indicator and Freedom House data.

Table 16.2 Environmental Performance Index, score 0–100

	EPI	Environmental health	Ecosystem vitality
2006	35.68	28.83	40.25
2008	35.97	29.11	40.55
2010	36.50	30.41	40.55
Change	*0.82*	*1.58*	*0.30*

Source: Environmental Performance Index from Yale and Columbia University.

Table 16.3 Water access and improved sanitation since settlement, in per cent

	Improved water source	Improved water source, rural	Improved water source, urban	Improved sanitation facilities	Improved sanitation facilities, rural	Improved sanitation facilities, urban
2006	83.2	81.4	92.9	31.5	28.3	48.6
2008	85.1	83.7	92.5	34.7	31.7	50.2
2010	87.0	86.0	92.0	37.9	35.1	51.9
Change	*3.8*	*4.6*	*–0.9*	*6.4*	*6.8*	*3.3*

Source: World Bank.

These improvements in environmental health relate among others to the access to improved water and sanitation (see Table 16.3). While progress in access to improved water sources is constant, one in eight people did not have access to improved water sources in Nepal five years after the conflict, especially in rural areas where 14 per cent remained without improved water sources. More significantly, access to improved sanitation was – while improving – still lagging behind, putting 62 per cent of the population at risk of waterborne disease.

The snapshot across these social, political, and environmental factors shows that Nepal made real improvements in the first five years after the conflict. However, it also shows the scale of the remaining challenges, with three out of five people still lacking access to improved sanitation facilities. One of the biggest challenges is the focus of the subsequent micro perspective – the provision of electricity especially to rural communities.

Environmental peacebuilding and micro-hydropower development in Nepal[2]

Energy remains one of the pivotal challenges for Nepal's development. In 2010, approximately 24 per cent of Nepal did not have access to electricity (World Bank n.d.). And even those who were connected did not receive continuous power. As shown in Table 16.4, for 2013/14 Nepal had an energy gap of over 1,200 GWh. The capital, Kathmandu, experienced scheduled power cuts of up to 14 hours a day during the drier winter season, and two to three hours a day in the water-rich monsoon months.

According to World Bank data (see Table 16.5), Nepal only managed to improve electricity provision to the population by 1.2 per cent within the first five years after the civil war. Nevertheless, Nepal has been able to develop a significant amount of micro-hydropower throughout the country. As a landlocked country in the Himalayas without its own fossil fuel resources, hydropower has been Nepal's key focus for energy production. On a positive note,

Table 16.4 Energy situation for Nepal

Total energy demand 2013/2014	5,909.96 GWh*
Total energy supply 2013/2014	4,631.51 GWh (78.4%)*
Energy gap 2013/2014	1,278.45 GWh (21.6%)*
Energy import from India 2013/2014	1,072.23 GWh (23.2%)*
Installed hydropower capacity 2013/2014	733.5 MW*
Total hydropower potential	40,000 MW**

Notes
* Nepal Electricity Authority Annual Report 2013/2014 (Nepal Electricity Authority 2014).
**Independent Power Producers Association, Nepal (IPPAN).

Table 16.5 Energy access and share of renewable energy, in per cent

	Proportion of population having access to electricity	Renewable electricity share of total electricity output
Settlement	74.8	99.5
2yrs	75.4	99.7
5yrs	76.3	99.9
Change 0–5	*1.2*	*0.4*

Source: World Bank.

this gives Nepal an outstanding score regarding the renewable electricity share of electricity production, with 99.9 per cent (Table 16.5). However, given the extremely remote and difficult terrain of Nepal, getting electricity to the rural population is tremendously challenging. In recent years micro-hydropower has become one of the only reliable ways of providing small communities with electricity.

Funding of these projects is administered through the Nepali state. The projects are implemented through the Alternative Energy Promotion Centre (AEPC) of the Ministry of Environment, Science and Technology in cooperation with the UNDP and World Bank as principle donors (Alternative Energy Promotion Center (AEPC) Rural Energy Development Programme 2011). However, the funding sources for these projects are more complex. Funding is divided between the state through AEPC, the World Bank, District Development Committees (DDCs), Village Development Committees (VDCs), and local households. This is similar to other development policies in Nepal, where households have to contribute a share of the costs, for example to be connected to the national grid.[3] According to experts in Kathmandu, the most successful district of micro-hydropower development has been Baglung district located in the Western Development Region of Nepal.[4] Here the efforts have been particularly successful and given the district national prominence for their successful electrification of these remote communities ("As Darkness Lurks. . ." 2013).

The following analysis provides a micro perspective into the workings of two of these communities with the aim of understanding what the socioeconomic and political consequences have been of (1) the Daram Khola Micro Hydro Project Rishmi (henceforth Rishmi) and (2) the Girindi Khola Micro Hydro Project (Kharbang). The analysis is structured by first assessing the socioeconomic impact on these communities. Afterwards, the influence on political legitimacy is described. In the last section I bring the findings on socioeconomic development and political legitimacy together in a section that aims to offer a discussion of the conduciveness of the micro-hydropower development in these two communities to building peace in Nepal. This section builds primarily on household interviews and personal observations. Short quotes from the interviews are used to illustrate or highlight key findings.

Impact on rural livelihood

There have been substantial socioeconomic changes in the two villages following the completion of the micro-hydropower projects. The improvement of livelihood is directly observable when walking through the villages. According to locals as well as experts interviewed in Kathmandu the economic development has been positive in Kharbang in particular, where the central street is lined by small workshops.[5]

My observations show that both villages have experienced very similar developments. Access to electricity has made life easier in many ways. Electricity has especially changed the situation of women in these villages. The reduced need for firewood, the capacity to use electrical cooking appliances such as rice cookers, as well as electric rice mills, has reduced villagers' exposure to hard and time-consuming labour. These changes give women more time to interact with other members of the community. In particular, the participation of women in gender-separated village groups, a donor demand by UNDP, has empowered women. These groups are focused on different tasks and give members power to decide, for example, on the type of seeds that should be ordered.

Further effects of electrification that are immediately visible when walking through both communities are the presence of electronic appliances like occasional fridges in small shops and televisions, a good mobile phone connection including Internet access, and lighting in all households, which has increased learning possibilities for students through allowing studying in the evenings. All this has opened new economic opportunities for the two communities. However, the economic outcomes differ between both villages.

In Rishmi, following the completion of the Daram Khola micro-hydropower dam and powerhouse in 2009, the 50 KW scheme began providing electricity for about 450 households. As a result, locals tell of new business opportunities that opened up, like poultry farms and furniture shops that require electricity. But most significant are the visible changes in terms of agricultural production and food security. Villagers reported that they initially feared that the micro-hydropower station would reduce the water available for irrigation. However, the real effect has been a significant improvement of irrigation through bigger and improved channels. Two older women who had lived in the village for over four decades mentioned that food security has improved tremendously. Today the villagers can get up to three harvests of different grains per year, while before they were only able to get one.[6] The combination of improved agricultural performance, food availability, as well as food storage in fridges, has tremendously positively affected food durability and security for most villagers in this community.[7] These developments have visibly increased socioeconomic status in Rishmi, especially of women.

In case two, Kharbang, the 75 KW Girindi Khola Micro Hydro Project station is providing electricity to about 688 households. Satish Gautam, Director at UNDP Nepal, refers to the case as the key example of successful micro-hydropower development and rural electrification in Nepal.[8] In comparison to Rishmi's agricultural successes, the socioeconomic change in Kharbang is related to a boost in small enterprises and factories. The national media featured a listing of the achievements that gives an impression of the conducive environment that micro-hydropower development has provided to bring various other services to the community level:

a local FM station, a telecommunication centre, a cable TV network, health services with x-ray and ultrasound facilities, a pathology laboratory, agro-processing mills, a mechanical grill industry, a furniture factory, electronic repairs shops, restaurants and hotels, a herbal shop factory, meat shops with deep freezes, a dairy industry, a noodle factory and several poultry farms.

("As Darkness Lurks. . ." 2013)

The attention that Kharbang has received from the beginning of the project through state and non-state actors is important when assessing its socioeconomic development. Without this attention, the village would likely have never received advanced equipment. For example, the local school received computers during the visit of the World Bank director to the village that continue to expose students to modern technology. The effects are further amplified by Kharbang's beneficial location at the crossroads of the road from Baglung to the east, and the road from Butwal, passing the village from south to north. Its geographic location has made it easier to connect Kharbang to the Internet and TV cable network. This has also increased demand and opportunities for further development in the service sector leading, for example, to more guesthouses.[9]

As expected, there have been changes in socioeconomic development that came with electrification through the micro-hydropower stations and these changes are reported by locals as well as directly visible in both villages. The improved socioeconomic status of households in these two communities reflects a clear reduction of vulnerability.[10] In addition to micro-hydropower development various other public and private services have reached the community level like cable Internet and television. However, as the following analysis shows, despite the increased reach of many services to communities and conducive environment, many public services are still absent.

Impact on political legitimacy

The previous section has briefly illustrated the local socioeconomic impact of the micro-hydropower projects. In this section, the focus will be on the question of the legitimacy of state actors and as such the state. To recall, I understand state actors as individuals acting on behalf of the state. In the specific context of the two villages, state actors are typically, but not limited to, representatives of AEPC, the Nepal Electricity Authority, and the District Development Committees.

In general, all people interviewed in the two villages gave similar answers in regard to perceived state actor performance. The performance of state actors especially in relation to the micro-hydropower projects was perceived as very poor. This is surprising, because, as previously mentioned, both projects were funded and implemented through state actors representing AEPC. In reflection of the field observations I will give two explanations for this unexpected result.

One reason for the perceived absence of Nepali state authorities is a failure of the government agencies to successfully communicate that the government was actually a key actor in the implementation of the project. When asked about interactions with actors in the implementation phase, all households and even station managers in Rishmi expressed the view that there was no interaction with state actors. Neither the government nor its institutions, such as the Nepal Electricity Authority (NEA), were perceived as having been involved in the implementation of the micro-hydropower project. This might indicate a communication problem, because, on further enquiry, it is clear that state actors certainly visited the community and were directly involved. However, these actors have not been recognised as state actors and providers of public good. One villager even suggested that the Nepali Alternative Energy Promotion Centre, the key government agency for micro-hydropower development in Nepal, was an international NGO.[11]

It is likely that the financial details of the project implementation may have been elusive to villagers. Yet, it is unexpected that the actual interactions with state actors from AEPC and DDC during the planning and implementation of the project did not translate into a positive perception of the state actors' performance. The distance between rural and central actors is certainly not a new problem in Nepal. However, it is surprising that this was not different in regard to the micro-hydropower development where service was actually provided and significantly funded by the state, and was successfully implemented to a large extent with the help of Nepali state actors.

The reason for this may lie within the particular local viewpoint regarding the implementation of the micro-hydropower projects. Especially local actors with responsibility in the projects, such as the station managers, mention that the successful implementation of the project is an achievement of the community. It was on the initiative and through the labour of the Rishmi community, not state actors, that the hydropower project was started and implemented.[12] This seems consistent with the perception of many villagers in both cases who communicate that there is no representation of their political interest at the district or national level. That is why people feel that they need to take care of themselves, as no one else is.

Even in Kharbang, which received more frequent visits by different state actors, and as such had more interaction than Rishmi, the perception of these actors is similar. Except for a visit during the opening of the dam, in combination with UNDP and the World Bank, people express the view that they had not experienced much interaction with state actors. It is conceivable that especially visits of multiple state and non-state actors at the opening diluted perceptions of who was actually in charge of the project. However, clearly there was more interaction than during the opening of the micro-hydropower station. The problem is rather that in those moments when there were actions by state actors, those were not perceived as positive, but rather as having complicated life for the community.[13] For example, villagers talk with anger about the construction of roads by the government, which damaged some of the channels leading to the micro-hydropower station, thus necessitating extensive repairs and caused a stop of electricity. Again, also in terms of transport infrastructure, the provision of service has not translated into more legitimacy for state actors.

In both cases, state actors are perceived as largely absent. If state actors are perceived as active their performance is generally perceived as negative. This amplifies the view that authorities are not interested in the villagers' needs and problems and inhibits a positive effect on state legitimacy. This view is widely held and stretches from the utility sector to the security sector. The owner of a guesthouse in Kharbang expressed his concern over the local police force, which is corrupt and mostly absent.[14] Rishmi does not even have a police station.

The negative views in terms of government performance and presence are not caused by the micro-hydropower project. Nepal, like many developing nations, suffers from a strong legitimacy gap between state and society. What is surprising, however, is that the observations from both cases indicate that the micro-hydropower projects, in the short term, did not have any impact on state legitimacy that would narrow the gap between state actors and society. This is contrary to the anticipated positive relation between the provision of services by the state and increased perceptions of legitimacy by society. As the state actors are not perceived as active in the implementation of the micro-hydropower projects, this has added to the experience of households that the government is not present. This is problematic since it challenges compliance of local communities with state actors' policies.

The provision of services through state actors did not reduce the deep-rooted distrust against state actors. For instance, the experience of the Maoist insurgency remains deeply ingrained in the minds of villagers. This distrust continuously shapes the perceptions of the state, particularly towards those rebels turned state actors. This is visible though the strong framing of particular Maoists in terms of violence by some villagers.[15] There is no distinction between the Maoists as rebel group and the Maoists as state actors building the government. It is a clear dismissal of the Maoist government and contests the legitimacy of the current political order. However, interviewees who said that they stand politically close to the Maoists also expressed disconnect and distrust towards the post-war state. This reemphasises that the low legitimacy of the post-war state actors is not just a conflict-related issue, but that the problem is rather the long experience of marginalisation of these villages.

As mentioned, the interactions with state actors differ between the cases. Kharbang is notably different to Rishmi. Interestingly, however, in Kharbang the observations mirror many of the expressed attitudes from Rishmi. There is, however, one significant difference. The more frequent interaction with state and non-state actors in Kharbang has resulted in socioeconomic development as shown before. The connectivity of the village to modern information technology like the Internet and cable television has significantly impacted individuals' knowledge and awareness about political processes, through access to social and traditional media. A high degree of awareness about current national political processes is notable throughout all interviews and conversations experienced in Kharbang. This has not been the case in Rishmi, where a lot of infrastructure like the Internet is still lacking.

Despite the notably higher degree of interactions that Kharbang experienced, residents and even local elites in Kharbang still feel neglected by state actors. Mitra Bahadur Pun who is the chairman of the Girindi Khola Micro Hydro Project and previously was VDC chairman, as well as a candidate for the Communist Party of Nepal–Unified Marxist Leninist (UML) in the election to the constituent assembly in 2008, said: "I have some requests. As I said earlier, we don't have any place to go for proper support by explaining our problems."[16] If even politically active local elites are lacking a connection to central state actors, it is not surprising that the normal households in both cases express that they have no one in the government or administration who would represent their interests.

While there is a desire to have a more active state, people in both villages have learned to live in quasi-autonomy in the absence of state actors. Despite the frustration it is because of the long-term marginalisation that locals are not dependent on state actors in their everyday life. The bureaucracy just matters when official papers are required. And then contact with state actors is associated with long travels to the central municipality representation, in this case Baglung Bazar (about 6 to 8 hours by bus).

This local autonomy is a critical challenge to the legitimacy of the post-war state actors, because it reduces interest in political participation. People in both communities claimed that they did not intend to vote in the November 2013 elections – a claim that could not be verified. As stated before, the problem was not because of negative sentiments towards the Maoist government. The observations indicate rather that there was little hope that the relation between state actors and society would change after the elections, no matter who won.

In summary, despite differences in both cases regarding the presence and intervention of state actors, both cases are surprisingly coherent in their experiences and expressed attitudes towards state actors. There is no indication that legitimacy of state actors has improved in the short term through the provision of electricity to these communities. In the following analysis, I will attempt to bring the specific local socioeconomic development and views on state legitimacy in relation to the micro-hydropower project together to offer an explanation why the theorised mechanism is not working as suggested and what that means for the Nepali peace process.

Community resilience and the Nepali state

It is difficult to be sure with certainty that these negative perceptions are solely the consequence of interactions around the micro-hydropower stations. Nevertheless, the arrival of electricity in these villages had the most significant impact on locals' life, making it a powerful moment that had the potential to influence local perceptions. Therefore, there are some important intermediate conclusions that can be drawn that contribute to our understanding of peace processes. There is clearly successful socioeconomic development in both cases. But, equally, there is a clear problem in the political development. It is remarkable that the economic flourishing has not translated into more legitimacy of the post-war state. Considering the significance that is ascribed to socioeconomic development in peacebuilding, this finding strengthens the need to consider and use state legitimacy more thoroughly as an analytical tool when studying peace processes. Identifying nuances and discrepancies between local perceptions and state actors would otherwise be more difficult, if not impossible.

The above empirical data illustrate a challenge to the theoretical assumption that service provision will increase both socioeconomic and state legitimacy and support peace processes to progress from negative towards a positive peace. In the following analysis, I explore more deeply the particular dynamics that were observed in the two cases surrounding the socioeconomic and political impact of the hydropower projects. I argue that the socioeconomic development and the interactions among villagers themselves have manifested local informal governance structures that highlight local autonomy and thus amplify the already existing divide between rural communities and central state actors.

The main reason for the weak state legitimacy is the high degree of local autonomy, which stands in opposition to a reciprocal relationship between local and state actors. While this is a historical legacy of Nepali politics and a failure to hold community level elections in the last decade, the experiences around the micro-hydropower project have amplified the divide between rural and central actors by strengthening the cohesion of autonomous local networks. For example, in Rishmi, the success of local cooperation has reaffirmed the community's ability to take charge of their own interests and confirmed that they can successfully do so. Yet, this has contributed to the local perception of a widened gap between state actors and the community, while also contributing to the community's mistrust of those actors. In particular, the successful implementation of the project through locals' labour and own financial contribution has been an important factor that strengthened the sense of being able and responsible for themselves: "The people from the village brought this. We all contribute money in this. We all brought it together. We all worked for it."[17] This expression of local solidarity and cohesion is expressed with similar strength in Kharbang: "In my experience, we can do it."[18]

The findings indicate that the high level of socioeconomic status in both cases is the result of the micro-hydropower projects. Yet, the successful local interaction during the implementation of the micro-hydropower project has created and consolidated new informal governance structures. These are locally legitimate structures that operate informally and appear as distinguished forms of self-governance. More frequent interaction and cooperation within the communities has replaced formal state actors with local informal actors. These receive a high degree of local support and legitimacy, because they are perceived as having been the actual provider of socioeconomic development. Hence, trust and interaction with these local structures is strong and they are frequently referenced in the interviews. These actors are certainly important in stabilising the local communities in the absence of legitimate state actors. The formation of "governance without government" (Menkhaus 2006) has been seen before. As such, the findings from Nepal indicate a similar process to that seen by Kappler in Bosnia, despite an absolutely different context: if the post-war state actors are not accepted, legitimacy finds new spaces and actors (Kappler 2012).

In the case of Nepal, these informal governance structures are perceived as highly legitimate among the villagers. Of course, a strong local community is a positive development. It empowers actors and increases resilience to cope with disturbances to the community. It reduces vulnerabilities and contributes to socioeconomic development and status. There is a tendency in recent peacebuilding research to look more favourably at such alternative traditional developments in peace processes (Clements et al. 2007). For instance, Richmond argues that such local developments are indicative of an alternative post-liberal peace, especially since locals show a strong tendency to transform external support according to their own necessities (Richmond 2012).

However, taking the larger state–society relationship into account, as argued in this chapter, a widened distance between state actors and the local community is more likely to have negative implications for the peace process, because it calls the legitimacy of the post-war state into question. Nepal as a state exists despite its weak government actors and it also exists in the heads of villagers. Thus, the observed "governance without government" inadvertently complicates the consolidation of the post-war order. The legitimacy of informal self-governance is an acknowledgement of a local order and as such challenging to the overall national post-war order. Certainly, the question if local legitimacy versus central legitimacy of the post-war order has to be a zero-sum game depends highly on how the government is reacting to the challenge.

Migdal argues "that state leaders may purposely weaken their own state agencies that could apply and enforce rules, and that the state may purposely strengthen those who apply and enforce rules in contradiction to those of the state" (Migdal 2001:64). Yet this is unlikely in the case of Nepal. Central political figures in Nepal referenced the emergence of informal governance structures as a problem. The former prime minister Baburam Bhattarai stated that governing is becoming more difficult since the local demands are being expressed with increasing strength. Bhattarai argues that the problem has been exacerbated through other, external actors in both cases, because locals get what they need through other channels. He says that because of external involvement locals "are getting ideas".[19]

Indeed, my observations suggest that external actors like NGOs are perceived positively in communities as a consequence of the government's inability to provide for the communities. Locals consider these NGOs as a way to fund their own community development. People are aware of potentially normative agendas brought by these actors, but simply disregard them as long as they do not interfere with the community's interest:

> *Translator*: They see the NGOs as someone to help. And as long as their interest is fulfilled they are pretty happy about their presence. And they discuss among themselves now, that is something they didn't tell me, but the discussion is going on [discussion among respondents is ongoing in the background] saying obviously there is interest, they have an interest, but it's something that we might neither care or understand, as long as we have what we want.[20]

This means that whoever serves the community's interest and needs is welcome, be it the Nepali government, NGOs, or international aid agencies. And, contrary to Bhattarai's statement, the actual development is not imposed from outside, but is an agenda deeply driven by agency in the communities.

This agency is amplified through the informal governance structures that are continuously, in turn, reconfirmed and strengthened on a local level through so far constant successful socioeconomic development and increased local interaction and solidarity. For example, in Rishmi, the community created their own social services. Poorer families that were unable to contribute financially to the construction of the micro-hydropower station are receiving free electricity. Still some households are unable to buy the electricity pole necessary to connect their house to the local grid. In such cases the community forest provides poor households with wooden poles for free. This initiative is managed locally by the community itself. As such, the local informal structures provide governance through effective informal regulation and are highly relevant to villagers' everyday life.

The observations suggest that the micro-hydropower project has facilitated local interactions and autonomy. This effect continues to play an instrumental role for the current local social order. Cooperation helps form and reinforces new informal governance structures. In fact, they are manifestations of a functioning legitimate sub-system that is reproduced through dynamic interaction effects with local cooperation and development success. Interestingly, this confirms the suggested mechanism and Lipset's argument that the provision of instrumental needs "maintains the belief that existing political institutions are the most appropriate or proper ones for the society" (Lipset 1959). The difference is that these institutions and actors are on an informal local level, not on a formal state level.

In the recent peacebuilding literature, scholars have argued that local substructures are a representation of a peace, and they may even be indicative of an alternative post-liberal peace for locals (Boege, Brown and Clements 2009; Richmond 2012; Kappler 2014). On a theoretical level, this argument is certainly interesting; however, empirically, the local understanding of peace challenges this argument. Asked if there is peace in Nepal today, all interviewed people answered the question unanimously that there was not (Krampe and Swain 2016) – a clear indication that the local informal governance structures are not improving perceptions of peace.

The case analysis suggests a more complex relationship between state and society. The disconnect between socioeconomic change and state legitimacy offers insight into the simultaneous possibilities and risks of this form of development policy for the peace process in Nepal.

The successful socioeconomic development within the communities has to be seen as positive and as contributing to peace and stability. It is appeasing communities as the increase in livelihood and de facto autonomy from the state is reducing the likelihood of members of these local communities joining violent uprisings. Even though locals would like a stronger state, the overall satisfaction and socioeconomic status of households have improved according to locals. Considering that the dissatisfaction of villagers with their daily life was, as Eck argues, a favourable condition for Maoist mobilisation during the civil war (Eck 2010), we can say with some certainty that the socioeconomic development has contributed to a more stable, peaceful constellation.

The failure of increasing state legitimacy in the short term, however, is concerning. Not on the community level, but on the state level, as it emphasises a long-term dilemma for states that attempt to use development through service provision to gain legitimacy among the population. As such, it is uncertain how Nepali state actors will react to the de facto autonomy of communities. It is the political actors that are of concern, rather than institutional actors or security forces like the army. Since the end of the conflict the political actors in Kathmandu have been engaged in their personal power struggles that are responsible for the overall paralysis. The question is if this will remain this way. As the statement of the former prime minister Bhattarai suggests, there is increasing pressure on political elites. This likely has to do with higher socioeconomic status in rural communities. But the question is how the political elites will act in regard to the local autonomy and informal governance structures. It is reasonable to believe that the political leadership will not allow autonomous local structures to continue in their current form because, as argued before, they threaten the foundation of the state and its leadership if they hinder mobilisation through state actors. The uncertainty that the micro-hydropower development has emphasised in terms of the relationship between the state and society, raises the question of whether this type of service provision in its current form is conducive to building peace in Nepal.

Conclusion

The aim of this chapter has been to assess the possibilities of environmental peacebuilding interventions for facilitating the building of peace in Nepal. As such, the focus has been placed first on studying the socioeconomic impacts of micro-hydropower development for rural communities and second on the political effects, specifically how the provision of renewable energy sources has affected the political legitimacy of the post-war state. The micro level analysis of two localities in Nepal highlights important dynamics between state and society actors that are an important contribution to a broader understanding of environmental peacebuilding interventions. The consistency of the views expressed across the two cases indicates that the general dynamics outlined might be specific to community-based micro-hydropower projects. Yet, it was highlighted that other background variables, like the long-term marginalisation of rural populations, play a significant role for households interviewed in Rishmi and Kharbang.

The analysis shows an interesting dynamic that offers valuable insight for the design and implementation of environmental peacebuilding interventions as it points to the interlinkage of intended and unintended consequences of the intervention. There is certainly a need to acknowledge the long-term interplay of social, political, and ecological processes in post-war countries and to understand the potential and dynamics of natural resources and environmental issues in this context. The interactions of these processes decisively shape the post-war landscape. It is therefore prudent to help build a peace that is ecologically sensitive and socially and politically relevant and desirable.

The study of two localities in rural Nepal shows that micro-hydropower development has had many positive effects for rural communities, especially in regard to socioeconomic development. This improved socioeconomic status of households reflects a clear reduction in vulnerability to poverty and even food security as the improved channels diverting water to the micro-hydropower station have improved irrigation of nearby fields. Though it does not immediately translate into improving the legitimacy of the Nepali state, by helping to bring overall sustainable development to its citizens, the state is most likely going to reap the benefit in the future. The experiences from the study of micro-hydropower development in Nepal show that the state needs to actively pursue and project the ownership of the water sector development process in a post-war period in order to legitimise itself.

Notes

1 India/Nepal: Floods and Landslides – June 2013 http://reliefweb.int/disaster/fl-2013-000070-ind [Accessed 11 November 2016].
2 The following analysis builds on the analysis published in Krampe (2016).
3 Interview with Dilli Ghmiri, Director, National Association of Community Electricity Users-Nepal (NACEUN), Sanepa, Nepal, 6 September 2013.
4 Author interview Dilli Ghmiri, Director, National Association of Community Electricity Users-Nepal (NACEUN), Sanepa, Nepal, 6 September 2013. Author interview with Satish Gautam, Director Programme "Rural Electrification for Rural Livelihood", UNDP. Kathmandu, Nepal, 16 September 2013.
5 Author interview Dilli Ghmiri, Director, National Association of Community Electricity Users-Nepal (NACEUN), Sanepa, Nepal, 6 September 2013. Author interview with Satish Gautam, Director Programme "Rural Electrification for Rural Livelihood", UNDP. Kathmandu, Nepal, 16 September 2013.
6 Author interview Rishmi, HH3&4, 252–266.
7 This claim is based on statements by villagers. It could not be verified how many fridges are present in the community, beyond those visible in some of the street side shops and a guesthouse. According to the 2011 census no refrigerator was available in the community. However, there are no data regarding the change since then.

8 Author interview with Satish Gautam, Director Programme "Rural Electrification for Rural Livelihood", UNDP. Kathmandu, Nepal, 16 September 2013.
9 Author interview Kharbang, HH3, 176–208.
10 An assessment of the equity of these changes is a valid and important question, although it is beyond the scope of this study.
11 Author interview Rishmi, HH2, 156–164.
12 Author interview Rishmi, 01_Bedi Lal Sapkota and Prem Sapkota, 83–82.
13 Author interview Kharbang, HH2, 181–188.
14 Author interview Kharbang, 04_HH3, 282–284.
15 Author interview Rishmi, HH3&4, 329–343.
16 Author interview Kharbang, Mitra, 236–238.
17 Author interview Rishmi, HH3 & HH4, 156.
18 Author interview Kharbang, 03_Mitra.
19 Author interview with Baburam Bhattarai, former Prime Minister of Nepal, Senior leader UCPN–M. 19 July 2013, Sanepa, Kathmandu.
20 Author interview Rishmi, Bedi Lal Sapkota and Prem Sapkota, 195–196.

References

Alternative Energy Promotion Center (AEPC) Rural Energy Development Programme (2011) *Achievements of REDP*.

"As Darkness Lurks around Capital, Baglung Glitters" (2013) *Ekantipur.com*. Available at: www.ekantipur. com/2013/03/07/related-article/as-darkness-lurks-around-capital-baglung-glitters/368075.html

Baral, L. R. (2012) *Nepal – Nation-State in the Wilderness*. Sage, Los Angeles.

Boege, V., Brown, M. A. and Clements, K. P. (2009) "Hybrid Political Orders, Not Fragile States" *Peace Review* 21(1):13–21.

Clements, K. P., Boege, V., Brown, A., Foley, W. and Nolan, A. (2007) "State Building Reconsidered: The Role of Hybridity in the Formation of Political Order" *Political Science* 59(1):45–56.

Dahal, D. R. and Bhatta, C. D. (eds.) (2010) *Building Bridges of Peace in Nepal*. Friedrich-Ebert-Stiftung (FES), Kathmandu. Available at: www.fesnepal.org/publications/book_reviews/book_on_peace.htm

Eck, K. (2010) "Recruiting Rebels: Indoctrination and Political Education in Nepal" in Lawoti, M. and Pahari, A. (eds.) *The Maoist Insurgency in Nepal*. Routledge, London.

Kappler, S. (2012) "Everyday Legitimacy in Post-Conflict Spaces: The Creation of Social Legitimacy in Bosnia-Herzegovina's Cultural Arenas" *Journal of Intervention and Statebuilding* 7(1):1–18.

Kappler, S. (2014) *Local Agency and Peacebuilding*. Palgrave Macmillan, Basingstoke.

Krampe, F. (2016) "Empowering Peace: Service Provision and State Legitimacy in Nepal's Peace-Building Process" *Conflict, Security & Development* 16(1):53–73.

Krampe, F. and Swain, A. (2016) "Human Development and Minority Empowerment" in Richmond, O. P., Pogodda, S. and Ramovic, J. (eds.) *The Palgrave Handbook of Disciplinary and Regional Approaches to Peace* Palgrave Macmillan, Basingstoke.

Lipset, S. M. (1959) "Some Social Requisites of Democracy: Economic Development and Political Legitimacy" *American Political Science Review* 53(1):69–105.

Menkhaus, K. (2006) "Governance without Government in Somalia: Spoilers, State Building, and the Politics of Coping" *International Security* 31(3):74–106.

Migdal, J. S. (2001) *State in Society*. Cambridge University Press, Cambridge.

Nepal Electricity Authority (2014) *Nepal Electricity Authority Annual Report*. NEA, Kathmandu. Available at: www.nea.org.np/images/supportive_docs/Annual%20Report-2014.pdf

Pyakurel, U. (2015) "Maoist Insurgency and Peace Process in Nepal" in Chandran, D. S. and Chari, P. R. (eds.) *Armed Conflict, Peace Audit and Early Warning 2014*. Sage, Los Angeles, 247–270.

Richmond, O. P. (2012) *A Post-Liberal Peace*. Routledge, Abingdon.

United Nations Security Council (UNSC) (2007) Resolution 1740 (2007). 2.

World Bank (n.d.) Access to Electricity (% of Population) Data. World Bank. Available at: http://data. worldbank.org/indicator/EG.ELC.ACCS.ZS/countries/1W-NP?display=graph

17

Environmental peacebuilding in post-conflict Colombia

Pedro Valenzuela and Servio Caicedo

Introduction

On 24 November 2016, after four years of negotiations, the Colombian government and the largest rebel organization, the Revolutionary Armed Forces of Colombia–People's Army (FARC-EP),[1] signed the "Final Accord for the Ending of the Conflict and the Building of a Stable and Lasting Peace."[2] The Accord ends a five-decade-old conflict that by 2012 had claimed around 220,000 lives and left 25,000 disappeared, 6,000 forcibly recruited minors, 27,000 kidnapped, and 5,000,000 internally displaced persons (CNMH 2013).

The armed conflict and related economic dynamics have also negatively affected a country that, with only 0.22 percent of the earth's surface, holds more than 10 percent of currently known species, has more than half of its territory covered by natural forests (Naciones Unidas Colombia 2014) and a wealth of natural resources, including extensive freshwater and a variety of minerals, and is in terms of species per land unit the second most biodiverse country in the world (USAID 2010).

This chapter identifies central environmental issues related to the armed conflict, examines the Accord's potential contribution to the positive transformation of environmental problems, and concludes by discussing challenges to the implementation of the peace agreement and environmental peacebuilding.

Armed conflict and the environment

From its inception, the armed conflict has been closely linked to environmental issues. The struggle for land and control of territories and population has given rise to guerrilla, self-defense, and paramilitary organizations, strengthened legal and illegal economies around licit and illicit resources, and severely affected biodiversity-rich areas and fragile ecosystems.

Initially created as a self-defense organization with close ties to the Communist Party of Colombia, the FARC became an armed agrarian movement favoring the interests of landless peasants and poor farmers, promoting processes of "armed settlement" and the construction of alternative, autonomous structures of local power (Pizarro 1991; Ferro and Uribe 2002). Throughout the 1960s and 1970s, however, the conflict remained "rural and peripheral," and only experienced a "quantitative and qualitative leap" in the wake of the FARC's seventh conference in 1982, when the guerrillas adopted an offensive strategy, in an effort to bring the war closer to important economic, political, and administrative centers (Lair 2004). The decision to expand to every province of the country and consolidate power at the local level implied the need to increase the number of combat units and to find alternative sources of income, which in turn explains the guerrillas' presence in areas of economic boom around the exploitation of natural resources such as coal, oil, and gold, as well as livestock farming, commercial agriculture, and illicit crops (Echandía 1999).

The degree of insertion in different parts of the national territory largely determines the FARC's interaction with local economies. In areas of highly consolidated economy and society and areas of economic boom, where they normally do not have control, it tends to be "parasitic," mostly draining local resources and the economic surplus of the landowning class (Rangel 2000; Pizarro 1996). But in areas where they have settled for years, normally regions of low population density, weak state presence, and precarious commercial relations with the formal economy, such as areas with illicit crops, they have "symbiotically integrated themselves with production and the economic dynamic in general" (Rangel 2000:584).

The guerrillas' appropriation of resources has been used by sectors of the political class to discredit the rebel groups, presenting them as being guided by an economic rationality devoid of political objectives, negating thus any association with great social inequalities and exclusion within a political system that has been variously described as "illiberal democracy," "restricted democracy," or "low intensity democracy." Nevertheless, most academic analyses agree that predation of resources is not their main motivation and that their presence in the territories is explained by various political and social conditions (Valenzuela 2002).

The competition for resources, and the consequent impact on the environment, was compounded by the emergence of two additional illegal armed actors: paramilitary groups created by sectors threatened by the guerrillas' increased territorial control and influence at the local level, and a drug-related agrarian class bent on consolidating its own territorial dominance. The paramilitaries soon ceased to be a strictly private security apparatus for the protection of *haciendas*, adopted an offensive counterinsurgency strategy in cooperation with the armed forces, and sponsored a broader project of reconstruction of a rural order (Romero 2004).

The link between armed conflict and environmental deterioration has become all too evident. One of the most detrimental effects has been deforestation, as 42 percent of the forest areas of the country are located in municipalities where the armed conflict is being waged. According to estimates by the National Department of Planning, 4 out of 7 engines of deforestation are related to the conflict: illicit crops, illegal mineral extraction, illegal logging, and settlement of displaced populations. Between 1990 and 2013, 75 percent of deforestation was concentrated in municipalities affected by the conflict, and the annual rate of deforestation in those areas was almost three times larger than in the rest of the country (Gaviria 2016).

Drug trafficking, especially of cocaine, continues to be an important factor fueling the conflict. Coca crops increased by 39 percent between 2014 and 2015, especially in indigenous and black communities' territories (UNODC 2016). Some 87 percent of all areas with illicit crops are in regions affected by the armed conflict, and 42 percent of these are in natural reserves and national parks (Gaviria 2016).

The expansion of illicit crops has led to increased pressure on communities and territories, with detrimental impacts on ecosystems. The clearing out of areas for cultivation and the heavy use of pesticides, herbicides, fungicides, and highly toxic chemicals for the extraction of alkaloids result in deforestation, biodiversity loss, soil erosion, and loss of soil fertility, and contaminate waterways, affecting plant and animal species alike (Dourojeanni 1992).

The problem has been aggravated by some eradication policies. Close to 75 percent of the U.S. component of "Plan Colombia" was earmarked for the military and the police and was to be used in the "Push to Southern Colombia," where an estimated 50 percent of the country's cocaine production is located, and where the FARC are especially strong. After initially recognizing the need to keep the antinarcotics and counterinsurgency wars separate, the United States eventually pressed for a *merging* of the two wars (LeoGrande and Sharpe 2000). Most aerial fumigation in rebel-controlled areas was conducted by the Colombian armed forces and international private security companies (Armendáriz 2016).[3] The aggressive fumigation campaign has led to community displacement and affected legal and illegal crops alike, water sources, biodiversity, and the health of peasants, indigenous peoples, and Afro-Colombian communities.

A second factor related to environmental conflict has been the growth of extractive industries. Responding to high international demand for minerals, and in an effort to incorporate the Colombian economy into the global market, the Colombian government has made mining and energy one of the main "locomotives of development."[4] Especially important has been direct foreign investment in extractive industries such as oil, gas, coal, and gold. Some 38 percent and 20 percent (an increase of 92.8 percent in a year) of direct foreign investment in 2008 corresponded to the oil and mining sectors, respectively; 90 percent of direct foreign investment in the period 2009–2010 went to oil, hydrocarbons, and mining. While before 2001 between 80 and 100 mining permits were issued every year, an average of 400 per year have been issued since then. A total of 5067 permits covering 2.927.189 hectares had been issued by 2008 (Mantilla 2010). The Colombian police estimate that between 2010 and 2014 illegal exploitation of gold took place in 38 percent of the municipalities affected by the armed conflict, with the consequent destruction of water basins, rivers, and forests (Gaviria 2016). Mining titles have been issued in more than 80 percent of municipalities most affected by the armed conflict with the FARC (Naciones Unidas Colombia 2014).

The weakness of governance structures has led to uncontrolled systems of resource exploitation, a loss of accountability, and corruption. In some cases, opportunistic entrepreneurs, including large multinational corporations, have taken advantage of lax legislation and institutional vacuum to operate in mining areas, bypassing land management plans and violating environmental laws (Amnistía Internacional 2015). In addition, environmental institutions have experienced budget cuts, and their administrative capacity has been weakened by national, regional, and local pressures (Guhl 2014). In many instances, institutions have been coopted by illegal actors, as evidenced by the high number of criminal cases against public servants accused of having links with paramilitary groups.

The rapid expansion of mining has increased the number of conflicts, especially with peasant, indigenous, and Afro-Colombian communities whose territories and biological, social, cultural, and political capital have been threatened by exploration and exploitation activities. Conflicts have also emerged with ancestral–artisanal and illegal miners expelled by large mining companies or whose mines have been shut down by local authorities on charges of contamination, exploitation of child labor, and lack of adequate security conditions. Social mobilization and protests have increased accordingly. Pérez-Rincón (2015) documented 95 environmental conflicts affecting urban and rural communities: 36 percent are related to mining (especially gold), 23 percent to the exploration and extraction of fossil energy (coal and oil), and 14 percent to the monoculture of African Palm.[5] Between January 2001 and December 2011, about 274 collective actions related to the extraction of oil, coal, and gold were undertaken by indigenous, peasant, and Afro-Colombian communities (25 percent), workers of extractive companies (50 percent), urban dwellers (13 percent), and ancestral–artisanal miners (12 percent). These actions were motivated by a variety of reasons, including demands for social, cultural, and economic rights, a healthy environment and the collective enjoyment of natural resources, protests against policies regarding the management of hydrocarbons, and the defense of water sources and paramos (CINEP 2012).

The guerrillas' war strategies have caused additional environmental damage. Their attacks against oil infrastructure,[6] particularly pipelines, have resulted in the spilling of 4.1 million barrels in the last 35 years, affecting 129 municipalities (Gaviria 2016).[7] According to estimates, 723 attacks against oil infrastructure were carried out between 2007 and 2014. Spills and fires affect rivers, swamps, and soil, endangering the viability of the ecosystem, and putting the health and economic activities of communities at risk (Fundación Ideas para la Paz 2015).

Another serious problem associated with the conflict is displacement and land dispossession. The escalation of the armed conflict, state repression of illicit economies, and the expansion of extractive industries and agroindustrial production have resulted in the forced displacement of more than five million people (CNMH 2013). About 76 percent of internally displaced persons had some type of right to land, either as owners, occupants, or holders, which has compounded the problem of land concentration in the country: Less than 0.5 percent of large landowners own 62.91 percent of the land, while 57.87 percent of small and medium owners own 1.66 percent (Mantilla 2010). Many of the areas where internally displaced persons have settled experience environmental injustice, such as lack of access to drinking water, contamination, destruction of water sources, illegal mining, and location next to sanitary landfills.

The phenomenon of abandonment and dispossession of land is extremely complex, as it varies in terms of modalities, objectives, and agents, even within the same spatial and temporal context. In some cases, it is related to military strategies by armed actors, while in others, it is linked to political objectives or to legal and illegal productive projects by legal and illegal entrepreneurs. Estimates as to the amount of land abandoned or usurped also vary greatly among various sources (CNRR 2009; CNMH 2016). A case in point is the monoculture of African Palm, that, along with other agroindustrial farming projects, is part of the government and international entities' strategy of pacification, as well as the paramilitaries' strategy of territorial control. In some parts of the country where palm complexes were already established, palm companies invited and financed paramilitary groups as private security corps. In others, paramilitary presence and palm plantations expanded simultaneously, and in yet others, the paramilitaries invited the palm companies to establish themselves in areas under their control (Mingorance 2006).

The Peace Accord and environmental peacebuilding

Although the environmental impact of the armed conflict was not a priority in the Havana peace dialogues and the Accord does not contain a specific point regarding environmental issues,[8] they were nevertheless dealt with in a complementary manner in the agreements reached on Integral Rural Development (IRR) and illicit crops.

IRR is conceived as an instrument for the structural transformation of the countryside, in order to improve the living conditions of the rural population and narrow the urban–rural divide, reverse the negative effects of the conflict, change the conditions that have permitted the persistence of violence, and contribute to a lasting and sustainable peace. It aims to integrate different regions of the country, eradicate poverty, and promote the good life and equitable social and economic development.[9] Although structural transformation will eventually extend to the whole country, some areas will be given priority, depending on the level of poverty and unmet basic needs, the degree to which they have been affected by the armed conflict, the weakness of administrative institutions, and the presence of illicit crops and other illegal economies (Presidencia de la República de Colombia 2016).

Formalization of ownership and the updating of the land registry are important steps in this direction, considering that the lack of formal titles has been an obstacle to prevent land dispossession as well as restitution and reparation. The Accord also stipulates the creation of a Land Fund in order to democratize access to land, especially by rural dwellers with insufficient or no property, and a restitution program in favor of those who have been forcibly dispossessed.

Particularly important are the Environmental Zoning Plan, the creation of new Peasant Reserve Zones (PRZ), and the Development Plans with a Territorial Approach. The Environmental Zoning Plan aims at closing the agricultural frontier and protecting areas of special environmental interest, such as forest reserve zones, high biodiversity zones, fragile and strategic ecosystems, basins, paramos, wetlands, and other sources of hydric resources. The Peasant Reserve Zones promote new forms of organization of the territory and sustainable environmental development, strengthen peasant economies, and contribute to peacebuilding and reconciliation, guaranteeing the social, political, economic, and cultural rights of small farmers and indigenous and Afro-Colombian communities. The Development Plans with a Territorial Approach will protect multiethnic and multicultural diversity, promoting indigenous and Afro-Colombian communities' own modes of production.

The Accord calls for designing development plans that take into account environmental sustainability and preservation of water resources; the compatibility between the vocation of the soil and its use; and the social, cultural, and economic particularities of the territories, giving priority to food production. Benefits will also be extended to adjacent areas and areas that have experienced the armed conflict most intensely. Other topics related to the environment, such as sustainable agriculture and access to water, are also part of the agreement. Special attention will be given to women's property rights and participation.

The Accord also includes Environmental Conflict Resolution mechanisms to address conflicts related to land tenure and use. It specifically mentions Alternative Dispute Resolution mechanisms (conciliation), traditional community methods, and active community participation in the resolution of conflicts. In addition, it stipulates the creation of channels to facilitate dialogue between national, regional, and local governments, and peasant, indigenous and Afro-Colombian communities, and private sector enterprises, in order to promote consensus building around socio-environmental sustainability, the well-being of rural communities, and equitable economic growth. A new agrarian jurisdiction to facilitate access to justice, especially in priority areas, will be created. The creation of democratic institutional spaces for citizen participation in all stages of the plans and programs is intended to ensure the inclusion of rural communities in the political, social, economic, and cultural life of their territories and the nation.

The third part of the agreement deals with illicit drugs. The main point is the adoption of an Integrated National Plan of Substitution of Crops of Illicit Use. Priority will be given to areas with high population and illicit crops density, natural parks, and areas of implementation of the Development Plans with a Territorial Approach. The plan calls for a differential approach, depending on the conditions, needs, and economic, cultural, and social characteristics of each territory. Another important element is the voluntary participation of farmers in illicit crop substitution. Drug consumption will be treated as a public health problem, while the fight against drug trafficking will be intensified.

All in all, the Accord incorporates most of the recommendations found in the literature on environmental cooperation and peacebuilding. Environmental justice plays a key role, transcending the concern with preservation, in order to include change in the quality of life of populations and communities affected by economic growth and development. This implies recognition of local communities and the promotion of participation, equality, capacity building, and respect for the life options of local communities (Schlosberg 2007). Change is expected in terms of the impact on communities (generation of identity, sense of ownership, reconstitution of the social fabric, resilience, restored livelihoods), on state–community relations (increased trust, restored credibility, transparency, accountability), and on the broader context (support for peace, end to the recruitment by armed actors, reconciliation) (Mosulishvili 2016).

It also contemplates institutional reforms recommended for post-conflict situations where high-value natural resources are involved, in order to confront corruption and rentier practices, including appropriation of resources by illegal armed actors, and promotes consensus building between governments, enterprises, and civil society regarding responsible management of resources and mitigation of negative social and environmental effects, by establishing mechanisms for consultation with communities (Lujala and Rustad 2012).

Post-conflict and environmental peacebuilding: the challenges ahead

Colombia has made great strides in terms of legislation for reparation of victims, including land restitution and compensation, and schemes for the reintegration of demobilized combatants. In addition, the Peace Accord has stipulated important reforms to narrow the gap between city and countryside and to reduce social inequalities. However, the formidable challenges shared by countries that make the transition from war to peace will be compounded in Colombia by the fact that the end of the war with the FARC will not bring violence to an end. The "multiple sovereignty" that exists in the country as a result of the continued existence of other guerrilla organizations, criminal bands, and paramilitary organizations associated with drug trafficking and other illegal activities contradicts the liberal peace assumption of a unitary state governing a delimited territorial entity (Heathershaw and Lambach 2008).

The possibility that other armed actors will fill the power vacuum produced by the demobilization of the FARC, gravely endangering the capacity to implement the Accord, is all too real. The continued existence of these structures of domination may hinder the possibility of overcoming the traditional weakness of state institutions, including those in charge of environmental security, which is, in fact, a main explanatory factor of the protracted nature of the conflict (Boron et al. 2016).

According to the United Nations (Naciones Unidas Colombia 2014), at least 125 Colombian municipalities of high environmental relevance that have been given priority for the implementation of the Accord will face environmental challenges in the post-conflict. To the weakness of public institutions and the presence of parallel structures of authority must be added the government's plans for the mining sector. Already at the beginning of the Santos administration, the Minister of Mining and Energy announced the great potential of 17.6 million hectares for the extraction of strategic minerals such as uranium, coltan, gold, iron, and platinum (CINEP 2012). The government aims to triple the areas of basic exploration and mining, to double and triple the exploitation of coal and gold, respectively, and to make mining one of the main sources of revenues (UPME 2014).

It remains to be seen if a balance between these objectives and the environmental agenda of productive, responsible, and competitive mining can be achieved, or whether institutional weakness, the presence of powerful criminal structures and legal interests, in combination with the government's and international financial institutions' plans will promote a "resource rush" that will increase pressure on new areas or on territories already experiencing environmentally predatory activities. Of special concern are the building of infrastructure, legal and illegal mining, and agricultural activities in fragile ecosystems and biodiversity-rich conservation areas where the Accord will be implemented (Naciones Unidas Colombia 2014).

Preserved areas formerly protected to some degree by the presence of guerrillas may be negatively transformed. This potential impact can be illustrated by cases such as the Macarena Special Management Area (*Área de Manejo Especial de la Macarena*) and the Sumapaz paramo, where agroindustrial cultivation of African Palm and livestock farming by investors external to the area bloomed after the expulsion of the FARC as a result of the implementation of "Plan Colombia" and the "Consolidation Plan" between 2003 and 2010. Forced displacement of communities, "social cleansing," and destruction of ecosystems typical to the area ensued, in some cases stimulated and financed by the national government. With the argument that they responded to national security reasons, these decisions were made with little environmental consideration and minimum or no participation of local stakeholders and environmental authorities.

The expectation of environmental peacebuilding through horizontal cooperation and the active participation of citizens in defense of the autonomy of local development may also be at risk.[10] The "Colombian anomaly," as argued by Gutiérrez (2012:78), is that the country is at the same time too democratic and too repressive, as a result of "the tension between institutional stability and solidly established liberal designs, on one hand, and high levels of violence, on the other." The Peace Accord opens up spaces that will strengthen social and community organizations; as in the past, increased mobilization and collective action may bring them into conflict with powerful local, national, and international economic interests.[11] The murders of 153 social leaders between 2014 and June 2016 (Garzón 2016) are ominous signs in a country where peace still has powerful enemies and reconciliation is resisted by some sectors. The elimination of "multiple sovereignty" is a necessary condition for the consolidation of peace; but the existence of a widespread antidemocratic political culture that stigmatizes social movements and political dissent shows that it is by no means a sufficient condition (Valenzuela 2016).

Notes

1 In 1982 the FARC added People's Army to their name, signaling the purpose of making the transition from a guerrilla organization to an army capable of taking power. However, as is common practice in Colombia, we will continue to refer to them simply as the FARC.

2 This is the second, definitive version. A first agreement signed in September 2016 was rejected by an extremely narrow margin in a referendum.

3 The number of military and private security enterprises grew sharply in the mid-1990s, and increased constantly in the period 2002–2010. The Colombian state and private transnational companies hire their services, in an attempt to provide security in rural areas affected by increased guerrilla activity (Armendáriz 2016).

4 The other engines of growth identified by President Santos are infrastructure, agriculture, housing, and innovation. The plan is to create 2.4 million jobs in a four-year period and formalize 500,000 jobs, in order to reduce unemployment to less than 9 percent by 2014 and to less than 6 percent by 2020 (Cárdenas 2010).

5 The rest are related to infrastructure, especially the building of ports and roads (9 percent), energy generation (8 percent), and the management of solid residues, tourism, and aerial fumigation (6 percent) (Pérez-Rincón 2015).

6 Oil companies have been subjected to extortion since the 1960s, and as early as 1965 the National Liberation Army (ELN) carried out the first attack against a pipeline. Economic considerations, however, are not the only motivation behind the targeting of oil companies and other extractive industries. The attacks are also motivated by a nationalist political position opposed to "giving away" national wealth to foreign companies and to joint ventures that overwhelmingly benefit transnational companies (Fundación Ideas para la Paz 2015).

7 In one of the last serious episodes, a FARC attack in the context of a dispute for land for the cultivation of illicit crops and agroindustrial cultivation of African Palm resulted in an oil spill on the Mira and Caunapi rivers in the city of Tumaco. The consequences of the damage to the ecosystems and the

destruction of the sources of livelihood of the Afro-Colombian and indigenous communities of the surrounding areas will be felt for at least 10 years (UN OCHA 2015).

8 Agreement was reached on the following points: 1) integrated rural development, 2) political participation, 3) end of the conflict, 4) solution to the problem of illicit drugs, 5) victims, and 6) implementation, verification, and ratification.

9 Evidently, this reference to the good life is not related to positions advanced in countries such Bolivia and Ecuador (Delgado 2014), where it implies maintenance of the lifestyles of peasant and indigenous communities, very close to the proposal of economic decrease (D'Alisa et al. 2014).

10 Successful cases of environmental peacebuilding based on cooperation between communities, the government, and enterprises are not unknown in Colombia. Motivated by the need to recover the territory's ecosystems, the rural community of Otanche switched from cultivating coca to a sustainable cultivation of butterflies (Mosulishvili 2016). Displaced rural communities that settled in marginal areas of Bogotá successfully engaged with local authorities and enterprises to manage the streams in their area (Caicedo 2016).

11 In the past few months the government has expressed the need to put limits to the currently operating Environmental Public Audiences.

References

Amnistía Internacional (2015) *Colombia: restituir la tierra, asegurar la paz. Los derechos territoriales de las comunidades indígenas y afrodescendientes.* Amnistía Internacional noviembre.

Armendáriz, L. (2016) "La fuerza invisible en Colombia. Análisis del rol y el impacto de las Empresas Militares y de Seguridad Privada (EMSPs) en los derechos humanos y en el proceso de construcción de paz en Colombia" *International Institute for Nonviolent Action, The Privatization of War Series*, No. 4.

Boron, V., Payán, E., MacMillan, D., and Tzanopoulos, J. (2016). "Achieving sustainable development in rural areas in Colombia: Future scenarios for biodiversity conservation under land use change" *Land Use Policy* (59):27–37.

Caicedo, S. (2016) *Agua y territorio en la Bogotá Humana.* Editorial Bonaventuriana, Bogotá.

Cárdenas, M. (2010) "Locomotoras para el desarrollo" *Portafolio*, julio 7.

Centro de Investigación y Educación Popular (CINEP) (2012) *Minería, conflictos sociales y violación de derechos humanos en Colombia.* CINEP, Bogotá.

Centro Nacional de Memoria Histórica (CNMH) (2013) "¡Basta ya! Colombia: Memorias de Guerra y Dignidad" Impenta Nacional, Bogotá.

Centro Nacional de Memoria Histórica (CNMH) (2016) *Tierras y conflictos rurales. Historia, políticas agrarias y protagonistas.* CNMH, Bogotá.

Comisión Nacional de Reparación y Reconciliación (CNRR) (2009) *El despojo de tierras y territorios. Una aproximación conceptual.* IEPRI, CNRR, Memoria Histórica, Bogotá.

D'Alisa, G., Demaria, F., and Kallis, G. (eds.) (2014) *Decrecimiento, un vocabulario para una nueva era.* Icaria, Barcelona.

Delgado, G. (2014) *Buena vida, buen vivir: imaginarios alternativos para el bien común de la humanidad.* Universidad Nacional Autónoma de México.

Dourojeanni, M. (1992) "Environmental impact of coca cultivation and cocaine production in the Amazon region of Peru" *Bulletin on Narcotics*, UNODC.

Echandía, C. (1999) "Expansión territorial de las guerrillas colombianas: geografía, economía y violencia" in Deas, M. and Llorente, M. (eds.) *Reconocer la guerra para construir la paz.* CEREC, Ediciones Uniandes, Editorial Norma, Bogotá, 99–149.

Ferro, J. and Uribe, G. (2002) *El orden de la guerra. Las FARC-EP: Entre la organización y la política.* Centro Editorial Javeriano, CEJA, Bogotá.

Fundación Ideas para la Paz (FIP) (2015) "El ELN y la industria petrolera: Ataques a la infraestructura en Arauca" *Área Dinámicas del Conflicto y Negociaciones de Paz, abril.*

Garzón, J. (2016) "El futuro de la violencia política sin las FARC" *Fundación Ideas para la Paz*, Septiembre 9.

Gaviria, S. (2016) *Dividendos ambientales de la paz. Oportunidades para construir una paz sostenible.* Departamento Nacional de Planeación.

Guhl, E. (2014) *Evolución del Ministerio de Ambiente de Colombia en sus primeros veinte años.* Foro Nacional Ambiental/FESCOL, Bogotá.

Gutiérrez, F. (2012) "El déficit civilizatorio de nuestro régimen político. La otra anomalía en una perspectiva comparada" *Análisis Político* 25(76):59–82.

Heathershaw, J. and Lambach, D. (2008) "Introduction: Post-conflict spaces and approaches to statebuilding" *Journal of Intervention and Statebuilding* 2(3):269–289.

Lair, E. (2004) "Transformaciones y fluidez de la guerra en Colombia: un enfoque militar" in Sánchez, G. and Lair, E. (eds.) *Violencias y estrategias colectivas en la región andina: Bolivia, Colombia, Ecuador, Perú y Venezuela.* IFEA, IEPRI, Editorial Norma, Bogotá.

LeoGrande, W. and Sharpe, K. (2000) "Two wars or one? Drugs, guerrillas, and Colombia's new 'violencia'" *World Policy Journal* 17(3):1–11.

Lujala, P. and Rustad, S. (2012) "High-value natural resources: A blessing or a curse for peace?" in Lujala, P. and Rustad, S. (eds.) *High-Value Natural Resources and Post-conflict Peacebuilding.* Routledge, London, 3–18.

Mantilla, A. (2010) "La política agraria en Colombia, desigualdad y despojo" *Equipo de Tierras y Territorios* CEDINS, agosto.

Mingorance, F. (2006) "El flujo del aceite de palma Colombia–Bélgica/Europa. Acercamiento desde una perspectiva de derechos humanos" *Human Rights Everywhere*, Estudio realizado por HREV para la Coordination Belge pour la Colombie.

Mosulishvili, A. (2016) *From Coca to Butterflies: Managing Natural Resources for Post-Conflict Peacebuilding. A Case Study of Otanche Community, Colombia.* Lund University Master of Science in International Development and Management.

Naciones Unidas Colombia (2014) *Consideraciones ambientales para la construcción de una paz territorial estable, duradera y sostenible en Colombia.* Naciones Unidas, Cooperación Alemana, Bogotá.

Oficina de Las Naciones Unidas para las Drogas y el Crime (UNODC) (2016) *Colombia, monitoreo de territorios afectados por cultivos ilícitos.* UNODC, Bogotá.

Pérez-Rincón, M. (2015) "Conflictos ambientales en Colombia: actores generadores y mecanismos de resistencia comunitaria" *Ecología Política*. Available at: www.ecologiapolitica.info/?p=1980

Pizarro, E. (1991) *Las FARC. De la autodefensa a la combinación de todas las formas de lucha.* Tercer Mundo Editores, Bogotá.

Pizarro, E. (1996) *Insurgencia sin revolución. La guerrilla en Colombia en una perspectiva comparada.* Tercer Mundo Editores/IEPRI, Bogotá.

Presidencia de la República de Colombia (2016) *Acuerdo final para la terminación del conflicto y construcción de una paz duradera.*

Rangel, A. (2000) "Parasites and predators: Guerrillas and the insurrection economy of Colombia" *Journal of International Affairs* 53(2):577–601.

Romero, M. (2004) "Democratización política y contra reforma paramilitar en Colombia" in Sánchez, G. and Lair, E. (eds.) *Violencias y estrategias colectivas en la región andina: Bolivia, Colombia, Ecuador, Perú y Venezuela.* Editorial Norma, Bogotá.

Schlosberg, D. (2007) *Defining Environmental Justice: Theories, Movements, and Nature* Oxford University Press, Oxford.

Unidad de Planeación Minero Energética (UPME) (2014) "Indicadores de la minería en Colombia" Versión preliminar, Ministerio de Minas y Energía.

United Nations Office for Coordination of Humanitarian Affairs (OCHA) Equipo Humanitario Colombia (2015) *Derrame de crudo en ríos Mira y Caunapí Tumaco (Nariño) 01/07/2015.* OCHA, Pasto, Colombia.

United States Agency for International Development (USAID) (2010) "Country profile." Property rights and resource Governance.

Valenzuela, P. (2002) "Reflections on recent interpretations of violence in Colombia" in Rudqvist, A. (ed.) *Breeding Inequality – Reaping Violence. Exploring Linkages and Causality in Colombia and Beyond.* Collegium for Development Studies, Uppsala, 77–97.

Valenzuela, P. "El fin del conflicto armado en Colombia y retos para la paz y la reconciliación" in KAAS, forthcoming.

18

From curse to blessing – how natural resources affect peace and conflict in the Philippines

Colin Walch

Introduction

Under what conditions do natural resources become opportunities for peace in countries affected by civil wars? While natural resources could generate important economic development for the country and build peace, they can also fuel violence if not properly managed. This variation is found in the case of the Philippines where natural resources management has been a source of conflict and peace.

On the one hand, natural resources have played a positive role in the conflict opposing the Government of the Philippines and the Moro Islamic Liberation Front (MILF). In the negotiations that led to the Bangsamoro Basic Laws, a more equal sharing of the natural resources in the Bangsamoro region played an important role to sustain the peace negotiation. Natural resources were thought of as a way to contribute to peacebuilding through economic development and sustainable livelihoods. The focus during peace negotiation on more cooperation and equal sharing of the resources in the region served as an effective platform for building confidence and for exploiting shared interests between segmented and conflicting groups. While the fate of the Bangsamoro Basic Law remains unclear since the 2016 election, President Duterte's agenda for more regional autonomy is favorable to the Bangsamoro Basic Law and to a more common management of the natural resources in Mindanao.

On the other hand, natural resources did not have any peacebuilding effect between the New People's Army (NPA) and the government. Natural resources did not play a significant role in the previous and unsuccessful peace negotiations with the NPA, and there is increasing evidence of NPA involvement in illegal mining to finance their armed struggle. It is estimated that most of the NPA revenues come from their illegal mines and extortion from mining and other companies in their regions of control. In addition, some elements in the army and a growing number of paramilitary and private security groups have been paid by corporations to defend their mines and other interests. The result has been an increased level of violence in some parts of the country, especially in Eastern Mindanao. Natural resources in Eastern Mindanao have therefore sustained the armed conflict between the NPA and the government and generated inter-elite and intercommunal violence at the local level.

In trying to understand this variation, this chapter suggests that cooperation around natural resources is likely to occur when rebel groups and the government see the common sharing of the natural resources as mutually beneficial. This switch from a "zero-sum" view regarding the sharing of natural resources to a win–win one is explained by three main factors that relate to the changing nature of the relationship between the government and the rebel group. First, this chapter suggests a decreasing level of hostility between the rebel group and the state opens up for more cooperation around natural resources. Second, cooperation around natural resources is likely to occur when the rebel group has established a strong social contract with the local population. Low hostility makes cooperation less costly and the quality of the social contract creates obligations towards the civilians in terms of fair redistribution of these natural resources. Finally, the group's goals and ideology regarding the economy in general and the management of natural resources in particular represent the third factor that helps to explain cooperation around natural resources.

The case study of the Philippines is chosen because it provides an interesting variation in how natural resources fuel conflict, or, on the contrary, build peace. By exploring the case of the Philippines and comparing the use of natural resources by the two largest rebel groups in the country, this chapter hopes to reveal some of the conditions under which cooperative actions are expected. Understanding better these conditions can help provide a framework to prevent or moderate resource conflicts in other cases and contribute to diffusing cooperative behavior to other disputed issues. The empirical analysis is based on a series of interviews that took place in the Philippines between 2013 and 2015.

This chapter starts with a small theory section summarizing the main theories in the field and proceeds with the presentation of the theoretical arguments. The theoretical arguments are then explored through the case of the Philippines, examining particularly the MILF and the NPA. A conclusion closes the chapter by discussing the results and highlighting the possible pathways by which cooperation around natural resources management are expected.

Previous research

Previous research suggests that the abundance of natural resources has negative effects on the socio-economic situation of a country through greed and grievances. The greed mechanism focuses on the sources of finance of civil war. Income from the exploitation of natural resources represents an important source of revenue for rebel movements, particularly when the state is weak and unable to protect these resources (Collier and Hoeffler 1998). While important natural resources make rebellion easier to launch, they can also lengthen the armed rebellion and fuel the conflict. For example, Le Billon (2001) and Ross (2004) claim that the vulnerability of a mining company to extortion, and the likelihood of it making payments to armed groups (given its high fixed costs and immobility) increase the duration of the armed conflict violence. What facilitates attacks upon mines by armed groups is the fact that mineral deposits originate in mountainous areas, which are ideal terrain for guerrilla warfare (Holden and Jacobson 2007). The revenue extorted from mining projects can be used to buy more weapons and hire more combatants. In addition, with lucrative payments from mining companies, insurgents have a reduced incentive to stop their activities, increasing conflict intensity.

The grievance mechanism suggests that the unequal sharing of the wealth extracted from mining can motivate people to start a rebellion or join rebel groups to address this inequality (Gurr 1970). The abundance of natural resources can also strengthen separatist groups that fight for more equal redistribution of these resources. Mining has also environmental effects that disrupt people's livelihood, or displace them, which further generate grievances among the people (De Soysa 2000). The greed and the grievance mechanisms are not mutually exclusive and most of the rebel groups tend to use a mix of both.

The environmental peacebuilding literature goes beyond this dichotomy between greed and grievances to focus on the conditions under which natural resources can build peace. There is a consensus in the environmental peacebuilding literature that (re)establishing the rule of law and fair, orderly process for resource access and extraction is crucial for sustaining peace (Kovach and Conca 2016). Indeed, failure to respond to environmental needs of war-torn societies may trigger tensions regarding natural resources management and greatly complicates the difficult tasks of peacebuilding (Conca and Wallace 2009). The next section presents some factors that seem to explain when natural resources management becomes part of a peacebuilding process. This chapter looks at how negotiations processes in the Philippines have included the management of natural resources, with a particular focus on mining activities. Therefore, the study examines the management of natural resources during ongoing civil wars, as most existing literature on environmental peacebuilding explores post-war societies.

Cooperation around natural resources: when and how

Hostility

While the relationship between the rebel group and the state is by definition contentious, it varies across space and time; creating different levels of hostility. Tacit alliances with the so-called enemy happen more often than one would assume. Armed conflicts involve elements of cooperation and collusion to limit violence (Keen 2000) and rebel groups have a "variable rather than unflinchingly hostile relation to the state" (Gregory 2010:167). The management of natural resources between the government and the rebel group is affected by their changing relationship and level of hostility. When hostility is high, war objectives take precedence over cooperation around the management of natural resources. These resources are instead used to fight the enemy. However, the demands and goals of the rebel groups may change over time and therefore create different relations and varying levels of hostility. Hostility in this chapter is defined by a combination of conflict intensity (the number of battle-related deaths) and how the use of violence against the state or the rebel group respectively is considered as justifiable by the supporters of both camps. The level of hostility therefore determines the costs of cooperating with the enemy, not only in terms of warfare but also in terms of public support. Staniland (2012) discusses this varying relation between rebel groups and the state, which he conceptualizes as wartime political order. Depending on the type of territorial control by the actors and the level of hostility, Staniland (2012:244) identifies six wartime political orders: collusion, shared sovereignty, sphere of influence, tacit coexistence, clashing monopolies and guerrilla disorder. These orders are not static as they vary over time within and across conflicts.

When the relation between the rebel group and the state is characterized by delimited control over the territory, ordering of the use of violence and regular communication, shared management of natural resources is likely to take place. In this situation, the relations between the rebel groups and the state start to normalize, more links are created and cooperation becomes easier. Both sides find an agreement for a division of influence for the pursuit of mutual gains where the use of force is minimized, despite maintaining their military capacities (Staniland 2012). By getting out of a "zero-sum" context, rebel groups and government realize the mutual benefits to commonly manage natural resources.

Goals and ideology

The ideology and the goals of the rebel groups also determine the level of hostility and margin for cooperation around natural resources. Rebel groups that are fighting to gain some autonomy for a specific region in the country might be easier to accommodate for the state than groups that want to gain total independence for a region or overthrow the central government. More particularly with the exploitation of natural resources, the state and the rebel group need to share a similar view on the benefits of commercializing and liberalization of the natural resources. When the state and the rebel group believe that revenue they can get from natural resources is higher through cooperation, there is high chance that natural resources become an opportunity for peace. Therefore, the benefit of liberalization and foreign investment needs to be clear for both the state and the rebel group to trigger cooperation around these resources. Yet, when the government or the rebel group shares a very different ideology, for example free market vs. nationalization, mutual benefits of common natural resources management are greatly reduced.

Dependency on civilian population

In addition to the level of hostility determining the cooperation between the rebel groups and the state, the strength of the social contract between the rebel group and the local population is also important. Indeed, a rebel group that cares about its local legitimacy is more likely to cooperate with the government to manage natural resources to make sure that the local population benefit from these revenues. Rebel governance is sustained through a strong contract with the local population (Mampilly 2011). The popular legitimacy of the rebel group depends on the type of social contract it has been able to establish with the local population. Similar to the state, the rebels try to create a social contract whereby they offer public goods, such as justice and security, in exchange for taxation and collaboration from the local communities, resulting in the emergence of mutual obligations. The ways through which the rebel group is able to establish such a social contract vary according to the context. Some groups rely on kinship or ethnic networks while others focus on ideology and political indoctrination of local communities. Groups that have been successful in developing a strong social contract with the civilians are indirectly obliged to indicate to their constituents that their fight or cooperation regarding natural resources will benefit them directly.

The next section explores these two propositions in the case of the Philippines where it examines the use of natural resources by two armed groups.

The case of Mindanao in the Philippines

In addition to being the fruit basket of the Philippines, Mindanao is "a treasure trove" of mineral resources, including gold, copper, nickel, manganese, chromite, silver, bauxite, marble and limestone (Bracamonte 2015). According to estimates from the Filipino Mines and Geosciences Bureau, the Philippines holds the fifth largest mineral deposits in the world, and up to 70 percent of these mineral resources may be in Mindanao (Bracamonte 2015). While rich in natural resources, Mindanao is among the poorest and most conflict-affected regions in the Philippines. The conflict in Mindanao is complex and multilayered and involves at least five major rebel groups. These include the Moro Islamic Liberation Front (MILF), the Moro National Liberation Front (MNLF), the Bangsamoro Islamic Freedom Fighters (BIFF), the Abu Sayaf group (ASG) and the New People's Army (NPA). In addition, there is a high number of self-defense groups created as a consequence of the inter-elite competition and clan conflict.

As a result, conflict dynamics in Mindanao vary considerably from one community to another and, even within the same province, depend on the configuration of local elite political networks, and the presence or absence of insurgent groups (Adriano and Parks 2013). Mining in the region is therefore affected by these localized dynamics of violence.

A large number of legal and illegal mines in the region of Mindanao have paid and still pay money to the NPA, the MILF and other armed groups to protect them from violent attacks against their personnel and facilities. Since the ceasefire in 2003 and the peace talks with the government, the MILF has greatly reduced its extortion activities on companies and the rebel group has instead placed the sharing of the natural resources in the agenda of peace talks. The NPA however has a long history of extorting money from businesses, such as logging companies and mining companies, which it refers to as "revolutionary taxation" (Santos and Santos 2010). This section first examines how the NPA has used natural resources in its armed struggle before turning to the case of the MILF. This section relies on interviews made between 2013 and 2015 with rebel leaders, government officials, local and international NGOs, indigenous leaders and academics.

NPA and natural resources

The communist insurgency in the Philippines is divided into three organizations – the Communist Party of the Philippines (CPP) as the "brain" of the insurgency, the New People's Army (NPA), as "the weapon," and the National Democratic Front (NDF), as the political representation or the "shield" (Interview rebel, April 2013). The aim of the insurgency (CPP–NPA–NDF) is to overthrow the Government of the Philippines, seen by the group as "a reactionary bourgeois regime," and replace it with a "national democratic system," in other words a socialist system, through a "protracted people's war" (Santos and Santos 2010). The communist insurgency consists of around 4500 fighters, although they insist that they are more numerous and stronger than government estimates (Interview rebel, April 2013). The CPP–NPA–NDF is primarily active in poor rural and mountainous regions in most parts of the country. The armed wing of the movement uses guerrilla tactics, such as hit-and-run attacks, sabotage and political assassinations.

In Mindanao, the CPP–NPA–NDF is especially strong in the Eastern part, which is a strategic region for the rebellion since it provides the rebels with most of their financial resources. Such resources stem mainly from their "revolutionary taxation" on mining, logging and fruit companies (Interview professor, April 2013).

One of the main sources of revenue of the NPA is its "taxation" on mining companies in the territory where the rebel group has some presence. A mining company that fails to pay revolutionary taxes to the NPA may find its facilities attacked, equipment destroyed and personnel killed. As a result, most companies in Mindanao have a "budget line" to account for the taxes paid, also called protection money, to the NPA and avoid any problem (Interview mining company, January 2015). The amount of revenue from these extortions is estimated by the military intelligence at three million dollars a year (Interview military official, January 2015).

The opportunities for extortion that mines present, and the grievances they generate, are complementary processes; the former provides funds to purchase weapons, the latter provides the grievances to recruit combatants (Holden and Jacobson 2007). Small-scale mining operations represent not only a significant source of revenue for the NPA but also an important recruitment ground and employment opportunities for NPA rebels (Interview former NPA rebel, 2015).

The NPA justifies these revolutionary taxes by arguing that it is "a legitimate act and a right of the state of the people's democratic government" (Holden and Jacobson 2007). The NPA claims that it uses these taxes for development projects in the poorest community or for people who have been displaced because of these companies. Rebel leaders have often accused mining companies (both foreign and national) of being "land grabbers," "foreign plunderers," "imperialist plunderers" and "greedy capitalists" (Interviews with NPA leaders, 2013). According to the NPA, foreign mining projects are a clear manifestation of the capitalist order the rebels are fighting against. An extract from the NPA website in 2012 is rather clear:

> The grave losses suffered by the people highlights the need to stop environmental plunder by indiscriminate large-scale mining, expanding large-scale plantations, and logging operations that are being abetted by the US Aquino regime's pro-capitalist economic policies.
>
> *(Philippinesrevolution.net 2012)*

The rebels argue that their attacks are always meant to punish the mining firms for allegedly destroying the environment and the livelihood of farmers. However, authorities believe the attacks are most usually triggered by the refusal of the companies to pay the "revolutionary tax" demanded by the rebels. By benefiting from their taxes on mining companies, the communist insurgency is caught in a paradoxical trap: on the one hand, they pretend to protect the people and the environment by using the taxes from the mining corporation for social projects but, on the other, these extortions are also their main source of revenue.

There has been virtually no cooperation between the government and the NPA regarding the management of natural resources. Instead, it has been another battlefield where both the rebels and the government accused each other of destroying the environment and displacing communities. Aware of the government interest in providing several generous incentives to encourage national and foreign mining in the country, the NPA has tried to prevent this plan by attacking and extorting companies in Mindanao (Interview indigenous leader, January 2015).

While the NPA targets legal companies related to the state, it allows and sometimes encourages small-scale mining in communities where the group has a strong control because it represents a source of income, employment and recruitment (Interview local NGOs, January 2015). However, when territorial control is divided or under government control, mines are more likely to be attacked especially if the protection money is not paid or if the mining company is financing paramilitary groups (Interview rebel leader, January 2015). Since the 1980s, the NPA has gradually lost its support base in the population, and the NPA has been less able to create a governance and redistribution system (Interview former rebel, January 2015).

Since the beginning of the armed conflict, the objective of the CPP–NPA–NDF has remained the same: the defeat of the government through the people's protracted war. This unflinchingly hostile position has been addressed by the state with hardbitten counterinsurgency, accompanied with numerous extra-judicial killings. This high and consistent level of hostility between the government and the NPA has prevented any type of cooperation around natural resources. Following Staniland's (2012) typology on wartime political order, the "guerrilla disorder" particularly well applies to describe the relationship between CPP–NPA–NDF and the government. Indeed, every opportunity to impose costs is taken by both sides creating a context where the state, the civilian and the rebel group are locked into a situation of violence difficult to predict (Staniland 2012). While there is evidence of collusion between certain local elites and the NPA in order to share the revenue from the mining, the high level of hostility and strong ideological differences on how to manage the country's natural resources have prevented any common management of natural resources between the government and the NPA.

However, the election of Rodrigo Duterte in 2016 has changed the ideological and hostility context between the government and the NPA, paving new ways toward more cooperation in the country. Considered by the NPA to be the first "leftist president not beholden to US imperialism," Duterte has moved towards more cooperation with the rebel group. Following his election, he offered to communist leaders several positions in his administration, including the leadership of the Department of Agrarian Reform (DAR), the Department of Labor and Employment (DOLE), the Department of Environment and Natural Resources (DENR) and the Department of Social Welfare and Development (DSWD) as a way to revive the peace talks, which were later launched in Oslo on August 22, 2016. The communist rebel group responded to the offer and suggested a number of candidates for these positions.

The decreasing level of hostility with the new government following the election of Duterte – ideologically closer to the rebel group – seems to have started a new process of cooperation, particularly around the management of natural resources. For example, the new secretary for Department of Environment and Natural Resources, Gina Lopez, has been praised by the historic leader of the rebel group as "a dedicated activist against abusive mining that ruins the indigenous communities, environment, agriculture, and our chances of processing the mineral ores and industrializing our country" (Tupaz 2016). While it is too early to predict to what extent natural resources will be commonly managed during and after the peace negotiations, there are many positive signs that indicate increased cooperation for natural resources management in the country.

This section indicates how hostility and cooperation can change over time and how wartime political orders may be short-lived or deeply enduring. The relationship between the government and the rebels can change rapidly and open up new opportunities to manage natural resources in common.

MILF and natural resources

By contrast to the NPA, the MILF has been more open to finding ways to share and manage natural resources in common in Mindanao for a long time. While there are also instances of the MILF extorting money from businesses, the MILF has tried to indicate its willingness to attract companies in order to use the revenue to develop the Bangsamoro region. Since the 2003 ceasefire between the MILF and the Government of the Philippines, the MILF has argued that peace and a more equal sharing of the natural resources under its authority will help the socio-economic development of the Bangsamoro people (Interview negotiating panel member, January 2015).

This is clearly reflected in the Bangsamoro Basic Law – the final accord between the MILF and the government – which mentions explicitly in several articles the importance of fair sharing of natural resources. For example, under the section on natural resources, there is clear reference to common management of natural resources:

> The Bangsamoro Government and the Central Government shall jointly exercise the power to grant rights, privileges and concessions over the exploration, development and utilization of fossil fuels, natural gas, and coal and uranium in the Bangsamoro. The Central Government, through the Department of Energy (DOE), and the Bangsamoro Government shall adopt a competitive and transparent process for the grant of rights, privileges and concessions in the exploration, development and utilization of fossil fuels and

uranium. The DOE and the Bangsamoro Government will identify and select prospective contract areas to be offered for exploration and development. A qualified Filipino citizen who is bona fide resident of the Bangsamoro will receive a rating higher than other proponents during the evaluation process. The award of the service contract shall be made jointly by the DOE and the Bangsamoro Government.

(Bangsamora Basic Law 2014:93–94)

The government and the MILF during the peace negotiation understood that natural resources are a highly emotive issue that is intertwined with identity-based conflicts in the Bangsamoro region (Interview government negotiating panel member, 2015). Both the MILF and the government agreed that clarity regarding ownership rights and regulatory authority is critical for political stability and investor confidence. Indeed, ambiguity about who owns natural resources can become a source of ongoing dispute between national governments and the new Bangsamoro autonomous region (Interview academic professor, 2015). Guaranteeing regional governments or indigenous communities a voice in development plans for natural resources management (including employment) and a share of revenues was essential to make the "zero-sum" ownership debate around natural resources a win–win one (Interview Asia Foundation, 2015).

How can this level of cooperation around natural resources be explained? What factors explain this switch to a win–win cooperation?

The government and the MILF understood that an ambiguous ownership provision can be a major source of political risk for potential investors. This can lessen the attractiveness of an investment opportunity in the country's resources, resulting in difficulties in attracting capital, and in turn reducing the amount of revenue. Technical experts from the World Bank, the EU and various international NGOs have accompanied the process and indicated to the parties the possible outcomes of more cooperation to illuminate the mutually beneficial growing of the pie (Interview negotiating panel, January 2015). Ideologically, the MILF has been open to the commercialization of the resources and was effective in securing grants and loans from the World Bank to develop its institutions, such as the Bangsamoro Development Agency.

This was made possible due to a gradually reducing level of hostility between the government and the MILF since the 2003 ceasefire. Before this increased cooperation around natural resources, the MILF and the government collaborated closely on counterterrorism issues (Santos and Santos 2010). The MILF shared intelligence with the Philippines military, expelled "terrorists" from its territory and even allowed the Philippines military to operate in its area during counterterrorism actions, most notably for the rescue of kidnapping-for-ransom victims and missions designed to "terminate" Abu Sayyaf and Jemaah Islamiah (JI) elements. This increased level of collaboration was a way to avoid being listed as a terrorist group, in strong contrast with the NPA. This move in cooperating against terrorism with Manila provided legitimacy to the MILF and created trust in the relationship with the government. More recently, the MILF and the government have collaborated in disaster relief following devastating typhoons (Walch 2014).

The objective of the MILF is fundamentally different from those of the NPA, as it only challenges a part of the Philippines territory, which it views as having a different history and religion. The principal goals of the MILF include the creation of a Bangsamoro autonomous region, more political and economic power at the regional level and the development of the poor Bangsamoro communities. According to MILF leaders, this objective of improving the living conditions of the Bangsamoro people, who have been marginalized by the

Philippines government for a long time, has made the MILF open to any collaboration with the government around natural resources, as long as it benefits the communities (Interview rebel, May 2013).

The MILF seeks to show that it is better at responding to the needs of the communities than the government. As a result, the failure to efficiently manage natural resources and redistribute the revenues may imply a loss of support for the movement and in turn damage the social contract with the local population. With the creation of the Bangsamoro Development Agency (BDA), a joint effort from the MILF and the government to coordinate national and international aid for developing the Bangsamoro region, the MILF has indicated it is open to collaboration with the government and international actors. Although the agency suffers from a lack of financial resources, the mere presence of this organization implies that the development of the region is a common problem to be resolved conjointly (Interview government official, November 2013). This joint mechanism opened up a new avenue for collaboration. "Over the course of the peace talks, the Aquino government gradually became willing to see the MILF not just as its adversary across the negotiating table but as a partner for the years ahead" (International Crisis Group 2012:2). According to the government, the MILF has been very clear in identifying the needs of the communities. "They have become partners and they are sincere about their interest in developing the Bangsamoro communities. The good relationship between the two parties is likely to lead to a lasting peace" (Interview government, November 2013).

The process of normalization between the MILF and the government since 2004 has placed the conflicting actors in a situation of shared sovereignty, involving active cooperation in which each side has a delimited control over a particular territory (Staniland 2012). The MILF–government relationship is a strong fit within the shared sovereignty typology as both actors have negotiated a political order with a clear division of influence and authority that is mutually satisfactory. While both sides keep their coercive military capacities, this clear negotiated arrangement allows for more sophisticated cooperation (Staniland 2012).

While it remains unclear whether the Bangsamoro Basic Law will be approved in Congress or redefined by the Duterte government, it represents in itself a milestone for collaboration between the MILF and the government.

Conclusion

This chapter has shown how the common management of natural resources between rebel groups and the government can vary across groups and time in the same country. While the MILF has been collaborating with the government to manage natural resources, the NPA has not behaved similarly. Strong ideological differences and goals in a context of high hostility have prevented any type of collaboration around natural resources. Following the election of Duterte, however, the level of hostility and ideological difference between the government and the NPA has decreased, opening up new opportunities for a common management of natural resources.

The findings of this chapter indicate that the conditions for cooperation are not constant as they mainly depend on the changing relationship between rebel groups and the government. The level of hostility is the factor most supported by the empirical analysis where evidence suggests that reduced level of hostility can lead to new avenues for cooperation. The rebel group's stated goals and its relationship to its constituencies are important factors but they do not explain by themselves the variation between the MILF and the NPA. While most research in environmental peacebuilding focuses on the post-conflict period, this chapter highlights the importance of examining the management of natural resources before and during the peace process in order to be better prepared to manage natural resources in the post-conflict and adopt a more comprehensive approach to peacebuilding. While the integration of a natural resources sharing agreement in peace accords is crucial for post-conflict development, it needs to be properly implemented and accompanied by policies on economic diversification, institutional innovation and anti-corruption.

While other types of cooperation between the government and the MILF around disaster relief and counterterrorism seem to further support the finding of this study, it is not clear if the theoretical arguments presented in this chapter are applicable to countries other than the Philippines. Yet, anecdotal evidence from other cases seems to support the findings of this chapter. The sharing of the natural resources was an important factor fueling the conflict between the Indonesian government and the GAM in Aceh. However, the election of a president more favorable to negotiation and good collaboration between the GAM and the military during the humanitarian response to the tsunami led to a decreased level of hostility, in turn leading to a successful peace accord and common natural resources management.

This chapter has shown that cooperation between the state and the rebels on common challenges, such as counterterrorism or disaster relief, are likely to be strong basis for making the management of natural resources an opportunity for peace. Indeed, previous collaboration can serve as an effective platform for enhancing dialogue, building confidence, exploiting shared interests and broadening cooperation between segmented and conflicting groups. Future research should explore the specific factors that can lead to a decrease of hostility between belligerents. This could help external actors in their peacebuilding interventions.

References

Adriano, F. and Parks, T. (2013) *The contested corners of Asia: The case of Mindanao, Philippines*. The Asia Foundation, San Francisco.

Bangsamoro Basic Law (2014) Office of the Presidential Adviser on the Peace Process. Available at: www.opapp.gov.ph/milf/news/draft-bangsamoro-basic-law

Bracamonte, N. (2015) Development a shared agenda for mining development in the Philippines, International Mining for Development Centre (IM4DC), June.

Collier, P. and Hoeffler, A. (1998) "On the economic causes of civil war" *Oxford Economic Papers* 50:563–573.

Conca, K. and Wallace, J. (2009) "Environment and peacebuilding in war-torn societies: Lessons from the UN Environment Programme's experience with postconflict assessment" *Global Governance* 15(4):485–504.

De Soysa, I. (2000) "The resource curse: are civil wars driven by rapacity or paucity?" in Berdal, M. and Malone, D. M. (eds.) *Greed and grievance: Economic agendas in civil wars* Lynne Rienner, Boulder, CO.

Gregory, D. (2010) "War and peace" *Transactions of the Institute of British Geographers* 35(02):154–186.

Gurr, T. R. (1970) *Why men rebel?* Princeton University Press, Princeton, NJ.

Holden, W. and Jacobson, D. (2007) "Mining amid armed conflict: Nonferrous metals mining in the Philippines" *Canadian Geographer* 51(4):475–500.

International Crisis Group (2012) The Philippines: Breakthrough in Mindanao, Asia Report No. 240, 5 December.

Keen, D. (2000) "War and peace: What's the difference?" *International Peacekeeping* 7(4):1–22.

Kovach, T. and Conca, K. (2016) "Environmental priorities in post-conflict recovery: Efficacy of the needs-assessment process" *Journal of Peacebuilding and Development* 11(2):4–24.

Le Billon, P. (2001) "The political ecology of war: Natural resources and armed conflicts" *Political Geography* 20:561–584.

Mampilly, Z. (2011) *Rebel rulers: Insurgent governance and civilian life during war*. Cornell University Press, Ithaca, NY.

Philippinesrevolution.net. Page accessed in August 2016. Available at: www.philippinerevolution.net/

Ross, M. (2004) "What do we know about natural resources and civil war?" *Journal of Peace Research* 41(3):337–356.

Santos Jr., S. M. and Santos, P. V. M. with Dinampo, O., Kraft, H., Paredes, A., and Quilop, J. (2010) *Primed and purposeful: Armed groups and human security efforts in the Philippines* edited by Rodriguez, D. Small Arms Survey, Geneva, and South–South Network for Non-State Armed Group Engagement, Quezon City, RP.

Staniland, P. (2012) "State, insurgents, and wartime political orders" *Perspectives on Politics* 10(2):243–264.

Tupaz, V. (2016) "Joma Sison: Gina Lopez as DENR chief is acceptable" *The Rappler*, June 22. Available at: www.rappler.com/nation/137268-joma-sison-gina-lopez-denr-chief-acceptable

Walch, C. (2014) "Collaboration or obstruction? Rebel group behavior during natural disaster relief in the Philippines" *Political Geography* 43:40–50.

Part IV

Analytical challenges and future-oriented perspectives

19

Environmental conflict and peacebuilding in Africa

Connecting resources, issues, and ongoing governance initiatives

Timothy Adivilah Balag'kutu, Jeremiah O. Asaka,
Linda Holcombe, Jason J. McSparren,
and Stacy D. VanDeveer

The ongoing acceleration of climate change, and debate raging about the massive human impacts on ecosystems from local to global sometimes denoted by the "Anthropocene" concept, are making the connections between human security, environmental change and resource exploitation and consumption increasingly apparent (Adger et al. 2014; Andrews-Speed et al. 2015; VanDeveer 2015). As such, environmental and resource-based factors seem likely to proliferate, with influences on violent conflict, conflict mitigation and peacebuilding activities. Research on environmental and resource-related causes of conflict, and on the peacebuilding opportunities presented by greater attention to environmental and resource-related cooperation, has produced a rich analytical literature over the last twenty-plus years (Krampe 2016, 2017; Ali 2007; Weinthal et al. 2013; Chalecki 2013; Matthew et al. 2010). However, many ongoing peacebuilding and conflict mitigation initiatives – and many existing transnational governance initiatives – remain unconnected to these areas of inquiry and uninformed by them. This chapter seeks to illustrate both this lack of attention to existing initiatives and the tremendous potential for learning in research and practice by making such connections more explicit.

The next section briefly introduces the "resource nexus" perspective, focusing on its relationship to governance. After that, three short sections illustrate both the challenges and opportunities of connecting resource nexus, environmental conflict and peacebuilding, and existing governance initiatives. The illustrative cases presented below also seek to grapple with these connections across scales, from a focus on the northwest region of Kenya, to attention on one long-standing and one more recent global governance initiative with substantial regard to parts of Africa. These latter cases are centered around illicit trafficking in wildlife, connected to the decades-old Convention on the Trade in Endangered Species (CITES), and the younger transnational Extractive Industries Transparency Initiative (EITI). These illustrative cases cover a great deal of geographic, human security and governance "territory" in an attempt to demonstrate that many existing and ongoing transnational governance initiatives could benefit from more explicit attention to practices and research related to environmental conflict and peacebuilding. Furthermore, we hope to illustrate that environmental conflict and peacebuilding research can also benefit from greater attention to governance initiatives across scales that may not be explicitly framed in environmental conflict or peacebuilding terms.

Linking environmental conflict and peacebuilding: across resources and pre-existing initiatives

In both research and practice, the environmental conflict and peacebuilding agenda has grown substantially over twenty-plus years, making connections to the causes of violent conflict, post-conflict reconstruction, peace parks and natural resource management, cooperative institutions from local to global scales, defense and military operations and planning, security analyses and threat assessments, and so on (as the contributions to this volume make clear). But among the challenges facing contemporary environmental conflict and peacebuilding research are: (1) how to enhance connections with the huge number of ongoing inter-state and transnational governance initiatives – those not explicitly framed as having connections to violent conflict and peacebuilding; and (2) how to grapple with the increasing complexities of accelerating environmental and resource-related change. The first challenge is illustrated below by attention to CITES and EITI, one initiative framed mostly in environmental terms and another framed mostly around financial transparency in the extractives sector. But these are only two of the now hundreds of inter-state initiatives or "regimes" and thousands of transnational governance arrangements that often combine forms of state, non-state and private sector governance in contemporary bilateral, regional and global governance (Bulkeley et al. 2014; Andonova et al. 2017; Van de Graaf and Colgan 2016).

The second challenge is perhaps best illustrated by debates about the arrival of "the Anthropocene" and the explosive growth in analytical work framed around "resource nexus" perspectives (Andrews-Speed et al. 2015). Analytical work framed around the resource nexus conceptualizes the terms as a "heuristic for understanding critical linkages between uses of different natural resources for systems of provision" such as energy, water, food, land and materials (or minerals) (Bleischwitz et al. forthcoming), often also trying to grapple with the connections of these to biodiversity, climate change and the atmospheric system, and so on. Probably the most common formulations are two-, three- or five-node combinations, such as food–energy–water or land–energy–food–water–minerals, for example.

Resource-based conflict and environmental peacebuilding in northwestern Kenya[1]

Throughout much of the 1980s and 1990s, state deployment of army and/or militarized police were the main responses to violent conflict in northwestern Kenya. Such military operations proved largely unsuccessful, and they were characterized by excessive use of force with resultant human rights abuses (TJRC 2013). While the state remains an actor in the region, today a growing number of non-state actors are engaged in conflict resolution and peacebuilding in the region. Multi-actor conflict resolution and peacebuilding initiatives are increasingly common. Moreover, environmental peacebuilding is emerging as a new approach to fostering cooperation among pastoralists in northwestern Kenya, albeit with mixed results, as awareness increases about the underlying roles in the violence of environmental and resource-based factors.

Geographically, northwestern Kenya is located within the Karamoja cluster – a conflict-prone region that sits astride the Kenya, Uganda and South Sudan border region (Simonse 2011). The region is prone to extreme climate variability, regularly experiencing recurrent droughts and flash floods. Administratively, northwestern Kenya falls within West Pokot, Turkana, Samburu and Baringo Counties. Demographically, it is home to about 1.6 million people mainly Pokot, Turkana and Samburu pastoralists (KNBS 2009).

Conflict between the Samburu, Pokot and Turkana dates back at least to the colonial period. Traditionally, the cultural practice of cattle rustling was considered the main driver of violent conflict in the region. Therefore, past efforts at conflict resolution and peacebuilding were mainly focused on getting rid of the culture/practice of cattle rustling through military action and promoting sedentarization, respectively. Today, however, violent conflict in the region is understood as a consequence of complex interplay of a variety of factors, including cattle rustling, moran (warrior) culture, resource competition, climate variability, proliferation of small arms, political incitement, banditry and marginalization (Okumu 2013; Njiru 2012; Opiyo et al. 2012; Schilling et al. 2012; Mkutu 2007, 2002). Moreover, climate change is emerging as a threat multiplier in this drought-prone region of Kenya (Basel et al. forthcoming; Adger et al. 2014).

Consequently, conflict resolution and peacebuilding are evolving with changing understandings of violent conflict causes and triggers. Instead of military action and sedentarization being center stage, the rise of new non-state actors – mainly NGOs and local elites –has resulted in the emergence of new approaches to conflict resolution and peacebuilding (Okumu 2013; Berger 2003). Laikipia Peace Caravan – a peacebuilding initiative of professionals from pastoralist communities in the Kenyan rangelands – is an excellent reflection of how much the understanding of conflict and the practice of conflict resolution and peacebuilding in the region have evolved. As Okumu (2013:40, italics added) explains,

> the publicity and awareness created through the Laikipia Peace Caravan has seen the birth of a multiplicity of other Peace Caravans and the registration of the Peace Caravan as a Trust in Kenya . . . *Further*, the original Laikipia Peace Caravan has further been restructured into Turkwel Peace Caravan (Turkana and Pokot professionals from Turkwel area), Suguta Peace Caravan (Turkana and Pokot), Waso Peace Caravan (*Samburu East*), Oasis Peace Caravan and Samburu North Peace Caravan to give more focus to professionals from these areas to deal more specifically with peacebuilding and conflict resolution efforts affecting their communities.

Of primary interest to this chapter is the emergence of environmental peacebuilding activities in the region in the past decade or so. The remainder of this section discusses community conservancies in the context of environmental peacebuilding. In the context of this chapter, these community conservancies are hereafter referred to as "peace conservancies."[2]

Emergence of environmental peacebuilding: NRT peace conservancies

Northern Rangelands Trust (NRT) is a non-governmental organization based in northwestern Kenya whose mission is "to develop resilient community conservancies that transform lives, secure peace and conserve natural resources" (NRT 2014:2). It was established in 2004 "by a coalition of local leaders, politicians and conservation interests."[3] By 2016 the organization had "33 conservancies across 11.8 million acres of northern Kenya," partnering with the region's county governments to promote environmental peacebuilding.[4]

The emergence of peace conservancies across northern Kenya continues to generate interest from scholars and practitioners alike, particularly with regard to the peacebuilding potential of environmental conservation in the conflict-prone region (Mbaaria and Ogada 2017;

Glew et al. 2010; Haro et al. 2005; Berger 2003). Since pastoralism is the main source of livelihood for most communities in northwestern Kenya, access to both pasture and water is critical to human well-being in the region. Therefore, if it is true that resource scarcity leads to competition, which sometimes results in violent conflict, then improving access to pasture and water for communities should adequately address the scourge of violent conflict in the region. Simply put, this is the logic behind NRT's peace conservancies. Through its rangeland management strategy, the NGO hopes its conservancies will ensure that pastoralists have year-round access to adequate pasture and water, as well as promote inter-community dialogue facilitated by what it calls "grazing committees."[5] Ultimately, when warring communities get to a point where they can hold peaceful dialogue on how to share pasture and water during periods of drought, the risk of violent conflict over these resources is greatly reduced.

In practice, peace conservancies have had mixed results to date. During 2016 fieldwork, I witnessed some progress in environmental peacebuilding courtesy of NRT peace conservancies. For example, I attended an inter-community dialogue meeting in Kom on the border of Samburu and Marsabit County. In attendance were warriors and elders from Samburu, Rendille, Borana and Somali communities from Samburu, Marsabit and Isiolo Counties of Kenya. Ordinarily, these communities would fight over pasture and water during such times, but instead they were gathered during drought season and engaging each other on (among other things) the need to chart a new path of mutual cooperation in both good times and bad.

On the flip side, for the better part of the first half of 2017, international and local (Kenya) media were awash with stories of deadly, violent conflict in Kenya's Laikipia area. While Laikipia is not in northwestern Kenya, the main antagonists in the conflict were Samburu herders and private landowners – including but not limited to white ranchers, thereby illustrating aspects of the colonial legacy. The nature of the conflict was such that herders not only attacked and razed tourist lodges owned by private ranchers, but also injured and killed some ranchers and engaged in mass killing of wildlife (Cruise and van der Zee 2017). In response, the government deployed a contingent of the Kenyan army and militarized police who unleashed lethal force on the herders, killing tens of them and hundreds of their livestock (Munyeki 2017; Ngirachu 2017).

Several points can be deduced from these events. Most relevant for this chapter may be evidence of an emerging new kind of violent conflict partly connected to the unparalleled rise of peace conservancies in the region, and perhaps comparable in nature to the Mau Mau uprising of the late 1950s (Asaka 2015). Notably, one aspect of the peace conservancy idea that may generate negative responses is the compartmentalization of hitherto commonly accessible communally owned land into zones that include a core conservation area. These core conservation areas are out of bounds to people and their livestock. Particularly in the context of climate change, without providing a viable alternative source of livelihood, such restrictions of access to previously accessible pastureland can lead to conflict as long as pastoralism remains the lifeline of communities living in northwestern Kenya. Such risks may be especially acute in a politically charged environment like northwestern Kenya that is emerging from a long period of socio-economic and political marginalization.

Living resources: trafficking in conflict

There are multiple ways to approach the resource nexus framework, in terms of what sets of resources to include in various frameworks. The new five-prong framing by Bleischwitz et al. (forthcoming) provides a more comprehensive and nuanced understanding of resource interactions than many former, more limited approaches. However, it remains insufficient to capture on-the-ground complexities in many parts of the world. The five-dimensional approach takes a decidedly anthropocentric approach, mostly considering natural resources in terms geared toward human use and consumption. This misses important implications relevant to discussions of resource interactions and conflict, as well as entire categories of resources not well represented in this framework. This biodiversity gap is illustrated by the example of wildlife crime.[6]

The five-prong framing of the resource nexus fails to provide for living resources beyond those used for food or energy. Existing categories encapsulate inanimate objects like minerals, water and land. Those categories which do provide for living resources, food and energy, are generally limited in their scope to resources directly consumed or used by humans. If we don't eat it or get energy from it, it is implicitly de-prioritized in this framing. This leaves blind spots, in terms of examining how resource interactions contribute to conflict. Illegal trading of wildlife is one such blind spot.

The illegal wildlife trade is here defined as the movement of animal or animal products across national boundaries in contravention of the Convention for International Trade in Endangered Species of Wild Fauna and Flora (CITES) and the national legislation based on its provisions. Some illegal wildlife trade is conducted for food, to be consumed locally or internationally, as is often the case with bushmeat (see e.g. Milner-Gulland and Bennett 2003; Bassett 2005; Herbig and Warchol 2011; IFAW 2013), and with delicacy foods like caviar (see Zabyelina 2014; Sellar 2014) or abalone (see Warchol and Harrington 2016). Other types of wildlife, namely plants, are illegally traded for energy. The illegal charcoal trade, for instance, is linked to funding rebel groups throughout Africa (UNODC 2011; Nellemann et al. 2014).

The relationship between the illegal trade in living resources, particularly wildlife, and conflict is an important yet under-researched area. Douglas and Alie (2014) provide one of the few attempts at exploring this connection, noting the failure to incorporate wildlife trade into discussions of natural resources and conflict. Several authors echo Douglas and Alie's (2014) observation that the illegal wildlife trade can be connected to armed conflict and other types of insecurity, such as organized crime and transnational criminal networks (Warchol et al. 2003; Zimmerman 2003; Wyatt 2011; Ayling 2013; Sellar 2014). Although the examples of ivory and rhino horn are overrepresented when compared to the volume and variety of species traded, ivory in particular illustrates the observed links between illegal wildlife resources and conflict. Ivory represents living resources not accounted for by existing resource nexus frameworks as it is consumed purely as a luxury and not as food or energy, and by itself does not contribute to water, land or materials/minerals. Despite its position outside of these categories, ivory is at the center of several ongoing conflicts throughout Africa, including the funding of armed rebel groups in DRC (Nellemann et al. 2014) and ongoing battles between rangers and poachers in South Africa (see Lunstrum 2014; White 2014; Duffy 2016).

It is important to note how the framing of the illegal wildlife trade influences the perceived connections to conflict and peacebuilding. Three main framings emerge from the wildlife trafficking literature: conservation, law enforcement and national security. The conservation literature, as noted by Douglas and Alie (2014), does not contribute much to the conflict–wildlife trade discussion. When wildlife trafficking is framed in a law enforcement or national security perspective, however, linkages become much more apparent. If the illegal wildlife trade is approached from a law enforcement framing, connections can be made to other types of crime, namely transnational organized crime. There are links and discussions related to various forms of organized crime and how it interacts with conflict and/or peacebuilding efforts, although few studies to date specifically examine how wildlife trade fits into this relationship. Outside of the potential for organized crime to serve as a funding mechanism for insurgency (described below), some authors note the potential for organized crime to serve as a complex spoiler for post-conflict and peacebuilding efforts (see e.g. Cockayne and Lupel 2009; Holt and Boucher 2009). Others note, however, that viewing organized crime as a spoiler may overlook underlying narratives of criminalization (Meagher 2014) or even undermine peacebuilding efforts through attempts at intervention (Reno 2009).

The connection between organized crime and terrorism (as described by Makarenko 2004; Shelley 2005; Shelley and Picarelli 2005), for example, highlights the process through which some have argued that wildlife trafficking finances insurgency (see IFAW 2013). Terrorist and/or insurgent groups have increasingly relied on illicit commodities in order to fund their operations, primarily the transnational drug trade (Makarenko 2004). Illegal wildlife or wildlife products have been used similarly, such as the ivory trade funding rebel groups in the DRC (Beyers et al. 2011) or the potential use of the illegal falcon trade to support Middle Eastern and other terror networks (Wyatt 2011). There is resistance, however, to the notion that the illegal wildlife trade should be viewed and treated as a threat to national security. Some are concerned with the perceived militarization of anti-poaching and trafficking strategies based on a national security framing, noting that such interventions can themselves be as problematic as or worse for security and conflict prevention than the crime they oppose (see e.g. Lunstrum 2014; White 2014; Duffy 2016).

The aim of the resource nexus approach is to broaden our scope beyond single-resource dynamics and understand the interactions, connections and conflicts inherent in resource use and governance (Bleischwitz et al. forthcoming). Accounting for living resources is critical if our goal is to understand how resources relate back to human conflict. Failing to account for living resources beyond those used by humans for food or energy denies the intrinsic value of non-human life (see Wyatt 2013 for further discussion), as well as creating a large blind spot for understanding single and inter-resource dynamics in relation to human conflict. Wildlife trafficking overlaps with several previously defined elements of the resource nexus, but also represents elements that cannot be neatly subsumed into existing categories. While the bushmeat trade incorporates concerns over land and food demands, as well as playing a role in sustaining some violent conflicts, the ivory trade also plays a large role in human violence but cannot be accounted for within the existing nexus structure.

An additional gap addressed by including living resources in nexus–conflict discussions is how utilization of other resources impacts ecosystems. Simply saying that mining activities disrupt "biomass" or "biodiversity" (Bleischwitz et al. forthcoming) does not account for the knock-on effects of losing species. While a connection between increasing poaching due to road construction for timber removal (energy) (see Van Solinge 2008b) or mining (minerals/materials) (Van Solinge 2008a) can be examined through a food lens if the motivation is bushmeat, when poaching is conducted for luxury or medicinal products, like ivory or pangolin scales, the relationships are missed because the activity falls outside the existing nexus categories. The illegal trade in wild living resources has demonstrated connections to conflict, whether through a law enforcement/crime or national security framing, and failure to include this category in discussions of resource nexus interactions and the resulting relationship to conflict creates a gap we cannot afford to overlook.

The global CITES regime and related scholarly research and activism often have been framed in terms of environmental values like conservation and species protection, as well as around national and international trade regulation and enforcement. However, the violence, human security, national security and international security concerns – and the corruption and the undermining of rule of law associated with these security concerns – that often accompany the illicit wildlife trade make it clear that the whole area of research and practice must more explicitly grapple with a broad set of human security challenges and goals, including conflict mitigation and peacebuilding needs and opportunities.

Resource extraction governance: peacebuilding potential?

How do global governance mechanisms contribute to mediating environmental conflict and building a sustainable peace within communities and regions where resource extraction takes place?[7] As previously mentioned, resource nexus approaches intertwine land and water use, energy and food production, mineral extraction and human livelihoods and lifestyles (Andrews-Speed et al. 2015). Resource extraction, whether mining for metals and minerals, drilling for oil and natural gas, clear-cutting timber or manipulating waterways and sources, creates change that has long manifested as negative impacts on local communities adjacent to these industrial activities that often lead to conflict and violence. Additionally, the products of natural resource exploitation have been ingrained in contemporary lifestyles, even as populations living in regions where these industrial activities take place are often excluded from benefiting from these products and the technology they produce due to prohibitive socio-economic structures. In a neoliberal era, when corporate interests are privileged above government regulation, and globalization of capital and value chains enforce these structures, the international community has responded by creating global governance initiatives (GGIs) to create a semblance of regulation and empower civil society in relation to the extractive multinational corporations (MNCs) and the state. The Extractive Industries Transparency Initiative (EITI) creates a multi-stakeholder working group to bring together representatives from a variety of interest groups to collaborate on expanding transparency, accountability and public ownership throughout the national extractive sector.

An international push for corporate oversight in the extractive sectors manifested around the turn of the twenty-first century, the result of an acknowledgement of corporate complicity in corruption, environmental degradation and violent conflicts in and around the sector (see Global Witness 1999; Human Rights Watch 1999). Out of the recognition of negative externalities associated with natural resource extraction came studies about the "Paradox of Plenty" (Karl 1997) and the "Resource Curse" (Mehlum et al. 2006; Sachs and Warner 1995; Ross 1999; McFerson 2010) which look most prominently at the structures of the sector. Other researchers (Basedau 2005) took a broader view of the problem and suggested looking at multiple factors that contribute to the socio-economic context in resource-rich states. The extractive sectors globally experience problems of violent conflict. These may be localized conflict at the site where community members obstruct mining operations or more broadly become civil wars where illicit trafficking of minerals funds the conflict as is the experience in Liberia.

The relationship between violent conflict and the resource nexus is extremely complex in nature and, therefore, requires assets and capacity from multiple societal sectors (government, industry and civil society) to alleviate such problems. In 2001, Lloyd Axworthy, the former Canadian foreign minister, observed that the extraction of natural resources had become a source of insecurity rather than livelihood (Axworthy 2001). The growing number of operations and changing nature of the sector had begun to cause extensive global insecurity in the form of social and environmental adversities. Conflict had become common and a major manifestation of insecurity in the extractive industry. Later, former United Nations Secretary-General Kofi Annan warned about possible negative effects of resource abundance. In commenting on the exploration and exploitation of natural resources on the African continent, Annan warns that the development of the extractive sector is often a "path leading to conflict, spiraling inequality, corruption and the failure of state institutions in Africa" (Annan 2012). Global governance initiatives, while not always explicitly designed to address violent conflict and peacebuilding processes, do have built-in mechanisms that could be utilized to confront conflict and promote peacebuilding.

The EITI, for instance, creates a forum for corporations and governments to consider the politics of the extractive industries, and to do so with the input of local actors. The negative externalities associated with the extractive sectors and thus part of the resource nexus can only be remedied through multi-stakeholder efforts; the interests among the stakeholders vary greatly, so dialogue and negotiations are imperative to identify the catalyst and categorize the type of conflict. As Gilpin (2016:24) points out, correct categorization helps "identify the trigger, underlying and sustaining causes of violent conflict" in addition to helping "frame more effective and realistic responses by national governments and external stakeholders. The design and implementation of remedial action and intervention strategies is critical to the success of efforts to address violent conflict" (Gilpin 2016:24). The EITI promotes norms of transparency and multi-stakeholder collaboration which contributes to a "universal" understanding of the core factors that cause conflict. While the interests of local communities are often disadvantaged in relation to capital-rich MNCs and host-country governments that rely on extractive sector revenues, the EITI empowers civil society by including representatives in the governance framework, thus providing a forum for unimpeded discourse as well as providing guidelines for improved governance practices across economic and societal structures.

To compound challenges in the extractive sector, in addition to industrial operations, a vibrant informal extractive sector has emerged. The rise in global gold prices, seen as a means to alleviate the impact of structural adjustment programs (SAPs), has triggered an increased interest in artisanal and small-scale gold mining (ASGM) globally (Armah et al. 2016; Banchirigah 2008; Hilson and Potter 2005). ASGM has become a major economic activity in many parts of the world, contributing significantly to total yearly gold production in states like Ghana (Minerals Commission 2014; Wilson et al. 2015) and Mali (Nampa-Reuters 2016) for instance, and about 30 percent of total global gold production (Seccatore et al. 2014).

Accompanying this rise and changing trend in mineral extraction, the incidence of violence, conflict and general human insecurity has also increased. In most states, the practice is illegal; where it is legal, some miners have resorted to practices that contravene the legal provisions for the sector, which aggravates the security (human and national) in resource-rich states. Conflicts take various forms, involve various actors and have, in recent times, triggered inter-state diplomatic tensions. Clashes often occur over working conditions, access to mining space and natural resources such as water, food, minerals and land. This turn of events in the extractive industry has a significant impact on the political economy of individual states and global markets.

A primary source of resource-based conflict in the modern extractive sector occurs between large-scale formal extractive companies and informal sector operators. In 2016, the BBC reported an incident in Obuasi, a mining community in Ghana, which involved clashes between artisanal and small-scale miners (ASM) in the community and Anglo-Gold Ashanti, a multinational mining company (BBC 2016). In this conflict, the MNC complained of encroachment on its concession by ASM operators in the community. In the bid to protect its property, the company employed the protection of state security forces. Contesting the company's claim over the concession, the ASM operators defied these efforts and continued to mine, counterclaiming that the company was encroaching on their ancestral lands. This led to clashes resulting in the death of an official from Anglo-Gold Ashanti. Although the issue appeared to have been resolved later through government intervention, relations remain volatile and thus threaten peace and security in the community.

In a recent incident, members of Denkyira-Obuasi, another Ghanaian mining community, lynched a military officer. According to news accounts, the military detail had been stationed in the community to help curb the illegal activities of ASM operators (Ghanaweb 2017a). Angered by the presence of the military personnel, members of the mining community ambushed and attacked the officer, resulting in his death. The incident triggered a widespread national outcry and further undermined national peace.

Violence and conflict have become common features of the extractive industry across Africa. A recent case is the Marikana Massacre in South Africa, in which 34 protesting platinum mine workers were shot and killed by state police on August 16, 2012 (Alexander 2013). Dissatisfied with working conditions, the mine workers undertook to register their displeasure to their employers in a peaceful demonstration. The mine owners felt threatened and would not countenance the action so they sought the intervention of the state. The result was a mass murder of defenseless mine workers, which has become known as the Marikana Massacre.

Mining-related conflicts are not specifically an African issue. In Latin America, for instance, the Observatory of Mining Conflicts, a coalition of civil society organizations, compiled a list of 215 conflicts spread over 19 regional countries in 2014 alone (Economist 2016). Leading the list were Mexico with 37 violent clashes, Peru with 36 and Chile with 35.

The informal artisanal and small-scale mining sector has also been at the center of inter-state diplomatic rows. Mineral extraction often involves the use of mercury and other deadly chemicals, which poison water, flora and fauna. In the West African sub-region operations have triggered tensions between neighboring states. Ghana's Tano River located in the western part of the country, where ASM activities are extensive, flows into Côte d'Ivoire's drinking sources (Ghanaweb 2017b). Illegal mining activities along the river have caused pollution which consequently impacted Côte d'Ivoirian citizens. Ivoirians raised concerns and registered their complaints, triggering ministerial level engagement by the governments, which has not been an entirely smooth reconciliation process.

The diplomatic implications of and tensions arising from ASM have in recent times also extended beyond the African continent. Relations between Ghana and China have experienced some unpleasant moments owing to the involvement of Chinese nationals in the perpetuation of illegal and environmentally unfriendly mining activity. Ghana's ASM sector is replete with Chinese nationals who use heavy equipment to mine on restricted lands. Ghanaian stakeholders and the media have focused attention on these illegal miners and security agencies have also arrested several Chinese operators for engaging in illegal mining practices (Ghanaweb 2017c). Following these developments, the Chinese Mission in Ghana reacted in a press release to media reportage on the involvement and treatment of Chinese nationals (Ghanaweb 2017d); the Mission further threatened diplomatic action (Ghanaweb 2017e, 2017f). This position in turn tested relations with the newly elected Ghanaian government, whose response had to manage domestic outcry and diplomatic relations with China (Ghanaweb 2017g, 2017h, 2017i).

As these examples show, extractive sector-related conflicts take various forms, involve various actors and manifest at different levels. They are sometimes localized among actors within a particular community; they could also have a national character involving state agencies; in some instances, they induce inter-state (regional and global) diplomatic rows. Resource-related conflicts also have the potential of escalating into civil wars as in the cases of Liberia, DR Congo and Colombia among others (Ross 2004). The manifestation of inter-state conflicts or tensions is indicative of the sector's potential adverse impact on global relations, peace and security. At the national and subnational level, the situation is even more complex. This underscores the imperative for a widening of the scope of resource governance mechanisms to address such social issues as conflict.

Global governance initiatives, while not always explicitly designed to address violent conflict and peacebuilding processes, do have built-in mechanisms that could be utilized to confront conflict and promote peacebuilding. The Voluntary Principles on Security and Human Rights (VPs) provide a series of strategies that corporations may utilize to avoid inciting conflict. The Kimberly Process Certification Scheme (KPCS) was established to discourage trade in "conflict diamonds" – that is diamonds from territories engaged in civil war and/or used to fund violence. Publish What You Pay (PWYP) and the Extractive Industries Transparency Initiative (EITI) both promote the good governance initiative based on transparency of revenue flows between MNCs and governments to cultivate public ownership of the sector and use public data to hold officials accountable. Ultimately, this effort addresses corruption and fiscal mismanagement that has the potential to trigger conflict.

Membership of these governance initiatives is mostly voluntary. However, their ability to focus public awareness on issues endemic in the extractive sector is significant and enhances their capacity to impact governance at various levels. Their embedded multi-stakeholder engagement is a key aspect of the operations that enable this capacity. GGIs assist in empowering civil society actors by creating forums for interaction with state and corporate actors as well as providing guidelines for improved governance practices across economic, social, security and environmental issues.

The EITI, a multi-stakeholder governance initiative focusing on transparency and accountability in the resource value chain, has the capacity to perform some conflict mediation roles in the extractive sector. Its membership involves states, extractive companies and civil society groups, all of which are central actors to addressing resource-related conflicts at various levels. The rise in the informal extractive sector and its contribution to the global political economy as well as its impact on global security further necessitate the conflict mediation role of EITI. Indeed, some scholars have suggested the imperative for the EITI to extend its focus to the informal ASM sector (Garrett 2007). Hence, the 2016 EITI Progress Report re-emphasized the need to incorporate ASM in its operations (EITI 2016:6). The significance of a governance model to mitigate (potential and actual) conflict that emanates from an evolving extractive sector adds to the essence of these suggestions. A conflict mediation component in the operation of the EITI can boost the impact of the extractive industry on human security, well-being and development. A key feature of the EITI is the multi-stakeholder arrangement which creates a trust-building forum for disparate actors. Scholars have observed that through its multi-stakeholder engagement, the EITI has the potential to improve trust and ultimately enhance peaceful coexistence among the various actors in the extractive sector and the larger global economy (Rich and Warner 2012:207).

The relationship between violent conflict and the resource nexus is complex. Conflict undermines the industry's potential to improve human well-being. Yet, most mechanisms of resource governance often overlook or de-prioritize this. Intergovernmental resource governance mechanisms offer opportunities to effectively mediate or even curb resource-related conflicts. Addressing insecurities in the extractive sector requires multiple actor engagements. Global or transnational governance initiatives, while not always explicitly designed to address violent conflict, have in-built mechanisms that could be utilized to confront conflict and promote peace. As Cyril Obi asserted: "The notion of peace building as being synonymous with exorcising Africa of the resource curse has to go beyond calls for market reforms or stronger and more efficient institutions. The reality is that zero-sum politics, without paying attention to issues of equity, culture, equal participation and justice, lie at the heart of the resource-conflict nexus" (Obi 2016:100).

A multi-stakeholder engagement can facilitate better understanding of the varied interests and concerns that have the potential to generate conflict and violence among actors (Gilpin 2016).

The EITI provides the forum for a variety of actors to engage on the social, political, environmental, economic and cultural issues of the extractive industry that affect national, regional and global peace, security and well-being. The EITI framework holds potential for peacebuilding in conflict affected societies because transparency provides data that can inform discourse among multiple stakeholders. Such a process can in effect build trust among various stakeholders. The EITI empowers civil society to engage state and corporate actors on a balanced platform. For instance, Zambia is using the EITI to better inform the public regarding revenue transfers as well as clarify information regarding mining contracts. In post-conflict countries, such as the Democratic Republic of Congo, Liberia and Sierra Leone, the EITI is a component of a wider peace and reconciliation process because it is bringing stakeholders to the table to discuss revenue allocation and environmental protection as well as supporting societal ownership of the nation's mineral wealth. The goal of the EITI is to mainstream the good governance agenda within resource governance regimes. As the norms of transparency, official accountability and public ownership are institutionalized within extractive governance regimes, the variety of stakeholders will build the capacity and become better equipped to make decisions in a democratic fashion as opposed to fracturing into conflicting camps.

Conclusions

Florian Krampe (2017) argues that the impressive accomplishments of environmental peacebuilding practices and research are manifest in, for example, the explicit inclusion of peace as one of the Sustainable Development Goals and the increasing attention to environmental and resource issues by more traditional peacebuilding and post-conflict reconstruction programs and research communities. He argues that the next generation of research should be aimed at both understanding and enhancing the prospects for "sustainable peace" by grappling with more of the endemic complexities of the interactions between environmental factors and resources with a larger set of critical social processes occurring in post-conflict societies. Similarly, this chapter seeks to demonstrate – with its three brief illustrative cases – that there are enumerable opportunities in the worlds of research and practice to better connect and integrate environmental conflict and peacebuilding research to existing and ongoing governance initiatives across scales, world regions and issues areas.

The section on northwestern Kenya suggests that there are many existing governance initiatives at local and other scales clearly engaging resource cooperation and institution building as part of conflict mitigation strategies – and that research on why such strategies have mixed results might teach us a lot about environmental peacebuilding across contexts. Furthermore, while neither the CITES regime nor EITI (and the host of other transparency initiatives) were launched and built primarily with violent conflict mitigation and peacebuilding as central goals, both illustrate the substantial potential that improved attention to environmental and resource-based peacebuilding might realize if both decades-old and comparatively young intergovernmental and transnational initiatives would more explicitly engage environmental conflict and peacebuilding issues, practices and research. In addition, drawing on resource nexus frameworks helps avoid the limitations of focusing on only one or two resources – such as water or water and energy, for example. Of course, no one nexus framework should become a straitjacket. Grazing land and illicit species trade both illustrate that violence can be connected to resources other than water, food, energy, land and minerals. Environmental conflict and peacebuilding practice and research have much to contribute – and much to learn – by inquiring about the unrealized environmental conflict and peacebuilding potential embodied in a host of existing governance institutions at and across scales.

Notes

1 This section draws on Jeremiah O. Asaka's doctoral research.
2 A peace conservancy refers to a community conservancy that is explicitly focused on, among other things, contributing towards the achievement of peace and security.
3 How NRT works: www.nrt-kenya.org/about/
4 County government partnerships: www.nrt-kenya.org/county-government/
5 Each NRT conservancy forms a grazing committee charged with, among other things, the responsibility of planning community livestock grazing including but not limited to initiating conversations with other communities on pasture sharing during periods of drought.
6 This section draws on Linda Holcombe's ongoing research on the illegal wildlife trade, and its implications.
7 This section draws on research and fieldwork conducted by Timothy Adivilah Balag'kutu and Jason J. McSparren.

References

Adger, W.N., Pulhin, J., Barnet, J., Dabelko, G. D., Hovelrud, G. K., Levy, M. and Vogel, C. (2014) "Human Security" in Field, C. B., Baros, V. R., Dokken, D. J., Mach, K. J., Mastrandrea, M. D., Bilir, T. E. and White, L. L. (eds) *Climate Change 2014: Impacts, Adaptation, and Vulnerability. Part A: Global and Sectoral Aspects. Contribution of Working Group II to the Fifth Assessment Report of the Intergovernmental Panel on Climate Change* Cambridge University Press, New York, 755–791.

Alexander, P. (2013) "Marikana, turning point in South African history" *Review of African Political Economy*, 40(138):605–619. Available at: <http://dx.doi.org/10.1080/03056244.2013.860893>

Ali, S. H. (ed.) (2007) *Peace Parks: Conservation and Conflict Prevention* MIT Press, Cambridge, MA.

Andonova, L., Hale, T. and Roger, C. (2017) "National policy and transnational governance of climate change: Substitutes or complements?" *International Studies Quarterly*, 61(2):253–268. Available at: https://doi.org/10.1093/isq/sqx014

Andrews-Speed, P., Bleischwitz, R., Boersma, T., Johnson, C., Kemp, G. and VanDeveer, S. D. (2015) *Waste, Want or War? The Global Resource Nexus and the Struggle for Land, Energy, Food, Water and Minerals* Routledge/Earthscan, Abingdon.

Annan, K. (2012) "Momentum rises to lift Africa's curse" *New York Times*, 12 September. Available at: <www.nytimes.om/2012/09/14/opinion/kofi-annan-momentum-rises-to-lift-africas-resource-curse.html?_r=0>

Armah, F. A., Boamah, S. A., Quansah, R., Obiri, S. and Luginaah, I. (2016) "Unsafe occupational health behaviors: Understanding mercury-related environmental health risks to artisanal gold miners in Ghana" *Frontiers in Environmental Science*, 4(1):29. Available at: <http://journal.frontiersin.org/article/10.3389/fenvs.2016.00029>

Asaka, J. O. (2015) "Colonial Kenya observed: British rule, Mau Mau and the wind of change" *The Round Table: The Commonwealth Journal of International Affairs*, 104(5):631–633. Available at: <https://doi.org/10.1080/00358533.2015.1090790>

Axworthy, L. (2001) "Human security and global governance: Putting people first" *Global Governance: A Review of Multilateralism and International Organizations*, 7(1):19–23. Available at: <www.jstor.org/stable/27800284>

Ayling, J. (2013) "What sustains wildlife crime? Rhino horn trading and the resilience of criminal networks" *Journal of International Wildlife Law & Policy*, 16(1):57–80. Available at: <http://dx.doi.org/10.1080/13880292.2013.764776>

Banchirigah, S. M. (2008) "Challenges with eradicating illegal mining in Ghana: A perspective from the grassroots" *Resources Policy*, 33(1):29–38. Available at: <https://doi.org/10.1016/j.resourpol.2007.11.001>

Basedau, M. (2005) "Context matters – rethinking the resource curse in Sub-Saharan Africa" *GIGA Working Paper No. 1.* <http://dx.doi.org/10.2139/ssrn.906983>

Basel, D., Lee, S., Mohtar, R., Asaka, J. O. and VanDeveer, S. (2018 forthcoming) "Security, climate change and the nexus" in Bleischwitz, R., Hoff, H., Spataru, C., van der Voet, E. and VanDeveer, S. (eds) *Routledge Handbook of the Resource Nexus* Routledge, Abingdon.

Bassett, T. J. (2005) "Card-carrying hunters, rural poverty, and wildlife decline in northern Côte d'Ivoire" *Geographical Journal*, 171(1):24–35. Available at: <http://dx.doi.org/10.1111/j.1475-4959.2005.00147.x>

BBC World Service (2016) Ghana: The Obuasi Stand-Off, Assignment (www.bbc.co.uk/programmes/p03tw2nj) [Accessed 7 July 2017].

Berger, R. (2003) "Conflict over natural resources among pastoralists in northern Kenya: A look at recent initiatives in conflict resolution" *Journal of International Development*, 15(2):245–257. Available at: <http://dx.doi.org/10.1002/jid.985>

Beyers, R. L., Hart, J. A., Sinclair, A. R. E., Grossmann, F., Klinkenberg, B. and Dino, S. (2011) "Resource wars and conflict ivory: The impact of civil conflict on elephants in the democratic republic of Congo – The case of the Okapi reserve" *PLoS ONE*, 6(11):e27129. <https://doi.org/10.1371/journal.pone.0027129>

Bleischwitz, R., Hoff, H., Spataru, C., van der Voet, E. and VanDeveer, S. D. (2018 forthcoming) *Routledge Handbook of the Resource Nexus* Routledge, Abingdon.

Bulkeley, H., Andonova, L., Betsill, M., Compagnon, D., Hale, T., Hoffman, M., et al. (2014) *Transnational Climate Change Governance* Cambridge University Press, Cambridge.

Chalecki, B. (2013) *Environmental Security: A Guide to the Issues* Praeger, Santa Barbara, CA.

Cockayne, J. and Lupel, A. (2009) "Introduction: Rethinking the relationship between peace operations and organized crime" *International Peacekeeping*, 16(1):4–19. Available at: <http://dx.doi.org/10.1080/13533310802485567>

Cruise, A. and van der Zee, B. (2017) "Armed herders invade Kenya's most important wildlife conservancy" *The Guardian*, 2 February. Available at: <www.theguardian.com/environment/2017/feb/02/armed-herders-elephant-kenya-wildlife-laikipia>

Douglas, L. R. and Alie, K. (2014) "High-value natural resources: Linking wildlife conservation to international conflict, insecurity, and development concerns" *Biological Conservation*, 171(1):270–277. Available at: <https://doi.org/10.1016/j.biocon.2014.01.031>

Duffy, R. (2016) "War, by conservation" *Geoforum*, 69(1):238–248. Available at: <https://doi.org/10.1016/j.geoforum.2015.09.014>

Economist (2016) "Mining in Latin America: From conflict to co-operation" *The Economist* 6 February. Available at: <www.economist.com/news/americas/21690100-big-miners-have-better-record-their-critics-claim-it-up-governments-balance> [Accessed 7 July 2017].

Extractive Industries Transparency Initiative (EITI) (2016) *2016 Progress Report: From Reports to Results* (K. Andreasen and V. Ponsford eds, EITI International Secretariat), EITI International Secretariat, Oslo, Norway. <www.eiti.org>

Garrett, N. (2007) *The Extractive Industries Transparency Initiative (EITI) and Artisanal and Small-Scale Mining (ASM): Preliminary Observations from the Democratic Republic of the Congo (DRC)*. EITI.

Ghanaweb (2017a) "Diaso lynching: Captain Mahama was deployed to fight galamsey – Uncle". Available at: <www.ghanaweb.com/GhanaHomePage/NewsArchive/Diaso-lynching-Captain-Mahama-was-deployed-to-fight-galamsey-Uncle-542625> [Accessed 1 July 2017].

Ghanaweb (2017b) "Ivory Coast mad at Ghana over galamsey". Available at: <www.ghanaweb.com/GhanaHomePage/NewsArchive/Ivory-Coast-mad-at-Ghana-over-galamsey-525490> [Accessed 1 July 2017].

Ghanaweb (2017c) "Clampdown on galamseyers: Another 4 Chinese arrested". Available at: <www.ghanaweb.com/GhanaHomePage/NewsArchive/Clampdown-on-galamseyers-Another-4-Chinese-arrested-527811> [Accessed 1 July 2017].

Ghanaweb (2017d) "Chinese Mission cries over galamsey fight; demands fair reportage". Available at: <www.ghanaweb.com/GhanaHomePage/NewsArchive/Chinese-Mission-cries-over-galamsey-fight-demands-fair-reportage-526879> [Accessed 1 July 2017].

Ghanaweb (2017e) "Chinese Embassy threats won't stop fight against galamsey – Minister". Available at: <www.ghanaweb.com/GhanaHomePage/NewsArchive/Chinese-Embassy-threats-won-t-stop-fight-against-galamsey-Minister-528028> [Accessed 1 July 2017].

Ghanaweb (2017f) "Chinese mission demands fair reportage on galamsey". Available at: <www.ghanaweb.com/GhanaHomePage/NewsArchive/Chinese-Mission-demands-fair-reportage-on-galamsey-526871> [Accessed 1 July 2017].

Ghanaweb (2017g) "We don't hate Chinese; our laws must work – Akufo-Addo". Available at: <www.ghanaweb.com/GhanaHomePage/NewsArchive/We-don-t-hate-Chinese-our-laws-must-work-Akufo-Addo-529271> [Accessed 1 July 2017].

Ghanaweb (2017h) "Respect our laws – Nana Addo to Chinese galamsey operators". <www.ghanaweb.com/GhanaHomePage/NewsArchive/Respect-our-laws-Nana-Addo-to-Chinese-galamsey-operators-529268> [Accessed 1 July 2017].

Ghanaweb (2017i) "China cannot tell us what to do to abate galamsey – Lloyd Amoah" Available at: <www.ghanaweb.com/GhanaHomePage/NewsArchive/China-cannot-tell-us-what-to-do-to-abate-galamsey-Lloyd-Amoah-527494> [Accessed 1 July 2017].

Gilpin, R. (2016) "Understanding the nature and origins of violent conflict in Africa" in Aall, P. and Crocker, C. A. (eds) *Minding the Gap: African Conflict Management in a Time of Change* CIGI Publications, Waterloo, Ontario, 21–33.

Glew, L., Hudson, M. D. and Osborne, P. E. (2010) *Evaluating the Effectiveness of Community-based Conservation in Northern Kenya: A Report to The Nature Conservancy* University of Southampton, Southampton.

Global Witness (1999) *A Crude Awakening: The Role of Oil and Banking Industries in Angola's Conflict* London.

Haro, G. O., Doyo, G. J. and McPeak, J. G. (2005) "Linkages between community, environmental, and conflict management: experiences from northern Kenya" *World Development* 33(2):285–299.Available at: <https://doi.org/10.1016/j.worlddev.2004.07.014>

Herbig, F. J. W. and Warchol, G. (2011) "South African conservation crime and routine activities theory: A causal nexus?" *South African Journal of Criminology*, 24(2):16.

Hilson, G. and Potter, C. (2005) "Structural adjustment and subsistence industry: Artisanal gold mining in Ghana" *Development and Change*, 36(1):103–131. Available at: <http://dx.doi.org/10.1111/j.0012-155X.2005.00404.x>

Holt, V. and Boucher, A. (2009) "Framing the issue: UN responses to corruption and criminal networks in post-conflict settings" *International Peacekeeping*, 16(1):20–32. Available at: <http://dx.doi.org/10.1080/13533310802485492>

Human Rights Watch (1999) *The Price of Oil: Corporate Responsibility and Human Rights Violations in Nigeria's Oil Producing Communities* New York.

International Fund for Animal Welfare (IFAW) (2013) *Criminal Nature: The Global Security Implications of the Illegal Wildlife Trade* Yarmouth Port, MA. Available at: <www.ifaw.org/sites/default/files/ifaw-criminal-nature-UK.pdf>

Karl, T. L. (1997) *The Paradox of Plenty: Oil Booms and Petro-states* University of California Press, London.

Kenya National Bureau of Statistics (KNBS) (2009) *Kenya: 2009 Population and Housing Census Highlights* Kenya National Bureau of Statistics, Nairobi. Available at: <www.scribd.com/doc/36672705/Kenya-Census-2009>

Krampe, F. (2016) Building sustainable peace: Understanding the linkages between social, political and ecological processes in post-war countries. Department of Peace and Conflict Research, Uppsala University Report 110. Doctoral Dissertation. Uppsala University.

Krampe, F. (2017) "Toward sustainable peace: A new research agenda for post-conflict natural resource management" *Global Environmental Politics*, 17(4):1–8.

Lunstrum, E. (2014) "Green militarization: Anti-poaching efforts and the spatial contours of Kruger National Park" *Annals of the Association of American Geographers*, 104(4):816–832. Available at: <http://dx.doi.org/10.1080/00045608.2014.912545>

McFerson, H. M. (2010) "Extractive industries and African democracy: Can the resource curse be exorcised?" *International Studies Perspectives*, 11(4):335–353. Available at: <http://dx.doi.org/10.1111/j.1528-3585.2010.00410.x>

Makarenko, T. (2004) "The crime–terror continuum: tracing the interplay between transnational organised crime and terrorism" *Global Crime* 6(1): 129–145.

Matthew, R., Barnett, J., McDonald, B. and O'Brien, K. (2010) *Global Environmental Change and Human Security* MIT Press, Boston.

Mbaaria, J. and Ogada, M. (2017) *The Big Conservation Lie* Lens & Pens Publishing, Auburn, WA.

Meagher, K. (2014) "Smuggling ideologies: From criminalization to hybrid governance in African clandestine economies" *African Affairs*, 113(453):497–517. <https://doi.org/10.1093/afraf/adu057>

Mehlum, H., Moene, K. and Torvik, R. (2006) "Institutions and the resource curse" *Economic Journal*, 116(508):20. Available at: <http://dx.doi.org/10.1111/j.1468-0297.2006.01045.x>

Milner-Gulland, E. J. and Bennett, E. L. (2003) "Wild meat: The bigger picture" *Trends in Ecology & Evolution*, 18(7):351–357. Available at: <https://doi.org/10.1016/S0169-5347(03)00123-X>

Minerals Commission (2014) *Artisanal and Small-scale Mining (ASM) Framework*, Ministry of Finance Accra, Ghana.

Mkutu, K. A. (2002) "Pastoralism and conflict in the Horn of Africa" *Africa Peace Forum/Saferworld*, University of Bradford.

Mkutu, K. A. (2007) "Small arms and light weapons among pastoral groups in the Kenya–Uganda border area" *African Affairs*, 106(422):47–70. Available at: <https://doi.org/10.1093/afraf/adl002>

Munyeki, J. (2017) "Security forces shoot 500 cows in Laikipia as herders protest" *The Standard*, 30 March. Available at: <www.standardmedia.co.ke/article/2001234496/security-forces-shoot-500-cows-in-laikipia-as-herders-protest>

Nampa-Reuters. (2016) "Mali produces 50 tonnes gold in 2015, expects more in 2016" *The Namibian*, 4 January. Available at: www.namibian.com.na/index.php?page=archive-read&id=145770

Nellemann, C., Henriksen, R., Raxter, P., Ash, N. and Mrema, E. (eds) (2014) *The Environmental Crime Crisis – Threats to Sustainable Development from Illegal Exploitation and Trade in Wildlife and Forest Resources* A UNEP Rapid Response Assessment, United Nations Environment Programme and GRID-Arendal, Nairobi <www.grida.no>

Ngirachu, J. (2017) "Britain's Foreign Secretary Boris Johnson welcomes KDF deployment to Laikipia" *Daily Nation*, 17 March. Available at: <www.nation.co.ke/news/Britain-Boris-Johnson-military-KDF-deploy-Laikipia/1056-3853870-147ytcc/index.html>

Njiru, B. N. (2012) "Climate change, resource competition and conflict amongst pastoral communities of northern Kenya" in Scheffran, J., Brzoska, M., Brauch, G. H. and Schilling, J. (eds) *Climate Change, Human Security and Violent Conflict* Springer-Verlag, Berlin, 513–527.

Northern Rangelands Trust (NRT) (2014) *NRT State of the Conservancies Report* Northern Rangelands Trust, Kenya.

Obi, C. (2016) "Understanding the resource curse effect: Instability and violent conflict in Africa" in Aall, P. and Crocker, C. A. (eds) *Minding the Gap: African Conflict Management in a Time of Change* CIGI Publications, Waterloo, Ontario.

Okumu, W. (2013) *Trans-local Peacebuilding among Pastoralist Communities in Kenya: The Case of Laikipia Peace Caravan* Cologne Africa Studies Center, Cologne.

Opiyo, F. E. O., Wasonga, O. V., Schilling, J. and Mureithi, S. M. (2012) "Resource based conflicts in drought prone northwestern Kenya: The drivers and mitigation mechanisms" *Wudpecker Journal of Agricultural Research*, 1(11):442–453.

Reno, W. (2009) "Understanding criminality in West African conflicts" *International Peacekeeping*, 16(1):47–61. Available at: <http://dx.doi.org/10.1080/13533310802485542>

Rich, E. and Warner, T. (2012) "Addressing the roots of Liberia's conflict through the Extractive Industries Transparency Initiative" in Lujala, P. and Rustad, S. A. (eds) *High-Value Natural Resources and Post-Conflict Peacebuilding* Earthscan, London, 200–209. Available at: <https://environmentalpeacebuilding.org/assets/Documents/LibraryItem_000_Doc_096.pdf>

Ross, M. L. (1999) "The political economy of the resource curse" *World Politics*, 51(2):297–322. Available at: <https://doi.org/10.1017/S0043887100008200>

Ross, M. L. (2004) "What do we know about natural resources and civil war?" *Journal of Peace Research*, 41(3):337–356. Available at: <https://doi.org/10.1177/0022343304043773>

Sachs, J. and Warner, A. M. (1995) "Natural resource abundance and economic growth" *Center for International Development*, Harvard University, Cambridge, MA.

Schilling, J., Opiyo, F. E. O. and Scheffran, J. (2012) "Raiding pastoral livelihoods: Motives and effects of violent conflict in north-western Kenya" *Pastoralism: Research, Policy and Practice*, 2(25).

Seccatore, J., Veiga, M., Origliasso, C., Marin, T. and De Tomi, G. (2014) "An estimation of the artisanal small-scale production of gold in the world" *Science of the Total Environment*, 496:662–667. Available at: <https://doi.org/10.1016/j.scitotenv.2014.05.003>

Sellar, J. M. (2014) *The UN's Lone Ranger: Combating International Wildlife Crime* Whittles Publishing, Caithness.

Shelley, L. (2005) "The unholy trinity: Transnational crime, corruption, and terrorism" *Brown Journal of World Affairs*, 11(2):101–112.

Shelley, L. I. and Picarelli, J. T. (2005) "Methods and motives: Exploring links between transnational organized crime and international terrorism" *Trends in Organized Crime*, 9(2):52–56.

Simonse, S. (2011) *Human Security in the Borderlands of Sudan, Uganda and Kenya: Key Advocacy Issues from the Perspective of a Grassroots Peace Building Programme for Warrior Youths* Cross-border Peace & Sports Programme for Youth Warriors/IKV PAX CHRISTI/Seeds of Peace Africa International, Kenya. Available at: <www.bibalex.org/Search4Dev/files/393711/335360.pdf>

Truth, Justice and Reconciliation Commission (TJRC) (2013) *Report of the Truth, Justice and Reconciliation Commission.* TJRC, Kenya. Available at: <http://digitalcommons.law.seattleu.edu/tjrc/>

United Nations Office on Drugs and Crime (UNODC) (2011) *Organized Crime and Instability in Central Africa: A Threat Assessment* UNODC, Vienna. Available at: <www.research.ed.ac.uk/portal/en/publications/organized-crime-and-national-security(9a9dc8b7-515d-4f51-a813-261474b81d35).html>

Van de Graaf, T. and Colgan, J. (2016) "Global energy governance: A review and research agenda" *Palgrave Communications*, January.

Van Solinge, T. B. (2008a) "Crime, conflicts and ecology in Africa" in Sollund, R. (ed.) *Global Harms: Ecological Crime and Speciesism* Nova Science Publishers, Oslo, 13–34.

Van Solinge, T. B. (2008b) "Eco-crime: The tropical timber trade" in Siegel, D. and Nelen, H. (eds) *Organized Crime Culture Markets and Policies* Springer-Verlag, Berlin, 97–111.

VanDeveer, S. D. (2015) "Consumption, commodity chains and global and local environments" in Axelrod, R. and VanDeveer, S. D. (eds) *The Global Environment: Institutions, Law and Policy*, 4th Edition. CQ Press, Los Angeles, 350–372.

Warchol, G. L. and Harrington, M. (2016) "Exploring the dynamics of South Africa's illegal abalone trade via routine activities theory" *Trends in Organized Crime*, 19(1):21–41.

Warchol, G. L., Zupan, L. L. and Clack, W. (2003) "Transnational criminality: An analysis of the illegal wildlife market in Southern Africa" *International Criminal Justice Review*, 13(1): 27. Available at: <https://doi.org/10.1177/105756770301300101>

Weinthal, E., Troell, J. and Nakayama, M. (2013) *Water and Post-Conflict Peacebuilding* Earthscan/Routledge, London.

White, N. (2014) "The 'White Gold of Jihad': Violence, legitimisation and contestation in anti-poaching strategies" *Journal of Political Ecology*, 21:452–474.

Wilson, M. L., Renne, E., Roncoli, C., Agyei-Baffour, P. and Tenkorang, E. Y. (2015) "Integrated assessment of artisanal and small-scale gold mining in Ghana – Part 3: social sciences and economics international" *Journal of Environmental Research and Public Health*, 12(7):8133–8156. Available at <http://dx.doi.org/10.3390/ijerph120708133>

Wyatt, T. (2011) "The illegal trade of raptors in the Russian Federation" *Contemporary Justice Review*, 14(2) 103–123. Available at <http://dx.doi.org/10.1080/10282580.2011.565969>

Wyatt, T. (2013) *Wildlife Trafficking: A Deconstruction of the Crime, the Victims, and the Offenders* Palgrave Macmillan, New York.

Zabyelina, Y. G. (2014) "The 'fishy' business: A qualitative analysis of the illicit market in black caviar" *Trends in Organized Crime*, 17(3):181–198.

Zimmerman, M. E. (2003) "The black market for wildlife: Combating transnational organized crime in the illegal wildlife trade" *Vanderbilt Journal of Transnational Law*, 36:1657–1689.

20

The role of water diplomacy in peacebuilding

Maria Vink

Introduction

This chapter explores the links between water diplomacy and peacebuilding. It describes competing interests around water and looks at how political power influences cooperation. It then highlights the gap between how water is treated in the different policy domains of development and foreign affairs and argues that these domains need to be considered simultaneously for water cooperation to lead to sustainable development and peacebuilding. It concludes that well-designed water diplomacy approaches would serve to connect the two policy domains and could therefore contribute to more effective and sustainable peacebuilding.

Water diplomacy is defined here as a *process* addressing the political and social aspects that hinder or enable cooperation on water resources that are shared between states. A water diplomacy approach can be especially useful in situations where there are competing or even conflicting interests on how water should be allocated or managed. Water diplomacy can also be applied to support peacebuilding in situations characterized by conflict and hostile relations between countries over issues other than water. In such situations, the shared water resources can serve as an entry point for dialogue that over time can lead to the identification of mutual gains and confidence building beyond the water sector.

Work on water diplomacy, as in other areas of diplomacy, is often divided into different 'tracks' based on the formality, the actors involved, and its purpose: official, governmental actions to resolve conflicts fall under track one, and unofficial, informal interaction between members of adversary groups to resolve conflicts within and between states is referred to as track two (Montville 1991). The terms track three diplomacy and 'multi-track diplomacy', are increasingly being used to capture the complexity or breadth of unofficial diplomacy. The broadening of the term diplomacy has evolved from the increasing realization that inclusive approaches, engaging many actors from different parts of the system simultaneously, are needed to build sustainable peace. Such inclusive approaches are especially relevant in a water context as water interconnections stretch over geographical scales and political levels, and are often interwoven with culture and identity.

The term peacebuilding here refers to efforts to change beliefs, attitudes and behaviours that can transform the short- and long-term dynamics between individuals and groups towards a more stable, peaceful coexistence. Peacebuilding deals with establishing political arrangements at government level that address the political needs and manage the boundaries of a peace system. It also deals with establishing structures and institutions at various levels that support nonviolent resolution of conflict and implementation of a peace culture. Social infrastructure is another key component of peacebuilding, addressing peoples' and groups' feelings, attitudes, beliefs, values and skills to build commitment towards a 'peace culture' (Notter and Diamond 1996). Peacebuilding in this chapter is applied in its broadest sense: comprising the continuum from preventive diplomacy, peacemaking, peacekeeping, to post-conflict peacebuilding.

Hydrological interdependencies between states sharing the same water also bring with them political, economic, social and environmental interdependencies. Transboundary water resources therefore have the potential to foster cooperation through a variety of entry points. However, while cooperation over international waters can be a crucial element in both regional peacebuilding and sustainable development it must also be acknowledged that what falls under the ambit of cooperation often includes both positive and negative (asymmetric and coercive) interactions (Zeitoun and Mirumachi 2008). Peacebuilding in transboundary water contexts is more complex than promoting cooperation between states as it needs to take into account the socio-political context in which transboundary water interactions take place and be based on an understanding of the role water plays in society with competing uses and interests by basin actors.

Water in society – competing uses and interests

Rivers, lakes and aquifers have multiple uses and are a source for drinking water, fishing, navigation, flood control, industrial uses, irrigation and hydropower generation. Water is also at the core of global change, and in geographic areas with rapid population growth the available water resources per capita are constantly decreasing. Water scarcity affects more than 40 per cent of the global population and is projected to rise. In addition, climate change and the resulting increased variability of water flows has resulted in increasing the stress on available water resources.

Complicating matters further, most of the world's freshwater resources come from rivers, lakes and aquifers that are shared between countries. Approximately 40 per cent of the world's population lives in river and lake basins that comprise two or more countries and, perhaps even more significantly, over 90 per cent lives in countries that share basins. The existing 286 transboundary lake and river basins cover nearly one-half of the Earth's land surface and account for an estimated 60 per cent of global freshwater flow. A total of 148 states include territory within such basins, and 21 countries lie entirely within them. In addition, about 2 billion people worldwide depend on groundwater, which includes over 500 transboundary aquifer systems.

Coordinated management of internationally shared waters is crucial and covers a broad spectrum of issues, including water quantity, quality and economic development, and can often aggregate benefits that are larger than if water is managed at country level only. Examples of benefits from such cooperative management include: possibility to build on comparative advantages linking the hydrology of each country to water uses, such as coordination of irrigation and hydropower, to reduce evaporation losses; economies of scale for example in reduced electricity costs through hydropower and power pools; and coordinated management of infrastructure such as controlling water flows in cascades of dams to maximize power generation.

Yet, few transboundary water systems have well-functioning cooperation mechanisms that enable them to take advantage of such cooperation benefits. In many cases formal cooperation between riparians is weak, and only one-third of multilateral rivers are covered by treaty provisions that regulate cooperation and water uses. Over 1.7 billion people are currently living in river basins where water use exceeds recharge, and it is not unusual that different actors and countries have legitimate yet competing needs and interests over water allocations and use, making transboundary disputes inevitable.

Specifically, large infrastructure projects that reduce or alter water flows, such as water diversion for irrigated agriculture and construction of dams, often provoke disagreement and can be a main trigger for conflict-laden events between riparian states. Approximately 70 per cent of the water abstracted globally is used for irrigation, and water scarcity and irregularity of supply are among the biggest threats to agricultural production and global food security. For the majority of the 2.5 billion people living in low-income countries, agriculture is the most important sector of employment and any policy decisions that affect the water availability for food production will have a large impact on their livelihood opportunities. The potential political costs or gains of such decisions would hence need to be carefully assessed by riparian governments.

With climate change and increased efforts to reduce the use of fossil fuels, hydropower has regained attention and can be an attractive alternative for energy generation. But although hydropower is non-consumptive (except for increased evaporation), it can have major environmental impacts and affect ecology, fish and livelihoods. The International Energy Outlook 2016 (USEIA 2016) forecasts an increased worldwide energy demand by 48 per cent in year 2040 compared to 2012, with more than half of the projected increase in global energy consumption from 2012 to 2040 occurring among non-OECD nations in Asia. Hydropower is expected to provide nearly 40 per cent of the growth in energy generation in the non-OECD regions. It is not unreasonable to think that conflicts between states over initiatives to expand the use of water for the production of food and energy in the future will increase in both multitude and magnitude.

The politics of water

Many of the larger shared basins – the Nile, the Indus, the Ganges, the Euphrates–Tigris, the Amu Darya and Syr Darya, and the Mekong – are also regions that are characterized by substantial inter- and intra-state tensions and have a history of armed conflict. Out of 55 countries involved in major conflict, 41 share at least one basin with one or more nations. As such, transboundary water issues need to be viewed through a national security lens and embedded within a broader set of economic and geopolitical issues (Wolf 2005).

Even though there are many underlying challenges for transboundary water cooperation, tension between states over water issues has seldom by itself led to violent conflict. It is more likely that the deterioration of water sources affects intra-state stability, which may over time also affect the inter-state relations. Early coordination among riparian states can, however, serve to ameliorate these sources of friction (Wolf 2007).

Several explanations for this absence of water wars exist. One such explanation is that market forces manage to even out deficiencies in water-scarce and arid countries through the import of water-intense food products, which if produced locally would draw on scarce water resources. Such hidden flows of water in food and other commodities that are traded from one place to another are often referred to as virtual water (Allan 1998). An example is the Middle East and North Africa, which by the year 2000 were importing fifty million tons of grain annually (Allan 2003). However, a country's ability to import water through agriculture products depends on the strengths of its economy and capacity to benefit from global markets. Hence, poor countries have an increased dependency on global markets, with fluctuating food prices also risking increasing local tensions and conflict potentials as seen during the 2007–2008 world food price crisis. Allan also warns that the availability of virtual water has slowed the pace of implementing necessary water policy reforms for improved water efficiency.

Another explanation for why the control over water resources is seldom achieved through water wars refers to the imbalance of power between the riparians, where a powerful state manages to impose solutions on other states in the same basin. In this context, the term hydro-hegemons is often used referring to states that assert power over other riparian states in a shared river basin. The hegemon would often be the state with stronger economic and military capability and is often, but not always, upstream in relation to other riparians. The hegemon defines the 'rules of the game', establishing what are issues and what are non-issues, and non-hegemonic states usually comply with the order preferred by the hegemon. Hard power is seldom used in hydropolitics as a hegemon's superior power position effectively discourages any violent resistance against the order. Instead, the hegemon typically uses soft power such as trying to persuade subordinate actors not just to accept the hegemon's authority, but also to adopt and internalize its values and norms, for example to impose one solution over others. In many cases this use of soft power can be perceived as consensual cooperation between basin states (Zeitoun and Warner 2006).

The non-hegemonic states may in turn try to improve their situation by pushing against the perceived negative influence of the hydro-hegemon through counter-hegemony strategies. Such strategies also mainly rely on the use of soft powers such as reference to international law principles and delaying agreements, de-securitization and use of alternative funding sources (Zeitoun and Warner 2006). An interesting case in point of counter-hegemony action is the Nile basin where Egypt, although being the most downstream state, has through its stronger economic and military capability played the role of hydro-hegemon. However, this situation has been challenged in recent years as the strengthened cooperation among upstream countries has led to more unified positions, with the signing by six upstream states of a Cooperative Framework Agreement (CFA). Furthermore, Ethiopia took the initiative to build Africa's largest dam, the Grand Ethiopian Renaissance Dam (GERD), and to finance it through domestic means.

Even though regional power relations clearly have a strong impact on the cooperation and conflict climate of transboundary waters there is often a tendency among both riparian governments and external financing institutions to try to de-politicize transboundary water management. A common approach in programmes aimed at supporting cooperation on transboundary waters in environments affected by conflict is to focus on the technical track of cooperation, trying to separate it from the political context. The programmes that support cooperation via the political track are typically relatively limited in scope and often focused on encouraging riparian states to develop and sign international agreements and subsequently establish international river basin organizations. The strong focus on technical solutions has indeed brought remarkable success, especially those solutions targeting infrastructure and economic development, but has limitations as it often misses out on the opportunities to build a more inclusive and stable cooperation climate.

An increasing realization is also that the provision of external support to building institutional capacity for technical cooperation risks being unsustainable in the longer term as political disagreements sooner or later tend to impact on the institutions driving the technical cooperation. Examples are the Nile and the Mekong basins where development partners have invested substantial financial resources to develop the institutional and technical capacity of the Nile Basin Initiative and the Mekong River Commission, respectively, but where external support has reduced largely in recent years, partly due to unmet expectations on the impact these institutions have had on building an inclusive peacebuilding agenda. The fact that key riparians (Egypt and China) have chosen to stay outside the formal cooperation mechanisms points to the need to pay larger attention to the political interests and risks when designing support to transboundary cooperation in regions affected by conflict.

Water in development and security policy domains

A reason for separation of the political and technical tracks can be found in the divide between the policy domains of development and peacebuilding in governments. Water is hence looked at with two different lenses:

a) Water in the development agenda: water for poverty reduction and economic development, with a strong focus on infrastructure development.
b) Water in the foreign policy and security agenda: water as a security risk and a factor for regional stability.

Both domains have different objectives and methodologies. Development programmes usually rely on relatively rigid long-term planning, with strong requirements to set measurable goals and show results accordingly, while security and diplomacy work in a more flexible manner, seeing dialogue and cooperation as an objective in itself.

The gap between these policy domains concerns both riparian states sharing common water resources and external governments supporting transboundary cooperation. Usually neither riparian ministries responsible for water nor international development agencies supporting the water sector have the mandate to enter into the formal diplomacy domain, while ministries of foreign affairs often lack the capacity and expertise to fully understand water-sharing dynamics required to facilitate cooperation around shared water resources.

However, there is a growing understanding that relying solely on technically focused solutions for water management is not enough because basin management is often eclipsed by basin politics. Water scientists and practitioners have increasingly over the last decade argued that the 'systems engineering' practice is insufficient to deal with complex water problems and that water resources management must be put into its relevant natural, societal and political context (Islam and Susskind 2012). Transboundary water initiatives would benefit from stronger consideration of asymmetric power in their design.

> Water has been integral to war since before the Belgians manipulated the dykes of the Yser River to halt a German advance, in the muddy and blood-ridden trenches of World War I. With this in mind, the fight to control dams in Syria and Iraq – as with tensions spilling over transboundary rivers around the world – are entirely predictable, and well within our grasp to resolve. Yet water continues to be misunderstood by pundits, diplomats and politicians alike as a natural resource devoid of politics; a matter for environmental scientists and engineers.
>
> *(Zeitoun 2017)*

Although the gap between these two policy domains is a challenge in the implementation of transboundary water programmes, transboundary water by its nature of reaching over horizontal and vertical boundaries also offers a unique opportunity to practically combine the areas of development and security in context-specific settings. This chapter argues that a stronger focus on water diplomacy approaches would be a means to better explore the potential of shared water resources for peacebuilding and implement such initiatives.

Even though the formal decision making over international transboundary waters lies within the responsibility of state governments, international financial institutions and development partners also play a key role as third parties, influencing agendas by supporting certain regional initiatives. Realizing the value of water diplomacy, the EU Foreign Affairs Council in 2013 adopted the 'Council conclusions on EU water diplomacy'. A concrete objective of this policy was for the EU to proactively engage in transboundary water security challenges with the aim of promoting collaborative and sustainable water management arrangements and encouraging and supporting regional and international cooperation in the context of agreed policies and programmes (Council of the European Union 2013). However, the implementation of the Council conclusions on water diplomacy has turned out to be challenging and the results have so far been limited, pointing to a gap between policy formulation and implementation.

According to the Stockholm International Peace Research Institute (SIPRI) (Mobjörk et al. 2016), a reason for the EU's limited implementation of such preventive conflict work lies in the culture within EU institutions of neglecting upstream and strategic thinking in favour of more immediate crisis response. The problem with limited policy implementation is not restricted to the EU institutions, but is widespread to most foreign policy and development partners. SIPRI also concludes that both the UK Department for International Development (DfID) and the German development agency GIZ have high level policies in place to link climate change and security, but that these links are not integrated systematically into analytical tools and implementation procedures. Furthermore, the British Independent Commission for Aid Impact (ICAI) in its evaluation of DfID's work in fragile states concludes that DfID's work on security and justice needs to be far more realistic, rigorous and holistic in its approach (ICAI 2015).

The evaluations of policies and implementation of foreign aid to peacebuilding interventions show the need for stronger focus on comprehensive analysis in the design of such interventions. Economic and technical analyses need to be combined with analysis of power and the larger political economy to find solutions that are both technically desirable and politically feasible. It needs to be acknowledged, however, that assessments of water-related conflict risks and the design of appropriate measures to support peacebuilding can be difficult to perform, and access to the right expertise and proper analytical tools is essential for responding effectively to water-related security risks.

Water diplomacy – a useful approach in peacebuilding

An analytical approach highlighting the links between politics, power and human behavioural factors that influence the implementation of development projects is required to identify and develop strategies that are both holistic and realistic. It is important, therefore, to develop analytical tools that can help overcome organizational silos, and increase synergies between the efforts of different policy communities (Mobjörk et al. 2016). A number of such tools that can help the analysis in transboundary water contexts have been developed, and three are briefly described next.

Political Economy Analysis (PEA) can be a useful starting point in engaging in water diplomacy in a specific basin. Realizing the importance of the role that political power plays in transboundary relations, the World Bank and development partners supporting the programme Cooperation on International Waters in Africa (CIWA) identified the need to develop a framework for PEA relating to transboundary waters (World Bank 2017). The PEA should identify a range of water-related issues which assist or hamper effective cooperation, map the institution and actor landscape and describe the power and influence of those actors in the process. An iterative deployment of PEA can increase the understanding of power dynamics and how changes in this dynamic influence the relations between key stakeholders as well as the hegemonic and counter-hegemonic trends in inter-state transboundary relations.

Islam and Susskind (2012) argue that continued efforts to apply analytical tools such as cost–benefit analysis and optimization theory to complex water problems are not likely to help in finding solutions to transboundary conflicts and propose an alternative approach through their "Water Diplomacy Framework" that seeks to bridge scientific objectivity and contextual understanding. The framework shows how open and constantly changing water networks can be managed using collaborative adaptive techniques to build informed agreements among disciplinary experts, water users with conflicting interests, and governmental bodies with countervailing claims.

The work by Mirumachi (2007, cited in Zeitoun and Mirumachi 2008) on the Transboundary Waters Interaction Nexus (the TWINS matrix) offers a tool for simultaneous consideration of the intensity of conflict and cooperation in a specific basin. This tool analyses the different elements characterizing conflict and cooperation by considering positions on a two-dimensional matrix. It highlights that coexisting conflict and cooperation can change over time, thereby providing an insight into the physical, socio-economic and political reasons for water use and management.

While the analytic tools described above provide a means for better understanding of the context within which water diplomacy operates, there are also important experiences to draw from the practical implementation of peacebuilding interventions. Literature evaluating peacebuilding efforts (UN 2011; ICAI 2015; Mobjörk et al. 2016) and the effectiveness of different diplomacy tracks (Böhmelt 2010, Fisher 2006) points to some common characteristics of the most successful programmes. The characteristics of successful peacebuilding interventions resonate well with the ideas behind water diplomacy, and in adapting these characteristics to a water diplomacy context some of the conclusions that can be drawn are that:

- The most convincing peacebuilding designs are relatively modest in their objectives and focus on finding solutions to specific problems, rather than aiming for across-the-board improvements in one sector. A transboundary water basin provides by its nature an opportunity to focus on specific and targeted challenges. Solutions would then not only be found through a traditional water sector approach but through an integrated approach combining the expert fields of water and diplomacy.
- Peacebuilding interventions to prevent, transform, manage or resolve conflict must be flexible and able to adapt to a changing political context. Using the analytical tools developed for water diplomacy in an iterative way, analysing the situation on the ground with subsequent redesign of interventions, water diplomacy programmes can integrate lessons learnt and address windows of opportunity.
- Different diplomacy tracks can complement each other and coordination between tracks improves efficiency and effectiveness. Official and non-official tracks have distinct and unique roles and if efforts are combined the different actors can make complementary contributions. Interventions by third parties could also benefit from the sharing of information about analysis, coordination and sequencing of interventions by different actors. A closer cooperation between academics, diplomats and water practitioners would be a way to ensure appropriate design and implementation of water diplomacy interventions.

Water diplomacy in practice

There are a number of strategies, approaches and tools that fall under the umbrella of water diplomacy. One interesting strategy is the engagement of third parties as facilitators, and sometimes also as mediators, in water diplomacy processes. The third parties engaged can typically be representatives from non-riparian governments, policy institutes or NGOs and are commonly engaged to arrange meetings, set agendas and guide discussions, and/or to facilitate the development of legal, technical and financial instruments to reduce the perceived risk of cooperation. Such parties can also play a role in bridging the development and foreign policy domains by informing and involving different actors in joint dialogues. This can be achieved through activities identified and designed based on the in-depth analysis of a specific situation, and the needs articulated by the different actors and stakeholders in a basin.

Some examples of water diplomacy activities include:

- Knowledge and skills expansion: tailor-made activities would aim at providing basin actors with specific knowledge needed to enable them to constructively contribute to dialogue and cooperation. Such knowledge could, for example, include water governance options, application of international water law, benefits of cooperation, and technical issues such as management options for hydropower dams, and also skills to support constructive negotiations and dispute resolution.
- Joint fact finding: it is not unusual that perceptions rather than facts drive the discourse in conflict-affected basins. It would therefore be important to ensure that knowledge is shared among basin stakeholders and that dialogue is based on agreed knowledge. For example, access to good hydrological data is essential to develop a shared view of the challenges and opportunities and to create the foundation for evidence-based decision making.
- Dialogue among riparians at different levels: water diplomacy can promote the exchange of perspectives among riparian parties, clarify divergent views and the reasons for those views, and try to get parties to develop a common understanding of the situation, contribute to humanizing conflict parties and serve as a confidence-building measure. Dialogue opportunities can also serve to identify capacity gaps, identify concrete opportunities for continued engagement and over time to identify solutions which satisfy the interests of all parties.

Key elements of water diplomacy

In addition to the characteristics of water diplomacy described above there are other key elements to successful water diplomacy approaches. Three key issues to consider in the design of water diplomacy interventions would be: i) inclusion of stakeholders, ii) transboundary water governance structures, and iii) principles of international water law.

Inclusion of stakeholders

To achieve sustainable results, peacebuilding activities need to consider political, social as well as structural aspects and hence encompass several levels of actors and institutions (Notter and Diamond 1996). In many cases the focus on peacebuilding activities is limited to government actors, with the risk that the affected population does not approve the agreements made at central level. The same could be said for many programmes aimed at supporting transboundary cooperation. In cases of protracted conflicts or disagreements the conflicts have become deep-rooted and become part of the social system and to change such patterns many parts of the system need to be engaged in a process of transformation. In some situations, shared water resources can open up an avenue for more sustainable peace through inclusion and engagement of different parts of the system, including grassroots, in dialogues aimed at identification of shared concerns and benefits that can be drawn from cooperation around the shared water source. Successful water diplomacy efforts would hence work at different levels involving a multitude of actors such as political leaders, academics, political advisers, parliamentarians, journalists and water user associations. Track two diplomacy can hence serve to complement track one diplomacy in water-related conflicts by involving grassroots and middle leadership who are in direct contact with the conflict, giving them a platform to air views and ideas on solutions to conflicts (Mapendere 2005).

An example of the potential benefits of engagement of stakeholders can be taken from the Mekong basin, where a survey and interviews done with stakeholders show that they perceive that their livelihoods are threatened by large infrastructure and that they are unsatisfied with their opportunities to get involved in the transboundary dialogue and decision making that takes place at government level and within the Mekong River Commission (SIWI 2016). The stakeholders are seeking to strengthen their involvement by establishing a Multi-Stakeholder Platform, with the expectation that this platform would bring in important peacebuilding aspects including:

- the development of a shared vision among countries and stakeholders;
- adding regional level perspectives to national level consultations;
- identification and promotion of shared benefits that can be achieved through cooperative approaches;
- bringing in high quality information – for science and policy to inform each other and for joint learning; and
- reconciliation of conflictual conservation and development agendas.

Governance structures

Experience has shown that institutional capacity for dialogue and management of disputes is an important factor in predicting conflict (Wolf 2007). Wolf concludes that "the likelihood of conflict rises as the rate of change within the basin exceeds the institutional capacity to absorb that change", defining institutional capacity as water management bodies or treaties, or generally positive international relations. Hence, very rapid changes that cannot be managed by the existing institutional capacity are at the root of most water conflicts. An example is the rapid institutional change of water resources management occurring when states are becoming independent. This has resulted in disputes in the Nile, Jordan, Tigris–Euphrates, Indus, and Ganges–Brahmaputra river basins. On the physical side, rapid change often includes the construction of large dams for hydropower and irrigation that can lead to conflict if decisions are taken unilaterally in the absence of cooperative regimes.

The establishment of River Basin Organizations (RBOs) can be an important measure to create sustainable structures that promote cooperation and peacebuilding. RBOs can lay the ground for improved governance systems of shared basins by providing technical capacity and by providing platforms for dialogue and decision making based on shared knowledge. Ideally the governance structure should also provide for the involvement of different stakeholders in the dialogue and decision making. However, the reality is that the engagement of stakeholders in transboundary water management is an area that has so far achieved limited attention by many

RBOs. However, the establishment of institutional frameworks for cooperation meets several challenges. Schmeier (2013) has identified that only 116 (of the 286) shared watercourses are covered by RBOs. The mere existence of an RBO, however, does not guarantee sustainable management of a river basin. An RBO can come in many different formats and with many different mandates that deal with a variety of different collective action problems. Some RBOs succeed in managing the watercourse in a sustainable and equitable way while others fail.

A serious challenge in establishing collaborative governance structures is that hydro-hegemons frequently choose not to be a member of cooperative multilateral basin fora, preferring to deal with riparian partners individually on a bilateral basis. For example, China is not part of the Mekong River Commission (MRC), although it is a key riparian in the Mekong river basin and Egypt has frozen its cooperation with the Nile Basin Initiative since 2011. In situations where not all riparians are included in the River Basin Organization, these governance structures have a limited impact on basin-wide development. Furthermore, RBOs often focus mainly on technical issues and have a limited mandate to intervene in the political track of cooperation.

International water law

International Water Law (IWL) has gradually evolved since the adoption of the 'Helsinki Rules on the Uses of International Rivers', by the International Law Association in 1966. The rules covered drainage basins and included issues related to pollution, navigation, timber floating and dispute prevention procedures. They introduced equity criteria for shared use of the river basin. The Helsinki rules have been followed by a number of important instruments to promote equitable, sustainable and integrated management of transboundary water resources, namely: the 1997 UN *Convention on the Law of the Non-Navigational Uses of International Watercourses*; the 1992 UN Economic Commission for Europe *Convention on the Protection and Use of Transboundary Watercourses and International Lakes* (amended in 2003 to allow all states to join); and the 2008 UN International Law Commission (ILC*) Draft Articles on the Law of Transboundary Aquifers.*

The 1997 UN Watercourses Convention is the one most often referred to internationally in contexts of water disputes and sets out norms for cooperation and sensible ways to resolve tensions. The key principles of the Convention serve as good reference points for dialogue on principles of cooperation and include: i) equitable and reasonable utilization of shared watercourses, ii) an obligation not to cause significant harm, iii) the general obligation to cooperate, iv) regular exchange of data and information, v) the principle of prior notification of planned measures that may have significant adverse effects on another riparian, vi) provisions on the protection and preservation of international watercourses, and vii) peaceful settlement of disputes (Rieu-Clarke 2017).

The UN Watercourses Convention was elaborated over a long time trying to interpret and codify customary law (McCaffrey 2008). In that sense, the historic evolution of the Convention differs from more modern multiparty environmental treaties, for example on climate change, which are negotiated by an intergovernmental negotiating committee where power politics is an integral part of the initial negotiation process. The Convention was signed by 103 countries at the United Nations General Assembly in May 1997 with three countries voting against it (Burundi, China and Turkey). However, it only entered into force in August 2014 after the required 35 countries had formally joined the Convention.

International Water Law provides important frameworks for water diplomacy in that it establishes key principles of cooperation and could institutionalize water law globally. The principles of equitable and reasonable utilization and no significant harm limit the territorial sovereignty and could also be said to be a tool that can contribute to countering hydro-hegemonic approaches (Farnum, Hawkins and Tamarin 2017).

There are however shortcomings with the UN Convention on International Water Law as it has only been ratified by about one-fifth of the world's countries, not including any hydro-hegemon on a water-scarce basin. It also has a clause that prevents its retroactive application to existing international treaties on water bodies and has no Conference of the Parties to ensure that it becomes a living treaty. Nevertheless, it is not unimaginable that with an appropriate follow-up to this Convention, it could be converted into a stronger framework convention in the future.

Conclusion

This chapter sheds light on the challenges and opportunities of water diplomacy. Although wars over water are uncommon, disagreements and conflicts over the allocation and use of transboundary water resources are common. The interaction between riparian states is highly influenced by power imbalances and often conflict and cooperation occur simultaneously. The impact of power structures and the broader political context often receive insufficient attention in the design of transboundary water programmes, and a reason for this is the divide between the policy domains of development and security in government structures. Well-designed water diplomacy approaches can serve to bridge the gap and provide opportunities to practically connect the two policy domains. A focus on transboundary water sources in conflict-affected regions offers exciting opportunities to combine the expert fields of water and diplomacy and to engage different tracks of diplomacy for effective and sustainable peacebuilding.

The chapter further points out the importance of in-depth understanding of the political economy in a specific river basin in the design of efforts to promote transboundary water management. It briefly describes a few analytical tools developed to be used in transboundary water contexts. Experiences from peacebuilding programmes outside the water sector are useful in designing water diplomacy efforts. A focus on finding solutions to specific problems, rather than aiming for across-the-board improvements in one sector, and ensuring flexibility to adapt to a changing political context have shown to be useful approaches. Other key elements to consider in promoting transboundary water cooperation are: the principles elaborated in international water law that can provide a framework for dialogue, the role of shared governance structures, as well as the opportunities provided through the inclusion of different parts of the water governance system, including grassroots.

Taking into consideration that the majority of countries involved in conflict share water resources with one or more neighbouring nations, there is plenty of room to further explore the opportunities that water diplomacy and cooperative management of transboundary waters offer in peacebuilding agendas. An aspect that is not included in this chapter is the human behavioural dimension and factors influencing decisions by individuals engaged in inter-state negotiations on water allocation and management. This is a research area that deserves more attention and that can help shed further light on how to reach peaceful cooperation on transboundary waters.

References

Allan, J. A. (1998) "Virtual water: a strategic resource" *Ground Water* 36(4):545.

Allan, J. A. (2003) "Virtual water eliminates water wars? A case study from the Middle East" in Hoekstra, A. (ed.) *Virtual Water Trade: Proceedings of the International Expert Meeting on Virtual Water Trade. Delft, the Netherlands, 12–13 December 2002*. Research Report Series No. 12. Delft: IHE, 137–145.

Böhmelt, T. (2010) "The effectiveness of tracks of diplomacy strategies in third-party interventions" *Journal of Peace Research* 47(2):167–178.

Council of the European Union (2013) "Council conclusions on EU water diplomacy" Foreign Affairs Council meeting Brussels, 22 July.

Farnum, R. L., Hawkins, S., and Tamarin, M. (2017) "Hydro-hegemons and international water law" in Rieu-Clarke, A., Allan, A., and Henry, S. (eds.) *Routledge Handbook of Water Law and Policy* Routledge, London, 297–310.

Fisher, R. J. (2006) "Coordination between track two and track one diplomacy in successful cases of pre-negotiation" *International Negotiation* 11: 65–89.

Independent Commission for Aid Impact (ICAI) (2015) "Assessing the impact of the scale-up of DFID's support to fragile states" Report 40, London.

Islam, S. and Susskind, L. (2012) *Water Diplomacy: A Negotiated Approach to Managing Complex Water Networks* Routledge, New York.

McCaffrey, S. C. (2008) *The 1997 UN Watercourses Convention: Retrospect and Prospect* Scholarly Article, Pacific McGeorge School of Lae.

Mapendere, J. (2005) "Track one and a half diplomacy and the complementarity of tracks" *Culture of Peace Online Journal* 2(1):66–81.

Mobjörk, M., Gustafsson, M-T., Sonnsjö, H., van Baalen, S., Dellmuth, L.M., and Bremberg, N. (2016) *Climate-related Security Risks – Towards an Integrated Approach* SIPRI, Stockholm.

Montville, J. (1991) "Track two diplomacy: the arrow and the olive branch: a case for track two diplomacy" in Volkan, V. D., Montville, J., and Julius, D. A. (eds.) *The Psychodynamics of International Relations: Vol. 2. Unofficial Diplomacy at Work* Lexington Books, Lexington, MA, 193–204.

Notter, J. and Diamond, L. (1996) "Building peace and transforming conflict: multi-track diplomacy in practice", Occasional Paper Number 7, October, Institute for Multi-Track Diplomacy, Arlington, VA.

Rieu-Clarke, A. (2017) "The treaty architecture for the governance of transboundary aquifers, lakes and rivers" in Rieu-Clarke, A., Allan, A., and Henry, S. (eds.) *Routledge Handbook of Water Law and Policy* Routledge, London, 193–204.

Schmeier, S. (2013) *Governing International Watercourses. The Contribution of River Basin Organizations to the Effective Governance of Internationally Shared Rivers and Lakes* Routledge, Abingdon.

Stockholm International Water Institute (SIWI) (2016) "Stakeholder mapping for a regional multi-stakeholder platform for the Mekong River Basin", unpublished report, SIWI, Stockholm.

United Nations (UN) (2011) *Preventive Diplomacy: Delivering Results*, Report of the Secretary General, S/2011/552, 26 August.

U.S. Energy Information Administration (USEIA) (2016) International Energy Outlook 2016, DOE/EIA-0484. Available at: www.eia.gov/outlooks/ieo/pdf/0484%282016%29.pdf

Wolf, A. (2005) Transboundary Freshwater Dispute Database, Oregon State University, www.transboundarywaters.orst.edu/

Wolf, A. (2007) "Shared waters: conflict and cooperation" *Annual Review of Environment and Resources* 32:241–269.

World Bank (2017) "Political Economy Analysis for Transboundary Water Resources Management in Africa: Practical Guidance" World Bank, Washington, DC.

Zeitoun, M. (2017) "Water and war" *Helsinki Times*, 16 March. Available at: www.helsinkitimes.fi/columns/columns/viewpoint/14615-water-and-war.html

Zeitoun, M. and Warner, J. (2006) "Hydro-hegemony – A framework for analysis of trans-boundary water conflicts" *Water Policy* 8(5):435–460.

Zeitoun, M. and Mirumachi, N. (2008) "Transboundary water interaction I: Reconsidering conflict and cooperation" *International Environmental Agreements* (8):297–316.

21

Climate diplomacy and peace

Dennis Tänzler

Introduction: climate diplomacy – more than international negotiations

The Paris Agreement reached at the COP21 in December 2015 is a landmark climate agreement – and the successful culmination of years of complex negotiations. Diplomats were able to break the long-standing divide between developed and developing countries by building a coalition that agrees that it is really time to aim at high ambition. The agreement is considered unique for its ambition to keep global warming well below 2 degrees Celsius compared to pre-industrial levels, its inclusiveness, its transparency requirements, and the fact that each country will own and be held accountable for their own climate targets. The agreement is also the result of a long-lasting process that collapsed in 2009 during the climate conference in Copenhagen. This slow progress in further developing the international climate regime convinced diplomats after 2009 that urgent action is needed that complements and stretches beyond international climate negotiations. So it was no surprise after the Copenhagen failure that climate change has gained increasing prominence among foreign policy makers and diplomats (Tänzler and Carius 2012).

In part this can be explained by the fact that climate change represents a vital challenge for international politics. Flooding, droughts, a shift of climate zones, and increasingly frequent and intense extreme weather hazards will have serious economic and social consequences for entire regions. In addition, there is a broad consensus that countries with low adaptation capacities will be hit the hardest, among them many of the so-called fragile states (Corendea et al. 2012). This also led the G7 foreign ministers to ask in 2013 "do we need a new climate for peace?" and they commissioned a study on climate-fragility risks and how to deal with them (Rüttinger et al. 2015).

Already, starting in 2007, a number of analyses have revealed a growing potential for conflict and an increase in social tension as a result of the impending changes in the climate (Campbell et al. 2007). Conflicts may arise as a result of water and food shortages, caused in turn by an increase in extreme weather events and climate change-induced mass migration. Weak and fragile states are considered particularly vulnerable because of their already limited political capacities. The main assumption is that a further weakening of the key services provided by the public sector is likely to lead to national and regional destabilization, with societal and political tensions potentially developing into violent conflict. Seen in this light, it is not surprising that the foreign policy community has been concerned about the slow progress of the international climate negotiations and welcomed the outcome of the Paris conference (Wolters et al. 2016).

However, the role of foreign policies in a changing climate is complex. When assessing whether there will be an increase of violent conflicts related to the distribution of natural resources such as water and land, we should avoid a one-dimensional causal explanation (Harris 2012). Possible conflicts will not be caused by climate change alone; rather climate change is seen as a factor that multiplies the deficits in other areas such as poverty, a lack of rule of law, and social and economic injustice (WBGU 2007; Carius et al. 2008). In addition, a worsening of conflict situations as a result of climate change is only one possible pathway. Another is the peaceful avoidance of new conflict situations through early action and cooperation. The latter interpretation is based on research findings about how environmental cooperation toward common challenges could support confidence-building between former antagonists and support peace-building efforts (Conca and Dabelko 2002; UNEP 2009).

This constellation opens a different entry point for climate diplomacy to contribute to peace and to promote a stronger foreign policy engagement. In other words, not only an appropriate reflection of potential security-related impacts of climate change is needed, but also appropriate policy measures timely enough to avoid, in the worst case, a further destabilization of already weak or fragile states. It seems to be more than obvious that such approaches must go beyond traditional climate policy as we have known it for some time.

By encompassing the full range of available policies, including development cooperation, conflict prevention, and humanitarian assistance, as well as climate change adaptation and mitigation, a new profile of climate diplomacy is evolving. This new profile most likely requires new strategic alliances beyond the conference halls of Copenhagen, Paris, or Marrakesh. In the following we describe the major risks associated with climate change and fragility to illustrate the scope of the challenge. We then discuss selected political processes on climate change, international security and foreign policies initiated in recent years. These processes can illustrate the importance of moving from risk analysis to preventive action and how to integrate climate change concerns into development, foreign, and security policies.

Peace and climate diplomacy – conceptual reflections

The interrelationship between climate, peace, and stability has been subject to a number of reports and studies. "A New Climate for Peace: Taking Action on Climate and Fragility Risks" (Rüttinger et al. 2015), an independent report commissioned by members of the G7 foreign ministries and published in 2015 aimed at a comprehensive reflection on already ongoing or potential climate change-related impacts on conflict-prone settings. Overall the report identified seven compound climate-fragility risks that pose serious threats to peace and stability of states and societies. These compound risks reach from the local to the international level and are often overlapping.[1]

Climate change can increase local resource competition: As the pressure on natural resources increases at the local level, competition can lead to instability and even violent conflict in the absence of effective dispute resolution. The resource competition will be influenced on the one hand by reduced access to natural resources, particularly water and arable land. On the other hand, resource demand is increasing in areas with growing populations and rapid economic development. This competition is likely to be particularly disruptive in regions that rely on a narrow resource base, have a history of conflict, or are home to marginalized groups. Among the examples are conflicts at the local level in Afghanistan, Egypt, Haiti, and Tajikistan (ibid.:16–25).

Climate change can trigger livelihood insecurity and migration: Climate change is likely to increase the human insecurity of people who depend on natural resources for their livelihoods. This could push them to migrate or turn to illegal sources of income. People who depend directly on natural resources will find their livelihoods endangered by the impacts of climate change because of reductions of grazing land, drying up of water sources, and threatening of jobs connected to climate-sensitive economic sectors. These changes can combine with other problems such as unequal land distribution, insecure land tenure, poorly developed markets, trade barriers, and inadequate infrastructure to push populations to seek alternative livelihoods. Some will move to urban areas that already suffer from high levels of unemployment and poor living conditions, while others may be forced to turn to more informal or illegal sources of income. Examples could be found in Mali, Syria, Sierra Leone, among others (ibid.:30–32).

Climate change is likely to intensify the challenge of extreme weather events and disasters: Extreme weather events can exacerbate fragility challenges and can increase people's vulnerability and grievances, especially in conflict-affected situations. The relationship between disasters and fragility is often mutually reinforcing: Disasters put additional stress on already stretched governance systems, decrease economic opportunities, reduce resources, and displace people. A lack of safety nets, preparedness, insurance mechanisms, and other methods to cope with the impacts of disasters can fuel grievances, especially if government or international assistance is inadequate or inequitably distributed. Cases from Thailand, Sri Lanka, Indonesia, and Pakistan offer some empirical insights on this compound risk (ibid.:38–41).

Climate change is highly likely to disrupt food production in many regions due to decreases in yields. As a result there is the risk of increasing prices and market volatility, and heightening the risk of protests, rioting, and civil conflict. Combined with increasing global pressures – including population growth and changing energy demands – food insecurity is likely to increase and food prices to become more volatile. As exemplified by the 2007–2009 food riots in more than 40 countries, food price volatility and high prices can increase the risk of public unrest, democratic breakdown, and civil and local conflict, particularly when combined with poverty, poor governance, and a weak social contract. States that depend on food imports and spend a significant proportion of household income on food are particularly vulnerable. Examples in the Middle East or in Myanmar illustrate the complex interrelationship between increasing scarcity, higher demand, and price volatility (ibid.:48–50).

Climate change can increase the tensions on transboundary water management: Water is frequently a source of tension; as demand grows and climate impacts affect availability, increased competition over water use will likely increase the pressure on existing governance structures. Many transboundary water basins are located in regions with a history of armed conflict and significant interstate tensions. Though historically, armed conflicts between states over water are nearly unprecedented, the future may not look like the past. Competition over water use will likely increase. Managing the effects of climate change on water resource use will be particularly complicated in transboundary basins affected by fragility or conflict, where water management is often eclipsed by political considerations or affected by power asymmetries. The Nile and the Indus River basin are only two examples where climate change is likely to have profound impacts on the political economy of the region (ibid.:56–57).

Climate change can lead to significant sea-level rise and coastal degradation: Rising sea levels already threaten the economic and physical viability of low-lying areas. As land and coastal resources are gradually lost, the economic viability of many coastal areas will significantly decrease; damage from cyclones and storm surges will become more severe; and the risk of future land and resource loss will become more pressing. These changes may displace people or push them to migrate, which also increases the risks of tension and conflict in the receiving areas. As seas rise, changing coastlines may also alter border demarcations and trigger disputes over maritime boundaries, territorial seas, sea lanes, and ocean resources. Kiribati and other small island states are important examples where already today significant impacts of sea-level rise become visible. In addition, countries with low-lying coastlines like Bangladesh face major challenges (ibid.:61–63).

Additional risks due to unintended effects of climate policies: The seventh risk complex identified by "A New Climate for Peace" is already shifting the focus to the response side. As climate adaptation and mitigation policies are more broadly implemented, the risks of unintended negative effects – particularly in fragile contexts – will also increase. If designed and implemented without considering broader impacts, even well-intentioned climate change policies could undermine economic development, contribute to political instability, and exacerbate human insecurity. In fragile situations, the unintended consequences may include increased insecurity of land tenure, marginalization of minority groups, increased environmental degradation and loss of biodiversity, and accelerated climate change (Tänzler and Ries 2012; Tänzler et al. 2013).

We already know from the environmental security literature that equitable and effective natural resource management can help reduce tensions and prevent environmental change from being a major driver of increased competition over limited resources which escalates into violence. A peace-promoting effect of climate policy is also one of the potential pathways into the future. Ambitious climate mitigation can reduce the overall risks of unmanageable climate change. Climate change adaptation holds a great potential to strengthen resilience and to offer alternative livelihoods. In addition, disaster risk reduction and effective disaster management efforts can provide opportunities to improve resilience to climate-fragility risks and build peace. One of the prerequisites is, however, to consider the cross-sectoral nature of responding to the climate and disaster risk challenges and to apply conflict-sensitive policy approaches.

In addition, decision makers need to avoid a one-dimensional cause–effect relationship which becomes clear, for example, with respect to the debate on climate and migration. Climate change will alter both existing migration patterns and an increasing number of people are likely to move. While the increased movement of people driven by climate change impacts could, if migration and resettlement are poorly managed, lead to local and regional instability, migration is also a traditional way to cope with climate stress. In other words, migration is an adaptation strategy and deserves more attention from the adaptation community and less a framing as a security issue.

Selected initiatives and approaches related to climate and peace

During the last decade, a number of processes have been initiated to address the challenges of climate change and peace. The UN took the climate change issue seriously right after its appearance on the international agenda. The United Nations Framework Convention on Climate Change (UNFCCC) from 1992 as well as the Kyoto Protocol from 1997 have been highly influential in establishing a portfolio of policy innovations worldwide to mitigate greenhouse gas emissions and to adapt to unavoidable climate changes. However, an increasingly complex and slow process of international negotiations and the collapse of the Copenhagen climate conference in 2009 caused some concerns that the UNFCCC cannot achieve its main objective according to Article 2, namely to avoid dangerous climate change. This is especially understandable from a perspective of Small Island States as well as other Least Developing Countries (LDCs) with low-lying coastlines like Bangladesh that are already today witnessing the severe impacts of climate change.[2] With the Paris Agreement of 2015 a major normative framework for ambitious climate policy was established. However, not only because of the announced intention in June 2017 of US withdrawal from the Paris Agreement, there are still major concerns that the ambition level will be insufficient to avoid dangerous climate change and that further activities are needed to encourage the international climate community to take more decisive steps – e.g. as part of the G20 (Li et al. 2016).

As a result, the issue of climate security has also gained increasing attention in recent years in other UN fora. In 2007, the UN Security Council held a first debate on the impact of climate change on global peace and security. The discussions among UN member states revealed broad uncertainty regarding the question of an appropriate international framework for action on responding to the security risks of climate change. The General Assembly of the UN on 3 June 2009 adopted a resolution on "Climate change and its possible security implications" (A/63/281), which was proposed by the Pacific Small Island Developing States (UN General Assembly 2009). The resolution was adopted by a consensus and 101 states supported it. For the first time in the history of the UN, the United States co-sponsored a climate-protection resolution. The resolution urged the UN bodies to strengthen their efforts to combat climate change and to avoid intensifying potential security risks. This was also the first time that a UN resolution established a direct link between climate change and international peace and security.

On the basis of 35 contributions from member states and relevant regional and international organizations, the UN Committee for Economic and Social Affairs published a comprehensive report in September 2009 (United Nations Secretary-General 2009). The report defined "security" in a broader sense, where vulnerable individuals and communities are the primary concern and security is understood in terms of protection from a range of threats, i.e. disease, unemployment, political repression, disasters, and violence. It further acknowledged that the security of individuals and communities was important in shaping the security of nation states, which is typically framed in terms of threats of external aggression. The most important aspect of this report was the strong focus on potential threat minimizers such as climate mitigation and adaptation, economic development, democratic governance and strong institutions, international cooperation, and preventive diplomacy and mediation. In addition, it highlighted the importance of timely availability of information and increased support for research and analysis in order to improve the understanding of links between climate change and security and to build up early warning capacities.

Despite the clear mandate of the report, it only received minor attention as reference for further activities. It took until July 2011, when the German government, under its Security Council presidency, brought the topic of climate change and security again on to the agenda of high-level discussions – the UN Security Council. The open debate in the Council resulted in a presidential statement not only confirming the concern of climate change affecting security but also asking for a systematic and regular review of and reporting by the UN Secretary-General to the UN Security Council on the likely security implications of climate change (United Nations Security Council 2011). This result is remarkable since Russia, China, and several countries among the G77 expressed their concerns about linking climate change to security.[3] The unanimous adoption of the Presidential Statement on climate change and security at the Security Council meeting of 20 July, however, has lent new momentum to the debate on a renewed climate diplomacy spirit at international level – in particular because also the UNFCCC was endorsed as the major UN forum to discuss comprehensive climate policy actions by all participating representatives.

In the aftermath of the Security Council meeting, not only has the German government taken further initiatives to design preventive climate diplomacy but the United Kingdom and other governments are also involved in further establishing climate change as a key issue of foreign policies (Thölken and Börner 2012). In addition, the UN Security Council has repeatedly covered the issue – most recently in March 2017. Overall, the discussions in the Security Council have mainly served as important awareness-raising instruments.

An early approach to address the potential security implications of climate change was initiated by the European Union. Under the 2007 German EU Presidency, the European Council and the European Commission were asked to prepare a joint paper on climate change and international security. The respective report, published in March 2008, summarized potential security risks associated with climate change (High Representative/European Commission 2008). Broadly, climate change has the potential of becoming a "threat multiplier," exacerbating existing tensions and potentially creating new ones over time. Among the main security-relevant threats of climate change that the EU identified were conflicts over depleting resources such as water and food, and the economic damage and risks caused by an increase in sea levels and in the strength and frequency of extreme weather events. According to the paper, situations of fragility and radicalization may become exacerbated due to the amount of environmental stress and a lack of coping capacity.

Against the backdrop of these risks, the Council stated in its conclusions from December 2009 that climate change and its international security implications are part of the wider EU agenda for climate, energy, and its Common Foreign and Security Policy (Council of the European Union 2009). It stressed the need to strengthen the EU's comprehensive efforts to reduce emissions as one aspect of conflict prevention. In the aftermath of the Council Conclusions, the main focus of the EU's activities has been directed to enhance EU capacities for early warning on one hand and to foster international cooperation with the aim of creating dialogue and a common awareness in relevant international fora, including the United Nations, on the other. However, due to the establishment process of the European External Action Service (EEAS) the initiatives to address climate change and security have only progressed very slowly.

In July 2011, the EEAS and the services of the Commission presented a conceptual outline of what should be considered as a climate diplomacy blueprint (EEAS/Services of the Commission 2011). Most importantly, the Joint Reflection Paper outlined three strands for action on EU climate diplomacy: the promotion of ambitious climate action, the support of implementation of climate policies and measures, and activities in the area of climate change and international security. Thirteen recommendations were outlined in the paper, such as, for example, to strengthen the capacities of the EEAS to report on climate change-related developments in priority partner countries. In addition, by suggesting climate action be mainstreamed in the multi-annual country and regional strategy papers, long-term processes should be initiated that may help to make climate change a cross-cutting issue on the EU foreign affairs agendas.

In principle, the approach of the EEAS can be interpreted as building a bridge between further improving the early warning capacities on climate change-related security threats and the diplomatic efforts needed to contribute to a global negotiation deal. The implementation of these recommendations still waits for an evaluation. However, it is fair to say that the ability of the EU and its member states to forge common messages and speak with one voice, including through the Green Diplomacy Network, played a key role in making European climate diplomacy a success in the lead-up to COP21 in Paris. They were able to mobilize diplomatic networks to broaden COP21 preparations, from technical negotiations to high-level political dialogue to public diplomacy efforts. The shared European message was strong, highly visible, and contributed to building a spirit of compromise across the entire UNFCCC process (Wolters et al. 2016).

With respect to the future, EU climate diplomacy can build on this significant political capital to make sure the foundations laid with the Paris Agreement turn into a true success story. This will require continued intensive and inclusive dialogue to maintain the momentum, help build capacities, and further the integration of climate change into development and energy policies. Right after the Paris conference, the Foreign Affairs Council of February 2016 indicated the importance of a proactive climate diplomacy agenda. The Council recognized the need for prolonged engagement, encouraged keeping climate change and implementation of the Paris Agreement as a strategic priority, and called for increased action to address the climate–security nexus. One outstanding example in this regard is the decision by the European Commission initiated together with UNEP in 2015 for a multi-year project to address the issue of adaptation in conflict-prone areas.

Finally, the G7 process on climate change and fragility needs to be mentioned. The Group of 7 (G7) has recognized the resulting challenges for sustainable economic development, peace, and stability. As a follow-up to the independent "New Climate for Peace" report (Rüttinger et al. 2015) mentioned above, the G7 foreign ministers established a working group on climate change and fragility. The working group met under German and Japanese G7 presidency with integrated risk assessments as a first focus area. To this end, in January 2017, the Ministry of Foreign Affairs of Japan hosted a roundtable seminar with international experts and country representatives to follow up on G7 efforts to address climate-fragility risks. As a next step, the working group is considering making Lake Chad the focus of a program to support preventive diplomacy in the light of major climate-fragility risks in this region.

Conclusions: towards a multi-level strategy on climate diplomacy

The UN, the EU, and also most recently the G7 have made some progress to describe how to address conceptually the challenges of climate change and peace. This can help to support international climate negotiations but also to strengthen peace and crisis prevention capacities. The definition of available threat minimizers as outlined by the UN Secretary-General from 2009 in principle opened the door to move from the stage of risk analysis to one of policy formulation and implementation, for which the parallel processes on this issue at the UN, G7, and EU levels can be used. These processes offer other governments the opportunity to engage in processes of strategy formulation as to how to deal with this challenge of climate security using different instruments of diplomacy. Again, this will hardly be solely a matter of international climate negotiations but requires the involvement of a broad spectrum of partners. In the following, we outline potential key areas of climate diplomacy that may deserve further examination which are in principle in line with the elements of the Paris Agreement but that aim at promoting integration of the climate and other agendas, especially the development, humanitarian, and crisis prevention ones.

Building transformative pathways

The concept of a low-carbon emission pathway is also relevant for the climate and peace debate because it aims to address different political key priorities: climate protection, energy security, and economic and social development. Comprehensive activities to mitigate greenhouse gas emissions in industrialized and developing countries are also needed to limit the risk of climate-induced conflicts and allow the global economy to shift towards lower emissions. Such transformative pathways should not only ensure compliance to ambitious climate change targets but also support sustainable growth and the creation of new employment opportunities. These co-benefits are also at the heart of two of the key instruments to support the implementation of the Paris Agreement. On the one hand, the Nationally Determined Contributions (NDCs) serve as the basis of the Paris Agreement and, on the other hand, there is the prominent role of the Green Climate Fund (GCF) established after the 2009 Copenhagen conference but fully operational only since 2015. The NDCs submitted by nearly all countries under the UNFCCC illustrate how countries intend to align climate priorities (mitigation and adaptation) with other national priorities. During the upcoming process of updating the NDC every five years it will be more and more important to outline the transformative pathway needed to ensure a low-carbon and climate-resilient development. This overall objective cannot be achieved without considering the importance of overall peace and security of a country. Those countries developing and submitting proposals to the GCF are asked to describe what kind of co-benefits a project will have – for example with respect to creating additional income opportunities. Overall, the projects under the GCF should contribute to transformative change and here is where also a debate on peace and security comes in.

The expansion of renewable energies is already today an important element of debates within the security and defense community: a major starting point to this end was the 2010 report by the Center for Naval Analyses (CNA) which outlined the potential opportunities for US national security that could result from the transition to a clean energy technology-based economy. According to the authors, innovation and commercialization of clean, low-carbon energy will directly contribute to America's future economic competitiveness and bolster national security (CNA 2010). Thus, well-designed mitigation policies have the potential to link climate protection, development, and conflict prevention to serve together as threat minimizers. To this end, however, some of the key mitigation questions need to be answered, e.g. how will mitigation efforts be distributed among the different countries, above all with respect to the key emitters? How can poorer countries be supported to link technological progress in strategic key areas such as energy supply, infrastructure development, or transportation with a low-carbon development pathway? The development of sustainable energy options is especially important to avoid locking in high-carbon technologies while the demand for energy rises and in turn often leads to costly energy import dependency. In addition, decentralized grids are likely to offer co-benefits between sustainable energy production and improved access to energy. The impact of mitigation policies will vary significantly by country due to varying sectoral composition, such as the energy supply or transportation infrastructures. Accordingly, there is no silver bullet but ongoing consultations are needed, not least on how to involve the private sector.

Designing conflict-sensitive climate policies

The discussion about appropriate policy frameworks is of strategic value and the development of low-carbon growth strategies needs further guidance and international cooperation. One possible option to support countries entering such a strategic discourse is to use the revenues generated from auctioning emission permits in carbon-trading programs or, more generally, as a result of any kind of carbon pricing approach. At the same time, a conflict-sensitive approach requires that international donors and recipient countries ensure funding is spent transparently and effectively to avoid the increasing of governance deficits such as corruption.

Apart from the energy sector, land use and forest protection have received increasing attention and can serve as an example how climate mitigation may be linked to development and stability. Efforts to systemically address the cost-effective emission reduction potentials in the forest sector have led to various approaches to conceptualize REDD+, a UN initiative to reduce emissions from deforestation and forest degradation. REDD+ can, in principle, contribute to economic recovery by generating new sources of income in the forest sector for often marginalized social groups. Depending on the concrete design of benefit-sharing agreements, central governments as well as local communities can receive income and use it, e.g. for building infrastructures and services. Additional employment opportunities may also be created for forest monitoring and law enforcement. However, whether sustainable forest management and extractive logging is compatible with REDD regulations will only be seen after a final agreement related to the overall relevance of REDD+ for international climate policy. In addition, implementation of REDD requires excellent governance capacities. Governments, communities, and project implementers need to develop sound concepts and implementation capacities to address the drivers of deforestation. When it comes to compliance with emission reduction commitments, countries need to provide the enforcement of forest protection (e.g. curb illegal logging) and build up sufficient capacities for measurement, reporting, and verification of their commitments. Last, but not least, sophisticated benefit-sharing mechanisms are needed in order to avoid conflicts on the national and local levels concerning the distribution of revenues generated through any kind of REDD mechanism (Rights and Resources Initiative 2011; Tänzler and Ries 2012).

Learning to adapt

The UNFCCC defines adaptation as "adjustment in natural or human systems in response to actual or expected climatic stimuli or their effects, which moderates harm or exploits beneficial opportunities." Seen through a more political lens, adaptation requires empowering people, securing their livelihoods, and building institutions to strengthen their resilience. Adaptation will require both effective local action and national and regional coordination for the design and implementation of appropriate action. To this end, international cooperation is needed, especially in the case of the most vulnerable developing countries, to provide for adequate resources (Tänzler et al. 2010; Tänzler et al. 2013). The processes of National Action Plans for Adaptation (NAPAs) for LDCs and later on the more comprehensive approach of a National Adaptation Plan process (NAP) already indicate that adaptation is moving from the margins towards the center of international climate diplomacy. Accordingly, adaptation priorities play also a major role in many NDCs and a balanced financial support through the GCF is one of the key governance principles of the fund.

The idea of adaptation has taken center stage in the debate on the security-related implications of climate change – in part, because greenhouse gas emissions to date have already triggered irreversible global warming. Adapting to a changing environment should help avoid negative effects such as water or food scarcity and consequently also social and political tensions. Ongoing activities have already made some progress in creating strategic support for future adaptation processes – including in some conflict-prone countries. Existing adaptation activities have already made some headway due to strong focus on adaptation needs in least developed countries: 45 NAPAs for LDCs have been submitted to the UNFCCC. Of these, 21 were developed in countries considered to be states at high risk of destabilization, and 19 in countries at increased risk of destabilization at the beginning of this decade (Tänzler et al. 2010). However, there is only a slow initiation of concrete projects, which not only illustrates as yet insufficient funding but also could contribute to an increasing loss of credibility for international climate-protection measures in those countries most severely affected by climate change. The Paris Agreement and especially the GCF is about to change this situation – not least because the topics of loss and damage and climate-induced displacement are also part of the overall Paris architecture.

Not only at the international but also at the national level significant capacities are needed to strengthen resilience to climate change. A coherent implementation of adaptation measures is likely to be facilitated by an institutionalization of responsibilities. If an appropriate national authority does not exist, this not only jeopardizes the integration of adaptation measures into other development processes but also makes it extremely difficult to incorporate conflict-sensitive considerations into national planning processes. As we learn from the research on environment and security, cooperation over scarce resources, such as shared waters, harnesses a great potential to facilitate sustainable development and political stability in riparian nations as well as within countries. One key factor for success is the establishment of strong institutions such as river commissions and other transboundary institutional arrangements. Cooperation between countries with bordering watersheds has long been a focus of the international donor community. As a result, it is often possible to make use of existing structures – also to address future adaptation needs. However, the stabilizing and trust-building potential often demonstrated by transboundary cooperation in the water sector is not yet reflected prominently in existing national adaptation activities. This suggests that there is a need to more systematically link and coordinate national and regional processes to provide for climate security, which also may be facilitated by appropriate institutions.

Notes

1 See for a comprehensive analysis of the compound risks the risk analysis in Rüttinger et al. 2015.
2 See the statements of then Minister for Environment and Forests of the People's Republic of Bangladesh, Hasan Mahmud, and then Minister of State for Housing and Environment of the Maldives, Mohamed Shareef, 2012.
3 The author's own observation during the open debate of the Security Council, 20 July 2011, New York.

References

Campbell, K.M, Gulledge, J., McNeill, J.R., Podesta, J., Ogden, P., Fuerth, L., et al. (2007) *The Age of Consequences: The Foreign Policy and National Security Implications of Global Climate Change*, www.csis.org/media/csis/pubs/071105_ageofconsequences.pdf [Accessed 3 August 2017].
Carius, A., Tänzler, D., and Maas, A. (2008) *Climate Change and Security – Challenges for German Development Cooperation*, GTZ, Eschborn.
CNA (2010) *Powering America's Economy: Energy Innovation at the Crossroads of National Security Challenges*, Center for Naval Analyses, Alexandria, VA.
Conca, K. and Dabelko, G. (eds.) (2002) *Environmental Peacemaking*, Johns Hopkins University Press, Baltimore, MD.
Corendea, C., Warner, K., and Yuzva, K. (2012) *Social Vulnerability and Adaptation in Fragile States*. InterSecTions Report 11/2012, United Nations University Institute for Environment and Human Security (UNU-EHS), Bonn.
Council of the European Union (2009) *Council Conclusions on Climate Change and Security*, 2985th Foreign Affairs Council meeting, Brussels, December 8.

EEAS/Services of the Commission (2011) *Towards a Renewed and Strengthened EU Climate Diplomacy*, Joint Reflection Paper, Brussels, 9 July.

Harris, K. (2012) *Climate Change in UK Security Policy: Implications for Development Assistance?* Working Paper 342, Overseas Development Institute, London.

High Representative/European Commission (2008) *Climate Change and International Security*, Joint Paper to the European Council, Brussels.

Li, L., Melnikowa, J., and Tänzler, D. (2016) *The Climate–Energy Nexus and the G20: Compatible or Mutually Exclusive?* Climate Diplomacy Brief, Adelphi, Berlin.

Mahmud, H. (2012) "Climate Change and Security: The Challenges for Bangladesh" in Tänzler, D. and Carius, A. (eds.) *Climate Diplomacy in Perspective. From Early Warning to Early Action*, Wissenschaftsverlag, Berlin, 25–29.

Rights and Resources Initiative (2011) *The End of the Hinterland. Forests, Conflict, and Climate Change*, www.rightsandresources.org/documents/files/doc_1400.pdf. [Accessed 27 July 2017].

Rüttinger, L., Stang, G., Smith, D., Tänzler, D., Vivekananda, J., et al. (2015) *A New Climate for Peace – Taking Action on Climate and Fragility Risks*. Adelphi, International Alert, The Wilson Center, EUISS, Berlin/London/Washington/Paris.

Shareef, M. (2012) "Climate Change and Security: The Challenges for Small Island States" in Tänzler, D. and Carius, A. (eds.) *Climate Diplomacy in Perspective. From Early Warning to Early Action*, Wissenschaftsverlag, Berlin, 31–32.

Tänzler, D. and Carius, A. (eds.) (2012) *Climate Diplomacy in Perspective. From Early Warning to Early Action*, Wissenschaftsverlag, Berlin.

Tänzler, D. and Ries, F. (2012) "International Climate Change Policies: The Potential Relevance of REDD+ for Peace and Stability" in Scheffran, J., Broszka, M., Brauch, H.G., Link, P.-M., and Schilling, J. (eds.) *Climate Change, Human Security and Violent Conflict. Challenges for Societal Stability*, SpringerVerlag, Berlin, 695–706.

Tänzler, D., Maas, A., and Carius, A. (2010) "Climate Change Adaptation and Peace" *Wiley Interdisciplinary Reviews Climate Change*, 1(5):741–750.

Tänzler, D., Mohns, T., and Ziegenhagen, K. (2013) *Adaptation to Climate Change for Peace and Stability. Strengthening of Approaches and Instruments as well as Promotion of Processes to Reduce the Security Risks Posed by Climate Change in the Context of Climate Change Adaptation*, Umweltbundesamt, Dessau.

Thölken, H. and Börner, W. (2012) "Climate Change and International Security: Why Foreign Policy Must Meet the Challenge" in Tänzler, D. and Carius, A. (eds.) *Climate Diplomacy in Perspective. From Early Warning to Early Action*, Wissenschaftsverlag, Berlin, 7–8.

United Nations Environment Programme (UNEP) (2009) *From Conflict to Peacebuilding: The Role of Natural Resources and the Environment*, UNEP, Nairobi.

United Nations General Assembly (2009) *Climate Change and its Possible Security Implications* (A/63/281), New York, 3 June.

United Nations Secretary-General (2009) *Climate Change and its Possible Security Implications* (A/64/350), United Nations, New York.

United Nations Security Council (2011) *Statement by the President of the Security Council. S /PRST/2011/15. 20 July*. United Nations, New York.

WBGU (2007) *World in Transition – Climate Change as a Security Risk*, Springer, Berlin.

Wolters, S., Tänzler, D., Stang, G., and Ribera, T. (2016) *Climate Change and European Foreign Policy after COP 21*. Climate Diplomacy Brief, Adelphi, Berlin.

22

The role of the military in environmental peacebuilding

Saleem H. Ali and Rebecca Pincus

Introduction: the greening of security

Discourse on how adverse environmental changes and climate-induced resource scarcity may give rise to armed conflicts between and within states has been increasing remarkably; and it is having a considerable impact on how environmental change is being securitized in public policy (Floyd and Matthew 2012). Yet frequently overlooked in environmental security debates are how adverse environmental and ecological conditions can actually create conditions for the *resolution* of conflicts and *peaceful interactions* between parties to ongoing or potential conflicts. The role of existing militaries in this context deserves particular attention from an instrumental perspective of peacekeeping, as well as from a strategic goal of repurposing the military–industrial complex. Past scholarship in human geography has particularly focused on the ways the military shapes environmental processes through entrenched power structures and infrastructure impacts (Woodward 2004; Davis 2015). No doubt the negative impact of militaries cannot be underestimated or diminished. However, the opportunities to consider a positive transformative role for the military nevertheless deserves greater attention, given the enormous resource base of military establishments and continuing public investment in militaries worldwide.

An emerging body of literature suggests that environmental conditions may be important in how conflict processes are mediated and resolved (Ali 2007) and that shared environmental stressors have the potential to encourage cooperative interactions between parties on either side of a conflict (Barquet 2015), or greater understanding, trust, and potential reconciliation of underlying conflicts (Harari and Roseman 2008). Therefore, conceptualizing scarcity-driven interactions as existing on a spectrum between cooperation and conflict enables a shift away from discretely considering environmental scarcity as a driver of conflict and allows it to be seen as playing a role in peacebuilding initiatives. Of particular policy interest is how environmental issues play a role in mediation and diplomatic processes that occur during conflict resolution and peacebuilding activities. Moreover, underlying assumptions about the precise role that environmental issues play in relation to how peacebuilding initiatives are framed in discussions among mediators are either understood implicitly or remain poorly conceived or unexamined. As such, research on this topic has largely been confined to anecdotal expository accounts of individual case studies without detailed analyses of diplomatic processes across cases that may contribute to mediating disputes and building theoretical foundations in the field, and several weaknesses are evident in the scarce literature that exists (Ide and Scheffran 2014). Environmental issues thus remain confined to low politics, being framed as a peace *dividend* rather than as *instrumental* to peacebuilding processes.

Consequently, current questions about global environmental concerns and the relative failure of many environmental governance systems such as the climate change convention make such a research approach highly salient. Rather than focusing on the threat of conflict from resource scarcity to gain security traction, such an approach posits a more positive connection to peacebuilding itself as a motivating force for ecological linkages in security decision making.

Following on from environmental security literatures that gained prominence toward the end of the cold war, environmentalists have often sought to highlight linkages between resource scarcity, ecological degradation, and conflict (for example see Homer-Dixon 1991, 1994; Barnett and Adger 2007). Solutions presented in this vein have tended to focus on how to improve environmental conditions as a means of addressing conflicts. While certainly a laudable goal where environmental factors are part of the conflict, improving environmental conditions often remains an acute policy challenge. Moreover, critics often infer that environmental factors play only a subsidiary role in conflict dynamics to political, economic, ethnic, or demographic factors.

Yet as Ali (2007) clearly lays out, environmental security may be driven by processes of both scarcity and abundance, and lead to various cooperative or conflictual outcomes. Therefore, instead of trying to tease out environmental causality in conflicts and thereby accentuate the importance of conservation, environmental issues can also be viewed as playing a constituent role in cooperation – regardless of whether they are part of the original conflict. The key premise of environmental peacemaking narrative therefore suggests that key attributes of environmental concerns would lead acrimonious parties to consider them as a means to address common environmental threats; and that mutual knowledge of resource depletion and a positive aversion to such depletion leads to cooperation (for example, see United Nations "Natural Resources and Conflict" 2015). Supported by the International Union of Conservation of Nature (IUCN) and the United Nations Environment Programme (UNEP), pioneering approaches by Conca and Dabelko (2002) presented logics where environmental issues could play instrumental roles even in cases where conflicts do not involve environmental issues. They argued this was further possible as the old model of the Westphalian State was being transformed by non-state actors. Moreover, as water resource theorists have frequently observed, this pathway often occurs despite perceived disputes of ownership or rights to water that may occur locally (Lowi 1995; also see Scholz and Stiftel 2005). Even adversaries who are aware of the dire impact of depletion are forced to be cooperative on water and avert any "water wars" (Islam and Susskind 2012). Despite this growth in interest around environmental cooperation, tangible institutional structures such as peace parks have only been largely studied from a conservation management perspective. There is thus a need to connect the "low politics" of micro-level border cooperation around environmental management to the "high politics" of war and peace.

Militaries as instruments of conservation and peacebuilding

The following section will review military involvement in environmental conservation, from the micro level of wildlife conservation on individual military bases to the macro-level contributions military strategists are making to climate change adaptation and mitigation through linking national security to climate. At levels ranging from local to global, militaries play an important role in shaping the natural environment and government mediation in human–environment relationships. While the military is frequently an agent of environmental destruction, also from local to global scales, we argue that it is important to consider both positive and negative impacts flowing from military–environment encounters in order to advance comprehension and support more effective policy approaches for maximizing social goods.

Military and conservation

One of the most enduring and simplest ways in which militaries have contributed to instrumental environmental conservation is through the establishment and enforcement of buffer zones. The US Department of Defense's Dictionary of Military and Associated Terms defines "buffer zone" in the following terms:

1   A defined area controlled by a peace operations force from which disputing or belligerent forces have been excluded.
2   A designated area used for safety in military operations.

More extended scholarly analysis of buffer zones has provided a complex understanding of the role of these areas in military strategy and operations (see Beehner and Meibauer 2016); however, less attention has been paid to their impacts on the natural environment.

One of the most widely cited examples of instrumental conservation flowing from military buffer zones is in the Korean DMZ, or demilitarized zone, a permanent buffer established between North and South Korea. Kim (1997) argued that the preservation of the DMZ offered a "monumental opportunity" for North and South Korea to "preserve the last of Korea's natural landscapes and native biodiversity." In fact, recent decades have seen the emergence of dialogue on morphing the DMZ into a peace park or similar space (Ali 2007).

Buffer zones have historically been primarily terrestrial, but it is also possible to understand contemporary no-fly zones, as well as areas within a naval blockade, as quasi-buffer zones, in that the enforced halt to typical traffic in these areas of military interdiction creates unintended positive ecological effects. No-fly zones decrease air pollution and noise pollution; naval blockades also reduce underwater noise pollution and temporarily halt fishing pressure. For example, Rolland et al. (2012) used fecal sampling to demonstrate that the temporary drop in undersea noise pollution linked to a drop in marine traffic following the September 11, 2001 attacks led to significant reductions in stress hormones in the coast-hugging North Atlantic right whale.

In addition to wartime buffer zones, whether land, sea, or air, the military sets aside or protects land on an ongoing basis during peacetime, generally around military installations and particularly sensitive defense-related infrastructure. For example, the Hanford defense nuclear weapons production site in the Columbia River basin has surrounding lands and waterways which are fairly well conserved due to development restrictions in the area. There have been suggestions made by ecologists and military geographers to use such buffer areas around military sites such as Hanford as wildlife refuges (Gray and Rickard 1989; Havlick 2011).

Of course, the unintentional positive impacts of buffer zones, whether temporary or more permanent, cannot be disassociated from, and are dwarfed in comparison with, the harmful environmental impacts of war and military complexes. Nevertheless, these occasional benefits demonstrate that instrumental benefits to conservation do occur in a militarized context, and consideration of these benefits may inform discussions of policy and planning.

Military and peacebuilding

Starting from an analysis of organizations such as the US Army Corps of Engineers, this section will analyze how the military can help with technical mechanisms in environmental peacebuilding. Specific analysis of various Pentagon units that have linkages to environmental factors will be presented as an example.

The United States Department of Defense (DoD) recognized the importance of environmental issues to relationship-building and the identification of common ground. This movement grew out of a dark period during the Vietnam conflict, when the US military directly attacked the natural environment of Vietnam and Laos. Confronted with a growing stockpile of chemical weapons and munitions, the US Army created the US Army Environmental Command (US-AEC) in 1972, originally under the title Demilitarization of Chemical Material. Over the course of the 1970s, the AEC gradually expanded its portfolio until its responsibilities included installation restoration, research and testing, and pollution control technology. The command achieved its modern form in 2005, when it received the formal name of Army Environmental Command. The AEC is currently housed in the Installation Management Command, a major subcomponent of the Department of the Army. It is based out of Fort Sam Houston, Texas. The USAEC mission states that it is "committed to delivering environmental solutions in support of U.S. Army readiness and sustainability" (USAEC).

In the international context, the US military also recognizes the importance of ecological integrity to stabilization and nation-building efforts. In Afghanistan, the use of Agribusiness Development Teams (ADTs) and similar tools has been lauded. The US Army describes ADTs as a unit composed of National Guard soldiers with backgrounds in agriculture and related fields, which "provide training and advice" to community institutions, local governments, and individual community members in targeted areas (US Army 2008). The Army has sent ADTs to Central America for almost thirty years, and began deploying ADTs to parts of Afghanistan in 2008. According to the Army, the first ADT deployed to Afghanistan was "very well received," and provided a helpful mix of agricultural knowledge, military security, and "hard work" (US Army 2008). One of the first ADTs deployed to Afghanistan was a unit of the Kansas National Guard, which conducted an effort in 2012 to purchase 2,400 fruit and nut tree saplings for distribution to village elders in Alingar District (Goble 2012). These trees, which will provide ecosystem benefits, will also improve community food security, and improve US–Afghan community relations. A unit of the Iowa National Guard worked with local Amish farmers before deploying to Afghanistan, in order to prepare for the largely non-mechanized agricultural techniques in Afghanistan (Shinn 2010).

The work of the ADTs can clearly be seen as part of a multi-pronged approach to achieving US military and security objectives, an approach which includes the "winning hearts and minds" concept – and including sustainable agricultural practices that have carry-on ecological benefits, like planting local fruit tree species, is a wise strategic move. The US Army handbook that guides ADT preparation states, "[r]evitalizing Afghanistan's agricultural sector is critical to building the government's capacity and to stabilizing the country" (US Army 2009:1) It goes on to note the environmental benefits of enhancing agricultural health: "ADTs will continue to serve US and Afghan interests by helping farmers return the fertile Afghan countryside to the green and productive environment it was" (US Army 2009:2).

Military role in environmental response

As an institution, the military's functionality is often perceived by the public as an insurance policy to address security challenges through defensive or offensive mechanisms. There can thus often be some level of excess capacity within military establishments during periods of relative peace. To remain relevant to its public mandate, particularly in these periods, the military can provide important services in other non-combat crises. Historically, countries with large militaries have used such excess capacity by volunteering troops for peacekeeping through the United Nations system. Countries such as Bangladesh and Pakistan, which have very large militaries, have often been key providers of military human capital for peacekeeping missions with the United Nations, that are often labeled "blue helmet" missions. In a similar vein, there can also be an important role for militaries in international environmental conservation, remediation, and enforcement missions. The mechanisms by which "green helmets" could be mobilized by the United Nations Security Council has been discussed in detail by Malone (1996), but since then there have also been specific initiatives to develop regional "green armies" against imminent threats such as wildlife poaching (Wasley 2008).

Domestically, governments often deploy military forces to respond to natural disasters. In the United States, this often takes the form of the National Guard, which has been described as "critical in the maintenance of civil order," as well as "the provision of logistical support, and the coordination of rescue and relief effort" (Bowman, Kapp, and Belasco 2005). For example, following Hurricane Katrina in 2005, both National Guard and active-duty Army troops were mobilized to assist response efforts in New Orleans. A Forward Command Post was established, and units of signal battalions, airborne, and field artillery troops were deployed to assist with a variety of missions, including communications, airport functionality, and rescue missions (Berthelot 2010).

In addition, the US government also is quick to respond to natural disasters that occur in foreign countries. Forward-deployed forces and/or assets may be the quickest to respond; these might generally include US Navy or Coast Guard ships that happen to be in the area. For example, following the 2011 tsunami in Japan, the DoD launched Operation Tomodachi ("friend" in the Japanese language), a multipart relief effort that used the USS *Ronald Reagan*, as well as the Misawa airbase, as forward operating bases from which relief supplies could be dispatched and rescue helicopters refuel (Feickert and Chanlett-Avery 2011). The *Ronald Reagan* was accompanied by its carrier strike group, which had been conducting military exercises around Korea, and was therefore proximate to the tsunami zone.

The US Army Corps of Engineers (USACE) is one component of the Department of Defense that plays a critical role in environmental emergencies. In recent years, USACE teams have responded to the Haiti earthquake and the 2004 Indonesian tsunami. Under its statutory authority, USACE may engage in disaster preparedness, including advance measures; emergency operations; rehabilitation to flood management projects like levees and restoration of storm management projects; drought assistance; and emergency water assistance due to contamination. In responding to environmental emergencies, USACE works as part of the DoD enterprise, but may also respond directly to Department of State (USACE n.d.).

As climate change brings increasingly frequent and extreme weather events, the emergency response agencies of many nations – including the United States – are increasingly overstressed. Given growing strain on response agencies, which are generally quite small in comparison with militaries, it is no surprise that governments are increasingly turning to militaries for emergency environmental response. Militaries have the resources, skilled personnel, and grit required to manage dangerous and complex environmental emergencies, including hurricanes/typhoons, tsunamis, earthquakes, flooding, or similar.

Environmental emergency response is often characterized as humanitarian, and vice versa. This lack of clarity in the literature is partially due to the causes of humanitarian emergencies: according to one Congressional report, "the majority of humanitarian emergencies worldwide stem from natural disasters or from conflicts" (Margesson 2015). There is clearly overlap between the military's role in humanitarian response and environmental response. While attention to environmental issues may appear recent, due to heightened awareness of climate change, it should be remembered that military units have long been involved in humanitarian emergencies that often have had environmental components. A 2006 report by the Humanitarian Policy Group (HPG) outlined as much, noting the long history of humanitarian efforts by military actors – with the 1948 Berlin Airlift an early and notable example – while also underscoring the modern rise in "complex emergencies" that draw in military, peacekeeping, and humanitarian actors (HPG 2006, Abstract). More specifically, the HPG report identifies three major recent changes in military involvement in humanitarian response: first, increasing engagement by militaries in "activities and policy areas of humanitarian interest"; second, "structural and organizational changes" within militaries, initiated "in an attempt to combine civilian and military interests and assets in crisis response"; and third, an increased reliance on UN and regional missions for crisis response (HPG 2006:1). Perhaps it is more useful to refer to 'human–natural disasters,' which may serve to tie together the often conflated or artificially separated terms that are generally in use.

The role of the military in environmental enforcement mechanisms

There have been proposals to create a strong international-treaty-enforcement entity – or what might be called the "green police." Indeed, in recent years there have been calls to "green" the blue helmets – that is, to have the blue-helmeted peacekeeping forces of the United Nations take on expanded post-conflict roles including temporary control of natural resource management efforts (UNEP 2012). However, if we need an international police force to ensure compliance with global environmental treaties, we have probably failed to formulate agreements properly. Although countries insist that no one outside their borders ought to be empowered to second-guess them, the sovereignty argument does not apply to people and organizations within their own borders.

Thus, one way around the sovereignty problem is to create groups within each country to take responsibility for monitoring compliance. These groups, especially when they join forces on a worldwide basis, may be able to shame noncomplying nations into changing their behavior. By working together, highly motivated local activists can achieve the competence and credibility they need to bring the full weight of international opinion to bear on noncompliers. We have seen this model before; it is the approach that Amnesty International uses in pursuing noncompliance with United Nations human rights provisions. To build a parallel monitoring and enforcement system in the environmental field, all UN member states would have to sign a protocol equivalent to the Optional Protocol to the International Covenant on Civil and Political Rights. Countries that signed this agreement would be permitting their citizens to pursue individual complaints against violators of global environmental treaties. A UN environmental violations committee (perhaps with the same number of members, eighteen, as the UN Human Rights Committee) would adjudicate all complaints. A working group on noncompliance would receive information from what might be called the "Green Amnesty International" (GAI) as well as other nongovernmental organizations.

The GAI would not be a police force. Rather, it would offer a credible complaint system. There are parts of the world, though, particularly in Latin America, where the military is eager to take on additional environmental enforcement responsibilities (for example, patrolling the rain forest to prevent unauthorized burning of land), but UN peacekeeping forces are not looking for such an assignment. Moreover, it is unlikely that a "green police" force of sufficient size could be pieced together on a volunteer basis. It is also unlikely that the Security Council would authorize the use of UN forces to pursue compliance with environmental treaties.

Thus, if the threat of force is the only effective deterrent, and only deterrence or other direct measures are sufficiently powerful to produce compliance, then environmental treaty making is probably doomed. But, if indirect measures can encourage countries to define their self-interest in ways that produce compliance – without the threat of force – then the chances of successfully implementing these treaties are much greater. To the extent that compliance generates financial benefits, countries will make more of an effort to ensure that their citizens take these treaty requirements seriously. And, if a complaint system (along the lines of our Green Amnesty idea) can be put in place, citizens who care about sustainable development and environmental protection will be able to press their governments to comply with global environmental treaties.

Extensive monitoring of each signatory's compliance with the terms of all global environmental treaties is important, not just to ensure that no one gains an advantage through nonperformance but also because monitoring is the key to understanding the threats that motivated collective action in the first place and to successfully recalibrating the standards and timetables contained in each treaty. Continued improvement in treaty making depends on learning as much as possible about the ability of the parties to meet their obligations, and about the relative effectiveness of different strategies for managing or reducing environmental risks.

Although it seems to be true that most countries comply most of the time with most of the treaties they sign, this leaves lots of room for halfhearted compliance or inadvertent noncompliance. We need to track compliance with environmental treaties so that treaty effectiveness can be enhanced. In a 2011 opinion piece in the *Huffington Post*, German ambassador Peter Wittig took a skeptical approach to the concept of a green-helmeted UN force, writing, "repainting blue helmets into green might be a strong signal – but would dealing with the consequences of climate change – say in precarious regions – be really different from the tasks the blue helmets already perform today?" (Wittig 2011). Without effective monitoring to gauge compliance, such a green-helmet force would be neither needed nor effective.

Conclusion

The role of the modern military continues to evolve, as the nature of the threats confronting states in the international system also becomes more fragmented. The increasingly devastating impacts of climate change will draw militaries further into environmental security operations. The 2014 CNA report, "National Security and the Accelerating Risks of Climate Change," provides a thorough introduction to the security implications of climate change for militaries in both developed and developing states. By underscoring the important connections between environmental health and political stability (or lack thereof), the CNA report, which received widespread media attention, and other similar work has helped bring environmental integrity into security planning.

Environmental issues also open useful pathways to cooperation and relationship-building, as the involvement of military actors in environmental crisis response demonstrates. When a nation dispatches military units to assist another country stricken by disaster, the goodwill engendered by a positive contribution to disaster relief may strengthen the bonds between those countries, and pave the way for broader and more lasting cooperation. Therefore, the instrumental use of military structures to achieve environmental goals – relating to human–natural disasters – can have positive spillover effects on broader foreign policy strategic objectives.

Moreover, the increasing ties between climate change-driven natural disasters and humanitarian emergencies, which are often mediated by government competencies, offer a growing vector for increased military involvement in peacekeeping. While increased intervention and support to foreign countries struggling with emergency situations may offer broader opportunities to reap foreign policy dividends, it should be noted that public willingness to support such aid, even run through military channels, may eventually wane as the costs and impacts of climate change intensify. Proposals for environmental peacekeeping or treaty monitoring should be carefully considered in light of the complex effects and linkages already present in the military–environment nexus, which climate change promises to further complicate.

References

Ali, S. H. (ed.) (2007) *Peace Parks: Conservation and Conflict Resolution*, MIT Press, Cambridge, MA.

Barnett, J. and Adger, W. N. (2007) "Climate change, human security, and violent conflict" *Political Geography* 26(6):639–655.

Barquet, K. (2015) "'Yes to peace'? Environmental peacemaking and transboundary conservation in Central America" *Geoforum* 63:14–24.

Beehner, L. and Meibauer, G. (2016) "The futility of buffer zones in international politics" *Orbis* (Foreign Policy Research Institute), Spring.

Berthelot, R. (2010) The Army responds to Hurricane Katrina. US Army Military History Institute, Army Heritage Education Center.

Bowman, S., Kapp, L., and Belasco, A. (2005) Hurricane Katrina: DoD disaster response, RL33095. Congressional Research Service.

CNA Military Advisory Board. (2014) *National Security and the Accelerating Risks of Climate Change*, CNA Corporation, Alexandria, VA.

Conca, K. and Dabelko, G. (eds.) (2002) *Environmental Peace-building*, Johns Hopkins University Press, Baltimore, MD.

Davis, S. (2015) *The Empire's Edge: Militarization, Resistance and Transcending Hegemony in the Pacific*, University of Georgia Press, Athens.

Feickert, A. and Chanlett-Avery, E. (2011) Japan 2011 earthquake: U.S. Department of Defense (DoD) response, R42690. Congressional Research Service.

Floyd, R. and Matthew, R. (2012) *Environmental Security: Approaches and Issues*, Routledge, New York.

Goble, L. Spc. (2012) "Afghanistan: Kansas National Guard ADT gives Arbor Day gifts to locals" US National Guard, February 8.

Gray, R. H. and Rickard, W. H. (1989) "The protected area of Hanford as a refugium for native plants and animals" *Environmental Conservation* 16(3):251–260.

Harari, N. and Roseman, J. (2008) *Environmental Peacebuilding, Theory and Practice: A Case Study of the Good Water Neighbours Project and In-depth Analysis of the Wadi Fukin*, Friends of the Earth Middle East Project, Tel Aviv, Amman and Ramallah.

Havlick, D. G. (2011) "Disarming nature: Converting military lands to wildlife refuges" *Geographical Review* 101(2):183–200.

Homer-Dixon, T. (1991) "On the threshold: Environmental changes as causes of acute conflict" *International Security* 16(2):76–116.

Homer-Dixon, T. (1994) "Environmental scarcities and violent conflict: Evidence from cases" *International Security* 19(1):5–40.

Humanitarian Policy Group (2006) "Resetting the rules of engagement: Trends and issues in military–humanitarian relations" Wheeler, V. and Harmer, A., eds. Overseas Development Institute, London.

Ide, T. and Scheffran, J. (2014) "On climate, conflict and cumulation: Suggestions for integrative cumulation of knowledge in the research on climate change and violent conflict" *Global Change, Peace & Security* 26:263–279.

Islam, S. and Susskind, L. (2012) *Water Diplomacy: A Negotiated Approach to Managing Complex Water Networks*, RFF Press, New York.

Kim, K. C. (1997) "Preserving biodiversity in Korea's Demilitarized Zone" *Science* 278(5336):242–243.

Lowi, M. R. (1995) "Rivers of conflict, rivers of peace" *Journal of International Affairs* 49(1):123–144.

Malone, L. A. (1996) "Green Helmets: A conceptual framework for Security Council Authority in environmental emergencies" *College of William and Mary Faculty Publications*. Paper 599. Available at: http://scholarship.law.wm.edu/facpubs/599

Margesson, R. (2015) International crises and disasters: U.S. humanitarian assistance response mechanisms, RL33769. Congressional Research Service.

Rolland, R., Parks, S., Hunt, K., Castellote, M., Corkeron, P., Nowacek, D., et al. (2012) "Evidence that ship noise increases stress in right whales" *Proceedings of the Royal Society B* 279:2363–2368.

Scholz, J. T. and Stiftel, B. (eds.) (2005) *Adaptive Governance and Water Conflict: New Institutions for Collaborative Planning*, Resources for the Future/RFF Press, Washington, DC.

Shinn, P. Capt. (2010) "Iowa ADT trains with Amish before deployment" US National Guard, June 24.

United Nations Environment Programme (UNEP) (2012) *Greening the Blue Helmets: Environment, Natural Resources and UN Peacekeeping Operations*, UNEP, Nairobi.

United Nations (2015) "Natural Resources and Conflict: A Guide for Mediation Practitioners" UNEP, Nairobi.

US Army (2008) "Agribusiness Development Team" (ADT) Army Posture Statement, Information Papers.

US Army (2009) *Handbook: Agribusiness Development Teams in Afghanistan*, Center for Army Lessons Learned.

US Army Corps of Engineers (USACE) (n.d.) US Army Corps of Engineers: Emergency Response.

US Army Environmental Command. "About AEC." Available at https://aec.army.mil/index.php/about-aec.

Wasley, A. (2008) "A Green Army" *The Ecologist*, October. Available at: www.theecologist.org/investigations/society/269501/a_green_army.html

Wittig, P. (2011) "Facing the security challenge of climate change" *Huffington Post*, The Blog. Available at: www.huffingtonpost.com/dr-peter-wittig/post_2204_b_901967.html

Woodward, R. (2004) *Military Geographies*, Wiley-Blackwell, London.

23

Environmental resource governance and peace

A critical review

Larry Swatuk

Whether the issue is climate change, the loss of biodiversity, the spread of land degradation, water scarcity, or the continued strip-mining of coastal zone resources, regional approaches to adaptation have become increasingly important in human terms. Simply put, our failure to make global progress in preventing these problems in the twenty [five] years since Rio means we have an added moral responsibility to attend to their consequences in the next twenty. If so, then we are all regionalists now.

Ken Conca (2012:133)

The defining images of African environmental governance in this book are the road, which cuts swathes through protected areas of Africa's wilderness, and the periurban slum, which is wild but not wilderness. Both exemplify the hermaphrodite landscapes of contemporary Africa. These spaces are neither ungoverned nor conventional state territories. Instead, they are products of rhizome modes of state governance through which green land is shaped and represented in Africa. The green states of the future need to bring roads and slums as well as protected areas and agricultural land to the heart of debates over Africa's environmental governance.

Carl Death (2016:241–242)

Modern man is an animal whose politics places his existence as a living being in question.

Michel Foucault (1978:143)

Introduction

Managing (and mismanaging) the natural environment is as old as human community. The adoption of the Sustainable Development Goals (SDGs) appears as an attempt to make our way back toward less intrusive and destructive forms of resource use, and to situate our practices within a narrative of not 'man over nature' but 'humans in nature'. Aside from its massively destructive environmental impacts, humanity's access, use and management of natural resources have also engendered violent conflicts. How successful we will be in the effort to meet SDGs is the subject of extensive debate. In this chapter, I survey the landscape of environmental governance in relation to peace. 'Peace' is understood in its positive sense, i.e. as an enabler of constructive collaboration whereby just socio-ecological outcomes are realized. I critically reflect on the claims made in the name of environmental governance – at different scales – in relation to actually existing processes, practices and outcomes of 'environmental governance'. I argue that issue (in terms of complexity) and scale (in terms of authoritative actors involved) play a preeminent role in the character of environmental governance outcomes: the more complicated the issue and the greater number of authoritative actors, the less likely positive peace will be realized.

While global environmental governance may have failed to deliver on most of its promises, and while there may in some cases and instances be more purchase to collective action on common pool resources at regional scale (Conca epigraph above), there remain at least two problems with this notion. First, and as highlighted by Death (epigraph above), whereas 'environmentalism' in the Global North is a secondary issue, in the Global South – and in rural areas in particular – it is at the heart of life and death. Where access to natural resources is central to livelihoods (and state power), struggles over wildlife or forest conservation or transboundary water sharing are not just about getting the governance and management frameworks right; they are about shaping and controlling the framework from the start. Thus, while environmental governance creates complex global networks, the actors in the 'network' rarely agree on the rules of the game (cf. Rhodes 1996, 2007; Dietz et al. 2003), so spawning rival and competing networks (e.g. World Economic Forum versus World Social Forum). As highlighted by Broch-Due (2000) some years ago, in such a setting a resource management project quickly turns into the contextual basis for old-style politics. The second problem builds on the quotation from Foucault (epigraph above): where ever and more consumption constitutes the commonly accepted goal for all actors in the system, notions of 'conservation' or 'preservation' are bound to fail. Put simply: global or regional, we are largely kidding ourselves. Not only does the current system lead us away from appropriate forms of environmental governance, it leads us, almost by default, away from peace.

'Governance' in theory

Like any other concept whose application to the real world results in differential social outcomes, 'governance' is a highly debated idea defined in numerous ways. Governance, as a concept, emerged at the end of the Cold War to describe changes to ways and means of arriving at decisions regarding the authoritative allocation of values. Landell-Mills and Serageldin (1991) provided an early definitional starting point for arguments regarding 'governance': "The use of political authority and the exercise of control over society and the management of its resources for social and economic development." Roughly ten years later, Pierre (2000: 4; also, see Pierre and Stoker 2000) highlighted the discursive value of 'governance':

> Governance refers to a sustaining coordination and coherence among a wide variety of actors with different purposes and objectives, such as political actors and institutions, corporate interests, civil society and transnational organizations. The main point here is that political institutions no longer exercise a monopoly of the orchestration of governance . . . Governance is shorthand for the predominant view of government . . . It is also . . . more palatable than "government" which has become a slightly pejorative concept.

Rhodes (2007:1247) suggests that in the UK context, "the literature on governance explores how the informal authority of networks supplements and supplants the formal authority of government. It explores the limits to the state and seeks to develop a more diverse view of state authority and its exercise". Rhodes (2007:1246) argues that "the hierarchic Westminster model of responsible government is no longer acceptable". In its place, he feels is 'network governance',[1] a form of governance that seems to best express the processes of governing the environment as they have evolved over the last 50 years (Biermann 2014).

Apart from describing changes to the ways and means of deciding and acting upon 'the rules of the game', scholars of the intellectual Left critiqued 'governance' as a weasel word whose real intent was to legitimize World Bank and IMF meddling in the affairs of otherwise 'sovereign' state forms (see Moore 1995 and 1999). In the post-Cold War world, alongside economic structural adjustment programs (SAPs) foisted upon prostrate African governments, came the cross-conditionality of pressures for elections and the construction of liberal democracy. So, 'legitimacy' and 'authority' became tied to Western-defined measures of 'good governance' (World Bank 1997), which include the following criteria (UNESCO and UN Water 2003):

- Participation
- Transparency
- Equity
- Effectiveness and efficiency
- Rule of law
- Accountability
- Coherency
- Responsiveness
- Integration
- Ethical considerations.

Numerous measures of 'good governance' are now available across multiple platforms on the Internet. None, however, tell us exactly how we are to achieve these elements of governance. In other words, these are merely descriptive categories, not instructions on the ways and means of altering past systems of governance, some or all of which are deeply embedded in and reflective of particular social forms.

In my view, and as used in this chapter, governance is regarded as both outcome and process, involving a variety of legitimate and authoritative actors. As an outcome, it reflects settled social relations. If it is good, it suggests widespread – if not universal – social approval of its practices. Persistence of settled social relations, however, should not be automatically construed as reflective of 'good governance'. To the contrary, they may in fact reflect durable social inequalities (e.g. the caste system in India). Good governance can never reach an end point; as a process, it depends on the reiteration of activities that deepen trust. It is most readily constituted and observable at a local level, so raising questions about the fungibility of effective local governance, in particular the ways and means of moving from one socio-geopolitical scale to another. Let us now turn to an examination of environmental governance in relation to, first, water, and second, forests and protected areas.

Water

In his important 2006 monograph, Conca argues that the goal of global water governance is to embed contentious and conflicting interests and needs within 'institutional configurations and orientations', in other words, to create an institutional structure and process for dealing with multiple interests regarding a shared resource so as to minimize negative outcomes and to maximize shared benefits. Importantly, Conca (2006) highlights the gap between actually existing processes of governance (the 'is') relative to the idealized forms of governance envisioned by its architects (the 'ought').

In 2000, at the Second World Water Forum in The Hague, the Netherlands, King Willem Frederick, the then Prince of Orange, declared the world 'water crisis' to be a crisis of governance – not one of absolute physical scarcity. This statement opened the door for a re-examination of the ways and means of governing and managing the world's water. Conca, in relation to global water governance (2006:116) but which is valid for most other resources, describes the common pathway (the way things are; things as 'is') as follows:

> the sovereign state is the territorial reference point for water governance and management; the state (as represented by its government) is the acknowledged authority for decisions regarding access, use and management of water resources; decisions regarding access, use and management derive from expert/specialist knowledge deployed by the state in service of the national interest.

Such an approach to water governance and management has been common throughout the ages (Solomon 2010), especially during the high modern/industrial period where states, generally in competition with each other, engaged in a concerted 'hydraulic mission' to capture water resources in the interests of political and economic power (Allan 2003; Solomon 2010). This tendency to govern and manage a fugitive resource in terms of the needs of a spatially static state, a shared resource in terms of partial, 'national' interests (as determined by elites), and a resource essential to the functioning of a complex system in terms of highly specific expert knowledge designed to put a river 'to work', is now widely regarded as the source of environmentally unsustainable, socially inequitable and economically inefficient maldevelopment. These three, the 'triple E', comprised the 1990s rallying cry of Integrated Water Resources Management (IWRM) – Environmental sustainability, Economic efficiency, social Equity – but extend across the entire resource use landscape of the Sustainable Development Goals today.

Forests and protected areas constitute slightly different cases due to the fixed nature of their physical space, but highly dynamic nature of their ecosystems, biomass production, vulnerability to rapid degradation, and the varied interpretations of their 'value' to humans (multiple stakeholder groups) and nature itself (see the next section).

The Dublin Principles also articulated, among other things, the need for better governance, meaning, inter alia, participation of all stakeholders within a river basin. Thus, in direct response to the perceived negative cycle of unsustainability set in motion by the 'is', IWRM and good governance emerged as the twin meta-norms shaping the way water resource governance and management 'ought to be' (Allan 2003; Conca 2006). Not only is the global literature on IWRM and good water governance replete with the so-called 'triple E', it also adopts without question the ideas that: (i) the appropriate territorial space is not the sovereign state, but the river basin; (ii) the appropriate governing/managing authority is the stakeholder group (which includes the state as only one, albeit centrally important, actor); and (iii) decisions regarding resource access, use and management would be taken on the basis of inclusive forms of knowledge derived from stakeholders (e.g. indigenous knowledge and/or so-called 'citizen science'), wherein 'expert science' would constitute only one part of the knowledge tree.

Shaping the global water governance and management agenda in terms of the 'ought' immediately opened a Pandora's Box of problems and challenges, almost all of which stem from present beneficiaries' perceptions regarding anticipated future losses to be incurred through the new institutional configurations and orientations. Put simply: water is power, and to revise and rearticulate water institutions is to challenge existing forms and bases of power. Homer-Dixon's (1999) 'resource capture/ecological marginalization dynamic' is an elegant heuristic. It accurately describes the dynamics surrounding a scramble for resources due to one or a combination of supply side, demand side and structural pressures. In the context of the new water architecture, moving from the 'is' to the 'ought' aims to fundamentally alter extant structural conditions across the water world, so challenging in many cases the existing relations between states, the private sector and civil society. The same may be said for other both renewable (forests, fish, agricultural land) and non-renewable (minerals, gemstones, oil) resources. So, while there have been a plethora of governance mechanisms emerging across resources, industries, sectors, regions and societies in Africa (e.g. the Kimberley Process; West African Commission on Drugs; the African Mining Vision; Peace Parks initiatives; REDD+; Nile Basin Initiative; International Conference on the Great Lakes Region), there have been an equal number of monitoring and evaluation mechanisms created largely by forces external to the continent, but often with some linkages to government and/or the private sector and/or civil society: e.g. the Extractives Industries Transparency Index; Publish What You Pay; Freedom in the World (from Freedom House); Global Witness; TRAFFIC (Hanson et al. 2014). Whether any of this environmental governance adds up to 'peace' – be it positive or negative – is debatable, however (Conca and Dabelko 2002; Huggins et al. 2006).

More recently, a notable group of scholars have been lobbying for a more concerted approach to global water governance (Grey et al. 2013) through the lenses of security, vulnerability and risk. They argue that the absence of a global governance framework or mechanism derives in part from the fact that wealthy states perceive themselves to be water secure; hence, those with the capacity to drive the agenda fail to do so because they perceive their vulnerabilities differently than poor states. Their 'security' derives in part from what the authors describe as 'lower hydrological complexity' complemented by high investment in information, institutions and infrastructure. The opposite may be said for those suffering 'water insecurity' (Grey et al. 2013: figure 1).

> Air transport and shipping; infectious diseases; trade; crime; meteorology and weather forecasting; climate change – are all examples where global agreements and mechanisms have been established to manage potentially intolerable risks perceived by wealthy nations. Because water security challenges are complex and locally diverse, they are not adequately recognized or prioritized as policy challenges by most wealthy and currently water-secure nations. This explains the absence of specific global mechanisms to promote cooperation in water security monitoring, analysis and governance. Significant action is unlikely to be initiated through intergovernmental consensus mechanisms in the short term. Scientists have the obligation to recognize the policy challenge described here, and to move forward with building the evidence and knowledge base, catalysing the establishment of the global (and eventually intergovernmental) architecture required for water security.
>
> *(Grey et al. 2013:8–9)*[2]

In their opinion, much of the Global South is water insecure and so threatens the rest of the world (given water's ubiquity in natural, social, economic and cultural practices and processes at all scales). In my opinion, this reads very much like most of the literature emerging from Western think tanks and state houses on climate change (e.g. Moran 2011; Scheffran et al. 2012; USDS 2014) and harks back to governments' initial responses to Robert Kaplan's famous 1994 article in *The Atlantic Monthly* wherein he invokes the image of those inside and outside of 'the limousine'. This raises important questions about peace and security for whom?[3] It also raises serious questions regarding the 'networks of resource governance' emerging in response to these challenges: who is inside and outside of the governance limousine?

Forests and protected areas

When it comes to the world's forests and protected areas, it is quite clear who is 'inside' and who is 'outside' of Kaplan's limousine. As with water, parks and protected areas, those directly dependent upon forest resources for their survival are also the most vulnerable and least capable of determining their security. For millennia, forests have been central to social, economic and political power. De Jong, Donovan and Abe (2007) describe the changing fortunes of the world's forests as their values have shifted from being key pillars in the construction and expansion of civilization and empire to central components of sovereign state economies and for-profit private industry. Whereas, we are all dependent, albeit to varying degrees, upon forest products, there are significant numbers of people who are directly dependent upon access to the forest for their immediate livelihood needs. For example, it is estimated that there are 120–150 million forest dwellers in South Asia, of which some 70–90 million consist of tribal communities. It is further estimated that some 350–400 million South Asians are directly dependent upon forests for their products and environmental services. The World Wildlife Fund (WWF n.d.) estimates global numbers to be in the order of 300 million forest dwellers and 1.6 billion directly dependent upon forests.

Forests have been at the center of global governance initiatives since at least the 1980s. Arts and Buizer (2009) show how global governance approaches to forests have moved through three dominant discourses: biodiversity preservation during the 1980s, centered primarily on 'tropical rainforests'; sustainable development in the 1990s, focused on 'sustainable forest management'; and governance today, with a strong emphasis on indicators and monitoring (Mateo-Vega et al. 2017). Bennett (2015) argues that the 1980s resulted in a dualistic management approach: plantations for timber on the one hand; conservation through establishment of protected areas on the other. Such thinking may be seen in the latest FAO (2016) report on the state of the world's forests wherein the authors speak of 'net forest loss' as slowing in the last decade. According to FAO, between 2010 and 2015, loss of forest amounted to 7.6m ha and gain amounted to 4.3m ha, resulting in a net loss of 3.3m ha. In terms of aggregates, globally forest cover has declined by 129m ha between 1990 and 2015. An area, the FAO (2016) states, 'about the size of South Africa'. This translates into an estimated loss of global carbon stock over the same time period of 11 Gigatonnes. The specific geography of these net losses in forest cover and carbon stock shows increases across Europe, East Asia, North America, Oceania, the Caribbean and West/Central Asia; and decreases across Central America, South America, South and Southeast Asia, and all of Africa (FAO 2016: figure 5, p. 18; figure 22, p. 31). Juxtaposed to Peace Research Institute Oslo (PRIO) data on trends in armed conflict 1946–2015, and United Nations Development Programme (UNDP) data on the Human Development Index (HDI), one sees that these trends in deforestation, forest and other land degradation occur among low to lower-middle income countries, located at the lower end of the UNDP Human Development Index, stretching across the tropics, engaged in a wide array of organized violence.

Forests have featured extensively as sites of violent conflict, but less so as objects (De Jong et al. 2007). Throughout much of the 1990s and early 2000s, 'conflict timber' was a key issue in West and Central African civil wars, where the revenues derived from high value timber helped finance the activities of a variety of rebel movements (Swatuk 2007; De Koning 2007). Violent conflict in Liberia, Sierra Leone, Guinea and the Democratic Republic of the Congo (DRC) featured centrally in the 'greed and grievance' literature (Richards 1996; Ellis 1999; Collier and Hoeffler 2004). At the time, Richards asked whether Africa's forest wars were resource wars. That most of these conflicts have waned seems to me to have answered that question. The ongoing conflicts in the eastern Congo, northern Uganda and South Sudan are less about 'greed' or resource capture than they are about ideology, identity and political power.

Missing from the PRIO survey of armed conflict are the myriad instances of seemingly incessant and more spontaneous intra-communal violence between forest dwelling people and farmers[4] and forest dwelling people and the state in league with private or state-owned companies.[5] From the 1970s, indigenous peoples in the Amazon attached their direct interests to international human rights organizations such as Survival International. Environmental activists concerned with Amazon deforestation and its impact on biodiversity also became involved with tribal groups, the logic being, in part, that these NGOs could exercise a kind of soft power not available to indigenous people on their own. Most of this conflict takes place on state land. Globally, an estimated 77 percent of forests are managed by the state. However, in the areas identified above, state ownership and management is in the region of 90 percent or more. Across large sections of South and Southeast Asia, endemic conflict between local communities and the state has resulted in a resurgence of community-managed forestry programs (Jeffery and Vira 2001). Forest dwelling tribal groups around the world, however, have fared badly.

These phenomena – of large-scale organized violence dependent upon forest-based revenues; of small-scale organized but also anomic sorts of violence focused on land use – have given rise to two forms of environmental governance for peace making and building: (i) certification programs interested in encouraging best practice by the many different actors located along the forest product value chain; (ii) sustainability management plans. Each of these governance approaches emphasizes appropriate forms of stakeholder engagement, in particular the inclusion of groups most dependent upon the forest for their livelihoods.

Parks and protected areas have also adopted these approaches, both within states (through, for example, community-based natural resources management – CBNRM – programs) and across states (through, for example, transfrontier peace parks) (see Swatuk 2005; Child 2004; Fabricius and Koch 2004; Duffy 2000; Buscher 2013; Ali 2007). International organizations, such as the International Union for Conservation of Nature (IUCN) and UNEP, and NGOs, such as Conservation International and the WWF, serve as lead organizations in knowledge production and dissemination as well as advocacy. While forests, parks and protected areas have historically been 'managed' by states or, at best, elite coalitions led by states most often in alliance with international financial institutions (IFIs) such as the World Bank, the governance landscape has changed dramatically over the last 25 years. Van der Ven et al. (2017:3) state that "non-state and subnational climate governance has exploded in recent years and has contributed to an increasingly fragmented governance landscape". They argue that states continue to drive the agenda by managing 'orchestration platforms'; however, in their view, citing Kramarz and Park (2016), there is a serious 'accountability deficit in global environmental politics'. Kramarz and Park (2017), building on their 2016 paper, highlight the seeming contradiction that in the face of ever increasing numbers and mechanisms of global environmental governance, the state of the environment has only worsened. One could rightly add to that, that global and local inequalities have also worsened despite claims of 'best practice' and 'inclusive' forms of decision-making.

Najam and Halle (2010) suggest that part of the problem derives from the fact that global environmental governance is largely 'declaratory not regulatory'. Kramarz and Park (2016:19) show

how environmental governance "involves biases that determine what counts as an appropriate response". In emphasizing 'monitoring, compliance and enforcement' without meaningfully involving those most seriously and negatively affected by decisions, global environmental governance looks more like policing than co-management from the perspective of the poor.

Donovan, De Jong and Abe (2007:2) state that "ultimately if the forest suffers, society suffers". One would rightly amend that to include the following: "If the forest-dependent societies suffer, global society suffers." However, the problem is that we do not all suffer equally. This is especially the case where governments across the tropics ignore 'accountability' to the citizenry because they are dependent upon resource rents (from, for example, timber exports or tourist revenues) and not on taxes. They may be accountable to extra-state actors – donor states, multinational corporations, even influential NGOs such as WWF – and be deemed by these authoritative actors as well performing despite realities on the ground.

Peace: positive and negative

Following Galtung (1971), 'negative peace' is the absence of wide-scale violent conflict. It is often argued that this is the prerequisite for all forms of progressive and productive social interaction. While negative peace may be a necessary component of positive peace, it is by no means sufficient to guarantee it. Indeed, negative peace can mask deeper, structural forms of violence. For example, where a peacekeeping exercise has stopped warring parties from killing each other, it may have facilitated new forms of gender-based violence and oppression such as prostitution.[6] Positive peace may be defined as a condition wherein all members of society are enabled to lead fulfilling and meaningful lives of their own determination without causing harm to others. Positive peace thus aligns quite closely with Sen's understanding of development as freedom; as the conditions which enhance an individual's life within a communal setting (Sen 1999: chapters 1 and 2).

Global environmental governance may openly or implicitly seek to foster positive peace: a healthy natural environment is necessary for all; non-socially or -ecologically destructive production processes must be the aim of all economic activities. Litfin (2000) highlights the interaction between scientific and political forms of authority in establishing appropriate practices. In some cases, robust science is necessary to make a compelling case for collective action – acid rain, ozone depletion. In other cases, the negative impacts are more obvious, direct and easily exposed – conflict timber, conflict diamonds. In still other cases, the net benefits may be debatable – large-scale dams which displace many and disrupt their lives in the short term but yield demonstrable social benefits over the long term.

In addition, particular negative effects on the natural environment yield corresponding negative social effects: land degradation may create competition for limited resources and lead to physical violence; exclusion from a needed resource may likewise lead to physical violence. So, enhancing the resource base is thought to create an environmental pathway toward both negative and positive peace: an end to the fighting and the beginning of the realization of broad social benefits (UNEP 2009). Uncertainty is also thought to be a driver of violent conflict, which is especially important in the context of the discourse on climate change (Gemenne et al. 2014).

Violence, environmental degradation and prospects for peace

When you conduct a google search using terms such as 'conflict in the world', 'regional conflict', 'biodiversity loss', 'land degradation' and 'vulnerability to climate change', you quickly discover that those areas currently engaged in violent conflict are the same areas that are most likely to be worst affected by climate change, and are already suffering extensive losses of biodiversity, land degradation in drylands and net forest loss: i.e. the land between the tropics. Numerous studies have been conducted interrogating the hypothesized links between environmental change and violent conflict (Gemenne et al. 2014; Gleditsch 2012; Hsiang and Burke 2014; Evans 2011; see Swatuk 2014 for an overview of this literature and Swatuk 2015 for an overview of this literature in relation to water resources in Africa). While the peer-reviewed literature is consistently inconclusive regarding the direct effects of environmental change on violent conflict, the policy-oriented, think-tank driven literature is equally consistent in presenting hypotheses regarding climate change, land degradation, extreme events, mass migration and social instability (Salehyan 2008:317). These documents tend to present cases such as Darfur, and the ongoing Syrian refugee crisis, as emblematic of future social instability: a taste of things to come requiring, in the main, powerful state responses to ensure their safety from 'climate refugees' (Schwartz and Randall 2003; Gleick 2014).

While the debates in academia continue, the architects of global environmental governance keep cobbling away. There are a variety of workshops dispersed around the world. UNEP functions as the primary aggregator and disseminator of knowledge across UN member states (Haas 2007). A visit to www.unep.org reveals the extent to which the organization is engaged in knowledge production, aggregation and dissemination. According to UNEP, "Policy making 'in the dark' – under high levels of uncertainty and without concrete data – carries high risks and transactional costs which need to be minimized. End users must be able to access data in a meaningful way" (UNEP 2017). To this end UNEP has created 'Environment Live' which, it claims, is "the dynamic UN knowledge platform, designed to collect, process and share the world's best environmental science and research". This, UNEP says, will help "review progress towards the implementation of the Sustainable Development Goals" (ibid.).

There are numerous hubs for knowledge gathering related to particular resources with a focus on practice: on forests (Center for International Forestry Research – CIFOR), on water (International Water Management Institute – IWMI), on mountains (International Centre for Integrated Mountain Development – ICIMOD), on agriculture and aquaculture (CGIAR), to name just the most obvious. There are an endless array of think tanks, research institutes and university centers related to these same resources at different scales. Annual or biannual meetings of various scientific organizations provide nodal points for scholars, policy makers and practitioners to come together. These same organizations provide one or more publishing outlets for the dissemination of their members' and associates' research. What would be particularly revealing is a stakeholder analysis and social network analysis with these various organizations at the heart of the data (see, for example, Prell et al. 2009). While this is beyond the scope of this chapter, it is nevertheless accurate to point out that multi-nodal forms of networked environmental governance have recorded remarkable achievements at the regional scale, especially in the European Union (Carter 2001). EU successes in issues related to water and land have spun off a sort of global governance activism, that has been particularly effective among EU development cooperation recipient states (Howarth and Roos 2017).

Globally, the institutional and organizational response to environmental stress has been remarkable over the last several decades. Whereas 30 years ago, few governments had a Ministry of the Environment, today most have a Ministry or a Department of the Environment and Climate Change. There is quite an organic feel to the linkages developed from the global to the regional, sub-regional, national and sub-national levels as well as across world regions and sub-regions. While most of these entities are state-centric, all provide space for civil society organizations and private sector actors, often extra-national as well, to participate in policy-making deliberations.

Let me just present one example, that of WaterNet – the Southern (and now also Eastern) African Water Network. In its infancy, WaterNet was a co-creation of the Netherlands (as then President of the EU) and the Southern African Development Community (SADC), as part of the biannual special cooperative project undertaken by the EU and SADC. As initially conceived, WaterNet was a teaching and research network anchored in a six-country partnership to jointly deliver a Master of Science in Integrated Water Resources Management (IWRM) funded by the Government of the Netherlands, and a water research arm (WARFSA – Water Research Fund for Southern Africa) initially funded by the Government of Sweden. The year 2017 marks 20 years since WaterNet was conceived. Today there are 72 members, including 61 university departments and institutes located in tertiary institutions in 16 southern and eastern African countries, six private sector/NGO members, two IGOs (SADC, the Global Water Partnership-Southern Africa), two Dutch tertiary education institutions and the Government of the Netherlands. In addition, there are numerous linkages between private sector, NGO and university actors within the region and around the world. WaterNet was also the model for Cap-Net, a UNDP-associated entity currently funded by the Government of Brazil devoted to network building and capacity development for IWRM. Many of these actors, institutions and individuals within them meet at various global forums such as the annual Stockholm World Water week hosted by Stockholm International Water Institute (SIWI), and the biannual World Water Forum. Through its MSc, WaterNet partner universities have graduated nearly 400 young water professionals over the last 18 years. This is a remarkable achievement and constitutes one small node in a complex and interdependent world of water governance and management. It is just as easy to present examples from forestry, common property management, parks and protected areas, marine ecosystems, and so on.

The question remains, does all of this environmental governance and management lead to peace, either negative or positive? Across southern and eastern Africa, where WaterNet is active and where dramatic changes have taken place in national and regional water resources governance and management practices, mostly for the better, it can be seen that there is limited overt physical violence. As one crosses the equator, one encounters numerous persistent violent clashes in the Great Lakes region as well as intermittent terrorist actions in Kenya and northern Uganda. Is this violence the result of environmental degradation; or of extreme climatic events; or of resource capture and environmental marginalization? As suggested by several researchers in the 2012 special issue of the *Journal of Peace Research* devoted to climate change and conflict, the answer might be yes (Adano et al. 2012; Theisen 2012; Koubi et al. 2012; Devitt and Tol 2012) especially to the last factor: given structural inequalities and different capacities to react to environmental stressors, certain groups are better able to capture resources for their security than are others, so triggering limited conflict. However, many of the same stressors exist across the sub-equatorial SADC region, yet, there, violence is at best anomic, mostly urban if manifest, and/or latent. In order to understand the presence and absence of violent conflict across this region, despite similar environmental stressors, one would need to undertake extensive and systematic research. Perhaps this will be an area for future research. To this point in time, however, and as shown in the various special issues of regional environmental governance (Balsiger and VanDeveer 2012) and of climate change and conflict (Gemenne et al. 2014; Gleditsch 2012; Nordas and Gleditsch 2007), the cases are suggestive but there is little empirical basis to make substantive claims regarding the effectiveness (or not) of environmental governance on peace (see also Conca and Dabelko 2002).

Conclusion

As suggested by Conca (2012), and as seems intuitively correct, shared resources that are necessary to the shared and complementary livelihoods of people are more likely to be collectively governed and adequately managed as the scale decreases. This is especially so when there is little room for defection (i.e. access to alternative resources), as well as clear rights of access. One of the biggest environmental governance problems on the horizon is the redefinition of forest and land value according to the interests of large, influential actors external to the physical environment (Swatuk 2017). Some of the negative consequences arising from state-to-state or state-to-private sector actor engagement around land use are unintended. For example, it seems unlikely that governments deriving benefits from forest conservation for carbon sequestration (as part of REDD+ and COP21 ideas and agreements) through carbon markets anticipated backlash from local communities in places such as Brazil, Ethiopia and Indonesia. It is equally unlikely that state actors could have anticipated local community resistance to large-scale sales of land to extra-continental third parties interested in biofuel or food production – e.g. Brazilian interests in Mozambique; Indian interests in Ethiopia; Chinese interests in Malawi – especially when framed in terms of 'benefit sharing' and 'income generation' (Cotula et al. 2009; Brautigam and Xiaoyang 2011; Brautigam and Zhang 2013).

This takes us back to Carl Death's epigraph regarding the green state in Africa. His observations hold, however, for most the rest of the Global South. Where global governance mechanisms trigger local or regional actions in support of a global good – such as climate change mitigation – if these actions impinge on the ability of sub-national groups (who may also be transnational in their lived spaces) to pursue their livelihood strategies, then violent conflict may result from well-intended environmental governance activities. Dabelko and colleagues have labelled this 'backdraft'.[7]

So, does environmental governance lead to positive peace? Without doubt, the landscape of resource access, use and management has changed dramatically over the last 45 years, since the initial 'Man and the Biosphere' meeting in Stockholm in 1972. Arts and Buizer (2009:346) suggest, in the context of global forest governance, that "the sustainable development, biodiversity and governance discourses 'materialized' in the form of new partnerships, certification programs, voluntary instruments and an empowerment of non-state actors". These efforts, while important, have had uneven outcomes especially where the social–ecological landscape is most vulnerable and threatened. Do the SDGs, as another macro-organizing framework, offer some hope in relation to putting economic processes back into their environmental context? Without doubt, trying to 'save' the environment without confronting the facts of production and consumption will continue to fail. Maybe, as Conca claims above, we are all regionalists. But it would be better if we were all political economists and political ecologists too.

Notes

1 The four core characteristics of network governance are: "1) interdependence between organizations . . .; 2) continuing interactions between network members, caused by the need to exchange resources and negotiate shared purposes; 3) game-like interactions, rooted in trust and regulated by rules of the game negotiated and agreed by network participants; 4) a significant degree of autonomy from the state . . . Although the state does not occupy a privileged, sovereign position, it can indirectly and imperfectly steer networks" (Rhodes 1996:653).

2 The 'call to science' is interesting, given the close collaboration between scientific knowledge and state power through the ages (for a not dissimilar argument see Turton et al. 2007; for a nuanced critique see Litfin 2000).

3 This is most clearly seen in the literature on climate change and energy security, where the discourse on climate change and arguments regarding the need to ween ourselves off fossil fuels constitutes the threat as perceived by powerful states and transnational actors (see King and Gulledge 2014; Johnson and Boersma, 2013).
4 See, for example: www.theguardian.com/world/2017/may/01/brazilian-farmers-attack-indigenous-tribe-machetes
5 See, for example: www.irinnews.org/report/95443/indonesia-forests-remain-source-conflict
6 See: www.politico.eu/article/my-body-was-not-mine-but-the-u-s-militarys/
7 See, for example: www.wilsoncenter.org/event/the-conflict-potential-climate-change-adaptation-and-mitigation-backdraft-revisited

References

Adano, W., Dietz, T., Witsenburg, K. and Zaal, F. (2012) "Climate Change, Violent Conflict and Local Institutions in Kenya's Drylands" *Journal of Peace Research* 49:65.

Ali, S. (ed.) (2007) *Peace Parks: Conservation and Conflict Resolution*, Cambridge, MA: MIT Press.

Allan, J. A. (2003) *IWRM/IWRAM: A New Sanctioned Discourse?* Occasional paper 50. SOAS Water Issues Study Group, School of Oriental and African Studies/King's College, London (April).

Arts, B. and Buizer, M. (2009) "Forests, Discourses, Institutions: A Discursive-Institutional Analysis of Global Forest Governance" *Forest Policy and Economics* 11:340–347.

Balsiger, J. and VanDeveer, S. D. (2012) "Navigating Regional Environmental Governance" *Global Environmental Politics* 12(3):1–17.

Bennett, B. (2015) *Plantations and Protected Areas: A Global History of Forest Management*, Cambridge, MA: MIT Press.

Biermann, F. (2014) "Global Governance and the Environment" in Betsill, M., Hochstetler, K. and Stevis, D. (eds.) *Advances in International Environmental Politics*, 2nd edition, Basingstoke: Palgrave Macmillan, 245–272.

Brautigam, D. and Xiaoyang, H. (2011) "African Shenzhen: China's Special Economic Zones in Africa" *Journal of Modern African Studies* 49(1):27–54.

Brautigam, D. and Zhang, H. (2013) "Green Dreams: Myth And Reality in China's Agricultural Investment in Africa" *Third World Quarterly* 34(9):1676–1696.

Broch-Due, V. (2000) "Producing Nature and Poverty in Africa: An Introduction" in Broch-Due, V. and Schroeder, R. (eds.) *Producing Nature and Poverty in Africa*, Uppsala: Nordic-Africa Institute.

Buscher, B. (2013) *Transforming the Frontier: Peace Parks and the Politics of Neoliberal Conservation in Southern Africa*, Durham, NC: Duke University Press.

Carter, N. (2001) *The Politics of the Environment: Ideas, Activism, Policy*, Cambridge: Cambridge University Press.

Child, B. (ed.) (2004) *Parks in Transition: Biodiversity, Rural Development and the Bottom Line*, London: Earthscan.

Collier, P. and Hoeffler, A. (2004) "Greed and Grievance in Civil War" *Oxford Economic Papers* 56(4):563–595.

Conca, K. (2006) *Governing Water*, Cambridge, MA: MIT Press.

Conca, K. (2012) "The Rise of the Region in Global Environmental Politics" *Global Environmental Politics* 12(3):127–133.

Conca, K. and Dabelko, G. (eds.) (2002) *Environmental Peacemaking* Baltimore, MD: Johns Hopkins University Press.

Cotula, L., Vermeulen, S., Leonard, R. and Keely, J. (2009) *Land Grab or Development Opportunity? Agricultural Investment and International Land Deals in Africa*, London and Rome: IIED/FAO/IFAD.

Death, C. (2016) *The Green State in Africa*, New Haven, CT: Yale University Press.

De Jong, W., Donovan, D. and Abe, K-I. (eds.) (2007) *Extreme Conflict and Tropical Forests*, Dordrecht: Springer.

De Koning, R. (2007) "Greed or Grievance in West Africa's Forest Wars?" in de Jong, W., Donovan, D. and Abe, K-I (eds.) *Extreme Conflict and Tropical Forests*, Dordrecht: Springer, 37–56.

Devitt, C. and Tol, R.S.J. (2012) "Civil War, Climate Change and Development: A Scenario Study for Sub-Saharan Africa" *Journal of Peace Research* 49:129.

Dietz, T., Ostrom, E. and Stern, P. C. (2003) "The Struggle to Govern the Commons" *Science* 302:1907–1912.

Donovan, D., de Jong, W. and Abe, K-I. (2007) "Tropical Forests and Extreme Conflicts" in de Jong, W., Donovan, D. and Abe, K-I (eds.) *Extreme Conflict and Tropical Forests*, Dordrecht: Springer, 1–16.

Duffy, R. (2000) *Killing for Conservation: Wildlife Policy in Zimbabwe*, London: James Currey.

Ellis, S. (1999) *The Mask of Anarchy*, New York: New York University Press.

Evans, P. (2011) *Resource Scarcity, Climate Change and the Risk of Violent Conflict*, Background paper, Washington, DC: World Bank.

Fabricius, C. and Koch, E. with Magome, H. and Turner, S. (eds.) (2004) *Rights, Resources and Rural Development: Community-based Natural Resources Management in Southern Africa*, London: Earthscan.

Food and Agricultural Organization (FAO) (2016) *State of the World's Forests 2016. Forests and Agriculture: Land-use Challenges and Opportunities*, Rome: FAO.

Foucault, M. (1978) *The History of Sexuality, Volume 1: Introduction*, New York: Vintage Books.

Galtung, J. (1971) "A Structural Theory of Imperialism" *Journal of Peace Research* 8(2):81–117.

Gemenne, F., Barnett, J., Adger, W. N. and Dabelko, G. (2014) "Climate and Security: Evidence, Emerging Risks, and a New Agenda" *Climatic Change*, online at DOI 10.1007/s10584-014-1074-7.

Gleditsch, N. P. (2012) "Whither the Weather? Climate Change and Conflict" *Journal of Peace Research* 49(1):3–9.

Gleick, P. H. (2014) "Water, Drought, Climate Change and Conflict in Syria" *American Meteorological Society* 6:331–340.

Grey, D., Garrick, D. E., Muller, M. and Sadoff, C. W. (2013) "Water Security in One Blue Planet: Twenty-first Century Policy Challenges for Science" *Philosophical Transactions of the Royal Society* (September).

Haas, P. M. (2007) "Turning Up the Heat on Global Environmental Governance" *The Forum* 5(2): Article 8.

Hanson, K. T., D'Alessandro, C. and Owusu, F. Y. (eds.) (2014) *Managing Africa's Natural Resources: Capacities for Development*, Basingstoke: Palgrave Macmillan.

Homer-Dixon, T. (1999) *The Environment, Scarcity and Violence*, Princeton, NJ: Princeton University Press.

Howarth, D. and Roos, M. (2017) "Pushing the Boundaries: New Research on the Activism of EU Supranational Institutions" *Journal of Contemporary European Research* 13(2):1007–1024.

Hsiang, S. M. and Burke, M. (2014) "Climate, Conflict and Social Stability: What Does the Evidence Say?" *Climatic Change* 123:39–55.

Huggins, C., Chenje, M., Mohamed-Katerere, J. and Attere, F. (2006) "Environment for Peace and Regional Cooperation" in Africa Environment Outlook 2, UNEP.

Jeffery, R. and Vira, B. (eds.) (2001) *Conflict and Cooperation in Participatory Natural Resource Management*, Basingstoke: Palgrave.

Johnson, C. and Boersma, T. (2013) "Energy (In)security in Poland: the Case of Shale Gas" *Energy Policy* 53:389–399.

Kaplan, R. (1994) "The Coming Anarchy: How Scarcity, Crime, Overpopulation; Tribalism, and Disease Are Rapidly Destroying the Social Fabric of Our Planet" *The Atlantic Monthly*, February.

King, M. D. and Gulledge, J. (2014) "Climate Change and Energy Security: An Analysis of Policy Research" *Climatic Change* 123:57–68.

Koubi, V., Bernauer, T., Kalbhenn, A. and Spilker, G. (2012) "Climate Variability, Economic Growth and Civil Conflict" *Journal of Peace Research* 49:113.

Kramarz, T. and Park, S. (2016) "Accountability in Global Environmental Governance: A Meaningful Tool for Action?" *Global Environmental Politics* 16(2):1–22.

Kramarz, T. and Park, S. (2017) "Introduction: The Politics of Environmental Accountability" *Review of Policy Research* 34(1):4–9.

Landell-Mills, P. and Serageldin, I. (1991) "Governance and the External Factor" Staff paper, World Bank Annual Conference on Development Economics, Washington, DC: World Bank.

Litfin, K. (2000) "Environment, Wealth, and Authority: Global Climate Change and Emerging Modes of Legitimation" *International Studies Review* 2(2):119–148.

Mateo-Vega, J. et al. (2017) "Full, Effective Participation of Indigenous People in Forest Monitoring for Reducing Emissions from Deforestation and Forest Degradation (REDD+): Trial in Panama's Darien" *Ecosphere* 8(2):1–19.

Moore, D. (1995) "Development Discourse as Hegemony: Towards an Ideological History, 1945–95" in Moore, D. and Schmitz, G. (eds.) *Debating Development Discourse: Institutional and Popular Perspective*, London: Macmillan.

Moore, D. (1999) "'Sail On, O Ship of State': Neo-liberalism, Globalization and the Governance of Africa" *Journal of Peasant Studies* 27(1):61–96.

Moran, D. (ed.) (2011) *Climate Change and National Security: A Country-Level Analysis*, Washington, DC: Georgetown University Press.

Najam, A. and Halle, M. (2010) "Global Environmental Governance: The Challenge of Accountability" *Sustainable Development Insights*. Available at: www.bu.edu/pardee/files/2010/UNsdkp005fsingle.pdf

Nordas, R. and Gleditsch, N. P. (2007) "Climate Change and Conflict" *Political Geography* 26:627–638.

Pierre, J. (2000) *Debating Governance: Authority, Steering and Democracy*, Oxford: Oxford University Press.

Pierre, J. and Stoker, G. (2000) "Towards Multi-level Governance" in Holliday, I. (ed.) *Developments in British Politics*, 6th edition, London: Macmillan.

Prell, C., Hubacek, K. and Reed, M. (2009) "Stakeholder Analysis and Social Network Analysis in Natural Resource Management" *Society and Natural Resources* 22:501–518.

Rhodes, R.A.W. (1996) "The New Governance: Governing without Government" *Political Studies* 44:652–667.

Rhodes, R.A.W. (2007) "Understanding Governance: Ten Years On" *Organization Studies* 28(8):1243–1264.

Richards, P. (1996) *Fighting for the Rainforest: War, Youth and Resources in Sierra Leone*, Oxford: James Currey.

Salehyan, I. (2008) "From Climate Change to Conflict? No Consensus Yet" *Journal of Peace Research* 45:315.

Scheffran, J., Brzoska, M., Kominek, J., Link, P. M. and Schilling, J. (2012) "Climate Change and Violent Conflict" *Science* 336(6083):869–871.

Schwartz, P. and Randall, D. (2003) *An Abrupt Climate Change Scenario and Its Implications for the United States National Security*, Washington, DC: Environmental Media Services.

Sen, A. (1999) *Development as Freedom*, Oxford: Oxford University Press.

Solomon, S. (2010) *Water: The Epic Struggle for Wealth, Power and Civilization*, New York: HarperCollins.

Swatuk, L. A. (2005) "From 'Project' to 'Context': Community Based Natural Resource Management in Botswana" *Global Environmental Politics* 5(3):95–124.

Swatuk, L. A. (2007) "Seeing the Forest for the Trees: Tropical Forests, the State and Violent Conflict in Africa" in de Jong, W., Donovan, D. and Abe, K-I (eds.) *Extreme Conflict and Tropical Forests*, Dordrecht: Springer, 93–116.

Swatuk, L. A. (2014) "Environmental Security" in Betsill, M., Hochstetler, K. and Stevis, D. (eds.) *Advances in International Environmental Politics*, 2nd edition, Basingstoke: Palgrave Macmillan, 211–244.

Swatuk, L. A. (2015) "Can IWRM Float on a Sea of Underdevelopment? Reflections on Twenty-plus Years of 'Reform' in Sub-Saharan Africa" in Munck, R., Asingwire, N., Fagan, H. and Kabonesa, C. (eds.) *Water and Development: Good Governance after Neoliberalism*, London: Zed Books, 60–83.

Swatuk, L. A. (2017) "The Land–Water–Food–Energy Nexus: Green and Blue Water Dynamics in Contemporary Africa–Asia Relations" in Raposo, P., Arase, D. and Cornelissen, S. (eds.) *The Routledge Handbook on Contemporary Asia–Africa Relations*, Abingdon: Routledge.

Theisen, O. M. (2012) "Climate Clashes? Weather Variability, Land Pressure, and Organized Violence in Kenya, 1989–2004" *Journal of Peace Research* 49:81.

Turton, A. R., Hattingh, H., Maree, G., Roux, D., Claassen, M. and Strydom, W. (eds.) (2007) *Governance as Trialogue: Government–Society–Science in Transition*, Berlin: Springer for the CSIR.

United Nations Environment Programme (UNEP) (2009) *From Conflict to Peacebuilding: The Role of Natural Resources and the Environment*, Nairobi: UNEP.

United Nations Environment Programme (UNEP) (2017) *Live-tracking Progress towards Global Goals Now Possible Thanks to a Cutting-edge UN Knowledge Platform*. Available at: http://web.unep.org/newscentre/live-tracking-progress-towards-global-goals-now-possible-thanks-cutting-edge-un-knowledge-platform [Accessed 16 February 2017].

UNESCO and UN Water (2003) *Water for People, Water for Life*. Available at: www.unesco.org/new/en/natural-sciences/environment/water/wwap/wwdr/wwdr1-2003/ [Accessed 21 August 2017].

United States Department of State (USDS) (2014) *United States Climate Action Report 2014*, Washington, DC: US Dept. of State.

Van der Ven, H., Bernstein, S. and Hoffman, M. (2017) "Valuing the Contribution of Non-state and Subnational Actors to Climate Governance" *Global Environmental Politics* 17(1):1–20.

World Bank (1997) *World Development Report: The State in a Changing World*, New York: Oxford University Press.

The World Wildlife Fund (n.d.) *Forest Habitat*. Available at: www.worldwildlife.org/habitats/forest-habitat

Index

Page locators in **bold** refer to tables and page locators in *italics* refer to figures.

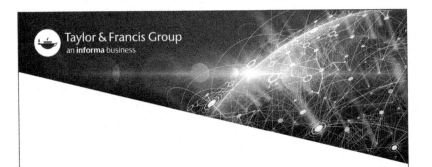